KT-488-027

Skill Acquisition in Sport
Research, theory and practice

Edited by
A. Mark Williams and Nicola J. Hodges

Routledge
Taylor & Francis Group

LONDON AND NEW YORK

First published 2004
by Routledge
2 Park Square, Milton Park, Abingdon, Oxon, OX14 4RN

Simultaneously published in the USA and Canada
by Routledge
270 Madison Avenue, New York, NY 10016

Reprinted 2005

Routledge is an imprint of the Taylor & Francis Group

© 2004 A. Mark Williams and Nicola J. Hodges

Typeset in Goudy by
Newgen Imaging Systems (P) Ltd, Chennai, India
Printed and bound in Great Britain by
MPG Books, Bodmin, Cornwall

British Library Cataloguing in Publication Data
A catalogue record for this book is available from the British Library

Library of Congress Cataloging in Publication Data
A catalog record for this book has been requested

ISBN 0–415–27074–X (hbk)
ISBN 0–415–27075–8 (pbk)

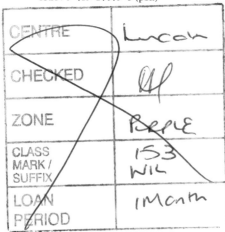

Skill Acquisition in Sport

The acquisition of skill is fundamental to human existence and throughout life we are continuously trying to develop new skills and refine existing ones. Success in sport depends upon the athlete's ability to develop and fine-tune a specific set of perceptual, cognitive and motor skills.

This book examines how we learn such skills and, in particular, considers the crucial role of practice and instruction in the process. Leading authorities within the field provide a comprehensive review of current research and theory on skill acquisition. Potential avenues for future work are highlighted and, where possible, implications for instruction and practice are discussed.

Skill Acquisition in Sport will be of interest to those involved in motor behaviour work in the sport and movement sciences, as well as physical therapy, ergonomics and human factors. This book will appeal to students, academics and practitioners, given both its discussion of current and complex issues in motor behaviour and recommendations for effective practice in the field.

A. Mark Williams is Professor of Motor Behaviour at the Research Institute for Sport and Exercise Sciences, Liverpool John Moores University, UK.

Nicola J. Hodges is a Senior Lecturer in Motor Behaviour at the Research Institute for Sport and Exercise Sciences, Liverpool John Moores University, UK.

Contents

Contributors

Phillip L. Ackerman
School of Psychology
Georgia Institute of Technology
Atlanta, Georgia, USA

Duarte Araújo
Faculty of Human Kinetics
Technical University of Lisbon
Lisbon, Portugal

Peter J. Beek
Faculty of Human Movement Sciences
Vrije Universiteit
Amsterdam, The Netherlands

Sian L. Beilock
Department of Psychology
Miami University
Oxford, Ohio, USA

Simon J. Bennett
Department of Optometry and
    Neuroscience
University of Manchester Institute of
    Science and Technology
Manchester, UK

Mary O. Boyle
School of Psychology
Georgia Institute of Technology
Atlanta, Georgia, USA

Chris Button
School of Physical Education
University of Otago
Dunedin, New Zealand

Thomas H. Carr
Department of Psychology
Michigan State University
East Lansing, MI, USA

Richard G. Carson
School of Human Movement Studies
The University of Queensland
Brisbane, Australia

Kristine L. Chambers
Faculty of Kinesiology
University of Calgary
Calgary, Alberta, Canada

Graham Chapman
Department of Exercise and Sport
    Science
Manchester Metropolitan University
Manchester, Crewe, UK

Stephen A. Coombes
Department of Exercise and Sport
    Sciences
University of Florida
Gainesville, Florida, USA

John D. Cullen
Department of Kinesiology
McMaster University
Hamilton, Ontario, Canada

Andreas Daffertshofer
Faculty of Human Movement Sciences
Vrije Universiteit
Amsterdam, The Netherlands

Keith Davids
School of Physical Education
University of Otago
Dunedin, New Zealand

John Dickinson
School of Kinesiology
Simon Fraser University
Burnaby, BC, Canada

Aaron R. Duley
Department of Exercise and Sport
  Sciences
University of Florida
Gainesville, Florida, USA

Ian M. Franks
School of Human Kinetics
University of British Columbia
Vancouver, BC, Canada

David Goodman
School of Kinesiology
Simon Fraser University
Burnaby, BC, Canada

Nicola J. Hodges
Research Institute for Sport and
  Exercise Sciences
Liverpool John Moores University
Liverpool, UK

Robert R. Horn
College of Education and Human
  Services
Montclair State University
Upper Montclair, NJ, USA

Raôul Huys
Faculty of Human Movement
  Sciences
Vrije Universiteit
Amsterdam, The Netherlands

Christopher M. Janelle
Department of Exercise and Sport
  Sciences
University of Florida
Gainesville, Florida, USA

John van der Kamp
Faculty of Human Movement
  Sciences
Vrije Universiteit
Amsterdam, The Netherlands

Michael A. Khan
School of Sport, Health and Exercise
  Sciences
University of Wales-Bangor
Bangor, Wales, UK

Timothy D. Lee
Department of Kinesiology
McMaster University
Hamilton, Ontario, Canada

Clare MacMahon
Department of Kinesiology
McMaster University
Hamilton, Ontario, Canada

Steve Martell
Faculty of Kinesiology
University of Calgary
Calgary, Alberta, Canada

Richard S.W. Masters
Institute of Human Performance
The University of Hong Kong
Hong Kong, China

Jonathan P. Maxwell
Institute of Human Performance
The University of Hong Kong
Hong Kong, China

Raôul R.D. Oudejans
Faculty of Human Movement
  Sciences
Vrije Universiteit
Amsterdam, The Netherlands

Bill Randall
School of Kinesiology
Simon Fraser University
Burnaby, BC, Canada

Mary-Ann Reeves
National Coaching Institute-Calgary
Calgary, Alberta, Canada

Stephan Riek
School of Human Movement Studies
The University of Queensland
Brisbane, Queensland, Australia

Geert J.P. Savelsbergh
Faculty of Human Movement Sciences
Vrije Universiteit
Amsterdam, The Netherlands

Mark A. Scott
Research Institute for Sport and
    Exercise Sciences
Liverpool John Moores University
Liverpool, UK

Charles H. Shea
Department of Health &
    Kinesiology
Texas A & M University
Texas, USA

Jonathan Shemmell
School of Human Movement Studies
The University of Queensland
Brisbane, Queensland, Australia

Dominic A. Simon
Department of Psychology
Nex Mexico State University
Las Cruces, NM, USA

Nicholas J. Smeeton
Research Institute for Sport and
    Exercise Sciences
Liverpool John Moores University
Liverpool, UK

Janet L. Starkes
Department of Kinesiology
McMaster University
Hamilton, Ontario, Canada

Jeffery J. Summers
School of Psychology
University of Tasmania
Hobart, Tasmania, Australia

James R. Tresilian
School of Human Movement
    Studies
The University of Queensland
Brisbane, Queensland, Australia

Joan N. Vickers
Faculty of Kinesology
University of Calgary
Calgary, Alberta, Canada

Paul Ward
Department of Psychology
Mississippi State University
Mississippi State, MS, USA

Daniel Weeks
School of Kinesiology
Simon Fraser University
Burnaby, BC, Canada

A. Mark Williams
Research Institute for Sport and
    Exercise Sciences
Liverpool John Moores University
Liverpool, UK

Gabriele Wulf
Department of Kinesiology
University of Nevada
Las Vegas, NV, USA

Biographies

Phillip L. Ackerman is Professor of Psychology at Georgia Institute of Technology. He has published widely in the areas of individual differences in learning and skilled performance, human abilities and human factors/engineering psychology. He is the Editor of *Journal of Experimental Psychology: Applied*. In 1992, he was the recipient of the American Psychological Association's Distinguished Scientific Award for Early Career Contribution to Psychology (in the field of Applied Research/Psychometrics) for his work on the cognitive determinants of complex skills of air traffic controllers. He is a Fellow of the American Psychological Association, the Human Factors and Ergonomics Society, and a Charter Fellow of the American Psychological Society.

Duarte Araújo is Assistant Professor at the Faculty of Human Kinetics, Technical University of Lisbon. His research involves the study of expert decision-making in sport, which led to his receiving a Young Researcher Award at the European College of Sport Science in 2001 and also at the Association des Chercheurs en Activités Physiques et Sportives (ACAPS) in 2002. He was elected member of the Managing Council of the International Society of Sport Psychology in 2001, and has been a performance consultant for the Portuguese Sailing Federation since 1995.

Peter J. Beek is Professor of Coordination Dynamics at the Faculty of Human Sciences, Vrije Universiteit, Amsterdam. His research interests include the dynamics of bimanual rhythmic coordination and the perceptual control of movement in interceptive actions. In addition, he is engaged in research on the learning and development of perceptual-motor skills. Building on his early studies of juggling and other bimanual skills, he is seeking applications of dynamical systems theory to the study of learning expertise in the domain of sport. He is currently the Editor of *Human Movement Science*.

Sian L. Beilock is an Assistant Professor in Cognitive Psychology at Miami University, Ohio. She received a doctoral degree in kinesiology and psychology from Michigan State University in 2003. This degree reflects her interest in the acquisition and maintenance of complex skills across both cognitive and sensorimotor skill domains. By examining skill performance across a number of different task types and performance environments, she hopes to gain a better understanding of the nature of successful skill execution and why, at times, it fails to occur.

Simon J. Bennett is working as a Senior Research Fellow in the Department of Optometry and Neuroscience at the University of Manchester Institute of Science and Technology. He has a range of interests in the area of perceptual-motor behaviour and skill acquisition. Currently, he is researching oculomotor prediction of extrapolated object motion, and the role of perceptual information in timing interceptive action.

Mary O. Boyle is an I/O Psychology Graduate Student at Georgia Institute of Technology, where she received a President's Fellowship award and completed a Masters degree in Psychology in 2003. She has been involved in research efforts to develop and validate computerized perceptual speed tests and contributed to a meta-analytic examination of the relationship between perceptual speed and other cognitive abilities. Her interests include the identification of individual differences that are instrumental for vocational selection and/or task performance.

Chris Button is Director of the Human Performance Centre and a Senior Lecturer at the University of Otago. His research interests include movement coordination and interception skills, skill learning, coaching, variability and individual differences and dynamical systems theory. A common theme of his published work is the application of movement science to sport within an Ecological framework.

Thomas H. Carr is Professor of Cognitive Psychology at Michigan State University. He investigates attentional, perceptual, and memorial influences on real-time skilled performance, using the behavioral methods of cognitive psychology and the neuroimaging methods of cognitive neuroscience. Recent research has focused on how instruction, practice, motivation and emotion, and development mediate the acquisition and expression of skill in linguistic, mathematical, and sensorimotor task domains. He is a past Editor of the *Journal of Experimental Psychology: Human Perception and Performance*, and is currently the Editor of *Perception & Psychophysics* and an Associate Editor of *Cognitive Psychology*.

Richard G. Carson is a Professorial Research Fellow in the School of Human Movement Studies at the University of Queensland. He joined the School in 1993 after completing his postgraduate education at Simon Fraser University in British Columbia. He completed his undergraduate degree at the University of Bristol. The focus of his basic research program is upon the fundamental mechanisms of sensori-motor control including corticospinal mediation of inter- and intra-limb coordination, motor skill acquisition, and the cross-modal integration of sensory information. The emphasis of his applied research program is upon the changes in sensori-motor coordination that occur during childhood development and ageing, and the remediation of deficits exhibited by stroke survivors and the elderly.

Kristine L. Chambers is a Sessional Instructor at the University of British Columbia, Canada (Faculty of Education); and the University College of the Fraser Valley (Kinesiology). She completed a Masters degree at the University of Calgary, in Alberta, Canada, in the area of applied cognitive psychology and motor learning. She is currently applying this research in Triathlon as head coach of a junior club. She is a coordinator of provincial and national youth development programs, and leader of the new Triathlon NCCP (National Coaching Certification Program) program development.

Graham Chapman has a Masters degree from Manchester Metropolitan University and is currently a Ph.D. Student in Motor Control at the University of Birmingham. His research interests include the study of skill acquisition, gaze behaviour during locomotion and the role of eye and head movements in the control of gait and posture.

Stephen A. Coombes is a Doctoral Student and Laboratory Assistant in the Department of Exercise and Sport Sciences, University of Florida. His research interests focus on linking emotion with motor control by mapping psychophysiological measures onto corresponding performance characteristics. He has an undergraduate degree from Liverpool John Moores University and a Masters degree from the University of Florida.

John D. Cullen is a Doctoral Candidate in Human Biodynamics in the Department of Kinesiology at McMaster University. He has a Masters degree from McMaster University and an undergraduate degree from the University of Waterloo. His Masters thesis examined bimanual coordination in aiming and currently he is researching expert perception and cognition in ice hockey coaches.

Andreas Daffertshofer is an Associate Professor at the Faculty of Human Movement Sciences, Vrije Universiteit, Amsterdam. He received his Ph.D. in theoretical physics at Stuttgart University in 1995. His primary interest is in complex dynamics in biological systems and its formal and conceptual assessment in terms of synergetics. At present, his research activities focus on spatio-temporal aspects of neural synchronization phenomena during perceptual-motor tasks.

Keith Davids is Professor and Dean of the School of Physical Education at the University of Otago. His research interests include the application of dynamical systems theory to the study of processes of coordination, control and their acquisition in human movement systems. His publications have examined the implications of these theoretical ideas for understanding the design of practice programmes and the structure of learning activities in sport and exercise settings. He is a member of the Editorial Board for the *Journal of Sports*

Sciences, Psychology of Sport and Exercise and *Infant Behavior and Development*, and an Associate Editor for *Behavioral and Brain Sciences*.

John Dickinson is Professor and Director of the School of Kinesiology, Simon Fraser University. His undergraduate studies were completed at the University of Birmingham and his doctoral degree was awarded by the University of Nottingham. He taught at Loughborough College of Education before immigrating to Canada. His research focus has been on motor learning and control and he is the author of fifty research articles and two books in the field.

Aaron R. Duley is a Doctoral Student in the Department of Exercise and Sport Sciences at the University of Florida. He is currently a Research Associate in the Motor Behavior and Performance Psychology Laboratories, and his research interests involve the psychophysiological nature of emotion and attention as related to human performance. He is involved in several diverse pursuits, examining the nature of short-lead prepulse startle modification as an index of automatic attentional processing in motor control, and he is the recipient of a National Science Foundation grant to create course modules for students in motor learning, control and biomechanics domains.

Ian M. Franks is a Professor of Human Kinetics at the University of British Columbia. He is a researcher in the areas of motor learning and control. His basic research deals with the preparation and execution of simple voluntary movements while his applied research focuses upon the analysis of coaching behaviours with particular reference to the effective use of feedback in the acquisition of sport skills. These research programmes have been funded by the Natural Sciences and Engineering Research Council of Canada, the Social Sciences and Humanities Research Council of Canada and Sport Canada.

David Goodman is Professor in the School of Kinesiology, Simon Fraser University. He has taught and carried out research in the area of motor learning and control since the early 1970's when he completed a Masters degree at the University of British Columbia. After lecturing for two years at York University in Toronto, he moved to the United States to carry out his doctoral studies at the University of Iowa. After spending a year at Haskins Laboratories, he was appointed at Simon Fraser University in 1981. He has published in a broad range of areas including motor learning, motor control, human factors, sport analysis and coaching.

Nicola J. Hodges is a Senior Lecturer in Motor Behaviour at the Research Institute for Sport and Exercise Sciences, Liverpool John Moores University. Her research interests include the study of skill acquisition and the attainment of expertise and she has published extensively in these areas. She has a doctoral degree from the University of British Columbia and a Masters degree from McMaster University. She was recently awarded a Young Scientist Award by The European College of Sport Science.

Robert R. Horn is an Assistant Professor at the Department of Health Professions, Physical Education, Recreation and Leisure Studies at Montclair State University. His research focuses on the impact of demonstration on skill acquisition, and on visual search and the perception of critical information for learning. He completed his Ph.D. in Motor Behaviour at Liverpool John Moores University. He also has an M.Sc. in Kinesiology from the University of West Chester, Pennsylvania, and a B.Sc. (Hons) in Human Movement Science from the University of Liverpool.

Raôul Huys is a Doctoral Student at the Faculty of Human Movement Sciences, Vrije Universiteit, Amsterdam. The focus of his project, supervised by Andreas Daffertshofer and Peter Beek, concerns the interaction among multiple subsystems (e.g., manual, posture, vision, respiration) as they become embedded into a functional dynamical organization in the course of learning.

Christopher M. Janelle is Associate Professor of Sport and Exercise Psychology in the Department of Exercise and Sport Sciences, University of Florida. His research interests focus on the interactive nature of emotion and attention as related to human performance and health issues, and is currently funded by the National Institute of Mental Health for his work in these areas. He was awarded the Dorothy Harris Memorial award for early career excellence in sport psychology scholarship by the Association for the Advancement of Applied Sport Psychology (AAASP) in 2002. He is a Section Editor for the International Journal of Sport and Exercise Psychology, and currently serves as the Program Chair for Division 47 (Exercise and Sport Psychology) of the American Psychological Association.

Michael A. Khan is Lecturer in Motor Control and Learning at the School of Sport, Health and Exercise Sciences, University of Wales, Bangor. His research interests include visuo-motor control in manual aiming movements, motor programming and attention demands of movement control. He has a doctoral degree from the University of British Columbia and Masters degree from the University of Western Ontario.

Timothy D. Lee is a Professor in the Department of Kinesiology at McMaster University in Hamilton, Ontario. Since 1984 his research has been sponsored by grants from the Natural Sciences and Engineering Research Council of Canada. He has published extensively in motor behaviour and psychology journals and has served as an Editor for both the *Journal of Motor Behavior* and the *Research Quarterly for Exercise and Sport*. He is the co-author (with Richard Schmidt) of *Motor Control and Learning: A Behavioral Emphasis*.

Clare MacMahon is a Doctoral Candidate in Human Biodynamics in the Department of Kinesiology at McMaster University. She has a Masters degree from the University of Ottawa and an undergraduate degree from McGill University. Her research at the Masters level examined perceptual and cognitive skill in rugby referees, whilst in her doctoral thesis she is exploring the nature of expertise and career development of highly skilled basketball referees and World Cup soccer officials.

Steve Martell is a Doctoral Candidate in the Faculty of Kinesiology at the University of Calgary. His research interests include topics related to gaze behaviour, decision-making, skill acquisition, expertise, motor control and sport psychology. As a former hockey player who has had international and professional level experience, he worked extensively with the National Sport Centre, National Coaching Institute, Olympic Oval and numerous other developmental programs in ice hockey. He is an elite level coach with the University of Calgary Men's ice hockey team.

Richard S.W. Masters is Assistant Director (Research) at the Institute of Human Performance, The University of Hong Kong. He has an undergraduate and a Masters degree in psychology from the University of Otago and a doctoral degree from the University of York. He is interested in understanding the knowledge mechanisms which support skill acquisition and skilled performance, particularly in relation to the phenomenon of implicit motor learning. He is presently an Associate Editor for *Psychology of Sport and Exercise*.

Jonathan P. Maxwell is an Assistant Professor at the Institute of Human Performance, The University of Hong Kong. He completed his undergraduate and doctoral degrees in sports science at the University of Birmingham. His research involves the cognitive processes underlying the acquisition of motor skills and their subsequent performance in demanding situations, the effect of instructions on learning and the evolution of verbal and motor processes.

Raôul R.D. Oudejans is a Lecturer at the Faculty of Human Movement Sciences, Vrije Universiteit, Amsterdam. His Ph.D. was on the optics and actions of catching fly balls in baseball. His current research involves perceptual-motor learning and performance in sports (e.g., visual control of basketball jump shooting, judging offside in football) and sport psychology (e.g., effects of anxiety and fatigue on perception and action in sport climbing).

Bill Randall is currently a Rehabilitation Equipment Specialist with Motion Specialties BC Ltd, and holds RESANA certification as an Assistive Technology Supplier. He completed his B.Phed at Brock University in 1993, and a B.A. in health studies the following year. He then earned his Masters in Kinesiology from Simon Fraser University in 1999. He re-opened the area of one-trial learning with papers and presentations, and initiated the research on the topic in the motor field.

Mary-Ann Reeves is Director of the National Coaching Institute at the University of Calgary. She founded and was Head Coach of the Calgary Aquabelles Synchronized Swimming Club, one of Canada's most successful teams. She acted as a consultant in over a dozen countries, presented papers at numerous international seminars and clinics and served as a Team Leader at many World Championships and Olympic Games.

Stephan Riek is a Principal Research Fellow in the School of Human Movement Studies at The University of Queensland, and holder of the Australian Research Council QEII Fellowship. He completed his Ph.D. at Simon Fraser University in Canada in musculo-skeletal modelling. His current research is focused on the neuro-mechanical basis of coordination with an emphasis on how the neuromuscular system adapts in response to novel mechanical tasks.

Geert J.P. Savelsbergh is Professor of perceptual-motor development at the Institute for Biophysical and Clinical research into Human Movement, Manchester Metropolitan University, and Associate Professor at the Institute for Fundamental and Clinical Human Movement Sciences, The Vrije University in Amsterdam, where he is Head of the Perceptual-Motor Control: Development, Learning and Performance Research Group. He has special interest in the visual regulation of movements and is Editor of *Infant Behavior and Development*.

Mark A. Scott is a Principal Lecturer at the Research Institute for Sport and Exercise Sciences at Liverpool John Moores University. His research interests include the visual regulation of interceptive actions and factors that affect the acquisition of skilled behaviour.

Charles H. Shea is a Professor of Kinesiology in the Human Performance Laboratories at Texas A&M University. He has published extensively in the area of motor skill learning and transfer. He is a member of the Editorial Board for the *Journal of Motor Behavior* and currently the President Elect of the North American Society of Psychology of Sport and Physical Activity.

Jonathan Shemmell is a Ph.D. Student in the School of Human Movement Studies at the University of Queensland. His doctoral work focuses on the neuromuscular-skeletal constraints associated with skill acquisition in complex tasks and the role of the primary motor cortex in the consolidation of acquired skill. His research interests include the neuro-mechanical basis of coordination and the corticospinal mechanisms of motor learning and consolidation.

Dominic A. Simon is an Assistant Professor in the Department of Psychology, New Mexico State University. His research interests include skill acquisition and memory, with particular interest in scheduling of practice and metacognition. He received his Ph.D. in Psychology from the University of California at Los Angeles, followed by a Post-Doctoral Fellowship in Kinesiology at McMaster University. His undergraduate degree is from St. Mary's College, Twickenham, UK.

Nicholas J. Smeeton is a Postgraduate Researcher at the Research Institute for Sport and Exercise Sciences, Liverpool John Moores University. His research interests focus on training perceptual skills and transfer of learning. He has a Masters degree from Liverpool John Moores University and is currently working in professional sport.

Janet L. Starkes is Professor and Chair of the Department of Kinesiology at McMaster University. She has published extensively in the areas of expert performance in athletes and surgeons as well as the visual control of manual aiming. She has been President of the North American Society for the Psychology of Sport and Physical Activity, the Canadian Society for Psychomotor Learning and Sport Psychology, and the Canadian Deans and Directors of Kinesiology and Physical Education. She has also been honoured as an International Fellow of the American Academy of Kinesiology and Physical Education.

Jeffery J. Summers is Professor and Head of the School of Psychology at the University of Tasmania. He has published extensively in the field of human motor control and learning, particularly in the area of interlimb coordination. In recent years his research focus has shifted to the study of movement disorders and movement rehabilitation. He is currently on the Editorial Boards of *Human Movement Science, Acta Psychologica* and the *International Journal of Sport and Exercise Psychology*, and a Consulting Editor for the *Journal of Motor Behavior*.

James R. Tresilian is Principal Research Fellow and Associate Professor in the School of Human Movement Studies, The University of Queensland. He has published widely in the areas of visual control of movement, the control of upper limb movements and the interaction of perception and action. He is currently a Consulting Editor for the *Journal of Experimental Psychology: Human Perception and Performance*.

John van der Kamp is a Lecturer in Perceptual-Motor Control at the Faculty of Human Movement Sciences, Vrije Universiteit, Amsterdam. His research interests include the development and learning of perceptual-motor skills.

Joan N. Vickers is Professor of Kinesiology in the Faculty of Kinesiology, University of Calgary. She has published extensively in the areas of cognition, vision, gaze behaviour and decision making/training. She completed her doctoral degree in psychology at the University of British Columbia. She divides her time between research in the laboratory where the focus is understanding the gaze of motor performers in ecologically valid settings and in the field applying decision training in the coaching setting.

Paul Ward is a Post Doctoral Researcher in the Skill Acquisition Laboratory, Department of Psychology, Mississippi State University. His research focuses upon the study of expert performance and skill acquisition in applied domains. He has a doctoral degree from Liverpool John Moores University and a Masters degree from Manchester Metropolitan University. He received the American Psychological Association, Division 21 (Applied Experimental Psychology) Dissertation Award in 2003 for his doctoral thesis which examined the development of perceptual-cognitive expertise in soccer.

Daniel Weeks is an Associate Professor and Chair of the Department of Psychology, Simon Fraser University. He earned his Ph.D. in experimental psychology from Auburn University. He is interested in spatial cognition and the role of cognitive coding and translation mechanisms in processing spatial information and has an ongoing program of research examining cerebral specialization and information processing in individuals with intellectual challenges. He is a past recipient of the Distinguished Scholar Award from the North American Society for the Psychology of Sport and Physical Activity and in 2003 he received the Distinguished Research Service Award from the Down Syndrome Research Foundation.

A. Mark Williams is Professor of Motor Behaviour at the Research Institute for Sport and Exercise Sciences, Liverpool John Moores University. He has published extensively in the areas of motor expertise, skill acquisition and sport psychology and is currently a member of the Editorial Board for the *International Journal of Sport and Exercise Psychology* and the *Journal of Sports Sciences*. He has been honoured with Early Career Distinguished Scholar Awards by the International Society of Sport Psychology and the North American Society for the Psychology of Sport and Physical Activity.

Gabriele Wulf is an Associate Professor in the Department of Kinesiology at the University of Nevada. She has published extensively in the area of motor learning and serves as a Section Editor for *Research Quarterly for Exercise and Sport* and *Women in Sport and Physical Activity Journal*. She is a Consulting Editor for *Journal of Motor Behavior*, and is an Editorial Board Member for *Human Movement Science*. She also serves as the Secretary/Treasurer of the North American Society for the Psychology of Sport and Physical Activity. In 2001, she received a Research Writing Award from the Research Consortium of the American Alliance for Health, Physical Education, Recreation and Dance.

Preface

The acquisition of perceptual-motor skills is fundamental to human existence. At each stage within the cycle of life, humans continuously strive to acquire new skills or to refine existing ones in the hope that productivity and quality of life is enhanced. This is particularly the case within the domain of sport where individuals are judged almost exclusively by their ability to reproduce such skills, often in a diverse range of performance contexts. Skilled athletes spend many hours practicing and refining these skills with the aim of improving performance and achieving excellence. The practice history profiles of experts in a variety of sports suggest that an investment of over 10,000 hours of practice is required to reach elite levels of performance. It appears that the commitment to engage in practice, and practice itself, are the most important factors in the development of expertise.

Despite the perceived importance of practice, relatively little effort has been devoted to the process of identifying those factors underpinning effective practice or how the acquisition of skills can be facilitated through the instruction process. This fact is particularly disappointing when one considers the amount of time and resources devoted to other factors assumed to be important to performance enhancement in sport, such as physical training, diet and nutrition and mental skills training. Questions relating to practice and instruction have historically been viewed as the preserve of the practitioner, with current practice often driven by intuition and anecdote rather than empirical evidence.

The aim in this book is to partly redress the balance by highlighting the importance of practice and instruction in the acquisition of sports skills. A combination of established authorities and up and coming researchers from around the world provide contemporary reviews within their specific areas of expertise. Attempts are made to integrate current research and theory, highlighting potential avenues for future work and, where applicable, implications for instruction and practice. The book 'kicks off' with a chapter from Jeff Summers, who chronicles the historical development of the field. The material covered provides a useful backdrop to the remaining chapters in the book, putting the ensuing topics into a broader historical context. The book is then divided into three somewhat distinct parts encompassing prevalent theoretical frameworks from the perspectives of information processing, the expertise approach, and ecological/dynamical systems theory. It is acknowledged that there is some overlap and theoretical integration across the parts.

In Part I the authors mainly, but not exclusively, adopt an information-processing theoretical framework. The chapters are further sub-divided into those that focus on the scheduling and organization of practice sessions and those that consider how best to provide instruction and feedback. Timothy Lee and Dominic Simon provide a detailed review of literature on practice scheduling. In particular, they highlight how the phenomenon of contextual interference impacts upon the skill acquisition process. Mike Khan and Ian Franks discuss the importance of specificity within the practice environment and whether different sources of sensory information become more or less important as practice progresses. John Dickinson and colleagues consider whether learning is a cumulative process with gradual improvements in performance as a function of practice or whether it can occasionally be immediate as illustrated by the phenomenon of 'one-trial' learning. Mary Boyle and Phillip Ackerman focus on the importance of individual differences in skill acquisition. They argue that individual differences in abilities, personality, and motivation should be considered when predicting those individuals likely to benefit from systematic training and practice. In the final chapter on the scheduling and organization of practice sessions, Joan Vickers and colleagues outline the decision training approach that they have used to enhance skill acquisition in various sports.

The next group of chapters outline how learning can be facilitated through the provision of instruction and feedback. Gabriele Wulf and Charles Shea examine the importance of augmented feedback in motor learning and, in particular, question the validity of the 'guidance hypothesis' that has governed recent work in this area. Nicola Hodges and Ian Franks examine the theoretical and practical implications of pre-practice information and evaluate the effects of verbal instructions and demonstrations on motor learning in view of these considerations. In a similar vein, Robert Horn and Mark Williams review research and theory relating to observational learning and examine questions surrounding when and how visual information is used to enhance learning. Richard Masters and John Maxwell close the section by considering the relative value of instructional procedures that encourage explicit and implicit processes during skill acquisition and highlight potential difficulties when learners 're-invest' attention in task performance.

In Part II the authors focus more on the acquisition of expert performance, rather than the skill acquisition process per se, although in the sporting domain the acquisition of expertise is generally the desired end product of practice and instruction. The first three chapters provide a theoretical backdrop to the area whereas the final two chapters focus more on application. Paul Ward and colleagues provide a critical overview of deliberate practice theory and its implications for skill acquisition. Janet Starkes and colleagues then address a shortcoming in the study of expertise by proposing a descriptive model to account for the acquisition and retention of perceptual-motor skills. Chris Janelle and colleagues complete the theoretical overview by examining the psychophysiology of attention as related to skill acquisition. Sian Beilock and Thomas Carr adopt a more applied perspective by examining the implications of automaticity for skilled performers and identify the phenomenon of 'expertise-induced amnesia', whereby knowledge becomes more subconscious or automated with increasing levels of skill. Mark Williams and colleagues then provide a critical review of research relating to the trainability of 'game reading' skills in sport.

The chapters presented in Part III consider the merits and potential implications of theoretical perspectives encompassing ideas from ecological psychology/dynamical systems theory and the central notion of behaviour emerging under various constraints. Raoul Huys and colleagues provide a tutorial review of the dynamical systems approach and its relevance to the study of skill acquisition in sport. Using the framework of ecological psychology, Geert Savelsbergh and colleagues explain how freezing, freeing, and exploiting the important couplings between perception and action variables may facilitate the skill acquisition process. Jonathan Shemmell and colleagues then discuss some of the neuromuscular constraints that impact upon motor performance and learning. Finally, Duarte Araújo and colleagues consider the relative merits of a constraints-based perspective on skill acquisition in comparison with more traditional prescriptive approaches.

The book is aimed primarily at academic staff and research students in the sport and movement sciences. The material covered should also be of interest to high-level practitioners within the field and to those undertaking taught courses in the areas of motor learning and motor behaviour. Whilst acknowledging that the main focus of the book is on the acquisition of sports skills, the material presented is of equal value to those involved in the skill acquisition process in other domains such as physical therapy, the armed services and in human factors. The processes involved in (re)learning skills in clinical and work settings are likely to be very similar to those involved in the acquisition of sports skills. The intention is to highlight the vibrancy currently evident within the field and to encourage others to 'take up the mantle' and extend understanding of the important factors underpinning the effective acquisition of sports skills.

A. Mark Williams
Nicola J. Hodges
Research Institute for Sport and Exercise Sciences
Liverpool John Moores University

Acknowledgements

The editors would like to thank all the authors for their contributions to this book. We would also like to acknowledge Mark Scott for his help in reviewing selected chapters and Daniel Eaves for his assistance with copy-editing and proof reading.

A. Mark Williams – to my wife Sara and two sons Thomas and Matthew who continue to inspire and help maintain a sense of perspective. For your patience, love and support I am eternally grateful.

Nicola J. Hodges – to Ian Franks, Tim Lee, Digby Elliott and Janet Starkes my mentors in the field of motor behaviour. These people inspire me through their knowledge and enthusiasm for the area and desire to know and share more with the community. I would also like to thank Stuart, for his love and companionship and his welcomed editorial advice during many months of reviewing and writing. Finally, I dedicate this book to my mum and dad for their unconditional love and support always.

1 A historical perspective on skill acquisition

Jeffery J. Summers

Despite the fact that skilled behaviour underlies nearly every human activity, our understanding of the factors that contribute to attainment of expertise is far from complete. The study of skill learning has a long and somewhat chequered history. Long, in that interest in the acquisition of perceptual-motor skills can be dated back to the late 1800s. Chequered, in the sense that the importance of skill acquisition as a major research agenda item has waxed and waned and its relationship with the sub-field of motor control has at times been quite tenuous. One of the problems inherent in the field has been agreeing on what we regard as a skilled behaviour. While most would agree that a perfectly executed high bar routine in gymnastics is a highly skilled activity that only a few can accomplish, whether a simple action that few cannot achieve, like reaching for a glass is a skilled behaviour is more contentious. The problem is that while the reach and grasp action is a simple automatic action for an adult, it poses a complex motor control problem for a young child.

A further issue in defining the field of study relates to the types of activities that a theory of skilled behaviour should try to explain. Although the primary focus of skills research has been on perceptual-motor skills in which the production of movement is a crucial ingredient, some (e.g. Bartlett, 1958; Proctor and Dutta, 1995; Welford, 1976) have argued that a broad definition of skill should also encompass cognitive activities such as thinking and problem solving. For example, many of the insights into expertise and the development of the expert–novice approach, to be discussed later, have come from studies of chess masters (e.g. Chase and Simon, 1973). However, the skill in chess lies mainly in pattern recognition processes and decision rules rather than in the movements used to shift pieces on the chessboard (Holding, 1985). In the following review of the history of skill learning, the primary concern will be to identify the key concepts/landmarks that shaped our thinking with regard to the acquisition of skill in the sport domain.

The beginnings

Although it is difficult to define the area of skill acquisition and identify a 'founding father', it is clear that for most of its history the field can be regarded as a sub-branch of experimental psychology (Bilodeau and Bilodeau, 1969). It is not surprising, therefore, that Ebbinghaus's (1885/1964) classic work on the rote learning and retention of nonsense syllables provided a framework for the study of skill acquisition. In particular, Ebbinghaus emphasized the examination of learning curves, the distribution of practice sessions, the savings evident in relearning a previously learned list, and transfer of learning from one list to another. These issues also became important research topics in the motor skill acquisition area.

There appears to be general consensus that the earliest formal study of motor skill acquisition can be traced back to the work of Bryan and Harter (1897, 1899) on the sending and receiving of Morse code messages. In a telegraphy task, the sender has to translate a message written in English into Morse code and send it as a series of taps of long and short duration on a telegraph key. The receiver must re-translate the tap series into English and type out the message on a typewriter for the intended recipient. Skill in this task, therefore, relates to the speed with which operators can translate and retranslate between English and Morse code and execute the required key taps.

The work of Bryan and Harter was important in that they studied a real-world skill, compared expert and novice telegraphers and, in the later study, examined the learning curves of several operators over a 40-week practice period. Among the significant findings of their research was that the attainment of expertise in telegraphy requires at least two-and-a-half years, and that skill acquisition proceeds through distinct phases including periods of no improvement (plateaus). In the task of receiving, learning seemed to involve the acquisition of a hierarchy of units from individual letters, to words to phrases. It was suggested that plateaus represent periods of consolidation of lower-order units and the development of automaticity before progress on the higher-level units can be made. Interestingly, the development of automaticity was later to feature as a key concept in information processing models of skill acquisition. Likewise, Bryan and Harter emphasized the examination of variability of motor responses both within a message and, more importantly, across repetitions of the same message by an operator. Low repetition variability was seen as a characteristic of the expert performer. As discussed later in this chapter, the issue of performance variability is again seen as a key factor in understanding motor control and learning by current proponents of the dynamical systems perspective (see Newell and Corcos, 1993; Riley and Turvey, 2002).

Although subsequent research on the acquisition of typing (Book, 1908/1925) showed similar learning curves to those obtained for telegraphy, the meaning of performance plateaus (i.e. motivational, due to measurement, result of resource limitations) and their existence for other skills has been topic of considerable debate. What is undeniable, however, is the influence of Bryan and Harter's work on subsequent and current research on skilled performance (see Lee and Swinnen, 1993).

The early period of motor skills research extended from 1880 to 1940 (Adams, 1987). This period also included the classic research of Woodworth (1899) analysing simple repetitive movements (for a recent evaluation of Woodworth's contribution, see Elliott *et al.*, 2001). In the discipline of psychology the writings of Thorndike (1874–1949), the father of instrumental learning, on the role of reward in strengthening behaviour (Law of Effect) stimulated interest in the use of error information (knowledge of results) to enhance motor learning. For example, in a study by Woodworth involving the drawing of lines of specific lengths by blindfolded participants, the provision of simple 'right' or 'wrong' feedback after each movement dramatically improved performance. Mere repetition without knowledge of results (KR) showed no improvement in accuracy over the drawing of 5,400 lines. A detailed investigation of the form and timing of KR for the optimal learning of motor skills, however, had to wait until the 1970s when the first independent models of the motor learning process were proposed (e.g. Adams, 1971).

Another issue that has become of major importance within motor learning theories, to which Thorndike also gave impetus, is transfer of training. In applied research the degree to which the learning of skills in one situation (e.g. flight simulator) influences/transfers to another situation (e.g. flying a plane) is the key issue in determining the worth of a training programme. Thorndike argued that transfer only occurs when there are identical elements in the two situations. A related aspect of transfer to which later researchers would devote considerable effort was part–whole task transfer. That is, whether some tasks may be best learned by breaking them down into sub-tasks that are practised before the whole task is attempted.

Although little systematic work in skill acquisition was conducted during the early period, many of the issues that still occupy the minds of researchers were formulated. These include KR, practice scheduling and transfer of training (for a detailed discussion of these and other issues, see Adams, 1987). The area of skill acquisition remained fairly dormant until the advent of the Second World War brought with it the need for the selection and training of military personnel and a renewed interest in the learning of motor skills. During the period 1940–1970, labelled by Adams (1987) as the Middle Period, much of the research was task-centred and continued to investigate the influence of various practice variables (e.g. scheduling of knowledge of results, distribution of practice sessions). Tracking, involving the following of a target with a cursor, became an exemplar task for study. It allowed for a detailed examination of eye–hand coordination, a skill fundamental to many real-world activities such as flying an aircraft, steering a boat or driving a car (see Poulton, 1974).

Of particular note during this period were the supposed insights into understanding human behaviour gained through the adoption into psychology of theoretical perspectives from other domains, particularly engineering and computer science. The research orientation in the early part of the period, however, was strongly influenced by the publication of Hull's (1943) general learning theory in the book *Principles of Behaviour*. The work in the behaviourist tradition covered both animal and human learning through the process of conditioning and emphasized the build up of inhibitory-like processes during long practice periods. Within the field of motor skills, Hull's predictions stimulated numerous studies examining the influence of various practice schedules on inhibitory and recovery processes during skill learning. For example, it was speculated that having practice periods close together with no or brief rest intervals in between (massed practice) leads to the build up of inhibitory or fatigue-like processes that impair performance. In contrast, performance is better when long periods of rest are inserted between practice periods (distributed practice) because the inhibition has time to dissipate. Although the research indicated that distributed practice produces better performance (but not learning) than massed practice, by the 1960s Hull's theory had been shown to be an inadequate description of motor skill learning and his ideas are rarely cited in current literature.

There were, however, two more enduring ideas that stem from this period. Both can be seen as consequences of the rapid advances associated with the war years in technology and the development of mechanisms for the control of complex systems. In this context, conceiving of human behaviour as the output of a complex machine seemed a profitable avenue to pursue. Craik (1948) in England was the first to propose that the brain should be considered as a type of computer in which information is received, processed, and output in the form of overt actions. He also suggested that the human, because of limitations in processing information, was not able to respond continuously but rather in discrete bursts, the idea of *central intermittency*. A number of aspects of human behaviour are consistent with the intermittency notion such as the delay in responding to the second of two closely spaced signals, known as the *psychological refractory period* (PRP). To explain the PRP and related phenomena, Welford (1952, 1967) proposed the *single-channel hypothesis* for processing (attending) to information. The brain–computer metaphor and the development of a mathematical theory of communication (information theory) by Shannon and Weaver (1949) provided the conceptual framework for a view of the human organism as an information-processing system with limited channel capacity. The information-processing models that had their beginnings in the late 1950s went on to dominate the psychological and skill acquisition literature in the 1970s and 1980s and still maintain a significant influence in the field today.

The second important 'discovery' in another domain that became incorporated into the psychology of learning was the closed-loop system. Originating in engineering as servo theory and termed cybernetics by Wiener (1948), the feedback control system or servo mechanism became a useful model in the training of pilots, gunners and operators of other complex machines. The main feature of the servo mechanism idea is that such systems possess a controlling or error detection device capable of continuously monitoring the state of the system for discrepancies between a desired and the present state and automatically correcting for any discrepancy or error. Under this view, motor behaviour is conceived as essentially an error-nulling activity. The operation of a thermostat controlling the heating of a house is the usual analogy made for this type of control (see Figure 1.1). The application of servo mechanism principles from engineering to the human system led to the view that a central component of skill learning is the development of

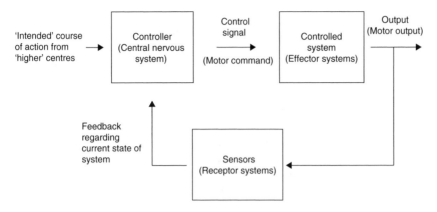

Figure 1.1 A closed-loop control system (adapted from Kelso, 1982a).

the capability to detect and correct errors. Not surprisingly, the importance of feedback processes in closed-loop models of learning re-vitalized research on knowledge of results and provided the foundation for the first major theory of learning (Adams, 1971) specifically focused on motor skills.

Brief mention should be made of other observations from that time that continue to influence research and theorizing about motor learning. One observation was that performance on most tasks appears to improve indefinitely with the greatest performance gains being evident early in practice. Snoddy (1926) was the first to recognize that learning could be described as a power function and proposed the general learning equation: $\log C = \log B + n \log x$, where C is a measure of performance, x is the number of trials or time on task, and B and n are constants. This relationship was observed in many studies and became known as the power law of practice. Perhaps the most famous 'real-world' example of the power law was Crossman's (1959) study of the operation of a cigar-making machine. Plotting the log speed of operation of the machine against the log number of cigars produced resulted in a straight line of improvement up to three million cigars or about 2 years on the job. The machine's minimum cycle time, rather than limitations in human performance however, limited further improvement in performance time in this task. The existence and interpretation of the power law of practice is still a matter of debate today (e.g. Heathcote *et al.*, 2000).

Another important observation made around the turn of the century by William James (1890) was that we should distinguish between skills, such as walking, that are under automatic control (i.e. require little mental effort) and those activities that demand high levels of concentration for their execution as when the diver performs a high difficulty triple somersault. The role of attentional processes in skill acquisition and, in particular, the development of automaticity through practice became key issues in information processing models of motor learning.

One final strand of research worth mentioning that gained impetus during the Second World War and has had some influence on the thinking about skill acquisition was the research of E. A. Fleishman on individual differences and learning. The initial work was concerned with designing new motor tests to improve personnel selection in the US Air Force. Using a factor-analytic approach, Fleishman (1953, 1956) administered a battery of tasks measuring different skills to hundreds of participants, usually airmen, and examined patterns of correlations between the tasks. Fleishman identified some eighteen psychomotor and physical proficiency factors or 'abilities' that underlie the performance of most tasks. Most important, for skill learning, was the finding that the number of factors contributing significantly to performance decreases from early to late in practice and also the nature of the factors changes from perceptual to motor abilities (e.g. Fleishman and Hempel, 1954, 1955). For example, while visual abilities appear important early in practice, kinesthetic abilities become more dominant as practice progresses. Whether the change from external (visual) to internal (kinesthetic) control with training is the normal process of skill learning, has been a subject of considerable debate. Proteau (1992), for example, has argued that the role of visual feedback does not diminish with practice. Criticisms of the factor-analytic methodology used in identifying human abilities, however, has limited the impact of Fleishman's ability taxonomies (see Adams, 1987). The notion that there are small sets of general abilities underlying motor expertise has been revived from time to time in more recent research. Keele and Hawkins (1982), for example, searched unsuccessfully for the existence of attention-related abilities, such as time-sharing and attentional flexibility, as components of highly skilled performance. Likewise, Jones (1993) in his modular approach to skill acquisition suggested that, in addition to the amount of task-specific practice, the level of performance ultimately achieved in a task may be determined by individual differences in a small number of abilities controlled by different modules (anatomically distinct neural computations) in the brain. Some experimental support was outlined for modular functions identified as sequencing, timing and force regulation with general coordination and attention switching abilities being proposed also for complex tasks.

It's all in the head

While the 1960s were a time of rapid change in experimental psychology, interest in skill learning declined as many psychologists became preoccupied with other topics more central to the upcoming 'cognitive revolution'. The somewhat sombre mood of motor behaviour psychologists of the time was captured in the *Acquisition of Skill*, a volume edited by E. A. Bilodeau (1966). However, as the number of psychologists in the area declined, an important factor in the future development of motor learning research occurred. This was the expansion of physical education and doctoral research programmes in the university and college sector in the United States and the United Kingdom. Under the leadership of F. M. Henry, A. W. Hubbard and A. T. Slater-Hammel, the study of motor behaviour as a laboratory science became a popular research topic for graduate students. Naturally, there was greater concern for the study of gross motor tasks and activities that appeared direct correlates of skills required in sports. Particularly noteworthy during the late 1960s and early 1970s was the publication of a number of textbooks written for physical education students and teachers. These included in the United Kingdom, books by Knapp (*Skill in Sport*, 1963) and Whiting (*Acquiring Ball Skill*, 1969), and in the United States, works by Cratty (*Movement Behaviour and Motor Learning*, 1964) and Singer (*Motor Learning and Human Performance*, 1968). The research and models of motor behaviour, however, were still strongly influenced by the theoretical frameworks and methodology being adopted in experimental psychology.

The information-processing perspective

Growing dissatisfaction with the ability of the behaviourist approach to deal with higher mental processes led to the rise in experimental psychology of the cognitive information-processing approach, based on the brain–computer analogy first coined by Craik (1948). Ulric Neisser's (1967) book *Cognitive Psychology* opened the door to the study of those aspects of human behaviour such as attention, memory and decision making previously denied by the behaviourist tradition. A basic assumption of this approach is that the processing of information occurs through discrete stages that can be isolated and studied through appropriate chronometric methods. Using flow-diagram techniques borrowed from computer programming, the flow of information is typically traced through three primary stages involving perceptual processes, decision making and response selection and response programming and execution. An attentional system responsible for selecting between sources of information for further processing and memory systems (long-term and short-term or working memory) for the storage of information are also part of most information-processing models (see Figure 1.2).

This general framework has dominated experimental psychology for the past thirty or so years. It has also led to compartmentalization of the study of human behaviour into the areas of perception, cognitive processes and motor processes. Few cognitive psychology texts, for example, contain chapters on motor skills. As a consequence of this separation, the linking of perception to action was rarely dealt with or assigned to a homunculus-like entity termed the 'executive'. The study of skill acquisition within the information-processing framework assumed that similar cognitive processes underlie the learning of motor skills as for other skills such as language and chess. Accordingly, Posner and Keele (1973) argued that the central issue in the study of skilled movements:

> becomes how the laborious, conscious movements of the novice come to be performed with a minimal involvement of attention. What changes as skill learning progresses and when and how are central attentional mechanisms brought into the control of highly skilled movements?
>
> (Posner and Keele, 1973, p. 806)

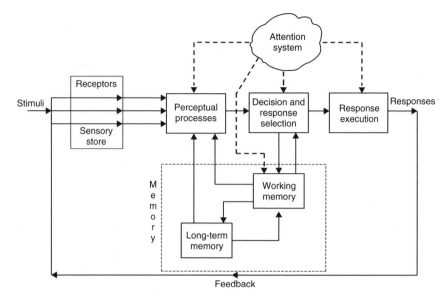

Figure 1.2 A generic information-processing model (adapted from Wickens, 1992).

The approach emphasizes internal mental processes involved in the control of skill. Although these processes cannot be directly observed, it is argued that there are two basic limitations of information processing that can be measured. These are the limitations of time and space (Keele, 1973). All processes involved in the control of movement take time and they may also take space within a limited capacity central attention system (Posner and Keele, 1973). While reaction time and movement time measures are used to study the temporal aspect of skill, interference techniques, such as dual-task performance assess the space demands of activities. With regard to skill acquisition, a basic premise is that the skilled performer has found some way of overcoming or circumventing the limitations on human performance.

During the 1960s and 1970s the unquestioning adoption of information-processing models from cognitive psychology lead to the proliferation of studies on issues such as short-term motor memory, the planning (pre-programming) of simple movements using reaction time methodology and the attentional demands of movement. A second influence operating against skill learning research came from the growing interest in issues of motor control, rather than learning, among movement scientists located in physical education departments. Partly driven by the development and limitations of techniques for the recording and analysing movements, such as muscle activity through electromyography and kinematics derived from three-dimensional motion analysis systems, movement scientists focused on the elementary control processes underlying simple, often one-dimensional, movements. The expansion of research activity in motor control, particularly at the university level in the United States, lead to the founding by Richard Schmidt in 1969 of the first specialist journal in the field, the *Journal of Motor Behavior*. In the United Kingdom, John Whiting launched the *Journal of Human Movement Studies* in 1972. Despite the growth in the movement behaviour field, some reviews of motor learning research have argued that neither motor control, 'a child of physiology' (Adams, 1987, p. 41), nor information processing, based on a digital computer analogy, contributed much of substance to the understanding of skill learning.

Certainly, issues of motor control in the form of the centralist–peripheralist (open-loop versus closed-loop) debate dominated the early 1970s. The debate centred on the relative importance of pre-planned efferent commands and ongoing afferent information in the control of movement. As with many similar 'strawman' debates in psychology (e.g. early versus late selection models of attention), it eventually became acknowledged that both open-loop and closed-loop processes are involved in motor control and their relative contribution depends on a number of factors including the type of movement and stage of learning. The debate, however, did produce the first theories to emerge from psychology devoted to explaining motor learning. Of particular importance were Adams' (1971) closed-loop theory, Keele's (1968) motor program model and Schmidt's (1975) schema theory. Adams' theory emphasized the role of response-produced feedback and knowledge of results in the detection and correction of errors, a capability that was seen as central to the learning process. Although the theory generated a great deal of research, it had limited appeal as it only dealt with the learning of slow positioning movements. Motor program theory, in contrast, was particularly concerned with the representation and execution of well-learned sequences of movements and the possibility that such sequences could be produced in open-loop mode. Implicit in early motor program models (e.g. Keele, 1968) was a one-to-one mapping between stored programs and specific movements making the storage of programs within the limited capacity human memory system a problem. Schema theory attempted to incorporate both closed- and open-loop modes of control and to overcome the storage problem by borrowing from memory and perception research the concept of the schema (Bartlett, 1932). In Schmidt's model a generalized motor program was, like the schema, an abstract representational structure containing the general characteristics of a class of movements. Although more encompassing than Adams' theory, schema theory was primarily a model of discrete motor skill learning and provoked much laboratory research using simple motor tasks that seemed to have little immediate relevance to sport scientists.

While the theories differed mainly in regard to the extent that feedback information is essential for the ongoing control of movement, they all share basic assumptions from psychological theory of the time. The first was the adoption of the cybernetic analogy between human behaviour and servo mechanisms described earlier. That is, a central component of the three models was a comparator system in which the intended outcome is compared with the actual output achieved with any resulting discrepancy being used in the control of future behaviour. The similarity in the 'architecture' of Adams closed-loop theory and Keele's motor program model can be seen in Figure 1.3. Both models contain a referent or model (the template or perceptual trace) specifying the sensory consequences of performing the skill correctly. Inherent in both models is some sort of transducer mechanism that compares the intended with the actual consequences and feeds back any resulting error into the controlling system. In the Keele model, the system that generates movements (the motor program) and the system that evaluates feedback (the template) are seen as separable entities. Implications of the dual representation of movement include; the execution of a highly learned skill in open-loop mode, the use of an artificial template and feedback source (e.g. loop films and videotape feedback) to establish a motor program, and the establishment of the template before actually performing the skill through the use of mental practice (for details, see Keele, 1977; Keele and Summers, 1976).

The second major influence on the models of motor learning developed in the 1970s, was the notion of the hierarchical organization of behaviour. This view of behaviour stemmed from the analogy between the human and computer in which higher-order (executive) programs control lower-order sub-routines and Miller *et al.*'s (1960) notions of plans as the basis of human activity. The plan or executive program was seen as containing a hierarchically ordered set of instructions represented at a high level in the brain. In the spirit of Miller *et al.*, models of skill acquisition placed great emphasis on the development of plans incorporating at the highest level a broad plan of action representing the goal and various operations involved in the skill. The plan is then broken down into

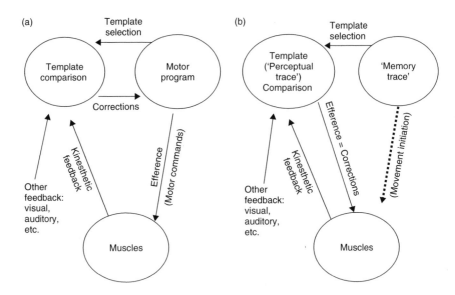

Figure 1.3 Comparison between (a) a motor program model (Keele and Summers, 1976) and (b) a closed-loop model (Adams, 1971) [from Neill, W. T. (1977). Input and output coding in motor control: a review. *Unpublished manuscript, University of Oregon*].

the sequence of specific components or sub-routines that allow the plan to be executed. For example, making an overhead smash in tennis could be broken down into the grip, stance, back-swing, forward swing, contact and follow-through. At the next lower level the operations involved in the execution of each component in the sequence can be specified, such as the actions of the arm, shoulders, hips and legs in the forward-swing component. Each of these operations could then be broken down into even more basic movements if desired. The adoption of the computer analogy and principles of hierarchical organization also had implications for the teaching of skills. It was advised, for example, that instructors should first break down a skill into its hierarchically organized elements and then begin the learner at a level in the hierarchy commensurate with their past experience (Marteniuk, 1976). Progression to the next more complex level of the hierarchy occurs once the operations at the lower level have been mastered, much as Bryan and Harter (1897) had proposed.

The concepts imported from the disciplines of engineering and computer science, that human behaviour involves an error-nulling mechanism and is hierarchically organized, have dominated models of movement behaviour through the 1970s and 1980s. Attempts were also made to map the terminology of executive programs and sub-routines onto central nervous system structures (e.g. Paillard, 1960; Requin *et al.*, 1984). Hierarchical, multilevel control was especially predominant in models of cognitive motor skills such as handwriting, typing, speech and musical performance (Mackay, 1982; Rumelhart and Norman, 1982; Shaffer, 1980; van Galen, 1980). The motor program itself became viewed as a multilevel system in which an abstract representation of the skill at the highest level is elaborated into its more specific components at lower levels (e.g. Keele, 1981). An advantage of multilevel control is to reduce the computational burden of higher control centres by allowing the details of movements to be specified by lower-level organizational units. The programming process was seen as the selection, ordering, timing and parameterization of autonomous subsystems such as reflexes (Easton, 1972). Identifying those features of movements that are contained in the abstract representation at the highest level and those that are the mutable parameters specified at lower levels became the main research issue for proponents of the motor programming perspective during the 1980s and remains a topic of current interest. For example, Schmidt and colleagues have proposed that skills involving a sequence of movements (e.g. serving in tennis) are composed of a string of programs or units of action, a unit being a segment of behaviour that exhibits relative timing, can be used repeatedly in a variety of skills, and be scaled to the environmental context. In a series of studies involving coincident-timing and bimanual coordination tasks, such units of action have been identified by examining, within each participant over trials, correlations or covariances among intervals designated as landmarks in an action (see Schmidt *et al.*, 1998).

While the establishment of a motor program has been regarded as the end-state of the learning process, with the exception of Keele and Summers (1976), little discussion has been devoted to how motor programs are learned (see also Summers, 1981). Rather motor program theorists seemed to adhere to the three-stage model of skill acquisition proposed by Paul Fitts in 1964. He argued that skill learning was a continuous process with gradual shifts in the nature of the processes as learning progresses. In the spirit of Bryan and Harter (1899), the learning process was characterized by the organization of behaviour into larger and larger units. Fitts proposed that the learner moves through three general phases in the learning of a skill. In the early or cognitive stage the learner attempts to understand the task requirements through watching someone perform the skill and verbal instructions. Performance is quite variable during this phase as the learner tries out different performance strategies. In the intermediate or associative stage, the movement patterns are refined, errors are reduced and verbal mediation of movements is diminished. This stage can last for varying periods of time depending on the complexity of the skill to be learned and the adoption of optimal practice conditions for skill acquisition. The final or autonomous phase is achieved after extensive practice and is characterized by the performance of the skill with minimal mental effort (i.e. automatically). A skilled soccer player, therefore, can dribble the ball without needing to attend to this activity and can concentrate on whether the next action should be to pass the ball (where and to whom), shoot or continue dribbling. In the motor domain, the development of automaticity was associated with the establishment of a motor program. For example, Keele (1973) in his 'gearshift analogy' suggested that motor programs/automaticity might be achieved by chaining together over practice small units of behaviour that eventually become controlled as a single unit, much as appears to happen when learning to shift gears in a car.

Because of the general nature of Fitts' description of skill learning, little research has been generated to directly test the model. The basic assumption of three phases leading to the development of automaticity, however, has been incorporated into most information-processing models of skill learning. For example, Anderson's (1982) framework for the acquisition of cognitive skills had three stages similar to those of Fitts. The first stage involves the formation of declarative knowledge (i.e. facts and information about the skill); a second transition stage in which declarative knowledge is converted into a set of productions (i.e. condition–action pairs); and a final procedural stage involving the refining and strengthening of the productions.

Bring in the experts

Although the information-processing approach has prompted extensive research into the factors that influence motor skill learning, such as the type and scheduling of practice sessions (see Schmidt and Bjork, 1992), much of this work has limited application to the acquisition of sports skills. To a large extent this was due to the adoption of research paradigms from experimental psychology that emphasized carefully controlled laboratory experiments involving simple 'novel' tasks (e.g. unidirectional arm movements, sequences of finger movements, tracking). Furthermore, because of the use of simple tasks and the research philosophy of testing large numbers of participants to 'control' for individual differences in past learning experiences, very few studies examined changes in performance over long practice periods.

To overcome the limitations of the laboratory-based approach to skill learning some cognitive psychologists began studying expert performance in real-life domains. The study of expert–novice differences and how the knowledge and strategies exhibited by experts are acquired promised new insights into the skill acquisition process. The impetus for this direction came from a classic study by Chase and Simon (1973) of expert/novice distinctions in the game of chess. In this study, chess players of different skill levels were briefly (5 seconds) shown chessboards with the pieces arranged from the middle of a real chess game or randomly distributed across the board. Following removal of the board from view, the players attempted to reconstruct the arrangement of the pieces. As expected, chess experts were able to recall more accurately the positions of the chess pieces from real games. However, on recall of the randomly arranged boards experts performed slightly worse than novices, indicating the highly specific nature of expertise. The methodology and findings have been replicated across a variety of sports including basketball, volleyball, football and field hockey (see Ericsson and Lehmann, 1996), leading to the view that 'sport experts possess cognitive skills very similar to experts in other skill domains...' (Allard and Burnett, 1985, p. 295). Thus, experts are able to easily perceive and recall complex, meaningful patterns within their domain. This ability, however, is not due to a superior memory capacity but rather to use of strategies such as chunking to encode information into large meaningful units.

The cognitive expert–novice approach has also generated a great deal of research into how sport experts overcome the limitations of time on human performance. Given that experts and non-experts do not differ on measures of basic reaction time, it has been assumed that in sports requiring fast reactions skilled performers have developed an ability to recognize advanced cues in the environment allowing for anticipation of what will happen next and thereby reducing processing time. To examine this issue numerous studies have attempted to identify the cues used for anticipation by experts in a variety of racket and team sports (for a review, see Cauraugh and Janelle, 2002; Williams *et al.*, 1999). In this research, occlusion techniques have typically been used in which expert and novice players watch a film or video sequence of a particular activity (e.g. an opponent executing a squash shot) and the film is stopped at a particular point (temporal occlusion) or a particular cue (e.g. racket arm) is blanked out (see Abernethy, 1991). The task is to indicate the landing position of the ball. Another technique has been to use eye movement recording devices to analyse visual search patterns to determine whether experts fixate on different parts of the visual display than novices. In general, this research has shown that experts pick up earlier advanced cues and exhibit different visual search patterns than novices (see Williams *et al.*, 1999).

As McLeod and Jenkins (1991) aptly noted, however, the finding of expert–novice differences in these laboratory tasks is to be expected but what is surprising is that the effects are quite small given the vast differences in skill level of the participants in the studies. Sport scientists were encouraged not to engage in an endless stream of studies examining expert–novice differences in every sport possible, but rather to focus on determining whether the cognitive strategy differences identified are sufficient to account for expertise. In recent years the criticisms and concerns about the ecological validity of the early occlusion studies have led researchers to seek more realistic techniques, such as life-size interactive video displays involving activity related motor responses by the subject and the tracking of eye movements during actual sport situations (for reviews of recent work, see Davids *et al.*, 2002; Williams *et al.*, 1999).

Deliberate practice theory

Taking the study of skill acquisition out of the laboratory and into the real world highlighted the importance of practice in the attainment of expertise. It has been argued that at least 10 years of intensive practice is needed to become an expert in a variety of cognitive and physical skills. The most extreme version of the practice hypothesis was put forward by Ericsson and colleagues (e.g. Ericsson *et al.*, 1993; Ericsson and Charness, 1994) based on an in-depth study of skilled and lesser-skilled individuals in the music domain. Similarities in the practice profiles of violinists and pianists led to the general conclusion that experts in many domains are characterized as individuals that started practice at an early age and continued to maintain a high level of daily domain specific practice throughout their career. In deliberate practice theory innate abilities play little role in determining who will become an 'expert', rather the level of performance obtained by an individual is monotonically related to the cumulative amount of time spent undertaking deliberate practice. Deliberate practice is defined as any activity designed to improve the current level of performance (Ericsson *et al.*, 1993). It is also practice that is active, effortful and not intrinsically enjoyable. Although not explicitly stated, the theory seems to share with other cognitive models the assumption that the acquisition of expertise involves the development, through deliberate practice, of domain-specific knowledge structures.

Deliberate practice theory has considerable intuitive appeal and has enjoyed some success in its application to the sport domain (see Starkes, 2000). One concern with the theory, however, is its reliance on retrospective estimates of the amount of time spent engaged in deliberate practice during an experts' career. A direct relationship between expertise and the actual amount of deliberate practice has not been demonstrated and retrospective estimates have been shown to be subject to inflation bias (for further problems, see Davids, 2000). Perhaps, the major concern with the theory is its lack of clear testable assumptions. As such it shares similar status to other 'non-disconfirmable' theories, such as multiple resource theory in the attention field.

Coupling perception to action

Without doubt the greatest impact on notions of skill acquisition in recent times has come from the emergence of the ecological approach to perception and action that, to some, placed the motor control and learning field in the midst of a full scale paradigm crisis (see Abernethy and Sparrow, 1992; Meijer and Roth, 1988; Summers, 1992). The ecological approach developed partly in response to the perceived inadequacies of the cognitive approach to explain movement behaviour without invoking the concept of a homunculus-like 'executive' who selects motor programs from a 'library' (memory) and then orchestrates movements on a cortical keyboard. That is, 'when trying to explain how it is that a person, can for instance, play tennis, you do not want in your explanation a person inside the head playing tennis' (Turvey *et al.*, 1982, p. 243). Researchers were admonished to 'trim down the homunculus' in their models of control and coordination of movement and to stoically defend the principle of ecological realism (Turvey and Carello, 1981). The ecological approach sees skill as an emergent consequence of the direct mapping between the biomechanical system and environment information, rather than residing in the acquisition of internal knowledge structures.

In the early 1980s, a series of seminal papers outlining the philosophical underpinning and agenda of the ecological approach were produced by three researchers working in Haskins Laboratories, University of Conneticut; Peter Kugler, Michael Turvey and Scott Kelso (Kelso *et al.*, 1981; Kugler *et al.*, 1980, 1982; Turvey and Kugler, 1984).

> The ecological approach to perception and action incorporates psychology as a companion endeavor to physics and biology for the purpose of studying the epistemological relationship between an animal, as agent and perceiver, and its environment. The goal of a theory of action and perception is to explicate the organizational principles relating animal and environment on the basis of energy and informational transactions.
>
> (Kugler *et al.*, 1982, p. 69)

It is interesting to note that as with the previous shift from the behaviourist to the cognitive approach, the 'new' paradigm shift has been precipitated by the importing of ideas and concepts from other fields of science, in this case mathematics, biology and physics. In order to solve the homunculus problem proponents of the ecological approach have turned to the writings of Nicolai Bernstein (1896–1966) on movement coordination and James Gibson (1904–1979) on direct perception. Bernstein (1967) coined the now famous 'degrees of freedom problem' suggesting that the central issue for any theory of motor control is to account for how the multiple degrees of freedom (i.e. the separate independent dimensions that are free to vary, such as joints, muscles and limbs) of the motor system are regulated during the course of action. To solve the degrees of freedom problem, the concept of constraint was introduced. Constraints are seen as boundaries or features that limit the number of states or configurations that a dynamical system can take at any one time. On the motor side, for example, to keep the degrees of freedom that need to be individually controlled to a minimum, elements in the system are linked together into autonomous self-regulating task specific functional units. These units were called coordinative structures, defined as 'a group of muscles often spanning several joints that is constrained to act as a single functional unit' (Tuller *et al.*, 1982, p. 253). The development of a task-specific coordinative structure, therefore, was seen as an important part of the skill learning process. A key theoretical advance in providing a mechanism by which the coordination between coordinative structures can be achieved for 'free' without mediation by an executive was the modelling of the functional units as non-linear limit-cycle oscillators. Such oscillatory systems exhibit self-sustaining properties and when they interact they mutually synchronize or entrain each other. To illustrate the existence of self-organization in biological systems, the early writers used compelling examples such as horses changing gaits (Tuller *et al.*, 1982), termites building mounds (Kugler, 1986) and fish schooling (Kelso, 1982b).

To address the problem of linking perception to action, that is, how perceptual information modulates coordinative structures without the intervention of a homunculus-like entity, proponents of the ecological approach have incorporated concepts from direct perception theory. Gibson (1979) argued that energy patterns (perceptual flow fields) within the environment provide information directly and unambiguously about the layout of the environment (e.g. objects, surfaces and edges) and about the environment in relation to movement of the perceiver. Our perceptual systems become sensitive to higher-order properties (invariants) of the environment that remain constant across changes associated with the perceiver, the environment or both. For example, one higher-order invariant of the visual flow field, termed the optic array, that has received a great deal of attention and current debate is the time-to-contact (*tau*) between an object and an observer (e.g. Lee, 1976, 1980; Tresilian, 1999). Gibson further argued that rather than perceiving directly the invariant energy patterns in the environment, the organism perceives the affordances between objects or events (Gibson, 1979). As affordances represent the possibilities for action in the environment, they are not exclusively a property of the perceiver or the environment but result from their interaction. According to the direct perception perspective, it is the energy patterns specifying affordances (termed *information*) that are detected by the perceptual systems and underlie the coupling of actions to objects and events (Michaels, 1993). The affordance concept has been, and continues to be, the topic of much discussion ranging from labelling it '...a pure cheat: an attempt to have all the goodness of intentionality without paying any of the price' (Fodor, 1980, p. 107), to discussing whether affordances and events are qualitatively distinct properties (Stoffregen, 2000).

In terms of the skill acquisition process, ecological theorists have suggested a three-stage process dealing with the degrees of freedom problem comprising *coordination*, *control* and *skill*. In the first stage, the learner attempts to gain control over the redundant degrees of freedom produced by movement of the various body parts. Initially, the learner solves this problem by the freezing of degrees of freedom, keeping as much of the body as possible rigid, leading to inflexible and inefficient performance. Eventually, coordination is achieved through the constraining of the degrees of freedom into a temporary coordinative structure in which a few parameters are free to vary. The establishment of the basic movement pattern leads to the control phase in which the free parameters are manipulated, the appropriate *control parameters* that drive the system through its stable states are discovered, and the tuning of the interface between perception and action occurs. The attainment of skill is characterized by the exploitation of non-muscular reactive forces by the performer and the ability to flexibly adapt to changes in environmental conditions and task goals.

The most influential general framework for examining skill acquisition from an ecological perspective was presented by Newell (1986). As shown in Figure 1.4, this constraints-led view suggests that motor learning is a function of the interaction between constraints arising within the organism (e.g. intrinsic dynamics, anxiety), in the environment (e.g. perceptual flow fields) and in the task (e.g. goals, rules). The learning process involves a search for an appropriate solution to the specific task demands through a perceptual-motor workspace, which is constrained by the three sources of constraints. Implications of this general framework for the analysis of sports skills and the role of the teacher/coach in the learning process have been of great interest to sports scientists (see Davids *et al.*, 2002).

In recent years, differences in how the relation between perception and action should be conceptualized have led to the emergence of a bifurcation between researchers remaining within the ecological psychology umbrella and researchers adopting dynamical systems theory. Those researchers adhering to the tenets of ecological psychology have been primarily concerned with identifying the key 'higher-order' invariants available in the structured energy gradients of perceptual flow fields (optical, acoustic, haptic) that constrain movements (i.e. environmental constraints) (e.g. Turvey, 1996; Warren, 1998). Although the dynamical approach emerged from the ecological movement, its ecological pedigree has been questioned (Carson, 1998; Pressing, 1998). Dynamical systems theory applies the concepts and tools of non-linear dynamics to study the stability properties of self-organized movement patterns. The approach is ostensibly phenomenological, as through the language of dynamics it is hoped to identify general laws and principles that operate across levels of analysis (metabolic, neural, biomechanical,

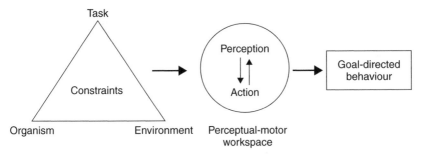

Figure 1.4 Skill acquisition from a constraints-led perspective (adapted from Newell and McDonald, 1994).

psychological) and movement systems with different architectures and structures (see Beek *et al.*, 1995; Haken, 1990; Kelso, 1995). It has enjoyed considerable success in describing inter-limb coordination dynamics and the identification of intrinsic constraints (or attractor states) that an individual brings to the learning situation. Skill learning is seen as behavioural information, specifying the to-be-learned pattern, acting on (cooperating or competing with) the already existing behavioural patterns (intrinsic dynamics). The approach has been criticized for its failure to examine how neuromuscular–skeletal constraints influence the behavioural dynamics (Carson, 1998) and its inability to account for the cognitively mediated aspects of skill learning, such as strategic planning, decision making, attention, mental and observational practice (Summers, 1998; Wulf *et al.*, 1999). It remains to be seen whether this radically different approach to the study of motor behaviour can deliver its promise as an all-encompassing theory of perception and action.

Where to from here?

Abernethy and Sparrow (1992) predicted that the motor control and learning field was in for protracted period of paradigmatic debate and division. They further argued that reconciliation between the two approaches seemed unlikely as hybridization could only meaningfully be achieved by some compromise of their conceptual and philosophical differences. At that time it was acknowledged that the difficulty for the ecological perspective would be to provide a unified theory of learning devoid of cognitive constructs such as representation and memory. Ingvaldsen and Whiting (1997) even suggested that the marrying of Skinnerian principles of operant conditioning with the dynamical systems approach may allow for a more complete explanation of motor skill learning without the need to incorporate representations.

In the ensuing ten years, there has been a growing interest in examining the link between cognition and dynamics. To some researchers this has involved incorporating concepts and methods from cognitive psychology into the dynamical paradigm, such as using dual-task methodology to examine the role of attention (mental effort) in stabilizing coordination patterns (e.g. Summers *et al.*, 1998; Temprado *et al.*, 1999). Other researchers have been concerned with remapping cognitive constructs into the language of dynamics, that is, into the development of cognitive dynamics. For example, the concept of intention has been described as a specific perturbation or supplementary force that can modulate or override the intrinsic dynamics and move the system towards a desired attractor (e.g. Davids and Button, 2000).

The last decade has also seen the beginning of a systematic attempt by researchers working within an ecological psychology/dynamical systems framework to build a comprehensive theory of motor skill learning that has specific implications for practice organization. In the area of coordination dynamics, the research has largely focused on the learning of single-degree-of-freedom rhythmic bimanual coordination patterns (e.g. Kelso and Zanone, 2002; Summers *et al.*, 2003; Zanone and Kelso, 1992, 1997). A key feature of this work has been the recognition that all learning occurs against a background of existing capabilities. Of particular interest, therefore, has been the mapping of an individual's attractor landscape prior to learning and monitoring changes to the landscape during the learning of a 'new' coordination pattern. The attractor landscape is like a movement signature reflecting a person's behavioural history and pre-existing abilities that are brought to the learning situation. This research has clearly illustrated the influence of constraints within the learner (intrinsic dynamics) on the acquisition of new coordinations and vice versa.

With regard to the acquisition of multiple-degree-of-freedom movements that are typical in sports skills, the bringing together of concepts from ecological psychology and dynamical systems theory within a constraints-led perspective is promising. Davids and colleagues, in particular, have invoked an interdisciplinary neo-Darwinian perspective to understand how various interacting constraints within the individual, the task, and the environment influence the emergence of functional muscle synergies in the neuro-skeletomuscular system to solve the task problem (e.g. Davids *et al.*, 1999). In the spirit of Newell's (1986) model (see Figure 1.4), learning is seen as a process of searching through a perceptual-motor landscape shaped by the interacting constraints and selecting appropriate goal-directed patterns of behaviour. The role of the instructor in this scheme is to assist learners by directing their search to the most important sources of information within the perceptual-motor landscape. An important research issue is the identification of key constraints that shape the emergence of task specific coordination patterns. One approach to this issue has been to examine in detail the coordination patterns exhibited under various task constraints by skilled sportspersons. In a number of recent studies this approach has been applied to interceptive actions in a variety of sports, such volleyball, table tennis, soccer and long jumping (see Davids *et al.*, 2002). For example, the volleyball serve has been used to study the coordination between task-related joints and limb segments within the motor system and the coupling between environmental information and movement necessary to contact the ball successfully (Davids *et al.*, 1999; Temprado *et al.*, 1997). Although the neo-Darwinian approach emphasizes individual differences among learners and task-specific constraints, an important issue for future research will be to determine principles of skill acquisition that generalize across different sports.

The other clear direction for future research is the need to integrate our understanding of the neural basis of behaviour into theoretical accounts of behaviour (see Keil and Bennett, 2002). Although Pressing (1999) has argued that the integration of cognitive and dynamical systems approaches is best realized by a unified mathematical form, it has been pointed out that all constraints on motor behaviour (perceptual, cognitive or musculo-skeletal) are mediated by the integrative action of the central nervous system (Carson and Kelso, 2003). In recent years, the recognition of the dynamic nature of biological nervous systems has led to attempts to model cognitive processes in terms of interactions between populations of neurons (e.g. Edelman, 1992; Freeman, 1999). Through the development of sophisticated brain imaging techniques there has been an explosion of knowledge about the dynamics of brain activity (see Bressler and Kelso, 2001). Techniques such as multielectrode electroencephalography (EEG), magnetoencephalography (MEG) and functional magnetic resonance imaging (fMRI) have provided important insights into the neural correlates of behavioural phenomena, such as phase transitions that occur in bimanual coordination tasks (e.g. Jirsa *et al.*, 1998; Meyer-Lindenberg *et al.*, 2002; Swinnen, 2002). Of particular importance have been recent studies showing neural reorganization accompanying motor skill learning (e.g. Ghilardi *et al.*, 2000; Hund-Georgiadis and von Cramon, 1999; Jantzen *et al.*, 2001, 2002). Jantzen *et al.* (2002), for example, found that practice of a difficult coordination task (syncopation) led to a decrease in the number of cortical networks active, possibly reflecting a reduction in attentional demands with practice. The on-line monitoring of cortical activity during the learning of more complex skills is the next exciting step in understanding the neural basis of learning. What is clear is that future theories of skill acquisition will need to integrate information at both the psychological and physiological levels.

References

Abernethy, B. (1991). Visual search strategies and decision-making in sport. *International Journal of Sport Psychology*, 22, 189–210.

Abernethy, B. and Sparrow, W. A. (1992). The rise and fall of dominant paradigms in motor behaviour research. In J. J. Summers (Ed.), *Approaches to the study of motor control and learning*. Amsterdam: North-Holland.

Adams, J. A. (1971). A closed-loop theory of motor learning. *Journal of Motor Behaviour*, 3, 111–150.

Adams, J. A. (1987). Historical review and appraisal of research on the learning, retention, and transfer of human motor skills. *Psychological Bulletin*, 101, 41–74.

Allard, F. and Burnett, N. (1985). Skill in sport. *Canadian Journal of Psychology*, 39, 294–312.

Anderson, J. R. (1982). Acquisition of cognitive skill. *Psychological Review*, 89, 369–406.

Bartlett, F. (1932). *Remembering: a study in experimental and social psychology*. Cambridge: Cambridge University Press.

Bartlett, F. (1958). *Thinking: an experimental and social study*. New York: Basic Books.

Beek, P. J., Peper, C. E. and Stegeman, D. F. (1995). Dynamical models of movement coordination. *Human Movement Science*, 14, 573–608.

Bernstein, N. A. (1967). *The coordination and regulation of movements*. Oxford: Pergamon Press.

Bilodeau, E. A. (1966). *Acquisition of skill*. New York: Academic Press.

Bilodeau, E. A. and Bilodeau, I. McD. (1969). *Principles of skill acquisition*. London: Academic Press.

Book, W. F. (1908). *The psychology of skill*. University of Montana Studies in Psychology, Vol. 1. (Reprinted, New York: Gregg, 1925.)

Bressler, S. L. and Kelso, J. A. S. (2001). Cortical coordination dynamics and cognition. *TRENDS in Cognitive Sciences*, 5, 26–36.

Bryan, W. L. and Harter, N. (1897). Studies in the physiology and psychology of the telegraphic language. *Psychological Review*, 4, 27–53.

Bryan, W. L. and Harter, N. (1899). Studies on the telegraphic language. The acquisition of a hierarchy of habits. *Psychological Review*, 6, 345–375.

Carson, R. G. (1998). Ecological psychology and movement dynamics: a plea for biological realism. In J. P. Piek (Ed.), *Motor behaviour and human skill: a multidisciplinary approach*. Champaign, IL: Human Kinetics.

Carson, R. G. and Kelso, J. A. S. (2003). Governing coordination: behavioural principles and neural correlates. *Experimental Brain Research* (in press).

Cauraugh, J. H. and Janelle, C. M. (2002). Visual search and cue utilisation in racket sports. In K. Davids, G. Savelsbergh, S. J. Bennet and J. Van der Kamp (Eds), *Interceptive actions in sport* (pp. 64–89). London: Routledge.

Chase, W. G. and Simon, H. A. (1973). Perception in chess. *Cognitive Psychology*, 4, 55–81.

Craik, K. J. W. (1948). The theory of the human operator in control systems: II. Man as an element in a control system. *British Journal of Psychology*, 38, 142–148.

Cratty, B. J. (1964). *Movement behaviour and motor learning*. Philadelphia: Lea and Febiger.

Crossman, E. R. F. W. (1959). A theory of the acquisition of speed skill. *Ergonomics*, 2, 153–166.

Davids, K. (2000). Skill acquisition and the theory of deliberate practice: it ain't what you do it's the way that you do it! *International Journal of Sport Psychology*, 31, 461–466.

Davids, K. and Button, C. (2000). The cognition–dynamics interface and performance in sport. *International Journal of Sport Psychology*, 31, 515–521.

Davids, K., Bennett, S., Handford, C. and Jones, B. (1999). Acquiring coordination in self-paced, extrinsic timing tasks: a constraints-led perspective. *International Journal of Sport Psychology*, 30, 437–461.

Davids, K., Savelsbergh, G., Bennett, S. J. and Van der Kamp. J. (Eds) (2002). *Interceptive actions in sport*. London: Routledge.

Easton, T. A. (1972). On the normal use of reflexes. *American Scientist*, 60, 591–599.

Ebbinghaus, H. (1964). *Memory: a contribution to experimental psychology*. New York: Dover (Original work published 1885).

Edelman, G. (1992). *Bright air, brilliant fire: on the matter of mind*. New York: Penguin.

Elliott, D., Helsen, W. F. and Chua, R. (2001). A century later: Woodworth's (1899) two-component model of goal-directed aiming. *Psychological Bulletin*, 127, 342–357.

Ericsson, K. A. and Charness, N. (1994). Expert performance: its structure and acquisition. *American Psychologist*, 49, 725–747.

Ericsson, K. A. and Lehmann, A. C. (1996). Expert and exceptional performance: evidence of maximal adaptation to task constraints. *Annual Review of Psychology*, 47, 273–305.

Ericsson, K. A., Krampe, R. and Tesch-Romer, C. (1993). The role of deliberate practice in the acquisition of expert performance. *Psychological Review*, 100, 363–406.

Fitts, P. M. (1964). Perceptual-motor skills learning. In A. W. Melton (Ed.), *Categories of human learning* (pp. 243–285). New York: Academic Press.

Fleishman, E. A. (1953). Testing for psychomotor abilities by means of apparatus tests. *Psychological Bulletin*, 50, 243–262.

Fleishman, E. A. (1956). Psychomotor selection tests: research and application in the United States Air Force. *Personnel Psychology*, 9, 449–467.

Fleishman, E. A. and Hempel, W. E., Jr. (1954). Changes in factor structure of a complex psychomotor test as a function of practice. *Psychometrika*, 19, 239–252.

Fleishman, E. A. and Hempel, W. E., Jr. (1955). The relation between abilities and improvement with practice in a visual discrimination reaction task. *Journal of Experimental Psychology*, 49, 301–312.

Fodor, J. A. (1980). Methodological solipsism considered as a research strategy in cognitive psychology. *Behavioural and Brain Sciences*, 3, 63–110.

Freeman, W. J. (1999). *How brains make up their mind*. London: Weidenfield & Nicolson.

Gibson, J. J. (1979). *The ecological approach to visual perception*. Boston: Houghton Mifflin.

Ghilardi, M.-F., Ghez, C., Dhawan, V., Moeller, J., Mentis, M., Nakamura, T., Antonini, A. and Eidelberg, D. (2000). Patterns of regional brain activation associated with different forms of motor learning. *Brain Research*, 871, 127–145.

Haken, H. (1990). Synergetics as a tool for the conceptualisation and mathematization of cognition and behaviour – how far can we go? In H. Haken and M. Sadler (Eds), *Synergetics of cognition* (pp. 2–31). Berlin: Springer.

Heathcote, A., Brown, S. and Mewhort, D. J. K. (2000). The power law repealed: the case for an exponential law of practice. *Psychonomic Bulletin and Review*, 7, 185–207.

Holding, D. H. (1985). *The psychology of chess skill*. Hillsdale, NJ: Erlbaum.

Hull, C. L. (1943). *Principles of behaviour*. New York: Appelton-Century-Crofts.

Hund-Georgiadis, M. and von Cramon, D. Y. (1999). Motor-learning-related changes in piano players and non-musicians revealed by functional magnetic-resonance signals. *Experimental Brain Research*, 125, 417–425.

Ingvaldsen, R. P. and Whiting, H. T. A. (1997). Modern views on motor skill learning are not 'representative'! *Human Movement Science*, 16, 705–722.

Jantzen, K. J., Fuchs, A., Mayville, J. M., Deecke, L. and Kelso, J. A. S. (2001). Neuromagnetic activity in alpha and beta bands reflect learning-induced increases in coordinative stability. *Clinical Neurophysiology*, 112, 1685–1697.

Jantzen, K. J., Steinberg, F. L. and Kelso, J. A. S. (2002). Practice-dependent modulation of neural activity during human sensorimotor coordination: a functional magnetic imaging study. *Neuroscience Letters*, 332, 205–209.

Jirsa, V. K., Fuchs, A. and Kelso, J. A. S. (1998). Neural field theory connecting cortical and behavioural dynamics: bimanual coordination. *Neural Computation*, 10, 2019–2045.

Jones, S. K. (1993). A modular approach to individual differences in skill and coordination. In J. L. Starkes and F. Allard (Eds), *Cognitive issues in motor expertise* (pp. 273–293). Amsterdam: Elsevier.

Keele, S. W. (1968). Movement control in skilled motor performance. *Psychological Bulletin*, 70, 387–403.

Keele, S. W. (1973). *Attention and human performance*. Pacific Palisades, CA: Goodyear.

Keele, S. W. (1977). Current status of the motor program concept. In D. M. Landers and R. W. Christina (Eds), *Psychology of motor behaviour and sport*, Vol. 1. Champaign, IL: Human Kinetics.

Keele, S. W. (1981). Behavioural analysis of motor control. In V. B. Brooks (Ed.), *Handbook of physiology*, Vol. 2: Motor control (pp. 1391–1414). Bethesda, MD: American Physiological Society.

Keele, S. W. and Hawkins, H. L. (1982). Explorations of individual differences relevant to high level skill. *Journal of Motor Behaviour*, 14, 3–23.

Keele, S. W. and Summers, J. J. (1976). The structure of motor programs. In G. E. Stelmach (Ed.), *Motor control: issues and trends* (pp. 109–142). New York: Academic Press.

Keil, D. and Bennett, S. J. (2002). Perception and action during interceptive tasks: an integrated modelling approach. In K. Davids, G. Savelsbergh, S. J. Bennett and J. Van der Kamp (Eds), *Interceptive actions in sport* (pp. 212–224). London: Routledge.

Kelso, J. A. S. (1982a). The process approach to understanding human motor behaviour. In J. A. S. Kelso (Ed.) *Human motor behaviour : an introduction*, Hillsdale, NJ: Erlbaum.

Kelso, J. A. S. (1982b). Epilogue: two strategies for investigating action. In J. A. S. Kelso (Ed.), *Human motor behaviour: an introduction* (pp. 283–287). Hillsdale, NJ: Erlbaum.

Kelso, J. A. S. (1995). *Dynamic patterns: the self-organization of brain and behaviour.* Cambridge, MA: MIT Press

Kelso, J. A. S. and Zanone, P.-G. (2002). Coordination dynamics of learning and transfer across different effector systems. *Journal of Experimental Psychology: Human Perception and Performance*, 28, 776–797.

Kelso, J. A. S., Holt, K. G., Rubin, P. and Kugler, P. N. (1981). Patterns of human inter-limb coordination emerge from the properties of non-linear, limit-cycle, oscillatory processes: theory and data. *Journal of Motor Behaviour*, 13, 226–261.

Knapp, B. (1963). *Skill in sport: the attainment of proficiency.* London: Routledge.

Kugler, P. N. (1986). A morphological perspective on the origin and evolution of movement patterns. In M. Wade and H. T. A. Whiting (Eds), *Motor development in children: aspects of coordination and control.* Dordrecht: Martinus Nijhoff.

Kugler, P. N., Kelso, J. A. S. and Turvey, M. T. (1980). On the concept of coordinative structures as dissipative structures: I. Theoretical lines of convergence. In G. E. Stelmach and J. Requin (Eds), *Tutorials in motor behaviour* (pp. 3–47). Amsterdam: Elsevier.

Kugler, P. N., Kelso, J. A. S. and Turvey, M. T. (1982). On the control and coordination of naturally developing systems. In J. A. S. Kelso and J. E. Clark (Eds), *The development of movement control and coordination* (pp. 5–78). New York: Wiley.

Lee, D. N. (1976). A theory of visual control of braking based on information about time-to-collision. *Perception*, 5, 437–459.

Lee, D. N. (1980). Visuo-motor coordination in space–time. In G. E. Stelmach and J. Requin (Eds), *Tutorials in motor behaviour* (pp. 281–295), Amsterdam: North-Holland.

Lee, T. D. and Swinnen, S. P. (1993). Three legacies of Bryan and Harter: automaticity, variability, and change in skilled performance. In J. L. Starkes and F. Allard (Eds), *Cognitive issues in motor expertise* (pp. 295–315). Amsterdam: Elsevier.

Mackay, D. G. (1982). The problems of flexibility, fluency and speed–accuracy trade-off in skilled behaviour. *Psychological Review*, 89, 483–506.

Marteniuk, R. G. (1976). *Information processing in motor skills.* New York: Holt, Rinehart and Winston.

McLeod, P. and Jenkins, S. (1991). Timing accuracy and decision time in high-speed ball games. *Inetrnational Journal of Sport Psychology*, 22, 279–295.

Meijer, O. G. and Roth, K. A. (Eds) (1988). *Complex movement behaviour: 'the' motor-action controversy.* Amsterdam: North-Holland.

Meyer-Lindenberg, A., Ziemann, U., Hajak, G., Cohen, L. and Berman, K. F. (2002). Transitions between dynamical ststes of differing stability in the human brain. *Proceedings of the National Academy of Sciences*, 99, 10948–10953.

Michaels, C. F. (1993). Destination compatibility, affordances, and coding rules: a reply to Proctor, Van Zandt, Lu, and Weeks. *Journal of Experimental Psychology: Human Perception and Performance*, 19, 1121–1127.

Miller, G. A., Galanter, E. and Pribram, K. H. (1960). *Plans and the structure of behaviour.* New York: Holt, Rinehart and Winston.

Neisser, U. (1967). *Cognitive psychology.* New York: Appelton-Century-Crofts.

Newell, K. M. (1986). Constraints on the development of coordination. In M. Wade and H. T. A. Whiting (Eds), *Motor development in children: aspects of coordination and control.* Dordrecht: Martinus Nijhoff.

Newell, K. M. and Corcos, D. M. (Eds) (1993). *Variability and motor control.* Champaign, IL: Human Kinetics.

Newell, K. M. and McDonald, P. V. (1994). Learning to coordinate redundant biomechanical degrees of freedom. In S. Swinnen, H. Heuer, J. Massion and P. Casaer (Eds), *Interlimb coordination: neural, dynamical, and cognitire constraints*. New York: Academic press.

Posner, M. I. and Keele, S. W. (1973). Skill learning. In R. M. Travers (Ed.), *Handbook of research on teaching*. Chicago, IL: Rand-McNally.

Paillard, J. (1960). The patterning of skilled movement. In J. Field (Ed.), *Handbook of physiology: neurophysiology*, Vol. III. Baltimore, MD: Williams & Wilkins.

Poulton, E. C. (1974). *Tracking skill and manual control*. New York: Academic Press.

Pressing, J. (1998). The scope of ecological designs. In J. P. Piek (Ed.), *Motor behaviour and human skill: a multidisciplinary approach*. Champaign, IL: Human Kinetics.

Pressing, J. (1999). The referential dynamics of cognition and action. *Psychological Review*, 106, 714–747.

Proctor, R. W. and Dutta, A. (1995). *Skill acquisition and human performance*. Thousand Oaks, CA: Sage.

Proteau, L. (1992). On the specificity of learning and the role of visual information for movement control. In L. Proteau and D. Elliott (Eds), *Vision and motor control* (pp. 67–103). Amsterdam: Elsevier.

Requin, J., Lecas, J.-L. and Bonnet, M. (1984). Some experimental evidence for a three-step model of motor preparation. In S. Kornblum and J. Requin (Eds), *Preparatory states and processes* (pp. 259–284). Hillsdale, NJ: Lawrence Erlbaum.

Riley, M. A. and Turvey, M. T. (2002). Variability and determinism in motor behaviour. *Journal of Motor Behaviour*, 34, 99–125.

Rumelhart, D. E. and Norman, D. A. (1982). Simulating a skilled typing: a study of skilled cognitive–motor performance. *Cognitive Science*, 6, 1–36.

Schmidt, R. A. (1975). A schema theory of discrete motor skill learning. *Psychological Review*, 82, 225–260.

Schmidt, R. A. and Bjork, R. A. (1992). New conceptualizations of practice: common principles in three paradigms suggest new concepts for training. *Psychological Science*, 3, 207–217.

Schmidt, R. A., Heuer, H., Ghodsian, D. and Young, D. E. (1998). Generalized motor programs and units of action in bimanual coordination. In M. L. Latash (Ed.), *Progress in motor control*, Vol. 1. Champaign, IL: Human Kinetics.

Shaffer, L. H. (1980). Analysing piano performance: a study of concert pianists. In G. E. Stelmach and J. Requin (Eds), *Tutorials in motor behaviour*. Amsterdam: North-Holland.

Shannon, C. E. and Weaver, W. (1949). *The mathematical theory of communication*. Urbana, IL: University of Illinois Press.

Singer, R. N. (1968). *Motor learning and human performance*. New York: Macmillan.

Snoddy, G. S. (1926). Learning and stability: a psychophysical analysis of a case of motor learning with clinical applications. *Journal of Applied Psychology*, 10, 1–36.

Starkes, J. (2000). The road to expertise: is practice the only determinant? *International Journal of Sport Psychology*, 31, 431–451.

Stoffregen, T. A. (2000). Affordances and events. *Ecological Psychology*, 12, 1–28.

Summers, J. J. (1981). Motor programs. In D. H. Holding (Ed.), *Human skills* (pp. 41–64). Chichester: Wiley.

Summers, J. J. (1992). Movement behaviour: a field in crisis? In J. J. Summers (Ed.), *Approaches to the study of motor control and learning*. Amsterdam: North-Holland.

Summers, J. J. (1998). Has ecological psychology delivered what it promised? In J. P. Piek (Ed.), *Motor behaviour and human skill: a multidisciplinary approach*. Champaign, IL: Human Kinetics.

Summers, J. J., Byblow, W. D., Bysouth-Young, D. F. and Semjen, A. (1998). Bimanual circle drawing during secondary task loading. *Motor Control*, 2, 106–113.

Summers, J. J., Davis, A. and Byblow, W. D. (2003). The acquisition of bimanual coordination is mediated by anisotropic coupling between the hands. *Human Movement Science*, 21, 699–721.

Swinnen, S. P. (2002). Intermanual coordination: from behavioural principles to neural-network interactions. *Nature Neuroscience*, 3, 350–361.

Temprado, J. J., Della-Grasta, M., Farrell, M. and Laurent, M. (1997). A novice–expert comparison of (intra-limb) coordination subserving the volleyball serve. *Human Movement Science*, 16, 653–676.

Temprado, J. J., Zanone, P. G., Monno, A. and Laurent, M. (1999). Attentional load associated with performing and stabilizing preferred bimanual patterns. *Journal of Experimental Psychology: Human Perception and Performance*, 25, 1575–1594.

Tresilian, J. R. (1999). Visually timed action: time-out for 'tau'? *TRENDS in Cognitive Sciences*, 3, 301–310.

Tuller, B., Turvey, M. T. and Fitch, H. L. (1982). The Bernstein perspective: II. The concept of muscle linkage or coordinative structure. In J. A. S. Kelso (Ed.), *Human motor behaviour: an introduction* (pp. 253–270). Hillsdale, NJ: Lawrence Erlbaum.

Turvey, M. T. (1996). Dynamic touch. *American Psychologist*, 51, 1134–1152.

Turvey, M. T. and Carello, C. (1981). Cognition: the view from ecological realism. *Cognition*, 10, 313–321.

Turvey, M. T. and Kugler, P. N. (1984). An ecological approach to perception and action. In H. T. A. Whiting (Ed.), *Human motor actions: Bernstein re-assessed*. Amsterdam: Elsevier.

Turvey, M. T., Fitch, H. L. and Tuller, B. (1982). The Bernstein perspective: I. The problems of degrees of freedom and context-conditioned variability. In J. A. S. Kelso (Ed.), *Human motor behaviour: an introduction* (pp. 239–252). Hillsdale, NJ: Lawrence Erlbaum.

van Galen, G. P. (1980). Handwriting and drawing: a two stage model of complex motor behaviour. In G. E. Stelmach and J. Requin (Eds), *Tutorials in motor behaviour*. Amsterdam: North-Holland.

Warren, W. H. (1998). The state of flow. In T. Watanabe (Ed.), *High-level motion processing: computational, neurobiological and psychophysical perspectives*. Cambridge, MA: MIT Press.

Welford, A. T. (1952). The 'psychological refractory period' and the timing of high speed performance – a review and a theory. *British Journal of Psychology*, 43, 2–19.

Welford, A. T. (1967). Single-channel operation in the brain. *Acta Psychologica*, 27, 5–22.

Welford, A. T. (1976). *Skilled performance: perceptual and motor skills*. Glenview, IL: Scott, Foresman.

Whiting, H. T. A. (1969). *Acquiring ball skill: a psychological interpretation*. London: G. Bell & Sons, Ltd.

Wickens, C. D. (1992). *Engineering psychology and human performance* (2nd ed.). New York: Harpers Collins.

Wiener, N. (1948). *Cybernetics: or control and communication in the animal and the machine*. New York: Wiley.

Williams, A. M., Davids, K. and Williams, J. G. (1999). *Visual perception and action in sport*. London: E & FN SPON.

Woodworth, R. S. (1899). The accuracy of voluntary movement. *Psychological Review Monographs, 3* (Whole No. 13).

Wulf, G., McNevin, N., Shea, C. H. and Wright, D. L. (1999). Learning phenomena: future challenges for the dynamical systems approach to understanding the learning of complex motor skills. *International Journal of Sport Psychology*, 30, 531–557.

Zanone, P.-G. and Kelso, J. A. S. (1992). Evolution of behavioural attractors with learning: nonequilibrium phase transitions. *Journal of Experimental Psychology: Human Perception and Performance*, 18, 403–421.

Zanone, P.-G. and Kelso, J. A. S. (1997). The coordination of learning and transfer: collective and component levels. *Journal of Experimental Psychology: Human Perception and Performance*, 23, 1454–1480.

Part I

Information processing perspectives

2 Contextual interference

Timothy D. Lee and Dominic A. Simon

Two old sayings, one mostly correct, the other mostly incorrect, still dominate many opinions regarding the effects of practice. The first saying is that 'practice makes perfect' and has a ring of truth to it – all other factors being equal, the development of skill is generally and positively related to the amount of practice. For example, the *power law of practice* (Crossman, 1959; Fitts, 1964; Newell and Rosenbloom, 1981; Snoddy, 1926) characterizes how performance improvements continue to emerge over hours, days, months or years of accumulated time in practice. In general, there are few, if any, exceptions to the law of practice and to the essence of this old adage.

On the surface the other saying, 'perfect practice makes perfect', appears also to have merit. The idea is that the optimization of performance during practice will lead to the best 'memory' for what has been learned. Conversely, making errors in practice leads to learning of these errors and, generally, degrading the overall potential benefit of practice. The adage suggests that conditions of practice that lead to good performance should lead to good learning when compared to conditions of practice that lead to poor performance. In this chapter, we describe the effect of a practice variable called *contextual interference* that contradicts the wisdom of this saying. Moreover, in our discussion of the reasons for this effect, we explain why attempts to optimize both performance and learning in practice are generally doomed to failure.

Early studies

Most motor learning researchers attribute the first demonstration of the contextual interference effect to Shea and Morgan (1979). This may be true, but important antecedents to the publication of their research heightened the impact of Shea and Morgan's findings. An early study by Pyle (1919), involving the sorting of cards, illustrated how a difficult practice condition could degrade performance during practice. In the Pyle study, two groups of participants practised a card-sorting task. A trial consisted of placing each card from a deck of 150, one at a time, into compartments (similar to sorting mail). Five cards of each number (1–30) occurred in the deck. The compartments were physically arranged in six rows of five compartments per row. The compartments, each numbered from 1 to 30, were not ordered consecutively, but rather, were arranged unsystematically. Two different compartmental spatial arrangements were used in the experiment. The 'blocked' group used one arrangement for the first 15 days of the study and the second arrangement for the next 15 days. The 'alternating' group switched between arrangements on every other day. The results of the experiment are illustrated in Figure 2.1. With the exception of the first trial on the new spatial arrangement (day 16), the blocked group outperformed the alternating group throughout the practice period. These findings led Pyle (1919, p. 109) to comment that 'The group that alternated from one (arrangement) to the other from day to day was at a great disadvantage in its method .... The inference from this experiment is that it is not economical to form at the same time two mutually inhibitory sets of habits. The better procedure is to form one, and then the other'.

Notice in Pyle's comments that the influence of the practice variable on learning was being assessed *during* the trials in which the variable had been manipulated in these groups. This emphasis on making assessments about learning based on practice performance was common at the time, despite theoretical arguments to the contrary (e.g. Blodgett, 1929; Hull, 1943). A problem similar to this one concerned the role of augmented feedback, often presented as knowledge of results (KR). The manipulation of KR, like the scheduling of reward in animal conditioning experiments, was believed to have an important impact on learning. Reviews of the many human motor learning experiments in which KR was manipulated often focused on the effects that these manipulations had during the time in which these variables were influencing performance. That is, the effects of these KR variables were often attributed to an influence on *learning* (Ammons, 1956).

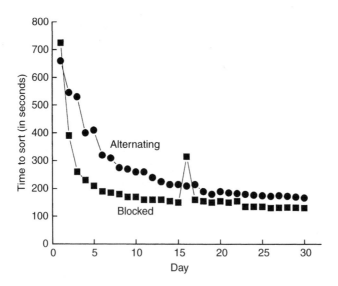

Figure 2.1 Results of the Pyle (1919) experiment.

Other researchers have argued differently. In the motor learning literature, the problem of (mis)attributing the influence of practice variables during practice to a learning effect was discussed frequently by Schmidt (1971, 1972) (see also Salmoni *et al.* 1984). He argued that retention or transfer trials were the only reliable means to assess the impact on learning of those various practice conditions. All individuals previously undergoing different practice manipulations should be examined under similar test conditions. The soundness of these theoretical arguments was also supported when considered in the context of learning daily activities. For example, the true test of practice is not how a golfer hits the ball on the driving range, but rather how practice impacts performance during a round of golf on the course.

Shea and Morgan (1979)

In the historical context of discussions regarding the performance/learning distinction and the perceived effect of practice variables in motor learning theory (Adams, 1971; Schmidt, 1975), the timing was perfect for the impact of Shea and Morgan's (1979) findings. In their study, Shea and Morgan compared two groups of individuals who practised three versions of a laboratory task for a total of fifty-four trials (eighteen trials per version). The task required participants to respond to the illumination of one of three coloured lights by picking up a tennis ball, knocking over three (of six) small wooden barriers and replacing the tennis ball, all as quickly as possible. The three different task versions differed in terms of the specific barriers to be struck during the movement. Both groups received the same number of total trials, the same number of trials per version, the same quality and quantity of KR, and took roughly the same amount of time to complete their practice trials. The only difference between the groups was the *order* in which these practice trials were conducted. The *blocked* group practised all eighteen trials of one task version before switching to a second version (then completing those eighteen trials), and then on to the third version. In contrast, the *random* practice group had a much less systematic practice order. The order of practice for this group was randomized with the restrictions that no more than two trials of any one task version could be completed in succession and that three trials of each version were completed in each set of nine trials.

The results from the Shea and Morgan study are presented in Figure 2.2. The total time elapsed in response to an imperative signal was the primary dependent measure (i.e. the sum of reaction time plus movement time). The fifty-four acquisition trials were grouped into six blocks of nine trials each, and represent the progress made by each group during practice. Two retention tests were given for each group: the three task versions were performed both in a random and in a blocked retention order. These retention trials were conducted by one-half of the participants in the blocked and random acquisition groups following a 10-minute rest, and by the remaining participants in each group 10 days after the acquisition trials.

As can be seen in Figure 2.2, the impact of these two orders on performance in practice was predictable: compared to random practice, the blocked practice

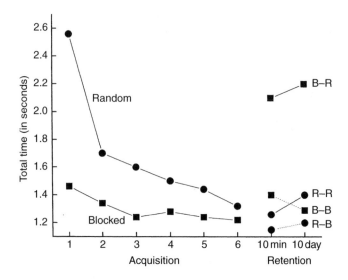

Figure 2.2 Results of the Shea and Morgan (1979) experiment.

order facilitated a rapid reduction in response time during acquisition performance (especially so during the first block of nine trials). Clearly, the blocked group resulted in a much faster *rate* of improvement on the task and a greater overall *amount* of improvement than random practice. The retention results, however, revealed a very different effect. The filled circles represent the randomly ordered acquisition practice and the filled squares represent the blocked-ordered acquisition practice. Dotted lines connect the trials in which the participants performed the retention trials in a blocked sequence and solid lines illustrate the randomly ordered retention trials. Figure 2.2 illustrates the following findings: random practice resulted in better retention performance than blocked practice when compared in both randomly ordered retention trials and in blocked-ordered retention trials, and when compared in retention tests both 10 minutes and 10 days following the practice period. Random practice had facilitated retention (learning) compared to blocked practice.

The blocked practice schedule, which had facilitated a rapid performance improvement, appeared to be poor for learning compared to the random schedule, which had resulted in much slower and more modest improvements during practice. The second adage that was discussed at the beginning of this section, that 'perfect practice makes perfect', had been violated by these results.

A note on comparing Pyle with Shea and Morgan

The blocked practice group in the Pyle (1919) study shows a very different acquisition practice 'profile' than the blocked group in Shea and Morgan (1979). There is a simple, statistical reason for this difference that has gone relatively

unnoticed over the years. In Figure 2.1, Pyle's blocked data are plotted chrono-
logically; trials 1–15 are performed with one compartment order, trials 15–30 are
performed with a different order. For Shea and Morgan (1979), however, trial
block one represents the average performance of the first three trials for each task
version; trial block two represents the average of trials 4, 5 and 6 for each task version, and so on. Notice that while this is a true chronological representation of
the order by which the random group performed their acquisition trials, this is not
so for the blocked group. Rather, trial block one in Figure 2.2 illustrates the average performance of trials 1, 2, 3 (the first three trials of task version one), trials
19, 20 and 21 (the first three trials of task version two), and trials 37, 38 and 39
(the first three trials of task version three). Trial block two is the average of trials
4, 5, 6, 22, 23, 24, 40, 41 and 42. Trial blocks three to six are calculated similarly.
The deterioration in performance seen in the blocked group when switching
between compartments in the Pyle study (i.e. between Days 15 and 16) is not
replicated in how Shea and Morgan presented their blocked data (Figure 2.2).

The artefactual nature of the difference between the Pyle and Shea/Morgan
results is illustrated in Figure 2.3. These data are taken from Lee (1982), which
were subsequently published in Lee and Magill (1983; Experiment Two). In many
respects, this experiment replicated the task and procedures used by Shea and
Morgan. In Figure 2.3, we have replotted the individual trial performance for each
participant in the blocked and random groups as a function of the chronological

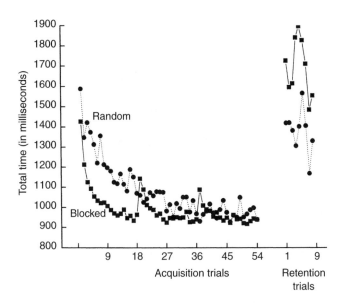

Figure 2.3 Results of Lee (1982). Individual trial data are plotted in chronological
order (see text for details). [Originally, these data were presented in a
manner similar to Shea and Morgan (1979), replicating their findings
(see Lee and Magill, 1983). In the present illustration, the individual trial
data have been re-plotted in chronological order. See text for details.]

order in which each trial was performed in practice. Presentation of the results in this way shows an effect similar to that seen in Pyle (1919). There is a marked deterioration in performance of the blocked group in trials 19 and 37, the trials in which there was a change from one pattern to a new pattern.

Replications and extensions of Shea and Morgan (1979)

The implications of Shea and Morgan's findings for theory and practice were staggering. Why should a practice order be good for performance, but poor for learning? Conversely, why should a practice order retard performance, but boost learning? What processes underlying performance and learning were being affected by these practice orders? And, if the findings were reliable and externally valid, what were the practical implications? Before these important questions could be addressed, the Shea and Morgan findings needed to be replicated elsewhere.

Extensive reviews of the contextual interference literature have been published by Brady (1998) and Magill and Hall (1990), and document numerous task, participant and methodological considerations that moderate the magnitude of the contextual interference effect. In some cases, blocked practice produces much better acquisition performance than random practice (replicating Shea and Morgan), and in some cases, the difference is minimal or non-existent. We feel, it is, therefore, safe to conclude that *in the acquisition of a motor skill, a blocked practice schedule is very likely to facilitate performance when compared to the performance of individuals in a random practice schedule.*

Reviews of the contextual interference literature regarding the influence of practice schedules in retention and transfer also have reported mixed results (see Brady, 1998; Magill and Hall, 1990). In some cases, the benefit of random practice is as large, or larger, than was found by Shea and Morgan. In other cases, there have only been small or null differences between blocked and random schedules. However, rarely, have there been reliable learning advantages that favour blocked practice. Thus we feel confident in making the following conclusion: that *in the learning of a motor skill, when differences due to practice schedules are found, these differences will favour retention or transfer following a random acquisition schedule.*

A matter of clarification

The effects of random, blocked and other types of practice schedules in which the effects of trial practice order are the main concern, are often confused with a related, but different issue regarding the effects of *variability of practice.* This latter theoretical concern was motivated by schema theory (Schmidt, 1975), which predicted that transfer to a novel parameterization of a generalized motor program (GMP) would be facilitated following practice involving many parameter variations of the GMP compared to practice following only one or a limited number of parameter variations. Schema theory offered no provision regarding how the order of these practice trials might be conducted, only that 'variable' practice should be better for transfer than 'non-variable' practice. In studies of contextual interference, however, the typical experimental protocol is to compare groups that experience the same amount of practice on the same number of task variations, the only difference being the order of practice trials.

Thus, it seems as though these two practice variables are distinct and separate lines of investigation. However, some have argued that there is more overlap than appears at first. In their review of the variability of practice literature, Lee *et al.* (1985) discovered that tests of the schema theory prediction (better transfer following many task variations in practice versus a few or only one task variation) was supported only when those task variations had been conducted in a random practice sequence. Studies in which task variations had been conducted in a blocked order most often resulted in transfer that was no better than constant (single variation) practice. The conclusion of Lee *et al.* (1985), based on the literature review and their own empirical evidence, suggested that random practice was necessary in order to maximize the benefits of variable practice when comparisons are made to transfer following non-variable practice conditions.

Theoretical concerns

A variety of theoretical accounts have been advanced to explain the contextual interference effect. Of course, any satisfactory account needs to explain the relative performances observed for blocked and random practice not only in retention, but in acquisition also. It is relatively easy to postulate mechanisms that predict an ordering of performance of two practice conditions. Less easy is to explain the interaction effects observed in contextual interference: blocked practice with superior performance in acquisition, but random practice with superior performance in tests of delayed retention or transfer. In the following, we outline theories that have been advanced, though we feel that it is important to recognize the possibility that many of the accounts are not mutually exclusive, and that contextual interference may represent the confluence of a set of concurrently acting mechanisms. The two most commonly cited explanations of contextual interference are the elaboration-and-distinctiveness view and the forgetting-and-reconstruction view.

The elaboration–distinctiveness view

Borrowing heavily from the work of William Battig (1972, 1979), the elaboration–distinctiveness view was put forward by Shea and Morgan to account for their original findings. The basic idea is that random practice, by virtue of the interspersing of the to-be-learned tasks, affords the learner many opportunities to compare and contrast the tasks. As a result of these comparisons and contrasts, the learner develops rich representations of the tasks and thus more elaborate and more distinctive memories are established. The need to keep the patterns unambiguous and to avoid confusion during practice is what causes the disadvantage during acquisition. In blocked practice, the continued repetition of long series of the same task makes it less important to keep track of which task is which, except perhaps for the first few trials of a new block. Although more demanding during acquisition, the need to compare and contrast, leading as it does to more elaborate and distinctive memorial representations of the practiced tasks yields superior performance in retention tests. In transfer tests, the argument is essentially that random practice has made learners more adept at identifying the relevant features of the to-be-performed transfer task, providing an advantage on these tasks, even though they are novel.

The forgetting–reconstruction view

The forgetting–reconstruction view of contextual interference (Lee and Magill, 1983, 1985) draws more heavily on the preparatory processing involved in practice. The idea here is that random practice forces the learner to 'dump' a given pattern from working memory in order to plan and execute successive practice trials. Because a given pattern is dumped and superceded by planning and execution of trials of one of the other patterns, it is not immediately available and must either be drawn out of long-term memory, or constructed from scratch (or more likely some hybrid of the two). In blocked practice, a given movement pattern can be planned and maintained in working memory across an entire series of trials. Although modifications may be made to the movement in that period, this practice schedule generally affords the learner only one opportunity to bring up, or construct, each movement pattern, once for each pattern. This need (or lack of need) for forgetting–reconstruction in the two practice schedules is the basis for both the acquisition and retention effects seen in contextual interference: uninterrupted repetitions of the same pattern in blocked-practice makes for relatively high-quality performance, but the lack of practice at constructing the movement patterns anew supports relatively poor learning. In random practice, the opposite is seen: the need to continually reconstruct the to-be-performed action pattern from one trial to the next makes for lower quality performance, but affords an advantage in delayed tests of learning, which make high demands on such reconstruction abilities.

On the surface, the distinction between the elaboration–distinctiveness view and the forgetting–reconstruction view comes down to working memory. In elaboration–distinctiveness, the argument is that concurrent presence of the to-be-learned patterns in short-term memory (STM) allows opportunities for comparison and contrast. In the forgetting–reconstruction view, it is the loss of an action plan from working memory and the consequent need to generate it anew that is the hallmark of random practice. These distinctions suggest that working memory should be the basis for distinguishing the theories. It seems plausible, however, that both accounts are tenable. Upon constructing one action pattern, it seems likely that one could make comparisons and contrasts with the previous action, whilst essentially replacing it as the 'loaded' response. In other words, the two accounts need not be at odds with one another, but could simply reflect different aspects of the same cognitive process.

Alternative views

Drawing on ideas from the verbal learning literature, some investigators have proposed that contextual interference effects may be due to retroactive interference. Retroactive interference is a phenomenon where later experiences affect memory for earlier learned associations. As an example, learning someone's new phone number would hopefully have a retroactively interfering effect on one's tendency to call the old number. The parking spot chosen this morning will, hopefully, retroactively interfere with your recollection of yesterday's parking spot. The suggestion by Poto (1988) is that later learned patterns in blocked practice tend to act backwards to attenuate the memory strength of earlier learned patterns. In random practice, there is less scope for the patterns to 'undo' earlier learning because the practised patterns are all carried on throughout practice. The prediction arising from the retroactive interference view is thus, not that blocked practice is bad for learning per se. The later practised patterns should fare well, while earlier practised patterns should be less well learned, so that the blocked practised patterns would, on average, not be so well learned. Detailed, pattern-by-pattern analyses in retention are obviously needed to test these predictions. In a relevant modelling simulation by Horak (1992), a neural network was trained on different patterns in blocked or random fashion and it was observed that after random training, the network was optimized for the three trained associations, whereas at the end of blocked training, the network was essentially better for the later practised patterns and weaker for the earlier trained patterns. Data from studies by Meeuwsen and Magill (1991) and Poto (1988) are consistent with an influence of proactive and retroactive interference for blocked practice.

Magill and Hall (1990) cite the doctoral work of Wright as providing evidence against a retroactive interference interpretation for contextual interference. Wright had people engage in different types of information processing between blocked learning trials: viewing another to-be-learned pattern and stating the commonalities between it and the task being practised, viewing the current practice task and verbalizing the movement sequence involved, viewing another to-be-learned task and verbalizing the movement sequence involved in it, or no intervening task. Magill and Hall (1990, p. 273) state, '... retention performance showed that only the group that made comparisons between the new and present patterns was better than the other groups. Thus, reducing retroactive interference during practice did not necessarily improve retention performance, which is counter to what a retroactive interference explanation would predict.' However, it is debatable as to whether or not the intervening cognitive activity truly reduced retroactive interference in these practice schedules. Indeed, in what is presumably the publication of those same data, Wright (1991) makes no reference to retroactive interference issues.

Del Rey *et al.* (1994) also searched for possible contributions of retroactive interference to contextual interference effects. Their data supported such a contribution, but for reaction times and not for movement times. Again then, it seems to be debatable as to whether the contributions to actual performance effects (movement execution) as opposed to pre-performance delays (movement planning) in contextual interference are related to retroactive interference. Overall, this theoretical explanation is worthy of further consideration, along with the others we mention. Contextual interference may well be the result of multiple concurrent processes. Perhaps it should also be pointed out that, in principle at least, proactive interference effects could be argued for as well, and thus should be considered when evaluating the effects of contextual information.

Wulf and Schmidt (1994) have suggested that feedback dynamics may play a role in the contextual interference effect. Their idea is that random practice may be beneficial because feedback for a given trial cannot be used on the very next trial, thus making it less immediately useful. In contrast, for blocked practice, the inferential benefits of feedback can be applied on the very next trial. At first blush, this reasoning may appear somewhat backwards: *less* useful feedback supports better learning? However, as mentioned above, contrary to early ideas of the mechanistic benefits of feedback in motor learning, there are a number of findings primarily attributable to Schmidt and colleagues (e.g. Salmoni *et al.*, 1984; Schmidt *et al.*, 1989; Winstein and Schmidt, 1989) in which conditions of practice that make feedback less immediately available/useful to learners, may have a detrimental impact on performance, but a beneficial impact on learning.

Although not a theory per se, the contextual interference effect may also be seen as an instance of spacing effects. The individual trials in a random schedule are spaced compared to those in a blocked practice schedule. There is considerable evidence to suggest that spacing of learning opportunities can facilitate learning as compared to massing of such opportunities (see, e.g. Crowder, 1976). Some investigators have considered spacing as the basis for contextual interference effects (Meeuswen and Magill, 1991) though based on their data, these authors suggest that the phenomena may be independent of one another. It is unlikely, however, that the standard spacing effect is attributable to time per se, but rather due to the cognitive activity that is afforded by spacing delays. Attempts to somehow equate the amount of interference due to a given amount of temporal spacing with that due to practice of other to-be-learned movements may prove useful in answering this interesting question.

Gabriele *et al.* (1989) have investigated the influence of a random schedule in mental practice. Their data suggest that physical practice is not necessary for beneficial interference to occur. Similarly, data from Simon and Bjork (2002) also show potential benefits of watching models performance different rather than the same response within a block of trials. Findings such as these lend weight to the role of cognitive processes in the contextual interference effect, but in and of themselves do not support any one information processing-based account.

In a study by Wright (1991) inter-trial processing during blocked practice made acquisition poorer but helped retention. Thus, blocked practisers were made to look more like random practisers by this intervention (see also Simon and Bjork, 2002). However, no direct comparison between the impact of these intervening cognitive activities and the interposition of actual physical practice of other movement patterns is afforded by Wright's data (and the Simon and Bjork data yielded an additive effect of the blocked/random manipulation and the form of between-trial processing, rather than an interaction effect). As such, it seems possible that the inter-trial cognitive activities in these studies may be tapping different learning processes than are invoked by random practice. Further exploration of these issues is clearly warranted. A final explanation of the differential benefits in blocked and random practice is that random practice is simply more interesting than blocked practice and that consequent differences in learning are attributable to differential motivation levels in the two practice regimens (e.g. Wulf *et al.*, unpublished). As yet, however, this idea has not been rigorously tested.

Although each of these theories makes sense to some degree, it is not clear that any one of them can explain the phenomenon of contextual interference completely. It may well be that contextual interference represents the confluence of two or more of these contributing factors at any time. Experiments to address this issue need to be set up so that they not only provide evidence in favour of a particular theory, but that they also allow for the elimination of other explanations. If only one of these conditions is met, as usually seems to be the case, the evidence may support the pet explanation of the investigator, but will fail to rule out the other accounts. Such an approach represents something of a challenge for those interested in understanding the phenomenon of contextual interference.

Applications

Although research on the contextual interference effect has generated significant interest for reasons related to learning theory, perhaps of greater importance have been the studies conducted using tasks of everyday living and the potential application of these results in other life events. For example, effects of random versus blocked practice have been found using a number of sport-related skills specific to badminton (e.g. Goode and Magill, 1986), baseball (Hall *et al.*, 1994), rifle-shooting (Boyce and Del Rey, 1990), kayaking (Smith and Davies, 1995) and volleyball (Bortoli *et al.*, 1992). As well, contextual interference effects have been found in non-sport-related tasks such as automatic bank machine transactions (Jamieson and Rogers, 2000), foreign vocabulary learning (Schneider *et al.*, 1998), and in physical rehabilitation following stroke (Hanlon, 1996). It seems to be the case that, for tasks in which learning differences due to practice order are found, the advantage will favour a random practice schedule.

The study of the contextual interference effect as an empirical laboratory finding, as an important issue for learning theory, and as an empirical, applied finding, has been met with considerable interest in a wide number of applied disciplines in which ordering of 'task repetitions' are a daily practical consideration. Discussions of contextual interference effects in this context have been engaged in areas diverse as coaching (e.g. Vickers, 1999), the military (Druckman and Bjork, 1994; Schmidt and Bjork, 1992), speech rehabilitation

(Knock *et al.*, 2000; Verdolini and Lee, in press), physical therapy (Winstein, 1991; Lee *et al.*, 1991; Marley *et al.*, 2000), and occupational therapy (Jarus, 1994).

Summary and future directions

By now, it should go without need for comment that the publication of Shea and Morgan's (1979) classic experiment has had a major impact on research and application in fields that include, and far exceed, the motor learning area. Is there continued need for research and theory development regarding contextual interference? We think so and briefly conclude this chapter with two promising areas for continued investigation.

Accounting for variations in effect sizes. As highlighted in the reviews of Magill and Hall (1990) and Brady (1998), blocked practice does not *always* facilitate acquisition performance, and random practice does not *always* facilitate learning. Obvious goals for the future then must include a better understanding of the conditions (e.g. task, environment, individual differences) under which contextual interference effects might be expected to be large, small or non-existent and a better understanding of *why* these expectations are so. Regarding individual differences, some have suggested that since contextual interference effects are largely cognitively based, then effect sizes should be small or opposite to the norm in populations in which cognitive functioning has been compromised (e.g. Dick *et al.*, 2000). Regarding task differences, theoretical explanations of contextual interference suggest that larger effect sizes would be anticipated for discrete tasks (compared to continuous tasks) because of the greater reliance on planning processes prior to movement execution required in discrete tasks. However, despite the intuitive appeal of such proposals, there exists evidence to the contrary. For example, contextual interference effects remain strong in individuals with Down's syndrome (Edwards *et al.*, 1986) and for continuous tasks (e.g. Tsutsui *et al.*, 1998). Clearly, the influence of moderating variables remains an important area for investigation.

Optimizing performance and learning. Perhaps one of the most important, and overlooked, issues regarding contextual interference relates to *metacognitive* differences in judgements of performance versus learning. Quite simply, individuals are often poor judges of the state of their own learning, and misattribute feelings about how *learning* is proceeding instead to feelings about how changes in *performance* are proceeding (e.g. Koriat, 2000). For instance, participants undergoing blocked practice are likely to feel overconfident in their ability to perform a retention test compared to participants undergoing random practice (Simon and Bjork, 2001).

Metacognitive misattributions concerning performance and learning might be expected to have dire consequences if random practice schedules were to be strictly enforced in an applied setting, such as a rehabilitation clinic (although, to our knowledge, such applied metacognitive research has not been done). It is known that amount of practice is a key law of learning, and that motivation plays a very important role in the continuation of practice on a task. Therefore, it might be expected that random practice could be doomed to failure if the learner does not feel that improvement (learning) is progressing as well as might otherwise be expected (e.g. in a blocked order). Although random practice would be expected to facilitate learning, the metacognitive judgements about learning that might be anticipated to arise during a random practice schedule might lead to discouragement and perhaps, cessation of practice.

The question arises then, as to the possibility that there exists some *hybrid* practice schedule that combines the performance virtues of blocked practice with the learning advantages of random practice. There have been a few attempts to organize such a hybrid schedule, such as scheduling several blocked task variations before randomly switching to another task for a few blocked trials (Al-Ameer and Toole, 1993), or in which task to task changes are contingent on the individual's performance (Simon *et al.*, 2002). Such hybrid schedules show promise in terms of facilitating performance and learning, and possibly, too, the metacognitive attributions that might further engage the individual in practice. The design of different types of hybrid schedules, their influences on performance and learning, and the metacognitive attributions that arise from them reflect a significant promise for future theoretical and applied research on the contextual interference phenomenon.

References

Adams, J. A. (1971). A closed-loop theory of motor learning. *Journal of Motor Behaviour*, 3, 111–150.

Al-Ameer, H. and Toole, T. (1993). Combinations of blocked and random practice orders: benefits to acquisition and retention. *Journal of Human Movement Studies*, 25, 177–191.

Ammons, R. B. (1956). Effects of knowledge of performance: a survey and tentative theoretical formulation. *Journal of General Psychology*, 54, 279–299.

Battig, W. F. (1972). Intratask interference as a source of facilitation on transfer and retention. In E. F. Thompson and J. F. Voss (Eds), *Topics in learning and performance* (pp. 131–159). New York: Academic Press.

Battig, W. F. (1979). The flexibility of human memory. In L. S. Cernak and F. J. M. Craik (Eds), *Levels of processing and human memory* (pp. 23–44). Hillsdale, NJ: Erlbaum.

Blodgett, H. C. (1929). The effect of the introduction of reward upon the maze performance of rats. *University of California Publications in Psychology*, 4, 113–134.

Bortoli, L., Robazza, C., Durigon, V. and Carra, C. (1992). Effects of contextual interference on learning technical sports skills. *Perceptual and Motor Skills*, 75, 555–562.

Boyce, B. A., and Del Rey, P. (1990). Designing applied research in a naturalistic setting using a contextual interference paradigm. *Journal of Human Movement Studies*, 18, 189–200.

Brady, F. (1998). A theoretical and empirical review of the contextual interference effect and the learning of motor skills. *Quest*, 50, 266–293.

Crossman, E. R. F. W. (1959). A theory of the acquisition of speed-skill. *Ergonomics*, 2, 153–156.

Crowder, R. G. (1976). *Principles of learning and memory*. Hillsdale, NJ: Erlbaum.

Del Rey, P., Liu, X. and Simpson, K. J. (1994). Does retroactive inhibition influence contextual interference effects? *Research Quarterly for Exercise and Sport*, 65, 120–126.

Dick, M. B., Hsieh, S., Dick-Muehlke, C., Davis, D. S. and Cotman, C. W. (2000). The variability of practice hypothesis in motor learning: does it apply to Alzheimer's disease? *Brain and Cognition*, 44, 470–489.

Druckman, D. and Bjork, R. A. (1994). *Learning, remembering, believing: enhancing human performance*. Washington, DC: National Academy Press.

Edwards, J. M., Elliott, D. and Lee, T. D. (1986). Contextual interference effects during skill acquisition and transfer in Down's syndrome children. *Adapted Physical Activity Quarterly*, 3, 250–258.

Fitts, P. M. (1964). Perceptual-motor skill learning. In A. W. Melton (Ed.) *Categories of human learning* (pp. 243–285). New York: Academic Press.

Gabriele, T. E., Hall, C. R. and Lee, T. D. (1989). Cognition in motor learning: Imagery effects on contextual interference. *Human Movement Science*, 8, 227–245.

Goode, S. and Magill, R. A. (1986). Contextual interference effects in learning three badminton serves. *Research Quarterly for Exercise and Sport*, 57, 308–314.

Hall, K. G., Domingues, D. A. and Cavazos, R. (1994). Contextual interference effects with skilled baseball players. *Perceptual and Motor Skills*, 78, 835–841.

Hanlon R. E. (1996). Motor learning following unilateral stroke. *Archives of Physical Medicine and Rehabilitation*, 77, 811–815.

Horak, M. (1992). The utility of connectionism for motor learning: a reinterpretation of contextual interference in movement schemas. *Journal of Motor Behaviour*, 24, 58–66.

Hull, C. L. (1943). *Principles of behaviour*. New York: Appleton-Century-Crofts.

Jamieson, B. A. and Rogers, W. A. (2000). Age-related effects of blocked and random practice schedules on learning a new technology. *Journal of Gerontology: Psychological Sciences*, 55B, 343–353.

Jarus, T. (1994) Motor learning and occupational therapy: the organization of practice. *American Journal of Occupational Therapy*, 48, 810–816.

Knock, T. T., Ballard, K. J., Robin, D. A. and Schmidt, R. A. (2000). Influence of order of stimulus presentation on speech motor learning: a principled approach to treatment for apraxia of speech. *Aphasiology*, 14, 653–668.

Koriat, A. (2000). The feeling of knowing: some metatheoretical implications for consciousness and control. *Consciousness and Cognition*, 9, 149–171.

Lee, T. D. (1982). On the locus of contextual interference in motor skill acquisition. Unpublished PhD dissertation, Lousiana State University, Baton Rouge, LA, USA.

Lee, T. D. and Magill, R. A. (1983). The locus of contextual interference in motor-skill acquisition. *Journal of Experimental Psychology: Learning, Memory, and Cognition*, 9, 730–746.

Lee, T. D. and Magill, R. A. (1985). Can forgetting facilitate skill acquisition? In D. Goodman, R. B. Wilberg and I. M. Franks (Eds), *Differing perspectives in motor learning, memory, and control* (pp. 3–22). Amsterdam: Elsevier.

Lee, T. D, Magill, R. A. and Weeks, D. J. (1985). Influence of practice schedule on testing schema theory predictions in adults. *Journal of Motor Behaviour*, 17, 283–299.

Lee, T. D., Swanson, L. and Hall, A. L. (1991). What is repeated in a repetition? Effects of practice conditions on motor skill acquisition. *Physical Therapy*, 71, 150–156.

Magill, R. A. and Hall, K. G. (1990). A review of the contextual interference effect in motor skill acquisition. *Human Movement Science*, 9, 241–289.

Marley, T. L., Ezekiel, H. J., Lehto, N. K., Wishart, L. R. and Lee, T. D. (2000). Application of motor learning principles: the physiotherapy client as a problem-solver. II. Scheduling practice. *Physiotherapy Canada*, 52, 311–316.

Meeuwsen, H. J. and Magill, R. A. (1991). Spacing of repetitions versus contextual interference effects in motor skill learning. *Journal of Human Movement Studies*, 20, 213–228.

Newell, A. and Rosenbloom, P. S. (1981). Mechanisms of skill acquisition and the law of practice. In J. R. Anderson (Ed.), *Cognitive skills and their acquisition* (pp. 1–55). Hillsdale, NJ: Erlbaum.

Poto, C. C. (1988). How forgetting facilitates remembering: an analysis of the contextual interference effect in motor learning. Unpublished PhD Dissertation, Lousiana State University, Baton Rouge, LO, USA.

Pyle, W. H. (1919). Transfer and interference in card-distributing. *Journal of Educational Psychology*, 10, 107–110.

Salmoni, A. W., Schmidt, R. A. and Walter, C. B. (1984). Knowledge of results and motor learning: a review and reappraisal. *Psychological Bulletin*, 95, 355–386.

Schmidt, R. A. (1971). Retroactive interference and amount of original learning in verbal and motor tasks. *Research Quarterly*, 42, 314–326.

Schmidt, R. A. (1972). The case against learning and forgetting scores. *Journal of Motor Behaviour*, 4, 71–88.

Schmidt, R. A. (1975). A schema theory of discrete motor skill learning. *Psychological Review*, 82, 225–260.

Schmidt, R. A. and Bjork, R. A. (1992). New conceptualizations of practice: common principles in three paradigms suggest new concepts for training. *Psychological Science*, 3, 207–217.

Schmidt, R. A., Young, D. E., Swinnen, S. and Shapiro, D. C. (1989). Summary knowledge of results for skill acquisition: support for the guidance hypothesis. *Journal of Experimental Psychology: Learning, Memory, and Cognition*, 15, 352–359.

Schneider, V. I., Healy, A. F. and Bourne, L. E., Jr. (1998). Contextual interference effects in foreign language vocabulary acquisition and retention. In A. F. Healy and L. E. Bourne, Jr. (Eds) *Foreign language learning: psycholinguistic studies on training and retention* (pp. 77–90). Mahwah, NJ: Erlbaum.

Shea, J. B. and Morgan, R. L. (1979). Contextual interference effects on the acquisition, retention, and transfer of a motor skill. *Journal of Experimental Psychology: Human Learning and Memory*, 5, 179–187.

Simon, D. A. and Bjork, R. A. (2001). Metacognition in motor learning. *Journal of Experimental Psychology: Learning, Memory and Cognition*, 27, 907–912.

Simon, D. A. and Bjork, R. A. (2002). Models of performance in learning multisegment movement tasks: Consequences for acquisition, retention, and judgements of learning. *Journal of Experimental Psychology: Applied*, 8, 222–232.

Simon, D. A., Cullen, J. D. and Lee, T. D. (2002). Win-shift/lose-stay: contingent switching as an alternative to random practice. Paper presented at the annual conference of the North American Society for the Psychology of Sport and Physical Activity, Baltimore, MD.

Smith, P. J. and Davies, M. (1995). Applying contextual interference to the Pawlata roll. *Journal of Sports Sciences*, 13, 455–462.

Snoddy, G. S. (1926). Learning and stability: a psychophysical analysis of a case of motor learning with clinical applications. *Journal of Applied Psychology*, 10, 1–36.

Tsutsui, S., Lee, T. D. and Hodges, N. J. (1998). Contextual interference in learning new patterns of bimanual coordination. *Journal of Motor Behaviour*, 30, 151–157.

Verdolini, K. and Lee, T. D. (in press). Motor learning principles of intervention. In C. Sapienza and J. Casper (Eds), *For clinicians by clincians: vocal rehabilitation in medical speech–language pathology*. Austin, TX: Pro-Ed.

Vickers, J. (1999). *Decision training: a new approach to coaching*. Burnaby, BC: Coaches Association of British Columbia.

Winstein, C. J. (1991). Designing practice for motor learning: clinical implications. In M. J. Lister (Ed.), *Contemporary management of motor control problems: proceedings of the II step conference* (pp. 65–76). Alexandria: Foundation for Physical Therapy.

Winstein, C. J. and Schmidt, R. A. (1990). Reduced frequency of knowledge of results enhances motor skill learning. *Journal of Experimental Psychology: Learning, Memory, and Cognition*, 16, 677–691.

Wright, D. L. (1991). The role of intertask and intratask processing in acquisition and retention of motor skills. *Journal of Motor Behaviour*, 23, 139–145.

Wulf, G., Lee, T. D. and Schmidt, R. A. (unpublished). A motivational hypothesis for contextual interference effects.

Wulf, G. and Schmidt, R. A. (1994). Contextual interference effects in motor learning: evaluating a KR-usefulness hypothesis. In J. R. Nitsch and R. Seiler (Eds), *Movement and sport: psychological foundations and effects*. Vol. 2. *Motor control and learning* (pp. 304–309). Sankt Augustin, Germany: Academia Verlag.

3 The utilization of visual feedback in the acquisition of motor skills

Michael A. Khan and Ian M. Franks

The relative contribution of central planning and sensory information processing in movement control has been debated for a number of years. Researchers have developed models of limb control that are based predominantly on 'open-loop' processes (Plamondon and Alimi, 1997; Schmidt *et al.*, 1979), while others have stressed the importance of sensory information processing (Crossman and Goodeve, 1983). Related to this debate is the question of how the role of sensory information changes throughout the acquisition of a motor skill. During the early stages of learning a skill such as a dance routine or a golf swing, people will often look at their limbs to guide their movements. It has been suggested that the reliance on this sensory information decreases as learning progresses since motor programs are developed and refined which free the individual of the need to use time-consuming feedback-based control (Schmidt, 1975; Schmidt and McCabe, 1976). Others have suggested that there is no decrease in the importance of sensory information, but a shift in the importance of one source of sensory information to another, for example, from visual to proprioceptive feedback (Adams *et al.*, 1977; Fleishman and Rich, 1963). Although both of these viewpoints differ in their account of how the use of sensory information changes as a function of practice, common to both positions is the proposition that there is a decreasing reliance on visual feedback.

In contrast to these viewpoints, there is growing evidence that visual feedback remains important for movement control after extensive levels of practice (Proteau and Cournoyer, 1990; Proteau and Marteniuk, 1993; Proteau *et al.*, 1987). Furthermore, it has been shown that part of the learning process involves the discovery of specific control strategies that enable participants to optimize the utilization of visual feedback (Elliott *et al.*, 1995; Khan and Franks, 2000; Khan *et al.*, 1998). In this chapter, we present evidence to illustrate how the role of visual feedback changes throughout practice and discuss the implications of these findings for theories of skill acquisition and models of limb control. We begin with the work of Proteau and colleagues and their development of the specificity of practice hypothesis. This is followed by a discussion of evidence which points to a more flexible control system in which participants adapt their movements according to which sources of sensory information are available. Finally, we turn our attention to the role of visual feedback as a form of knowledge of results (KR). In this regard, the possibility that visual information from completed movements is used to improve motor programming on upcoming trials is discussed. Of specific interest is whether the use of vision as a form of KR has guidance-like qualities that subsequently lead to negative effects when it is removed (Salmoni *et al.*, 1984).

Specificity of practice

Much of the work of Proteau and colleagues has involved the use of a transfer paradigm in which participants received visual feedback during acquisition and were tested without vision after various levels of practice. The rationale for using this design was that reliance on visual feedback could be tested by examining the decrement in performance caused by withdrawing this information. In the first of a series of studies, Proteau *et al.* (1987) had four groups of participants perform an aiming task under two visual feedback conditions. Two groups of participants practiced the task under normal lighting (full vision), while the other two groups practiced in the dark with only the target visible (no vision). Under each visual condition, one group of participants practised for 200 trials (moderate practice) while the other group practised for 2000 trials (extensive practice). Verbal KR regarding the accuracy of movement was given after every trial. Following the training period, participants in all four groups were transferred to the no-vision condition without verbal KR. The results indicated that after both moderate and extensive practice, performance was better in the full vision compared to the no-vision condition. Furthermore, when participants in the full vision condition were transferred to the no-vision condition, there was a larger decrement in performance later in practice compared to when vision was removed earlier in practice. Therefore, instead of participants becoming less reliant on visual feedback processing, the reliance on vision increased as a function of practice.

Researchers have revealed that vision of the moving limb, target location and surrounding environment are important for aiming accuracy (Carlton, 1981; Prablanc *et al.*, 1979, 1986). However, it has been demonstrated that the increasing reliance on vision as a function of practice is primarily due to the ability of participants to effectively use online visual information from the moving limb (Proteau and Cournoyer, 1990; Proteau and Marteniuk, 1993). Proteau and colleagues proposed that learning is specific to the sources of sensory information available during practice. According to their early version of the specificity of practice hypothesis (Proteau, 1992), separate sensory stores were said to exist for vision and proprioception during the early stages of practice. When one source of sensory information was removed, participants could still rely on the other source of feedback. As learning progresses, vision and proprioception are integrated to form an intermodal representation of the expected sensory consequences, thereby mediating a shift from intramodal to intermodal sensory processing. At this point, the withdrawal of one source of information would cause performance to deteriorate because the incoming sensory information can no longer be compared to the single integrated sensory store.

Consistent with the idea that learning is specific to the sources of feedback available during practice, Proteau *et al.* (1992) have shown that providing additional sensory information has a detrimental effect on performance. Similar to their previous work (Proteau and Courneyer, 1990; Proteau *et al.*, 1987), participants practiced aiming movements either with or without visual feedback. However, instead of employing a no-vision transfer test, participants were transferred to a full vision condition in which KR was removed. As one might expect, there was no difference in performance between the acquisition and transfer phases for those participants who practiced with visual feedback. However, providing visual information to those participants who had extensive practice under the no-vision condition caused a significant decrement in performance. Furthermore, performance in the vision transfer test was worse than performance with visual feedback at pre-test level. The ability to utilize visual feedback was actually degraded by practice without vision (i.e. negative transfer).

Support for the specificity of practice hypothesis has been obtained from studies using more complex laboratory tasks such as waveform production (Ivens and Marteniuk, 1997). However, there has been some debate as to whether specificity holds for more 'real-world' tasks. Much of this evidence stems from research on expert–novice differences. The underlying assumption in these studies was that experts would have experienced extensive levels of practice using particular feedback sources. If specificity develops with practice, experts should experience greater decrements in performance compared to novices when sensory conditions are altered. Based on this rationale, Bennett and Davids (1995) examined the precision of a powerlift squat in expert and novice performers under varying sources of visual information. In one condition, participants performed the squat in front of a mirror (i.e. full vision). In a second condition, the mirror was occluded and participants were instructed to fixate on a marker placed overhead (i.e. ambient vision). In a third condition, participants were blindfolded throughout the testing session (i.e. no vision). The results showed that the experts were not affected by the manipulation of visual information. However, the performance of novices was best under the full vision condition and worst when no visual feedback was available. Bennett and Davids suggested that these findings were at odds with the specificity of practice hypothesis since expert weight lifters practice extensively under specific ambient vision conditions, but yet were unaffected by the addition or removal of visual feedback. They explained that for tasks such as the powerlift squat, where direct vision of the limbs is not encouraged, athletes may develop greater kinesthetic awareness with practice. This kinesthetic sensitivity may not be developed in novices and hence they are reliant on visual feedback to regulate their actions.

Similarly, Robertson *et al.* (1994) demonstrated that expert gymnasts are less dependent on visual feedback than novices. They showed that removing vision of the environment through the use of occlusion goggles had no effect on the time it took expert gymnasts to walk across a balance beam. However, novices took longer to complete their movements when visual feedback was not available. Also, while both groups increased the number of form errors when vision was removed, the increase in errors was significantly greater for novices. These findings implied that experts were able to rely on alternative sources of sensory information such as kinesthetic and/or vestibular signals. Noteworthy, is that although movement times were not affected by removing vision from the expert gymnasts, the number of steps to cross the beam did increase (also see Robertson and Elliott, 1996). This suggests that expert gymnasts did not rely on a set of open-loop motor commands developed through practice, but instead adapted their movement strategy to optimize the available sources of sensory information. We will return to this point later.

Proteau et al. (1998) have argued that the problem with testing the specificity of practice hypothesis with expert–novice paradigms is that experts have accumulated a considerable amount of practice without visual feedback and this would benefit their performance in a no-vision condition. For example, in tasks such as the powerlift squat, visual information from the limbs is not directly accessible and experts may rely more on proprioceptive feedback to regulate their movements (Bennett and Davids, 1995). Also, coaches have reported that gymnasts often practice walking across the balance beam with their eyes closed (Proteau et al., 1998). Therefore, in order to test specificity of practice, it is preferable to have more control over the actual sensory information that is available during practice.

In a re-examination of whether the specificity of practice hypothesis holds for the powerlift squat, Tremblay and Proteau (1998) had participants practice squatting movements in one of three conditions; no vision, ambient vision, and a laser condition. The no vision and ambient vision conditions were similar to those in the study of Bennett and Davids (1995). In the laser condition, an infrared penlight was attached to the participants' knees. This projected a beam onto a wall in front of the participants that provided concurrent visual feedback of their squatting position. For each participant, the experimenter noted the height on the wall that corresponded to an accurate squat position. Performance in the laser condition was found to be more accurate than in the no-vision condition throughout practice. When all participants were transferred to the no-vision condition without KR, performance was significantly worse for those who practised in the laser condition compared to the ambient and no-vision conditions. Therefore, consistent with the specificity of practice hypothesis, the source of information that resulted in the best performance during acquisition also lead to the largest decrement in performance when it was withdrawn.

Another important point raised by Proteau et al. (1998) is that in tasks such as beam walking, participants were able to evaluate their performance in the transfer tests by using intrinsic sources of feedback. For example, participants can sense the placement of their feet on the beam and any subsequent loss of balance through the vestibular system. Gaining information from these alternative sources could have reduced the effects of removing visual feedback by providing a basis upon which participants could modify their movements. In order to reduce the possibility of participants relying on alternative forms of feedback, Proteau et al. employed a precision walking task in which a target line was drawn on the floor that could not be detected from participants' foot placement. Participants practised walking across the target line with full visual feedback or blindfolded. When all participants were tested on a no vision transfer test, there was a significant increase in spatial error for participants who practised with visual feedback. Furthermore, this deterioration in performance was significantly greater after 100 compared to twenty trials of practice. These results were similar to those obtained in manual aiming studies and illustrated that the concept of 'specificity of practice' also holds for gross motor skills.

Another challenge to the specificity of practice hypothesis has come from the work of Whiting and colleagues (Whiting and Savelsbergh, 1992; Whiting *et al.*, 1995) on one-handed ball catching. They showed that performance improved when participants were provided with vision of the hand after training without vision of the hand. This was the case after moderate and extensive levels of practice. Changing the sensory conditions under which one practiced did not result in a decrement in performance as predicted by the specificity of practice hypothesis. Whiting and Savelsbergh (1992) noted that performance in a vision transfer test was similar for participants who practiced with vision of the hand and those who had practiced without vision of the hand. This differs from manual aiming in which practice under a particular sensory condition leads to negative transfer under a different sensory condition (see Proteau *et al.*, 1992). In ball catching, it seems that participants adjusted from one set of environmental conditions to another without any deleterious effects caused from practicing under specific feedback conditions.

In response to this evidence against the specificity of practice hypothesis, Tremblay and Proteau (2001) noted that in ball catching studies, participants receive KR about whether or not they have caught the ball from information derived from ball/hand contact. Therefore, similar to the balance beam walking studies of Robertson and colleagues, participants could easily evaluate their performance during both acquisition and in the transfer tests and hence did not suffer decrements in performance when sensory conditions were changed. In order to address this concern, Tremblay and Proteau employed a task in which balls were projected onto a Plexiglas screen placed in front of the participants. Participants were required to touch the screen at the location and time that the ball made contact. This task had many of the requirements of a normal catching task but information could not be derived from ball/hand contact. In support of the specificity of practice hypothesis, Tremblay and Proteau reported that there was a significant decrement in performance when vision of the hand was removed following practice with vision of the hand. However, performance in the transfer test was similar to that of participants who had practiced without vision of the hand. This was again in contrast to evidence from manual aiming studies where performance in a no-vision transfer test was significantly worse for participants who practised with visual feedback compared to participants who practised without visual feedback.

Although participants performing the touch screen task were not able to receive KR from proprioceptive sources, it was possible that participants did receive visual KR, dependent on whether or not the ball was in line with the hand (Proteau, personal communication). For example, participants could tell when they intercepted the ball accurately because the placement of the hand would block vision of the ball. In a recent study, Proteau *et al.* (in prep.) performed a video interception task where the position of the hand was represented as a cursor on a monitor. Removal of the cursor did result in a significant decrement in performance after an acquisition period with vision of the cursor. Also, performance in the no vision transfer test was worse for participants who practiced with vision of the cursor compared to those who practiced without. As for tasks involving movement to stationary targets, the specificity of practice hypothesis holds for tasks involving the interception of moving objects as long as KR is completely removed in transfer.

Although some studies have shown that removing vision results in a larger decrement in performance later in practice (Proteau *et al.*, 1987, 1992), other studies have shown that performance decrements were similar after moderate and extensive levels of practice (Proteau and Cournoyer, 1990; Proteau and Marteniuk, 1993). According to the original version of the specificity of practice hypothesis (Proteau, 1992; Proteau *et al.*, 1992), different sources of sensory information are integrated to form an intermodal sensori-motor representation. Removal or addition of one source of afferent information will cause performance to suffer because incoming sensory information is no longer compatible with the sensory store. Since it takes a considerable amount of practice for specificity to develop, decrements in performance are greater after extensive compared to moderate levels of practice. An alternative explanation recently suggested by Proteau *et al.* (1998) holds that with practice, the source of afferent information that is most likely to ensure optimal performance progressively dominates other sources of sensory information. The withdrawal of this information will lead to increasing decrements in performance as its dominance becomes established. This modified version of the specificity of practice hypothesis offers a viable account of why experts may not be as reliant as novices on vision in tasks such as powerlifting, gymnastic beam walking and catching. In these tasks, visual feedback from the limb may not be the dominant source of information and heavier weighting may be given to information such as proprioceptive feedback, efference copy and vestibular signals. Also, easy access to information as a form of KR may render visual feedback to be less critical for successful performance. While the importance of vision has been demonstrated under carefully controlled laboratory conditions, the development of expertise in more natural settings is likely to involve the use of alternative forms of information.

Optimal control strategies

The work of Proteau and colleagues has demonstrated that if participants practice with visual feedback they will remain dependent on this information after extensive levels of practice. According to their latest version of the specificity of practice hypothesis, the source of afferent information that is deemed to be the most appropriate progressively dominates the processing of other sources of information. Once this dominance is established, any change in sensory conditions will lead to a decrement in performance. Researchers have also proposed that part of the learning process involves the discovery of the most effective control strategy under a particular sensory condition. It has been suggested that when vision is available, participants adapt their movements to optimize its use and hence remain heavily reliant on this source of information after extensive levels of practice. Much of this evidence comes from research on manual aiming where the analysis of movement kinematics has allowed researchers to make inferences about movement programming and feedback processing as well as the interplay between these two processes.

Aiming movements have been said to consist of two phases, a centrally planned initial impulse and a sensory-based error correction phase (Abrams *et al.*, 1990; Meyer *et al.*, 1988; Woodworth, 1899). The initial impulse is assumed to be programmed to end at the location of the target and is characterized by a fairly rapid, continuous change in the position of the limb as it travels most of the distance from the home position to the target (see Figure 3.1). If the endpoint of the initial impulse misses the target, the limb movement may enter an error correction phase. Error corrections are indexed by discontinuities in kinematic profiles (e.g. reversals in direction, zero line crossings and significant deviations in acceleration), which are said to reflect the presence of online adjustments to movement.

In one of the most influential accounts of speed–accuracy trade-offs, Meyer *et al.* (1988) suggested that movement times are minimized through the realization of an optimum trade-off between the durations of the initial impulse and error correction phases. The stochastic optimized sub-movement model is based on the premise that noise exists in the neuromotor system that leads to systematic relationships between the velocity and endpoint variability of component sub-movements. Initial impulses that are too fast will be highly variable and will, therefore, yield long total movement times because of the extensive need for corrective sub-movements. On the other hand, initial impulses with low velocities will be highly accurate but will again result in long movement times because of the long initial impulse durations. An optimal velocity of initial impulses must be assumed so that the combined durations of the initial impulse and error correction phases will be minimized.

Meyer *et al.* (1988) suggested that when visual feedback is available, initial impulses may be programmed with higher velocities compared to when visual feedback is not available. This is because participants can compensate for the higher variability of initial impulse endpoints through effective visual feedback processing. When visual feedback is not available, it may be preferable to produce slow initial impulses to minimize the need for sensory based error corrections. However, Meyer *et al.* found that initial impulses were produced in the same manner regardless of feedback condition and hence the availability of visual information was not taken into account in the basic assumptions of the stochastic optimized sub-movement model. One reason that visual feedback had

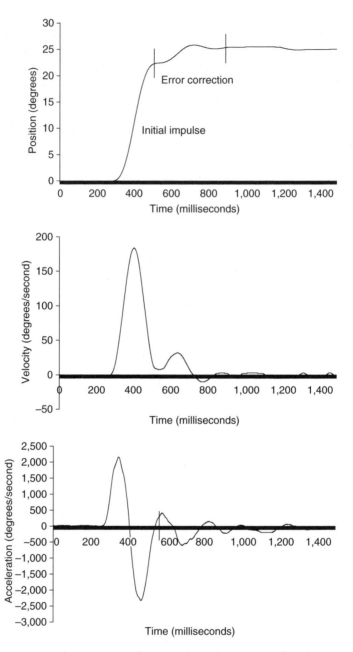

Figure 3.1 Example position, velocity and acceleration profiles showing the initial impulse (II) and error correction (EC) phases for a movement with a criterion movement amplitude of 25 degrees. The markers on the position profile represent the end of the initial impulse and error correction phases. In this particular example, the limb undershot the target in the initial impulse phase but reaccelerated during error correction to end the movement on the target. This type of error correction was indexed by a zero line crossing in acceleration.

relatively little impact in the studies of Meyer *et al.* was that vision and no vision conditions were alternated within trial blocks. Under such a feedback schedule, it was probably easier for participants to adopt similar strategies under the two feedback conditions.

In order to investigate whether different strategies emerge when participants acquire a task under separate visual conditions, Khan *et al.* (1998) had participants practice (i.e. 2,100 trials) rapid wrist rotation movements that translated to movement of a cursor on an oscilloscope screen. The required movement amplitude was 45 degrees and the width of the target was 2.25 degrees (index of difficulty = 4.3 bits). One group of participants practised with vision of the cursor (FV), while another group practiced without vision of the cursor (NV). We found that differences did exist between the initial impulse and error correction phases during the later stages of practice. Participants in the FV group showed a tendency to undershoot the target in the initial impulse phase, whereas there was no evidence for undershooting of the initial impulse for participants in the NV group. Also, the extent to which error corrections were produced was higher in the FV compared to NV condition with this difference increasing throughout practice. It seemed that participants in the FV group undershot the target in the initial impulse phase in order to enable visually based error corrections to proceed in the same direction in which the movement was originally programmed (Elliott *et al.*, 1999). This strategy has the advantage that uncertainty about the required direction of a corrective sub-movement is reduced and it prevents any need to change the order of agonist–antagonist muscle activation patterns in programming corrective sub-movements. In contrast, participants without visual feedback exhibited a progression towards a more open-loop mode of control, whereby they attempted to produce movements which were predominantly pre-programmed in order to avoid the use of less effective proprioceptive feedback.

Although Khan *et al.* (1998) showed that initial impulse *distance* was affected by the availability of visual feedback, the *duration* of initial impulses did not differ between visual conditions. Recall that Meyer *et al.* (1988) described optimal performance in terms of a trade-off between the duration of the initial impulse and error correction phases. However, in a subsequent study, Khan and Franks (2000) found that differences did exist in initial impulse durations under very high accuracy constraints. In this study, participants practiced elbow flexion movements with a required movement amplitude of 45 degrees to a target 1.5 degrees in width (index of difficulty = 5.1 bits). Participants in the FV group decreased the time spent in the initial impulse phase as a function of practice, while initial impulse movement times were relatively constant for participants in the NV group. It seemed that the participants in the FV group increased the speed of their movements such that they could get to the vicinity of the target quickly and then use visual feedback to 'home in' on the target. Participants in the NV group progressed towards a single sub-movement strategy in order to reduce reliance on online corrections. The extent to which error corrections were produced remained relatively high for participants in the FV group, while there was a more gradual decrease throughout practice for participants in the NV group.

The reliance on error corrections enabled participants in the FV group to be more accurate throughout practice than participants in the NV group. Of interest is the question of why participants with visual feedback adopt a strategy whereby they remained reliant on error corrections while there was a steady decline in the production of error corrections when visual feedback was not available? Examination of the consistency of initial impulse endpoints revealed that even after extensive levels of practice, the variability of initial impulses (i.e. within participant standard deviation) was still greater than 3 degrees of elbow rotation. Since the size of the target was 1.5 degrees, this meant that a large proportion of initial impulses missed the target. Due to noise in the neuro-motor system, it seems that participants could not decrease initial impulse variability to the extent that they could hit the target consistently on the initial impulse even after extensive levels of practice. When visual information was available, they adopted a strategy that enabled them to get to the vicinity of the target quickly so that they could optimize the processing of visual feedback to achieve high levels of accuracy. In the no-vision condition, since the threshold for proprioceptive sensitivity at the elbow is greater than 3 degrees (Bevan *et al.*, 1994), participants could not rely on proprioception to make the precise adjustments needed to hit the target. Since error corrections based on proprioception were ineffective in reducing error after the initial impulse, participants progressively reduced the production of corrective submovements with practice.

Elliott *et al.* (1995) provided further evidence that participants learn to adapt their movement trajectories to make optimal use of visual feedback. In their study, one group of participants practiced with visual feedback for the first 600 milliseconds of movement while a second group practiced with vision for the first 400 milliseconds. Both groups increased the velocity of their movements with practice while also being able to lower the variability of movement endpoints (see also Corcos *et al.*, 1993; Khan *et al.*, 1998; Moore and Marteniuk, 1986). Following acquisition, participants in each group were transferred to the visual condition in which the other group had practiced. When participants who practised with 600 milliseconds of visual feedback were transferred to the 400 milliseconds condition, they further increased the velocity of their movements, allowing them to get to the vicinity of the target even earlier. This strategy allowed them to maintain their accuracy level despite having less vision time since they were able to get closer to the target before vision was eliminated. Participants who practised with 400 milliseconds of vision became more accurate when transferred to the 600 milliseconds condition. This level of accuracy was accomplished primarily by increasing movement times to take advantage of the additional time for which vision was available. These results illustrate that participants learn to moderate their control strategies by adapting movement trajectories to accommodate for the available (or not available) sensory information under the given task constraints.

One factor that influences whether or not participants adopt different strategies under vision and no-vision conditions is the scheduling of visual feedback. Zelaznik *et al.* (1983) reported that when visual condition was known in advance of movement initiation, there were larger differences in spatial accuracy between vision and no-vision conditions compared to when participants did not know whether or not they would receive visual information. According to Zelaznik *et al.*, participants prepared to use visual feedback when they knew that it would be available on the upcoming trial and this preparation facilitated the efficiency of processing. When the availability of vision was uncertain, participants may have planned not to use vision in the event of it being absent and hence were not efficient at using vision when it was available. Consistent with the suggestions of Zelaznik *et al.*, Khan *et al.* (2002) have recently shown that prior knowledge of whether or not vision would be available had a significant impact on the strategies that participants adopted. When visual condition was not known in advance of movement initiation, participants adopted similar control strategies in the vision and no-vision conditions. However, when participants knew that they were going to receive visual feedback, they spent less time initiating their movements, less time reaching peak deceleration, but more time after peak deceleration compared to when they did not receive visual feedback. It appeared that when visual feedback was available, participants spent less time preparing the movement but made effective use of visual feedback by getting the limb to the vicinity of the target quickly and allowing time to adjust trajectories at the end of the movement. When visual feedback was not available, more time was spent preparing the movement prior to initiation in order to reduce the need for feedback-based corrections during movement execution. Also, the distance from the target at peak deceleration was greater when visual feedback was available. Participants optimized their use of visual feedback by leaving a window of space before the target in which adjustments to movements could take place (also see Worringham, 1991).

Consistent with the specificity of practice hypothesis, the discovery of optimal control strategies implies that if visual feedback is available during acquisition, this information will remain important for movement control after extensive levels of practice. However, the ability to adapt control strategies has also been viewed as detrimental to a strict version of the specificity of practice hypothesis that predicts that change in the available sources of sensory information will lead to a decrement in performance (i.e. negative transfer) (Bennett and Davids, 1996; Elliott *et al.*, 1995). One possible reason for these differing viewpoints is that in the studies of Proteau and colleagues, movement times were constrained, whereas in other studies (e.g. Elliott *et al.*, 1995), participants were given the freedom to manipulate movement times to optimize performance. It is possible that altering sensory conditions result in negative transfer effects only when other task variables are kept consistent between acquisition and transfer phases. The ability to develop and exhibit flexible control strategies may depend on the constraints imposed during practice and transfer.

Online versus offline control

Most of the research on the role of visual feedback in skill acquisition has focused on the utilization of vision to correct errors in the limb trajectory during movement execution. A prerequisite for online processing of visual feedback is that movement durations are long enough to encompass visuomotor delays. Typically, the use of vision during movement execution has been inferred from the presence of discrete adjustments in the kinematic profiles (i.e. reversals in the direction of movement, zero line crossings and significant deviations in acceleration profiles). The rationale for this was based on the assumption that visual feedback processing is intermittent whereby ballistic phases of movement are run to completion before visual control can take effect (Vince, 1948; for a review, see Elliott *et al.*, 2001). Researchers have also acknowledged that the benefit of vision may not only be due to online processing but that visual feedback from a completed trial may be processed offline as an enriched form of KR. That is, participants use visual information about the limb trajectory on trial '*n*' to adjust movement programming on trials '*n* + 1'. These offline processes would reveal significant differences in initial impulse endpoint accuracy between visual conditions in the absence of any kinematic evidence for online control.

Research has indicated that the variability of initial impulse endpoints and the extent to which error corrections were produced decreased with practice (Abrams and Pratt, 1993; Khan and Franks, 2000; Khan *et al.*, 1998; Pratt and Abrams, 1996). One interpretation of these findings is that improved programming of the initial impulse resulted in a decreasing reliance on visually based error corrections as a function of practice. However, consistent with the findings of Proteau and colleagues, Khan *et al.* (1998) showed that the removal of visual feedback in transfer tests resulted in a larger decrement in endpoint accuracy late in practice compared to early in practice. Despite a reduction in the production of discrete error corrections, the dependency on vision increased as a function of practice. This implies that the increasing reliance on vision may be a consequence of processing activities associated with the production of the initial impulse and not the error correction phases. Furthermore, we have shown that initial impulses were less variable when participants practiced aiming movements with visual feedback compared to when this information was not available (Khan and Franks, 2000; Khan *et al.*, 1998). Visual feedback had an effect on a movement phase that was assumed to be ballistic and, therefore, would not be expected to be influenced by the manipulation of visual feedback (see Abrams *et al.*, 1990; Meyer *et al.*, 1988). On the one hand, it is possible that vision was not playing a role during movement execution but was processed offline to improve movement programming. On the other hand, it is possible that the initial impulse is not ballistic but is open to online regulation. Elliott and colleagues (Elliott *et al.*, 1991, 1995) have suggested that visual guidance may be continuous rather than intermittent in nature taking the form of 'graded adjustment of muscle activity during deceleration' (Elliott *et al.*, 1995, p. 80). Such continuous visual regulation will not be reflected in discrete adjustments to kinematic profiles (also see Pélisson *et al.*, 1986; Proteau and Masson, 1997).

In order to assess the contribution of online and offline processing of visual feedback, Khan and Franks (2003) conducted an experiment in which participants performed aiming movements either without visual feedback, visual feedback from the first 50 per cent of the trajectory, visual feedback from the first 75 per cent of the trajectory or with visual feedback from the entire movement. In order to establish whether visual feedback was processed during the execution of the initial impulse and/or processed offline to improve the programming of initial impulses we examined the variability in distance travelled at various stages throughout the movement (i.e. peak acceleration, peak acceleration + 25 milliseconds, peak velocity, peak velocity + 25 milliseconds, negative peak acceleration, negative peak acceleration + 25 milliseconds, and the end of the initial impulse). The rationale was that if movements are programmed and not altered online, variability should increase as the movement progresses. If compensations for variations in the limb trajectory are made online, then variability profiles would deviate in form from those that describe movement which is programmed in advance and not moderated online.

We found evidence for *offline* control from the analysis of spatial variability at peak velocity. Spatial variability of the initial impulse was lower for the FV and 75 per cent conditions compared to the 50 per cent condition (see Figure 3.2). Since peak velocity occurred at about 50 per cent displacement, the additional visual information in the FV and 75 per cent conditions compared to the 50 per cent vision condition was provided after peak velocity. In order for this information to have an effect at peak velocity, it must have been used offline. Participants saw more of their movement trajectory in the 75 per cent and FV conditions and used this information to improve the programming of initial impulses.

The variability analysis also provided evidence for *online* processing of visual feedback during the production of the initial impulse. In all visual conditions, there was an increase in variability up to peak negative acceleration. Variability then decreased from peak negative acceleration to the end of the initial impulse in the FV condition, but not in the 75 per cent, 50 per cent and NV conditions. Hence, the form of the variability profile was significantly different in the FV compared to the other three conditions. This implies that when visual feedback was available over the duration of the initial impulse, participants compensated for early variations in the movement trajectory during the latter parts of the initial impulse. Therefore, the initial impulse, as defined by the absence of discrete discontinuities in the kinematic profiles, may not represent a ballistic phase of movement. As suggested by Elliott *et al.* (1995), visual regulation of this high-velocity phase may be continuous rather than intermittent in nature and hence would not be reflected in discrete adjustments in kinematic profiles. This evidence for online control during the initial impulse implies that the deterioration in performance caused by the removal of visual feedback was due to the withdrawal of information used in regulating the deceleration of the initial impulse. It has been shown that initial impulses considerably overshoot the target when vision is eliminated following practice with vision (Khan and Franks, 2000; Khan *et al.*, 1998). It is possible that participants develop the ability to use vision to bring the initial impulse to an end and that this information becomes more critical as the velocity of the initial impulse and hence the precision of the breaking process increases with practice.

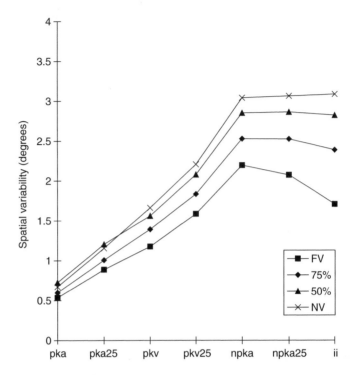

Figure 3.2 Variability in distance travelled at peak acceleration (pka), peak acceleration +
25 milliseconds (pka25), peak velocity (pkv), peak velocity + 25 milliseconds
(pkv25), negative peak acceleration (npka), negative peak acceleration +
25 milliseconds (npka25), and at the end of the initial impulse (ii) for the FV,
75 per cent V, 50 per cent V and NV conditions.

The evidence for offline processing of visual feedback suggests that visual
feedback provided an immediate and enriched form of KR (Abahnini *et al.*, 1997).
Providing frequent KR has been shown to improve performance during acquisition
but degrade learning. According to the guidance hypothesis, providing frequent
feedback would cause performers to be reliant on this information and prevent
the processing of other sources of feedback (Salmoni *et al.*, 1984). When visual
feedback was available during acquisition, participants may have relied on this
information for establishing the appropriate movement commands on subsequent movements. Withdrawing this information resulted in a decrement in
performance since participants could not use other sources of information for
movement planning. Similar to the specificity of practice hypothesis, the guidance
hypothesis can account for the decrements in performance when visual feedback is
removed.

Summary and implications

The evidence presented in this chapter indicates that when participants practise with visual feedback, this source of information remains important for both the planning and execution of movement after extensive levels of practice. This is the case for manual aiming tasks and more complex movements such as weight lifting, locomotion and catching. However, it should be kept in mind that the importance of visual feedback for well-practised performers has been demonstrated only when the sensory conditions during acquisition are carefully controlled. In many natural sporting situations, where vision of the limbs is not encouraged due to the demands of the task, performers may rely on other sources of sensory information such as proprioception. Hence, expert performers are not as reliant on visual feedback when compared to novices. According to the latest version of the specificity of practice hypothesis, the source of afferent information that is most suited to meet the demands of the task progressively dominates other sources of sensory information. Perhaps vision of the limbs is not the source of information that is most critical for optimal performance in many sporting environments and hence its dominance over other sources of information is not established. For example, in sports such as weightlifting, visual attention may be directed towards external frames of reference such as focal points in the environment to guide movement. In open sports such as cricket and tennis, visual information must be gained about the movements of players and the ball. Looking at the movement of the limbs by practicing without the ball may enhance the acquisition of technical skills early in learning when intrinsic sensory representations have not been established. The processing of visual information may provide a catalyst upon which the processing of intrinsic sources of information such as proprioception can be accurately calibrated (Proteau and Marteniuk, 1993). Providing concurrent visual feedback through video and biofeedback techniques has been shown to be successful in enhancing technical skills in sport and improving movement coordination in rehabilitation settings in which there has been damage to sensory pathways (see Magill, 2001). However, the continued and frequent availability of augmented visual feedback throughout the learning process would eventually lead to a reliance on this information and hence detract from the processing of intrinsic sources of feedback. Therefore, while the enhancement of visual feedback processing, either through instruction or artificial visual aids, may have beneficial effects in guiding limb movement during acquisition, this should be discouraged in those tasks where successful performance requires that vision is directed away from the limbs.

References

Abahnini, K., Proteau, L. and Temprado, J. J. (1997). Evidence supporting the importance of peripheral visual information for the directional control of aiming movement. *Journal of Motor Behaviour*, 29, 230–242.

Abrams, R. A., Meyer, D. E. and Kornblum, S. (1990). Eye–hand coordination: oculo-motor control in rapid aimed limb movements. *Journal of Experimental Psychology: Human Perception and Performance*, 16, 248–267.

Abrams, R. A. and Pratt, J. (1993). Rapid aimed limb movements: differential effects of practice on component submovements. *Journal of Motor Behaviour*, 25, 288–298.

Adams, J. A., Gopher, D. and Lintern, G. (1977). Effects of visual and proprioceptive feedback on motor learning. *Journal of Motor Behaviour*, 9, 11–22.

Bennett, S. and Davids, K. (1995). The manipulation of vision during the powerlift squat: exploring the boundaries of the specificity of learning hypothesis. *Research Quarterly for Exercise and Sport*, 66, 210–218.

Bennett, S. and Davids, K. (1996). Manipulating the informational constraints in one-handed catching: how generalisable is the specificity of learning hypothesis? *The British Psychological Society Sport and Exercise Psychology Section Newsletter*, 5, 21–25.

Bevan, L., Cordo, P., Carlton, L. and Carlton, M. (1994). Proprioceptive coordination of movement sequences: discrimination of joint angle versus angular distance. *Journal of Neurophysiology*, 71, 1862–1872.

Carlton, L. G. (1981). Processing visual feedback information for movement control. *Journal of Experimental Psychology: Human Perception and Performance*, 7, 1019–1032.

Corcos, D. M., Jaric, S., Agarwal, G. C. and Gottlieb, G. L. (1993). Principles for learn-ing single-joint movements I. Enhanced performance by practice. *Experimental Brain Research*, 94, 499–513.

Crossman, E. R. W. and Goodeve, P. J. (1983). Feedback control of hand-movement and Fitts' law. *Quarterly Journal of Experimental Psychology*, 35A, 251–278.

Elliott, D., Carson, R. G., Goodman, D. and Chua, R. (1991). Discrete vs continuous control of manual aiming. *Human Movement Science*, 10, 393–418.

Elliott, D., Chua, R., Pollock, B. J. and Lyons, J. (1995). Optimizing the use of vision in manual aiming: the role of practice. *Quarterly Journal of Experimental Psychology*, 48A, 72–83.

Elliott, D., Heath, M., Binsted, G., Ricker, K. L., Roy, E. A. and Chua, R. (1999). Goal directed aiming: correcting a force specification error with the right and left hand. *Journal of Motor Behaviour*, 31, 309–324.

Elliott, D., Helsen, W. F. and Chua, R. (2001). A century later: Woodworth's (1899) two-component model of goal directed aiming. *Psychological Bulletin*, 127, 342–357.

Fleishman, E. A. and Rich, S. (1963). Role of kinesthetic and spatial–visual abilities in perceptual-motor learning. *Journal of Experimental Psychology*, 66, 6–11.

Ivens, C. J. and Marteniuk, R. G. (1997). Increased sensitivity to changes in visual feed-back with practice. *Journal of Motor Behaviour*, 29, 326–338.

Khan, M. A. and Franks, I. M. (2000). The effect of practice on component submove-ments is dependent on visual feedback. *Journal of Motor Behaviour*, 32, 227–240.

Khan, M. A. and Franks, I. M. (2003). Online versus offline processing of visual feed-back in the production of component submovements. *Journal of Motor Behaviour*, 35, 285–295.

Khan, M. A., Franks, I. M. and Goodman, D. (1998). The effect of practice on the control of rapid aiming movements: evidence for an interdependency between programming and feedback processing. *Quarterly Journal of Experimental Psychology*, 51A, 425–444.

Khan, M. A., Elliott, D., Coull, J., Chua, R. and Lyons, J. (2002). Optimal control strate-gies under different feedback schedules: kinematic evidence. *Journal of Motor Behaviour*, 34, 45–57.

Magill, R. A. (2001). *Motor learning: concepts and applications* (6th ed.). New York, NY: McGraw-Hill.

Meyer, D. E., Abrams, R. A., Kornblum, S., Wright, C. E. and Smith, J. E. K. (1988). Optimality in human motor performance: ideal control of rapid aimed movements. *Psychological Review*, 95, 340–370.

Moore, S. P. and Marteniuk, R. G. (1986). Kinematic and electromyographic changes that occur as a function of learning a time-constrained aiming task. *Journal of Motor Behaviour*, 18, 397–426.

Pélisson, D., Prablanc, C., Goodale, M. A. and Jeannerod, M. (1986). Visual control of reaching movements without vision of the limb. II. Evidence of fast unconscious processes correcting the trajectory of the hand to the final position of a double-step stimulus. *Experimental Brain Research*, 62, 303–313.

Plamondon, R. and Alimi, A. M. (1997). Speed/accuracy trade-offs in target-directed movements. *Behavioural and Brain Sciences*, 20, 279–349.

Prablanc, C., Echallier, J. F., Jeannerod, M. and Komilis, E. (1979). Optimal response of eye and hand motor systems in pointing at a visual target: II. Static and dynamic visual cues in the control of hand movement. *Biological Cybernetics*, 35, 183–187.

Prablanc, C., Pélisson, D. and Goodale, M. A. (1986). Visual control of reaching movements without vision of the limb. I. Role of retinal feedback of target position in guiding the hand. *Experimental Brain Research*, 62, 293–302.

Pratt, J. and Abrams, R. A. (1996). Practice and component submovements: the roles of programming and feedback in rapid aimed limb movements. *Journal of Motor Behaviour*, 28, 149–156.

Proteau, L. (1992). On the specificity of learning and the role of visual information in movement control. In L. Proteau and D. Elliott (Eds), *Vision and motor control* (pp. 67–103). Amsterdam: North-Holland.

Proteau, L. and Cournoyer, J. (1990). Vision of the stylus in a manual aiming task: the effects of practice. *Quarterly Journal of Experimental Psychology*, 42A, 811–828.

Proteau, L. and Marteniuk, R. G. (1993). Static visual information and the learning and control of a manual aiming movement. *Human Movement Science*, 12, 515–536.

Proteau, L. and Masson, G. (1997). Visual perception modifies goal directed movement: supporting evidence from visual perturbation paradigm. *Quarterly Journal of Experimental Psychology*, 50A, 726–741.

Proteau, L., Marteniuk, R. G., Girouard, Y. and Dugas, C. (1987). On the type of information used to control and learn an aiming movement after moderate and extensive training. *Human Movement Science*, 6, 181–199.

Proteau, L., Marteniuk, R. G. and Lévesque, L. (1992). A sensorimotor basis for motor learning: evidence indicating specificity of practice. *Quarterly Journal of Experimental Psychology*, 44A, 557–575.

Proteau, L., Tremblay, L. and DeJaeger, D. (1998). Practice does not diminish the role of visual information in on-line control of a precision walking task: support for the specificity of practice hypothesis. *Journal of Motor Behaviour*, 30, 143–150.

Proteau, L., Veilleux, L.-N. and Gullaud, E. (in prep.). Seeing the incoming ball might be seeing one's hand in a manual interception task: support for the specificity of practice hypothesis.

Robertson, S. and Elliott, D. (1996). Specificity of learning and dynamic balance. *Research Quarterly for Exercise and Sport*, 67, 69–75.

Robertson, S., Collins, J., Elliott, D. and Starkes, J. (1994). The influence of skill and intermittent vision on dynamic balance. *Journal of Motor Behaviour*, 26, 333–339.

Salmoni, A. W., Schmidt, R. A. and Walter, C. B. (1984). Knowledge of results and motor learning: a review and reappraisal. *Psychological Bulletin*, 95, 355–386.

Schmidt, R. A. (1975). A schema theory of discrete motor skill learning. *Psychological Review*, 82, 225–260.

Schmidt, R. A. and McCabe, J. F. (1976). Motor program utilization over extended practice. *Journal of Human Movement Studies*, 2, 239–247.

Schmidt, R. A., Zelaznik, H., Hawkins, B., Frank, J. S. and Quinn, J. T., Jr, (1979). Motor-output variability: a theory for the accuracy of rapid motor acts. *Psychological Review*, 86, 415–451.

Tremblay, L. and Proteau, L. (1998). Specificity of practice: the case of powerlifting. *Research Quarterly for Exercise and Sport*, 69, 284–289.

Tremblay, L. and Proteau, L. (2001). Specificity of practice in a ball interception task. *Canadian Journal of Experimental Psychology*, 2001, 55, 207–218.

Vince, M. A. (1948). Corrective movements in a pursuit task. *Quarterly Journal of Experimental Psychology*, 1, 85–106.

Whiting, H. T. A. and Savelsbergh, G. J. P. (1992). An exception that proves the rule! In G. E. Stelmach and J. Requin (Eds), *Tutorials in motor behaviour II* (pp. 583–579). Amsterdam: North-Holland.

Whiting, H. T. A., Savelsbergh, G. J. P. and Pijpers, J. R. (1995). Specificity of motor learning does not deny flexibility. *Applied Psychology: An International Review*, 44, 315–332.

Woodworth, R. S. (1899). The accuracy of voluntary movement. *Psychological Review*, (3) (2, Whole No. 13).

Worringham, C. J. (1991). Variability effects on the internal structure of rapid aiming movements. *Journal of Motor Behaviour*, 23, 75–85.

Zelaznik, H. N., Hawkins, B. and Kisselburgh, L. (1983). Rapid visual feedback processing in single-aiming movements. *Journal of Motor Behaviour*, 15, 217–236.

4 One-trial motor learning

John Dickinson, Daniel Weeks, Bill Randall and David Goodman

An uncommon, but not rare, experience in the acquisition of skill is the occurrence of a sudden and dramatic change in level of performance. Typically, the phenomenon is displayed after a variable number of trials in which seemingly, and frustratingly, there is no change in performance. Then, on a single trial the skill is performed correctly and thereafter is often produced without error. Anecdotal descriptions of the process include statements such as: 'I suddenly got it'; or 'All at once I got the hang of it', or 'I got the knack that time'. The subjective perception is analogous to cognitive insights. When solving a cryptic crossword or some other intellectual puzzle, many solutions may be arrived at by logical progression, but occasionally an answer is achieved in a 'flash of inspiration' or an 'insight'. Often it is only after the correct response has been produced that the solver works out how and why it is appropriate. In the motor skills context we have received reports of such dramatic changes in performance in diverse skills including riding a bicycle, performing a kip on the parallel and high bars in gymnastics, in skiing and in raising the puck with a wrist-shot in hockey. While gradual improvement in skills appears to represent the normal experience of skill acquisition, a significant proportion of those questioned agreed that the step-function improvement characteristic of one-trial learning had formed a part of their acquisition history. It should be noted that we do not refer here to very simple tasks, which once observed or after instruction can be performed on the first trial. Rather we are examining those skills in which no apparent change in performance over a number of trials is suddenly replaced by success on a single trial.

Despite its frequency of occurence, the phenomenon has been largely ignored in the academic literature on motor learning. The rare exception is the work of Anderson (2000) who used modified gymnastic stunts to search for evidence of one-trial learning in motor skill acquisition. However, he conclude that minimal support was found for the one-trial learning phenomenon. Anderson (2000) further suggested that the 'one-trial learning phenomenon described in animal learning is quite different from the insights that are gained in human motor learning' (p. 46). Nevertheless, as we outline later in the chapter, there are strong lines of evidence from human verbal learning and conditioning that one-trial learning can occur. There have been other occasional instances where single trial acquisition effects have been noted, although this was not the focus of the research. For example, Weeks *et al.* (1996) found, in an elbow flexion task using a manipulandum, that participants could adjust to loads either assisting or opposing movement in a single trial. In the first trial following a change in the load condition, 63 per cent were able to perform the required movement to the target. For the remainder of the participants, success occurred on the subsequent trial. While this may be viewed in the context of transfer to a task variant, the observation, nevertheless, bears some similarity to a one-trial acquisition process. In general, however, research has been guided by an incrementalist view of the acquisition process in which improvement in performance is assumed to occur as the gradual establishment of correct responses and appropriate sub-routines combined with the elimination of errors. This has been true at both descriptive and theoretical levels.

In this chapter, we review the nature of the descriptions and theories of motor acquisition and trace the development of current incremental views. These are contrasted with earlier one-trial accounts of the learning process. Much of the early research in the controversy between one-trial and incremental learning involved paired-associate designs. These are reviewed and our replications with motor actions are described. We also provide an account of our investigation into one-trial effects in the acquisition of a complex motor task and finally try to draw some conclusions concerning the future of research in this area.

Acquisition theories and descriptions

The early description of the motor learning process by Bryan and Harter (1897, 1899) noted a systematic progression through a 'hierarchy of habits' as skill improved. Snoddy (1926) proposed a two-stage descriptive model of acquisition in which an 'adaptation' phase was succeeded by a 'facilitation' phase of increasing efficiency of movement. In their influential text, Fitts and Posner (1967) outlined three stages of acquisition: cognitive, associative and autonomous phases. They described a generic ogival relationship between trials and performance. While accepting that there are significant differences between tasks and between individual learners, the curve received general acceptance as an adequate account of progress in learning. Simple tasks may show an abbreviated or non-existent cognitive phase, and hence the performance curve may simply be a negatively accelerated function of practice. More complex tasks may require lengthy cognitive activity before any physical change in performance occurs, or considerable time spent in what Adams (1971) called the verbal-motor stage. Similarly, the nature of the task may influence later stages of learning. Gentile (1972) argued that what Fitts and Posner called the autonomous phase might be described as a process of fixation or diversification, depending on the skill's location on the open–closed continuum. Although there are significant differences between the descriptions of the course of the acquisition process, there is a common underlying assumption that there is an inevitable, predictable and gradual progression from novice to expert.

A similar assumption is present in theories, as well as descriptions, of motor learning. In Adams' (1971) closed-loop theory, the function of practice is the gradual accumulation of strength in the perceptual trace. Knowledge of results guides subsequent trials to closer and closer approximation to the desired movement goal. Knowledge of results also guides the selection of appropriate responses from the memory trace. In both cases, increments in performance appear as a function of experience, with the strengthening of traces and hence, quality of performance, directly related to the number of trials in which knowledge of results is provided. While Schmidt's (1975) schema theory solved a number of problems inherent in closed-loop theory, it maintained the same incrementalist perspective. Successive trials were assumed to refine the recognition and recall schemata enabling increasingly accurate responses, and again closer and closer approximation to desired outcomes. While not as explicit, dynamical conceptualizations of the acquisition process also assume an incremental position with coordinated patterns of movement 'emerging' as learners gradually solve such problems as the degrees of freedom inherent in the task (e.g. see Schmidt and Lee, 1999).

There are probably three reasons why the incrementalist position has achieved unquestioned acceptance. First, there is little dispute that the greater proportion of skills are acquired through gradual improvement, and it is therefore fitting that priority be given to the explanation of this phenomenon. Second, it may be argued that the existence of step-wise or one-trial acquisition is easily masked by conventional means of measuring and reporting in learning studies. For example, mean results presented on a per trial basis can reveal a negatively accelerated function which hides the fact that a proportion of the participants in the experiment acquired the skill in a single, although not necessarily the same, trial. It is also conceivable that *all* participants in an experiment could show one-trial learning, and the traditional performance curve result, when only mean scores are presented. Consider the example presented in Figure 4.1.

The superficial interpretation of such a graph is that it demonstrates an incremental process of acquisition, which is obviously belied by examination of individual scores. In addition, many of the tasks typical of a learning experiment may contain multiple components. If learning of each component occurs on a one-trial basis and this trial varies between participants, the probability that the process will be masked in gross outcome measures is exacerbated.

Third, it is our contention that the historical antecedents of current motor learning theorizing are partly responsible for the neglect of one-trial learning. Adams' (1971) paper, which proposed the closed-loop theory, was largely a reaction to the stimulus–response (S–R) connectionism of Clark L. Hull (Hull, 1943, 1951, 1952). In brief, Hull (1943) proposed that learning is a function of habit strength (sHr) linking stimuli and responses. Habit strength increases as a result of reinforced trials where reinforcement is a reward that reduces drive. The learning becomes overt and the response is produced when sHr exceeds some threshold value. This threshold value oscillates from moment to moment. Thus, for example, early in the acquisition process the organism may give the appropriate

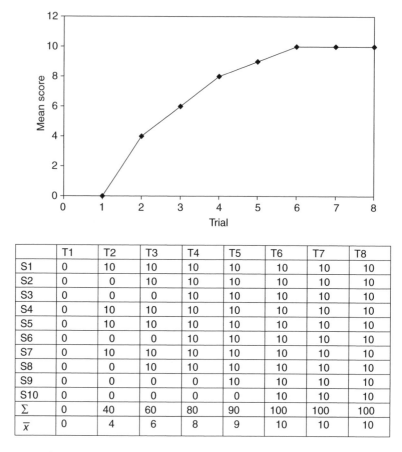

	T1	T2	T3	T4	T5	T6	T7	T8
S1	0	10	10	10	10	10	10	10
S2	0	0	10	10	10	10	10	10
S3	0	0	0	10	10	10	10	10
S4	0	10	10	10	10	10	10	10
S5	0	10	10	10	10	10	10	10
S6	0	0	0	10	10	10	10	10
S7	0	10	10	10	10	10	10	10
S8	0	0	10	10	10	10	10	10
S9	0	0	0	0	10	10	10	10
S10	0	0	0	0	0	10	10	10
Σ	0	40	60	80	90	100	100	100
$\overline{x}$	0	4	6	8	9	10	10	10

Figure 4.1 Illustrative example demonstrating incremental learning when examining mean performance.

response on one trial and fail to do so on the next. Hull's explanation was that sHr had increased but the threshold value was higher on the second trial and the increased level of learning failed to materialize in performance. In his rejection of this position, Adams focused on the error of equating knowledge of results in human learning and reinforcement in animal learning. Quite rightly, Adams pointed out that while knowledge of results may have some motivational function, it is the information given to the performer that guides subsequent attempts that is its important characteristic.

Nevertheless, while rejecting much of Hull's explanation of the acquisition process, Adams implicitly accepted Hull's proposition that learning is incremental in nature. Whereas Hull talked of increasing the 'habit strength' linking stimuli and responses as a function of reinforced trials, Adams proposed the incremental effect of trials with knowledge of results (KR) on the 'strength' of perceptual and memory traces. Therefore, in making the case for abandoning a previously influential Hullian perspective, Adams at the same time fostered Hull's assumption of incrementalism. Such was the impact of Adams' work and the reactions to it (including Schmidt's 1975 Schema Theory) that little reflection on the incremental assumption has occurred since.

This is perhaps surprising, in retrospect, since contemporary competing theories of learning during the 1940s and 1950s not only acknowledged that one-trial learning occurs, but in some cases argued that all learning occurs on a one-trial basis. In fact, in the noted text *Theories of Learning* by Hilgard and Bower (1966), the authors cited the controversy between incremental and one-trial learning as one of the central issues on which learning theorists are divided. Notable among the proponents of a one-trial view of learning was E. R. Guthrie (Guthrie, 1952).

Guthrie's writing places him in the S–R connectionist tradition with Hull, but with very different interpretations of many of the salient aspects of the learning and conditioning processes. The nature and function of motivation, reinforcement, punishment and intention were all approached in fundamentally and often antithetically different ways from those of Hull. Nowhere is this more apparent than in his discussion of the role of practice. Learning occurred in an all-or-none or one-trial fashion, according to Guthrie. Contiguity of stimulus and response were sufficient for acquisition to occur. The role of motivation was reduced to that of a simple activating system (i.e. it only had importance in determining the vigour of movement). Similarly, the function of reward or reinforcement was dismissed as merely an arrangement of circumstances that removed the organism from the preceding stimulus array and, hence, preserved the integrity of associations formed between those stimuli and the organism's responses. For example, Hull argued that hunger was a drive, which was reduced by the reinforcement of food and was partially responsible for increasing the habit strength of a response that preceded it. On the other hand, Guthrie contended that hungry animals were active and performed responses in a given stimulus environment. When presented with food, the environment was changed, so that the link between the responses and the preceding environment was preserved.

The ubiquitous observation of incrementalism in performance curves was explained with reference to the masking effect of averaging individual curves and, in more complex tasks, by arguing sub-components were learned in saltatory fashion which, when summed, gave an appearance of incremental improvement. Convincing evidence of the former explanation was provided by Guthrie's student Voeks (1954) in a study of eyelid conditioning. Using a puff of air to the eye as the unconditioned stimulus, Voeks found that once a participant produced a blink to the conditioned stimulus that conditioned response always occurred. That is, the learned response occurred on one-trial and thereafter always appeared. In the latter case, it was argued from the perspective of probability theory by Estes (1950) that skill represents a population of movement habits associated with a population of stimuli. Learning appears to accumulate with practice, but in actuality each sub-habit is acquired at full-strength on a single trial. The paper by Estes was theoretical in nature, but empirical support was found subsequently by Estes *et al.* (1960) using verbal paired-associate learning.

Cognitive psychologists of the era also devoted considerable attention to the issue of one-trial acquisition. The Gestalt psychologists (e.g. see Koffka, 1935) rejected much of S–R connectionism and particularly the trial-and-error assumptions left as a legacy to learning theory by Thorndike (1913). The Gestalt psychologists' position was that the laws of organization in perception, which they had developed over a number of years, could be applied to learning. In essence, they argued that a problem in learning may be solved by the restructuring of the perceptual field. A learner acts intelligently, reviewing the stimulus environment in the context of the goal to be achieved. On the basis of understanding, a solution is derived; there is an 'insight' that leads to appropriate action. The Gestalt psychologists did not deny that there may be some trial-and-error approaches preceding the solution or that a learner may resort to such an approach when the problem is too difficult, but in much of human learning, it was contended that restructuring and understanding were the precursors of success in learning.

The Gestalt psychologists identified four principal characteristics of insightful learning. First, the transition from pre-solution to the post-solution state is sudden. The transition occurs on an all-or-none basis. Second, the performance resulting from insightful solution will usually be error free. Third, such a solution will be retained for an extended period of time. Finally, they argued that solutions gained by insight may be transferred to other similar problems. In the context of one-trial motor learning, the Gestalt psychologists would have little problem with the description that after some trial-and-error attempts, the learner suddenly 'sees' the solution and performs the skill perfectly.

Paired-associate designs

After reviewing the literature we decided that the area merited some experimental investigation in the motor learning context. We chose as an initial study to replicate an experiment conducted in the domain of verbal learning by Rock (1957). Rock's experiment was an ingenious attempt to distinguish between one-trial and incremental learning hypotheses. He used a paired-associate protocol in which a list of twelve three-letter nonsense syllables in one experiment, and single or double letters in another, acted as stimuli and had to be paired correctly with number responses ranging from one to fifty in one experiment and from one to seventy-two in the second. Participants were presented with the pairs one at a time in the learning trial and with only the stimulus portion on the subsequent test trial displayed in random order, and were required to provide the response. For the control group, the learning and test trials were then repeated (with item order changed) until the complete list was recalled correctly. For the experimental group, the procedure was identical except that after each test trial any S–R pair that had not been recalled correctly was replaced with an entirely different S–R pair.

Rock's argument was that if an incremental view is correct there would be a gradual increase in the associative link between stimuli and responses until the threshold for overt production was passed and the correct response occurred. Hence, the incremental hypothesis would predict superiority for the control group who saw the same pairs repeatedly. Conversely, the prediction from a one-trial or all-or-none theorist would be that there would be no difference in the performance of the groups. If a participant responded incorrectly to a stimulus on the trial, the inference is made that no associative strength had been formed between the stimulus and its response on the preceding learning trial, and therefore no penalty would accompany the substitution of a different S–R pair.

The dependent variables were number of trials to reach the criterion of error-free performance and number of errors made before reaching criterion. In both cases there was no difference between the groups, which Rock suggested provided evidence for the one-trial perspective.

Our adaptation (Randall *et al.*, 1995) of the Rock study involved participants in learning a paired-associate list in which the stimuli were nonsense syllables and the responses were motor responses in the form of hand signs. On acquisition trials, the stimulus and response pairs were presented individually *via* a computer screen. On test trials, the stimulus was presented alone and the participant was required to physically produce the appropriate hand sign. The list consisted of eight pairs presented in random order on each trial. As in the Rock study, the control group received the same eight pairs throughout the experiment, whereas the experimental group followed the drop-out procedure in which any pair that was incorrect on a test trial was replaced with a new nonsense syllable–hand sign (S–R) pair on the subsequent learning trial. The dependent variables were again number of trials to reach the criterion of an error-free test trial and the number of errors committed in reaching criterion.

Our results closely replicated those of Rock. Mean number of trials to criterion was 5.38 for the experimental group and 4.75 for the controls, which was not significantly different. The median number of trials to criterion was identical (4.5 trials) for both groups. There were also no significant differences between mean and median errors between the groups in reaching the criterion.

In reviewing these results, we were conscious of the problems inherent in drawing conclusions from statistical support for the null hypothesis. Nevertheless, we were sufficiently encouraged by this evidence in support of one-trial learning using motor responses that we sought confirmation by modelling additional experiments on studies emanating from the debate of the 1950s.

Estes (1950, 1959), with collaborators and co-workers, developed the Stimulus Sampling Theory which was, in essence, a stochastic learning model and in many respects represented a mathematical formalization of Guthrie's S–R associationism. The probabilistic nature of the model is reflected in the use of probabilities as the dependent variable of interest in the study we replicated (Estes *et al.*, 1960). This study also used a paired-associate learning task.

We used a comparison between groups that experienced either two acquisitions and test trials of the same S–R pairings, or completed only one acquisition trial followed by two test trials (Randall, 1999). On the acquisition trials participants saw a nonsense syllable and hand sign on the computer screen. They physically produced the hand sign. On the test trials only the stimulus nonsense syllable was presented. The list of eight S–R pairs was the same for each group. Thus, the protocol for the control group consisted of an acquisition trial involving exposure to the eight S–R pairs, reproducing the response physically after viewing each pair. This group was then tested by providing them with the eight stimuli alone and requiring them to reproduce the appropriate hand position. This process was then repeated. In contrast, the experimental group experienced just one acquisition trial (pairing of S–R pairs) but this was followed by two test trials, where all eight stimuli alone were presented.

A number of hypotheses were developed based on one-trial and incremental perspectives. From an incrementalist position it was argued that on the first acquisition trial all S–R pairs would increase in habit strength. The extent to which this strength exceeded the oscillating momentary threshold would determine whether the response was made overt (i.e. was correct) on the test trial. For the experimental group, which experienced two test trials, it would be predicted that a similar number of pairs would be correct on the second test trial, but not necessarily the same pairs, since the threshold for overt production would be different on the second test trial. Conversely, for one-trial hypotheses a correct response on the first trial for the experimental group should lead to a correct response on the second trial and an incorrect response on the first trial should be followed by an incorrect response on the second for any particular pair. Put into terms of probability theory, the probability of a correct response on test trial two (CT2) following a correct response on test trial one (CT1) should be 1 and the probability of an incorrect response on test trial two (NT2) following an incorrect test on trial one (NT1) should also be 1.

In our study, $P(CT2\ CT1)$ was 0.875 and $P(NT2\ NT1)$ was 0.982. Both statistics are more in keeping with a one-trial perspective than an incrementalist perspective. Similarly, we found that $P(NT2\ CT1)$ was 0.125 (i.e. we found only one instance in which a pair that was correct on test one was incorrect on test two), supporting the one-trial view. The reverse probability also supported the one-trial hypothesis. The probability of being correct on the second test trial for the experimental group after being incorrect on the first test trial $P(C2\ NT1)$ was only 0.018. This conclusion is strengthened when a comparison is made with the control group whose result for $P(CT2\ NT1)$ was 0.274. The fifteen-fold difference between these probabilities suggests that the new correct pairs on T2 for the control group were learned in one-trial fashion on the second acquisition trial.

In comparing our results with the original data from Estes *et al.* (1960), we found that ours approximated to the hypothetical results predicted by one-trial learning. In light of this we decided to perform a third experiment replicating a paired-associate study emanating from the era. In this study we examined transfer of training from a one-trial versus incremental learning perspective. Two experiments (Rock and Heimer, 1959; Schwartz, 1963) that produced contradictory results, were the models for the experiment.

The phenomenon of positive transfer of training has proven easy to accommodate within theories of learning. Stimulus and response generalization hypotheses account for positive transfer in simple conditioning paradigms and Thorndike's (1911) 'identical elements' theory of transfer was accepted as a basis for accounting for transfer in more complex human skills. Adams' (1971) closed-loop theory and Schmidt's (1975) schema theory provided updated and more sophisticated descriptions, but fundamentally their explanations of positive transfer are very similar to Thorndike's view that the benefit of previous experience in learning a new skill is contingent on the similarities between the two skills. The greater the similarity between two skills, the greater the degree of positive transfer. While Thorndike referred only to similarities between the physical characteristics of stimulus and response, the interpretations of Schmidt focus on the similarities of relationships between parameters of the task; an amount of force applied, for example, produces a related impact on the environment and the knowledge of this relationship may be applied to a similar task.

Negative transfer has remained more intransigent as a phenomenon for inclusion in theoretical interpretations of learning. Why should previous learning impair subsequent acquisition of a similar, but different skill? The summaries of research on transfer by Holding (1976) and Osgood (1949) confirm that significant numbers of studies show that, particularly when stimulus conditions remain the same in two tasks but different responses are required, negative transfer is the likely result. Adams (1971) tended to ignore the phenomenon, whereas Schmidt (1988) minimized negative transfer, suggesting that it was relatively rare in real life skills and, moreover, that it was most frequently 'cognitive' rather than 'motor' in nature. Schmidt suggested that negative transfer resulted because participants did not know 'what to do' rather than 'how to do it'.

In the context of traditional paired-associate learning, negative transfer in AB–AD designs (same stimuli with different responses in the two tasks) was regarded differently by one-trial and incremental theorists. For the incrementalist, the first association (AB) would provide 'response competition' until the habit strength of the new association (AD) exceeded the association strength of AB. This process required more trials than necessary for a control group that learned AD without previous experience, and hence resulted in negative transfer (for an example of transfer surfaces, see Holding, 1976; Osgood, 1948). In the incremental view (see Postman, 1963) the gradual development of associative strength between the new S–R combination would eventually result in correct responding but response competition would still exist. By contrast, the one-trial view held that the new S–R combination would be acquired on a single trial, eliminating the original association (AB) and no 'response-competition' would be found. Again, negative transfer results from an AB–AD design according to one-trial theorists, but this is a function of the fact that a preceding association exists, which is not the case for a control group.

We again used a paired-associate test with nonsense syllables as stimuli and motor actions (hand signs) as responses. Participants in the experiment were divided into two groups and both groups learned two lists of stimulus–response pairs. For one group, three of the eight stimuli on the second list were changed but responses remained the same (an AB–CB design). For the other group, the stimuli were identical for the two lists, but three of the eight responses were different (an AB–AD design). In the former design zero or slightly positive transfer has been found in most paired-associate studies (see Holding, 1976), whereas negative transfer is typical of the latter. Both lists were learned to the criterion of one error-free trial. Following the acquisition phase of the second list, three test trials were given in which stimuli alone were presented.

As predicted from verbal paired-associate learning, there was evidence of negative transfer. The response-replaced group (AB–AD) required significantly more trials to reach criterion on the second list than the stimulus-replaced group (AB–CB). Similarly, the number of errors in reaching criterion was also significantly higher for AB–AD. More interesting, in the context of one-trial *versus* incremental explanations, was the nature of the errors in the test trials following acquisition of the second list. According to the incremental view response competition would exist between the two lists and it would be predicted that any errors in retention of second list responses would be 'intrusions' of first list responses. On the other hand, no such intrusions would be predicted by one-trial protagonists. It would be assumed that AD had simply replaced AB and eliminated the previous association on the first correct production of AD. Our results supported the one-trial hypothesis. Of the errors (seventeen in total) only one was an intrusion from the original list.

One-trial learning with complex tasks

These studies may be criticized in their reliance upon an experimental design (paired-associate learning) that is not part of the motor learning tradition. In addition, the motor responses used were dissimilar to modern research tasks and the dependent variables failed to take advantage of technical innovations that have emerged since the model experiments were performed. We therefore sought an exemplar of motor behaviour which did not conform to S–R protocols and would allow examination of kinematic variables during the learning process, as well as a criterion of success and failure. We decided to use a task similar to those developed by Heuer et al. (1995) and Swinnen et al. (1993). Both required participants to learn a bimanual coordination of extension–flexion around the elbow joint, breaking a natural pattern of functional synergy that normally couples actions of the limbs. Our variation of this task provided a complex and difficult task, which was amenable to kinematic analysis as well as having distinct criteria for success and failure (Randall, 1999). It also had the advantage of requiring rhythmical coordination. Many of the anecdotal accounts of one-trial motor learning cited tasks with this feature.

The task involved participants performing a pronation–supination–pronation movement of the right forearm while simultaneously producing a pronation–supination movement of the left forearm; a 3:2 ratio of right and left forearm movements. The range of movement was approximately 160°. Each trial was discrete. The constraints were made that movements of both arms were to be continuous and, in terms of timing, start and end points of both arms were to be simultaneous. The movements had to be completed in 600 milliseconds. The task was explained to participants and they were shown a videotape of a correct performance. The videotape was repeated after every fifteen trials and the learning phase constituted 200 trials. Participants did not receive feedback. Ten retention test trials were given after 24 hours.

Instrumentation of the manipulanda and appropriate transformation of the signals enabled us to examine velocity curves for both hands, points of movement initiation and termination, as well as the temporal locus of positive and negative peak values and zero crossings in velocity. Each trial was also video-taped. Using these data we established criteria to determine whether a response was correct. The videotapes were also used to produce a qualitatively assessed criterion of success. Trained observers scored the videotaped trials as successes and failures. Following the acquisition phase, participants were de-briefed concerning their experience.

In many respects, the results confirmed our expectations. Superficially, the data suggested that the skill was acquired incrementally. For example, Figure 4.2 shows the mean percentage of trials correctly performed by all participants over blocks of ten trials according to the qualitative analysis. This traditional method of reporting results reveals a familiar negatively accelerated relationship between trials and performance. Without further inspection it would be tempting to accept the incremental assumption that successive trials added some degree of correctness to the desired response. In Hullian terms, the curve suggests gradual enhancement of the 'habit strength' of the correct response. However, if details are examined, masking effects become apparent. The masking effects have three sources. First, an accurate reflection of progress towards success in the skill may be masked by presenting some average performance across participants, ignoring the fact that individual differences in the process of acquisition exist. Second, the data presented in Figure 4.2 are averages across trial blocks. That is, there is an inherent masking effect in which trial-by-trial variations are undetectable. Finally, masking can occur in the use of the global measure of successful completion of the task. It will be remembered that both Guthrie and Estes emphasized that a complex task is made up of sub-components and argued that these sub-components may be acquired in one-trial fashion on different trials by different participants. If only the global measure of success is used and each sub-component is acquired on different trials, a false impression of incrementalism may be generated.

By examining this type of masking in our experiment, we present data which convey a very different perspective. Four of the criteria we used for determining successful completion were: two left-hand peaks (one negative and one positive) in the velocity curve; three right-hand peaks (one negative and two positive) in the velocity curve; one left-hand zero crossing, and two right-hand zero crossings. A sample of a correct velocity profile illustrating these features is shown in Figure 4.3. The subsequent figures (Figures 4.4–4.7) show the results of all participants

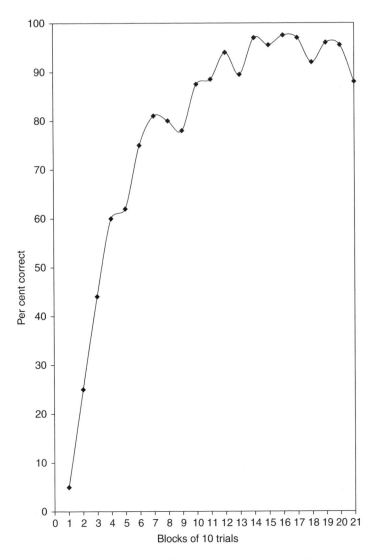

Figure 4.2 Mean percentage correct by block – qualitative analysis: all participants.

on these sub-components. Despite the fact that the measures are again averaged over participants and over blocks of trials, step functions in quality of performance in these sub-components are apparent. All four of these components were acquired early in the leaning process. In fact, the appropriate number of left-hand crossings was acquired in the first block of trials, three right-hand median peaks were acquired by the second block of trials and both correct left-hand peaks and right-hand zero crossings by the third block of trials. In other words, the essential movement sub-components of the task were acquired in a fashion consistent with

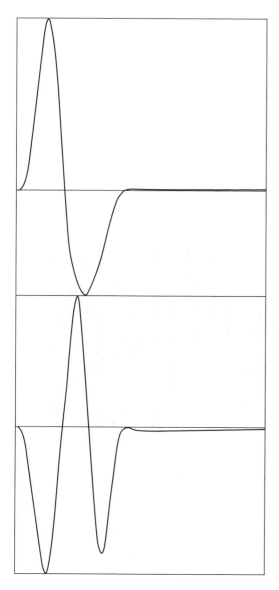

Figure 4.3 Sample of correct velocity profile.

a one-trial perspective. The fact that these step-function changes in important sub-components occurred in the first thirty trials generated the apparently negatively accelerated function in the early phases of acquisition displayed when only the global measure of success and failure was applied (Figure 4.2).

It needs to be admitted, however, that these step-functions may also be considered an artefact of the presentation method. Note that the dependent variable

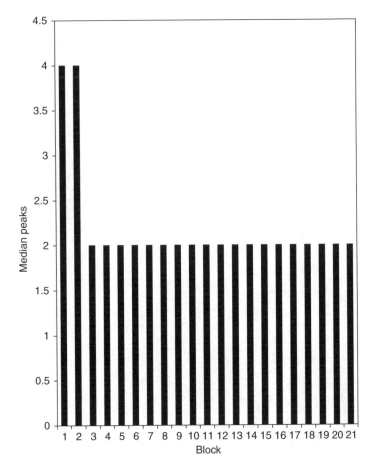

Figure 4.4 Left-hand median peaks by block – all participants.

is the median number of each movement parameter. That is, participants were not entirely consistent after initial success. For example, participant 1 showed frequent errors in terms of number of peaks until trial 32. After that his performance was consistently correct except on one trial. Other participants too showed similar occasional lapses after seemingly 'getting the hang of it'. Presenting the median as a statistic therefore masks these inconsistencies. Nevertheless, it may be argued that the occasional error was a function of attentional or motivational factors rather than an inherent phenomenon of learning.

Despite the apparent facility with which participants acquired the basic movements of the task, it proved as a whole to be difficult. The difficulty derived from the timing constraints placed upon successful completion. In order for a trial to be scored as correct, movements of both hands had to be initiated within

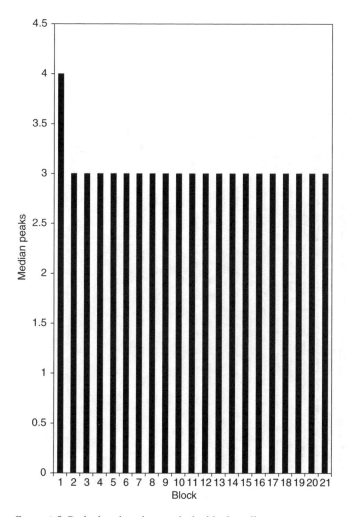

Figure 4.5 Right-hand median peaks by block – all participants.

30 milliseconds of each other and terminated within 100 milliseconds of each other. These criteria proved to be the source of difficulty. Figure 4.8 displays the mean onset and offset differences between the hands over blocks of trials for all participants. Off-set performance proved the more intractable of the two measures with essentially little improvement appearing over the two hundred acquisition trials. Conversely, onset timing did show improvement which, when regarded in the pooled data format of Figure 4.8 shows a negatively accelerated form.

Examination of individual participants' scores, however, provided some support for a one-trial hypothesis. One participant, for example, met the criterion of initiating movement simultaneously just occasionally in the first twenty trials.

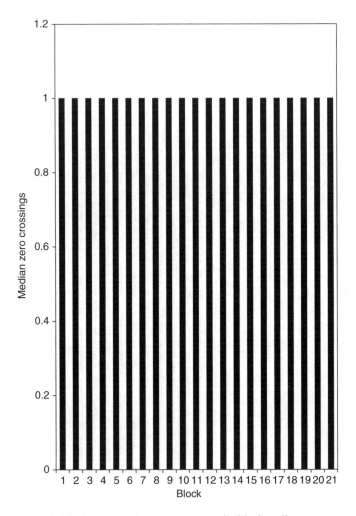

Figure 4.6 Left-hand median zero crossings by block – all participants.

After twenty trials he never made another error. Others began their sequence of error-free trials later, but again showed some consistency thereafter. But some participants still made occasional mistakes according to this criterion even in the last block of trials. Analysis of other parameters revealed similar results. Some participants appeared to 'get' a component of the movements on a single trial and never made another error on that measure. Others continued to produce errors throughout the course of the experiment, but with gradually diminishing frequency. In other words, their performance displayed characteristics typical of an incremental view of acquisition.

The difficulty of the task was best demonstrated by the fact that, according to our strict quantitative criteria, one participant did not produce a correct response

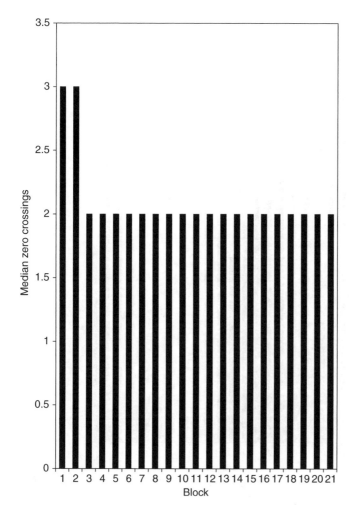

Figure 4.7 Right-hand median zero crossings by block – all participants.

over the 200 trials. The range of correct responses was 0–111 for the sixteen participants over the 200 trials. More to the point with respect to our hypotheses, there was no participant whose performance measured on all quantitative criteria revealed a step-function improvement on a single trial after which successful performance was consistent. While this was contrary to our predictions, we may still interpret the results within the context of one-trial theory. It is arguable that if we consider the task as consisting of components which are either movement or timing based, we have produced evidence that the *movement* components may be acquired on a one-trial basis. All *timing* components may not be acquired after 200 trials. It may therefore be postulated that either these components were simply too difficult for all but a very few individuals to achieve or that our training

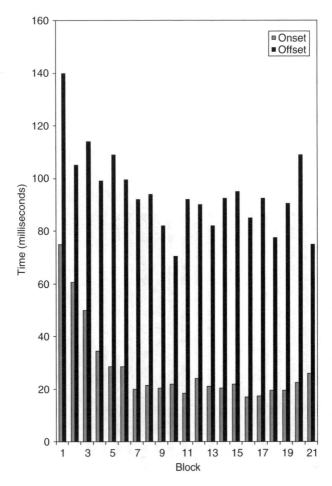

Figure 4.8 Mean absolute onset and offset differences by block – all participants.

period was insufficient for the skill to be learned in total. Given higher levels of practice, all timing components may have been learned on a one-trial basis, or it is also possible that in this particular skill, movement parameters may be acquired in a one-trial fashion and timing components acquired incrementally.

The results also highlight the further intriguing possibility that participants may vary in the way in which they achieve success. Some may show a gradual incremental approach to success, with slow elimination of errors in the sub-components of the task until correct responding is achieved. Others may experience a similar process for a number of trials and then undergo the 'Aha!' experience or sudden insight reported by the Gestalt psychologists. We found some support for this notion from the qualitative analysis and the debriefing of participants.

For the qualitative analysis three assessors were trained in the criteria for success and watched the video-recordings of all performances, rating them on a simple pass/fail basis. Agreement of two out of the three assessors determined whether the trial was labeled correct or incorrect. This qualitative assessment produced a greater percentage of 'correct' responses compared with the quantitative criteria based on the computer records. The range in terms of number of correct responses was from 62 to 206 using this qualitative criterion.

In de-briefing, nine of the sixteen participants felt they had learned the task in one-trial fashion. Of these, seven participants performed 90 per cent of the subsequent trials correctly, judged by the trained observers, after their first block of three correct trials. The other participants reported that they experienced an incremental approach to success. Only two of these participants achieved the 90 per cent success rate following a block of three correct trials. The concept that manner of acquisition may vary among individuals in the same skill therefore received some support from analysis of the qualitative assessments.

Implications

In terms of implications for teaching and coaching, obviously further experiments are required to elucidate on the conditions which one-trial learning is likely to be most evident, so that some degree of awareness of the learning process can be fostered. From the research so far, it seems that motor skills that require spatial–temporal coordination or consist of relatively complex motor components, for example, riding a bike, performing a wrist shot in ice-hockey, perhaps juggling, might be best characterized by this all-or-none learning process (at least at an observable level).

The challenge for the coach and teacher is then to find ways of bringing about these seemingly sudden changes or insights. Perhaps there is a need to change the type of information conveyed through demonstrations and instructions to encourage creative and novel ways of approaching the problem and the restructuring and understanding described by the Gestalt psychologists as precursors to learning. Early variability in initial practice attempts, or observations, might help performers gain insight into the motor processes necessary for task success. As with problems in the cognitive domain, distributed practice and time away from the problem (perhaps time on other tasks) might help to give a fresh approach on following motor attempts. The focus of future research in this area will be to identify how practice organization and instruction impacts on the learning process as a function of the type of skill.

Conclusions

The four studies summarized in this chapter provide the grounds for re-opening the issue of one-trial versus incremental approaches to motor learning. The three earlier studies certainly confirm that in any skill with a paired-associate format including simple motor responses, a one-trial description of the acquisition process is defensible. With more complex skills, our research suggests a more complicated picture. It may be the case that some learners experience the 'Aha!' phenomenon, but these may constitute a small minority. Others may show a step-function acquisition of some components of the task, but learn the remainder incrementally. Finally, a proportion of learners may gradually acquire all the components of the intended pattern, refining their performance until the desired outcome is achieved without any step-function changes. What is perhaps significant is that this research points out the wisdom of examining individual trial records when attempting to describe the acquisition process. Not all trials make an equal contribution to acquisition for all learners.

References

Adams, J. A. (1971). A closed-loop theory of motor learning. *Journal of Motor Behaviour*, 3, 111–150.

Anderson, D. E. (2000). Complex motor skill acquisition and the one-trial learning phenomenon. *Journal of Human Movement Studies*, 38, 23–56.

Bryan, W. L. and Harter, N. (1897). Studies in the physiology and psychology of the telegraphic language. *Psychological Review*, 4, 27–53.

Bryan, W. L. and Harter, N. (1899). Studies on the telegraphic language. The acquisition of a hierarchy of habits. *Psychological Review*, 6, 345–375.

Estes, W. K. (1950). Toward a statistical theory of learning. *Psychological Review*, 57, 94–107.

Estes, W. K. (1959). The statistical approach of learning theory. In S. Koch (Ed.), *Psychology: a study of a science*, Vol. 2. New York: McGraw-Hill.

Estes, W. K., Hopkins, B. L. and Crothers, E. J. (1960) All-or-none and conservation effects in the learning and retention of paired associates. *Journal of Experimental Psychology*, 60, 329–339.

Fitts, P. M. and Posner, M. I. (1967). *Human performance*. Belmont, CA: Brooks/Cole.

Gentile, A. M. (1972). A working model of skill acquisition with application to teaching. *Quest*, 17, 3–23.

Guthrie, E. R. (1952). *The psychology of learning*. New York: Harper & Row.

Heuer, H., Schmidt, R. A. and Ghodsian, D. (1966). Generalized motor programs for rapid bimanual tasks: a two level multiplicative-rate model. *Biological Cybernetics*, 73, 343–356.

Hilgard, E. R. and Bower, G. H. (1966). *Theories of learning* (3rd ed.). New York: Appleton-Century-Crofts.

Holding, D. H. (1976). An approximate transfer surface. *Journal of Motor Behaviour*, 8, 1–9.

Hull, C. L. (1943). *Principles of behaviour*. New York: Appleton-Century-Crofts.

Hull, C. L. (1951). *Essentials of behaviour*. New Haven, CT: Yale University Press.

Hull, C. L. (1952). *A behaviour system: an introduction to behaviour theory concerning the individual organism*. New Haven, CT: Yale University Press.

Koffka, K. (1935). *Principles of Gestalt psychology*. New York: Harcourt, Brace & World.

Osgood, C. E. (1949). The similarity paradox in human learning: a resolution. *Psychological Review*, 56, 132–143.

Postmann, L. (1963). One-trial learning. In C. N. Cofer and B. S. Musgrave (Eds), *Verbal Behaviour and Learning*. New York: McGraw-Hill.

Randall, W. E. (1999). One-trial motor learning. Unpublished master's thesis, Simon Fraser University, Burnaby, British Columbia, Canada.

Randall, W. E., Dickinson, J. and Goodman, D. (1995). Studies in one-trial motor learning. *Journal of Human Movement Studies*, 29, 229–249.

Rock, I. (1957). The role of repetition is associative learning, *American Journal of Psychology*, 70, 186–193.

Rock, I. and Heimer, W. (1959). Further evidence of one-trial associative learning. *American Journal of Psychology*, 72, 1–16.

Schmidt, R. A. (1975). A schema theory of discrete motor skill learning. *Psychological Review*, 82, 225–260.

Schmidt, R. A. (1988). Motor and action perspectives on motor behaviour. In O. G. Meijer and K. Roth (Eds), *Complex movement behaviour: the motor action controversy*. Amsterdam: Elsevier.

Schmidt, R. A. and Lee, T. (1999). *Motor control and learning*. Champaign, IL: Human Kinetics.

Schwartz, M. (1963). Transfer from failed pairs as a test of one-trial vs incremental learning. *American Journal of Psychology*, 76, 266–273.

Snoddy, G. S. (1926). Learning and stability: a psychophysical analysis of a case of motor learning with clinical applications. *Journal of Applied Psychology*, 10, 1–36.

Swinnen, S. P., Walter, C. B., Lee, T. D. and Serrian, D. J. (1993). Acquiring bi-manual skills: contrasting forms of information feedback for interlimb decoupling. *Journal of Experimental Psychology*, 19, 1328–1344.

Thorndike, E. L. (1911). *Animal intelligence*. New York: MacMillan.

Thorndike, E. L. (1913). *The psychology of learning*. New York: Teachers College.

Voeks, V. W. (1954). Acquisition of S–R connections: a test of Hull's and Guthrie's theories. *Journal of Experimental Psychology*, 47, 137–147.

Weeks, D., Aubert, M. P., Feldman, A. G. and Levin, M. F. (1996). One-trial adaptation of movement to changes in load. *Journal of Neurophysiology*, 75, 60–74.

5 Individual differences in skill acquisition

Mary O. Boyle and Phillip L. Ackerman

Questions about the nature of individual differences in learning and skill acquisition were raised early in the history of modern psychology. E. L. Thorndike (1908) was perhaps the first investigator to examine this issue, when he addressed the question of whether individuals become more alike or different in performance on a task after extensive practice. The underlying question that Thorndike and others sought to answer is a fundamental one about nature versus nurture. On the one hand, if nature (or genetic endowment) is the primary limiting determinant of skilled performance, then providing a group of individuals with extensive task practice should result in greater variability in performance, as each individual reaches his or her physiological or cognitive maximal efficiency. On the other hand, if nurture (e.g. training or experience) is the primary determinant of skilled performance, then providing a group of individuals with extensive task practice should result in reduced variability in performance, as individuals converge on a common level of task experience.

Over the past century, this question has been debated through developments of both theory and empirical research, with results suggesting that both nature and nurture have a role in determining skilled performance. Other research has focused on attempting to predict which individuals will perform best on skill learning tasks (e.g. for reviews, see Ackerman, 1987; Adams, 1987). This chapter will review some of the central issues of this field of investigation, and discuss major findings, along with a theoretical perspective that addresses the ability determinants of individual differences in task performance during skill acquisition. Current research seeking to extend theories of individual differences in skill acquisition will be presented, and topics appropriate for future research suggested.

Definition of skill

Among the issues that researchers have had to contend with is the problem of clearly defining the concepts of skill and learning. Adams (1987, p. 42), in his review of motor skills research, provided a description of *skill* in outlining three characteristics that delineate the scope of the domain, namely: (a) skill covers a broad domain of behaviours; (b) skill is learned (as opposed to merely defining performance at its peak); and (c) attainment of the goal is dependent on motor behaviour (rather than relying only on cognition and perception). In contrast to skills, *abilities* are of a more enduring nature and can be broadly applied across many different tasks. Thus, abilities and skills differ mainly in degree of generality and stability. Alternatively, the distinction between ability and skill can be one of the investigator's purpose. If a typing proficiency measure was included in a battery of motor tests, it might be considered an ability. However, if the measure was used as an index of achievement in a typing class, it might be considered a skill assessment. Schmidt and Wrisberg (2000) use the analogy of a toolbox, in which many motor abilities are available to perform specific skills, such as shooting a rifle or performing gymnastics. For the example of gymnastics, motor abilities might include strength, balance and coordination, while skills might include back tucks and flyovers.

Individual differences research

For those undertaking research in the area of individual differences in skill acquisition, there are three main concerns, as follows: (a) differences in initial performance; (b) differences in rate of skill acquisition; and (c) differences in asymptotic (maximum) skill levels. When considering individual differences in initial task performance, it is important to point out that, with the exception of the newborn infant, when individuals encounter a task, there is always some 'transfer' involved (Ferguson, 1956). The concept behind this notion of transfer is that individuals encounter a new situation with different degrees of prior knowledge and skills (not to mention different levels of relevant abilities). For example, a 50-year-old with 30+ years of driving experience and a 16-year-old driving novice can be expected to bring different levels of initial skills to the task of driving a rental agency car at an unfamiliar airport. Differential transfer can be expected to yield both differences in the amount of time needed to familiarize oneself with the unique characteristics of the rental automobile, and the degree of skill in operating the car on leaving the airport. Transfer can be positive (in the above example) or can be negative, such as when a driver from North America (where cars are supposed be operated on the right side of the road) sets out to negotiate roads in the United Kingdom (where cars are supposed to be operated on the left side of the road). When transfer is negative, performance can be impaired relative not only to the original skill, but also to a novice performer.

Subsequent to the concerns with determining individual differences in initial task performance are concerns with the rate of skill acquisition during practice or training. However, there are problems inherent in identifying who are the best learners in a given situation. A common finding for many skill acquisition tasks is that the individuals who perform the worst on a task tend to 'improve' the most with practice or training, in terms of the difference between initial and practiced task performance. Part of the explanation for such findings is that better performers at the start of practice are the ones who have a better repertoire of abilities and skills that can be usefully transferred to the new task. As such, individuals who start off a task with relatively good performance have a smaller distance to travel on a learning or skill acquisition curve than do individuals who start the task with little prior experience or transfer. Thus, the poorest initial performers have the greatest opportunity to improve with practice or training. From a psychometric (or statistical) standpoint, this creates a couple of difficult problems in using difference (or gain) scores between levels of performance before and after practice to assess degree of learning. Those individuals whose initial performance was worst will show the greatest 'gain', and those who performed the best initially will likely still perform the best after practice but show a smaller gain. Early researchers who did not appreciate this aspect of learning often concluded that abilities were negatively related to learning, or found that correlations between initial performance and the 'improvement' in performance were negative. There are also statistical problems with gain scores that discourage their use in studying individual differences. In particular, gain scores tend to be unreliable, because as the correlation between initial and post-practice scores increases, the reliability of the gain score decreases. For example, if the reliability of initial and post-practice scores are both equal to 0.80, and the correlation between the two scores is $r = 0.70$, then the reliability of the gain score is only 0.33 (for formulas for computing these reliabilities and a discussion of the problems associated with change scores in general, see Cronbach and Furby, 1970).

For selection purposes, such as deciding who should be recruited for a sports team or be hired for a job, we are often more interested in who performs the best after an extended period of training. According to Wechsler (1952), the typical ratio between the speed of skilled performance by job incumbents who are the best and the worst performers is around 3:1. That is, in a fixed period of time, the best performers (whether putting together items on an assembly line, type-writing or checking groceries) can complete three times as many items as the slowest performer, even after extensive practice or job experience. As a logical extension to the two areas of individual differences mentioned above, these final levels of performance are related to both the amount of prior knowledge that was able to transfer to the new situation and the amount of new learning that was gained through practice. If we measure only who has the highest performance after training or practice, we are unable to distinguish the separate influences of (1) the amount of transfer that assisted the current learning and (2) the quickness with which an individual progressed through the practice. A complete account of individual differences in skill acquisition will consider all of these elements: initial levels of performance, final levels of performance and the transition between them. We discuss these issues in the following sections.

The changing role of abilities

If we recognize that people perform at different levels at the outset of a new task, and that some differences remain after considerable practice, then how can we identify individuals who will perform best at each of these points? Early research indicated that the relation of an ability to performance changed with task experience. While some ability tests identified individuals who would perform well early in task training, different abilities became more important to performance late in practice (see, e.g. Ackerman, 1987; Adams, 1987). One theory stated that early performance on a skill task was determined by a general intellectual or cognitive ability, but in later performance a task-specific ability was most relevant (e.g. Fleishman and Hempel, 1954, 1955). According to this perspective, skilled performance on a task will only be well predicted from measures taken on that particular task, and not from other tasks or from abilities measured prior to task training or practice. The theory of task-specific abilities predicting final performance is problematic for two reasons. First, it suggests that general ability is only important at the outset and will not predict later performance in a task or job; this is a debate that continues (see Ackerman, 1989; Barrett *et al.*, 1992; Henry and Hulin, 1987; Hulin *et al.*, 1990). Second, the theory predicts that it is not possible to identify which individuals will be exemplary performers after practice, because performance after practice cannot be predicted from measures administered prior to task engagement. As we will see, however, recent research suggests that it may indeed be possible to develop measures that predict (to a reasonable degree) which individuals will be most likely to perform well or poorly after task practice or training.

In summary, a skill can apply to a broad set of behaviours, it is acquired over time and practice, and it has at least some dependency on motor actions. Learning has to do with performance at different levels of experience as an activity is repeated. An ability may promote performance in any of a number of skills, and the relation of an ability to performance may change through experience. Finally, the abilities that predict performance early in training may not be the same as the abilities that predict performance after skill development. This last issue of prediction is a difficult one, and will be revisited later in the chapter.

A theory of individual differences in complex skill acquisition

Individual differences research is driven by the premise that people do not have equivalent abilities, personality, or motivational traits, and that these differences may relate importantly to outcomes, such as skilled performance. By the same token, not all tasks are created equal. There is a difference between tasks whose processing demands change over repetition because the task is consistent and can become easily performed after practice and tasks that continue to be difficult to perform even after hours of experience. This distinction will be discussed below, followed by a theory of individual differences in skill acquisition for which this processing difference is fundamental.

Consistent tasks lead to different demands

From information-processing psychology, there is a distinction between tasks that are slow and effortful (particularly tasks new to the performer) and tasks that can be performed quickly and with less effort. Some tasks allow for a shift from effortful processing at the outset, when the task is unfamiliar, to more 'automatic' processing after the task has become well learned (e.g. Ackerman and Schneider, 1985; Schneider and Shiffrin, 1977). Such tasks are generally consistent in their input and response components, allowing for the task to eventually be performed as a 'procedure'. Classic examples of this type of task are the procedural aspects of driving a car or typing using a standard keyboard. Tasks do not allow for this shift if attention and control are continuously required, regardless of amount of practice. If the layout of a keyboard changed from time to time, where the current key for 'a' became the key for 'i' and the changes were unpredictable, then the hunt-and-peck method would be the only useful strategy available. It is unlikely that a typist would ever be able to exceed sixty words per minute. If the consistency of the key mapping that allows for memorization of letter positions were not present, then typewriting would become a quite different task, one that is not subject to the type of learning that allows for eventual quick and automatic execution.

A task that has rules and elements that are consistent permits the learner to move through different stages of learning. Initially, a person who encounters a novel activity is called on to identify the specific rules and individual elements that are important. In the typewriting example, early skill development is devoted to memorizing the location of each letter and learning how to strike a key to produce a response. Through practice, the association of a letter with its address on a keyboard becomes more familiar and is strengthened. With extended practice, not only do the letter positions become well learned, but also the typist can begin to learn sequences of letters that make up common words. This transition from having to identify and learn each component of a task, to strengthening the associations for consistent parts of the task, to becoming more fluid and efficient in performance, is typical of tasks that have consistent attributes (e.g. see Fitts and Posner, 1967). Thankfully, most skill-learning tasks have predominantly consistent underlying characteristics, which means that it is possible (though by no means certain) that individuals can reach an effortless and largely automatic level of task performance, at least within certain parameters. Skilled performance of many sports tasks, for example, would be essentially impossible without such automaticity, such as swinging the baseball bat in response to calculation of the initial trajectory of the ball released by the pitcher, or moving to anticipate a tennis ball hit by an opponent.

The three-phase theory of individual differences in skill acquisition

In an effort to account for the changing relations among abilities and task performance, Ackerman (1987) re-analysed data reported by Fleishman and colleagues from a series of tasks (including Complex Coordination, Discrimination Reaction Time and Rotary Pursuit) and their correspondence with ability factors across practice. For tasks of rotary pursuit and discrimination reaction time, there was an increased association over practice trials with ability factors representing rate of movement and motor reaction time. The re-analysed data supported the proposition that through consistent practice, tasks that could be made more automatic would change in how they related to ability. However, in contrast to the Fleishman (1972) perspective, the findings supported the controversial idea that individual differences in performance after practice in learning a skill could continue to be substantially related to cognitive, perceptual and/or psychomotor abilities. That is, individual differences in skilled performance may be predicted from measures administered prior to task practice, given that the appropriate ability measures are selected, and given that appropriate statistical procedures are applied (for a discussion of this issue, see Adams, 1987).

A theory of individual differences in skill acquisition that merged a three-phase framework of skill learning (Fitts and Posner, 1967) with the abilities required for task performance was proposed by Ackerman (1988); for a review, see Ackerman and Kyllonen (1991). The theory assumes performance of most consistent tasks can become more automatic with practice. In Phase 1, a task makes strong demands on attention and cognition; performance is slow and mistakes occur. The hypothesized relations of skill and ability are presented graphically in Figure 5.1. At this stage of learning, general intelligence is most important as a determinant of individual differences in performance as a novel situation is evaluated and reasoning skills are used. When an individual is introduced to a new situation, the basics must be learned, such as identifying where the controls are in driving a car, and those with higher general and broad content ability (e.g. spatial, verbal or numerical) will learn or infer these basics more quickly. For example, hitting a golf ball may have many consistent elements, especially when the player uses the same clubs, balls, and plays on the same course. Introducing novelty, such as changing to a new set of clubs, will put one element of the task back into the realm of controlled processing, but with substantial practice, the golfer may acquire new automatic processes with the new clubs.

In the second phase of skill acquisition, the elements of a task are combined into units that allow for streamlined performance and a reduction in attention and effort. During Phase 2, information is integrated and consolidated. Perceptual speed abilities that involve rapidly encoding consistent patterns and comparing symbols (such as making a same/different judgement for two numbers) are hypothesized to support this phase of learning. According to Ackerman (1988), perceptual speed was described as follows:

> In the language of skill acquisition, individual differences found on [perceptual speed] tests are directly attributable to the speed with which these productions can be implemented and compiled. The term 'perceptual' is perhaps a misnomer from a traditional usage of the term, because perceptual speed abilities involve a full system of encoding, perception, central processing, and response components.
>
> (p. 290)

Perceptual speed abilities have been categorized to include scanning, pattern recognition and memory as fundamental underlying components. During the

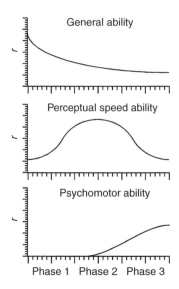

Figure 5.1 Ability–skill relations as hypothesized in the Ackerman framework. A task represented by this model is moderately complex, includes a moderate amount of transfer, and provides consistency in information processing (*r* = correlation). Figure 4 from Ackerman (1988, p. 294), Copyright American Psychological Association. Reprinted by permission.

second skill acquisition phase in auto driving, for example, the actions of turning on a directional signal, braking and steering will be integrated to negotiate a turn. Chaining of response patterns, such as going for a layup in basketball, or executing a gymnastics floor routine, are characteristic of this phase of skill acquisition. Although the early performance of these sequences can be effortful and error prone, with additional practice these movements become routine, quick and efficient.

Phase 3 of skill acquisition occurs late in practice, as skilled performance becomes more proceduralized and automatic (i.e. a fluid unit of action rather than a series of discrete cognitions and actions) and performance approaches asymptotic levels. At this final phase of skill acquisition, task responses become automatic and performance is generally rapid and free of errors. Psychomotor abilities become paramount. This class of ability is different from perceptual speed, in that the speed of processing is generally free of evaluation of information (mostly motor responses). At this stage, performance is based on how quickly and fluidly appropriate responses that are already known can be executed. Skills that have been acquired to this level are often effortlessly executed. A skilled pianist performs an entire concerto from memory in this fashion, similar to the gymnast or figure skater who executes a well-rehearsed and practised routine in a seamless fashion. One advantage of this autonomous level of skilled performance is that the individual does not need to devote attention to the routine portion of the actions, but can devote his or her attentional resources to other tasks, such as attending to style or unique aspects of the performance venue. A skilled fencer decides to initiate a particular move, and then can devote attention to competitive strategy even as the motor program proceeds with little needed supervision. Such a sequence is similar to how a typist automatically types a word after initiating the intention to type it, without having to worry about the location and sequence of the keys. While one word is being typed, the expert typist is already looking at future words in the text, and scheduling the intention to start the next motor program (e.g. see Shaffer, 1976).

This framework suggests that general ability correlates most highly with performance when the task is novel, and declines (but does not reduce to zero) over practice. Perceptual speed is not as highly related to performance initially, but increases during Phase 2 of learning as stronger associations are formed for task information and responses, eventually declining again in Phase 3. Psychomotor ability is not a determinant of performance early in practice (when reasoning skills are most valuable in appraising the requirements of the new task), but comes into play in the third phase of skill acquisition. Of the three ability classes, psychomotor ability is expected to be the most highly related to performance during the final stages of practice. At that point, the task requirements have been distilled to a procedure and performance is most dependent on rapid response.

This model of individual differences in skill acquisition applies to tasks that are moderately complex, that include a substantial motor component, that may reflect some transfer of prior skill and that allow for consistent processing of information. If a task is mostly cognitive in nature and does not require a physical response, such as adding numbers mentally, then the high relation with psychomotor ability at the end of practice will not be seen. By the same token, if a skill is extremely simple and only speeded reaction is needed, such as pressing a button when it lights up, then the ability–performance relation is described by the final phase, and psychomotor abilities will be the best predictors. If a task does not present consistency between input and appropriate response, then the task becomes familiar but not automatic with practice (the associations cannot be built to create a streamlined procedure). In this case, the ability–performance relations for the overall task are not expected to change dramatically (only the consistent sub-components of the task that can be automatized will result in a change in ability–performance associations). The overall success of the activity will continue to be described by the ability–skill relations in Phase 1, and general cognitive ability will continue to be highly related to performance even after extended experience, as long as the task is sufficiently complex.

Validation studies

Laboratory studies of simple to relatively complex skills generally support the three-phase approach to the ability determinants of individual differences in performance (e.g. see Ackerman, 1988, 1990). Most prominent among the results is the declining association between general intelligence (e.g. IQ, as measured by tests such as the Stanford–Binet, Wechsler or Wonderlic measures) and task performance as skills develop over practice or training. Results regarding perceptual speed abilities and psychomotor abilities have been less conclusive, partly because test developments in those areas have lagged in comparison to the development of general intelligence measures. However, recent research on both perceptual speed and psychomotor ability measures have provided generally encouraging results in terms of significantly predicting individual differences in task performance after extensive practice. For example, Ackerman and Cianciolo (2000) found that combinations of perceptual speed tests and psychomotor tests added incremental predictive validity over general intellectual ability in predicting skilled performance on a proceduralized skill task – the Kanfer–Ackerman Air Traffic Control simulation task.

In addition, research of many different skill learning tasks indicates that when the task is entirely consistent or mostly consistent in terms of the underlying information processing requirements, the magnitude of individual differences (the range of differences between the poorest and the best performers) declines with increasing task practice. That is, individuals start off with large differences in performance that decline as skills are developed. Whether this phenomenon is explained more by the diminished effects of prior transfer or the diminished involvement of general intellectual abilities with increasing skills is not fully determined, but the outcome tends to be that the range of individual differences in performance declines with increased task practice (Ackerman, 1987). Such effects are seen in 'real-world' performance, and would be reflected in the much smaller range of, for example, batting averages of professional baseball players in comparison to little-league players.

Relatively few field studies of individual differences in performance during skill acquisition have been conducted that shed light on the ability determinants of skilled performance, mainly because of the difficulty in performing large scale testing of many different kinds of abilities, and the difficulty in obtaining access to performance records over long periods of training and on-the-job skilled performance. Early studies by the military, however, demonstrated the validity of both perceptual speed and psychomotor abilities in providing significant incremental prediction (i.e. prediction over and above that provided by general intelligence measures) of skilled performance (see Guilford and Lacey, 1947; Melton, 1947). Psychomotor ability tests, in particular, have been found to be especially useful in predicting performance on skilled motor tasks, such as operative dentistry (Boyle and Santelli, 1986), industrial work performance (Salvendy and Seymour, 1973), clerical work (Andrew and Paterson, 1934) and various military specialties (Melton, 1947).

However, as noted by Fleishman (1956), traditional psychomotor tests use complex apparatus measures that involve substantial time and effort to administer. Due to these costs, such tests have been found to be impractical for many occupational selection situations. That is, traditional psychomotor tests include such measures as the Purdue Pegboard, the Minnesota Rate of Manipulation

Test, the Complex Coordination Test, Balance Tests, Steadiness tests, Maze Tracing and so on (e.g. see Melton, 1947). In many of these tests, there is a physical or electronic apparatus used to administer the test, and there are additional devices (e.g. impulse counters, stopclocks) used for assessment of test performance. The electronic devices are notoriously expensive to purchase or fabricate, and such apparatus tests usually require a one-on-one examiner-to-examinee setup, making group testing largely unfeasible. Nonetheless, recent developments in adapting psychomotor tests to desktop computers suggest that these difficulties may be relatively easily overcome, thus removing a major hurdle to implementing such tests in future selection applications (e.g. see Ackerman and Cianciolo, 1999). For example, Ackerman and Cianciolo report that psychomotor tests involving Tapping, Serial Reaction Time, Maze Tracing, Mirror Tracing and Rotary Pursuit can be implemented in a reliable and valid fashion, using off-the-shelf desktop computers, coupled with touch-sensitive displays (see also Ackerman and Cianciolo, 2000).

Practically speaking, however, the practice of professional football in North America provides a good example of the concerns with abilities and skilled performance. Although validity data are not generally available, the National Football League (NFL) in North America has administered a general intelligence measure, the Wonderlic, over the past 25 years to college players seeking to become professional football team members. Although there are demands of general intelligence when a new player must learn a playbook, the demands are somewhat diminished for some positions that, after skill acquisition, demand mostly motor skills (such as fullbacks and halfbacks). In contrast, other positions require more novel or inconsistent information processing, such as when a quarterback must make quick strategic decisions in the middle of a play. Given the difference in demands, we would expect higher scores on general intelligence measures from quarterbacks, and not necessarily higher scores from fullbacks and halfbacks. Data from the NFL are consistent with this proposition (e.g. see cbs.sportsline.com, 2002). Quarterbacks (mean = 24) obtained higher general intelligence scores than fullbacks (mean = 17), where a score of 20 corresponds to average intelligence (i.e. 100 on a typical IQ test). That is, even though general intelligence may be correlated with performance across each of these skills, it is apparently less important for skills that are primarily motor and more important for real-time problem-solving and decision-making skills. It should be noted, however, that for a variety of reasons there are relatively few empirical studies of the relationship between intellectual abilities of athletes and their performance levels. Thus, while these data are supportive of the general point, it remains to be seen how generalizable the relationships are with other sports.

In summary, the three-phase theory of individual differences in skill acquisition has helped to clarify the changing relations among abilities and performance through practice. More general classes of ability (such as spatial visualization or perceptual speed), rather than factors unique to the tests, have been shown to relate to skilled performance through all stages of learning. This approach to individual differences has helped to reconcile the observation that general ability loses its predictive usefulness after practice for some tasks, but remains important for others, even as individuals tend to perform more similar to one another after extensive task practice. Ultimately, ability measures may be used to predict individual differences in skilled performance, even after long periods of training or on-the-job experience.

Implications to prediction of skilled performance

The following issues are relevant in considering individual differences in the acquisition of skill regardless of domain.

Correct match of predictor and criterion

A primary issue is that the determinants of skilled performance are dynamic, depending on the stage of skill acquisition that is considered (see also Proctor and Dutta, 1995). The predictor ability should match the outcome that is targeted. If one is interested in performance early in training, then a more general ability should be used to predict individual differences in performance. Conversely, if one is most interested in performance after a skill has been acquired, then measures of psychomotor ability can be expected to correlate most highly with final performance.

Within classes of ability, there are different types of content and levels of precision that can be considered. One way of representing abilities is as a hierarchy, with broad group factors (such as verbal, numerical, spatial) and narrower or specific factors under a larger umbrella of general intelligence (see the extensive review and summary by Carroll, 1993). If we think of abilities in this way, then care must be taken to select an appropriate ability measure for predicting individual differences in skill acquisition. Conceptualizing psychomotor abilities as lower-order factors (i.e. in comparison to general intelligence), it is still necessary to identify the components that comprise the domain. Over the past few decades, there have been several attempts to develop a taxonomy of psychomotor abilities (e.g. see Guilford, 1958). At one point it was suggested that an adequate representation required eleven perceptual-motor factors (such as multi-limb coordination and manual dexterity) and nine physical proficiency factors (such as trunk strength and stamina; Fleishman, 1972). However, a recent investigation suggested that many psychomotor abilities (e.g. rotary pursuit, two-armed coordination, lane tracking, direction control) may be more simply organized with a general factor related across psychomotor tests and a unique learning factor associated with individual tests that have been practiced (Chaiken *et al.*, 2000).

One way of thinking about a resolution to this predictor–criterion alignment problem is in terms of *Brunswik symmetry* (Wittmann and Süß, 1999). The essence of this approach is that both the predictor and criterion domains are organized hierarchically and the strongest correspondence will be found at matching levels of related measures. On the predictor side, one such hierarchy might be the structure of intelligence discussed previously. On the criterion side, the lower levels of the hierarchy are individual acts (e.g. performance in a particular component of a sport, such as the long jump in the decathlon) while higher levels are aggregations across occurrences and tasks (such as overall decathlon performance). Least alignment will be found if the wrong predictor is selected and compared to a mismatched level of criterion performance (resulting in a combination that is both unrelated and asymmetric). Such a mismatch in sports science might be present, for example, if the rate of bouncing a basketball for a 5-minute session were used to predict performance in a triathlon. The challenge for maximizing the predictive utility of a battery of ability tests is in both the specification of the criterion task domain (the scope of the skill to be predicted) and the predictor domain (the individual characteristics that determine the criterion task performance). Matching both degree of overlap and the appropriate level of specificity are key to obtaining a useful prediction of individual differences in skilled performance.

Identification of the nature of the task

It is helpful to identify whether a task is one that continually makes demands on reasoning and general ability, or whether the qualities of the task allow for procedures to be developed. An analysis of the components of a task may be needed to identify the elements that are consistent and those that are not, and it should be recognized that a mixed task may behave more like a task that is inconsistent and difficult to automate (e.g. Ackerman, 1988). A caveat to this point is that while the task itself may provide associations that allow for easier execution, not everyone will choose the strategy that promotes the best performance. To return to the typewriting example, not everyone chooses to learn the hand and key positions, even though this clearly leads to faster typing in the long run. However, at least for consistent tasks used in the laboratory, it is possible to increase the use of beneficial strategies if an incentive is provided (e.g. Ackerman and Woltz, 1994).

For motor skills, the environment in which the skill takes place can be thought of as ranging from 'closed' to 'open' (see, e.g. Schmidt and Wrisberg, 2000). For a closed skill, the environment is predictable and the action to be taken can be determined in advance. Typing is such a skill, as it has the consistent and predictable qualities discussed earlier, as does archery or target shooting. Many elements of playing team sports, on the other hand, are open skills. In a football game, the environment is often unpredictable as there are many configurations of both the own team players and the other team players, and there are ranges of talents to be reckoned with on each play. This dimension of motor activities also has a bearing on the complexity of the task. Even though skills can be practiced and developed to expert level, the changing environment creates a more difficult task than a static and self-controlled situation. This complexity leads to longer practice periods to pass from beginner to intermediate to advanced levels of performance.

Understanding of amount of practice needed for near-asymptotic levels of performance

To accommodate the longer period of compilation for a highly complex task, researchers seeking to assess ability predictors of final performance must allow sufficient practice. For simple tasks, such as alternately tapping two squares on a computer screen, a dozen trials may be adequate for individuals to approach their maximum performance. For a more complex task with many rules and variations, additional task experience may be needed (e.g. the air traffic control task used by Ackerman, 1990). Due to cost and time constraints, practice often stops short of assessing final performance levels of a complex task (Ackerman, 1987; Adams, 1987). The problem is that early-training performance may be interpreted as well-learned performance, and a performance predictor may be abandoned or retained inappropriately. Skills in sports pose a special difficulty, if years of practice are required to reach maximal levels of performance (e.g. Ericsson *et al.*, 1993). Linking expert skill levels to the individual differences and practice styles that contributed to them is usually done retrospectively, after a decade or more of training has taken place.

Individual differences do matter when learning a new skill. But in trying to identify and select people who will successfully perform a task, it is important to keep in mind the three issues mentioned above, namely: (1) correct match of predictor and criterion; (2) identification of the nature of the task; and (3) understanding of amount of practice needed for near-asymptotic levels of performance. Also, the skill task should be understood, both for its level of consistency and the amount of practice needed to approach maximum performance. If months or years of practice are required to master a skill, then it is possible that individuals should be given opportunities to participate in practice, such as attending tennis lessons or joining the junior varsity football team. Over time, individuals may also 'self-select' if it becomes apparent that their performance is not improving and the activity is not one to which they are well suited (Schmidt and Wrisberg, 2000).

Extensions to individual differences in skill acquisition

The phases of complex skill learning and the dynamic nature of ability relations to those stages have been reasonably well established for tasks of varying complexity. The next section will introduce the concept of aptitude–treatment interactions, and suggest how such interactions may be applicable to skill acquisition in the sports domain.

Aptitude–treatment interaction (ATI)

Generally speaking, there is always a tension between individual differences approaches to predicting performance on skill acquisition tasks and more general educational/instructional approaches, which seek to provide overall improvements in how training is delivered or practice is conducted. That is, if improved training programmes or practice schedules can yield a result that all learners acquire expert-level skills, then assessments of individual differences in abilities or assessment of the prior transfer skills of individuals become largely irrelevant. In contrast, if training programmes are relatively ineffective at equalizing the performance of all learners, or if the goal is to select individuals who need minimal explicit training, then finding the underlying abilities that determine skilled performance can allow an organization to select those individuals who will perform the best on skill tasks.

Against this backdrop, one of the most difficult problems in translating individual differences approaches to skill acquisition applications has been an underlying belief of some practitioners and researchers that the 'best' training programme is one that is completely individualized to the learner (e.g. see Shute, 1993). That is, one learner might improve the most if given frequent encouragement, while another might improve the most if given corrective feedback when errors are made, and still another might learn best when left to his or her own devices. Tutors and coaches often take this particular perspective in deciding how much feedback to provide and when to provide it during skill learning. Part of what makes this approach relatively intractable, from a scientific viewpoint, is gaining knowledge of what particular individual characteristics are relevant for structuring instruction or training. To further complicate matters, it must be known what characteristics of tutors and coaches are important components to the equation (given that it is the rare coach or tutor who completely adapts his or her training methods to the individual learning). It would take an impossibly large investigation to randomly assign individuals and coaches to skill learning tasks in an effort to inductively determine which characteristics of both learner and coach represent optimal fits.

One partial approach to this general question was posed by Cronbach and Snow (1977). Cronbach described the general framework as one that investigates interactions between individual difference characteristics (called 'aptitudes') and instructional/training conditions (called 'treatments'). Cronbach (1957) suggested that investigators seek to find how aptitudes and treatments interact, so that it may be possible to, if not individualize instruction, at least assign groups of learners to instructional/training programmes that are more effective for their respective differences.

The purpose of ATI research is to identify whether a given learning environment is especially beneficial for a certain group of learners. For example, if learners benefit equally from a training regimen that breaks a skill down into components rather than practicing the 'whole' skill, regardless of the relevant aptitude measured prior to the training regimen, then part-task or component training is the best environment for everyone. However, if component training produces higher performance for learners who are low in general ability and whole-task training produces higher performance for individuals who are high in general ability, then overall performance can be enhanced if individuals are assigned to the condition that matches the training regimen with the ability levels of the learners. When an ATI is found, the goal of trainers should be to measure the relevant individual characteristics (the aptitudes, whether they are ability or non-ability traits, such as personality variables or interests), and then assign individuals according to the training condition (the treatment) that yields the best performance for each.

One type of ATI that has been reasonably well documented is the interaction between the amount of structure involved in instruction/training and the level of the learners' abilities. Specifically, it is generally found that learners of lower abilities benefit most from highly structured learning/training experiences, while learners of higher abilities benefit most from low-structured learning/training experiences (e.g. see Snow and Yalow, 1982). The reasons for this interaction are somewhat complex, but there are two underlying factors that appear to be most important. First, lower-ability learners are more likely to become frustrated when insufficient structure is provided during skill acquisition, as they may cast about in vain for appropriate strategies to accomplish the task. In contrast, higher-ability learners may become bored with repetitive drill and practice, when they have already acquired good strategies for task performance. Second, general intellectual abilities appear to be related to the degree of benefit from prior transfer experiences. That is, individuals with higher abilities are more likely to see opportunities for transfer of previously learned information and skills, and thus be more likely to maximize skill development opportunities when faced with a new task. Lower ability individuals often fail to transfer previous learning to a new situation, except when there are obvious similarities of the old and new task (Sullivan, 1964).

In one demonstration of this effect, Goska and Ackerman (1996) explored the effects of transfer distance and general ability on complex skill acquisition by using two types of pre-training for a computerized air traffic controller task. When initial training was indirectly related (far transfer) to the criterion task, the correlation between ability and performance was substantially higher than when initial training was directly related (near transfer) to the criterion task. That is, higher ability learners benefited most, relatively speaking, from training which encouraged distant transfer of training, but lower ability learners benefited most from a near transfer training condition.

Avenues for ATI research in sports

Although theory development and interest in ATI research is most common in education, such as how to maximize learning in physics, this approach can be applied in any domain. It has recently been suggested that coaching in sports be reconsidered as *instruction* in sports (Sherman *et al.*, 1997). Sherman *et al.* (1997) have re-framed the components of instructional theory in the context of sports psychology, defining aptitude as a learner's status with regard to the motor skills that are required. A treatment, in this case, is the form of instructional procedures used by a coach to promote performance in a sport from novice to expert levels. For example, different styles of teaching volleyball have been evaluated for their effectiveness depending on the beginning skill level of learners (Harrison *et al.*, 1995). Two instructional methods were used; the practice style allowed learners to set the order and pace of drills (e.g. serve or spike), while the command style was directed by the teacher and students moved to the next stage of practice only at the teacher's direction. Aptitude was assessed using approved tests for setting up, passing, serving and spiking the ball, and students were cat-egorized as having low, medium, or high skills overall. For students of low initial skill, the teacher-directed style produced greater improvement on the set, while the practice style was more effective for the spike. For the passing and serving components, it was suggested that either instructional style would be effective for learners of all initial skill levels (Harrison *et al.*, 1995). It is possible to explore such level and training style interactions for other sports, but to date there does not appear to be extensive research of this type.

Conclusions and future directions

The ability–skill relationships that are presented in Ackerman's (1988) theory are best supported at the early and late stages of training. That is, general or con-tent (such as verbal) abilities are most predictive of early performance on a new task, while psychomotor abilities have the highest correlations with performance after the task has been well learned. The relationship of perceptual speed abili-ties through practice has been less consistent (e.g. Ackerman and Cianciolo, 2000). Additional studies may lead to refinement of the perceptual speed factors and under what conditions certain factors continue to relate to performance after extensive practice.

The 'ideal' breakdown for psychomotor abilities has yet to be decided. As dis-cussed, recent research (Chaiken *et al.*, 2000) indicates that perhaps these abilities may be more general than had been thought (e.g. Fleishman, 1972). Whatever psychomotor structure is ultimately adopted for conducting research, the most use-ful results will adhere to the principles of Brunswik symmetry (Wittmann and Süß, 1999). That is, the aspect of psychomotor ability used to predict performance after training should be relevant to the outcome that is important, and should be at a level of generality that is consistent with the level of the outcome. A discrete skill such as bench-pressing weight may be best predicted by a specific measure of static strength, while a more complex skill such as downhill skiing likely requires a more comprehensive measure of motor abilities that includes strength, flexibility and coordination.

Individual differences include a wide variety of cognitive (ability), affective (personality) and conative (motivational) traits, although abilities have received the most attention in this chapter. Anxiety, self-efficacy and motivation are also aspects on which people differ, and may be particularly important in skill acqui-sition. Anxiety about learning a new task may be detrimental in early practice, when attention is required by the task and distracting thoughts may impact performance (e.g. Kanfer and Heggestad, 1999). Self-efficacy (the belief that one can accomplish a particular level of task performance) has been shown to be par-ticularly important in sports skills (e.g. see Feltz, 1988; Jourden *et al.*, 1991). Motivation is important throughout training, but is especially so late in training, when a task has become more familiar and somewhat monotonous. High moti-vation levels may result in the dedication to practice that moves an individual from advanced to truly expert levels of performance. These non-ability charac-teristics may also be considered for their interactions with certain training styles. Using the aptitude-treatment interaction framework, it may be possible to iden-tify coaching methods that are most beneficial to those high in anxiety about engaging in physical activities, particularly when participation is somewhat involuntary (such as in taking mandatory physical education classes).

Although within-individual changes as learners proceed from novice to expert levels of skill can be very large indeed, between individual differences at all lev-els of skill development are both substantial and significant. A ratio of 3:1 in performance times from best to worst skilled performers means that early identi-fication of those individuals who can develop the highest levels of skills can yield benefits to an organization interested in maximizing performance. Moreover, the early identification of talent potential for particular skills can aid vocational counseling, so that individuals are oriented to the tasks for which they have the highest likelihood of success. In the final analysis, though, identification of key individual differences can be integrated with developments in skill training/instruction, so that the type of training can be matched to the capabil-ities and limitations of learners. Much more research is needed, but the results of current and previous investigations suggest that substantial gains can be made to improve the performance of learners who have different levels of abilities, per-sonality, and motivational characteristics.

References

Ackerman, P. L. (1987). Individual differences in skill learning: an integration of psycho-metric and information processing perspectives. *Psychological Bulletin*, 102 (1), 3–27.

Ackerman, P. L. (1988). Determinants of individual differences during skill acquisition: cognitive abilities and information processing. *Journal of Experimental Psychology: General*, 117 (3), 288–318.

Ackerman, P. L. (1989). Within-task intercorrelations of skilled performance: implica-tions for predicting individual differences? (A comment on Henry and Hulin, 1987). *Journal of Applied Psychology*, 74 (2), 360–364.

Ackerman, P. L. (1990). A correlational analysis of skill specificity: learning, abilities, and individual differences. *Journal of Experimental Psychology: Learning, Memory, and Cognition*, 16 (5), 883–901.

Ackerman, P. L. and Cianciolo, A. T. (1999). Psychomotor abilities via touchpanel testing: measurement innovations, construct, and criterion validity. *Human Performance*, 12, 231–273.

Ackerman, P. L. and Cianciolo, A. T. (2000). Cognitive, perceptual-speed, and psy-chomotor determinants of individual differences during skill acquisition. *Journal of Experimental Psychology: Applied*, 6 (4), 259–290.

Ackerman, P. L. and Kyllonen, P. C. (1991). Trainee characteristics. In J. E. Morrison (Ed.), *Training for performance: principles of applied human learning* (pp. 193–229). New York: John Wiley & Sons.

Ackerman, P. L. and Schneider, W. (1985). Individual differences in automatic and controlled information processing. In R. F. Dillon and R. R. Schmeck (Eds), *Individual differences in cognition*, Vol. 2 (pp. 35–66). New York: Academic Press.

Ackerman, P. L. and Woltz, D. J. (1994). Determinants of learning and performance in an associative memory/substitution task: task constraints, individual differences, volition, and motivation. *Journal of Educational Psychology*, 4, 487–515.

Adams, J. A. (1987). Historical review and appraisal of research on the learning, retention, and transfer of human motor skills. *Psychological Bulletin*, 101 (1), 41–74.

Andrew, D. M. and Paterson, D. G. (1934). Measured characteristics of clerical workers. *Bulletins of the Employment Stabilization Research Institute, University of Minnesota*, 3 (1), pp. 7–19. Minneapolis: University of Minnesota Press.

Barrett, G. V., Alexander, R. A. and Doverspike, D. (1992). The implications for personnel selection of apparent declines in predictive validities over time: a critique of Hulin, Henry, and Noon. *Personnel Psychology*, 45, 601–617.

Boyle, A. M. and Santelli, J. C. (1986). Assessing psychomotor skills: the role of the Crawford Small Parts Dexterity Test as a screening instrument. *Journal of Dental Education*, 50, 176–179.

Carroll, J. B. (1993). *Human cognitive abilities: a survey of factor-analytic studies*. New York: Cambridge University Press.

Cbs.Sportsline.Com (2002). The wonderful Wonderlic. (http://cbs.sportsline.com/u/ce/feature/0,1518.5202529_59,00.html)

Chaiken, S. R., Kyllonen, P. C. and Tirre, W. C. (2000). Organization and components of psychomotor ability. *Cognitive Psychology*, 40, 198–226.

Cronbach, L. J. (1957). The two disciplines of scientific psychology. *American Psychologist*, 12, 671–684.

Cronbach, L. J. and Furby, L. (1970). How we should measure 'change' – or should we? *Psychological Bulletin*, 74 (1), 68–80.

Cronbach, L. J. and Snow, R. E. (1977). *Aptitudes and instructional methods: a handbook for research on interactions*. New York: Irvington.

Ericsson, K. A., Krampe, R. T. and Tesch-Römer, C. (1993). The role of deliberate practice in the acquisition of expert performance. *Psychological Review*, 100 (3), 363–406.

Feltz, D. L. (1988). Gender differences in the causal elements of self-efficacy on a high avoidance motor task. *Journal of Sport and Exercise Psychology*, 10, 151–166.

Ferguson, G. A. (1956). On transfer and the abilities of man. *Canadian Journal of Psychology*, 10, 121–131.

Fitts, P. M. and Posner, M. I. (1967). *Human performance*. Belmont, CA: Brooks/Cole.

Fleishman, E. A. (1956). Psychomotor selection tests: research and application in the U.S. Air Force. *Personnel Psychology*, 9, 449–467.

Fleishman, E. A. (1972). On the relation between abilities, learning, and human performance. *American Psychologist*, 27, 1017–1032.

Fleishman, E. A. and Hempel, W. E. (1954). Changes in factor structure of a complex psychomotor test as a function of practice. *Psychometrika*, 19 (3), 239–252.

Fleishman, E. A. and Hempel, W. E. (1955). The relation between abilities and improvement with practice in a visual discrimination reaction task. *Journal of Experimental Psychology*, 49 (5), 301–312.

Goska, R. E. and Ackerman, P. L. (1996). An aptitude–treatment interaction approach to transfer within training. *Journal of Educational Psychology*, 88 (2), 249–259.

Guilford, J. P. (1958). A system of psychomotor abilities. *American Journal of Psychology*, 71, 164–174.

Guilford, J. P. and Lacey, J. I. (Eds) (1947). *Army Air Forces Aviation Psychology Program Research Reports: Printed Classification Tests*. Report No. 5. Washington, DC: US Government Printing Office.

Harrison, J. M., Fellingham, G. W., Buck, M. M. and Pellett, T. L. (1995). Effects of practice and command styles on rate of change in volleyball performance and self-efficacy of high-, medium-, and low-skilled learners. *Journal of Teaching in Physical Education*, 14, 328–339.

Henry, R. A. and Hulin, C. L. (1987). Stability of skilled performance across time: some generalizations and limitations on utilities. *Journal of Applied Psychology*, 72 (3), 457–462.

Hulin, C. L., Henry, R. A. and Noon, S. L. (1990). Adding a dimension: time as a factor in the generalizability of predictive relationships. *Psychological Bulletin*, 107 (3), 328–340.

Jourden, F. J., Bandura, A. and Banfield, J. T. (1991). The impact of conceptions of ability on self-regulatory factors and motor skill acquisition. *Journal of Sport and Exercise Psychology*, 13, 213–226.

Kanfer, R. and Heggestad, E. D. (1999). Individual differences in motivation: Traits and self-regulatory skills. In P. L. Ackerman, P. C. Kyllonen and R. D. Roberts (Eds), *Learning and individual differences: process, trait, and content determinants* (pp. 293–309). Washington, DC: American Psychological Association.

Melton, A. W. (Ed.) (1947). *Army Air Forces Aviation Psychology Program Research Reports: Apparatus Tests*. Report No. 4. Washington, DC: US Government Printing Office.

Proctor, R. W. and Dutta, A. (1995). *Skill acquisition and human performance*. Thousand Oaks, CA: Sage.

Salvendy, G. and Seymour, W. D. (1973). *Prediction and development of industrial work performance*. New York: Wiley.

Schmidt, R. A. and Wrisberg, C. A. (2000). *Motor learning and performance* (2nd ed.). Champaign, IL: Human Kinetics.

Schneider, W. and Shiffrin, R. M. (1977). Controlled and automatic human information processing: I. Detection, search, and attention. *Psychological Review*, 84, 1–66.

Shaffer, L. H. (1976). Intention and performance. *Psychological Review*, 83, 375–393.

Sherman, C., Crassini, B., Maschette, W. and Sands, R. (1997). Instructional sport psychology: a re-conceptualisation of sports coaching as sport instruction. *International Journal of Sport Psychology*, 28, 103–125.

Shute, V. J. (1993). A comparison of learning environments: All that glitters….In S.-P. Lajoie and S. J. Deary (Eds), *Technology in education*. (pp. 47–73). Hillsdale, NJ: Erlbaum.

Snow, R. E. and Yalow, E. (1982). Education and intelligence. In R. J. Sternberg (Ed.), *Handbook of human intelligence* (pp. 493–585). Cambridge: Cambridge University Press.

Sullivan, A. M. (1964). The relation between intelligence and transfer. Unpublished doctoral dissertation, McGill University, Montreal.

Thorndike, E. L. (1908). The effect of practice in the case of a purely intellectual function. *American Journal of Psychology*, 19, 374–384.

Wechsler, D. (1952). *The range of human capacities* (2nd Ed.). Baltimore, MD: Williams & Wilkins.

Wittmann, W. W. and Süß, H.-M. (1999). Investigating the paths between working memory, intelligence, knowledge, and complex problem-solving performance via Brunswik Symmetry. In P. L. Ackerman, P. C. Kyllonen and R. D. Roberts (Eds.), *Learning and individual differences: process, trait, and content determinants* (pp. 77–104). Washington, DC: American Psychological Association.

6 Decision training

Cognitive strategies for enhancing motor performance

Joan N. Vickers, Mary-Ann Reeves,
Kristine L. Chambers and Steve Martell

The ability to make effective decisions, especially under conditions of stress, is a characteristic sought by all performers. One endeavour where this is valued is sport, where time and competitive pressure invariably leads to a right or wrong decision in the final moments of the contest. Coaches have long sought effective means by which they can train their athletes to make better decisions. Decision training is perhaps the first model of coaching based on research designed to facilitate this goal. The roots of decision training are in cognitive science and motor learning. Magill (2001) states that in motor learning we 'do not directly observe learning; we directly observe behaviour' and further 'we must make inferences about learning from the behaviour we observe' (p. 168). Similarly, Schmidt and Lee (1999) state that motor learning 'is not directly observeable... changes in the patterning of muscular activity are rarely directly observeable... and one must infer their existence from changes in motor behaviour' (p. 265). Traditionally, the difficulty for the coach therefore, has been to infer whether the perceptual and cognitive aspects of performance have been trained on the basis of observable behaviours.

Within decision training, learning is inferred when there is evidence that the performer is able to think and make effective decisions while physically performing. A decision trainer considers the extent to which the athlete is able to use his or her perceptual and cognitive abilities to anticipate events, attend to critical cues, retrieve from memory the best response, focus on the appropriate cues at the right time and overall make effective decisions in the field of play. A decision trainer assumes that the necessary perceptual and cognitive skills must be present *before* motor behaviour changes can occur in a consistent and reliable way. There is an attempt to increase the 'cognitive effort' of the athlete during practices, where cognitive effort is defined as the mental work that 'leads to high levels of decision making, anticipation, planning, regulation and interpretation of motor performance' (Lee *et al.*, 1994, pp. 328–329). As a result of this perspective, the decision trainer designs practice activities that reveal to *both* the coach and athlete the presence or absence of an ability to make the right decision at the right time under varying forms of pressure.

Our goal in this chapter is to explain how this is done in the decision training approach. We first review the literature on coaching effectiveness and highlight a circularity that exists in how coaching has traditionally been researched and coaches educated. We then explain how decision training has emerged during the past 15 years in the academic and coaching setting. We describe the three-step decision training process that has been developed to help coaches design practices with a balanced cognitive–physical training focus. We then conclude with two studies carried out to determine the effectiveness of decision training. In the first study, we assessed the extent to which experienced coaches continued to use decision training after being introduced to theory and methods underlying the approach. In study two, we determined if decision training contributed to improvements in performance of age group swimmers.

What makes an effective coach?

Coaching success, knowledge and expertise have traditionally evaded systematic approaches. Coaching has been described as being largely dependent on intuition, tradition and emulation (Abraham and Collins, 1998; Lyle, 1990; Reeves, 1999). A mystique surrounds coaching to this day and there exists a 'fallacy that an esoteric tradition of coaching skills lies awaiting the coaching initiate' (Lyle, 1990, p. 464). At the same time, coaching has emerged as a profession of importance as demonstrated by the growing number of coaching education and certification programmes around the world (MacLean and Chelladurai, 1995). The significant impact and influence of coaches upon athletes, athletic performance, talent development and sport organizations has seen a growth in research in the area (Saury and Durand, 1998; Smith et al., 1977). There is a concerted effort to have coaching recognized as a profession (Reeves, 1999), and an increased need for the field to be research based and directed by strong theoretical foundations.

As coaching has developed into a recognized profession, extensive attempts have been made to define the characteristics underlying coaching success (Bloom et al., 1999; Claxton, 1988; Cross and Lyle, 1999; Douge and Hastie, 1993; Fairs, 1987; Lacy and Darst, 1984; Lyle, 1990; Saury and Durand, 1998). Research in coaching effectiveness has focused primarily on identifying the behavioural components of successful coaches (Bloom et al., 1999; Smith et al., 1977, 1979; Solomon et al., 1996). Information is gained from observing coaches in the field with the goal of applying that knowledge to improve coach education programs and subsequently increase coaching expertise and effectiveness.

Coaching effectiveness research, in adhering to these trends, is rooted in the development of systematic observation. Bloom et al. (1999) explain that systematic observation allows a trained observer following stated guidelines and procedures to observe, record and analyze interactions with the assurance that others viewing the same situation would agree with the recorded data. This technique migrated from other social science domains into educational research in the early 1960s and soon after to physical education and sport settings in order 'to uncover what coaches and athletes were doing' (Bloom et al., 1999, p. 158; van der Mars, 1989).

For example, the Coaching Behavioural Assessment System (Smith *et al.*, 1977) was developed by observing coaches as they conducted their practices, and consists of twelve categories classified as either reactive (e.g. positive reinforcement, punishment) or spontaneous (e.g. game-related behaviours, general communication) behaviours. It has been used extensively to measure coaching behaviours and also to recommend coaching interventions to improve the climate in sport (Smoll *et al.*, 1993). Other instruments have evolved from similar foundations and been used to train future generations (Lacy and Darst, 1984, 1985; Salminen and Liukkonen, 1996; Wandzilak *et al.*, 1988). The result has been the evolution of coaching education programmes that emphasize the behavioural skills of the performer and where little heed is paid to coach's ability to perceive the perceptual and cognitive requirements of performance that are also critical.

Observing what? The circularity of coaching effectiveness research

Using the process of field observation, coaching effectiveness research has succeeded in defining an overwhelming list of recommended coaching behaviours (Cross and Lyle, 1999). These have also been described as 'idiosyncratic' when translated into each sport. Cross (1999) describes the problem aptly when he states: 'It is almost certain there is no one "best" method of coaching [that] exists…different sports, sports in different cultures, different kinds of athletes… and even the same athletes at the top of their form elicit a different coaching response' (Cross, 1999, p. 51). Lyle (1990) defines the more serious problem when he states that coaching will never be defined as a profession if it continues '…to claim that the skills of the coach are being enhanced when there is no consensus on what [those skills] are!' (Lyle, 1990, p. 467). Although many of the characteristics of expert coaches have been researched, there still lacks a substantial 'theoretical basis to enable praxis to take place' (Lyle, 1990, p. 463).

Since coach education has evolved from watching expert coaches in the field, a circularity exists from which coach education has not been able to extricate itself. The difficulties associated with this can be appreciated if one considers the consequences of a similar approach if used in the medical profession. The standards of the medical profession would be based on observing 'expert doctors' in their offices, at the bedside and in operating rooms, rather than on the progress of theory and science in medicine that has shown to foster health and wellness. There is ultimately a contradiction between the historical view of coaching and the goals of enhancing coach effectiveness. If coaching has been entrenched in tradition, governed by the intuition of coaches and techniques passed down from previous coaching generations, is it not counterproductive to study those coaches in order to advance coaching effectiveness? That would simply perpetuate the traditions, albeit in a more formal manner! In order to change this situation, a model of coaching is required that has at its heart sound theoretical and research foundations, which are applicable to all sports, coaches and age groups.

The origins of decision training

Decision training emerged during the early 1990s when one of us (Vickers) was asked to teach a course in coaching effectiveness at the National Coaching Institute (NCI) in Calgary. Coaches attending this institute are at the upper levels of certification and are actively coaching while in attendance. It was, therefore, common for them to take the content of classes and apply the material immediately in their practices. A major focus of the course was the presentation of intriguing new motor learning research on practice design and feedback that revealed a paradoxical reversal effect on motor performance (for reviews, see Christina and Bjork, 1991; Farr, 1987; Lee *et al.*, 1994; Schmidt, 1991; Vickers, 1994). One aspect of the research compared the effects of using blocked practice with that of variable and/or random practice (Goode and Magill, 1986; Hall *et al.*, 1994; Shea and Morgan, 1979), while another compared the effects of using high frequencies of feedback with that of delayed or bandwidth feedback (Sherwood, 1988; Winstein and Schmidt, 1990). When blocked practice was used, impressive gains in performance were found in the short term but these were not sustainable in the long-term; performance declined during later retention and transfer conditions. In contrast, when variable and/or random practice was used, a reversal in performance occurred; progress was slower at first, but long-term performance was enhanced. A similar result was observed when high levels of feedback were provided; impressive gains were observed during immediate practice but these were not sustainable following practice. In other words, the highly structured, high feedback styles that have traditionally been promoted in coaching actually produced results that were the opposite of what the coaches (and professors) intended. Schmidt and Lee (1999) explain that 'a practice variable can have opposite effects on temporary performance levels versus the relatively permanent levels that must be assessed' (p. 274). This research in motor learning has grown over the years with the central tenet emerging that permanent changes in sport performance occur when the athlete is cognitively engaged during the physical training process.

Two problems we encountered

During the initial years of working with the coaches, we encountered two problems that led, in part, to the creation of decision training. First, we found that experienced coaches were uncomfortable using variable and random practice as defined by Schmidt (1991), Magill (2001) and others. Schmidt (1991) defines variable practice as 'a schedule of practice in which many variations of a class of actions are practiced' (p. 287), while Magill (2001) states that variable practice occurs when there is a 'variety of movement and context characteristics a person experiences while practicing a skill' (p. 285). Random practice is defined as a 'practice sequence in which tasks from several classes of skills are experienced in random order over consecutive trials' (Schmidt, 1991), or 'a practice sequence in which individuals perform a number of different tasks in no particular order, thus avoiding or minimizing repetitions of a single task' (Schmidt and Wrisberg, 2000, p. 233). Our most experienced coaches had difficulty with the notion that skills could be trained in a variable and random manner without a conceptual or tactical reason openly governing the whole endeavour. We also found that some coaches with less experience interpreted a variable random practice environment as one where the athletes simply played the game without any overall goals or objectives to the training.

The second problem we encountered was in the use of bandwidth feedback. Studies showed that in order to increase long-term performance and reduce athlete dependence on the coach, feedback should be gradually reduced and delayed as skill level develops (Lavery, 1962; Sherwood, 1988; Swinnen *et al.*, 1990; Winstein and Schmidt, 1990). Many of our coaches reported that using bandwidth feedback often created communication problems between themselves and their athletes, clients, parents and administrators. Coaching is a profession often defined by the highly verbal coach, one who is seen to overtly direct and control the events of the practice. When these verbal behaviours are reduced or curtailed, it is difficult for the non-informed observer to understand what is happening in the coaching environment.

The three-step decision training process: decisions, triggers and tools

Our response to these two problems was to develop the three-step decision training process. In order to provide an overall conceptual framework for the practices, the content of each practice was oriented around the decision-making skills required to perform well in each sport. We adopted a decision-making focus in order to bring to the fore the cognitive skills required to perform at a high level as physical training occurred. In this perspective, random and variable practices are viewed as invaluable tools that facilitate the development of decision-making skills. In order to overcome the communication problems previously encountered when bandwidth feedback was used, we introduced questioning as a way of alleviating this problem.

The three-step decision training process provides coaches with a guide for designing practices that increase the decision-making abilities of their athletes. In step one, the goal is to frame practice events so that decision-making skills are at the fore. Each decision highlights a specific cognitive skill that is defined within the context of the sport, for example, to direct *attention* to specific cues, to *anticipate* a specific event, to *retrieve from memory* the correct solution, to *solve a problem* under time constraints and so on. Physical and tactical skills specific to each sport are, therefore, developed within the context of defined decision-making skills.

In order to facilitate this process, it is important that coaches understand how information is acquired when performing and how temporal and environmental constraints affect all athletic performance. We also emphasize new findings from eye movement and gaze control research that describes the visual control and focus that athletes use as they perform (Adolphe and Vickers, 1997; Harle and

Vickers, 2001; Holland *et al.*, 2002; Martell, 2001; Rodrigues *et al.*, 2002; Vickers, 1992, 1996; Vickers and Adolphe, 1997; Williams *et al.*, 1999, 2002a,b). In addition, research by Wulf *et al.* (2002) and others provides specific guidance for coaches in terms of how attention is best oriented when motor skills are performed (e.g. internal versus external). These are but a few of the cognitive skills that can assist coaches in the development of the decisions to be trained.

In step two, the coach designs a drill or sequence of drills that best trains the decision under conditions that simulate those found in competition. A decision training drill not only specifies the cognitive skills to be trained in a sport context but also a perceptual or 'cognitive trigger' that enables both the coach and athlete to determine if the correct decision is being made. This is a unique aspect of decision training, which we now illustrate through two examples.

Example 1

The ability to 'see' the movement of the opponent(s) is a critical perceptual skill important in all sports. Badminton is a sport where this is especially important. Quite often, athletes are so involved with executing the strokes in the game that they decide to focus solely on the technical aspects of performance and lose track of where the opponent(s) is over the net. In step one, the decisions trained are to develop an awareness of the movement of the opponent and to exploit the movements of the opponent. In step two, a continuity drill is selected to train the decision. Continuity drills are common in badminton and require a feeder to place the shuttle so that numerous repetitions of a tactical sequence of strokes can be performed. In traditional forms of coaching, the feeder is often stationary and places the shuttle in a predictable manner. Since this is not what occurs during competition, a decision training drill not only trains the correct physical skills but also contains a 'cognitive trigger' that lets the athlete and coach know if the right decision is being made. To be effective, the player has to develop the ability to know where the opponent is and exploit any errors they make in positioning. A continuity drill with a cognitive trigger, therefore, requires the feeder to move *after* the shuttle is set to the athlete, just before the stroke is made. Many players are not aware of the feeder movement until after the stroke and immediately their mental 'light bulb' comes on. These athletes know that they are unable to see what is occurring over the net and they must change their technique in order to develop this ability. Others athletes are able to 'see' the feeder move but have not developed the decision-making skills that effectively exploit the opponent's movements. A good decision training drill, therefore reveals, to both the coach and athlete, the extent to which effective decisions are made. What is the use of perfect technique drilled to perfection if the wrong decision is made?

Example 2

Our second example manipulates working memory load and reaction times and uses both as cognitive triggers to train the decisions needed in sports where athletes have to be able to make decisions on their own under time, competitive and environmental pressure. Used first in freestyle skiing, this type of decision training has been applied to a wide array of sports. Imagine a freestyle skier standing at the top of a jump site where the goal is to perfect the jumps used in competition. In traditional forms of coaching, the coach would decide the jump or jumps to be trained, the athletes would repeat each a number of times and receive feedback. With a decision training focus, the coach first asks the athlete to name a jump (e.g. a single) and then to hold in working memory a second jump (a double) that *may* be called during the in-run by the command 'double'. If the coach says nothing, then the original jump is performed, thus simulating competitive conditions where the choreography is maintained. If the coach calls a 'double', the athlete has to mentally throw out the first jump, retrieve the second from working memory, program it and perform the jump under time and environmental pressure. With this drill, the coach manipulates the athlete's time to react (i.e. the interval between commands). Beginners are given longer than highly trained athletes. The coach can also change the jump to any combination of a single to double, double to single, double to triple and so on. Very soon the coach says nothing and the athlete makes the right decision at the right time, which they discuss later. The randomness and variability that can be put into this type of drill is endless. More important, the coach and athlete develop a way to communicate during practices that serves them well in competition – the athlete, through decision training, develops the ability to make the needed decisions with the full support and understanding of the coach.

Once a decision has been defined and the drill or activity selected with the perceptual and cognitive triggers, then step three is added – that of the seven 'decision training tools'. The tools have been selected and/or adapted from motor learning research and include: variable practice (smart-variations), random practice (smart-combinations), bandwidth feedback, questioning, video feedback, hard-first instruction and modelling. All have an extensive research base and are effective in facilitating the training of the decisions identified in steps one and two. Together these tools provide coaches with a wide array of methods they can use to develop the decision-making abilities of their individual athletes. The tools are now explained within the context of study one.

Study 1: will experienced coaches change their coaching methods so that more decision training is used?

In Study 1, we followed thirteen experienced coaches over a full season and determined the extent they adopted the seven decision training tools in their regularly scheduled practices. The participants were full-time coaches (four females and nine males) enrolled in the NCI, Calgary. All were pursuing Level Four of the 3M National Coaching Certification Program. As well, most were vying for the National Diploma in High Performance Coaching that requires extra study beyond Level Four. The sports included were badminton, cross country skiing, short and long track speed skating, squash, men and women's ice hockey, track and field and wrestling. The athletes coached ranged in age from 11 to 30 years and their skill levels from developmental to seasoned international and Olympic competitor.

The coaches were videotaped during three regularly scheduled practices spaced across the season. Practice 1 (P1) occurred in the first month and was videotaped before the coaches received any formal education in decision training. Practice 2 (P2) was videotaped in months three or four, and followed a course given in decision training which was presented in month two. The three-step decision training process was taught during a 1-week, 40-hour course. The first 2 days were spent covering the underlying theory and research in a workshop setting, followed by 3 days of microcoaching where each coach assumed three roles: as coach, athlete and peer evaluator. By experiencing all three roles, the coaches were provided with the opportunity to (a) learn to implement decision training as a coach; (b) to experience the reception of decision training as an athlete; and (c) to develop skills in observing peer coaches and providing constructive feedback. Practice 3 (P3) occurred in months five or six, after all course requirements were completed and no evaluation pressures were present. In most sports, the season ended during months seven or eight. We expected the coaches to improve from P1 to P2 as a result of taking the decision training course, and also because of an evaluation component scheduled during P2 which added certification pressures to the practice. The critical comparison was, therefore, from P1 to P3, where no evaluation pressures or observers were present and the coaches were free to conduct their practices as they deemed appropriate.

Two coders familiar with decision training coded the videotapes using the Decision Training Instrument (Vickers, 2000). This instrument was developed over the years of working with the coaches and included the three-step decision training process and the seven decision training tools. Each of the tools is shown in Table 6.1 and includes four or five bi-polars as derived from (a) research in each area; (b) our experience in applying the tool in the field; and (c) our wish to achieve a balance between the cognitive and physical aspects of performance. A 5-point Likert scale was used in which a score of 5 was excellent, 4 good, 3 above average, 2 below average and 1 unacceptable. Practice management skills were also assessed and included measures of instruction time, active time, management time and verbal prompts (Vickers, 1990). Inter-observer agreements between the coders were determined. In the practice management category, these ranged from a low of 79 per cent for instruction time to a high of 89 per cent for management time. For the ordinal scales (1–5), the inter-observer agreements ranged from a low of 62 per cent for hard-first instruction to a high of 95 per cent for questioning. Each dependent measure was analyzed separately using repeated measures analysis of variance (ANOVA) to detect changes across the practice factor (P1, P2, P3). Table 6.1 presents the means for P1, P2 and P3, along with the significant differences found for P1 compared to P2, and P1 compared to P3. Of the fifty areas analysed, twenty-seven significant changes were found from P1 to P2, and fifteen from P1 to P3.

Table 6.1. Mean scores of thirteen coaches for practice management, variable practice, random practice, feedback, questioning, hard-first instruction and modelling during three practices (P1, P2, P3) scheduled over a season of coaching. Post hoc differences between P1 and P2, and P1 and P3 are also shown

Categories measured	Means			Comparisons	
	P1	P2	P3	P1–P2	P1–P3
Practice management					
Management %	7.0	7.1	5.0		
Instruction %	26.4	26.9	26.5		
Active %	67.5	67.6	72.1		
Verbal prompts (ratio/1)	1.9	2.1	2.3		
Variable practice overall	3.9	4.2	4.1	$p<0.0001$	
Smart variations	4.1	4.4	4.1	$p<0.0005$	
Technically sound	4.2	4.2	4.2		
Tactically sound	3.7	4.3	4.1	$p<0.0001$	$p<0.0006$
Competition-like	3.5	4.0	3.9	$p<0.0001$	$p<0.001$
Random practice overall	3.5	4.2	4.0	$p<0.0001$	$p<0.0001$
Smart combos	3.8	4.3	4.1	$p<0.0001$	
Technically sound	3.4	4.2	4.1	$p<0.001$	$p<0.0006$
Tactically sound	3.3	4.3	3.9	$p<0.0001$	$p<0.0001$
Competition-like	3.1	4.2	4.0	$p<0.0001$	$p<0.0001$
Feedback quantitative (per min)	0.5	0.2	0.6		
Individual corrective	8.7	6.3	8.2		
Group corrective	2.5	2.0	2.1		
Individual positive	5.2	4.2	4.2		
Group positive	1.7	1.5	1.1		
Negative	0.5	0.2	0.6		
Feedback qualitative overall	2.7	3.4	3.4	$p<0.0001$	$p<0.0001$
Frequent	2.7	3.3	3.3	$p<0.0001$	$p<0.0001$
Delayed/faded	2.1	3.1	3.2	$p<0.0001$	$p<0.0001$
Summary	3.2	3.6	3.5		
Bandwidth	2.7	3.6	3.6	$p<0.0003$	$p<0.0001$
Questions quantitative (per min)	0.3	0.5	0.4	$p<0.0001$	$p<0.0001$
To the individual	3.5	6.1	6.3	$p<0.0003$	$p<0.0001$
To the group	1.1	2.2	1.4	$p<0.0002$	
Questions answered	1.9	4.0	3.2	$p<0.0001$	
Athlete questions	1.1	1.2	1.4		
Questions qualitative (overall)	2.9	3.8	3.4	$p<0.0001$	$p<0.0003$
Frequent	2.5	3.3	2.8	$p<0.0001$	
Challenging/probing	2.7	3.5	3.0	$p<0.001$	
Appropriate	3.0	3.8	3.3		
Athlete-engaged	2.9	3.8	3.4	$p<0.0001$	$p<0.0003$
Hard-first instruction (overall)	3.6	3.8	3.4		
Concept clear	3.4	3.7	3.2		
Developmental/safe	3.9	3.9	3.6		
Top-down tactical	3.3	3.5	3.2		
Relevant to season	3.6	3.9	3.7	$p<0.0005$	
Modelling (Overall)	3.7	4.0	3.6	$p<0.0003$	
Organization	4.0	4.3	3.9	$p<0.0004$	
Cues explained	4.2	4.0	3.9		
Athletes questioned	2.6	3.0	2.6		
Athletes self-directed	3.6	3.9	3.4		
Model quality	4.0	4.3	4.0	$p<0.0001$	
Model timing	4.0	4.3	3.9		
Summary of practice					
Overall practice	3.7	4.4	3.9	$p<0.0001$	
The DT Index	2.7	4.0	3.5	$p<0.0001$	$p<0.0001$

Practice management skills

No significant differences were found from P1, P2 to P3 in any of the practice management skills. All values obtained were within the ranges expected (Seidentop, 1976: Vickers, 1990, 2000), thereby confirming the high level of skill of the coaches. The use of decision training did not adversely affect any of the management categories, active time increased from P1 to P3 (67.5–72.1 per cent), instruction time remained the same (26.4–26.5 per cent), and management time declined (from 7 to 5 per cent) from P1 to P3. The absence of any substantial change in these measures, therefore, allayed any fears that increasing cognitive effort during practices might take away from the time devoted to physical training (Cross and Lyle, 1999; Douge and Hastie, 1994; Siedentop, 1976).

DT Tool 1: Variable practice (smart-variations). Four of the five variable practice areas improved significantly from P1 to P2, while two improved from P1 to P3 (tactically sound and competition-like). The coaches improved over the season in their abilltiy to deliver training experiences that trained a single class of skills with many variations in tactically sound competitive settings.

DT Tool 2: Random practice (smart-combinations). Improvements occurred in all of the categories from P1 to P2, and in four of five from P2 to P3. The coaches improved over the season indicating the coaches improved in their ability to create training experiences that combined two or more skills in simulations of competitive events.

DT Tool 3: Bandwidth feedback. Significant improvements were found in the quality of feedback provided with improvements in the coaches' abilities to reduce the frequency of feedback, delay and fade and provide summary feedback. Overall, the coaches provided less corrective feedback as the season progressed.

DT Tool 4: Questioning. The results showed that the total number of questions increased significantly from P1 to P2, and from P1 to P3 in all areas except athlete questions to the coach. The results were consistent with the expectations of decision training, namely that the frequency of questions from athletes should increase in order to enhance decision-making skills and communication between the athlete and coach. Qualitatively, the coaches were observed to probe deeper and ask more challenging questions in P2 and P3 than in P1. Of all the tools, questioning was the one that the coaches consistently commented was most valuable. One of the coaches put it best when he stated: 'If an athlete comes up to me and asks a simple question I know he or she is looking for a simple answer and the athlete does not understand how decision making operates in our sport. I know now that this also translates into a bad or inconsistent performance in competition. On the other hand, if athletes ask for verification of their own discovery, then I know those athletes are engaged in developing the decision-making skills needed. Decision training encourages the process of self-discovery and starts the athletes on coming up with a well thought out questions and solutions and not just looking for answers'.

DT Tool 5: Video feedback. Only two coaches used video feedback, therefore, this category was not formally analysed.

DT Tool 6: Hard-first instruction. Unlike many traditional forms of coaching which begins each season with the teaching of easy first concepts, decision training reverses this practice and introduces the athletes to the complex knowledge they need about the sport as early as possible. This approach is supported by research by Doane *et al.* (1996) who show that participants exposed to 'easy-first' training conditions are never able to improve to the same extent as those that begin with 'hard-first'. One significant difference was found from P1 to P2, and this was an increase in the use of concepts relevant to the season, and none from P1 to P3. Although the amount of improvement from P1 to P2 was lower than desired, the results from P1 to P3 were as expected as by definition hard-first instruction should be provided early in the season and not later in order to maximize the amount of time the athletes had to cognitively incorporate the material into their motor performance.

DT Tool 7: Modelling. Modelling occurred when the coach demonstrated a skill or tactic using a demonstrator, a video of an elite or peer performer, or other model derived from a textbook, photograph, computer, kinematic or other illustration. Within decision training, modelling should be used early in the season as a method of developing analytical and cognitive skills that are sport-specific and most effective after long-term use. Three significant changes were found from P1 to P2 and none from P1 to P3. This was as expected as modelling is a method that should be used more early in the season more than later.

Overall rating and the DT index

The observers provided two omnibus measures for each practice. The first, overall rating, took into account all factors (including management time, variable-random practice, bandwidth feedback, questioning, hard-first instruction and modelling). A significant improvement was detected from P1 to P2, but not from P1 to P3, although the mean values were in the desired direction. The DT Index concentrated on the extent the coaches delivered practices that were perceived to increase athletes' cognitive effort and decision-making skills. In other words, did the decision training methods help the athletes develop the anticipation, attention, memory and problem-solving skills needed to perform under all competitive conditions? The DT Index increased significantly from P1 to P2 and from P2 to P3. In the opinion of the observers, the coaching environment improved significantly in terms of the extent that high-level decision-making abilities were being developed.

Follow-up

We followed the coaches for a period of 3 years after the study in terms of their employment as coaches. Of the thirteen who took part, four coached athletes at the Salt Lake Olympics and two of their athletes won medals even though they were relatively junior coaches at the time of being enrolled in the NCI. Eight went on to coach national and/or provincial teams, three at the university or college level, and two at the professional/club level.

Study 2: does decision training contribute to improvements in athlete performance?

Although the results of Study 1 were encouraging, one limitation was that we did not assess the performance of the athletes. In Study 2, our goal was to determine if the use of two of the decision training tools, bandwidth feedback and questioning would improve the performance of age group competitive swimmers (Chambers, 2001). To our knowledge, no studies in coaching have specifically examined the relation between delaying feedback and using questioning to increase athlete cognitive effort, although studies in medicine have shown that questioning is effective as a treatment intervention (House *et al.*, 1990; Knight *et al.*, 1997). Two adolescent competitive swim teams (age 13–17 years) were selected from the five available in City of Calgary and randomly assigned to two groups. The objective of the study was to determine if bandwidth feedback and questioning techniques would significantly improve the swim times and swim technique of the group receiving this instruction (BF-Q), as compared to a control (C) group.

Prior to the season, the coach of the BF-Q team participated in a 1-week programme that included theoretical and practical experiences using bandwidth feedback and questioning methods, while no attempt was made to influence the control coaches methods. Integrity of the BF-Q intervention was maintained over the 6-week intervention period using videotape and direct observation to measure feedback and questioning levels of the two coaches.

The study spanned one competitive winter season of 4 months. A pre-test was carried out, followed by a 6-week intervention, a post-test and a transfer test after 2 weeks. Competitive swim times were taken (pre-post-transfer) from regularly swim meets, while practice times were taken from simulated meets held during practices. Technical evaluations were carried out using videotape at similar intervals to determine changes in swim technique. Interviews with the athletes were also conducted.

Figure 6.1 shows the results for swim technique, which was assessed from the videotapes by two independent experts in swimming. The BF-Q group improved significantly during the pre- to post-intervention period, but showed no further improvements from post to transfer, while the C group improved less overall and their improvements occurred during the latter part of the season.

Figure 6.2 shows the results for competitive swim time (a negative score means a faster time). The BF-Q group did not improve in their times during the pre- to post-intervention period, but showed a significant improvement from post to transfer, while the C group recorded its greatest improvements during the early season

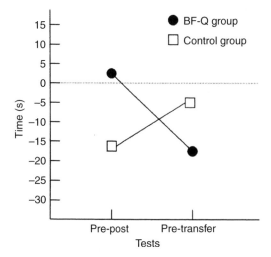

Figure 6.1 Mean difference in competitive swim time d-scores from pre to post and from post to transfer. A lower score indicates a greater improvement in time.

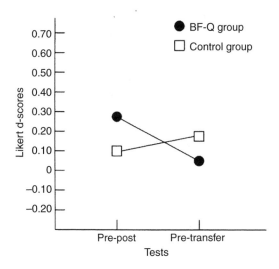

Figure 6.2 Mean difference in technique d-scores from pre to post and from post to transfer. A higher score indicates a greater improvement in swim stroke technique.

and less during the latter part of the season. In terms of absolute competitive swim times, mean times for the BF-Q group were equivalent to those of the C group during the first part of the season (pre-test) but by the end of the season (transfer) the BF-Q group was faster than the C group, although not significantly.

This study was one of the first to examine questioning methods and in particular, the interplay between bandwidth feedback and questioning. The intent of using bandwidth feedback and questioning in combination is to increase cognitive effort and thus assist the athletes in terms of understanding the technical and tactical requirements of the sport. Our results showed that the use of bandwidth feedback and questioning contributed to significant improvements in swim technique early in the season for the BF-Q group compared to the C group, but that benefits in competitive performance were not realized by the BF-Q group until later in the season. Overall, the BF-Q group improved more than the C group in both swim speed and technique. These results are consistent with those found in many of the motor learning studies in both the applied and laboratory setting; improvements in motor performance are often delayed but enhanced when methods are used that increase cognitive effort and decision making during training.

Conclusions

In this chapter, our goal was to present some of the foundations of decision training juxtaposed against the traditions of the coaching effective research, motor learning and cognitive science. Decision training is a new approach to coaching that has been used extensively in the field using the three-step decision training process. Two attempts to determine the effectiveness of the approach in the field were summarized in this chapter with the first showing that experienced coaches will adopt the decision training tools within their regularly scheduled practices, while the second showed that the use of two of the tools in combination, bandwidth feedback and questioning, improves both the technique and competitive swim times of age group swimmers.

Overall, the purpose of decision training is to provide coaches with workable strategies that increase the cognitive effort of their athlete within the physical training environment. The three-step decision training process is designed to increase the decision-making skills of the athlete through a judicious use of cognitive training in concert with physical training. The two cannot be separated in our mind, as often occurs when traditional or behavioural forms of coaching are used.

If the emerging profession of coaching is to extract itself from the circularity and idiosyncrasy still found today, then formal approaches to coach education must be developed that are substantiated in both research and practice. Decision training is grounded in theory and research, with increasing practical support. It presents a multifaceted approach to teaching and evaluating coaches that involves cognitive techniques underlying a process of mentorship, personal and peer evaluation, synthesis of sport/programme/practice goals and individual differences. One of the strengths of the approach is that the three-step decision training process and seven tools are the same for all sports, athletes and age groups and so offers a universal approach to coach education that has been lacking. Decision training recognizes that the emerging profession of coaching requires the use of a universal set of principles derived from research, while at the same time accommodating the specificity and diversity found in each sport.

Acknowledgement

The research reported in this paper was funded by the National Coaching Institute – Calgary, the Coaching Association of Canada and the Canadian Sport Centre – Calgary. We would like to thank John Bales, President of the Coaches Association of Canada, for his insight and long-standing support of this project.

References

Abraham, A. and Collins, D. (1998). Examining and extending research in coach development. *Quest*, 50, 59–79.

Adolphe R., Vickers, J. N. and LaPlante, G. (1997). The effects of training visual attention on gaze behaviour and accuracy: a pilot study. *International Journal of Sports Vision*, 4 (1), 28–33.

Bloom, G. A., Crumpton, R. and Anderson, J. E. (1999). A systematic observation study of the teaching behaviours of an expert basketball coach. *The Sport Psychologist*, 13, 157–170.

Chambers, K. L. (2001). The effect of bandwidth feedback and questioning on the performance, motivation and autonomy of age-group swimmers. Unpublished Masters Thesis, Faculty of Kinesiology, University of Calgary.

Christina, R. W. and Bjork, R. A. (1991). Optimizing long-term retention and transfer. In D. Druckman and R. A. Bjork (Eds), *In the mind's eye: enhancing human performance* (pp. 23–56). Washington, DC: National Academy Press.

Claxton, D. (1988). A systematic observation of more or less successful high school tennis coaches. *Journal of Teaching in Physical Education*, 7, 302–310.

Cross, N. (1999). Coaching effectiveness. In N. Cross and J. Lyle (Eds), *The coaching process: principles and practice for sport*. Woburn, MA: Reed Educational and Professional Publishing Ltd.

Cross, N. and Lyle, J. (Eds) (1999). *The coaching process: principles and practice for sport*. Woburn, MA: Reed Educational and Professional Publishing Ltd.

Doane, S., Alderton, D., Sohn, Y. and Pelligrino, J. (1996). Acquisition and transfer of skilled performance: are visual discrimination skills stimulus specific? *Journal of Experimental Psychology: Human Perception and Performance*, 22 (5), 1218–1248.

Douge, B. and Hastie, P. (1993). Coach effectiveness. *Sport Science Review*, 2 (2), 14–29.

Fairs, J. R. (1987). The coaching process: the essence of coaching. *Sports Coach*, 11 (1), 17–19.

Farr, M. J. (1987). *The long-term retention of knowledge and skills*. New York: Springer-Verlag.

Goode, S. and Magill, R. (1986). Contextual interference effects in learning three badminton serves. *Research Quarterly for Exercise and Sport*, 53, 308–314.

Hall, K., Domingues, D. and Cavazos, R. (1994). The effects of contextual interference on college level baseball players. *Perceptual and Motor Skills*, 78, 838.

Harle, S. K. and Vickers, J. (2001). Training quiet eye (QE) improves accuracy in the basketball free throw. *The Sport Psychologist*, 15, 289–305.

Holland, M. A., Patla, A. E. and Vickers, J. N. (2002). Look where you are going! Gaze behaviour associated with maintaining and changing direction. *Experimental Brain Research*, 143, 221–230.

House, B. M., Chassie, M. B. and Spohn, B. B. (1990). Questioning : an essential ingredient in effective teaching. *The Journal of Continuing Education in Nursing*, 21 (5), 196–201.

Knight, G. W., Guenzel, P. J. and Feil, P. (1997). Using questions to facilitate motor skill acquisition. *Journal of Dental Education*, 61 (1), 56–65.

Lacy, A. C. and Darst, P. W. (1984). Evolution of a systematic observation system: the ASU coaching observation instrument. *Journal of Teaching in Physical Education*, 3, 59–66.

Lacy, A. C. and Darst, P. W. (1985). Systematic observation of behaviours of winning high school football coaches. *Journal of Teaching in Physical Education*, 4, 256–270.

Lavery, J. J. (1962). The retention of simple motor skills as a function of type of knowledge of results. *Canadian Journal of Psychology*, 16, 300–311.

Lee, T. D., Swinnen S. and Serrien D. (1994). Cognitive effort and motor learning. *Quest*, 46, 328–344.

Lyle, J. W. (1990). Systematic coaching behaviour: an investigation into the coaching process and the implications of the findings for coach education. In T. Williams, L. Almond and A. Sparks (Eds), *Sport and physical activity: moving toward excellence*. Bury St. Edmonds, Suffolk: St. Edmondsbury Press Ltd.

Lyle, J. W. (1999). *The coaching process: an overview*. Woburn, MA: Reed Educational and Professional Publishing Ltd.

MacLean, J. C. and Chelladurai, P. (1995). Dimensions of coaching performance: development of a scale. *Journal of Sport Management*, 9, 194–207.

Magill, R. A. (2001). *Motor learning: concepts and applications* (6th ed.). Boston, MA: McGraw Hill.

Martell, S. T. (2001). Quiet eye as an indicator of decision making in ice hockey. Unpublished Masters Thesis. Faculty of Kinesiology, University of Calgary.

Reeves, M. A. (1999). Raising the bar in coach education. *Coaches Report*, 5 (4), 14–16.

Rodrigues, S. T., Vickers, J. N. and Williams, A. M. (2002), Head, eye and arm coordination in table tennis: an exploratory study. *Journal of Sport Sciences*, 20 (3), 171–186.

Salminen, S. and Liukkonen, J. (1996). Coach–athlete relationship and coaching behaviour in training sessions. *International Journal of Sport Psychology*, 27, 59–67.

Saury, J. and Durand, M. (1998). Practical knowledge in expert coaches: on-site study of coaching knowledge in sailing. *Research Quarterly for Exercise and Sport*, 69 (3), 254–266.

Schmidt, R. A. (1991). *Motor learning and performance: from principles to practice*. Champaign, IL: Human Kinetics.

Schmidt, R. A. and Lee, T. D. (1999). *Motor control and learning* (3rd ed.). Champaign, IL: Human Kinetics.

Schmidt, R. A. and Wrisberg, C. (2001). *Motor learning and performance: from principles to practice*. Champaign, IL: Human Kinetics.

Shea, J. and Morgan, R. (1979). Contextual interference effects on the acquisition, retention, and transfer of a motor skill. *Journal of Experimental Psychology: Human Learning and Memory*, 5, 179–187.

Sherwood, D. E. (1988). Effect of bandwidth knowledge of results on movement consistency. *Perceptual and Motor Skills*, 66, 535–542.

Siedentop, D. (1976). *Developing teaching skills in physical education*. Mountain View, CA: Mayfield Publishing Company.

Smith, R. E., Smoll, F. L. and Curtis, B. (1979). Coach effectiveness training: a cognitive–behavioural approach to enhancing relationship skills in youth sport coaches. *Journal of Sport Psychology*, 1, 59–75.

Smith, R. E., Smoll, F. E. and Hunt, E. (1977). A system for the behavioural assessment of athletic coaches. *The Research Quarterly*, 48 (2), 401–407.

Smoll, F. L., Smith, R. E., Barnett, N. P. and Everett, J. J. (1993). Enhancement of children's self-esteem through social support training for youth sport coaches. *Journal of Applied Psychology*, 78 (4), 602–610.

Solomon, G. B., Stringer, D. A., Eliot, J. F., Heron, S. N., Maas, J. L. and Wayda, V. K. (1996). The self-fulfilling prophecy in college basketball: implications for effective coaching. *Journal of Applied Sport Psychology*, 8, 44–59.

Swinnen, S., Schmidt, R. A. Nicholson, D. E. and Shapiro, D. C. (1990). Information feedback for skill acquisition: instantaneous knowledge of results degrades performance. *Journal of Experimental Psychology: Learning, Memory and Cognition*, 16, 706–716.

van der Mars, H. (1989). Systematic observation: *an introduction*. In P. W. Darst, D. B. Zakrajsek and V. H. Mancini (Eds), *Analyzing physical education and sport instruction* (2nd ed.). Champaign, IL: Human Kinetics Publishers.

Vickers, J. N. (1990). *Instructional design for teaching physical activity: a knowledge structures approach*. Champaign, IL: Human Kinetics.

Vickers, J. N. (1992). Gaze control in putting. *Perception*. 21, 117–132.

Vickers, J. N. (1994). Psychological research in sport pedagogy: exploring the reversal effect. *Sport Science Review*, 3 (1), 28–40.

Vickers, J. N. (1996). Visual control while aiming at a far target. *Journal of Experimental Psychology: Human Perception and Performance*, 22, 342–354.

Vickers, J. N. (1999). Decision training: a new coaching tool. *Insight: The FA Coaches Association Journal*, 4 (2), 18–20.

Vickers, J. N. (2000). *Decision training: a new approach in coaching*. Vancouver: Coaching Association of British Columbia.

Vickers, J. N. (in press). *Decision training in sport*. Champaign, IL: Human Kinetics.

Vickers, J. N. and Adolphe, R. A. (1997). Gaze behaviour during a ball tracking and aiming skill. *International Journal of Sports Vision*, 4 (1), 18–27.

Wandzilak, T., Ansgorge, C. J. and Potter, G. (1988). Comparison between selected practice and game behaviours of youth sport soccer coaches. *Journal of Sport Behaviour*, 11, 78–88.

Weeks, D. L. and Kordus, R. N. (1998). Relative frequency of knowledge of performance and motor skill learning. *Research Quarterly for Exercise and Sport*, 69 (3), 224–230.

Winstein C. J. and Schmidt, R. A. (1990). Reduced frequency of knowledge of results enhances motor skill learning. *Journal of Experimental Psychology: Learning, Memory, and Cognition*, 16, 677–691.

Williams, A. M., Davids, K. and Williams, J. G. (1999). *Visual perception and action in sport*. London: Routledge.

Williams, A. M., Vickers, J. N. and Rodrigues, S. T. (2002a). The effects of anxiety on visual search, movement kinematics and performance in table tennis: a test of Eysenck and Calvo's processing efficiency theory. *Journal of Sport and Exercise Psychology*, 24 (4), 438–455.

Williams, A. M., Singer, R. A. and Frehlich, S. (2002b). Quiet eye duration, expertise, and task complexity in a near and far aiming task. *Journal of Motor Behaviour*, 34, 197–207.

Wulf, G., McConnel, N., Gartner, M. and Schwarz, A. (2002). Enhancing the learning of sport skills through external-focus feedback. *Journal of Motor Behaviour*, 34 (2) 171–182.

7 Understanding the role of augmented feedback

The good, the bad and the ugly

Gabriele Wulf and Charles H. Shea

For nearly a century (see Thorndike, 1914, 1932), researchers have been concerned with the role of feedback in the learning of motor skills (for reviews, see Newell, 1977; Adams, 1987; Salmoni *et al.*, 1984; Schmidt, 1991; Swinnen, 1996). Recently, researchers have increasingly directed their attention to the effects of *knowledge of results* (KR). KR is terminal feedback provided to the performer after the completion of a response about the movement outcome in terms of an environmental goal (Adams, 1968, 1971). This source of information is thought to eliminate (or at least reduce) the need for error detection after a response is made and to serve as a basis for error correction on subsequent trials, presumably guiding the performer to the correct response. KR was viewed as integral in achieving more effective performance as practice continues. In fact, early accounts of the role of KR concluded that it was one of the most important learning variables such that learning did not occur in its absence (e.g. Bilodeau and Bilodeau, 1958; Bilodeau *et al.*, 1959). Practice without KR was thought to cause performance to drift away from the goal and to weaken the representation of the action in memory. The reason for this is that the representation [*perceptual trace* in Adams' (1971) theory; *recall* and *recognition schemata* in Schmidt's (1975) theory] was thought to develop as a function of previous experience with a task and the KR received. That is, the more trials with KR an individual had performed, the stronger the trace or schemata were assumed to be and, eventually, the ability to detect errors without KR. According to this view, learning was optimized when KR was provided more frequently, immediately or precisely (Adams, 1971; Schmidt, 1975; Thorndike, 1927). Recently, these ideas have been questioned, and researchers have suggested that a number of factors come into play when feedback is or is not provided during the learning of motor skills.

In recent years, researchers have tended to make a distinction between *knowledge of performance* (KP) and KR. KP refers to the 'nature of the movement produced' (Schmidt and Lee, 1999, p. 415), such as kinematic information about the movement pattern produced, whereas KR refers to the 'result produced in terms of the environmental goal' (Schmidt and Lee, 1999, p. 415), such as the overall movement time or spatial deviation from a target. Even though there might be situations, where KR and KP serve specific and differential functions in the learning process (e.g. Brisson and Alain, 1996, 1997), in general, it appears that both types of augmented feedback adhere to the same principles in the way they affect the learning of motor skills. Therefore, we will not distinguish between the two in the remainder of this chapter, but rather refer to both as (augmented) feedback, or simply KR.

The purpose of this chapter is to review the good, the bad and the ugly from the feedback literature. Salmoni *et al.* (1984) provided an important and influential review of the KR literature and put forward a theoretical view regarding the role of feedback for motor learning, termed the 'guidance hypothesis'. This hypothesis was based, in part, on KR experiments demonstrating a distinction between temporary acquisition effects, where different groups perform under different conditions, and more permanent learning effects assessed through delayed retention and/or transfer tests under common conditions (e.g. McGuigan, 1959; also see Schmidt, 1982). This distinction was particularly noteworthy because there were demonstrations in which the group/condition that performed worst during acquisition actually performed best on a common delayed test (e.g. Lavery, 1962). The advancement of these ideas resulted in a surge of new research and has clearly contributed to a better understanding of the various functions of feedback (the good). Yet, as we will demonstrate, the findings of the newer studies are not all consistent with the guidance notion (the bad). The biggest problem (the ugly part), however, has been a lack of a theoretical perspective that can provide a coherent framework capable of guiding future feedback research. After reviewing the guidance hypothesis (Salmoni *et al.*, 1984), we critically review the feedback literature resulting from the publication of this theoretical perspective and attempt to characterize those conditions or manipulations that are and are not consistent with the theory. Finally, we attempt to summarize what we feel are the stable principles that can be gleaned from the current literature and make suggestions for future research and theory.

Guidance hypothesis

A critical review and re-appraisal of the early KR literature was published by Salmoni *et al.* (1984). This review resulted in resurgence in KR research and provided a testable theoretical perspective that has guided the majority of that research. By the fall of 2003, the Salmoni *et al.* review had been cited approximately 260 times. Several shortcomings in the experimental designs used were highlighted and associated interpretations of the data from early KR studies questioned. More specifically, they noted that many of the early KR experiments failed to include retention and/or transfer tests, but rather inferred learning from acquisition data where participants were practicing under different experimental conditions. They argued that the use of delayed tests under common conditions was crucial for assessing stable learning effects. Performance differences during the practice phase may reflect temporary or transient effects associated with the various experimental manipulations, and therefore, may provide a distorted view of what has been learned. Delayed retention and/or transfer tests were argued to allow a cleaner assessment of what was learned uncontaminated by the temporary influences associated with the experimental manipulations. Based on their review, Salmoni *et al.* (1984) (see also Schmidt, 1991) proposed the guidance hypothesis.

The guidance hypothesis received its name from the role feedback was thought to play in *guiding* the performer to the correct movement during the learning process. According to the guidance hypothesis (Salmoni *et al.*, 1984; Schmidt, 1991; Schmidt *et al.*, 1989), KR effectively guides the performer to the correct response, resulting in enhanced acquisition performance. However, providing KR after every trial can result in a number of subtle negative effects. That is, the learner might become too dependent on the KR and bypass the processing of other important feedback sources that may be required to develop intrinsic error detection and correction mechanisms (e.g. Bjork, 1988; Landauer and Bjork, 1978; Schmidt, 1991). It has also been argued that frequent KR during practice results in less stable performance because KR prompts the performer to adjust even small response errors that may simply represent an inherent variability in the motor system. Bjork (see Winstein and Schmidt, 1990) has labelled these types of response corrections *maladaptive short-term corrections* because they result in unproductive response variability. In addition, providing feedback after each trial may facilitate the planning of the next response, thereby reducing the participant's need to perform memory retrieval operations thought to be critical for learning (Wulf and Schmidt, 1994). Thus, the guidance hypothesis suggests a positive influence of frequent KR during practice while it is present, but a detrimental impact on learning when it is withdrawn.

Several experiments using a variety of KR manipulations have provided support for the guidance hypothesis. These studies typically used feedback manipulations that in some way attempted to reduce the (negative) guidance effects of feedback and at the same time encourage the learner to attend to and utilize his or her intrinsic feedback. These experiments generally used reduced frequency of KR manipulations, where the percentage of trials after which KR is provided is reduced, bandwidth KR manipulations, where quantitative KR is provided only when errors are larger than a predetermined value, and summary or average KR manipulations, where KR, presented for individual trials or presented as an average, respectively, is delayed until a set of trials has been completed. Furthermore, KR delay and error estimation procedures have been used to examine predictions of the guidance view. Each of these KR manipulations will be reviewed in the following section.

Feedback manipulations used to examine the guidance hypothesis

Reduced frequency of KR

One of the most popular KR manipulations, but in our view the one that has yielded the least stable effects, to grow out of the guidance hypothesis is the reduced relative frequency of feedback manipulation. At least some of the experiments employing this technique found that reducing the proportion of trials for which augmented feedback was provided resulted in more effective learning than providing feedback after every single trial. However, this pattern of results seems to be qualified by whether constant or variable practice schedules were used. Thus, constant and variable practice studies will be reviewed separately in the following sections. In general, variable practice refers to a condition in which two or more task versions belonging to the same class of movements (see below for further explanation) are practiced, whereas under constant conditions, a single task is practised.

Constant practice

Several studies used single tasks to examine the effects of reduced KR frequencies in constant practice (e.g. Nicholson and Schmidt, 1991; Weeks and Kordus, 1998; Winstein and Schmidt, 1990). Winstein and Schmidt (1990, Experiment 2) had participants move a lever in an attempt to produce a goal movement pattern, consisting of several reversal movements, in 800 milliseconds under either 100 or 50 per cent relative frequency of KR conditions. The results of the delayed no-KR retention test indicated that the 50 per cent KR group produced significantly smaller errors than the 100 per cent KR group. Consistent with the predictions of the guidance hypothesis, Winstein and Schmidt suggested that lower relative frequencies might enhance learning because no-KR trials may cause the participant to engage in additional important cognitive processes such as those related to error detection and correction that may be bypassed when KR is presented. This effect was replicated by Nicholson and Schmidt (1991, Experiment 2), and Winstein and Schmidt (1990, Experiment 3).

However, a number of experiments (e.g. Dunham and Mueller, 1993; Kohl and Guadagnoli, 1996; Lai and Shea, 1998; Sparrow, 1995; Sparrow and Summers, 1992; Wishart and Lee, 1997; Wulf et al., 1998b) have produced results that are inconsistent with Winstein and Schmidt's (1990) findings. Sparrow (1995) conducted three experiments with a linear positioning task. Participants were assigned to one of five experimental conditions including two KR frequency (100 and 20 per cent) conditions. The results showed that the KR frequency manipulation during acquisition did not result in performance differences on either the immediate or delayed retention tests. In addition to the findings from the simple motor task used by Sparrow (1995), Wulf et al. (1998b) failed to find a benefit of 50 per cent KR frequency relative to 100 per cent KR with a complex ski-simulation task (also see Lai and Shea, 1999). These findings clearly question the utility of reducing the frequency of KR as a means of facilitating learning. Moreover, since the reduced KR frequency effect is the most commonly cited source of evidence in support of the guidance hypothesis, some of the proposals made in the guidance hypothesis should also be questioned. To further complicate this issue, Lai and Shea (1999) attempted to replicate the Winstein and Schmidt (1990) study using a similar task and fading schedule of feedback. Despite the similarities in the studies and manipulations, no benefits of reduced feedback were found.

Lai and Shea (1999) suggested that one reason for the lack of consistent findings relative to the reduced frequency of KR was the relatively weak effects of terminal feedback (i.e. KR) in guiding performers to the target response. For example, the acquisition data of Winstein and Schmidt (1990) (see also Nicholson and Schmidt, 1991) did not demonstrate strong guidance effects of frequent KR during acquisition relative to the reduced frequency conditions. Specifically, the analysis showed that there were no significant differences in acquisition between the 50 and 100 per cent relative frequency groups. Performers provided KR on all trials were no better in meeting the task demands during acquisition than those who received KR on only 50 per cent of the trials. These results indicate that terminal feedback may generally not have strong guidance properties. One feedback technique that does have very strong guiding effects is feedback that is presented concurrently with the movement. Studies examining this type of feedback are reviewed in a later section.

Variable practice

While the results of studies manipulating KR frequency in constant practice (one task version) have been somewhat equivocal in their support of the guidance view, studies employing variable practice of several task versions have generally provided more evidence for reduced KR benefits. For example, in a series of studies, Wulf and her colleagues (Wulf, 1992; Wulf and Schmidt, 1989; Wulf et al., 1993, 1994) manipulated the relative feedback frequency during practice of different task versions. These task versions had the same relative timing and relative force/amplitude characteristics (i.e. were thought to be governed by the same generalized motor program, GMP) but differed in terms of absolute time or absolute force/amplitude requirements (i.e. movement parameters). According to Schmidt (1975, 1985), the GMP is developed over practice and becomes the basis for generating responses within a movement class that share the same invariant features (e.g. sequencing, relative timing, relative force). Specific movements are produced by the assignment of parameters, such as absolute time or absolute force, via the recall schema. Importantly, Wulf and colleagues demonstrated that the locus of the reduced frequency of KR effect was at the level of the GMP and not at the level of parameter learning. For example, Wulf et al. (1994) asked participants to produce a four-key sequence in different absolute movement times (900, 1125 or 1350 milliseconds), with the relative timing structure of the three movement segments being identical for all three task versions (22.2, 44.4 and 33.3 per cent). They manipulated the relative KR frequency (50 versus 100 per cent) of relative and absolute timing KR during practice. The results indicated that GMP learning was enhanced (i.e. relative timing errors were reduced) for the groups that received a reduced KR frequency of relative timing, compared to the groups receiving 100 per cent KR about relative timing. In contrast, parameter learning was degraded (i.e. absolute timing errors were increased) for participants receiving 50 per cent KR about absolute timing, compared to those receiving 100 per cent KR. While the detrimental effects of reduced KR on parameter learning are in line with schema theory (Schmidt, 1975), according to which parameter learning only occurs when the movement outcome (KR) can be associated with the selected parameters, these findings are not in line with the guidance hypothesis.

At first glance, the findings of Wulf *et al.*'s (1994) investigations into GMP learning appear to be consistent with the guidance hypothesis. That is, GMP errors on retention and transfer tests were smaller for the groups receiving reduced frequency of KR pertaining to GMP errors. However, GMP errors were also smaller during *acquisition* for the reduced frequency of KR group than for the group receiving relative timing KR after each trial. The guidance hypothesis proposes that, because of the powerful effects of KR to guide the performer to the correct response, frequent KR should benefit performance during acquisition when feedback is present. Yet, in this case, more KR was not effective in guiding the performer to the correct response. On the contrary, more KR negatively affected acquisition performance. Similar GMP disruptions as a function of increased KR frequency (100 per cent) were found in the acquisition results reported by Wulf *et al.* (1993). That is, more KR resulted in poorer acquisition performance. This is clearly at odds with an important premise of the guidance hypothesis, according to which frequent KR serves to guide the performer to the correct response.

However, one aspect of a reduced KR frequency during acquisition does appear to be important in producing learning benefits. Response consistency, or more specifically GMP stability, appears to be increased under reduced KR frequency conditions in this series of experiments. While this measure is not specifically reported in the Wulf *et al.* (1994) paper, Wulf (1992), for example, reported increased GMP stability for the reduced KR frequency groups during acquisition relative to 100 per cent KR groups. Indeed, GMP stability is carried over to retention and transfer tests for the reduced frequency groups and may be associated with the increased precision of the GMP. This finding suggests that the GMP is developed more effectively when performance demands are more stable. This is consistent with the notion that trials without KR essentially prompt the participant to repeat the last trial providing the response stability that may be a requisite for GMP development.

In an attempt to determine more directly if a reduced KR frequency promotes GMP learning by enhancing response stability, Lai and Shea (1998) manipulated the frequency of KR about relative timing in constant and variable practice. Constant practice conditions were contrasted with variable practice because constant practice was also assumed to result in more stable acquisition performance relative to variable practice, independent of KR frequency. Thus, Lai and Shea (1998) predicted that a reduced KR frequency would enhance relative timing (GMP) performance not only during acquisition but also during retention and transfer. The effect of reduced KR frequency was assumed to be especially evident when multiple tasks were practiced (i.e. in variable practice) but less pronounced under constant practice conditions, as constant practice was predicted to engender sufficient response stability independent of the KR manipulation.

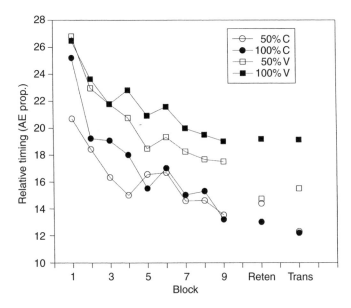

Figure 7.1 Relative timing performance of the 50 per cent KR-constant (50 per cent C), 100 per cent KR-constant (100 per cent C), 50 per cent KR-variable (50 per cent V), and 100 per cent KR-variable (100 per cent V) groups during practice (Day 1), retention and transfer (Day 2) in the Lai and Shea (1998) study.

The results indeed indicated that, while in variable practice reduced KR enhanced relative timing during acquisition, retention, and transfer, reduced KR frequency did not increment performance or learning in constant practice (see Figure 7.1). In addition, response stability was enhanced by constant practice or a reduced KR frequency. These findings provide support for the 'stability hypothesis' proposed by Lai and Shea (1999), according to which practice conditions that promote trial-to-trial stability enhance the learning of the movement structure (GMP) relative to conditions that promote trial-to-trial response variability.

Overall, findings related to KR frequency effects reviewed so far provide mixed support for the guidance hypothesis. While there is little evidence that KR provided after every practice trial causes learners to become dependent on it by preventing them from focusing on intrinsic feedback associated with the movement, it does appear that one benefit of a reduced KR frequency is that it promotes trial-to-trial stability, thereby enhancing learning of the fundamental movement structure. The augmented feedback (participant trace overlaid on the criterion trace) manipulated in the Nicholson and Schmidt (1991) and Winstein and Schmidt (1990) experiments characterized errors in the movement structure and not just the movement endpoint, as was typical in the early KR literature. Thus, the manipulation may have directly impacted the movement structure, as in the Lai and Shea (1999) experiment, such that the reduced frequency information about the movement structure resulted in increased response stability, the end result being enhanced performance and learning. That is, the effects of reduced KR frequency reported by Winstein and Schmidt (1990), for example, could perhaps be attributed to increased response stability rather than increased processing of important intrinsic information as proposed.

KR delay and error estimation

One feedback manipulation that has consistently provided evidence that appears to be in support of the guidance hypothesis is feedback that is concurrently provided with the movement. In particular, concurrent feedback typically has very strong performance-enhancing effects when it is present during practice, but results in clear performance decrements, relative to post-response (terminal) feedback, when it is withdrawn in retention or transfer tests (e.g. Park *et al.*, 2000; Schmidt and Wulf, 1997; Vander Linden *et al.*, 1993; Winstein *et al.*, 1996). Furthermore, delaying the feedback for a few seconds has been found to produce more effective learning than giving feedback immediately after each trial (e.g. Swinnen *et al.*, 1990). This suggests that feedback presented concurrently with or instantaneously after the completion of the movement provides strong guiding effects but blocks the processing of other important types of information (e.g. intrinsic feedback) and, therefore, is detrimental to learning.

Park *et al.* (2000, Experiment 1) attempted to take advantage of the powerful guiding effects of concurrent feedback (as compared to terminal feedback) while at the same time attempting to lessen participants' dependence on concurrent feedback by using a 50 per cent relative frequency of feedback. Although the reduced frequency, concurrent feedback condition did not enhance acquisition performance as much as 100 per cent concurrent feedback, the benefits during acquisition were substantially larger than for terminal feedback alone. On the no-KR retention test, the 50 per cent concurrent feedback condition performed similarly to the terminal-feedback-alone condition with both of these groups performing substantially better than the 100 per cent concurrent feedback condition. In Experiment 2, Park *et al.* (2000) manipulated both concurrent feedback and terminal feedback. The results indicated that learning could be enhanced by providing both concurrent and terminal feedback on one trial with no feedback on the subsequent trial (50 per cent). In this way, both the strong performance enhancing effects of concurrent feedback during acquisition and the more permanent beneficial effects of terminal feedback could be achieved.

In contrast to concurrent and instantaneous feedback, the presentation of feedback a few seconds after the end of the movement seems to result in learners' spontaneously evaluating the movement in the pre-KR interval based on the processing of intrinsic feedback. Such spontaneous error estimations, which according to the guidance hypothesis should benefit the learning process, might occur even under 100 per cent KR conditions, and this might be one reason why the effects of different frequencies of post-response feedback have generally been somewhat equivocal (at least in constant practice). Additional evidence for the learning benefits of subjective movement evaluations comes from studies in which participants were specifically instructed to error estimate after the completion of a movement. When compared with groups that were not asked to estimate their errors, these participants generally demonstrated superior retention performance (Guadagnoli and Kohl, 2001; Hogan and Yanowitz, 1978; Liu and Wrisberg, 1997; Swinnen *et al.*, 1990). For example, Hogan and Yanowitz asked one group of participants to estimate their timing error prior to receiving KR. No instructions were provided to the other group. In a no-KR transfer test, the participants in the estimate condition performed significantly better than participants in the no-estimate condition (although it is not clear whether these effects were temporary in nature or whether they were actual learning effects, as the estimate and no-estimate conditions were continued in transfer). Guadagnoli and Kohl (2001) found an interaction between KR frequency and error estimation/no-estimation for a force production task. Learning was enhanced for a low KR frequency condition (20 per cent) relative to 100 per cent KR when participants did not estimate, but when participants estimated, 100 per cent KR resulted in more effective learning than 20 per cent KR. The authors suggested that learning is enhanced to the extent that it allows individuals to test hypotheses regarding their performance. Such opportunities would be maximized if KR was always available *and* learners were encouraged to evaluate their movements (in addition to any evaluations that might occur spontaneously). In contrast, when error estimations are not specifically required, learners might be more indirectly encouraged to engage in such processing under reduced KR conditions, compared to a 100 per cent KR condition.

Thus, there is relatively clear evidence that feedback manipulations that prevent learners from evaluating their actions (e.g. when feedback is presented concurrently with or immediately after the movement) degrade learning. In these cases, participants might actually develop a dependency on external feedback, as suggested by the guidance hypothesis. In addition, it appears that requiring participants to estimate their errors is beneficial for learning. Yet, the fact that error estimation seems to be especially effective if frequent KR is available might be seen as being somewhat at odds with the guidance view.

Bandwidth KR

Bandwidth KR involves providing the participant qualitative KR (i.e. indicating that the response is 'correct') when performance is within a certain range of error (e.g. 15 per cent), and quantitative KR (e.g. 60 milliseconds too slow) when performance is outside the bandwidth. Consistent with the guidance hypothesis, several studies have demonstrated benefits of bandwidth KR relative to quantitative KR provided on every trial (e.g. Lai and Shea, 1999; Lee and Carnahan, 1990; Sherwood, 1988). The primary advantage of bandwidth KR for learning seems to be that it promotes response stability in acquisition, thereby reducing the occurrence of maladaptive short-term corrections. Therefore, bandwidth KR often results in more stable retention performance. For example, Lee and

Carnahan (1990) and Sherwood (1988) found that bandwidth KR led to reduced variable error. Yet, learning benefits of providing bandwidth KR have also been found for movement accuracy (i.e. reduced absolute constant error, Lee and Maraj, 1994).

Whereas most researchers have examined the effects of bandwidth KR in constant practice (e.g. Lee and Carnahan, 1990; Lee and Maraj, 1994; Reeve *et al.*, 1990; Sherwood, 1988; Wright *et al.*, 1997), Lai and colleagues (Lai and Shea, 1999; Lai *et al.*, 2000) compared the relative effectiveness of bandwidth KR in constant and variable practice. Lai *et al.* predicted that bandwidth KR, like reduced frequency KR, would enhance relative timing (GMP) performance in variable practice but not in constant practice. This would be expected if the important effects of bandwidth KR were related to response stability. If the effects were related to some additional processing and/or less dependence on the KR, then an additive effect would be expected. The results of both studies were consistent with the findings from the reduced KR frequency experiments (Lai and Shea, 1998) and the stability hypothesis. Bandwidth KR did not improve learning under constant practice but did under variable practice conditions.

Summary and average KR

Under both summary KR and average KR conditions, performers are provided with KR about a set of trials (e.g. five) after this set has been completed. Yet, whereas summary KR involves providing KR about every trial in the set, average KR refers to the average performance on a set of trials. Presumably, the first study to examine the effects of summary KR on the learning of motor tasks was done by Lavery (1962). Lavery used variations of a task, where a ball had to be propelled up an incline to a target by using a ballistic motion (e.g. by striking a rod with a hammer). The beneficial effects of summary KR relative to single-trial KR found by Lavery were replicated and extended in more recent studies (e.g. Guadagnoli *et al.*, 1996; Schmidt *et al.*, 1989, 1990; Yao *et al.*, 1994). The results generally confirmed the predictions of the guidance hypothesis, in that summary KR has been shown to be generally more effective than presenting KR immediately after every trial.

Yet, the optimal summary length (i.e. number of trials summarized) appears to depend on the relative task difficulty or the complexity of the task in relation to the performer's skill level (Guadagnoli *et al.*, 1996; Schmidt *et al.*, 1990; Yao *et al.*, 1994) (see also section on 'Complex skills and performer skill level'). Whereas in experiments using relatively simple tasks, the largest summary-feedback length proved to be the most effective for learning (e.g. a summary of sixteen trials in Gable *et al.*, 1991; twenty trials in Lavery, 1962; fifteen trials in Schmidt *et al.*, 1989), Schmidt *et al.* (1990) showed that the optimal number of summary trials for a more complex simulated batting task was lower than those found for more simple tasks. They used a coincidence-timing task that can be viewed as a laboratory analogue of a ball–batting task. The task required the participant to watch a series of light-emitting diodes (LEDs) being illuminated in succession while performing a reversal movement with a lever and trying to intercept a target LED when it was lit. In the Schmidt *et al.* (1990) study, a summary of five trials was more beneficial than longer (15) or shorter (1) feedback summaries. Also, Yao *et al.* (1994), using a movement timing task, found that both summary feedback and average feedback each five-trial block was more advantageous for learning than feedback every fifteen-trials or every-trial. Finally, Guadagnoli *et al.* (1996) directly demonstrated that task complexity, as well as task-related experience, interacted with the optimal number of trials summarized. Whereas relatively long feedback summaries benefited the learning of a relatively simple striking task for novice and experienced participants, as well as the learning of a more complex double-striking task for experienced participants, single-trial feedback was more effective than longer feedback summaries for novices trying to learn a complex task.

Average KR has not been studied as extensively as summary KR and the effects of this manipulation are also somewhat more equivocal (Wulf and Schmidt, 1996; Young and Schmidt, 1992). Young and Schmidt (1992, Experiment 2) used the coincidence-timing ('ball–batting') task and provided KR about the reversal point of the lever in relation to an optimal reversal point. They found that average KR resulted in superior learning (as measured by an overall performance score) compared to providing KR after every single trial. In another study, Yao *et al.* (1994) directly compared summary and average KR on a task requiring participants to move a stylus 40 cm in 500 milliseconds. KR provided for sets of five trials was more effective than every-trial KR or KR for sets of fifteen trials (independent of the type of KR), again suggesting that there is an optimal number of trials across which summary or average KR should be presented. Additional analyses revealed that participants who demonstrated high performance variability in practice were less accurate in retention than those with low variability on practice (at least for the fifteen-trial summary and average KR conditions). This finding points to the importance of performance consistency during practice.

While the results by Young and Schmidt (1992) and Yao *et al.* (1994) are in line with the guidance view, a subsequent study by Wulf and Schmidt (1996) found no advantages of average feedback. Participants practiced moving a lever to produce three versions of a movement pattern that had the same relative and absolute timing structure, as well as the same relative amplitudes, but differed in absolute amplitudes. Feedback was provided about the produced spatio-temporal pattern in relation to the goal pattern. The findings showed that average feedback affected the learning of the fundamental movement pattern (GMP) in a similar way to single-trial KR. Moreover, average feedback clearly *degraded* parameter learning compared to single-trial KR. Thus, there are obvious limitations to the effectiveness of average feedback.

Above all, the support for the guidance view, although intuitively pleasing, does not seem to be as unequivocal as it appeared in the early 1990s. In addition, several newer studies have used more motor complex tasks than those that are typically used in the laboratory (e.g. whole body movements), and investigated the attentional focus promoted by the feedback. The support these studies provide for the guidance hypothesis is even less convincing. These studies are reviewed next.

Complex skills and performer skill level

While there is at least some evidence that the learning of simple skills benefits from reducing or delaying the augmented feedback (despite some limitations, as discussed above), there is also evidence to suggest that more frequent feedback might be required for the learning of complex skills. We define skills as 'complex' if they generally cannot be mastered in a single session, have several degrees of freedom, and perhaps tend to be ecologically valid (see Wulf and Shea, 2002). Some support for the notion that complex skill learning requires more feedback, or at least is not degraded by frequent feedback, comes from the studies on summary (and average) feedback reviewed above.

Presumably one of the most complex tasks that has been used to examine the effects of a reduced feedback frequency is the ski-simulator task (Wulf et al., 1998b). The apparatus consists of bowed rails and a platform on wheels that is attached to it by elastic rubber belts. The goal of the performer standing on the platform is to move the platform sideways on the rails by making oscillatory, slalom-type movements, with the goal being to produce the largest possible amplitudes (and sometimes highest frequency). Thus, the task requires whole-body movements and the coordination of a large number of degrees of freedom (e.g. den Brinker and van Hekken, 1982; Durand et al., 1994; Vereijken, 1991; Wulf et al., 1998b). Wulf et al. (1998b; Experiment 2) provided learners with concurrent feedback (via an oscilloscope) about the so-called force onset, which indicates when the performer shifts her or his weight from one foot to the other. Force onset is a measure of movement efficiency and has been found to correlate with movement amplitude. Whereas one group of participants received feedback on all practice trials (100 per cent feedback), for another group the feedback was faded, with the average feedback frequency being 50 per cent. In addition, there was a control group without feedback. In delayed no-feedback retention, all groups showed very similar performances in terms of relative force onset on the first trial; however, the 100 per cent feedback group showed a clear performance improvement across trials, whereas the 50 per cent feedback group showed no performance gains, and the control group even demonstrated a performance decrement. By the end of the retention test, the 100 per cent group was significantly more effective than the control group, while the 50 per cent group did not differ significantly from either group. Thus, the 100 per cent feedback participants did not develop a dependency on feedback that reduced the learning effectiveness of this condition. It seems that participants in the 100 per cent feedback group developed the most effective error-detection-and-correction mechanism, which enabled them to demonstrate further performance improvements even when the feedback was withdrawn.

Contrary to studies that have used more simple tasks (e.g. Lai and Shea, 1999; Schmidt and Wulf, 1997; Winstein and Schmidt, 1990; Wulf and Schmidt, 1989; Wulf *et al.*, 1993), the learning of this more complex task was enhanced by 100 per cent feedback. This advantage occurred even though the feedback given in the Wulf *et al.* (1998b) study was continuous and concurrent. Similarly, Swinnen *et al.* (1997), who used a complex bimanual coordination task (phase offset of 90 degrees), also found benefits of concurrent visual feedback. Participants who received augmented visual information demonstrated more effective learning than those who were provided with reduced feedback and normal vision during practice. The strong dependency that this type of feedback typically promotes, at least for the learning of simple skills (Park *et al.*, 2000; Schmidt and Wulf, 1997; Vander Linden *et al.*, 1993; Winstein *et al.*, 1996), was therefore not found for these more complex tasks.

Overall, in contrast to the guidance view, reducing the relative feedback frequency does not seem to enhance the learning of complex tasks. Wulf and Shea (2002) argued that, whereas the learning of simple tasks might be enhanced by making practice more difficult or challenging for the learner (e.g. by reducing the feedback frequency), the learning of complex skills with inherently high attention, memory or control demands might not benefit from, and might even be degraded by increasing the demands imposed on the learner (see also Guadagnoli, 2001; Guadagnoli and Lee, in press).

As Wulf and Shea (2002) pointed out, feedback in complex tasks is generally not as prescriptive as it often is in many simple tasks. In complex tasks, there are often different components that have to be coordinated to produce skilled performance, making it much more difficult for a single feedback measure to be truly prescriptive. In attempts to improve performance, the learner has to rely on sources of intrinsic feedback. Thus, the likelihood of the learner becoming dependent on the extrinsic feedback and neglecting the processing of intrinsic feedback is reduced, compared to the learning of simple skills.

It should be noted that in these (Swinnen *et al.*, 1997; Wulf *et al.*, 1998b) and other studies (Shea and Wulf, 1999), feedback was provided (concurrently) on a computer screen or oscilloscope. This type of feedback might affect the performer's attentional focus such that his or her attention is directed away from the movements themselves and towards the movement effect seen on the screen. As we discuss in the following section, this aspect of feedback also seems to determine its effectiveness.

Feedback and attentional focus

A factor that appears to have an important influence on the effectiveness of feedback is what aspect of the task the performer's attention is directed towards. With regard to *instructions* given to learners, a number of studies in the past few years have demonstrated that the focus of attention induced by the instructions has a considerable effect on learning (e.g. Wulf *et al.*, 1998a, 1999, 2001a,b; for a review, see Wulf and Prinz, 2001). Specifically, these studies have shown that if the performer's attention is directed to his or her body movements (termed 'internal focus'), learning is less effective than when attention is directed to the movement effect on the environment (termed 'external focus'). It appears that when participants are asked to focus on their movements, they tend to actively intervene in the motor control processes. Yet, by attempting to actively control their movements, performers seem to inadvertently disrupt relatively automatic processes that normally control the movement. Focusing on the movement effect, on the other hand, has been argued to promote the utilization of more automatic control processes (Wulf *et al.*, 2001a,b; Wulf and Prinz, 2001). Two lines of evidence support this view. First, Wulf *et al.* (2001a; see also McNevin *et al.*, 2003; Wulf *et al.*, 2001b) found higher response frequencies for participants performing a balance task (stabilometer) under external relative to internal focus conditions. The former group of participants made more frequent and smaller corrections in maintaining their balance than the latter group, suggesting that their performance was based on more automatic (e.g. reflex-like) control processes. Second, faster probe reaction times were found for participants performing the balance task under external compared to internal condition, indicating a greater amount of spare attentional capacity, or a higher degree of automaticity (Wulf *et al.*, 2001a).

Studies examining the effects of attentional focus induced by feedback

In contrast to instructions, the effectiveness of external versus internal foci of attention has only recently been considered in the context of feedback. Shea and Wulf (1999) were the first to investigate whether the effectiveness of feedback was dependent on the focus of attention it induced. An interesting feature of that study was that the feedback presented to learners was actually identical and only the learner's interpretation of it was manipulated. Shea and Wulf used the stabilometer task and presented two groups with concurrent visual feedback – which essentially consisted of the platform movements displayed on a computer screen. One group of participants was informed that the feedback represented movements of their feet (internal focus), whereas the other group was told that the feedback represented lines attached to the platform in front of each of the performer's feet (external focus). In addition, there were internal and external focus (control) groups that were not provided feedback but were instructed to focus on their feet or the lines, respectively.

Several aspects of the results were interesting (see Figure 7.2). First, learning was more effective when performers adopted an external focus. Thus, even though the feedback display was identical for the two feedback groups, the group that interpreted the feedback as 'external' performed better than the group that interpreted it as 'internal'. This finding suggests that the effectiveness of feedback can be enhanced if it directs performers' attention to the movement effects, rather than to the movements themselves. Second, the concurrent feedback *generally* enhanced the learners' ability to maintain their balance compared to no feedback, even though it could be argued the feedback was redundant to their intrinsic

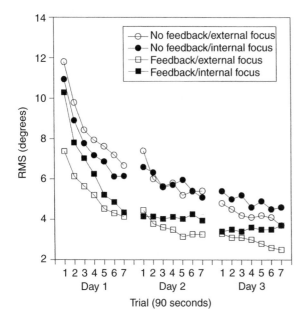

Figure 7.2 Root mean square (RMS) errors of the no-feedback/external focus, no-feedback/internal focus, feedback/external focus, and feedback/internal focus groups during practice (Days 1 and 2) and retention (Day 3) in the Shea and Wulf (1999) study.

(visual and kinesthetic) feedback (e.g. Magill *et al.*, 1991). Third, the beneficial effects of the feedback were not only seen during the 2 days practice when the feedback was present, but also in retention when feedback was withdrawn.

Why did the concurrent feedback enhance learning, if it did not really provide the learner with any information in addition to what he or she could see or feel? Shea and Wulf (1999) argued that the feedback served to induce an external focus of attention, independent of the (internal or external focus) instructions given to learners. That is, the display information might have provided a constant reminder to maintain an external focus. Furthermore, the withdrawal of the feedback display in retention had no detrimental effect on performance. This finding is in contrast to other studies, where the withdrawal of concurrent feedback resulted in clear performance decrements (e.g. Schmidt and Wulf, 1997; Vander Linden *et al.*, 1993; Winstein *et al.*, 1996). Both the performance-enhancing effects of this type of feedback and the lack of a performance decrement after the removal of feedback seem to suggest that feedback can have the capacity to induce an external focus of attention that benefits performance and learning.

The results of a recent study by Todorov *et al.* (1997) also suggest that feedback about the movement effect might be more beneficial than feedback related to the movements. Todorov *et al.* (1997) argued that the highest level of motor planning and control was in terms of the kinematics of the end-effector. Therefore, the feedback given to the learner should be most effective when it represents the movements of the end-effector, rather than the body movements. Even though they did not compare these two types of feedback, Todorov *et al.* (1997) showed that the learning of table tennis strokes was enhanced by providing performers with concurrent feedback about the trajectory of their paddle (in relation to the paddle trajectory of an expert). Participants receiving this type of feedback were more accurate in hitting the target than were participants who were provided verbal feedback (on gross errors) and who hit 50 per cent more balls. It is conceivable that at least part of the reason for the effectiveness of feedback about the paddle motion was that it induced an external focus of attention, whereas the control participants (without feedback) paid more attention to their own movement pattern.

While the results from the study by Shea and Wulf (1999) provided preliminary evidence that the learner's attentional focus induced by the feedback can have an influence on learning, their feedback manipulation was somewhat 'artificial' in that the feedback given to different groups of participants was actually identical. In contrast, in practical settings, coaches or instructors typically provide the learner with verbal feedback that refers to that aspect of performance that needs improvement the most. That is, based on what the coach considers to be the critical mistake or flaw, he or she gives feedback that will hopefully help the performer to make appropriate changes on subsequent attempts. With this in mind, Wulf *et al.* (2002) examined the effectiveness of external and internal focus feedback for the learning of sport skills. In Experiment 1, they had their participants practice a volleyball 'tennis' serve. For this purpose, different feedback statements were selected that are often used in volleyball training and that refer to the performer's body movements (internal-focus feedback). These statements were then 'translated' into statements that basically contained the same information but directed the learners' attention more to the movement effects (external-focus feedback). For example, instead of instructing learners to shift their weight from the back leg to the front leg while hitting the ball (internal focus), they were instructed to shift their weight toward the target (external focus). After every fifth practice trial, the performer was provided with the feedback statement that was deemed most appropriate based on his or her performance on the previous trials. The accuracy of the serves was greatly enhanced by the external relative to the internal focus feedback not only during practice, but also after a 1-week retention interval in a no-feedback retention test. This advantage in the movement outcome was not accomplished at the expense of movement form. As determined through expert ratings, both types of feedback led to similar improvements in form.

Implications for the guidance view

Wulf *et al.* (2002) argued that a high frequency of internal-focus feedback might be detrimental because it might encourage learners to focus *too much* on their movements, while these effects would be attenuated under reduced feedback conditions. This view contrasts with the guidance notion (e.g. Salmoni *et al.*, 1984; Schmidt, 1991), according to which frequent feedback prevents learners from attending to their movements.

Recent findings by Steinhauer and Preston Grayhack (2000) might be interpreted as support for the view that internal-focus feedback is detrimental for performance and learning. Using a voice motor task (vowel nasalization), they found that 100 per cent feedback about the degree of nasalance degraded both practice and transfer performance, relative to 50 and 0 per cent feedback, which did not differ from each other. Assuming that this type of feedback directed participants' attention to their articulators that typically function automatically and of which we are unaware during normal speech production, frequent feedback was clearly detrimental.

Similar findings were obtained in a study by Weeks and Kordus (1998), where participants practising a soccer throw-in were given feedback about various aspects of their technique. The feedback statements they used would clearly have to be considered 'internal' from an attentional-focus perspective; for example, 'The feet, hips, knees, and shoulders should be aimed at the target, feet shoulder width apart', or 'The back should be arched at the beginning of the throw'. The results showed superior movement form for participants who were given feedback on 33 per cent of the trials, compared to participants who were given 100 per cent feedback. The benefits for the 33 per cent feedback condition were not only seen in retention and transfer tests without feedback, but also during practice.

Wulf *et al.* (2002) argued that, while frequent internal-focus feedback should be detrimental, no degrading effects (or even benefits) of frequent feedback would be expected if it induced an external focus. Using a lofted soccer kick in Experiment 2, they indeed found the expected interaction between the attentional focus induced by the feedback and the frequency with which it was presented (see Figure 7.3). While 100 per cent internal focus feedback was detrimental for performance (practice) and learning (retention), relative to 33 per cent feedback, 100 per cent external focus feedback was no different from 33 per cent external focus feedback (and even tended to be more effective). Also, and importantly, both external feedback conditions were more beneficial for learning than the internal feedback conditions.

These results shed new light on the role of feedback for motor learning. They question the guidance explanation, at least as a complete account of how feedback functions. In particular, three sets of findings are difficult to explain from the guidance perspective: (a) the general benefits of external- over internal-focus feedback (Shea and Wulf, 1999; Wulf *et al.*, 2002); (b) the interactive effects of feedback frequency and attentional focus (Wulf *et al.*, 2002, Experiment 2); and (c) the lack of benefit of frequent relative to infrequent internal-focus feedback during practice (Wulf *et al.*, 2002, Experiment 2; see also Weeks and Kordus, 1998). However, these findings can be interpreted and predicted from an attentional focus perspective.

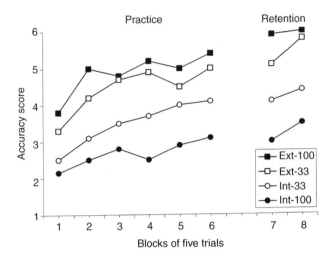

Figure 7.3 Accuracy scores of the external focus–100 per cent KR (Ext-100), external focus–33 per cent KR (Ext-33), internal focus–100 per cent KR (Int-100) and Internal focus–33 per cent KR (Int-33) groups during practice and retention (1 week after practice) in the Wulf *et al.* (2002) study.

What implications do these findings have for the validity of the guidance view? The guidance hypothesis was developed based on findings from experiments that used relatively simple laboratory tasks. In these situations, participants are often deprived of natural sources of feedback in order to examine various manipulations of experimenter-provided feedback. It is, therefore, entirely possible and likely that they develop a dependency on augmented feedback, if feedback is provided too frequently. Independent of whether the feedback induces an external or internal focus, detrimental effects of frequent feedback might be observed under such 'artificial' laboratory conditions, where performers are deprived of intrinsic feedback.

Studies examining attentional focus effects, on the other hand, have typically used relatively complex skills, performed under more 'realistic' conditions. In these situations, the focus of attention induced by the augmented feedback might have a greater impact (Wulf and Shea, 2002). For example, in the Shea and Wulf (1999) study, concurrent feedback about the movements of the stabilometer platform, provided *in addition* to the performers' intrinsic feedback, led to differential effects depending on whether performers interpreted it as internal or external feedback. Such a situation, where feedback is provided in addition to intrinsic feedback, is more representative of many real-life training situations, pointing to the need to examine more complex skills in motor learning experiments (Wulf and Shea, 2002). Only when we consider different levels of task complexity and different types of feedback will we be able to develop a better understanding of the various functions of feedback for motor learning.

Summary and conclusions

Based on our review of the post-guidance-hypothesis literature, there appears to be some support for the guidance hypothesis, especially for simple laboratory tasks where a single terminal error measure is provided. However, this theoretical proposal does not seem to provide a comprehensive and convincing description of how the processing of feedback enhances or retards the learning of motor skills. The following brief sections represent our summary of the current research with respect to the basic tenets of the guidance hypothesis.

- *KR plays a powerful role in guiding the performer to the correct response.* Some amount of KR is clearly required for learning to occur especially in those situations where intrinsic error information is not readily available. However, 100 per cent KR conditions do not consistently lead to better acquisition performance than reduced frequencies of KR conditions in constant practice. In variable practice, frequent KR sometimes leads to less effective performance both during acquisition and retention, as compared to less frequent KR. Only concurrent feedback seems to have the powerful guiding effects suggested by the guidance hypothesis.
- *Providing KR after every trial results in a dependence on the KR.* Particularly with regard to concurrent feedback, the withdrawal of feedback in retention or transfer typically results in large performance decrements, relative to performance at the end of practice. Often this is also the case for immediately presented KR (relative to delayed KR) and/or frequent KR (relative to reduced KR), although this evidence is less consistent. While the relative differences between end-of-practice and retention/transfer performance could be due to temporary performance-enhancing effects of KR (guidance, motivation) during practice and differences in the effectiveness of the processing under different KR conditions, the differences might also reflect a KR dependency. The evidence for this notion is not as strong as originally suspected, and is basically non-existent for complex motor skills. Also, because retention and transfer tests are most often given under no-KR conditions, it is difficult to attribute performance differences between the end of practice and retention/transfer to a dependence on KR. Although this may be an argument in semantics, we feel that dependence on KR per se has not been established in frequent KR conditions. This may be the case for concurrent feedback, where the information allows participants to control the movement differently than when terminal feedback is provided, but we feel that this supposition has not been demonstrated for terminal feedback. In fact, in one of the few examples where KR and no-KR retention tests were administered, Winstein and Schmidt (1990) demonstrated nearly identical patterns of results. This would not be expected if the presentation of frequent KR resulted in a stronger dependence on KR relative to reduced frequency KR (also see Schmidt *et al.*, 1990).

- *Providing KR after every trial blocks the processing of important intrinsic information.* Although this notion is intuitively plausible, there is insufficient direct experimental evidence to suggest that some unspecified, but important, processing is blocked by the frequent presentation of KR. What would be necessary to demonstrate this type of effect would be evidence linking enhanced intrinsic error detection capabilities, for example, to reduced KR frequency conditions relative to 100 per cent KR conditions or, alternately, impoverished error detection capabilities in frequent KR conditions. This could be accomplished by asking participants to estimate their errors during retention. Schmidt *et al.* (1990) used this type of procedure to determine if error estimation abilities were differentially improved with summary KR manipulations, but this method has not been used with other KR manipulations. They found that objective/subjective correlations and differences tended to favour the five-trial summary (optimal condition) although the authors noted that 'the correlations were all relatively low, indicating that none of the groups had developed particularly strong error-detection capacities' (p. 336). Using a somewhat less direct method, Guadagnoli and Kohl (2001), demonstrated improved performance for an error estimation group under 100 per cent KR relative to 20 per cent KR suggesting that error detection processes were not blocked by the presentation of KR, but rather were facilitated by the inclusion of KR.
- *Providing KR after every trial results in increased response variability.* It does appear that performers attempt to correct even small errors (i.e. maladaptive short-term corrections), detected via KR that may represent the inherent variability of the motor system, which may have been overlooked if KR had not been presented. This evidence comes from a number of KR manipulations including reduced frequency KR in variable practice, bandwidth KR, and summary/average KR. Increased response stability may be important for the learning of the movement structure, especially when variable practice conditions are used during acquisition (Lai and Shea, 1999).

Our conclusion is that the assumptions and boundary conditions of the guidance hypothesis need to be more directly examined in future studies. The results of a number of experiments emphasize the need to investigate task and performer factors that interact with KR to enhance performance and learning. Future research should view KR and other sources of feedback in terms of their interaction with factors such as the complexity of the task, the availability of intrinsic feedback, the learner's level of experience, and the degree to which KR promotes an internal or external focus of attention. These types of manipulations will allow us to fully appreciate the complex role feedback plays in the learning process. Clearly, the guidance hypothesis has had a great impact on motor learning research. Not only has it resulted in important changes in the way learning research, in general, is conducted (e.g. paradigm proposals related to providing delayed retention and transfer tests under common experimental condition), but it has also contributed to a much better understanding of how KR influences performance and learning. Yet, the last two decades or so of research have shown that human motor learning is somewhat more complicated than proposed by the guidance hypothesis. It is clear that various other factors need to be taken into account if we want to come to a more complete understanding of the role of KR in the learning process.

References

Adams, J. A. (1968). Response feedback and learning. *Psychological Bulletin*, 70, 486–504.

Adams, J. A. (1971). A closed-loop theory of motor learning. *Journal of Motor Behavior*, 3, 111–150.

Adams, J. A. (1987). Historical review and appraisal of research on the learning, retention, and transfer of human motor skills. *Psychological Bulletin*, 101, 41–74.

Bilodeau, E. A. and Bilodeau, I. M. (1958). Variable frequency of knowledge of results and the learning of a simple skill. *Journal of Experimental Psychology*, 55, 379–383.

Bilodeau, E. A., Bilodeau, I. M. and Schumsky, D. A. (1959). Some effects of introducing and withdrawing knowledge of results early and late in practice. *Journal of Experimental Psychology*, 58, 142–144.

Bjork, R. A. (1988). Retrieval practice and the maintenance of knowledge. In M. M. Gruneberg, P. E. Morris and R. N. Sykes (Eds), *Practical aspects of memory*, Vol. II (pp. 396–401). London: Wiley.

Brisson, T. A., and Alain, C. (1996). Should common optimal movement patterns be identified as the certain to be achieved? *Journal of Motor Behavior*, 28, 211–223.

Brisson, T. A., and Alain, C. (1997). A comparison of two references for using knowledge of performance in learning a motor task. *Journal of Motor Behavior*, 29, 339–350.

den Brinker, B. P. L. M. and van Hekken, M. F. (1982). The analysis of slalom-type movements using a ski-simulator apparatus. *Human Movement Science*, 1, 91–108.

Dunham, P. and Mueller, R. (1993). Effect of fading knowledge of results on acquisition, retention, and transfer of a simple motor skill. *Perceptual and Motor Skills*, 77, 1187–1192.

Durand, M., Geoffroi, V., Varray, A. and Préfaut, C. (1994). Study of the energy correlates in the learning of a complex self-paced cyclical skill. *Human Movement Science*, 13, 785–799.

Gable, C. D., Shea, C. H. and Wright, D. L. (1991). Summary knowledge of results. *Research Quarterly for Exercise and Sport*, 62, 285–292.

Guadagnoli, M. A. (2001). Motor behavior. In S. P. Brown (Ed.), *Introduction to exercise science* (pp. 334–358). Baltimore, MD: Lippincott, Williams & Wilkins.

Guadagnoli, M. A. and Kohl, R. M. (2001). Knowledge of results for motor learning: relationship between error estimation and knowledge of results frequency. *Journal of Motor Behavior*, 33, 217–224.

Guadagnoli, M. A. and Lee, T. D. (in press). Challenge point: framework for conceptualizing the effects of various practice conditions in motor learning. *Journal of Motor Behavior*.

Guadagnoli, M. A., Dornier, L. A. and Tandy, R. D. (1996). Optimal length for summary knowledge of results: the influence of task-related experience and complexity. *Research Quarterly for Exercise and Sport*, 67, 239–248.

Hogan, J. C. and Yanowitz, B. A. (1978). The role of verbal estimates of movement error in ballistic skill acquisition. *Journal of Motor Behavior*, 10, 133–138.

Kohl, R. M. and Guadagnoli, M. A. (1996). The scheduling of knowledge of results. *Journal of Motor Behavior*, 28, 233–240.

Lai, Q. and Shea, C. H. (1998). Generalized motor program (GMP) learning: effects of reduced frequency of knowledge of results and practice variability. *Journal of Motor Behavior*, 30, 51–59.

Lai, Q. and Shea, C. H. (1999). Bandwidth knowledge of results enhances generalized motor program learning. *Research Quarterly for Exercise and Sport*, 70, 79–83.

Lai, Q., Shea, C. H, Wulf, G. and Wright, D. L. (2000). Optimizing generalized motor program and parameter learning. *Research Quarterly for Exercise and Sport*, 71, 10–24.

Landauer, T. K. and Bjork, R. A. (1978). Optimal rehearsal patterns and name learning. In M. M. Gruneberg, P. E. Morris and R. N. Sykes (Eds), *Practical aspects of memory* (pp. 625–632). New York: Academic Press.

Lavery, J. J. (1962). Retention of simple motor skills as a function of type of knowledge of results. *Canadian Journal of Psychology*, 16, 300–311.

Lee, T. D. and Carnahan, H. (1990). Bandwidth knowledge of results and motor learning. *The Quarterly Journal of Experimental Psychology*, 42, 777–789.

Lee, T. D. and Maraj, B. K. V. (1994). Effects of bandwidth goals and bandwidth knowledge of results on motor learning. *Research Quarterly for Exercise and Sport*, 65, 244–249.

Liu, J. and Wrisberg, C. A. (1997). The effect of knowledge of results delay and the subjective estimation of movement form on the acquisition and retention of a motor skill. *Research Quarterly for Exercise and Sport*, 68, 145–151.

Magill, R. A., Chamberlin, C. J. and Hall, K. G. (1991). Verbal knowledge of results as redundant information for learning an anticipation timing skill. *Human Movement Science*, 10, 485–507.

McGuigan, F. J. (1959). Delay in knowledge of results: a problem in design. *Psychological Reports*, 5, 241–242.

McNevin, N. H., Shea, C. H. and Wulf, G. (2003). Increasing the distance of an external focus of attention enhances learning. *Psychological Research*, 67, 22–29.

Newell, K. M. (1977). Knowledge of results and motor learning. *Exercise and Sports Science Reviews*, 4, 195–228.

Nicholson, D. E. and Schmidt, R. A. (1991). Scheduling information feedback to enhance training effectiveness. *Proceedings of the Human Factors Society 35th Annual Meeting* (pp. 1400–1403). Santa Monica, CA: Human Factors Society.

Park, J.-H., Shea, C. H. and Wright, D. L. (2000). Reduced frequency concurrent and terminal feedback: a test of the guidance hypothesis. *Journal of Motor Behavior*, 32, 287–296.

Reeve, T. G., Dornier, L. A. and Weeks, D. J. (1990). Precision of knowledge of results: consideration of the accuracy requirements imposed by the task. *Research Quarterly for Exercise and Sport*, 61, 284–290.

Salmoni, A. W., Schmidt, R. A. and Walter, C. B. (1984). Knowledge of results and motor learning: a review and critical reappraisal. *Psychological Bulletin*, 95, 355–386.

Schmidt, R. A. (1975). A schema theory of discrete motor skill learning. *Psychological Review*, 82, 225–260.

Schmidt, R. A. (1982). *Motor control and learning: a behavioral emphasis*. Champaign, IL: Human Kinetics.

Schmidt, R. A. (1985). The search for invariance in skilled movement behavior. *Research Quarterly for Exercise and Sport*, 56, 188–200.

Schmidt, R. A. (1991). Frequent augmented feedback can degrade learning: evidence and interpretations. In J. Requin and G. E. Stelmach (Eds), *Tutorials in motor neuroscience* (pp. 59–75). Dordrecht, The Netherlands: Kluwer Academic Publishers.

Schmidt, R. A. and Lee, T. D. (1999). *Motor control and learning: a behavioral emphasis* (3rd Ed.). Champaign, IL: Human Kinetics.

Schmidt, R. A. and Wulf, G. (1997). Continuous concurrent feedback degrades skill learning: implications for training and simulation. *Human Factors*, 39, 509–525.

Schmidt, R. A., Lange, C. and Young, D. E. (1990). Optimising summary knowledge of results for skill learning. *Human Movement Science*, 9, 325–348.

Schmidt, R. A., Young, D. E., Swinnen, S. and Shapiro, D. E. (1989). Summary knowledge of results for skill acquisition: support for the guidance hypothesis. *Journal of Experimental Psychology: Learning, Memory, and Cognition*, 15, 352–359.

Shea, C. H. and Wulf, G. (1999). Enhancing motor learning through external-focus instructions and feedback. *Human Movement Science*, 18, 553–571.

Sherwood, D. E. (1988). Effects of bandwidth knowledge of results on movement consistency. *Perceptual and Motor Skills*, 66, 535–542.

Sparrow, W. A. (1995). Acquisition and retention effects of reduced relative frequency of knowledge of results. *Australian Journal of Psychology*, 47, 97–104.

Sparrow, W. A. and Summers, J. J. (1992). Performance on trials without knowledge of results (KR) in reduced relative frequency presentations of KR. *Journal of Motor Behavior*, 24, 197–209.

Steinhauer, K. and Preston Grayhack, J. (2000). The role of knowledge of results in performance and learning of a voice motor task. *Journal of Voice*, 14, 137–145.

Swinnen, S. P. (1996). Information feedback for motor skill learning: a review. In H. N. Zelaznik (Ed.), *Advances in motor learning and control* (pp. 37–66). Champaign, IL: Human Kinetics.

Swinnen, S., Schmidt, R. A., Nicholson, D. E. and Shapiro, D. C. (1990). Information feedback for skill acquisition: instantaneous knowledge of results degrades learning. *Journal of Experimental Psychology: Learning, Memory, and Cognition*, 16, 706–716.

Swinnen, S. P., Lee, T. D., Verschueren, S., Serrien, D. J. and Bogaerds, H. (1997). Interlimb coordination: learning and transfer under different feedback conditions. *Human Movement Science*, 16, 749–785.

Thorndike, E. L. (1914). *Educational psychology*. New York: Columbia University.

Thorndike, E. L. (1927). The law of effect. *American Journal of Psychology*, 39, 212–222.

Thorndike, E. L. (1932). *The fundamentals of learning*. New York: Teachers College.

Todorov, E., Shadmehr, R. and Bizzi, E. (1997). Augmented feedback presented in a virtual environment accelerates learning of a difficult motor task. *Journal of Motor Behavior*, 29, 147–158.

Vander Linden, D. W., Cauraugh, J. H. and Greene, T. A. (1993). The effect of frequency of kinetic feedback on learning an isometric force production task in nondisabled subjects. *Physical Therapy*, 73, 79–87.

Vereijken, B. (1991). *The dynamics of skill acquisition*. Meppel: Krips Repro.

Weeks, D. L. and Kordus, R. N. (1998). Relative frequency of knowledge of performance and motor skill learning. *Research Quarterly for Exercise and Sport*, 69, 224–230.

Winstein, C. J. and Schmidt, R. A. (1990). Reduced frequency of knowledge of results enhances motor skill learning. *Journal of Experimental Psychology: Learning, Memory, and Cognition*, 16, 677–691.

Winstein, C. J., Pohl, P. S., Cardinale, C., Green, A., Scholtz, L. and Waters, C. S. (1996). Learning a partial-weight-bearing skill: effectiveness of two forms of feedback. *Physical Therapy*, 76, 985–993.

Wishart, L. R. and Lee, T. D. (1997). Effect of aging and reduced relative frequency of knowledge of results on learning of a motor skill. *Perceptual and Motor Skills*, 84, 1107–1150.

Wright, D. L., Smith-Munyon, V. L. and Sidaway, B. (1997). How close is too close for precision knowledge of results? *Research Quarterly for Exercise and Sports*, 68, 172–176.

Wulf, G. (1992). The learning of generalized motor programs and motor schemata: effects of KR relative frequency and contextual interference. *Journal of Human Movement Studies*, 23, 53–76.

Wulf, G. and Prinz, W. (2001). Directing attention to movement effects enhances learning: a review. *Psychonomic Bulletin & Review*, 8, 648–660.

Wulf, G. and Schmidt, R. A. (1989). The learning of generalized motor programs: reducing the relative frequency of knowledge of results enhances memory. *Journal of Experimental Psychology: Learning, Memory, and Cognition*, 15, 748–757.

Wulf, G. and Schmidt, R. A. (1994). Feedback-induced variability and the learning of generalized motor programs. *Journal of Motor Behavior*, 26, 348–361.

Wulf, G. and Schmidt, R. A. (1996). Average KR degrades parameter learning. *Journal of Motor Behavior*, 28, 371–381.

Wulf, G. and Shea, C. H. (2002). Principles derived form the study of simple motor skills do not generalize to complex skill learning. *Psychonomic Bulletin and Review*, 9, 185–211.

Wulf, G., Schmidt, R. A. and Deubel, H. (1993). Reduced feedback frequency enhances generalized motor program learning but not parameterization learning. *Journal of Experimental Psychology: Learning, Memory, and Cognition*, 19, 1134–1150.

Wulf, G., Lee, T. D. and Schmidt, R. A. (1994). Reducing knowledge of results about relative versus absolute timing: Differential effects on learning. *Journal of Motor Behavior*, 26, 362–369.

Wulf, G., Höß, M. and Prinz, W. (1998a). Instructions for motor learning: differential effects of internal versus external focus of attention. *Journal of Motor Behavior*, 30, 169–179.

Wulf, G., Shea, C. H. and Matschiner, S. (1998b). Frequent feedback enhances complex motor skill learning. *Journal of Motor Behavior*, 30, 180–192.

Wulf, G., Lauterbach, B. and Toole, T. (1999). Learning advantages of an external focus of attention in golf. *Research Quarterly for Exercise and Sport*, 70, 120–126.

Wulf, G., McNevin, N. H. and Shea, C. H. (2001a). The automaticity of complex motor skill learning as a function of attentional focus. *Quarterly Journal of Experimental Psychology*, 54, 1143–1154.

Wulf, G., Shea, C. H. and Park, J.-H. (2001b). Attention in motor learning: preferences for and advantages of an external focus. *Research Quarterly for Exercise and Sport*, 72, 335–344.

Wulf, G., McConnel, N., Gärtner, M. and Schwarz, A. (2002). Feedback and attentional focus: enhancing the learning of sport skills through external-focus feedback. *Journal of Motor Behavior*, 34, 171–182.

Yao, W. -X., Fischman, M. G. and Wang, Y. T. (1994). Motor skill acquisition and retention as a function of average feedback, summary feedback, and performance variability. *Journal of Motor Behavior*, 26, 273–282.

Young, D. E. and Schmidt, R. A. (1992). Augmented kinematic feedback for motor learning. *Journal of Motor Behavior*, 24, 261–273.

8 Instructions, demonstrations and the learning process

Creating and constraining movement options

Nicola J. Hodges and Ian M. Franks

'Listen, watch and learn' are frequent words of wisdom from parents, teachers and coaches. The questioning learner might ask, 'What should we listen to, what should we watch?' and the questioning teacher must equally decide what to tell and what to show. The purpose of this chapter is to analyse how much we really know about providing instruction and demonstrations. What are the implications of motor learning theory for the provision of pre-practice information and how does the empirical evidence support the proposals?

We would not expect to visit a doctor and receive health prescriptions based on common sense, but we are often happy to receive coaching from practitioners who are unaware of the principles underlying the effective provision of instruction. There is a growing need for evidence-based practice in the coaching arena and classroom to validate the use of techniques that are too often administered based on implicit and explicit assumptions of how a skill should be performed, rather than how people learn (see Hodges and Franks, 2002b).

In this chapter, we attempt to understand how instructions work to affect the learning process, drawing upon theories of skill acquisition and empirical evidence supporting theoretical predictions. This will include discussions as to what information to provide, when and in what situations. We address the major components of instructional theory detailed by Glaser (1976, 1977) and more recently by Snow and Swanson (1992). These components include a description of the learning goals (achievement), the initial states of learners (aptitude), the process of learning in relation to instructions (i.e. learning and treatment design) and finally the assessment of learning.

Sources of augmented information

There are situations when instructions might be independent of or dependent on performance. The independent – dependent distinction is more of a continuum, rather than a dichotomy. There will be some types of instruction that might be based on performance generally, yet will be independent of a specific attempt, such as demonstrations. This type of information provision will be the major focus of this chapter. Instructions which are dependent on a person's performance are typically referred to as feedback. The second area where there is overlap is with the observational learning literature. It is extremely difficult to provide a review of instructions in motor skill acquisition without considering visual means of relaying information. Often the same type of information is conveyed in a demonstration as that provided through instructions, the only difference being the mode of presentation. Although we will examine the role of instructions and demonstrations, our primary focus will be on verbal and written instructions that are provided in isolation or in combination with demonstrations.

Goals of instruction

The goals of the learner and the teacher will, or should, influence the way a particular skill is taught. Typically, the primary goal is to encourage long-term learning. In motor skill acquisition, laboratory type tasks have often demonstrated dissociations between short-term improvements and long-term retention benefits. The general finding is that learning is enhanced if more effort (i.e. an increased level of processing of information) is devoted to the practice phase. However, there may be times when performance improvement in acquisition is the primary goal of instruction. Sometimes the coach and the performer will not be willing to trade-off short-term difficulties for long-term retention. Given that a slow rate of acquisition can be demotivating, the coach or teacher will need to strike a compromise as to short-term improvements and long-term gains. This would be particularly important in situations where learners can compare themselves to other groups within a practice session, which might be running repetitive drills and therefore taking the easier practice route. It will also be important for less mature learners who might have difficulty understanding that the long-term rewards will be worth more than any short-term costs.

The effectiveness of instruction also needs to be judged based on its ability to influence movement form and/or outcome success in situations where these two can be separated. For example, success at a corner kick in soccer will be judged on its outcome (i.e. was the ball delivered to the near or far post), although the skill might also be judged on the technique adopted to achieve this result. As with other sports, such as basketball shooting and golf, the goals of instruction might differentially impact on outcome success and technique and therefore effectiveness should be judged accordingly. Although there is of course a relationship between outcome and execution, the two variables are seldom in tune in early skill acquisition (see Halverson and Roberton, 1979; Higgins, 1991; van Rossum, 1987). When there are many performance goals, or the goals conflict, some method for prioritizing and guiding the learner is needed. It is important for the coach or teacher to effectively communicate his or her required goals to avoid confusion (Gentile, 1972; Whiting and den Brinker, 1982).

Motor learning theory, implications for instructions and a critique of the evidence

Many researchers have discussed the skill acquisition process as a series of stages or phases that the learner progresses in order to display skilled behaviour. These stages are rarely viewed as distinct and have been defined in many ways depending on the theoretical approach adopted. We start by briefly outlining descriptions and theories of skill acquisition, which have primarily been founded on cognitive theory and changes in information processing as a function of learning. In the second section we examine the implications of more dynamic, emergent-features based models for instruction. Typically, different types of movements (e.g. whole-body movements and multi-limb coordination) have been used to examine and develop these ideas of skill acquisition in comparison to those studied in cognitive theories, such that the predictions and implications for instruction of the two approaches are more complimentary rather than contradictory.

Information-processing accounts of skill acquisition

Changes in information-processing demands as a function of practice

One of the ways that the skill acquisition process has been defined is in terms of changes in information-processing demands as a function of increasing skill. Learning has been thought to progress from a more cognitive, declarative or verbal stage to a final automatic, procedural or non-verbal stage (e.g. Adams, 1971; Anderson, 1982, 1983; Fitts, 1964; Fitts and Posner, 1967; Schmidt, 1975; Shiffrin and Schneider, 1977; Snoddy, 1926). Declarative knowledge (i.e. rules and facts) becomes proceduralized so that it is less accessible to consciousness and more difficult to verbalize. This proceduralized form enables more automatic-type processing of information whereby certain conditions elicit, somewhat effortlessly, certain actions. The demands on working memory (i.e. attentional load) are decreased, due to the ability of the learner to bypass particular stages of processing and/or select the appropriate information more effectively (see Haider and Frensch, 1996). The notion that skills require less attention as practice progresses has positive implications for instructional methods that serve to decrease the attention load early in the skill acquisition process (e.g. attentional cueing). The mode of presentation also impacts on attention demands such that a consideration of verbal and visual techniques for conveying information (both written and demonstrations) is required.

Decreasing attention demands through verbal and visual cues

One method of decreasing the high attention demands during early skill acquisition is to provide verbal cues, which facilitate visual search of the environment and ability to extract useful information from a visual display (e.g. watching a skilled demonstration). Landin (1994, p. 299) defined verbal cues as 'concise phrases, often just one or two words, that either direct a student's attention to relevant task stimuli or prompt key movement pattern elements of a motor skill.' In this way, verbal cues help to simplify the learning context, such that only a limited amount of information requires attention.

In their review of the video-feedback literature, Rothstein and Arnold (1976) concluded that demonstrations are most effective when augmented by verbal cues. They also found that, generally, some degree of experience with the skill or sport was necessary for video replay to be successful on its own. Masser (1985, 1993) found that verbal cues had their greatest effect on the performance of a gymnastic move after an initial period of practice. Similarly, Scully and Carnegie (1998) argued that verbal cues help the learner perform a closer approximation to a model's movement, aiding the later refinement of the skill, rather than the acquisition per se.

One of the primary mechanisms underlying the effectiveness of verbal cues is that of attention allocation. While researchers have pointed out that the novice should be directed to relevant task stimuli (e.g. Abernethy, 1993; Magill, 2001; Newell *et al.*, 1985), the issue of what is relevant for different skills is problematic. Many aspects of performance, such as movement form, might emerge as a consequence of a focus on one specific cue and in many sport situations there is little research to help in understanding what exactly should be cued.

One potential way to decrease attentional load during motor performance is to only direct attention to a specific component of the action, or direct attention to the most difficult aspect. However, Sherwood and Rios (2001) failed to observe any benefits of an asymmetric attention focus when performing dual-limb movements of different amplitudes. Attention to one limb improved error on that limb, but led to increased error on the non-attended limb. Additionally, the benefits from attending to one limb during practice did not transfer to the dual-limb focus condition. Similar manipulations of attentional strategy by Temprado *et al.* (1999) showed that certain coordination patterns could be stabilized by attention to both limbs, or destabilized by attention to one limb. Instructors need to consider the potential trade-offs in performance from focusing attention on one component of the action at the expense of the other. Although one component might be improved (e.g. the height of the ball toss in preparing to serve in tennis; see Sherwood and Rios, 2001), the other component (e.g. the timing and execution of the racket swing) might suffer. More importantly, when the individual returns to a strategy that requires a focus on two components, no residual benefits from a simplified attention strategy have been observed.

It has been suggested by Landin (1994) that verbal cues can serve to artificially divide a skill into smaller components, such that the performer's attention is directed only onto specific aspects of a movement and not the general form and feeling and the integration of task components. Schmidt and Wrisberg (2000) only recommend breaking a skill down into separate parts when the relationship between the parts is relatively low. If cues are to be considered, those that help convey the general feel of the movement, or the gross action might be most effective (e.g. an auditory pattern to convey the temporal relationships between components). Indeed, in a number of studies examining face recognition, holistic methods for encoding faces, such as the assessment of personality, rather than feature-based methods, have been shown to lead to enhanced recognition at later presentations (e.g. Winograd, 1981). Schooler and Engstler-Schooler (1990) argue that feature-based processing may dominate the representation of the stimuli, such that specific features interfere with the holistic representation.

Despite these somewhat negative implications associated with verbal cueing, a number of empirical studies have shown quite significant benefits. For example, Carroll and Bandura (1990) found that augmenting demonstrations with sequence and relative timing cues of the components involved in hand sequences aided learning. The authors argued that this was achieved via a stronger cognitive representation of the task. Similar conclusions were reached by McCullagh *et al.* (1990), who argued that verbal cues helped to convey finer aspects of performance. There is considerable evidence that young children, who might have difficulty allocating and maintaining attention on a stimulus, benefit from the coupling of verbal cues with visual demonstrations during motor skill acquisition (see Landin, 1994; Weiss and Klint, 1987).

Due to the difficulty in knowing what to cue and differences in general ability and prior experiences among students in a classroom or gym, Rink (1994) recommended that teachers should provide verbal cues only if individuals do not automatically adjust their performance as a result of a demonstration or a change in task conditions. Inappropriate cues can be more harmful than not providing any cues. For example, Brown (1994) (cited in Rink, 1994) found that when teachers provided inappropriate cues to children learning to throw a ball, performance deteriorated post-practice. This finding shows that students learn what they are taught even when it is detrimental for performance.

A consistent principle in the verbal cueing literature is that cues should be kept short and simple (e.g. Rink, 1994; Rothstein and Arnold, 1976). However, if the goal is to aid the development of a new movement pattern, where components need to be related, verbal cues should be designed to convey as much information as possible with the minimum of words. Holistic instructions, such as providing analogies, can be a useful technique. For example, Swinnen (1996) suggests that a kip-up on the bars in gymnastics can be encouraged through the analogy of pulling on trousers. Masters (2000) has claimed that learning by use of analogy is not only effective in conveying a whole action, but also prevents breakdowns in performance under stress, due to a lack of detailed verbal knowledge about the task.

In summary, verbal cues serve to direct attention during observation of a demonstration and also when performing a motor skill. In situations where the skills have a number of task components that are spatially and temporally interrelated, there has been little evidence that dividing the skill into smaller parts is helpful for movement acquisition. For skills that are related in a more sequential fashion, information that helps to highlight the temporal order has been shown to be helpful. Verbal cues might be most effective after an initial period of practice or experience, aiding the refinement and improvement of subtle aspects of the movement, rather than its acquisition per se. However, if cues can be created that help convey general features of the movement, then, acquisition of more complex skills can be facilitated.

Conveying information effectively

Instructions can be provided in a visual mode, perhaps by a skilled model, in verbal form, or in written mode, so that the learner is required to read and retain. It is generally believed that demonstrations provide the simplest medium for conveying information about the action (see Newell *et al.*, 1985), especially for more complex, whole-body movement skills. There is also evidence that the processing demands associated with taking information from a visual display are somewhat decreased in comparison to ascertaining this same information from written or verbal instructions (see Craik and Lockhart, 1972). It is therefore important to consider the relative benefits of these methods for conveying information as a function of skill level and the type of movement.

In both cognitive (Paivio, 1969, 1979, 1986) and motor tasks, visual information has been shown to be better retained than verbal, although the manner of assessing retention mediates this effect (i.e. recognition versus recall). For example, Lavisse *et al.* (2000) found that visual instructions presented as photos of archery motions were better for performance than fleeting comments and gestures. The authors argued that the photos allowed the learners to construct enhanced mental representations of the motions. Similar conclusions were reached by Juaire and Pargman (1991), who found that photos led to a more accurate reproduction of a six-component dance piece than verbal instructions.

In a similar manner to the visual and verbal processing distinctions made by Paivio in cognitive psychology, Annett (1986, 1990, 1993) discussed different pathways underlying verbal instructions and demonstrations. Although the visual and verbal pathways were judged to be distinct, Annett provided a link between them through the mechanism of imagery. Accordingly, complex motor actions could be described in verbal terms only if a motor representation (i.e. image) was first activated (see Annett, 1993). Likewise, only if verbal instructions are capable of producing a motor image will they be useful in conveying a to-be-produced movement. Therefore, if visual and verbal information promote the same level of learning, perhaps because of the mechanism of imagery, there should be no differences in their effectiveness in the learning environment. However, because verbal codes can elicit an action through imagery, Annett proposed that the verbal coding of images would help to promote effective motor reproduction when an action needs to be recalled at a later date (see also Adams, 1990 and Paivio's dual-coding hypothesis, 1969).

In a study designed to test some of these proposals, Hall *et al.* (1997) required participants to watch or passively reproduce patterns on a graphics tablet. These patterns were high in terms of imagery potential but difficult to verbalise. They found that retention of movement patterns was improved when individuals combined verbal labelling with imagery. Imagery without encouragement to attach verbal labels did not lead to spontaneous strategies to do so. Comparisons of visual demonstrations to non-visually guided movements, where participants were blindfolded, showed that visual demonstrations were recalled more accurately.

The authors concluded that demonstrations generate more accurate and detailed motor images than guided movements, thereby enhancing movement recall. These findings support those of Lavisse *et al.* (2000) in addition to showing that memory can be further enhanced by a combination of imagery (i.e. visual coding) and verbal labelling.

The importance of verbal labelling to aid recall has also been demonstrated in children learning to reproduce a dance sequence. Cadopi *et al.* (1995) showed that different encoding strategies as a function of age were related to the visual and verbal nature of the children's representations. Eight-year-olds relied more on a visual representation of the demonstrated dance sequence, whereas 11-year-olds reported using verbal strategies to help encode the sequence. These dancers were also able to encode the rhythmic or quality aspects of the movement relating to the speed and transitions between segments. Strategy differences, as a function of age, support research that has demonstrated advantages for verbal coding instruction provided to young children (for a review, see McCullagh and Weiss, 2001).

It is worth noting that although verbalization of visual stimuli can aid recall, there is some evidence that the visual memory (as typically assessed through recognition) is somewhat disrupted by this re-coding procedure. Schooler and Engstler-Schooler (1990) showed that a degree of interference in visual memory resulted from allowing individuals time to verbally label faces and colours. The authors argued that the verbal mode of processing dominates the visual code. When there is not one or two particularly defining features differentiating between stimuli, verbal re-coding of visually complex images (i.e. face recognition) can negatively affect memory.

In some of our own work looking at the acquisition of novel bi-manual coordination movements, a combination of visual demonstrations with verbal instructions was found to be more beneficial than either one by itself. However, this combination is not always more helpful than withholding 'how to' pre-practice information and just providing task-relevant feedback alongside a reference template (Hodges and Franks, 2000). The verbal instructions had to encourage the learner to focus on the augmented feedback and the relationship between their movements and the feedback. Although verbal instructions and demonstrations were not directly compared, it was found that a somewhat similar pattern of results emerged across the studies, irrespective of the mode of presentation (see Hodges and Franks, 2002b). When a skill is difficult to label or understand, it seems the learner is unable to form an accurate image to aid production, even if the skill is presented visually. It has also been shown that individuals have difficulty imaging a novel action that they cannot perform (see Franks and Maile, 1991).

Instructions and demonstrations were explicitly compared in a study by Magill and Schoenfelder-Zohdi (1996). They found that a visual demonstration facilitated the acquisition of a rhythmic gymnastics' skill in comparison to verbal instructions and that feedback facilitated learning for the verbal instruction group only. The authors argued that feedback was redundant to the visual information provided via the demonstrations. The critical information for performing and acquiring movement skills relates to the required goals of the task (see Hodges and Franks, 2002b; Swinnen, 1996). The performer needs to know what it is they have to achieve. If the pre-practice information does not contain information concerning the task goal, or cannot specify this (as remarked by Annett, 1993, any verbal instructions need to be imaged for successful reproduction), then the task goal will not be achieved. For Magill and Schoenfelder-Zohdi (1996), the correct movement form and sequencing of components was the desired goal of the skill, but a somewhat complex set of instructions emerges when this movement is put into words. Therefore, for tasks which require the sequencing together of segments that are not easily captured by verbal labels, the requirements will not easily be conveyed by verbal instructions (see also Carroll and Bandura, 1982, 1985) and further feedback statements might be required.

To summarize, the mode of presentation is important in certain situations, particularly where it is difficult to attach a verbal label to a movement and when demonstrations are likely to be the one and only method of conveying a task goal. Also, when the level of cognitive development is such that verbal instructions are too complicated, or are not spontaneously used to aid recall, then the instructor should consider the mode of presentation. Perhaps a variety of methods might be most effective in aiding recall and ensuring that all the details are conveyed accurately (see Rink, 1994). Different modes of presentation could help to facilitate learning via such mechanisms as increased attention and deeper processing of information encouraged by multi-level processing of the various mediums. As discussed earlier, verbal instructions coupled with visual demonstrations help the learner encode and subsequently recall an action, in addition to drawing their attention to important sources of information. If many presentation modes are to be used then it is important that clarity of information is not sacrificed, the goal of the action is made clear and the learner does not suffer from attention overload. Perhaps the best advice for an instructor is to consider whether the mode of presentation can be verbalized and whether this verbal label promotes the same visual image across all skill levels and ages where the action is to be practised (Annett, 1993).

Development of error detection and correction mechanisms

The motor program account of skill learning provided by Schmidt (1975) and strongly influenced by Adams (1971) has led to a comprehensive description of the learning process after the basic movement form or topology has been acquired. The 'parameter' or 'refinement' stage of learning has received empirical verification from the variability of practice literature (see Shapiro and Schmidt, 1982). Refinement occurs through sensory experiences, which allow effective planning and execution of a movement. Mechanisms that detect and subsequently allow for the correction of error (through comparative processes) are critical to refinement, which has led to an important role for augmented feedback. However, the mechanisms responsible for initial acquisition are under developed. Important questions for theorists and practitioners is how skills such as swimming, juggling, riding a bike or serving in tennis are acquired and how this process can be made most effective? These shortcomings have been acknowledged by Schmidt (2001), who suggested that visual observations are likely to play the primary role in the initial formation of a program for action (see also Adams, 1987; Carroll and Bandura, 1982, 1985). The ability of pre-practice information to provide a reference-of-correctness (see Swinnen, 1996), enabling motor skill development in the absence of feedback is discussed below.

Providing a reference-of-correctness

There has been preliminary evidence that observation of a practised model helps the learner form an initial idea of the movement and encourages error-detection procedures similar to those developed through actual practice (Blandin *et al.*, 1999; Blandin and Proteau, 2000). Although the tasks were somewhat simple in terms of the motor response (i.e. barrier knock-down and coincident anticipation timing), observation facilitated the ability of participants to detect errors in subsequent presentations and among their own responses. These authors and others (e.g. Adams, 1986; Gentile, 1998; Vogt, 1996) argue that although observation can help shape the movement initially, physical practice is needed for effective implementation. This template or reference role for instructions and demonstrations has been particularly effective for skills that require the stringing together of different elements into a sequence and when the goal or criterion of the action is novel or unusual. As remarked earlier, demonstrations help form an image of the act which enhances memory for the correct sequence. Additionally, the benefits of movement templates are thought to be due to enhanced error-detection processes early in learning, brought about by comparisons across the desired and actual performance.

Newell *et al.* (1990) provided evidence that templates or criterions were critical to acquisition and performance when the requirements were unfamiliar (i.e. unusual two-dimensional shapes). They also found that feedback about the movement could only be used effectively when the shape was familiar (i.e. a circle) or a criterion was provided. The criterion provided a reference for the action (either in real or imagined form), which enabled comparisons with feedback about performance such that errors could be detected and corrected. As noted earlier, the learner needs information of some sort pertaining to what to do (i.e. the task goal), and as suggested by Annett (1993), if this information cannot be described in terms of a verbal label, or readily imaged, then a criterion needs to be provided. Given that there is a substantial body of research to show that performers become dependent on information available during practice, it is recommended that the criterion is provided after the movement has been performed (i.e. terminally), or in a fading schedule throughout the practice period (see Schmidt, 1991).

Caroll and Bandura (1982, 1985, 1990) have shown that demonstrations facilitate the spatial reproduction and temporal ordering of a complex sequence of arm movements. They argued that demonstrations help observers form a representation of correctness, as assessed through recognition measures, what they refer to as 'conceptual understanding', such that errors in performance can be detected and subsequently corrected. Carroll and Bandura (1982) found that visual feedback did not help performance until the participants had developed an understanding of what to do. Similarly to Newell *et al.* (1990), without a reference, it was not possible for the observers to use feedback to diagnose errors. Despite these interpretations, Hodges *et al.* (2003a) found that the coupling of feedback about performance with demonstrations helped the correct formation of a reference and therefore aided in conceptual understanding. For complex motor tasks, where the limb components are interrelated both spatially and temporally, feedback about performance appears to aid this error detection process. Measures of recognition showed that video feedback groups were better able to discriminate between correct and incorrect movement patterns, in comparison to demonstration-only groups. These findings are illustrated in Figure 8.1, where the mean proportion of correct discriminations as a function of type of demonstration is shown.

Symmetrical (i.e. in-phase), bi-manual movements were easily differentiated from limb movements with a 90° off-set for all groups, whereas groups who did not receive video feedback had difficulty discriminating alternating (i.e. anti-phase) movements from those off-set by 90°. Video demonstrations alone were not sufficient to encourage change in movement form unless they were accompanied by error-alerting information in the form of feedback, or verbal instructions. Feedback helps the learner to make comparisons across the two information sources, discriminate important information and develop an understanding of what to do. Therefore, the coupling of feedback with demonstrations aids both the formation and refinement of a novel motor action. This type of process can be seen in many complex skills, where the goal of the action might be difficult to understand (e.g. dance or martial art's moves that have complex spatial–temporal requirements). In teaching, mirrors might be employed not only to enhance learners' sensory awareness of their movements, but also to aid in the understanding of the requirements through comparisons of these movements with those demonstrated.

Although demonstrations can provide an important error-alerting role, they are not always the most effective way to convey the task requirements. In a number of experiments (for a review see Hodges and Franks, 2002b), we have found that a graphical template of the action, as illustrated in Figure 8.2, which simply relays information about the relationship between the limbs (i.e. relative phase), is a more effective constraining source of information than a demonstration or verbal instructions. Participants do not even need to know how the graphical template relates to their own movement (see Hodges and Franks, 2000), or even receive this information concurrently (see Hodges and Franks, 2002a; Hodges and Lee, 1999). As long as the learner is motivated to search out other movement options, error information is available and the task is sufficiently constrained that the movement solutions are not limitless, there is little or no advantage of knowing the specifics of the coordination pattern in advance (see also van Rossum, 1987).

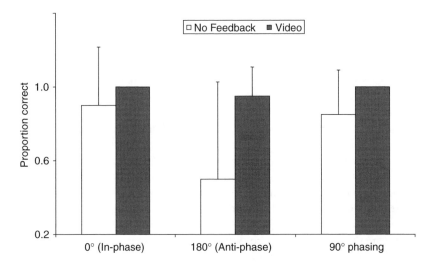

Figure 8.1 The mean proportion of correct discriminations of the demonstrated pattern (i.e. 90° phasing) from in-phase and anti-phase demonstrations for the Video and No Feedback (FB) groups. Between participant standard deviation bars are also included. These data are reproduced from Hodges *et al.* (2003a).

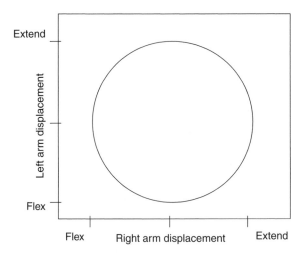

Figure 8.2 The graphical template used to provide reference information to participants in dual-limb coordination studies requiring a 90° phase offset between the limbs.

As a caveat, there are always individuals in experiments who, almost irrespective of the instructional manipulation and the amount of information provided, fail to show variability in performance indicative of a search for the required movement pattern. There has been some evidence that this is related to a difficulty discriminating between information sources and strong latent tendencies to perform more symmetrical-type movements. In these situations additional instructions might be required that, at the very least, try to encourage variability in initial movement attempts.

In summary, the reference role of pre-practice information is important. It is not the case that individuals need to be told what to do to achieve a goal, but that they need to receive information concerning attainment of the goal. Although error-detection mechanisms can be encouraged through pre-practice information such as a movement demonstration, the nature of the skill to be acquired will impact on the effectiveness of this information. Only for skills with relatively simple motor components will demonstrations be effective. As the motor component becomes more difficult, additional error information will be required to help guide the learner to successful reproduction.

Learning as a dynamic process dictated by constraints

There has been a move away from stage models of learning and development, which has most notably been evidenced by the publication of a popular motor development textbook by Haywood and Getchell (2001), towards the notion of learning as a product of constraints as described by Newell (1985, 1986). There has been greater emphasis on examining learning as a continual process of change, brought about by the interaction of constraints in the environment and changing skills of the performer. Accompanying this change in emphasis in skill development has been a shift to examining temporally and spatially complex movements, often involving coordination between limbs and with visual information in the environment.

Coordination dynamics

The coordination dynamics literature, which has grown out of dynamical systems theory, concerns itself with the process of change (for a review, see Kelso, 1995) and variables that capture and influence the organization of the system, whether this system refers to human movement, a colony of ants or the weather. In inter-limb coordination, the variable that best describes change of this system is relative phase, which captures the spatial–temporal relationship of the limbs, rather than the individual components in isolation. Speed is an example of a variable that influences relative phase. More specific influences on variables such as relative phase can be brought about by changes in visual information. Irrespective of the type of influences, these so-termed control variables act like constraints, shaping and guiding the unfolding movement.

The notion of change and the processes of stability and instability are important characteristics in the field of dynamics. Motor skill acquisition is
encouraged by variability within the system, allowing a new movement state to
emerge and develop. For the system to change from one stable state to a new
state, energy is needed; either physical, such as a change in the equipment; or
informational, in the form of a new movement goal brought about by intention
to change or visual information in the environment. This energy creates variability and a break from previously stable movements, such that a new movement
can emerge through experience of other task-relevant sensory information. This
concept of variability has been incorporated into methods of teaching where the
primary aim is to encourage the development of novel actions.

Encouraging acquisition through movement variability

There have been a number of experiments where control, or non-instructed/
discovery learning groups have demonstrated performance on certain tasks to
the same degree, or better, than instructed groups. For example, Vereijken and
Whiting (1989) and Whiting *et al.* (1987) found that in learning to perform fast
and wide movements on a ski-simulator, groups who were provided with a skilled
model to copy performed worse than those who practised without any instructional information. The authors argued that trying to copy the movement, rather
than directing attention to outcome success (i.e. keeping the apparatus moving
fast and wide), limited the performers' experience of the task environment and
the formation of adequate relations between their movements and its effects.
Copying a displayed movement can lead to a constrained movement, which
might be harmful to acquisition when this is not the desired goal. Nouritt *et al.*
(2000) also showed that a less constrained environment during practice on the
ski-simulator had later advantages in transfer. Constraining individuals to perform large amplitude movements had benefits in practice, but did not aid in
transfer to different amplitude movements. The authors argued that a high
constraint, whether this is physical, encouraged by feedback, demonstrations or
instructions, is detrimental to the development of an effective search strategy
and subsequently transfer to novel task conditions.

In developmental studies conducted by Vereijken and Thelan (1997), infants
who were most influenced by training methods to encourage walking (i.e. treadmill
interventions), were the ones whose initial performance was least stable. Arguably,
it was this instability, that allowed a new and efficient movement to emerge.
Introducing instability into action should be considered an important step when
trying to encourage acquisition of a novel skill. This instability affords the learner
opportunities to experience more varied sensory situations, both proprioceptive
and visual, promoting a better understanding of the relation between action and
environment and hopefully promoting adoption of a movement optimally suited to
the task and the characteristics of the learner. Instructions and movement demonstrations might help to encourage change and variability in performance, but only
if the performer is able to understand what change is required and receives some

sort of feedback as to whether that change has been achieved. Rather than creating choice, technique-based demonstrations or instructions might lead to perseverance type behaviour as a result of the learner trying to unsuccessfully copy.

We have shown that groups who are provided with 'how to' instructions and demonstrations before and during practice show less variability in their initial movement attempts and inhibit the selection of movement patterns that might be undesirable, but nevertheless encourage exploration (Hodges and Franks, 2000, 2001; Hodges and Lee, 1999). Similar to Vereijken and Thelan (1997), the degree of stability on a pre-practice coordination task predicted both acquisition rate and retention (e.g. Hodges and Franks, 2000). A failure or late decision to change from an in-phase mode (i.e. symmetrical flexion and extension of the arms) of coordination to an alternating mode when the task demands dictated a change, predicted ability to later acquire a novel movement. There was evidence that participants who failed to adapt their movements to changes in the task display, benefited from instruction that encouraged attention to the effects of their movements on the visual information (Hodges and Franks, 2000). Also, Hodges *et al.* (2003a) showed that video feedback helped to overcome these stable behaviours during acquisition of a new coordination pattern.

This learning to give up stability to progress and acquire new movement patterns can be illustrated in many sport situations. For example, when attempting to drive a golf ball up the fairway a beginner will have to learn how to swing their arms more freely, at least on the back-swing, so that the necessary momentum can be imparted to the ball. This might require the performer to initially forfeit a degree of consistency and accuracy, that is somewhat facilitated by a more rigid arm. In view of the above research, it might be more difficult to teach an effective swing to individuals who display greater consistency in components of their movements than others. Alternative, less direct methods for encouraging variability will need to be considered, such as changing attentional focus and physical parameters, such as the weight of the club. Despite the potential benefits of a more varied sensory experience of the environment, this unguided method is more often than not a time-consuming process and for some individuals might not result in success. For example, trying to learn how to swing the club in golf without any instructions concerning stance or hand-grip on the club is likely to be frustrating and somewhat unnecessary. The skill for the instructor is to determine how much direction should be given so that variability in initial attempts is not hindered, but the learner does not need to find out all the skills themselves. In this way, guided-discovery methods of instruction might be the most beneficial.

Learning to decouple

In many motor skills, such as catching and throwing balls when juggling, timing the movements of the arms and feet when playing the piano and coordinating the brush and dryer when hairdressing, simultaneous but non-synchronous movements are required of both arms. In a recent experiment, Hodges and Franks (2002a) tried to encourage acquisition of a difficult bi-manual coordination pattern through demonstrations and instructions, which built upon the learner's existing knowledge and behavioural preferences to perform synchronous, symmetrical (in-phase) or alternating (anti-phase) arm movements. Participants in two of the groups were both shown and told how these existing movements should be adjusted to perform a newly required coordination pattern (i.e. 90° relative phase). A third control group received only feedback at the end of a trial relating to the degree of coupling. The error data from these three groups across 2 days of practice and in retention are illustrated in Figure 8.3.

Despite the fact that the control group was not provided with any information concerning existing habits and how to perform the required movement, this group performed as well or better than the two instruction groups. Direct instruction did not facilitate the learning process. Instructions which conveyed information about how in-phase movements should be adopted were actually detrimental to the acquisition process. It was not the fact that participants in the in-phase instruction group stuck with these movements, but rather that they avoided symmetrical movements and subsequently could only perform anti-phase movements. The technique or strategy, which was intended by the instructions, was not that detected by the performer. For well-learnt or stable skills it is not sufficient, and may even be unhelpful, to merely tell people how old skills should be adjusted to perform new ones (e.g. adapting ways of responding with a racquet in tennis to responding in squash). It might be better to avoid this

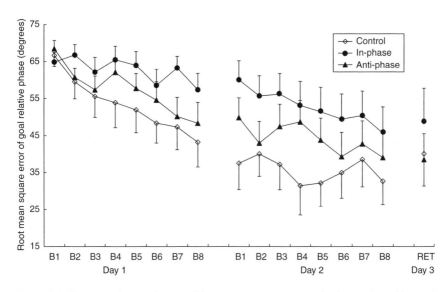

Figure 8.3 Error in relative phase and between participant standard error bars (degrees) across two days of practice and in retention for the Control (no-instruction) group and the In-phase and Anti-phase instruction groups who were told how to adjust these movements to perform the required 90° relative phase pattern. These data are reproduced from Hodges and Franks (2002).

method of instruction and to find creative methods that help to promote new links and encourage variability in initial attempts.

A creative method for encouraging this break from stable movement patterns was identifed by Walter and Swinnen (1992). They showed that decreasing the speed of the movement helped to decrease attraction to more stable movement and therefore aided skill acquisition. As shown by Temprado *et al.* (1999), the attention demands associated with bi-manual coordination are somewhat dependent on the speed and thus the underlying stability of movements. Hodges and Lee (1999) also found that acquisition of a new coordination pattern was almost completely prevented when attentional resources were allocated to a concurrent secondary task requiring mental arithmetic. Therefore, by decreasing speed, attention is freed to aid the break from stable movements and the discovery of new, initially unstable ones. Wishart *et al.* (2001) also found that elderly participants were only able to learn a novel coordination movement when speed was manipulated. Traditional instructed, guided-practice and observational learning techniques failed to encourage learning.

It has been shown that holistic–rhythmic methods of practice are beneficial for acquisition of novel coordination actions. For example, Summers and Kennedy (1992) required participants to learn a polyrhythm involving a 5 : 3 tapping ratio of the hands. Non-musicians had difficulty learning irrespective of whether the frequencies were practised separately by each hand or together. Skilled musicians, however, could learn the rhythm, but most effectively under whole-task conditions. Although the ability to integrate rhythms might only be realized after sufficient practice, Summers (2001) outlined a number of strategies that are typically adopted by individuals learning to produce polyrhythms. For example, most participants focused attention on the faster beat and then associated the slower beat to this guiding movement. Peters and Schwartz (1989) subsequently provided direct evidence that this was a useful strategy for coordinating tapping movements.

In summary, indirect methods of instruction, whereby constraints are manipulated to encourage change in a movement response, have been shown to be more effective at encouraging the acquisition of coordination movements than more direct methods of instruction. Cognitive understanding and a high degree of knowledge is unnecessary. Where the spatial and/or temporal relationship between stimuli is relatively complex, methods for encouraging the integration of rhythms might be encouraged through auditory techniques. For example, Franks and Stanley (1991) found that participants who learnt how to track a complex stimuli, used a rhythmic counting strategy to help them extract and remember the sequence complexities.

Levels of control within the sensori-motor system

The writings of the Russian physiologist, Nicolai Bernstein, have over the last 20 years had a strong influence over the way motor behaviour is viewed and studied. Although most of his ideas were formulated in the 1950s and 1960s, it is only more recently that these have been translated to influence Western thinking (see Latash, 1998; Latash and Turvey, 1996; Whiting, 1984). One of the compelling proposals to emerge from the readings of Bernstein, is the idea that the motor system functions as a hierarchy of action systems that have different roles to play in the control of movement (see Latash and Turvey, 1996). The primary function of the lowest level (A) is to maintain posture and tone. This level is virtually involuntary. Level B is believed to be critical for loco-motion and repetitive, rhythmic acts, but only semi-voluntary actions are con-trolled at this level (e.g. gestures). The level of space (C) is responsible for targeted and purposeful movements and at this level, processing of informa-tion (tactile, visual, auditory) is critical. Level C control is highly dominant in children. For example, Bekkering *et al.* (1996) showed that young children imitate the goal of the movement (i.e. moving the arm to the correct ear), but not the way the movement was achieved (i.e. left arm crossed over the body to touch the right ear). It is the highest level, the level of action plans, where conscious thought and high-level brain control systems are involved in planning and fine motor control, for example, painting, writing and solving a sequence of tasks.

Although this system is proposed as a hierarchy, control can take place at many levels. The role each level takes in controlling movement will change depending on the skill and perhaps the amount of practice. These differential roles of the action system have also been formalized by Gentile (1998) to describe the processes involved in skill acquisition. An explicit process is respon-sible for shaping and planning movements, whereas an implicit process involves low-level control processes (like those proposed by Bernstein). What is interest-ing about both these ideas is that higher, explicit levels do not need to have access to information from the lower, more implicit levels. Action planning might be formulated in terms of behavioural goals focused about the end-point of the action, rather than specific movement configurations required to achieve the goal.

Bernstein (1967) presented quite compelling arguments against the notion that movements were planned and organized in terms of efferent commands to the limbs (i.e. equifinality). Rather, through experience working within an environment and connections that are formed between input and output signals, movements are planned at a gross level, primarily directed towards goal attain-ment. Latash (1996) and Müller and Loosch (1999) made similar observations about dart throwing and basketball free-throw shooting. They showed that the variability during the movement itself was relatively large in comparison to the invariance in the trajectory of the dart and ball. Accordingly, the movements involved are seen as a by-product of the goal-focus and the achievement of con-sistent final trajectories. These ideas of movements as consequences of other fac-tors, or constraints, are germane to those of Newell (1985) and the coordination dynamics theory discussed earlier. In addition, there are other researchers work-ing within a more traditional information processing framework who explain learning in somewhat similar principles of common-coding mechanisms between efferent and afferent signals, whereby actions are planned in terms of their intended effects (Kunde *et al.*, 2002; Prinz, 1992, 1997). This view of motor control has implications for the nature of knowledge of certain skills at different stages of learning and for strategies that might benefit skill acquisition.

Accessibility of knowledge

Many motor skills may be acquired implicitly and later reinterpreted to aid instruction. In examination of children's drawing, Karmiloff-Smith (1992) proposed that for skill in drawing to progress, the child must engage in a process known as representational re-description. This process enables implicit knowledge to be re-described in explicit terms, subsequently aiding planning and drawing skills on future attempts. We know from work on visual perception that judgements in action are not as susceptible to top-down influences, which affect conscious perception and judgements out-of-action (see Goodale and Milner, 1992). Trying to control these low-level processes might be detrimental if accuracy and speed are sacrificed by bringing explicit knowledge to bear on processes normally controlled at a lower level of consciousness. These examples run contrary to the view of acquisition as a transition from a verbal, explicit stage to a more non-verbal, implicit stage. The implication of this work is that the information that is important changes with practice or the task demands, rather than the processes operating in a sequential fashion. Insights of experts and persons who have undergone training are probably based on this transformation of more implicit type knowledge. Because of the understanding developed through lower-level processes (i.e. attunement to sensory information), these insights into learning and control are unlikely to be very helpful to beginners. We have found that individuals who have learnt how to perform a relatively difficult spatial–temporal coordination pattern, explain their strategies after practice in ways that are unlikely to be understood or readily used by beginners. For example, participants report trying to 'get into the feel' of the movement, or 'finding the rhythm'. It can be difficult and frustrating for skilled performers to put their performance strategies into words.

There have been some studies where the verbalizations of skilled participants have been relayed to new learners as verbal instructions to determine whether they can bypass some of the practice needed to reach a skilled level. Stanley *et al.* (1989) used this procedure to determine whether individuals could learn to control a complex system, which required the learner to determine the relationship between an input and a response. Instructions written by practised participants only proved useful to learners near the end of testing, perhaps when they themselves had acquired a degree of understanding of the environment. However, Goode *et al.* (1998) provided verbal strategies obtained from experienced performers to a group of novices learning a throwing task and found that this information facilitated performance. Although a lot of knowledge belonging to highly experienced performers is likely to be implicit and difficult to convey to a beginner, especially if it relates to details of movement control, there are also likely to be a number of explicit strategies and cues that help facilitate the acquisition process (see also Kohl and Shea, 1992; Martens *et al.*, 1976).

Other evidence that knowledge might be somewhat inaccessible to performers until they themselves have reached a level of proficiency on a skill has been illustrated by Brooks *et al.* (1995). They differentiate strategy and tactical knowledge, whereby strategy knowledge contains information about what to do, but that knowing how to implement this is the role of tactical knowledge. Brooks *et al.* required participants to control a cursor onto a target that was manipulated to conform to the participant's velocity profile. The strategy component was learning to reverse the hand, whereas the tactical component required implementation of this strategy at the right time. Through examination of verbal protocols the authors found that within a couple of trials of the reversal strategy being performed, the participants expressed knowledge of this strategy. Voicing of tactics, however, were not made until after successful performance. A number of participants failed to perform the task although they were able to voice the correct strategy. The authors concluded that two distinct processes operate during motor learning and that in the absence of tactical control, strategic knowledge might prove unhelpful. Merely knowing what to do, or being told what to do is not sufficient to encourage the adoption of a required movement. Through experience and perhaps processing of information in a more implicit manner, the optimal movements are discovered. This does not mean that the process of learning cannot be facilitated by instruction, but that it is often not enough to merely tell people what to do.

Demonstrations, like verbal instructions, do not convey the important information to individuals until they themselves have developed an understanding of the task through experience. For example, we know when someone is juggling, or performing a butterfly stroke in the pool, perhaps a scissors-kick in soccer, but the level of understanding is not translated into a useable level whereby we can take this information and copy the complexities. As discussed earlier, some individuals face considerable difficulty understanding what is required when watching performance of a 90° relative phase pattern (Hodges *et al.*, 2003a). We have found that new learners realize very quickly from watching a demonstration and receiving step-by-step instructions that they should not move their arms symmetrically in-phase (e.g. Hodges and Franks, 2001; Hodges and Lee, 1999). It is typically only individuals who have had experience with bi-manual coordination skills such as drumming or playing the piano who are able to pick up the required coordination pattern from watching a demonstration. Knowing that something different from in-phase is required is not the same as understanding what that something actually is. It seems that the understanding of what to do and finding the ability to do it emerge in parallel (see also Brooks *et al.*, 1995).

The fact that learning can take place on many levels and that trying to exert conscious control over these levels can be detrimental to performance, has been illustrated in the perceptual-motor tracking literature. Invariance in perceptual displays during continuous manual tracking has been shown to benefit speed and accuracy without a corresponding change in explicit knowledge and awareness (e.g. Green and Flowers, 1991; Magill and Clark, 1997; Wulf and Schmidt, 1997). Green and Flowers (1991) found that instructions concerning the regularity of a stimulus–response pairing actually had a negative effect on performance in a video-game task.

To summarize, strategy knowledge is likely to be limited in its effectiveness unless some sort of physical response is incorporated into the training (see Berry, 1991) and the relayed strategy can be used effectively by individuals with low levels of experience of the practice domain. The insights of skilled performers might reflect the understanding of low-level processes, which are difficult to verbalize and therefore this type of information might be better provided after a period of practice without strategic knowledge.

End-point control of action

There is evidence that information which relates to the most important point or part of the movement, such as the toe in jumping hurdles, is sufficient to help shape the movement necessary to attain a behavioural goal. Gentile (1998) argues that, in attaining outcome goals, the learner attends only to key markers or 'turning points' that help to explicitly guide the unfolding movement. Therefore, in the early stages of acquisition, information that helps the learner find a fit between their movements and the action goal is important.

Wulf and colleagues have provided quite compelling support for the use of an attentional strategy in learning that is focused on a feature of the action that is not directly related to the body and the limbs. For example, Wulf et al. (1998) showed that a focus of attention onto the wheels of the apparatus rather than the feet when performing on a ski-simulator improved acquisition and retention. Because the externally directed attention group outperformed the non-instructed control group, it was concluded that an external focus is not automatically adopted and therefore participants benefit from instructions which encourage this end-point focus. Additionally, an effects-related focus was preferable to merely focusing attention externally and a far external cue was better for balance (on a stabiliometer) than a near external cue (for a review, see Wulf and Prinz, 2001).

In numerous sports there is evidence that the control focus of the performer is directed to an effects-related cue, such as the ball in basketball, volleyball and the putt or javelin in field-athletic events. Davids et al. (1999) examined the acquisition of a volleyball serve and noted invariance in the ball's peak height among skilled performers. The implication is that in teaching a volleyball serve, attention and instructions should be centred around controlling the ball, rather than the motions required to achieve a consistent serve. Indeed, Wulf et al. (2002) found that external feedback statements focused on the ball were more effective for teaching a volleyball serve than limb-related feedback statements. Davids et al. (1999) also found that it was important to actually strike the ball during practice and not merely throw the ball in the air. The implication is that learning the correct action emerges as a consequence of trying to achieve a particular external goal and maintaining the integral links between the movement and its effects. This outcome focus has also been incorporated into coaching strategies for self-paced acts such as golf putting, darts and serving in tennis (see Lidor *et al.*, 1996; Singer *et al.*, 1993).

Although Wulf and colleagues argue that these attentional strategies are not task dependent, there has been some evidence that only for skills performed in uncertain environments, for example a ground stroke in tennis in comparison to skills with no uncertainty such as a tennis serve, are environmental, externally focused cues better than internal, performance-related cues. In 'certain' environments, the reverse was true (see Kessler-Cooper and Rothstein, 1981). The contradictory nature of the findings to those of Wulf and colleagues might be the result of two factors. The tennis players in the study by Kessler-Cooper and Rothstein had undergone training before the experiment, which might have prompted the learners to spontaneously relate the performance /internal feedback to their actions. Second, the performance cues were not as 'internally based' as some of those in manipulations by Wulf and colleagues. Rather than directing attention to the movements in isolation, the statements were also related to movement outcomes.

We have recently attempted to examine the importance of end-point information during performance and learning through manipulation of ball trajectory information (Hodges *et al.*, 2000). If there is evidence that performers rely on this information when acquiring and producing complex movement skills, then this has important implications for instruction. In a first study we examined the acquisition of a golf chip. Beginner golfers practised this shot either with or without vision of ball flight, although both groups were shown the ball's final landing position. As illustrated in Figure 8.4, although there was no significant difference between the two groups in acquisition, when vision of the ball was removed in retention/transfer (i.e. PV), performance of the Full-vision group was negatively affected. In a second experiment, we also found some evidence that skilled golfers suffered from the withdrawal of ball flight information as performance progressed in the absence of this information. Due to the fact that the participants who had practised this skill in Experiment 1 were beginners and some had difficulty even lifting the ball, it is unlikely that participants in the Full-vision group were able to effectively relate this information to their movements early in practice. Without information prescribing an ideal ball trajectory, or sufficient practice with this information, the value of ball flight could not be sufficiently assessed.

We have begun to explore how end-point criterion templates attained from the ball trajectories of skilled performers can be used to facilitate learning. Data obtained from novices learning a soccer-chip shot has provided evidence that in terms of outcome attainment, ball-trajectory matching strategies are more effective than matching movement form (Hodges *et al.*, 2003b). Todorov *et al.* (1997) used a similar end-point type of instruction to teach table tennis and found that the experimental group who saw only the expert's paddle and ball outperformed a control group who received verbal instruction and demonstrations from a coach.

Perhaps if the goals of the task are two-fold, that is both a specified technique and outcome goal, as would be the typical aim when teaching a variety of

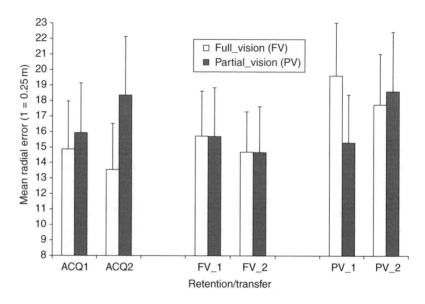

Figure 8.4 Mean radial error scores have been plotted for the Full-vision (FV) and Partial-vision (PV) groups for the 2 days of acquisition (ACQ1 and 2, 40 trials /day) and in two blocks (four trials/block) of retention and transfer with (FV) and without vision (PV).

self-paced skills including serving in tennis or putting in golf, then encouraging both outcome and a desired movement might take the invention of a more novel approach to teaching. For example, a video replay of an expert's free-throw shot in basketball could be shown in reverse, so that emphasis is placed on working backwards from the goal to the actions and forming relationships between them. This type of strategy could be compared to more typical approaches where the learner is encouraged to discover how their actions influence effects (e.g. playing a video forward), rather than how the effects are associated to the action. This strategy might be particularly important with children, who spontaneously adopt more external, outcome-based strategies (see Bekkering *et al.*, 1996). When children are asked to imitate a movement, they often ignore what they are shown if they are also provided with a task goal or outcome to achieve (Hayes *et al.*, 2003). These results with young children suggest that a goal focus is a spontaneous natural strategy that is replaced by more cognitively loaded strategies as adults learn. This indeed might be one of the reasons, at least anecdotally, why adults have greater difficulty acquiring motor acts as adults.

Conclusions

Instructions and demonstrations tell people what to do and directly or indirectly what not to do. In this way, this type of information serves to create options and to constrain choice. In many learning situations the choices are already constrained by physical and non-physical goals, for example, soccer players have to use their feet and need to score goals by getting the ball to cross the goal line. In this way, these constraints will dictate the use of certain strategies and ways of kicking the ball. Beyond these physical constraints, the instructor and learner will impose others that will determine the process of acquisition and the efficiency of the displayed movement.

What should be clear from the preceding discussion is that the information conveyed by instructions and demonstrations might not be that intended by the instructor. By telling people how to stand and place their hands on a golf club, the instructor might also be taking emphasis away from the ball and the golf club and the external effects of the action. The focus of the learner might change to one of the correct movement, rather than imparting enough force to get the ball up the fairway. It is important for the learner and the instructor to be clear of the learning goals and to prioritize task demands (e.g. technique versus distance). In addition, demonstrations that relay information concerning how an action is to be performed might also directly or indirectly relay a strategy which may or may not be beneficial for learning. Some strategies lead to relatively constrained movement attempts in the initial stages of acquisition and may be inappropriate for the level of skill of the learner, or in helping transfer of skills across similar activities. Tactical knowledge is also needed to successfully apply strategies and this knowledge might only be gained implicitly through experience on the task. The implication is that instructions and demonstrations should be combined with experiential learning so that the learner gains a better understanding of what the instructions mean and how they can be implemented. The instructor should think carefully as to the purpose of the information before supplying instructions so that it will be successfully conveyed to learners given their level of experience and the type of skill to be performed.

Elsewhere we have made recommendations for coaching based on our research and some of the literature reviewed in this chapter (see Hodges and Franks, 2002b, 2003). These recommendations were based on the need to encourage early variability to facilitate the acquisition of a novel action and the necessity to encourage search and the links between environmental information and the action. Attention also provided a guide for these recommendations, as methods associated with cueing and the directing of attention are major tools of a coach during practice and observation. As should be evident from this literature, attentional focus might depend on the goal of the skill (i.e. outcome or movement-form focused), but also on the level of experience of the learner. A certain cue, or strategy for directing attention, will only be useful once a certain level of experience with the skill has been acquired. Expert insights might reflect an understanding of implicit knowledge that cannot be passed on through explicit instruction and guidance.

Returning to the questions asked at the beginning of the chapter, we conclude by providing some general guidelines that help to answer these questions and summarize the points made in this chapter. The questions we set out to answer concerned: the informational content of instructions (i.e. what instructions should be provided?); the type of task, general conditions and point in the learning process when instructions should be provided (i.e. when and for whom should instructions be given?); and the method of delivering instruction (i.e. how should instructions be conveyed?).

In terms of what information to provide, it is critical that the learner understands the goal of the task. Therefore, some reference will be needed to guide performance. The learner does not need to know how to achieve the goal, just information concerning whether the goal was achieved. Discovery learning techniques have been shown to be somewhat effective at encouraging goal attainment and it might be that after a degree of familiarization with the task, some verbal cues and instructions could then be given to alter technique. Indirect instructional methods could also be used to change technique, such as changing the club, or using the hand as a barrier to control the extent of back-swing, which will lead to an overall change in movement form without the learner changing their focus from outcome attainment. Other strategies for encouraging the acquisition of a new movement might involve reducing temporal demands or encouraging change through the use of holistic-type instructions such as analogies.

The skill acquisition literature (both information-processing and constraints-based models) supports the need for varied experiences during the practice and acquisition phase of learning. Increased experience of the task domain and exposure to a variety of sensori-motor interactions aids long-term retention and transfer to new skills as a result of an increased repertoire of action situations and knowledge of general principles underlying skilled behaviour. This experience is likely to help learners implement strategy knowledge obtained from experts within the domain.

For movement skills that require the memory of certain skills and components, demonstrations and pictures seem to be the most effective method of conveying this information and enhancing memory for the correct sequence. Augmenting this information with verbal cues or instructions is likely to be helpful for the learner, especially when dealing with young children. A variety of methods and modes of instruction, which are typically employed by coaches and instructors, are effective, although whether the mechanism is one of motivation due to added variety or information is not entirely clear. In general, when considering how information should be relayed, the mode of presentation should be given particular attention when it is difficult to attach verbal labels to an action and when dealing with young and developmentally challenged learners. In both these cases, demonstrations are likely to be more effective than verbal instructions, although again verbal cues coupled with images and demonstrations will help with later recall.

References

Abernethy, B. (1993). Searching for the minimum essential information for skilled perception and action. *Psychological Research*, 55, 131–138.

Adams, J. A. (1971). A closed-loop theory of motor learning. *Journal of Motor Behaviour*, 3, 111–150.

Adams, J. A. (1986). Use of the model's knowledge of results to increase the observer's performance. *Journal of Human Movement Studies*, 12, 89–98.

Adams, J. A. (1987). Historical review and appraisal of research on the learning, retention, and transfer of human motor skills. *Psychological Bulletin*, 101, 41–74.

Adams, J. A. (1990). The changing face of motor learning. *Human Movement Science*, 9, 209–220.

Anderson, J. R. (1982). Acquisition of cognitive skill. *Psychological Review*, 89, 369–406.

Anderson, J. R. (1983). *The architecture of cognition*. Cambridge, MA: Harvard University Press.

Annett, J. (1986). On knowing how to do things. In H. Heuer and C. Fromm (Eds), *Generation and modulation of action patterns* (pp. 187–200). Berlin: Springer.

Annett, J. (1990). Relations between verbal and gestural explanations. In G. R. Hammond (Ed.), *Cerebral control of speech and limb movements* (pp. 295–314). Amsterdam: North-Holland.

Annett, J. (1993). The learning of motor skills: sports science and ergonomics perspectives. *Ergonomics*, 37, 5–16.

Bekkering, H., Wohlschläger, A. and Gattis, M. (1996). Motor imitation: what is imitated? *Corpus, Psyche et Societas*, 3, 68–74.

Bernstein, N. A. (1967). *The coordination and regulation of movements*. London: Pergamon.

Berry, D. C. (1991). The role of action in implicit learning. *The Quarterly Journal of Experimental Psychology*, 43A, 881–906.

Blandin, Y. and Proteau, L. (2000). On the cognitive basis of observational learning: development of mechanisms for the detection and correction of errors. *The Quarterly Journal of Experimental Psychology*, 53A, 846–867.

Blandin, Y., Lhuisset, L. and Proteau, L. (1999). Cognitive processes underlying observational learning of motor skills. *The Quarterly Journal of Experimental Psychology*, 52A, 957–979.

Brooks, V., Hilperath, F., Brooks, M., Ross, H.-G. and Freund, H.-J. (1995). Learning 'what' and 'how' in a human motor task. *Learning and Memory*, 2, 225–243.

Brown, S. (1994) (cited in Rink, 1994). The effects of limited and repeated demonstrations of the development of fielding and throwing in children. Unpublished doctoral dissertation, The University of South Carolina.

Cadopi, M., Chatillon, J. F. and Baldy, R. (1995). Representation and performance: reproduction of form and quality of movement in dance by eight and eleven-year-old novices. *British Journal of Psychology*, 86, 217–225.

Carroll, W. R. and Bandura, A. (1982). The role of visual monitoring in observational learning of action patterns: making the unobservable observable. *Journal of Motor Behaviour*, 14, 153–167.

Carroll, W. R. and Bandura, A. (1985). Role of timing of visual monitoring and motor rehearsal in observational learning of action patterns. *Journal of Motor Behaviour*, 17, 69–81.

Carroll, W. R. and Bandura, A. (1990). Representational guidance of action production in observational learning: a causal analysis. *Journal of Motor Behaviour*, 22, 85–97.

Craik, F. I. M. and Lockhart, R. S. (1972). Levels of processing: a framework for memory research. *Journal of Verbal Learning and Verbal Behaviour*, 11, 671–684.

Davids, K., Bennett S., Handford C. and Jones B. (1999). Acquiring coordination in self-paced, extrinsic timing tasks: a constraints-led perspective. *International Journal of Sport Psychology*, 30, 437–461.

Fitts, P. M. (1964). Perceptual-motor skills learning. In A. W. Melton (Ed.), *Categories of human learning* (pp. 243–285). New York: Academic Press.

Fitts, P. M. and Posner, M. I. (1967). *Human performance.* Belmont, CA: Brooks/Cole.

Franks, I. M. and Maile, L. J. (1991). The use of video in sport skill acquisition. In P. W. Dowrick (Ed.), *Practical guide to using video in the behavioural sciences* (pp. 231–243). Oxford, England: John Wiley & Sons.

Franks, I. M. and Stanley, M. L. (1991). Learning the invariants of a perceptual motor skill. *Canadian Journal of Psychology,* 45, 303–320.

Gentile, A. M. (1972). A working model of skill acquisition to teaching. *Quest,* 17, 3–23.

Gentile, A. M. (1998). Implicit and explicit processes during acquisition of functional skills. *Scandinavian Journal of Occupational Therapy,* 5, 7–16.

Glaser, R. (1976). Components of a psychology of instruction: toward a science of design. *Reviews of Educational Research,* 46, 1–24.

Glaser, R. (1977). *Adaptive education: individual diversity and learning.* New York: Holt, Rinehart and Winston.

Goodale, M. A. and Milner, D. A. (1992). Separate visual pathways for perception and action. *Trends in Neurosciences,* 15, 20–25.

Goode, S. L., Meeuwsen, H. J. and Magill, R. A. (1998). Benefits of providing cognitive performance strategies to novice performers learning a complex motor skill. *Perceptual and Motor Skills,* 86, 976–978.

Green, T. D. and Flowers, J. H. (1991). Implicit versus explicit learning processes in a probabilistic, continuous fine-motor catching task. *Journal of Motor Behaviour,* 23, 293–300.

Haider, H. and Frensch, P. A. (1996). The role of information reduction in skill acquisition. *Cognitive Psychology,* 30, 304–337.

Hall, C., Moore, J., Annett, J. and Rodgers, W. (1997). Recalling demonstrated and guided movements using imaginary and verbal rehearsal strategies. *Research Quarterly for Exercise and Sport,* 68, 136–144.

Halverson, L. and Roberton, M. (1979). The effects of instruction on overhand throwing development in children. In G. Roberts and K. Newell (Eds), *Psychology of motor behaviour and sport – 1978* (pp. 258–269). Champaign, IL: Human Kinetics.

Hayes, S. J., Scott, M. A., Hodges, N. J., Horn, R. R., Smeeton, N. J. and Williams, A. M. (2003). How do children extract and use information from point-lights when performing unfamiliar movements: effects of perceptual training and task constraints. Paper presented at the North American Society of Sport Psychology and Physical Activity Conference in Savannah, Georgia.

Haywood, K. M. and Getchell, N. (2001). *Life-span motor development,* (3rd ed.). Champaign, IL: Human Kinetics.

Higgins, S. (1991). Motor skill acquisition. *Physical Therapy,* 71, 123–139.

Hodges, N. J. and Franks, I. M. (2000). Focus of attention and coordination bias: implications for learning a novel bimanual task. *Human Movement Science,* 19, 843–867.

Hodges, N. J. and Franks, I. M. (2001). Learning a coordination skill: interactive effects of instruction and feedback. *Research Quarterly for Exercise and Sport,* 72, 132–142.

Hodges, N. J. and Franks, I. M. (2002a). Learning as a function of coordination bias: building upon pre-practice behaviours. *Human Movement Science,* 21, 231–258.

Hodges, N. J. and Franks, I. M. (2002b). Modelling coaching practice: the role of instruction and demonstration. *Journal of Sports Sciences,* 20, 1–19.

Hodges, N. J. and Franks, I. M. (2003). The nature of feedback. In M. Hughes and I. M. Franks (Eds), *Notational analysis of sport* (2nd ed.). London: E & FN Spon (in press).

Hodges, N. J. and Lee, T. D. (1999). The role of augmented information prior to learning a bimanual visual-motor coordination task: do instructions of the movement pattern facilitate learning relative to discovery learning. *British Journal of Psychology*, 90, 389–403.

Hodges, N. J., Chua, R. and Franks, I. M. (2003a). The role of video in facilitating perception and action of a novel coordination movement. *Journal of Motor Behaviour*, 35, 247–260.

Hodges, N. J., Hayes, S. J., Eaves, D. L., Horn, R., and Williams, A. M. (2003b). Teaching soccer skills through ball-trajectory matching strategies. Paper presented at the Fifth World Congress for Science and Soccer, Lisbon, Portugal.

Hodges, N. J., Oakey, M., Mussell, L. and Franks, I. M. (2000). The role of visual information pertaining to ball flight when learning and performing a golf chip. *Journal of Sport and Exercise Psychology*, 22, S52.

Juaire, S. and Pargman, D. (1991). Pictures versus verbal instructions to assist the learning of a gross motor task. *Journal of Human Movement Studies*, 20, 189–200.

Karmiloff-Smith, A. (1992). *Beyond modularity: a developmental perspective on cognitive science*. Cambridge, MA: The MIT Press.

Kelso, J. A. S. (1995). *Dynamic patterns: the self-organization of brain and behaviour*. Cambridge, MA: MIT Press.

Kessler-Cooper, L. and Rothstein, A. L. (1981). Videotape replay and the learning of skills in open and closed environments. *Research Quarterly for Exercise and Sport*, 52, 191–199.

Kohl, R. M. and Shea, C. H. (1992). Pew (1966) revisited: acquisition of hierarchical control as a function of observational practice. *Journal of Motor Behaviour*, 24, 247–260.

Kunde, W., Hoffman, J. and Zellman, P. (2002). The impact of anticipated action effects on action planning. *Acta Psychologica*, 109, 137–155.

Landin, D. (1994). The role of verbal cues in skill learning. *Quest*, 46, 299–313.

Latash, M. L. (1996). The Bernstein problem: how does the central nervous system make its choices? In M. L Latash and M. T. Turvey (Eds), *Dexterity and its development with 'On dexterity and its development' by N. Bernstein* (pp. 277–303). Mahwah, NJ: LEA.

Latash, M. L. (1998). *Progress in motor control, Vol I: Bernstein's traditions in movement studies*. Champaign, IL: Human Kinetics.

Latash, M. L. and Turvey, M. T. (Eds) (1996). *Dexterity and its development with 'On dexterity and its development' by N. Bernstein*. Mahwah, NJ: LEA.

Lavisse, D., Deviterne, D. and Perrin, P. (2000). Mental processing in motor skill acquisition by young subjects. *International Journal of Sport Psychology*, 31, 364–375.

Lidor, R., Tennant, L. K. and Singer, R. N. (1996). The generalizability effect of three learning strategies across motor task performances. *International Journal of Sport Psychology*, 27, 23–36.

Magill, R. A. (2001). *Motor learning: concepts and applications* (6th ed.). Singapore: McGraw-Hill International Editions.

Magill, R. A. and Clark, R. (1997). Implicit versus explicit learning of pursuit-tracking patterns. *Journal of Sport and Exercise Psychology*, 19, S85.

Magill, R. A. and Schoenfelder-Zohdi, B. (1996). A visual model and knowledge of performance as sources of information for learning a rhythmic gymnastics skill. *International Journal of Sport Psychology*, 24, 358–369.

Martens, R., Burwitz, L. and Zuckerman, J. (1976). Modeling effects on motor performance. *Research Quarterly for Exercise and Sport*, 47, 277–291.

Masser, L. (1985). The effect of refinement of student achievement in a fundamental motor skill K-6. *Journal of Teaching in Physical Education*, 6, 174–182.

Masser, L. (1993). Critical cues help first grade students' achievement in handstands and forward rolls. *Journal of Teaching in Physical Education*, 12, 301–312.

Masters, R. S. W. (2000). Theoretical aspects of implicit learning in sport. *International Journal of Sport Psychology*, 31, 530–541.

McCullagh, P. and Weiss, M. R. (2001). Modeling: considerations for motor skill performance and psychological responses. In R. N. Singer, H. A. Hausenblas and C. M. Janelle (Eds), *Handbook of sport psychology* (2nd ed.) (pp. 205–238). New York: Wiley.

McCullagh, P., Stiehl, J. and Weiss, M. R. (1990). Developmental modeling effects on the qualitative and quantitative aspects of motor performance. *Research Quarterly for Exercise and Sport*, 61, 344–350.

Müller, H. and Loosch, E. (1999). Functional variability and in equifinal path of movement during targeted throwing. *Journal of Human Movement Studies*, 36, 103–126.

Newell, K. M. (1985). Coordination, control and skill. In D. Goodman, R. B. Wilberg and I. M. Franks (Eds), *Differing perspectives in motor learning, memory and control*. Amsterdam. Elsevier Science.

Newell, K. M. (1986). Constraints on the development of coordination. In M. G. Wade and H. T. A. Whiting (Eds), *Motor developments in children: aspects of coordination and control* (pp. 341–360). Boston: Martinus Nijhoff.

Newell, K. M., Carlton, M. J. and Antoniou, A. (1990). The interaction of criterion and feedback information in learning a drawing task. *Journal of Motor Behaviour*, 22, 8–20.

Newell, K. M., Morris, L. R. and Scully, D. M. (1985). Augmented information and the acquisition of skill in physical activity. In R. L. Terjung (Ed.), *Exercise and sport science reviews*, Vol. 13 (pp. 235–261). Santa Barbara, CA: Journal Publisher Affiliates.

Nouritt, D., Deschamps, T., Lauriot, B., Caillou, N. and Delignieres, D. (2000). The effects of required amplitude and practice on frequency stability and efficiency in a cyclical task. *Journal of Sports Sciences*, 18, 201–212.

Paivio, A. (1969). Mental imagery in associative learning and memory. *Psychological Review*, 76, 241–263.

Paivio, A. (1979). *Imagery and verbal processes*. Mahwah, NJ: Lawrence Erlbaum Associates.

Paivio, A. (1986). *Mental representations: a dual coding approach*. New York: Oxford University Press.

Peters, M. and Schwartz, S. (1989). Coordination of the two hands and effects of attention manipualtion in the production of a bimanual 2 : 3 polyrhythm. *Australian Journal of Psychology*, 41, 215–224.

Prinz, W. (1992). Why don't we perceive our brain states? *European Journal of Cognitive Psychology*, 4, 1–20.

Prinz, W. (1997). Perception and action planning. *European Journal of Cognitive Psychology*, 9, 129–154.

Rink, J. E. (1994). Task presentation in pedagogy. *Quest*, 46, 270–280.

van Rossum, J. H. A. (1987). *Motor development and practice: the variability of practice hypothesis in perspective*. Amsterdam: Free University Press.

Rothstein, A. L. and Arnold, R. K. (1976). Bridging the gap: application of research on videotape feedback and bowling. *Motor skills: Theory into Practice*, 1, 35–62.

Schmidt, R. A. (1975). A schema theory of discrete motor skill learning. *Psychological Review*, 82, 225–260.

Schmidt, R. A. (1991). Frequent augmented feedback can degrade learning: evidence and interpretations. In G. E. Stelmach and J. Requin (Eds), *Tutorials in motor neuroscience*. Dordrecht: Kluwer Academic Publishers.

Schmidt, R. A. (2001). Motor schema theory after 26 years: some reflections and future directions. *Journal of Sport and Exercise Psychology*, 23, S4.

Schmidt, R. A. and Wrisberg, C. A. (2000). *Motor learning and performance: a problem-based learning approach* (2nd ed.). Champaign, IL: Human Kinetics.

Schooler, J. W. and Engstler-Schooler, T. Y. (1990). Verbal overshadowing of visual memories: some things are better left unsaid. *Cognitive Psychology*, 22, 36–71.

Scully, D. and Carnegie, E. (1998). Observational learning in motor skill acquisition. *The Irish Journal of Psychology*, 19, 472–485.

Shapiro, K. L. and Schmidt. R. A. (1982). The schema theory: recent evidence and developmental implications. In J. A. S. Kelso and J. E. Clark (Eds), *The development of movement control and coordination* (pp. 113–150). New York: Wiley.

Sherwood, D. E. and Rios, V. (2001). Divided attention in bimanual aiming movements: effects on movement accuracy. *Research Quarterly for Exercise and Sport*, 72, 210–218.

Shiffrin, R. M. and Schneider, W. (1977). Controlled and automatic human information processing: II. Perceptual learning, automatic attending and a general theory. *Psychological Review*, 84, 127–190.

Singer, R. N., Lidor, R. and Cauraugh, J. H. (1993). To be aware or not aware: what to think about while learning and performing a motor skill. *Sport Psychologist*, 7, 19–30.

Snoddy, G. S. (1926). Learning and stability: a psychophysical analysis of a case of motor learning with clinical applications. *Journal of Applied Psychology*, 10, 1–36.

Snow, R. E. and Swanson, J. (1992). Instructional psychology: aptitude, adaptation, and assessment. *Annual Reviews of Psychology*, 43, 583–626.

Stanley, W. B., Mathews, R. C., Buss, R. R. and Kotler-Cope, S. (1989). Insight without awareness: on the interaction of verbalization, instruction and practice in a simulated process control task. *The Quarterly Journal of Experimental Psychology*, 41A, 553–577.

Summers, J. J. (2001). Practice and training in bimanual coordination tasks: strategies and constraints. *Brain and Cognition*, 48, 166–178.

Summers, J. J. and Kennedy, T. (1992). Strategies in the production of a 5:3 polyrhythm. *Human Movement Science*, 11, 101–112.

Swinnen, S. P. (1996). Information feedback for motor skill learning: a review. In H. N. Zelaznik (Ed.), *Advances in motor learning and control* (pp. 37–66). Champaign, IL: Human Kinetics.

Temprado, J. J., Zanone, P-G, Monno, A. and Laurent, M. (1999). Attentional load associated with performing and stabilizing preferred bimanual patterns. *Journal of Experimental Psychology: Human Perception and Performance*, 25, 1579–1594.

Todorov, E., Shadmehr, R. and Bizzi, E. (1997). Augmented feedback presented in a virtual environment accelerates learning of a difficult motor task. *Journal of Motor Behaviour*, 29, 147–158.

Vereijken, B. and Thelan, E. (1997). Training infant treadmill stepping: the role of individual pattern stability. *Developmental Psychobiology*, 30, 89–102.

Vereijken, B. and Whiting, H. T. A. (1989). In defense of discovery learning. In P. C. W Wieringen van and R. J. Bootsma (Eds), *Catching up*. Selected essays of H. T. A. Whiting (pp. 155–169). Amsterdam: Free University Press.

Vogt, S. (1996). The concept of event generation in movement imitation – neural and behavioural aspects. *Corpus, Psyche et Societas*, 3, 119–132.

Walter, C. B. and Swinnen, S. P. (1992). Adaptive tuning of interlimb attraction to facilitate bimanual decoupling. *Journal of Motor Behaviour*, 24, 95–104.

Weiss, M. R. and Klint, K. A. (1987). 'Show and tell' in the gymnasium: an investigation of developmental differences in modeling and verbal rehearsal of motor skills. *Research Quarterly for Exercise and Sport*, 58, 234–241.

Whiting, H. T. A. (Ed.) (1984). *Human motor actions: Bernstein reassessed*. Amsterdam: Elsevier.

Whiting, H. T. A. and den Brinker, B. P. L. M. (1982). Image of the act. In J. P. Das, R. F. Mulcahy and A. E. Wall (Eds), *Theory and research in learning disabilities* (pp. 217–235). New York: Plenum.

Whiting, H. T. A., Bijard, M. J. and den Brinker, B. P. L. M. (1987). The effect of the availability of a dynamic model on the acquisition of a complex cyclical action. *Quarterly Journal of Experimental Psychology*, 39A, 43–59.

Winograd, E. (1981). Elaboration and distinctiveness in memory for faces. *Journal of Experimental Psychology: Human Learning and Memory*, 7, 181–190.

Wishart, L. R., Lee, T. D. and Cunningham, S. J. (2001). Age-related differences and the role of augmented visual feedback in learning a bimanual coordination pattern. *Acta Psychologica*, 110, 247–263.

Wulf, G. and Prinz, W. (2001). Directing attention to movement effects enhances learning: a review. *Psychonomic Bulletin & Review*, 8, 648–660.

Wulf, G. and Schmidt, R. A. (1997). Variabiltiy of practice and implicit motor learning. *Journal of Experimental Psychology: Learning, Memory and Cognition*, 23, 987–1006.

Wulf, G., Höß, M. and Prinz, W. (1998). Instructions for motor learning: differential effects of internal versus external focus of attention. *Journal of Motor Behaviour*, 30, 169–179.

Wulf, G., Gärtner, M., McConnel, N. and Schwarz, A. (2002). Feedback and attentional focus: enhancing the learning of the volleyball serve through external-focus feedback. *Journal of Motor Behaviour*, 34, 171–182.

9   Observational learning

Is it time we took another look?

Robert R. Horn and A. Mark Williams

The transfer of information from instructor to learner is crucial for effective skill acquisition. The mode of delivering this information may take many different forms, but coaches require methods that convey lasting information with maximal efficiency. Demonstration is one method that appears to meet these expectations, and coaches and researchers alike often invoke the notion that 'a picture paints a thousand words' to portray its potential. Not surprisingly, demonstration is estimated to be the most commonly used mode of instruction in skill acquisition (Magill, 2001), a fact reflected in recent physical education texts. The most common teaching technique in physical education settings is *direct instruction* (Graham *et al.*, 2001) or *interactive teaching* (Rink, 1998) both of which consider that a demonstration is the first and arguably most significant stage of the skill acquisition process. In this chapter, we review contemporary research and theory to determine whether such confidence in demonstrations is well founded. Prevalent theories from cognitive and ecological accounts of learning are considered, and a critical review of the associated research provided. Finally, we highlight recent neuroscience research that questions theoretical premises from both cognitive and ecological perspectives. It is not our intention to provide a detailed review of the research literature on developmental and psychosocial issues and the effectiveness of demonstrations (for detailed reviews of these areas, see McCullagh and Weiss, 2001; Williams *et al.*, 1999).

Concepts of imitation and observational learning

In theoretical terms, a demonstration changes behaviour through processes such as *observational learning, imitation, emulation* and *echokinesis*. In the psychology literature, *imitation* is the prevalent term for copying behaviours. According to Miller and Dollard (1941), there are two types of behaviour that fall under the process of imitation. The first is *matched-dependent* behaviour, in which the 'follower' is dependent on the 'leader' for action, as only the leader has access to relevant environmental information. The second is *copying* in which the copier must adapt his/her response to be more like the model. For motor skill acquisition, the second of these is more appropriate. Heyes (2001) defined imitation as the copying by an observer of a component feature of the body movement of a model. This definition implies a causal relationship between the observation of the component feature of the model's movement, and the execution of the feature by the observer.

In addition to copying the movements of the body, a learner can also reproduce the movement of an object. This has been labelled *emulation* (Heyes, 2001; Tomasello *et al.*, 1993). Prinz (1987) presented a similar distinction between the imitation of perceived movements as spatio-temporal events, and actions, for which the intention is to attain the same goal states as the model, independent of the movement performed. For the copying of perceived movements, Prinz (1987) preferred the term *echokinesis* used by Katz (1960) as a specific type of ideo-motor action in which movement is imitated. Because goals can be emulated independently of specific movement patterns, Byrne and Russon (1998) ascribe this the lowest level in their hierarchical account of imitation. For them, the next level of imitation is *program level*, in which an observer copies the structural organization (including sub-routines) of the action, but specific details are added on a trial-and-error basis. This process is assumed to account for the majority of imitation occurring on an everyday basis. In the highest, *action*, level of imitation, a comprehensive, linear description of the act is acquired from the model.

What then is the difference, if any, between imitation and observational motor learning? Observational motor learning (also known as *modelling*) should not be simply considered as imitation within the specific arena of motor behaviour. Williams *et al.* (1999) define observational learning as the process by which observers watch the behaviour of another, and adapt their own behaviour as a result of the interaction. Though imitation (or emulation) is clearly the core process, observational learning is more relevant for the study of skill acquisition because in measuring learning it accounts for long-term changes in behaviour. Observational learning and imitation are also assessed in a different manner. Imitation is typically measured using frequency counts as a dichotomous measure of whether or not the desired behaviour is present (e.g. Bandura's *Bobo Doll* experiments: Bandura *et al.*, 1961). In contrast, observational learning is assessed using specific qualitative and quantitative measures of performance. Furthermore, in observational learning, changes in behaviour are directional. Learning occurs if performance has improved with reference to a pre-determined criterion goal.

Cognitive accounts of observational learning

According to Bandura (1971), the earliest accounts of observational learning by Morgan (1896) and McDougall (1908) amongst others, described imitation as an innate propensity. As such, the empirical testing of observational learning was stifled. Following the denouncement of the instinct doctrine, imitation was described in connectionist terms. Miller and Dollard's (1941) *Social Learning and Imitation* theory applied behaviourism and reinforcement to the study of imitative behaviours. In their experiments, participants displayed matched-dependent behaviour. This describes the effect where the rewarding of a model's specific behaviour, coupled with the rewarding of the participant for repeating the behaviour, results in powerful imitation that can be generalized to other situations and models.

Behaviourist accounts were deemed inappropriate for observational learning due to their failure to recognize the influence of mediating factors that are internal to the organism. Moreover, behaviourism fails to explain how a new matching behaviour is acquired through observation in the first instance (Bandura, 1971). Finally, behaviourist accounts are not applicable to learning from observation where the observer does not overtly perform the model's actions in the environment in which they were demonstrated, where reinforcements are not administered, and when the acquired responses are not displayed until a later time when the model is not present (Bandura, 1971).

Sheffield (1961) first broke from traditional behaviourist accounts of stimulus–response reinforcement. His Systematic Representational Theory was developed to assess the effectiveness of filmed demonstrations in the learning of mechanical assembly tasks, and represents a vital step toward a testable theory of learning in complex human motor skills. It supposes that when observing a skill, the observer formulates a cognitive representation of the action through processes of association and contiguity. The cognitive representation subsequently acts as a *blueprint* to guide reproduction of the skill.

Bandura's (1986a,b) social cognitive theory

Although Sheffield's theory of cognitive symbolic representation preceded the work of Bandura, it is Bandura's Social Learning Theory (later revised to Social Cognitive Theory in 1986) that has been the foundation of the majority of research on observational learning. Bandura (1969, 1971, 1977, 1986a) incorporated Sheffield's idea of systematic representation, but expanded its scope to account for the acquisition and modification of behaviour and social skills (Williams *et al.*, 1999). Bandura concurred that behaviour is stored in representational form, with this representation being used to mediate the action response. However, unlike Sheffield, he considered that in many instances a learner observes a model without performing any concurrent response. The modelled response is acquired in representational, cognitive form before being acted out. Bandura (1965) designated this 'no-trial learning', and it echoes his rejection of behaviourist accounts of modelling through repeated reinforcement.

According to Bandura (1971), the sub-processes of *attention, retention (behaviour) production* and *motivation* govern the observational learning process. He also argued that a good theory of vicarious learning should explain why observers show different levels of response acquisition when exposed to the identical stimuli. Figure 9.1 highlights the four sub-processes and internal mediators such as cognitive capabilities and past experience.

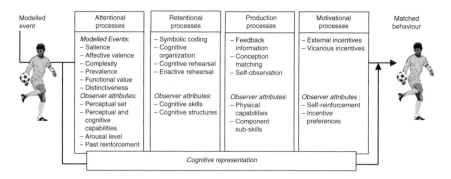

Figure 9.1 The sub-processes of observational learning according to Bandura's (1986) Social Cognitive Theory (adapted from Bandura, 1986).

Bandura (1977) believed that attention represents the start of the modelling process; we cannot learn unless we attend to and accurately perceive the significant features in the display. Attention was considered a selective mechanism that determines which information will constitute the cognitive representation of the skill. The basis of this selection of information was considered to be both externally and internally determined, based on various features of the demonstration (e.g. speed, distinctiveness) and the observer (e.g. level of arousal). Also relevant is the extent to which the learner can *associate* the observed behaviour with previous experiences, and the *functional value* of the display. Bandura (1977) hypothesized that observers pay closer attention to models that possess symbols reflecting status, are older and are highly skilled. This hypothesis has been the basis of the majority of research on observational learning.

The selective mechanisms of attention are redundant unless the observer can store the information in representational form. Bandura (1977) assumed two representational systems achieve this within the sub-process of retention, namely, the *imaginal and verbal systems*. Similar to Sheffield's (1961) concept of a perceptual blueprint, sequences of corresponding sensory experiences become associated or integrated in the imaginal system (Bower and Hilgard, 1981), resulting in the formation of enduring and retrievable representations. The cognitive processes that regulate behaviour are assumed to be verbal and are thus the domain of the *verbal system*. The process of verbal coding allows *chunking* of information in a format that facilitates memory.

Rehearsal is an additional factor in retention processes. Bandura (1971) argued that covert, mental rehearsal facilitates learning not through simple repetition, but through active processes. Overt physical practice was given little consideration in Bandura's analysis, although he did note that practice helps stabilize and strengthen the acquired response. According to Jeffrey (1976), effective observational learning is achieved by initially mentally organizing and rehearsing the skill and then by overt practice.

Collectively, the sub-functions of attention and retention represent a *response-acquisition* phase, in which the to-be-imitated behaviour is acquired and coded for action (Bandura, 1986b). The remaining two sub-functions of *motor production* and *motivation* were labelled as the *response production phase*, representing the translation of the acquired movement into action. The process of *motor (behavioural) production* refers to the conception-matching mechanisms that convert a cognitive representation of behaviour into approximate overt performance, and guide later reproductions of the skill. A feedback mechanism is employed to determine discrepancies between the symbolic representation and physical enactment of the skill, which in turn provides cues for corrective action (Bandura, 1977). Bandura (1971) indicated that the physical capabilities of the learner are a limiting factor in this sub-process. An observer may acquire a representation of the skill, but might not possess the physical attributes to replicate the task. Typically, researchers do not assess whether participants possess the necessary physical attributes, and assume that deficiencies in performance reflect problems in perception rather than action.

The final sub-process involved in observational learning is *motivation*. According to Bandura (1971), incentives act to regulate the overt expression of the matching behaviour, exert a selective control over the cues in the demonstration to which the observer attends, and aid selective retention by activating the deliberate coding and rehearsal of the response.

A review of research underpinned by social cognitive theory

The research work relating to Social Cognitive Theory includes manipulations of model type and tests of cognitive involvement in observational learning.

Model characteristics

The majority of observational learning research has manipulated the type of model presented to the participant. Particularly prevalent are tests of Bandura's (1977) prediction that observers pay closer attention to models that have a higher status, are more skilled and of the same gender as themselves.

STATUS

Lefkowitz *et al.* (1955) illustrated the impact of social status on imitative actions. A jaywalking model 'planted' on a busy street corner was followed by significantly more people when dressed in business attire than when dressed in soiled clothes. In a motor learning context, McCullagh (1986) found that participants performed significantly better on the *Bachman Ladder* task in response to a high compared with a low status model. The Bachman Ladder task involves a 6-foot wooden ladder with three uprights. The number of rungs climbed by the learner before the ladder falls to the ground is taken as a measure of performance.

SKILL LEVEL

In Bandura's analysis, the cognitive representation formed should correspond to a perfect performance of the skill. As such, a highly skilled model is recommended. In early tests of this prediction, Landers and Landers (1973) used the Bachman Ladder with fifth and sixth grade children. The model manipulations were skill level (skilled/unskilled) and status (teacher/peer). Participants who observed the skilled teacher climbed the most rungs on the ladder. However, a main effect for skill level was not observed. Participants who viewed the unskilled peer model recorded higher scores than the skilled peer model. Lirgg and Feltz (1991) replicated this study with sixth grade children, combining model skill level and status with videotaped rather than live models. Participants performed better after observing a skilled model. No model type by skill level interaction was reported.

Several authors have questioned whether expert models are more effective than learning models (e.g. see McCullagh and Caird, 1990; Pollock and Lee, 1992). They note that information processing based theories such as Adams' (1971) closed-loop theory and Schmidt's (1975) schema theory, view motor learning as a problem-solving process. In this process, feedback is received, and action is adjusted on a trial-and-error basis. As such, the provision of an expert model may be at odds with the problem-solving process, as no error information is provided (Pollock and Lee, 1992).

GENDER

Studies involving non-motor specific tasks suggest that elementary aged school-boys learn more about the behaviour of a same sex rather than an opposite sex model (e.g. Grusec and Brinker, 1972). Similar results have been found in the motor domain for ball-snatch tasks (Feltz and Landers, 1977; Gould, 1978). These results were explained in terms of motivation to emulate the model (Gould and Roberts, 1982). Gould and Weiss (1981) used a leg extension endurance test to investigate the effects of model–observer similarity in athletic ability and gender. Women observing a non-athletic, female (similar) model performed better than those watching an athletic, male (dissimilar) model. In an attempt to separate these factors, George et al. (1992) found that similarity in athletic ability, and not model gender, was responsible for the effects. However, Griffin and Meaney (2000) found that gender did influence learning in a scarf-juggling task. While no differences occurred in retention or transfer of the skill, female participants learned significantly more strategies as a result of viewing same sex rather than opposite sex models. Also, the authors replicated the finding that participants learned more strategies from a learning rather than a skilled model.

Research evidence for cognitive involvement in observational learning

REPETITION

There is evidence supporting the role of cognitive representations in observational learning, based upon the tenet that clearer or stronger cognitive representations will yield greater learning. In the last of a series of experiments using semaphore-like arm-paddle movements, Carroll and Bandura (1990) compared the effects of viewing two or eight demonstrations, with and without verbal coding of the pattern. Cognitive representation was assessed using a recognition test to detect correct photographs of the movement, and by pictorial arrangement tests to assess memory of the appropriate movement sequence. Eight presentations yielded a more accurate cognitive representation of the action than did two presentations. Reproductions of the movement were also significantly more accurate with the higher number of demonstrations. Moreover, verbal coding facilitated learning only when the higher number of demonstrations was provided, suggesting that a clear cognitive blueprint of the act is required before cognitive processes aiding retention can be effective.

Several researchers have indicated the benefit of multiple demonstrations with adult participants using the Bachman Ladder task (Feltz, 1982), perceptual modeling with the Bassin anticipation timer (Weeks, 1992; Weeks and Choi, 1992), and a wiffle-golf task (Sidaway and Hand, 1993). Similar results have been reported with children using a sequential movement task (Weiss and Klint, 1987) and a softball pitch (Weise-Bjornstal and Weiss, 1992). However, the relationship between performance and number of demonstrations is not monotonic. For example, Weeks and Choi (1992) found ten pre-practice demonstrations facilitated acquisition performance, while one or five demonstrations did not provide sufficient time or exposure for the formation of a usable cognitive representation.

COGNITIVE STRATEGIES

Researchers who have examined the effects on performance of cognitive strategies such as coding and imagery have also provided support for the cognitive nature of observational learning. Gerst (1971) found that imaginal coding, in which the learners imagine themselves performing the task, facilitated the acquisition of sign language. Similarly, Jeffrey (1976) found imaginal coding to aid learning of complex three-dimensional construction tasks. Assigning symbolic codes to movements (in the form of numbers or letters), and symbolic rehearsal have also resulted in significantly greater immediate and delayed retention of performance (e.g. Bandura and Jeffrey, 1973; Carroll and Bandura, 1990).

CONCURRENT MONITORING

According to Social Cognitive Theory, concurrent monitoring of performance and augmented feedback are presumed to improve reproduction via conception-matching processes. In support of this proposal, Carroll and Bandura (1985) found that concurrent monitoring of a movement skill facilitated learning, while delayed monitoring (shown after 100 seconds) was not facilitative, implying that the delay led to deterioration in the conception-matching process. McCullagh (1993) proposed that split-screen techniques could be employed to display the model's template movements simultaneously with the participant's own imitative attempts. However, assessment of this proposal has produced inconclusive results (see Laguna, 1996).

VARIABILITY OF DEMONSTRATION AND COGNITIVE LOAD

The cognitive processes underlying observational learning have also been addressed with reference to concepts of practice variability and contextual interference. According to Lee and Magill's (1985) *action plan reconstruction hypothesis*, high variability in practice leads to greater learning because the variability necessitates the reconstruction of action plans from one trial to the next. In observational learning, Lee and White (1990) suggested that observing a model performing under highly variable conditions mimics this process, leading to greater cognitive involvement on the part of the learner. Blandin *et al.* (1994) using a barrier knockdown task and Wright *et al.* (1997, 2001) using computer key sequencing tasks have provided support for this proposal. In the studies by Wright and colleagues, the contextual interference effect was replicated. Participants observing models performing under high variability showed better retention than those watching models performing under blocked practice.

Social cognitive theory: cause for concern

Social Cognitive Theory has undoubtedly advanced our understanding of the mechanisms involved in observational learning. Yet, there are some significant limitations with the theory and its supporting research. A fundamental concern has been that it is based on social rather than motoric learning (e.g. McCullagh *et al.*, 1989; Williams, 1993). Horn *et al.* (2002) have argued that the mechanisms of motoric and social learning are likely to be disparate. Social learning tends to prescribe to the aforementioned description of imitation, in that measurement tends to be dichotomous (present or not present), somewhat coarse, and non-directional. In contrast, motor learning involves a precise directional change in behaviour and in the qualitative mechanisms underpinning these changes.

Central to Social Cognitive Theory is the concept of a cognitive representation. Williams *et al.* (1999) have argued that this concept has never been fully elaborated, such that the nature and location of these representations are somewhat nebulous. There are also concerns with the use of recognition tests as valid measures of the existence of cognitive representations. In presenting images of the act from which participants must choose the one that they observed, this presupposes that the cognitive representation is some form of reference of correctness, similar to that suggested by Adams (1971). A recognition test performed after experimental trials naturally invokes memory of the task. Thus, it is a test of the subcomponent of retention. Bandura's notion of coding would suggest that the imaginal system accounts for matching between an internal representation and an external image. Yet, Bandura suggests that most coding occurs in verbal form. The conceptual links between the two systems have not been established.

While sequential tasks such as arm paddle movements lend themselves to memorial coding strategies, without which they perhaps could not be performed, an important question is whether such coding can guide the performance of complex multi-limb coordinative actions. If cognitive representations of these skills are found to be poorly developed, it suggests that the cognitive representations of the skills in Carroll and Bandura's studies may not be a kinematic representation of the act that covertly *guides* the skill, but a simple symbolic code.

Few studies have used kinematic measures of learning in conjunction with inference of cognitive representations via recognition tests. One notable exception by Weise-Bjornstal and Weiss (1992) measured kinematic variables and applied a recognition test at the end of each trial block during acquisition. The results suggest that for children at least, the addition of verbal cues to a pre-existing visual model resulted in the greatest increase in the recognition of correct form. No clear relationship between recognition and form scores was reported.

Research related to Social Cognitive Theory has typically measured learning by outcome rather than process measures of performance. Horn *et al.* (2002) suggest that this may have contributed to some equivocal findings in observational learning. Clearly, the addition of process measures increases measurement sensitivity. Moreover, if performance is measured by outcomes without reference to the movement pattern employed, then the model can become a redundant source of information. The learner may engage in emulative processes, or engage an existing movement pattern to maximize outcome performance under the guidance of intrinsic or extrinsically derived knowledge of results.

Byrne and Russon (1998, p. 668) describe novelty as a 'cardinal requirement of imitation'. However, in observational learning, several studies have ensured task novelty at the expense of ecological validity. Most of the tasks employed have been somewhat manufactured and simplistic. Such tasks include ball-rolling (Martens *et al.*, 1976), ladder climbing (Landers and Landers, 1973), knocking down barriers (Blandin and Proteau, 2000), horizontal positioning (Bird and Rickli, 1983), coincident anticipation (Weeks, 1992), and computer based tracking (Pollock and Lee, 1992) and sequencing (Wright *et al.*, 1997). It is also worth noting that when teaching sports skills to beginners, such skills are rarely 'novel' since it is likely that learners will already have had some exposure to the skill, mainly through the vicarious learning opportunities provided by watching others participating in the sport.

The social cognitive approach to observational learning emerged while information processing theory prevailed in motor behaviour. However, theoretical shifts toward ecological theories of perception and action have been commonplace in the last 20 years. To complement these developments, it has been argued that research should examine complex motor skills in settings mimicking their ecology. Outcome scores are discouraged in favour of the analysis of changes in coordination in an interdisciplinary manner (e.g. Christina, 1987; Williams *et al.*, 1999).

Scully and Newell (1985) have provided the most significant criticism of Bandura's work arguing that the theory merely focuses on *how* the process of observational learning occurs, and does not address the question of *what* information is perceived and used in the process. For example, even in Bandura's subprocess of attention, where *what* information ought to be a factor, concepts such as functional value, salience and distinctiveness relate to *how* much attention is allotted. An interest in the nature of information taken from the model was the driving force behind Scully and Newell's ecological view of modelling, known as the *visual perception perspective*.

An ecological alternative to cognitive accounts: the *visual perception perspective*

Direct perception and 'what' information

Scully and Newell's belief that a theory should focus upon what information is used rather than how the process works is a concept attributable to James Gibson's theory of direct perception (1950, 1979). Gibson rejected Helmholtz's notion that since the retina of the eye yields two-dimensional information of a three-dimensional world, information processing (epistemic mediation) is required to translate and make sense of incoming information. Gibson believed that the visual system has the ability to directly 'pick up' information in the visual field, via the structure of light in the 'optic array'. Features such as texture, relative position, and affordances (i.e. what the environment offers the perceiver in action-relevant terms; Williams *et al.*, 1999) are directly and unambiguously specified without recourse to information processing. Moreover, Gibson's notion of mutual interdependency, meaning that information perceived is functionally specific for the action that follows, promotes the concept of perception–action coupling.

Scully and Newell also drew upon Gibson's view that motion is essential to seeing. When we observe movement, three perceivable types of motion are available. Absolute motion describes the motion of a single element in a configuration relative to the perceiver. Common motion describes the motion common to all elements in the configuration relative to the perceiver. Relative motion is motion of all the elements in the configuration relative to each other. Considerable evidence from studies involving *biological* and non-biological motion points towards our preference for relative motion information.

Biological motion perception

To study the perception of human motion, Johansson (1971) revived Marey's (1895/1972) point-light technique. This procedure removes structural information, presenting only moving dots (point-lights) or strips (patch-lights) of light against a black background. Johansson (1971, 1973, 1975) found that events that were not discernable when the points of light were static were immediately salient when motion was introduced. When viewing point-light displays, humans can identify gender (Barclay *et al.*, 1978; Mather and Murdoch, 1994; Stevenage *et al.*, 1999), friends (Cutting and Kozlowski, 1977), different animal species (Mather and West, 1993), and American sign language (Poizner *et al.*, 1981). Intention and emotion may also be perceived from point-light displays. Bassili (1978) showed that patches of reflective tape placed on the face facilitated the recognition of expressions of emotion. Participants can also recognize emotion portrayed in dance (Brownlow *et al.*, 1997; Dittrich *et al.*, 1996), aesthetic quality from gymnastics (Scully, 1986), and affordances for actions (estimated optimal and maximal seat heights; Stoffregen *et al.*, 1999).

In Scully and Newell's (1985) analysis, relative motion has a fundamental role in observational learning. When observers watch a demonstration, they are assumed to perceive and minimize relative motion of the event. In subsequent attempts to re-enact the observed movement pattern, the relative motion is believed to constrain the emergence of coordination via its informational and instructional properties (see Warren, 1990). Scully and Newell's (1985) perspective is best understood in conjunction with Newell's (1985) embedded hierarchy of coordination, control and skill. Newell operationalized the concepts first presented by Kugler *et al.* (1980). Coordination represents the assembly of a novel movement topology. Control is the parameterization, or scaling of the movement pattern. Finally, skill represents the optimal, flexible scaling of the movement pattern. As an embedded hierarchy, learners do not progress serially through coordination and control *stages*. Instead, they operate synergistically such that coordination is the organization of control. However, in early learning of an observed movement pattern, the dominant function appears to be coordination. As such Scully and Newell (1985) estimate that the influence of a model's relative motion pattern is greatest at this stage. When a learner approximates the model's relative motion pattern within 'certain bandwidths', this is considered to indicate that the action has been modelled (Scully and Newell, 1985). Learners are assumed to emphasize the scaling of the movement pattern with extended practice. In this period of skill acquisition, the exploration of the dynamics of the task is emphasized and demonstration is presumed to be less effective (Scully and Newell, 1985).

Few researchers have tested Scully and Newell's predictions. A credible reason for this is that it requires kinematic data for the direct comparison of model and learner movement patterns. While measures of movement form have been calculated, the typical method has been to analyse movement qualitatively or, at best, using subjective measures of movement form such as rating scales (e.g. see Cadopi *et al.*, 1995;

Ille and Cadopi, 1995; Magill and Schoenfelder-Zhodi, 1996; McCullagh and Meyer, 1997). Although this type of analysis provides a gross estimation of changes in movement form, objective and quantitative assessment of movement kinematics is required to identify specific changes in timing and spatial orientation as a function of practice. An additional concern is that many researchers have used pre-existing movement patterns for which the task for the learner is to scale an existing movement pattern (Southard and Higgins, 1987). Newell (1985) argues that these studies do not address the acquisition of coordination.

Comparisons of learning by modelling and discovery methods

Some evidence for the visual perception perspective is provided in studies where the performance of a group that observes a model is compared to that of a control group encouraged to learn through discovery. Whiting *et al.* (1987) found that observing a model was more beneficial than discovery learning on a ski-simulator task. Participants in the modelling group were more fluent and consistent in their movements. Using the same task, Schoenfelder-Zhodi (1992) compared participants' relative motion changes with the model's pattern. Those who observed a model illustrated changes in relative motion to become more like the model after practice than those learning by discovery methods.

For an underarm dart throw, Al-Abood *et al.* (2001a) found that a model conveyed the relative motion more effectively than discovery learning or verbal guidance. This study made a considerable contribution to observational learning research by quantifying coordination relative to the model using chain encoding and cross-correlation techniques. Finally, Horn *et al.* (in press) found that in the absence of intrinsic visual knowledge of results, observers of models in video or point-light form rapidly and enduringly imitated the relative motion of a soccer chip. The authors adapted the normalized root mean square (NoRMS) error technique (Sidaway *et al.*, 1995) that assesses variability in movement patterns, to quantify coordination in terms of proximity to the model's relative motion. This measure is termed normalized root mean difference (NoRM-D). No change in proximity to the model's relative motion at the knee–hip or knee–ankle was reported for those participants who did not see the model (for a recent review of techniques for quantifying coordination, see Mullineaux *et al.*, 2001).

The coordinative versus control-based role of demonstration

In accordance with the predictions of the visual perception perspective, Scully and Carnegie (1998) found evidence in support of the role of demonstration in conveying coordinative rather than control-based information. Participants observing a ballet sequence successfully approximated the model's landing position, angular displacement and relative timing, but were unable to replicate forces at take-off or landing.

Horn *et al.* (submitted) found that while control-based information was picked up from a demonstration, the model's relative motion pattern contributes to neither the perception nor reproduction of the event. Participants were presented with point-light displays of a model bowling a medicine ball to four unknown, evenly spaced distances. The participants' perceived and re-enacted distances were highly correlated with actual distances. The model's four relative motion plots were analysed for a consistent, systematic pattern that could act as the basis for this accurate perception. In Figure 9.2(a), shoulder–elbow relative motion shows no such systematic pattern. With the addition of velocity information in (b), the shoulder phase-portrait yields a more consistent pattern around ball release. However, an organized pattern is most evident in shoulder angular velocity (c) around ball release (d). Participants appeared to abstract systematic velocity information from this small window of time rather than relative motion information per se. In addition, the role of relative motion was further negated in this study when slow motion presentations significantly affected perceived distances, despite the fact that in these images relative motion information was maintained.

This study, and others involving the perception of lifted weight (e.g. Shim and Carlton, 1997), suggests that the role of demonstration in conveying control-based dynamic information may be less limited than proposed by Scully and Newell (1985). They argue that demonstration does not act to parameterize a movement since this requires practice to overcome specific individual constraints. The opposing view of Runeson *et al.* (2000) is that it may be more meaningful to perceive the underlying *dynamic* rather than the kinematic properties of movement, since the causal dynamics contain action-relevant information that is more enduring in nature. Although research is required to clarify this issue, Horn *et al.* (submitted) suggest that while relative motion acts to constrain the assembly of a movement, it may have no role in its parameterization.

The role of motion

There is evidence in support of the importance of motion in observational learning. Gray *et al.* (1991) reported significantly better reproduction of ballet sequences from point-light displays than from a series of still images. Furthermore, in instances when the original speed of demonstration is reduced, but relative timing is intact, the learning of complex multi-limb coordination has not been affected in some cases (e.g. Fehres and Olivier, 1986, gymnastic movements; Scully and Carnegie, 1998, ballet routine). In contrast, in tasks where the absolute speed of the movement is a critical feature, movement reproduction is impeded by changes in demonstration speed (e.g. Al-Abood *et al.*, 2001b; Williams, 1989b).

Video versus point-light models

Runeson (1984) has hypothesized that the absence of structural information in point-light facilitates the perception of motion because the removal of non-essential information leaves relative motion salient. Pellechia and Garrett (1997)

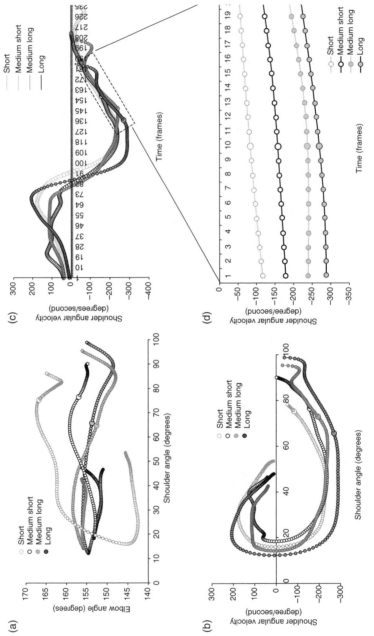

Figure 9.2 Model's relative motion (a), shoulder phase portrait (b), shoulder angular velocity throughout the motion (c), and around ball release (d), when bowling to four evenly distributed points (oversized markers represent ball release).

have presented some support for this notion in physical therapy. The assessment of lumbar stabilization was shown to be more reliable from point-light rather than video displays. In learning studies though, a clear pattern of results has not emerged. Romack (1995) found a detrimental impact of a point-light model for children learning to dribble a basketball. After 6 days of acquisition, those observing the point-light model completed fewer consecutive bounces than those observing a video model or no model. They also illustrated poorer phasing between the ball and the hand. This result was questionable due to differences in the phasing information afforded in the video and point-light conditions.

A follow-up study designed to eradicate this inconsistency continued to show superior outcome scores from the video rather than point light (PLD) display (Romack and Briggs, 1998). Scully and Carnegie (1998) obtained more favourable results for learning of a ballet movement. Participants observing a point-light model demonstrated more accurate landing positions, and closer imitation of the model's angular displacement and relative timing than those observing a video model. In our own work, looking at the acquisition of a soccer-chip, both video and point-light models have yielded similar findings in terms of outcome attainment and the reproduction of movement form. Horn et al. (2002) compared the effects of viewing a point-light model, a video model, and no model on the outcome (radial and variable error) and movement form. Coordination was assessed at a *local* intra-limb level (knee–hip and knee–ankle), and at a more global level the number of steps adopted in approach to the ball was measured. Although participants learned to reduce error and variability in their outcomes, no differences were found between groups. For measures of coordination, no differences were found at the intra-limb level. However, both modelling groups learned the correct approach to the ball, while the control group showed no change with practice.

Horn et al. (2002) considered that the presence of intrinsic feedback (i.e. vision as to where the ball landed) acted as the constraining source of information guiding learning. Therefore, to constrain participants to use the model as their primary information source, Horn et al. (in press) removed intrinsic visual and auditory knowledge of results (KR) by occluding vision immediately after contact with the ball. In comparison to the pre-test scores, participants who observed a model changed their knee–hip and knee–ankle relative motion to become more like the model. In contrast, no changes were found for the control group. Data from a single participant from the video group, and her corresponding proximity (NoRM-D) and variability (NoRMS) data are presented in Figure 9.3. At each test period, three of the participants' trials are superimposed over the model's (darker) criterion plot. Each angle–angle plot represents relative motion at the knee (y-axis)–ankle (x-axis). Graph (a) indicates proximity to the model's pattern (where lower NoRM-D represents closer modelling) and illustrates that a large change in proximity of the participants' coordination to the model occurred from the pre-test to the first period of acquisition and this change was maintained across remaining periods. Graph (b) indicates variability, where lower NoRMS represents greater consistency. Despite maximizing the saliency of the model (and perhaps, therefore, access to relative motion

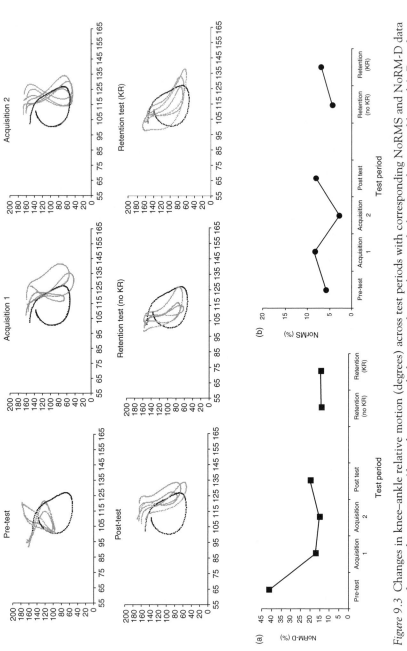

Figure 9.3 Changes in knee–ankle relative motion (degrees) across test periods with corresponding NoRMS and NoRM-D data for a single participant (for each test period, the vertical axis = knee angle, horizontal axis = ankle angle). Data from Horn *et al.* (in press). *Journal of Motor Behavior.*

information) by removing intrinsic KR, no differences were found between participants observing video and point-light models.

Techniques to determine 'what' information

In addition to comparing learning from point-light and video sources, researchers have employed two techniques common to the expertise literature to elucidate what information is picked up from demonstrations. These are visual search and event occlusion techniques (for a detailed review of these methods, see Williams *et al.*, 1999). Typically, visual search behaviour is assessed using an eye movement registration technique. For example, Williams (1989c) classified participants as trackers or saccaders based on their natural observation patterns. Prior to viewing a demonstration of a dart-throwing movement, participants were instructed to observe the action in the manner opposite to their natural tendency. Those who typically used visual saccades used smooth pursuit movements, while those typically using smooth pursuit eye movements performed saccades. Participants illustrated more error in reproducing the movement sequence compared to matched controls. de la Pena *et al.* (2000) reported some evidence for differences in visual search behaviours in response to observation of point-light, video and stick-figure models of a basketball free throw. The point-light model was purported to produce the optimal search pattern.

Horn *et al.* (2002) assessed visual search during observation of a soccer chip. The design alternated three periods of observation (point-light and video models) with three periods of acquisition. In the presence of intrinsic KR, participants showed a pattern of progressive refinement of visual search, evidenced by longer fixations to fewer areas of the display (Horn *et al.*, 2002). The suggestion is that the perceptual system first seeks an overall or, global representation of the task, before later seeking information with which to refine the movement. No significant differences in search patterns were found between participants who viewed the PLD model and those who observed the video model, contrary to the initial prediction that participants viewing a PLD model would employ a more refined search pattern.

In a follow-up study without intrinsic visual KR, Horn *et al.* (in press) did not find evidence for progressive refinement of search across viewing periods. This may be explained in tandem with changes in coordination. Participants in the original study failed to show significant change in intra-limb relative motion in the presence of intrinsic KR. However, in the follow-up, without intrinsic KR, changes in relative motion were immediate. As a result of the increased salience of the demonstration, participants were assumed to be immediately refining an established movement pattern, and consequently, there were no subsequent changes in search behaviour.

The spatial or event occlusion technique has been used relatively infrequently in observational learning research. In this approach, sources of information that are presumed to be important are occluded for the duration of the trial. If performance is degraded when a particular area or information cue is occluded, then it is inferred that this region is important for successful task performance. The scale of performance decrement is assumed to be indicative of the relative importance of different information cues. The paucity of work using this technique is disappointing because by systematically removing sources of information in the display, and assessing changes in imitative behaviour, this method can directly address the sources of information used by the learner. Mather et al. (1992) used this approach to illustrate that perception of gait in point-light form was more dependent on points that travelled furthest than points such as the hips and shoulders. Similarly, Scully and Carnegie (1998) adapted their point-light display of ballet movement by removing the markers representing the toes and ankle. The removal of these markers was detrimental to the skill acquisition process indicating that information from the ankles and toes was critical to perceiving and reproducing the movement.

The visual perception perspective: cause for concern

As with Social Cognitive Theory, the visual perception perspective may be criticized for providing few testable hypotheses. It has also been portrayed as providing a simplistic and incomplete account of learning (e.g. Bandura, 1997). The key shortcoming is its description of how the pick-up of relative motion is translated into action. Al-Abood et al. (2001b) breached this gap using concepts common to ecological accounts of learning. They argued that the informational and instructional constraints imposed by the relative motion pattern guide a learner's search for motor solutions in the 'perceptual motor workspace' (defined as 'a metaphorical description of the emergence of coordination as a movement system flows through its state space seeking stability', Williams et al., 1999, p. 260). The concept of the learner 'searching for' and 'assembling' an optimal task solution is, however, at odds with some recent findings. Horn et al. (in press) found that when intrinsic KR was removed, participants significantly changed their relative motion pattern to become more like the model within the first three trials of acquisition. Horn et al. (in prep.) reported similar results using a novel throwing action (based upon a reverse baseball pitch). These studies imply that when constrained to use a model as the primary source of information, early acquisition (i.e. the first three trials after the demonstration) may involve the process of refining an existing movement pattern (i.e. control) rather than searching for a new one (i.e. coordination).

Finally, Scully and Newell's (1985) concept that learning occurs when relative motion approximates the model within 'certain bandwidths' remains unclear. This may represent one of the most important challenges for researchers in the visual perception perspective. At present, the perceptual system's degree of sensitivity to relative motion is not known. Several authors suggest that imitation of action primarily operates in a manner described variously as holistic (Scully and Carnegie, 1998), global (Bertenthal and Pinto, 1994; Horn et al., 2002) or program level (Russon and Byrne, 1998). These imply that perception of relative motion in a localized sense may not be well developed. In corroboration, Oram and Perett (1994) found cells in anterior temporal lobe that were sensitive only to whole body motion and not localized motion in single arm articulation. The authors suggested that sensitivity to biological motion is not readily accounted for in terms of isolated patterns of relative motion. Attempts to determine the boundaries of perceptual sensitivity are underway (e.g. Sparrow *et al.*, 2002). A systematic analysis using the methods of psychophysics may better define what action responses are attainable based on the sensitivity of the perceptual system.

From motor imagery to mirror neurons: the impact of recent neuroscience developments on observational learning theory

Of great significance to theories of observational learning are concepts of shared neural substrates for perception, action-imitation, motor imagery and enactive mediation. Jeannerod (1994) suggested that in light of evidence for shared processes of visual imagery and actual vision, mental simulation of motor action (i.e. motor imagery) may share neural substrates with execution of the actual motor action. In support of this argument, Decety *et al.* (1994) and Stephan *et al.* (1995) have employed positron emission tomography and functional magnetic resonance imaging to indicate the complex involvement of the cerebellum, pre-motor cortex and inferior parietal lobe during imagery. Decety and Grezes (1999) report that implicit motor imagery also shares a common neural network with perception of the motor act. If there are common neural structures for perception and motor imagery and for motor imagery and actual motor action, it is reasonable to imagine shared substrates between the perception and subsequent re-enactment of a demonstration. Jeannerod's (1994) idea of 'representation neurons' has since been substantiated, evolving into a 'mirror system'.

Mirror neurons: the evidence

Di Pelligrino *et al.* (1992) found a portion of pre-motor cortex in the macaque monkey to be activated during both observation and execution of manipulative actions such as grasping and tearing. This area, called F5, is known to selectively discharge in response to these manipulative tasks, but not to elementary movements (Umilta *et al.*, 2001). A follow-up by Gallese *et al.* (1996) showed that these 'mirror neurons' served an apparently emulative function, in that they discharged only when the action was object-oriented. Considerable evidence now exists for mirror neurons in humans and they do not appear to require emulation of objects in order to discharge. For example, Rizzolatti *et al.* (1996) found activation in Broca's region of the cerebral cortex (Brodmann's area 44) during observation and execution of grasping movements using positron emission tomography. This area is the homologue of F5 in the macaque. Using functional magnetic resonance imaging, Iacoboni *et al.* (1999) found activity not only in Broca's area, but also in the parietal cortex. The parietal cortex is differentially activated when observing meaningful actions for imitation, rather than watching meaningless pantomimes (e.g. Grezes *et al.*, 1998). It is proposed that Broca's area is involved in action relative to its goal (Koksi *et al.*, 2002), while the parietal cortex is presumed to code precise kinesthetic properties for how to move the body (Iacoboni *et al.*, 1999). For example, Lacquaniti *et al.* (1995) showed the parietal cortex to code limb position. In addition to the cortical areas, new evidence suggests that cerebellum has mirror properties (Leggio *et al.*, 2000) and has shared neural circuitry for imagined and executed action (Luft *et al.*, 1998).

Activation in the aforementioned areas during observation and execution of action does not directly indicate the role of mirror neurons in imitative behaviour. However, Iacoboni *et al.* (1999) reported that finger movements evoked by imitation induced greater activation in the mirror system than movements evoked symbolically by highlighting the index finger on a picture of a static hand. Behavioural evidence in support of a mirror system has also been presented in chronometric studies (e.g. Brass *et al.*, 2000; Wohlschlager and Bekkering, 2002).

There is speculation that mirror neurons are also involved in the recognition of actions. Umilta *et al.* (2001) reported that neurons illustrating mirror properties still fire when the action was occluded part way through the reach, suggesting that even without full visual information the mirror neurons internally represent the (missing) action. Could the mirror system therefore be involved in the recognition of biological motion? Oram and Perett (1994) and Servos *et al.* (2002) showed that both the anterior temporal lobe and lingual gyrus are responsive to biological motion in monkeys. These studies suggest little or no overlap with Broca's area. However, Rizzolatti has recently suggested a functional relationship between Broca's area and the temporal areas involved in biological motion recognition (see Morrison, 2002).

The tight coupling of perceived and re-enacted events also extends to motor output in the form of *enactive mediation*. Observation of action results in heightened electrical activity serving the muscles involved in the action (e.g. Berger *et al.*, 1979). In a recent experiment using transcranial magnetic stimulation, participants observing actions were found to exhibit increased motor evoked potential in the muscles used to execute the action (see Fadiga *et al.*, 1995).

Implications for observational learning theory

With regard to the theories of observational learning presented in this chapter, these neurological studies put forward the paradoxical position that both the direct and mediated accounts have credible components, but neither can be sufficient in their current form. On the one hand, in support of Bandura's position, the studies show clear evidence for internal representation mediating action, a concept considered anathematic to ecological views (Hommel *et al.*, 2001). Yet, conversely, the direct mapping of perception and action through shared neural substrate does support theories inextricably coupling perception and action. Al-Abood *et al.* (2001b) conceived the conversion of perception of relative motion to action via the informational and instructional constraint it imposed. Yet it appears even less involved than this. The constraint to match observed and executed movements perhaps could not be more intimate than shared neural substrate.

What is apparent is that Social Cognitive Theory overestimates the role of retention, motor production and motivation in *forming* the cognitive representation.

The simplicity of the mirror system is such that the representation is present even without being forearmed with the explicit knowledge that one must imitate. The mirror system acts as an effortless version of conception matching, such that unlike Bandura's (1986a,b) vision of it, it does not necessarily require higher cognitive processing (through deliberate matching of a mental template with feedback of one's own performance) to operate. Bandura's other sub-processes may fine tune action, rather than form the representation, and their involvement is likely to reflect the memory components of the tasks.

Prinz (1997) occupies the theoretical middle ground via his common-coding model, which is allied to direct matching hypotheses. This model assumes that translation from the sensory code of a perceived event to a motor code for action occurs via a commensurate representational region. This has more recently been advanced into the *theory of event coding* (Hommel *et al.*, 2001). Grounded in ideomotor views, these approaches also emphasize the representation of goals, and Chaminade and Decety (2001) take the position that higher order representations of the goals of action are used rather than lower-level motor neural representations. Given this position, and evidence from an evolutionary perspective, whereby the mirror system in monkeys requires an object and emulation, further theorizing in observational learning should incorporate the imitation of goals rather than just actions.

On variations in the effectiveness of observational learning

A review of observational learning literature suggests that demonstrations are not always effective in facilitating skill acquisition. Variations in task type and novelty contribute to the conflicting nature of the research findings (e.g. see Gould and Roberts, 1982), as has the learning of pre-existing movement patterns (Southard and Higgins, 1987). In terms of information, the extent to which the demonstration conveys a strategy for action (Burwitz, 1975), the degree of redundancy in information provided (Newell, 1981), and informational load (Gould and Roberts, 1982) have all been proposed as factors contributing to the effectiveness of a demonstration. In light of recent research, additional factors such as the interaction between demonstration and feedback should also be considered, and the type and sensitivity of the measures collected.

KR is considered to be a potent learning variable and is present in many observational learning studies. The studies of Horn *et al.* (2002 and in press) suggest that intrinsic visual KR competes with the model as a constraining source of information. In the first study, with KR available, participants decreased error in their outcomes, at the expense of failing to change their movement pattern relative to the model. In the follow-up study, with intrinsic visual KR occluded, the exact opposite occurred. Participants' learned to more closely match the model's coordination, but failed to learn to decrease error on their outcomes. For illustration, we have compared the angle–angle plots (i.e. inter-limb coordination) for one participant from each of the studies in Figure 9.4. Graphs (a) and (b) show the participant's closest attempts at reproducing the model's knee (vertical) – ankle (horizontal) relative motion (represented by the dark plot) in the pre-test and retention test. Note that

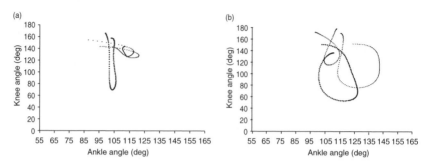

Figure 9.4 Pre-test to retention test changes in knee–ankle relative motion to match a model from in the presence (a) and absence (b) intrinsic visual knowledge of results (for each test period, the vertical axis = knee angle, horizontal axis = ankle angle). Data from Horn *et al.* (in press). *Journal of Motor Behavior.*

there is little change in relative motion for the participant with KR available in (a), whilst in (b) considerable improvement occurs without KR.

The second factor is level of sensitivity of the measure. As previously mentioned, we do not know the sensitivity of human perception to subtle variations in relative motion. If we do predominantly imitate at a holistic or program level, as suggested by Byrne and Russon (1998) and others, then measures that reflect the global organization of the task (e.g. number of steps taken in approaching a ball) may be more likely to be sensitive to demonstration manipulation than measures reflecting higher, localized levels (e.g. intra-limb relative motion during the kick).

A related issue is the distinction between imitation of the kinematic properties of the model's action and the emulation of the action of an object. With neuroscience evidence in support of emulatory processes, some original positions should be revisited. For example, positive modelling effects in tasks such as geometric assembly, arm-paddle movements, and computer tracking have all been attributed to the cognitive properties of the task. Yet, the tasks also lend themselves to emulation. Furthermore, when participants were asked to imitate a movement pattern while also emulating the landing position of the ball, they showed preference for emulating outcomes at the expense of change in movement pattern (Horn *et al.*, 2002). A systematic analysis is required to elucidate the impact of the level (i.e. global/local) and type (imitation/emulation) of observational learning, in addition to the strategic value and novelty of the demonstration.

The final consideration regards our very concept of the role of demonstration. Researchers have tended to estimate the effects of demonstration by retention measures. Yet, several authors have pointed to the benefits of demonstration as a means of accelerating the skill acquisition process (e.g. Carroll and Bandura, 1985). The efficiency of demonstrations in facilitating skill acquisition has been illustrated by way of the reduced number of trials to achieve a correct movement sequence (Williams, 1989a), and rapid changes in relative motion early in practice (Horn *et al.*, in press). In traditional studies of observational learning, this early advantage is not measured and may fade as discovery learners 'catch-up' over the course of long acquisition periods. Although one could argue that long-term changes are the benchmark for skill acquisition, there is an important practical implication here. In realistic learning environments, the efficiency of demonstration may put learners in a position to receive further augmented information or coaching to guide skill acquisition earlier than those not receiving demonstration.

Prescriptive advice for the use of demonstration in coaching and teaching

It is an onerous task to reduce observational learning research to ostensible, prescriptive advice due to wide variations in type of task, participant and performance goal. McCullagh and Weiss (2001) have suggested that a task analysis may solve this problem and suggest Gentile's (1987) classification system as a viable tool. This is a sixteen-category system that takes two considerations into account; the stability and trial-by-trial variation in environment (regulatory conditions), and the action performed, in terms of body transportation and manipulation of objects.

Although Gentile's system is currently the most complete classification, we would argue that is not appropriate for observational learning. First, it does not account for the goal of the task. This chapter has reported evidence suggesting that whether or not one performs a skill while in transit, or manipulating an object, is less significant than the whether the performance criterion is defined by its outcome or its process (i.e. technique). Second, it does not account for variations in the cognitive element of the task. The theoretical implications and research reported in this chapter indicate that the use of demonstration for tasks with high cognitive demand may be very different to those for which it is a minor element.

Table 9.1 presents prescriptive advice based upon the goals of the task. Four task categories are presented. For *outcome-defined* tasks, performance criteria are based on outcomes, without regard to the qualitative processes of achieving them. These tasks tend to have strong perceptual and strategic elements. *Outcome-dominated* tasks involve greater impact of technique on outcomes, but still use outcome-based performance criteria. For example, consider taking a penalty in soccer. The criterion for performance is clearly outcome based, but likelihood of success is heavily influenced by technique. This is an example of an outcome-dominated task with lower cognitive demand. Outcome-dominated tasks with higher cognitive demand often require memory of sequential information. *Process-dominated* tasks involve task outcomes, but performance measures emphasize technique. An example of this is working on golf technique at a driving range. Although there is an outcome derived from the ball's flight, the practice is designed to improve form. Finally, *process-defined* tasks have no outcomes outside of technique, or are practiced in the absence of an object or target. In the absence of outcome elements, demonstrations here are likely to convey specific technical information. As such, demonstrations may benefit from enhancement of key information by highlighting, verbal cueing and slow motion.

Table 9.1 Research-based prescriptive advice

Type of task	Description	Examples	Advice	Research support
Outcome-defined	The outcome of the action defines performance. The process used to achieve the outcome is irrelevant	Computer tracking and game tasks, mechanical assembly, perceptual anticipation	Use multiple demonstrations for perceptual anticipation Make the strategy salient Alternate demonstration with practice Emphasize the action of objects rather than the model	Weeks (1992); Weeks and Choi(1992) Burwitz (1975) Blandin et al. (1994) Hodges and Franks (2002)
Outcome-dominated	The process or technique contributes to achieving the outcome, but outcome dominates the assessment of task performance	Higher cognitive: Semaphore and manual alphabet, movement sequence activities. Lower cognitive: Weight lifting; performing complex motor skills for successful outcomes	Demonstrations before practice Encourage mental rehearsal Increase cognitive engagement by alternating demo and practice Lower cognitive: Include learning models Provide model's KR	Bandura and Jeffrey (1973) Weeks et al. (1996) McCullagh and Caird (1990) Herbert and Landin (1994)
Process-dominated	Outcomes contribute, but process dominates the assessment of performance outcomes	Performing complex actions such as kicking, throwing, or hitting with outcomes, but emphasizing technique	Minimize early intrinsic KR to induce rapid improvements in form Use demonstration retrospectively as a reference of correctness	Horn et al. (2002 and in press) Richardson and Lee (1999)
Process-defined	The process defines performance	Diving, trampolining, gymnastics	Guide learners' attention to key elements of the demonstration with verbal guidance	Champenoy and Janelle (1999)
	Technique is the measured outcome, or no outcome is included	Performing techniques such as kicking, throwing, or hitting in absence of object or target	Use slow motion to enhance relative motion	Scully and Carnegie (1998) Fehres and Olivier (1986)

Increasingly process-driven →

← Increasingly outcome-driven

Given the delimitations of this chapter, Table 9.1 is meant to be neither all encompassing nor definitive. However, it may be helpful in providing research-driven guidelines for practitioners and bring attention to the importance of the goal of the task.

Summary

Observational learning is the process by which we watch the actions of a model and adapt our behaviour to more closely match the outcomes or process of the event. The traditional theoretical explanation implies that this process is mediated by cognition and mental representation. Considerable evidence exists in support of this position, albeit in research studies using tasks with considerable cognitive demands. The ecological alternative questions the need for cognitive mediation, suggesting that we perceive and become constrained by the relative motion in the display. In complex coordinative tasks, there is mounting evidence for changes to more closely match the model's relative motion at intra- and inter-limb levels. By quantifying coordination changes, these studies suggest that demonstration can meet the twofold challenge of accelerating the acquisition of skill, while providing a stable platform for enduring behavioural change. This appears to be facilitated by the removal of intrinsic visual KR. Recent neuroscience advances provide evidence for imitation via an elegant and simple mechanism: neurons that selectively fire during observation and subsequent re-enactment. This pivotal development should provide a timely rethink of both theoretical positions. Current cognitive accounts may be overly complex, while ecological accounts may need to be revised to incorporate this representation mechanism. Future developments in the neurosciences should shed further light on the mechanisms of 'how' observational learning occurs. To address the question of 'what' information is used in the process, techniques such as event occlusion and the recording of eye movement data should be used in tandem with the systematic quantification of coordination. Finally, a threshold-based analysis of perceptual sensitivity to relative motion may provide a framework within which to better set our expectations of imitative processes.

References

Adams, J. A. (1971). A closed-loop theory of motor learning. *Journal of Motor Behaviour*, 13, 111–150.

Al-Abood, S. A., Davids, K. and Bennett, S. J. (2001a). Specificity of task constraints and effects of visual demonstrations and verbal instructions in directing learner's search during skill acquisition. *Journal of Motor Behaviour*, 33, 295–305.

Al-Abood, S. A., Davids, K., Bennett, S. J., Ashford, D. and Martinez, M. M. (2001b). Effects of manipulating relative and absolute motion information during observational learning of an aiming task. *Journal of Sports Sciences*, 19, 507–520.

Bandura, A. (1965). Vicarious processes: the case of no-trial learning. In. L. Berkowitz (Ed.), *Advances in experimental social psychology II* (pp. 1–55). New York: Academic press.

Bandura, A. (1969). *Principles of behaviour modification*. New York: Rinehart-Winston.

Bandura, A. (1971). *Principles of behaviour modification*. London: Holt, Rinehart & Wilson.

Bandura, A. (1977). *Social learning theory*. Englewood Cliffs, NJ: Prentice Hall.

Bandura, A. (1986a). *Social foundations of thought and action: a social cognitive theory*. Englewood Cliffs, NJ: Prentice Hall.

Bandura, A. (1986b). Social cognitive theory. *Annals of Child Development*, 6, 1–60.

Bandura, A. (1997). *Self-efficacy: the exercise of control*. New York: Freeman.

Bandura, A. and Jeffrey, R. W. (1973). Role of symbolic coding and rehearsal processes in observational learning. *Journal of Personality and Social Psycholgy*, 26, 122–130.

Bandura, A., Ross, D. and Ross, S. A. (1961). Transmission of aggression through imitation of aggressive models. *Journal of Abnormal and Social Psycholgy*, 63, 575–582.

Barclay, C. D., Cutting, J. E., and Kozlowski, L. T. (1978). Temporal and spatial factors in gait perception that influence gender recognition. *Perception and Psychophysics*, 23, 145–152.

Bassili, J. N. (1978). Facial motion in the perception of faces and of emotional expression. *Journal of Experimental Psychology: Human Perception and Performance*, 4, 373–379.

Berger, S. M., Carli, L. L., Hammersla, K. S., Karshmer, J. F. and Sanchez, M. E. (1979). Motoric and symbolic mediation in observational learning. *Journal of Personality & Social Psychology*, 37, 735–746.

Bertenthal, B. I. and Pinto, J. (1994). Global processing of biological motions. *Psychological Science*, 5, 221–225.

Bird, A. M. and Rickli, R. (1983). Observational learning and practice variability. *Research Quarterly for Exercise and Sport*, 54, 1–4.

Blandin, Y. and Proteau, L. (2000). On the cognitive basis of observational learning: development of mechanisms for the detection and correction of errors. *The Quarterly Journal of Experimental Psychology*, 53A, 846–867.

Blandin, Y., Proteau, L. and Alain, C. (1994). On the cognitive processes underlying contextual interference and observational learning. *Journal of Motor Behaviour*, 26, 18–26.

Bower, G. H. and Hilgard, E. R. (1981). *Theories of learning* (5th ed.). Englewood Cliffs, NJ: Prentice Hall.

Brass, M., Bekkering, H., Wohlschlager, A. and Prinz, W. (2000). Compatibility between observed and executed finger movements: comparing symbolic, spatial, and imitative cues. *Brain & Cognition*, 44, 124–143.

Burwitz, L. (1975). Observational learning and motor performance. *FEPSAC Conference Proceedings*, Edinburgh.

Byrne, R. W. and Russon, A. E. (1998). Learning by imitation: a hierarchical approach. *Behavioral and Brain Sciences*, 21, 667–721.

Brownlow, S., Dixon, A. R., Egbert, C. A. and Radcliffe, R. D. (1997). Perception of movement and dancer characteristics from point light displays of dance. *Psychological Record*, 47, 411–421.

Cadopi, M., Chatillon, J. F. and Baldy, R. (1995). Representation and performance: Reproduction of form and quality of movement in dance by 8-year old and 11-year old novices. *British Journal of Psychology*, 86, 217–225.

Carroll, W. R. and Bandura, A. (1985). Role of timing of visual monitoring and motor rehearsal in observational learning of action patterns. *Journal of Motor Behaviour*, 17, 69–81.

Carroll, W. R. and Bandura, A. (1990). Representational guidance of action production in Observational Learning: a causal analysis. *Journal of Motor Behaviour*, 22, 85–97.

Chaminade, T. and Decety, J. (2001). A common framework for perception and action: neuroimaging evidence. *Behavioural and Brain Sciences*, 24, 879–882.

Champenoy, J. D. and Janelle, C. M. (1999). Video modeling with auditory cueing facilitates learning of a self-paced task. *Journal of Sport and Exercise Psychology*, 21, S26.

Christina, R. W. (1987). Motor learning: future battlefronts of research. In: H. Eckert (Ed.), *The Cutting edge in physical education and exercise science research. American Academy of Physical Education Papers*, 20 (pp. 26–41). Champaign, IL: Human Kinetics.

Cutting, J. E. and Kozlowski, L. T. (1977). Recognising friends by their walk: gait perception without familiarity cues. *Bulletin of the Psychonomic Society*, 9, 353–356.

Decety, J., Perani, D., Jeannerod, M., Bettinardi, V., Tadary, B., Woods, R., Mazziotta, J. C. and Fazzio, F. (1994). Mapping motor representations with positron emission tomography. *Nature*, 371, 600–602.

Decety, J. and Grezes, J. (1999). Neural mechanisms subserving the perception of human actions. *Trends in Cognitive Sciences*, 5, 172–178.

de la Pena, D., Janelle, C. M., Hass, C. J. and Ellis, S. R. (2000). Video-modeling of a self-paced task: attentional considerations. *Research Quarterly for Exercise and Sport*, 71, A-55.

di Pelligrino, G., Fadiga, L., Fogassi, L., Gallese, V. and Rizzolatti, G. (1992). Understanding motor events: a neurophysiological study. *Experimental Brain Research*, 91, 176–180.

Dittrich, W. H., Troscianko, T., Lea, S. E. G. and Morgan, D. (1996). Perception of emotion from dynamic point-light displays represented in dance. *Perception*, 25, 727–738.

Fadiga, L., Fogassi, L., Pavesi, G. and Rizzolatti, G. (1995). Motor facilitation during action observation: a magnetic study. *Journal of Neurophysiology*, 73, 2608–2611.

Fehres, K. and Olivier, N. (1986). The effects of videotaped repetitive presentations and slow-motion presentations on the acquisition of a complex motor skill. *Proceedings of the AIESEP World Congress*, Heidelberg, Germany.

Feltz, D. L. (1982). Effects of age and number of demonstrations on modelling of form and performance. *Research Quarterly for Exercise and Sport*, 53, 291–296.

Feltz, D. L. and Landers, D. M. (1977). Information-motivational components of a model's demonstration. *Research Quarterly*, 48, 525–533.

Gallese, V., Fadiga, L., Fogassi, L. and Rizzolatti, G. (1996). Action recognition in the premotor cortex. *Brain*, 119, 593–609.

Gentile, A. M. (1987). Skill acquisition: action, movement and neuromotor processes. In J. H. Carr, R. B. Shepherd, A. M. Gentile and J. M. Hinds (Eds), *Movement science: foundations for physical therapy in rehabilitation* (pp. 93–154). Rockville, MD: Aspen.

George, T. R., Feltz, D. L. and Chase, M. A. (1992). Effects of model similarity on self-efficacy and muscular endurance: a second look. *Journal of Sport and Exercise Psychology*, 14, 237–248.

Gerst, M. S. (1971). Symbolic coding processes in observational learning. *Journal of Personality and Social Psychology*, 19, 7–17.

Gibson, J. J. (1950). *The perception of the visual world*. Boston, MA: Houghton-Mifflin.

Gibson, J. J. (1979). *The ecological approach to visual perception*. Boston, MA: Houghton-Mifflin.

Gould, D. R. (1978). The influence of motor task types on modeling effectiveness. Unpublished doctoral dissertation, University of Illinois.

Gould, D. R. and Roberts, G. R. (1982). Modeling and skill acquisition. *Quest*, 33, 214–230.

Gould, D. R. and Weiss, M. R. (1981). The effects of model similarity and model talk on self-efficacy and muscular endurance. *Journal of Sport Psychology*, 3, 17–29.

Graham, G., Holt-Hale, S. A. and Parker, M. (2001). *Children moving: a reflective approach to teaching physical education* (5th ed.). Mountain View, CA: Mayfield Publishers.

Gray, J. T., Neisser, U., Shapiro, B. A. and Kouns, S. (1991). Observational learning of ballet sequences: The role of kinematic information. *Ecological Psychology*, 3, 121–134.

Grezes, J., Costes, N. and Decety, J. (1998). Top–down effect of strategy on the perception of human biological motion: a PET investigation. *Cognitive Neurophysiology*, 15, 553–582.

Griffin, K. and Meaney, K. S. (2000). Modeling and motor performance: An examination of model similarity and model type on children's motor performance. *Research Quarterly for Exercise and Sport*, 71, A-56, 67.

Grusec, J. E. and Brinker, D. B. (1972). Reinforcement for imitation as a social learning determinant with implications for sex-role development. *Journal of Personality and Social Psychology*, 21, 149–158.

Herbert, E. P. and Landin, D. (1994). Effects of a learning model and augmented information on tennis skill acquisition. *Research Quarterly for Exercise and Sport*, 65 (3), 250–257.

Heyes, C. M. (2001) Causes and consequences of imitation. *Trends in Cognitive Sciences*, 5, 253–261.

Hodges, N. J. and Franks, I. M. (2002). Modelling coaching practice: the role of instruction and demonstration. *Journal of Sports Sciences*, 20, 793–811.

Hommel, B., Musseler, J., Aschersleben, G. and Prinz, W. (2001). The theory of event coding (TEC): a framework for perception and action planning. *Behavioural and Brain Sciences*, 24, 849–937.

Horn, R. R., Williams, A. M. and Scott, M. A. (2002). Learning form demonstrations: the role of visual search during observational learning from video and point-light models. *Journal of Sports Sciences*, 20, 253–269.

Horn, R. R., Williams, A. M., Scott, M. A. and Hodges, N. J. (in press). Visual search and coordination changes in response to video and point-light demonstrations in the absence of intrinsic knowledge of results. *Journal of Motor Behavior*.

Horn, R., Williams, A. M., Scott, M. A., Hayes, S. J. and Hodges, N. J. (in prep.). On the immediacy of changes in relative motion in observational learning.

Horn, R. R., Greenwood, J., Scott, M. A. and Williams, A. M. (submitted). The role of relative motion to the perception and replication of dynamics.

Iacoboni, M., Woods, R. P., Brass, M., Bekkering, H., Mazziotta, J. C. and Rizzolatti, G. (1999). Cortical mechanisms of human imitation. *Science*, 286, 2526–2528.

Ille, A. and Cadopi, M. (1995). Reproducing choreographic walks from the observation of a kinematic point light display: Effect of skill level. *Journal of Human Movement Studies*, 29, 101–114.

Jeannerod, M. (1994). The representing brain: neural correlates of motor intention and imagery. *Behavioural and Brain Sciences*, 17, 197–245.

Jeffrey, R. W. (1976). The influence of symbolic and motor rehearsal on observational learning. *Journal of Personality and Social Psychology*, 10, 116–127.

Johansson, G. (1971). Visual motion perception: a model for visual motion and space perception from changing proximal stimulation. Report from the Department of Psychology, University of Uppsala, Number 98.

Johansson, G. (1973). Visual perception of biological motion and a model for its analysis. *Perception and Psychophysics*, 14, 201–211.

Johansson, G. (1975). Visual motion perception. *Scientific American*, 232, 76–88.

Katz, D. (1960) Social Psychology. In D. Katz and R. Katz (Eds), *Handbook of psychology* (2nd ed.). Basel/Stuttgart: Schwabe.

Koksi, L., Wohlschlager, A., Bekkering, H., Woods, R. P., Dubeau, M. C., Mazziotta, J. C. and Iacoboni, M. (2002). Modulation of motor and premotor activity during imitation of target-directed actions. *Cerebral Cortex*, 12, 847–855.

Kugler, P. N., Kelso, J. A. S. and Turvey, M. T. (1980). On the concept of coordinative structures as dissipative structures: Theoretical lines of convergence. In G. E. Stelmach and J. Requin (Eds), *Tutorials in motor behaviour* (pp. 3–47). Amsterdam: North Holland.

Lacquiniti, F., Guigon, E., Bianchi, L., Ferriana, S. and Caminiti, R. (1995). Representing spatial information for limb movement: role of area 5 in the monkey. *Cerebral Cortex*, 5, 391–409.

Laguna, P. L. (1996). The effects of model demonstration strategies on motor skill acquisition and performance. *Journal of Human Movement Studies*, 30, 55–79.

Landers, D. N. and Landers, D. M. (1973). Teachers versus peer models: effects of model's presence and performance level. *Journal of Motor Behaviour*, 5, 129–139.

Lee, T. D. and Magill, R. A. (1985). Can forgetting facilitate skill acquisition? In: D. Goodman, R. B. Wilberg and I. M. Franks (Eds), *Differing perspectives in motor learning, memory and control* (pp. 3–22). Amsterdam: North Holland.

Lee, T. D. and White, M. A. (1990). Influence of an unskilled model's practice schedule on observational motor learning. *Human Movement Science*, 9, 349–367.

Lefkowitz, M., Blake, R. R. and Mouton, J. S. (1955). Status factors in pedestrian violation of traffic signals. *Journal of Abnormal and Social Psychology*, 51, 704–705.

Leggio, M. G., Moliari, M., Neri, P., Graziano, A., Mandolesi, L. and Petrosini, L. (2000). Representation of action in rats: the role of the cerebellum in learning spatial performances by observation. *Proceedings of the National Academy of Sciences USA*, 97, 2320–2325.

Lirgg, C. D. and Feltz, D. L. (1991). Teacher versus peer models revisited: effects on motor performance and self-efficacy. *Research Quarterly for Exercise and Sport*, 62, 217–224.

Luft, A. R., Skalej, M., Stefanou, A. Klose, U. and Voigt, K. (1998). Comparing motion- and imagery-related activation in the human cerebellum: a functional MRI study. *Human Brain Mapping*, 6, 105–113.

Magill, R. A. (2001). *Motor learning and control: concepts and applications* (6th ed.). Boston, MA: McGraw-Hill.

Magill, R. A. and Shoenfelder-Zhodi, B. (1996). A visual model and knowledge of performance as sources of information for learning a rhythmic gymnastics skill. *International Journal of Sport Psychology*, 27, 7–22.

Marey, E. J. (1972). *Movement*. Arno Press/New York Times, New York (first published in 1895).

Martens, R., Burwitz, L. and Zuckerman, J. (1976). Modeling effects on motor performance. *Research Quarterly for Exercise and Sport*, 47, 277–291.

Mather, G. and Murdoch, L. (1994). Gender discrimination in biological motion displays on dynamic cues. *Proceedings of the Royal Society of London B* 259, 273–279.

Mather, G. and West, S. (1993). Recognition of animal locomotion from dynamic point-light displays. *Perception*, 22, 759–766.

Mather, G., Radford, K. and West, S. (1992). Low-level visual processing in biological motion. *Proceedings of the Royal Society of London B*, 273–279.

McCullagh, P. (1986). Model status as a determinant of observational learning and performance. *Journal of Sport Psychology*, 8, 319–331.

McCullagh, P. (1993). Modeling: learning, developmental and social psychological considerations. In R. N. Singer, M. Murphey and L. K. Tennant (Eds), *Handbook of research on sport psychology* (pp. 102–125). McMillan: New York.

McCullagh, P. and Caird, J. K. (1990). Correct and learning models and the use of model knowledge of results in the acquisition and retention of a motor skill. *Journal of Human Movement Studies*, 18, 107–116.

McCullagh, P. and Meyer, K. N. (1997). Learning versus correct models: Influence of model type on the learning of a free-weight squat lift. *Research Quarterly for Exercise and Sport*, 68, 56–61.

McCullagh, P. and Weiss, M. R. (2001). Modeling: considerations for motor skill performance and psychological responses. In R. N. Singer, H. A. Hasenblaus and C. M. Janelle (Eds), *Handbook of sport psychology* (2nd ed., pp. 205–238). New York: Wiley.

McCullagh, P., Weiss, M. R. and Ross, D. (1989). Modeling considerations in motor skill acquisition and performance: an integrated approach. In K. B. Pandolf (Ed.), *Exercise and Sport Science Reviews*, Vol. 17. Baltimore, MD: Williams & Wilkin.

McDougall, W. (1908). *An introduction to social psychology*. London: Methuen.

Miller, N. E. and Dollard, J. (1941). *Social learning and imitation*. New Haven, CT: Yale University Press.

Morgan, C. L. (1896). On modification and variation. *Science*, 4, 733–403.

Morrison, I. (2002). Genuine imitation. *Trends in Cognitive Sciences*, 6, 367–368.

Mullineaux, D. R., Bartlett, R. M. and Bennett, S. (2001). Research design and statistics in biomechanics and motor control. *Journal of Sports Sciences*, 19, 739–760.

Newell, K. M. (1981). Skill learning. In D. Holding (Ed.), *Human skills* (pp. 203–226). New York: Wiley.

Newell, K. M. (1985). Coordination, control and skill. In D. Goodman, R. B. Wilberg and I. M. Franks (Eds), *Differing perspectives in motor learning, memory and control*. Amsterdam: Elsevier.

Oram, M. W. and Perett, D. I. (1994). Responses of anterior superior temporal polysensory (STPa) neurons to biological motion stimuli. *Journal of Cognitive Neuroscience*, 6, 99–116.

Pellechia, G. L. and Garrett, G. E. (1997). Assessing lumbar stabilization from point-light and normal video displays of manual lifting. *Perceptual and Motor Skills*, 5, 931–937.

Poizner, H., Bellugi, U. and Lutesdriscoll, V. (1981). Perception of American Sign Language in dynamic point-light displays. *Journal of Experimental Psychology: Human Perception and Performance*, 7, 430–440.

Pollock, B. J. and Lee, T. D. (1992). Effects of the model's skill level on observational motor learning. *Research Quarterly for Exercise and Sport*, 63, 25–29.

Prinz, W. (1987). Ideo-motor action. In H. Heuer and A. F. Sanders (Eds), *Perspectives on perception and action* (pp. 47–76). Hillsdale, NJ: Erlbaum.

Prinz, W. (1997). Perception and action planning. *European Journal of Cognitive Psychology*, 9, 129–154.

Richardson, J. R. and Lee, T. D. (1999). The effects of proactive and retroactive demonstrations on learning of signed letters. *Acta Psychologica*, 101, 79–90.

Rink, J. E. (1998). *Teaching physical education for learning* (3rd ed.). Boston, MA: McGraw-Hill.

Rizzolatti, G., Fadiga, L., Matelli, M., Bettinardi, V., Paulesu, E., Perani, D. and Fazio, F. (1996). Localization of grasp representation in humans by PET: 1. Observation versus execution. *Experimental Brain Research*, 111, 246–252.

Romack, J. L. (1995). Information in visual event perception and its use in observational learning. In: B. G. Bardy, R. J. Bootsma and Y. Guiard (Eds), *Studies in perception and action II*. Hillsdale, NJ: Erlbaum Associates.

Romack, J. L. and Briggs, R. S. (1998). Relevant visual information in a demonstration and its subsequent use in learning how to dribble a ball. *Journal of Sport and Exercise Psychology*, 20, S79.

Runeson, S. (1984). Perception of biological motion: the KSD principle and the implications of a distal versus proximal approach. In G. Jansson, S. Bergstom and W. Epstein (Eds), *Perceiving events and objects* (pp. 383–405). Hillsdale, NJ: Erlbaum.

Runeson, S., Jusslin, P. and Olsen, H. (2000). Visual perception of dynamic properties: heuristic cues versus direct perceptual competence. *Psychological Review*, 107, 525–555.

Schmidt, R. A. (1975). A schema theory of discrete motor skill learning. *Psychological Review*, 82, 225–260.

Schoenfelder-Zhodi, B. (1992). Investigating the informational mature of a modelled visual demonstration. Unpublished doctoral dissertation, Louisiana State University, Baton Rouge.

Scully, D. M. (1986). Visual perception of aesthetic quality and technical execution in biological motion. *Human Movement Science*, 5, 185–206.

Scully, D. M. and Carnegie, E. (1998). Observational learning in motor skills acquisition: a look at demonstrations. *The Irish Journal of Psychology*, 19, 472–485.

Scully, D. M. and Newell, K. M. (1985). The acquisition of motor skills: toward a visual perception perspective. *Journal of Human Movement Studies*, 12, 169–187.

Servos, P., Osu, R., Santi, A. and Kawato, M. (2002). The neural substrates of biological motion perception: an f MRI study. *Cerebral Cortex*, 12, 772–782.

Sheffield, F. D. (1961). Theoretical considerations in the learning of complex tasks from demonstrations and practice. In A. A. Lumsdaine (Ed.), *Student response in programmed instruction* (pp. 13–32). Washington, DC: National Academy of Science National Research Council.

Shim, J. and Carlton, L. G. (1997). Perception of kinematic characteristics in then motion of lifted weight. *Journal of Motor Behaviour*, 2, 131–146.

Sidaway, B. and Hand, M. J. (1993). Frequency of modelling effects on the acquisition and retention of a motor skill. *Research Quarterly for Exercise and Sport*, 64, 122–125.

Sidaway, B., Heise, G. and Schoenfelder-Zhodi, B. (1995). Quantifying the variability of angle–angle plots. *Journal of Human Movement Studies*, 29, 181–197.

Southard, D. and Higgins, T. (1987). Changing movement patterns: effects of demonstration and practice. *Research Quarterly for Exercise and Sport*, 58, 77–80.

Sparrow, W. A., Shinkfield, A. J., Day, R. H., Hollitt, S. and Jolley, D. (2002). Visual perception of movement kinematics and the acquisition of "action prototypes". *Motor Control*, 2, 146–65.

Stephan, K. M., Fink, G. R., Passingham, R. E., Silbersweig, A. O., Ceballos-Baumann, A. O., Frith, C. D. and Frackowiak, R. S. J. (1995). Functional anatomy of the mental representation of upper extremity movements in healthy subjects. *Journal of Neurophysiology*, 73, 373–386.

Stevenage, S. V., Nixon, M. S. and Vince, K. (1999). Visual analysis of gait as a cue to identity. *Applied Cognitive Psychology*, 13, 513–526.

Stoffregen, T. A., Gorday, K. M., Sheng, Y. Y. and Flynn, S. B. (1999). Perceiving affordances for another person's actions. *Journal of Experimental Psychology: Human Perception and Performance*, 25, 120–136.

Tomasello, M., Kruger, A. C. and Ratner, H. H. (1993). Cultural learning. *Behavioural and Brain Sciences*, 16, 495–552.

Umilta, M. A., Kohler, E., Gallesse, Fogassi, L., Fadiga, L., Keysers, C. and Rizzolatti, G. (2001). I know what you are doing: a neurophysiological study. *Neuron*, 31, 155–165.

Warren, W. H. (1990). The perception–action coupling. In H. Bloch and B. I. Bertenthal (Eds) *Sensory-motor organizations and development in infancy and early childhood* (pp. 23–37). Dordrecht: Kluwer.

Weeks, D. L. (1992). A comparison of modelling modalities in the observational learning of an externally paced skill. *Research Quarterly for Exercise and Sport*, 63, 373–380.

Weeks, D. L. and Choi, J. (1992). Modelling the perceptual component of a coincident-timing skill: the influence of frequency of demonstration. *Journal of Human Movement Studies* 23, 201–213.

Weise-Bjornstal, D. M. and Weiss, M. R. (1992). Modeling effects on children's form kinematics, performance outcome, and cognitive recognition of a sport skill: an integrated perspective. *Research Quarterly for Exercise and Sport*, 63, 67–75.

Weiss, M. R. and Klint, M. R. (1987). "Show and tell" in the gymnasium: an investigation of developmental differences in modelling and verbal rehearsal of motor skills. *Research Quarterly for Exercise and Sport*, 22, 234–241.

Whiting, H. T. A., Bijlard, M. J. and Brinker, B. P. L. M. (1987). The effect of availability of a dynamic model on the acquisition of a cyclical action. *Quarterly Journal of Experimental Psychology*, 39A, 43–59.

Williams, A. M., Davids, K. and Williams, J. G. (1999). *Visual perception and action in sport.* London: E & FN Spon.

Williams, J. G. (1989a). Throwing action from full-cue and motion only video models of an arm movement sequence. *Perceptual and Motor Skills*, 68, 259–266.

Williams, J. G. (1989b). Visual demonstration and movement production: effects of timing variations of a model's actions. *Perceptual and Motor Skills* 68, 891–896.

Williams, J. G. (1989c). Motor skill instruction: visual demonstration and eye movements. *Physical Education Review*, 12, 49–55.

Williams, J. G. (1993). Motoric modeling: theory and research. *Journal of Human Movement Studies*, 25, 237–279.

Wohlschlager, A. and Bekkering, H. (2002). Is human imitation based on a mirror-neuron system? Some behavioural evidence. *Experimental Brain Research*, 143, 335–341.

Wright, D., Black, C. and Breuckner, S. (2001). Identifying and correcting error following physical and observational practice. *6th Annual Congress of the European College of Sport Science*, Cologne, Germany, p. 127.

Wright, D. L., Li, Y. and Coady, W. (1997). Cognitive processes related to contextual interference and observational learning: a replication of Blandin, Proteau, and Alain (1994). *Research Quarterly for Exercise and Sport*, 68, 106–109.

10 Implicit motor learning, reinvestment and movement disruption

What you don't know won't hurt you

Richard S.W. Masters and Jonathan P. Maxwell

Motor skill acquisition can be thought of as the gradual harmonizing of a number of complicated processes in order to achieve a consistent output. Typically, the harmonizer (learner) gains insight into the performance of the skill by analysis of the motor problem, and formulates strategies based on the accumulation of 'declarative' knowledge of the task. This knowledge is manipulated in working memory to support performance and the efficacy of the strategies is evaluated using outcome feedback. Successful attempts tend to be repeated and eventually stored in long-term memory, whereas unsuccessful attempts tend to be disregarded. These processes are often augmented by additional instructions, conveyed verbally, perhaps, by a *well-intentioned* coach or therapist. The performer practices and develops the skills until they become second nature or automatic; that is, they no longer rely on the action recipes that were formulated during the early stages of learning. At this point, the competent performer may engage in competition against other individuals, or exhibit his or her special abilities publicly. Unfortunately, the motor output of even the most well-practiced performer can sometimes be disrupted.

In this chapter, we discuss one of the acknowledged contributors to performance disruption – verbally accessible, task relevant knowledge – and articulate an addendum to the traditionally accepted cognitive view of motor learning (Anderson, 1983; Fitts and Posner, 1967; Schneider and Schiffrin, 1977). Our view is based on the premise that motor skills can be acquired without an early dependence on working memory (Baddeley, 1999; Baddeley and Hitch, 1974), and that the recruitment of working memory resources in explicitly learned skills can interfere with the efficient control of movement. Working memory provides a temporary storage space where incoming information is held and manipulated, and from which verbal mediation of knowledge emanates. It is made up of a central executive, which controls attention, overseeing cognition, and subordinate 'secretarial' systems, which hold verbal or visual information until it can be acted upon. We review work undertaken over the past decade that has attempted to develop, and validate, methods for acquiring motor skills, which preclude, minimize or circumvent contributions from working memory during motor output. These methods prevent working memory from forming hypotheses, either by involving it in alternative activities, occluding or diminishing environmental information available to the performer about his actions (which working memory needs in order to form hypotheses) or by presenting to the learner information that requires little or no involvement from working memory in motor output. Finally, we describe a preliminary working model of implicit motor learning, debate the advantages and disadvantages of explicit as opposed to implicit control of motor output and discuss the implications of the evolution of verbal skills for motor learning.

Reinvesting the wheel

Explanations of disruption to performance as a result of, for want of a better description, conscious control, can be tracked clearly through the literature (e.g. Baumeister, 1984; Bliss, 1895; Boder, 1935; Borkovec, 1976; Henry and Rogers, 1960; Reason and Mycielska, 1982; Weinberg and Hunt, 1976; Wulf *et al.*, 2001). This literature has witnessed considerable reinvention of the wheel over the years. For example, the 'constrained action hypothesis' (Wulf *et al.*, 2001) proposes that when performers focus attention on their movements they may 'constrain or interfere with automatic control processes that would normally regulate the movement' (Wulf *et al.*, 2001: 1143). There is little to differentiate this hypothesis from Deikman's (1969) concept of 'deautomatization', the 'undoing of automatization, presumably by *reinvesting actions and percepts with attention*' (Deikman, 1969: 31).

The automatic/non-automatic conception is a much revisited building block of cognitive theories of learning (Tracy *et al.*, 2001). Once skilled, the performer is said to execute complex responses with minimal attention to the specific 'declarative' knowledge involved, because the underlying information processing has become automatized (Bryan and Harter, 1897; Salmoni, 1989). In certain circumstances, however, the declarative knowledge that initially supported performance, can, in a sense, be recovered by attention (voluntarily or otherwise) and reapplied to the task in hand. This knowledge is manipulated by working memory and may interfere with the execution of automatic processes, regressing the normally fluent movements of the expert to the rather erratic style of the beginner.

Masters (1992) attempted to unite various descriptions of this process under one expression – 'reinvestment', which refers to the propensity for manipulation of conscious, explicit, rule-based knowledge, by working memory, to control the mechanics of one's movements during motor output. Masters *et al.* (1993) went on to develop the Reinvestment Scale; a twenty-item questionnaire intended to measure individual predispositions for reinvestment. It was predicted that high scores on the scale would predict a greater propensity for reinvestment than low scores. A significant negative correlation ($r = -0.59$, $p < 0.05$) was reported between participant scores on the Reinvestment Scale and performance of a putting task under pressure, supporting Masters *et al.*'s (1993) predictions. Supplementary evidence was reported in the form of coaches' appraisals of their athletes' ability to perform under pressure. Squash and tennis players whose coach rated them more likely to 'choke under pressure' possessed higher reinvestment scores than those rated unlikely to choke ($r = 0.64$, $p < 0.01$).

Additional support for Masters *et al.*'s (1993) contention has recently been reported. Bawden *et al.* (2001) showed that high self-conscious golfers, identified using the Self-Consciousness Scale (Fenigstein *et al.*, 1975), which shares twelve items with the Reinvestment Scale, were more likely to break down under self-focused attention than low self-conscious golfers. Maxwell *et al.* (2000) reported evidence that not only do high reinvesters perform poorly under pressure but they may also exhibit performance decrements during learning. Maxwell *et al.* (2000) had novice golfers putt 3000 golf balls over five sessions and found that success on the golf-putting task was negatively correlated with the score on the Reinvestment Scale. High reinvesters were less successful during learning than low reinvesters. The reinvestment score was also positively correlated with the number of technical rules learners reported using to control their putting action, suggesting that high reinvesters rely on explicit knowledge to control their actions more than low reinvesters.

Recently, Maxwell and Masters (submitted) replicated the work of Masters *et al.* (1993). Identical findings were observed which greatly increase support for the predictive validity of the Reinvestment Scale. Maxwell and Masters (submitted) found that high reinvesters reported using more explicit information to control their actions than low reinvesters during a stressed performance phase, suggesting that conscious processing mediates skill breakdown. Further evidence is provided by Liao and Masters' (2002) work, which showed that learning to perform basketball free throws under self-focused attention resulted in the build up of a large pool of explicit knowledge about the skill. Regression analysis was employed to show that the more technical rules the learner acquired during learning the worse he or she performed under pressure, implying that people who pick up more explicit knowledge of their movements during learning are under greater threat of disruption from reinvestment. In line with this finding, Wulf and Weigelt (1997) demonstrated that the use of verbal instruction to convey information about the task requirements during skill acquisition both hindered learning and performance under stress.

The principle of reinvestment and the ability to quantify the tendency for reinvestment has implications for a number of domains of motor performance not previously considered. Stroke patients, for example, score more highly than age-matched controls on a movement specific version of the Reinvestment Scale (Orrell *et al.*, 2002). Additionally, the difficulties in movement initiation and execution, which typify Parkinson's disease, may cause patients to consciously monitor the mechanics of their actions in order to arbitrate effective motor output. Pall *et al.* (2001) assessed the propensity for reinvestment in a sample of fifty-six patients using the Reinvestment Scale. Unexpectedly, the duration of disease predicted reinvestment, suggesting that, over time, patients monitor the mechanics of their movements increasingly. Pall *et al.* suggested that this might occur as a result of constant anxiety to perform effectively. They cited similarities in the sporting world, where athletes become so conscious of flaws in their movement output that performance is severely disrupted (e.g. the 'yips' in golf, Lees, 1998).

Reinvestment prevention

Disruption to motor output as a result of reinvestment is clearly a problem for many individuals. Over the past decade, Masters and colleagues have used the distinction between explicit and implicit processes to construct a series of paradigms designed to combat reinvestment. Explicit processes rely on working memory for the storage and manipulation of information and are, therefore, verbally based and open to introspection. In other words, we are consciously aware of the information being processed and can share that information with others (Seger, 1994). Implicit processes, conversely, are typically unavailable for conscious inspection and difficult to verbalize (Kellogg, 1982). Several criteria have been identified which dissociate implicit from explicit processes. Lack of verbalizable knowledge has been taken as the primary indication of implicitly held knowledge (Berry and Broadbent, 1984). Additionally, implicit processes are more resistant to the effects of psychological stress, disorders and dysfunctions (Abrams and Reber, 1988; Reber, 1993; Schacter, 1987) and may be more durable, or less prone to forgetting over time than explicit processes (Allen and Reber, 1980). Implicit processes are also non-attentionally demanding or independent of working memory (Berry and Broadbent, 1988; Berry and Dienes, 1993; Curran and Keele, 1993; Hayes and Broadbent, 1988) and relatively independent of age and IQ, whereas explicit learning and memory degrade with age and are closely correlated with IQ (Light and Singh, 1987; Reber, 1993; Reber *et al.*, 1991).

During the unskilled, declarative stages of learning, motor output is characterized by a predominance of explicit processing. In the highly skilled, autonomous stages, implicit processes predominate as a result of the gradual release from explicit control during the course of learning (Anderson, 1983; Fitts and Posner, 1967; Schneider and Schiffrin, 1977). Reinvestment, therefore, can be seen as an abandoning of elusive implicit processing in favour of explicit processes, which offer the performer a sense of security as a result of their availability for conscious inspection in working memory.

Preventing the use of working memory

Early attempts to prevent reinvestment focused on limiting the build up of verbal knowledge resources available to reinvest. Masters (1992) argued that the learning experience should reduce the amount of explicit knowledge that the learner accumulates so that implicit processing predominates and the possibility for reinvestment is eliminated or, at least, reduced. Capitalizing on the fact that implicit learning had previously been shown to bypass conscious awareness (Jacoby *et al.*, 1988, 1989), Masters based his original implicit *motor* learning paradigm on the simple premise that by (over)loading working memory capacity with a demanding second task the accumulation of accessible task-relevant knowledge could be prevented. Participants learned a complex motor skill, golf putting, either *without* simultaneous performance of a secondary task, to permit the use of working memory, or *with* simultaneous performance of a secondary task, to preclude the use of working memory. The secondary task, random letter generation (Baddeley, 1966), was hypothesized to prevent the acquisition of explicit knowledge by preventing the rehearsal/storage of task-relevant information in working memory. Learners who performed the secondary task during practice of the primary putting task failed to amass as much verbalizable knowledge of the putting skill as learners who performed the putting task only. Additionally, the putting performance of the secondary task group improved over trials, demonstrating that learning occurred. By showing learning in the presence of only very limited verbal knowledge, Masters demonstrated the possibility for implicit motor learning.

This work is of particular interest in motor learning as a result of Masters' (1992) claim to have demonstrated that implicitly learned motor skills were robust to disruption from evaluation-induced anxiety to perform well, whereas explicitly learned skills were not. He claimed that breakdown in these circumstances was due to the processing of explicit, verbal knowledge related to the mechanics of the movements, which accumulated during learning. In other words, these participants 'reinvested'. Participants with implicitly learned skills, on the other hand, had little explicit knowledge with which to reinvest and were, therefore, immune to the effects of this form of anxiety. Sceptical of the claims made by Masters (1992) regarding implicit motor learning, Hardy *et al.* (1996) replicated this study. Their initial proposal was that robust performance in the implicit learning condition during the stress phase was due to release from the secondary task load and not implicit learning *per se*. To test this possibility, they had two implicit groups learn the golf-putting task whilst performing the letter generation task. However, during the stress phase one implicit learning group continued performing the secondary, articulatory suppression task (ILAST), whereas the other implicit learning group performed the putting task only (IL). Hardy *et al.* argued that the IL group would show an increase in performance during the stress phase, but the ILAST group would not, indicating that release from the secondary task load was responsible for the robust performance of Masters' IL group during the stress phase. Despite their predictions the performance level of both groups improved during the stress phase, lending support to what Hardy *et al.* termed Masters' conscious processing hypothesis.

Mullen and Hardy (2000) recently provided further support for the conscious processing hypothesis by comparing the effects of processing task-relevant and irrelevant information on the putting performance of skilled golfers. They found that, under conditions that generated high anxiety, the processing of task-relevant information by skilled players led to a greater decrement in performance than was apparent when processing task-irrelevant information. This finding supports Masters' belief that it is the reinvestment of task-relevant knowledge that is responsible for breakdown of performance under pressure, rather than a general overload of processing capacity.

It is not only pressure conditions that can bring about reinvestment. Beilock and Carr (2001), for example, caused reinvestment by introducing novel task demands in a putting skill. Novice and experienced performers were asked to use an unusually shaped, 'funny', putter in one condition and a regular putter in a second condition. Verbal protocols were collected of their episodic memory for putting performance in both conditions. While novices, as one would expect, had a high degree of episodic recall in both funny putter and regular putter conditions (after all, they were manipulating verbal, declarative information in working memory when performing), experts exhibited significantly more recollection of the mechanics of their movements in the funny putter condition than the regular putter condition. It would appear that the funny putter condition led experts to become explicitly aware of the mechanics of their movements. The funny putter is perhaps an instrumental form of Potter's (1947) cognitive tactic of 'gamesmanship', in which reinvestment is caused by a passing comment on the uniqueness of an opponent's grip or stance.

Circumventing working memory during early learning

A method for reducing reliance on working memory during the learning period was recently developed by Maxwell *et al.* (2001). Based on a suggestion by Baddeley and Wilson (1994), they proposed that explicit processes deploy working memory to identify and correct errors during learning and performance, whereas implicit processes encode frequency information without the involvement of working memory and are unable to correct errors – accounting for the poor performance of implicit learners. If errors are absent, the contribution from working memory should be correspondingly low, and learning should be more implicit in nature.

Numerous studies have demonstrated that providing guidance or prompting during learning leads to better performance than trial and error learning (Holding, 1970; Hunkin *et al.*, 1998; Prather, 1971; Robinson and Storm, 1978; Singer, 1977; Wulf *et al.*, 1998). In the majority of these studies, performance during delayed retention and transfer tests was poorer for guided or errorless learners (Singer, 1977). However, in these studies errorless learners have performed the retention and transfer tests without the guidance received during learning. For example, Wulf *et al.* (1998) had participants learn a slalom ski-simulator task with the help of ski poles. During subsequent retention tests these poles were removed, crucially altering the requirements of the task and, thereby, reducing performance level. It is likely that during performance with the poles the upper body was able to supplement force production through weight-bearing activity, but when the poles were removed the upper body was no longer able to contribute to force production. Hence, performance was seen to deteriorate.

Prather (1971) observed that participants learning under errorless conditions appeared to acquire their skill in a passive manner, reminiscent of implicit learning, whereas learners in trial and error conditions seemed to actively test hypotheses, reminiscent of explicit modes of learning. Typically, when errors occur the learner will conceive and trial hypotheses about how to correct them

(Ohlsson, 1996). A visit to the local golf driving range should be enough to convince the reader of this phenomenon. A glance along the bays should reveal potential Open winners contorting their motor apparatus into the most biomechanically awkward positions, as working memory goes into overdrive to test various hypotheses aimed at correcting the location the ball previously landed in. Working memory serves to manipulate the explicit information required for the hypothesis testing process (Berry and Broadbent, 1984, 1988). When errors are absent, hypotheses are less likely to be tested because the movement is effective (successful). Errorless learners are, therefore, more likely to adopt a passive, implicit mode of learning by default and are not reliant on the availability of working memory. Reliance on working memory can be measured in two ways. First, the generation of verbalizable rules should be possible when working memory has been involved in skill acquisition, consistent with previous findings. Second, if working memory is not utilized to perform the primary task it should be available to perform a secondary task; however, if working memory is being utilized to perform the primary task, the introduction of a secondary task should result in a decrement in the performance of the primary task, the secondary task or both. Subsequently, Maxwell *et al.* (2001) compared an errorless with an errorful motor learning protocol in order to test these proposals.

Maxwell *et al.*'s (2001) experiments showed that when errors were prevented, or considerably reduced, during the learning of a task where task difficulty gradually progressed from easy to hard, an implicit mode of acquisition was adopted. On the other hand, when errors occurred as the task difficulty decreased, an explicit mode of acquisition was adopted. Errorful learners formed hypotheses about how to correct their errors during acquisition of the skill (golf putting), and this resulted in the accumulation of explicit, verbalizable rules and the breakdown of performance under secondary task loading. In contrast, the errorless learners acquired the golf-putting skill passively, without testing hypotheses, because there were no errors to correct. Participants accumulated little verbal knowledge and demonstrated robust performance under dual task conditions, characteristic of implicit learning. The performance of errorless learners was also superior to those of errorful learners throughout, suggesting that this method may prove useful in applied settings.

Prevention of hypothesis testing by withholding outcome feedback

Maintaining the concept that reduced hypothesis testing will inhibit the accumulation of explicit task-relevant knowledge, Maxwell *et al.* (1999) and Maxwell and Masters (submitted) investigated the consequences of manipulating the presence of outcome feedback during learning. Visual, auditory, proprioceptive and tactile sensory feedback is normally available to performers for appraising the outcome of their actions (Magill, 1993). In most motor learning situations (at a golf driving range, for instance), the learner predominantly relies upon visual feedback to assess whether the relationship between the intention/action and the outcome is satisfactory. In fact, the saliency of proprioceptive (and other) stimuli may be overridden by the dominant visual information (Kelso, 1982). Maxwell *et al.* (1999) and Maxwell and Masters (submitted) hypothesized that performing a novel movement without access to visual sensory feedback pertaining to the outcome would result in the adoption of an implicit learning strategy, because without information about the outcome of their actions the performer would be unable to formulate hypothetical rules or appraise performance strategies. Thus, two processes were proposed, one dependent, the other independent, of working memory. Working memory dependent learning should be characterized by reportable (declarative) knowledge and subsequent performance breakdown under secondary task loading, due to reliance on working memory for control of the primary task. In contrast, working memory independent learning should be characterized by poor explication of the (motor) processes required to accomplish the task and robust performance under secondary task loading.

Maxwell *et al.* (1999) carried out three experiments in which verbal protocols were collected following a learning phase where outcome feedback regarding the success of a golf putt was either present (Working Memory Dependent, WMD) or absent (Working Memory Independent, WMI). Participants then completed a test phase comprising two retention tests, one before and one after a secondary task transfer test. All forms of feedback were available during the test phase. During the transfer test, the performance of the primary putting task was accompanied by a concurrent tone counting task in order to examine whether support was required from working memory for performance of the primary task.

In Experiment one, participants who learned with and without visual outcome feedback were aware of numerous aspects of their motor output and were consequently able to verbally report them. This finding was expected in the WMD condition, but not in the (reduced feedback) WMI condition. Unimpeded by having visual sources of information to process, the resources of WM in this condition appeared to be diverted to manipulate proprioceptive and tactile feedback information associated with motor output, which resulted in explicit rather than implicit learning. The number of rules reported by the WMI group, which were not significantly different from those reported by the WMD group, provided support for this conclusion. Further support was provided by the performance of the groups under secondary task loading. Both groups of participants showed a similar degradation in performance when required to perform the secondary task whilst putting, suggesting that participants learnt in an explicit, selective manner, utilizing working memory.

Participants in Experiment two performed the putting task either with (WMD) or without (WMI) visual sensory feedback, but were also asked to perform a visual search task between trials. The visual search task was designed to replace the absent visual and auditory feedback in the WMI condition and so avoid diversion of the attentional resources of working memory to the proprioceptive and tactile sensory information associated with putting. It was anticipated that the visual search task would have no effect on performance in the (full feedback) WMD condition, as the absence of time constraints allowed the outcome of the putt to be registered before the visual search task was attempted.

The combination of absent visual feedback and surrogate attentional load (visual search task) between trials prevented the build up of declarative knowledge in the WMI treatment condition. Verbal protocols indicated that at the end of the learning phase participants in this condition had accrued significantly fewer rules than those in the WMD condition. This result supports the contention that they did not utilize working memory to process primary task information during the learning phase.

During the Transfer Test, all participants performed a secondary tone-counting task whilst putting. The performance level of the WMI group continued to rise, supporting the hypothesis that there was no manipulation of explicit, declarative knowledge by working memory to support performance of the primary task. The WMD group, however, suffered a drop in performance while performing the secondary task, reflecting their reliance on working memory.

Further support was evident in the third experiment when the acceleration profile of the club was assessed during the putting movement. As learning proceeds, movements generally become smoother and less jerky and trial-to-trial variability decreases (Hogan, 1984; Schneider and Zernicke, 1989; Young and Marteniuk, 1997). On this basis, the reduced feedback (WMI) group was expected to demonstrate changes in their acceleration profile similar to those produced while learning with feedback. In particular, jerk and between trial variability was expected to decrease and smoothness expected to increase. Additionally, it was predicted that changes in performance due to the imposition of a secondary task would be reflected in the kinematic profile produced by the acceleration of the club head. For example, the jerkiness of the movement was expected to increase, suggesting a mechanism through which performance deteriorates. Analysis of kinematic data derived from the acceleration of the club head, 100 milliseconds prior to and after contact with the ball, illustrated that during learning the WMI and WMD conditions experienced similar changes in acceleration profile, jerk and smoothness. Under secondary task loading, however, the WMD condition exhibited adverse changes in jerk associated with disrupted performance, whereas performance remained robust in the WMI condition, with no changes in smoothness or jerkiness (see Figure 10.1).

It was concluded that the replacement of visual outcome feedback with an irrelevant visual search task during learning prohibits the build up of task-relevant explicit information. Motor output improves, but is independent of working memory, as demonstrated by robust performance under secondary task loading.

Behavioural adaptation to unconsciously perceived environmental information

The major theoretical drawback with the 'no-feedback paradigm' is the lack of noticeable performance improvement during the learning stage, not to mention the lack of ecological validity of such a technique. This issue raises the question of whether outcome feedback can be presented in such a way that the learner does not have access to explicit information regarding the outcome of the

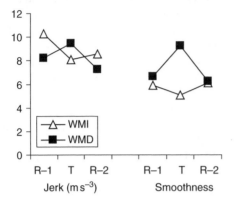

Figure 10.1 Jerk and smoothness profiles for the WMI and WMD groups in the no feedback experiment (higher values indicate increased jerk but decreased smoothness. R, retention test; T, secondary task transfer test).

movement (and by implication, cannot use working memory to test hypotheses), yet still modifies his or her motor behaviour to learn. There is no doubt that information in the environment has the potential to influence behaviour without us becoming consciously aware of that information. Henry (1953), for example, showed that learners could respond to random pressure changes in order to hold a lever in a constant position, despite the fact that the pressure changes were so low that they could not be consciously perceived. More recently, Haffendon and Goodale (1998) provided a neat illustration of the effect of unconsciously perceived information on subsequent actions. Their study was based on the observation that grip aperture is consistently scaled to the size of an object that is about to be grasped (Goodale and Servos, 1996). When presented with a version of the Ebbinghaus or Titchner illusion (see Figure 10.2), participants verbally indicated that one circle/line appeared bigger than the other, consistent with the normal response to such illusions. However, when asked to position their thumb and forefinger as if they were about to pick up the line/circle, the aperture was scaled to the physical size of the disc and not the apparent size. The dissociation between perceived size and grip size remained when the central circles were adjusted so that they appeared identical, but were not. Participants stated that the circles were the same size, yet, altered the dimension of their grip to the actual size of the circle (Aglioti *et al.*, 1995).

Haffendon and Goodale (1998) suggested that the information used to guide prehension is unavailable to consciousness because it is processed in a separate pathway from the information of which we become aware. They argued that the ventral pathway transmits 'what' information to the inferior temporal cortex and results in conscious awareness of environmental cues, whereas the dorsal pathway transmits 'how' information to the posterior parietal cortex, which remains unconscious and is used to guide action (Servos *et al.*, 2000).

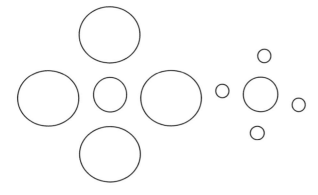

Figure 10.2 Ebbinghaus illusion, the centre circles are of the same size but the one surrounded by larger circles is usually perceived as smaller than the one surrounded by small circles.

Accurate action in the face of distorted conscious perception of the environment has been replicated a number of times with different tasks. For example, the trajectory of movements directed at targets can be altered on the basis of unperceived changes in target location (Goodale *et al.*, 1986). In addition, the subjective physical ability of the performer may affect conscious judgements but not action driven judgements. For example, Bhalla and Proffitt (1999) reported that low physical fitness, carrying a heavy backpack, fatigue and age all affected verbal reports of the steepness of a hill – the hill was perceived to be steeper in these conditions than controlled conditions. Haptic estimations of steepness, however, using hand inclination to mimic the slope of the hill, were not altered.

Ghahramani *et al.* (1996) examined the effects of manipulating visual feedback on perceptions of felt arm position. Using a virtual feedback system, they were able to introduce a 10 cm discrepancy between the true position of the hand and a target representing the position of the hand, such that they appeared to be in the same place but were actually 10 cm apart in the *x* or *y* direction. Participants quickly adapted their movements, but post-experimental interviews revealed that they were unaware of the incongruity. In a later study, Goodbody and Wolpert (1999) surreptitiously introduced an 8 cm displacement (2 mm per trial over forty trials) to the right or left of actual hand position. Participants adapted their hand movements to accommodate the inconsistency but were unaware of the displacement. A similar study introduced visual displacement, using small-displacement prisms (five dioptres), of a target that was to be touched with the index finger (Jakobson and Goodale, 1989). Participants adjusted their arm position to reach the target but were unaware that their visual field had been displaced.

These demonstrations of successful visually-guided actions, despite a misguided conscious perception of the environment, provide evidence that adaptive behaviour need not depend on awareness of the precise perceptual stimuli that instigate movement, and establishes the basic premise that we can act upon feedback of which we are not fully aware. This raises the question of whether *motor learning* is possible if visual outcome feedback is presented below the awareness threshold. Clearly, if the learner is unaware of the outcome feedback, there will be little likelihood that working memory will be able to oversee hypothesis testing. Consequently, there should be no declarative stage to the learning process and *implicit* motor learning should occur.

Presentation of marginally perceptible outcome feedback

Cheesman and Merikle (1984) made a distinction between subjective and objective thresholds of stimulus identification following considerable debate in the literature regarding the objectivity/subjectivity of measures of subliminal perception (e.g. Fowler *et al.*, 1981; Marcel, 1983). The Cheesman and Merikle distinction is now an accepted method by which to present marginally perceptible (subliminal) stimuli (Greenwald *et al.*, 1995; Kemp-Wheeler and Hill, 1988). In typical studies, one of several target stimuli is presented through a tachistoscope for various stimulus durations. At long stimulus durations, the observer can report the target identity, they are aware of what they see and can confidently estimate their accuracy. As the stimulus duration is reduced, confidence decreases and eventually observers will report that they can no longer see the stimulus and are guessing its identity. Typically, at this subjective threshold, participants perform at above chance levels, despite their apparent lack of conscious awareness. If the stimulus duration is further reduced to the objective threshold, performance will drop to chance levels, at which point the observer is truly guessing the identity of the stimulus (Cheesman and Merikle, 1984; Holender, 1986).

Masters *et al.* (2001) adopted this notion of a subjective threshold to test whether complex skills, such as golf putting can be acquired without conscious awareness of outcome feedback. It was hypothesized that presentation of outcome feedback at the subjective threshold would result in learning even though performers believed that they were not receiving useful information. It was argued that, due to the lack of conscious access to the outcome information, working memory would be unable to generate explicit, task-relevant information. Learning in the subjective threshold condition was expected to be implicit.

The experimental apparatus was arranged in such a way that participants had no knowledge of the outcome of their putts immediately after the point at which they struck the ball with the putter. The only outcome feedback they received, and hence the only impression they had of target location, was presented through a tachistoscope, at either a subjective or objective threshold. Both the objective and the subjective threshold of each participant was established prior to commencing the motor learning task. Each participant performed 500 learning trials and then provided a verbal account of the rules or strategies they had developed to accomplish the task. The group that received feedback at their objective threshold reported that they were unaware of using any strategies and that they had no idea of how well they had performed. Their performance did not increase over trials, which suggests that learning did not occur. The group which received feedback at its subjective threshold was also unable to provide verbal accounts of its performance; however, its putting performance increased over trials. These findings were replicated in two further experiments, which also demonstrated that the performance of subjective threshold learners was robust under secondary task loading, suggesting independence from working memory.

Heuristic instruction

By now, the more practically minded reader may have begun to ask how any of the techniques described can be used in an applied setting, over the many years that it takes to become proficient in motor skill. Masters (2000) and Liao and Masters (2001) have recently proposed an alternative, more user friendly technique that, paradoxically, relies on explicit instruction. This technique, termed analogy learning, is designed to reduce the amount of information consciously processed in working memory during learning by repackaging (or chunking) task-relevant 'rules' and knowledge into a single, all encompassing, biomechanical metaphor or heuristic. In the domains of pedagogy and problem-solving, it has been argued that knowledge conveyed in this way is not rule-based, but represents a higher order relationship among the rules of the concept (Gentner, 1982, 1983). Donnelly and McDaniel (1993), for example, showed that analogy learners had the facility to apply the concept described by the analogy despite an inability to answer questions about the rules underlying the concept. This same phenomenon is regarded as a defining characteristic of implicit learning (Berry, 1991; Berry and Broadbent, 1984; Hayes and Broadbent, 1988).

Liao and Masters (2001) asked novices to acquire a table tennis forehand shot with topspin under Analogy, Explicit Instruction or Implicit (dual task) conditions. The Analogy group was instructed to draw a right angle triangle (hypotenuse uppermost) with the bat and to strike the ball as the bat passed up the hypotenuse of the triangle. The Explicit Instruction group was provided with a set of twelve rules adapted from a table tennis coaching manual. The Implicit group was given no instructions and was required to perform a secondary, random letter generation task while learning to perform the table tennis task. All participants performed 300 learning trials, followed by a fifty-trial secondary task transfer test and a fifty-trial delayed retention test. No differential effect of learning condition on performance was observed during the learning phase or in the delayed retention test. However, the performance of the Explicit Instruction group was impaired by secondary task loading, whereas the performances of the other two groups remained robust. These results were interpreted as support for the assertion that, as a simple heuristic, learning by analogy places fewer demands on working memory than learning by more complex, explicit algorithms of instruction.

In a second experiment, Liao and Masters (2001) evaluated the efficacy of analogy learning, relative to explicit learning, by measuring performance under psychological stress. Performance in the explicitly instructed condition deteriorated under pressure, consistent with previous findings; however, performance in the analogy learning condition remained robust. This finding was recently replicated using supportive versus adversarial audience conditions as the stressor (Law *et al.*, in press). Limiting the amount of accessible, explicit knowledge of the motor task, by introducing an analogy that implicitly conveys a substantial amount of information, would appear to reduce the possibility for reinvestment. This idea extends well from the work of Todd and Gigerenzer (2000), who argued that simple rules or heuristics are as effective as complex rules and algorithms for imparting new data. In motor learning terms, the analogy is a simple instructional heuristic with which to present new rules and techniques to novice learners implicitly. It is expected to perform comparably with the highly complex algorithms (see Masters, 2000) traditionally used to instruct novices acquiring a motor skill.

A working model of implicit and explicit learning

In this chapter we opened with a description of the traditional view of how motor skills are acquired by a novice performer (e.g. Anderson, 1983; Fitts, 1964). Hypotheses are derived by the learner and evaluated against performance outcomes, leading to the formation of conscious, verbalizable bits of knowledge that are manipulated in a temporary information processing work space, commonly described as working memory, to support motor output. These bits of knowledge are gradually compiled or chunked (e.g. Anderson, 1982, 1987; Newell and Rosenbloom, 1981) through repeated direction of the motor system by working memory, until performance proceeds in an uninterrupted, automatic fashion. This account portrays a progression from motor output supported by predominantly explicit, declarative knowledge that is dependent on the availability of working memory to output supported by predominantly implicit, procedural knowledge that can be applied independently of working memory. The model presented in Figure 10.3 takes as its basic structure this fundamental progression, mimicking traditional memory system models (e.g. Anderson, 1982; Atkinson and Shiffrin, 1968; Colley, 1989), but provides an alternative avenue for progression. All of the components of the model can contribute to motor output to varying degrees, depending on the nature of the learning experience, the amount of practice and concurrent demands within the performance environment (e.g. fatigue, injury, anxiety, distraction). The novice who has received a set of verbal instructions from a coach, for example, will utilize predominantly explicit control of output, represented on the left side of the diagram. As learning progresses, the balance tends to shift to the right side as implicit knowledge accumulates. Implicit motor learning interventions are designed to promote *primarily* right-sided control (even in the early stages of acquisition) by diminishing the role of working memory and preventing the accumulation of unwieldy explicit knowledge. Working memory remains accessible, however, and can be re-introduced into control of output strategically (as represented by the dashed arrow). For example, an anxious performer may manipulate available explicit knowledge via working memory, hoping

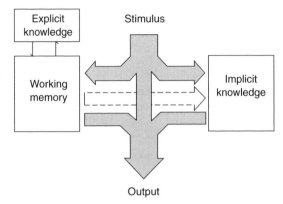

Figure 10.3 A model outlining the role of working memory in implicit and explicit motor learning.

that this will ensure successful performance, or a performer carrying an injury may choose to strategically alter control of their motor apparatus in order to reduce the impact of that injury. Eventually, the performer may rely exclusively on implicit processes; in fact, action (output) might be initiated directly by perception (stimulus), consistent with ecological views of movement control (Gibson, 1979; Summers, 1998).

The dynamical systems approach (Kelso, 1982, 1995) attempts to describe physical principles that underlie complex interactions, such as motor coordination (Beek *et al.*, 1995). Groups of muscles are hypothesized to work together in coordinated units or structures independent of metacognition. For example, when one abducts the arm, postural adjustments automatically occur to compensate for the change in centre of gravity. The arm and postural muscles form a functional unit. It is possible that conscious control of action breaks down these functional synergies into their component parts. This would result in a dramatic increase in the number of degrees of freedom that have to be controlled by the performer. The increased complexity that additional degrees of freedom incur is likely to exceed the attentional resources available to the performer, thus disrupting performance.

The evolution of verbal and motor skills

Reber (1993) developed the case for a biological approach to the theory of implicit learning, taking into account the evolutionary history of the species. This view was echoed by Cosmides and Tooby (1994), who argued that psychologists should view the functioning of the brain in the light of what it was designed to accomplish. Motor function is almost certainly an evolutionary predecessor of cognitive functioning, in that action came before words. After all, it is unlikely that the motor system developed to enable verbal communication or that verbal communication systems developed in order to control action, although they are clearly able to cooperate to produce speech. If our ancestors were capable of learning prior to the arrival of verbal communication, and they undoubtedly were, then motor skills must have been acquired/communicated by some non-verbal (implicit) process. Whatever that process, it was clearly effective (since the species survived) and is likely to have endured to the present day (Reber, 1993). It is our contention that this process is implicit motor learning.

Similar concepts are addressed in Donald's (1991) conjecture that the earliest memory system was procedural (Mathews and Roussel, 1997) and that declarative memory evolved later. Donald proposed a transition from mimetic skill (or copying), as a means of communication, to the replacement of overt action with symbols that represented actions and events (i.e. words). These symbols are unlikely to represent the full richness that visual appraisal of an event allows. Instead, they provide a degraded, yet highly manipulable, approximation. The ease with which symbols, such as words, can be conveyed ensured their success but did little to enhance the already well-developed motor control system. Based on their evolutionary development and the tasks that they were designed to accomplish, it is no surprise that dissociations and interference, as well as limited cooperation, between verbal (explicit) and motor (implicit) processes should be discovered. What is surprising is the absence of attempts to incorporate evolutionary theory in motor learning theory. Extensive integration is apparent within cognitive and social psychology (e.g. Tooby and Cosmides, 1990, 1992) and consciousness (e.g. Dennett, 1995; MacPhail, 1998), yet a recent introduction to evolutionary psychology (Badcock, 2000) makes no reference to motor learning or control.

In response to our own criticism, taking Donald's contention that mimicry was an evolutionary antecedent of verbally-based communication, we predict that observation should have an advantage over verbal instruction during motor learning, particularly if verbally-based working memory resources are prevented from interfering with the mimetic process. Observation is clearly beneficial for learning in certain circumstances (Bandura, 1971; Scully and Newell, 1985) and this may be due to some property endowed by the earlier evolutionary development of the mental processes that mediate its use. The zombie within (Chalmers, 1996) may yet relearn some old tricks.

Summary and future directions

As a whole, the evidence suggests that motor actions can be adapted to accomplish a goal without the performer being consciously aware of what has changed or how. The performer may be aware that his or her performance has improved but consistently is unable to describe what it is that they are now doing. It is clear that these findings add credibility to the argument that motor learning and performance can proceed without contributions from conscious processing. Although it is equally clear that conscious processing does affect the acquisition of motor skills. For generations, verbal instructions have, understandably, been utilized as a primary tool for passing on knowledge about how to perform physical skills. The employment of verbal instruction is often justified by the premise that conscious control of actions is an important aspect of a novice's (un)skilled behaviour. The evidence presented here, however, suggests that conscious processing may not be up to the job and that the provision of declarative knowledge may, in some cases, be detrimental to skill acquisition and performance.

Future research should focus on the delineation of implicit from explicit processes and their relative contributions to performance of motor skills. Quite simply, when should conscious control be used and when should we allow the implicit system to get on with the job unheeded? To answer this question, a clear understanding is required of what constitutes implicit and explicit knowledge and of the extent to which we can expect implicit processes to cope with task demands. Explicit processes probably evolved because they allow a phenomenal degree of flexibility that was not already available. Beek (2000), for example, argues that in extreme cases it is a '...blessing rather than a curse to be able to consciously develop alternative motor strategies on the basis of explicit knowledge' (p. 553), but presents no evidence that implicit processes cannot cope in such cases. If implicit (motor) processes can cope, what is conscious control really for?

References

Abrams, M. and Reber, A. S. (1988). Implicit learning: robustness in the face of psychiatric disorder. *Journal of Psycholinguistic Research*, 17, 425–439.

Aglioti, S., DeSouza, J. F. X. and Goodale, M. A. (1995). Size-contrast illusions deceive the eye but not the hand. *Current Biology*, 5, 679–685.

Allen, R. and Reber, A. S. (1980). Very long term memory for tacit knowledge. *Cognition*, 8, 175–185.

Anderson, J. R. (1982). Acquisition of cognitive skill. *Psychological Review*, 89, 369–406.

Anderson, J. R. (1983). *The architecture of cognition*. Cambridge, MA: Harvard University Press.

Anderson, J. R. (1987). Skill acquisition: compilation of weak-method problem solutions. *Psychological Review*, 94, 192–210.

Atkinson, R. C. and Shiffrin, R. M. (1968). Human memory: a proposed system and its control processes. In K. W. Spence (Ed.), *The psychology of learning and motivation: advances in research and theory*. New York: Academic Press.

Badcock, C. (2000). *Evolutionary psychology*. Cambridge: Polity Press.

Baddeley, A. D. (1966). The capacity for generating information by randomisation. *Quarterly Journal of Experimental Psychology*, 18, 119–129.

Baddeley, A. D. (1999). *Essentials of human memory*. Hove: Psychology Press Ltd.

Baddeley, A. D. and Hitch, G. (1974). Working memory. In G. A. Bower (Ed.), *Recent advances in learning and motivation*, Vol. 8. New York: Academic Press.

Baddeley, A. D. and Wilson, B. A. (1994). When implicit learning fails: amnesia and the problem of error elimination. *Neuropsychologia*, 32, 53–68.

Bandura, A. (1971). *Social learning theory*. New York: General Learning Press.

Baumeister, R. F. (1984). Choking under pressure: self-consciousness and paradoxical effects of incentives on skilful performance. *Journal of Personality and Social Psychology*, 46, 610–620.

Bawden, M. A. K., Maynard, I. W. and Westbury, T. (2001). The effects of conscious control of movement and dispositional self-consciousness on golf putting performance. *Journal of Sports Sciences*, 19, 68–69.

Beek, P. J. (2000). Toward a theory of implicit learning in the perceptual-motor domain. *International Journal of Sport Psychology*, 31, 547–554.

Beek, P. J., Peper, C. E. and Stegeman, D. F. (1995). Dynamical models of movement coordination. *Human Movement Science*, 14, 573–608.

Beilock, S. L. and Carr, T. H. (2001). On the fragility of skilled performance: what governs choking under pressure? *Journal of Experimental Psychology: General*, 130, 701–725.

Berry, D. C. (1991). The role of action in implicit learning. *Quarterly Journal of Experimental Psychology*, 43, 881–906.

Berry, D. C. and Broadbent, D. E. (1984). On the relationship between task performance and associated verbalisable knowledge. *Quarterly Journal of Experimental Psychology*, 36, 209–231.

Berry, D. C. and Broadbent, D. E. (1988). Interactive tasks and the implicit–explicit distinction. *British Journal of Psychology*, 79, 251–272.

Berry, D. C. and Dienes, Z. (1993). *Implicit learning: theoretical and empirical issues*. Hove, England: Lawrence Erlbaum Associates, Inc.

Bhalla, M. and Proffitt, D. R. (1999). Visual-motor recalibration in geographical slant perception. *Journal of Experimental Psychology: Human Perception and Performance*, 25, 1076–1096.

Bliss, C. B. (1895). Investigations in reaction time and attention. *Studies from the Yale Psychological Laboratory*, 1892–1893, 1, 1–55.

Boder, D. P. (1935). The influence of concomitant activity and fatigue upon certain forms of reciprocal hand movement and its fundamental components. *Comparative Psychology Monographs*, 11, 4.

Borkovec, T. D. (1976). Physiological and cognitive processes in the regulation of anxiety. In G. E. Schwartz and D. Shapiro (Eds), *Consciousness and self-regulation: advances in research I*. New York: Plenum Press.

Bryan, W. L. and Harter, N. (1897). Studies in the physiology and psychology of the telegraphic language. *Psychological Review*, 4, 27–53.

Chalmers, D. J. (1996). *The Conscious mind: in search of a fundamental theory*. Oxford: Oxford University Press.

Cheesman, J. and Merikle, P. M. (1984). Priming with and without awareness. *Perception and Psychophysics*, 36, 387–395.

Colley, A. M. (1989). Learning motor skills: integrating cognition and action. In A. M. Colley and J. R. Beech (Eds), *Acquisition and performance of cognitive skills*. London: John Wiley & Sons.

Cosmides, L. and Tooby, J. (1994). Beyond intuition and instinct blindness: Towards an evolutionarily rigorous cognitive science. *Cognition*, 50, 41–77.

Curran, T. and Keele, S. W. (1993). Attentional and nonattentional forms of sequence learning. *Journal of Experimental Psychology: Learning, Memory and Cognition*, 19, 189–202.

Deikman, A. J. (1969). Deautomatization and the mystic experience. In C. T. Tart (Ed.), *Altered states of consciousness*. New York: Wiley.

Dennett, D. C. (1995). *Darwin's dangerous idea: evolution and the meanings of life*. New York: Simon and Schuster.

Donald, M. (1991). *Origins of the modern mind: three stages in the evolution of culture and cognition*. Cambridge, MA: Harvard University Press.

Donnelly, C. M. and McDaniel, M. A. (1993). Use of analogy in learning scientific concepts. *Journal of Experimental Psychology: Learning, Memory and Cognition*, 19, 975–987.

Fenigstein, A., Scheier, M. F. and Buss, A. H. (1975). Public and private self-consciousness: assessment and theory. *Journal of Consulting and Clinical Psychology*, 43, 522–527.

Fitts, P. M. (1964). Perceptual-motor skill learning. In A. W. Melton (Ed.), *Categories of human learning*. New York: Academic Press.

Fitts, P. M. and Posner, M. I. (1967). *Human performance*. Belmont, CA: Brooks/Cole.

Fowler, C. A., Wolford, G. T., Slade, R. and Tassinary, L. (1981). Lexical access with and without awareness. *Journal of Experimental Psychology: General*, 110, 341–362.

Gentner, D. (1982). Are scientific analogies metaphors? In D. S. Miall (Ed.), *Metaphor: problems and perspectives*. Brighton, England: Harvester Press.

Gentner, D. (1983). Structure-mapping: a theoretical framework. *Cognitive Science*, 7, 155–170.

Ghahramani, Z., Wolpert, D. M. and Jordan, M. I. (1996). Generalization to local remappings of the visuomotor coordinate transformation. *Journal of Neuroscience*, 16, 7085–7096.

Gibson, J. J. (1979). *The ecological approach to visual perception*. Boston, MA: Houghton Mifflin.

Goodale, M. A., Pélisson, D. and Prablanc, C. (1986). Large adjustments in visually guided reaching do not depend on vision of the hand or perception of target displacement. *Nature*, 320 (6064), 748–750.

Goodale, M. A. and Servos, P. (1996). Visual control of prehension. In H. Zelaznik (Ed.), *Advances in motor learning and control* (pp. 87–121). Champaign, IL: Human Kinetics.

Goodbody, S. J. and Wolpert, D. M. (1999). The effect of visuomotor displacements on arm movement paths. *Experimental Brain Research*, 127, 213–223.

Greenwald, A. G., Klinger, M. R. and Schuh, E. S. (1995). Activation by marginally perceptible ('subliminal') stimuli: dissociation of unconscious from conscious cognition. *Journal of Experimental Psychology: General*, 124, 22–42.

Haffendon, A. and Goodale, M. A. (1998). The effect of pictorial illusion on prehension and perception. *Journal of Cognitive Neuroscience*, 10, 122–136.

Hardy, L., Mullen, R. and Jones, G. (1996). Knowledge and conscious control of motor actions under stress. *British Journal of Psychology*, 87, 621–636.

Hayes, N. A. and Broadbent, D. E. (1988). Two modes of learning for interactive tasks. *Cognition*, 28, 249–276.

Henry, F. M. (1953). Dynamic kinaesthetic perception and adjustment. *Research Quarterly*, 24, 176–187.

Henry, F. M. and Rogers, D. E. (1960). Increased response latency for complicated movements and a 'memory drum' theory of neuromotor reaction. *Research Quarterly*, 31, 448–458.

Hogan, N. (1984). An organizing principle for a class of voluntary movements. *Journal of Neuroscience*, 4, 2745–2754.

Holding, D. H. (1970). Repeated errors in motor learning. *Ergonomics*, 13, 727–734

Holender, D. (1986). Semantic activation without conscious identification in dichotic listening, parafoveal vision, and visual masking: a survey and appraisal. *The Behavioural and Brain Sciences*, 9, 1–66.

Hunkin, M. H., Squires, E. J., Parkin, A. J. and Tidy, J. A. (1998). Are the benefits of errorless learning dependent on implicit memory? *Neuropsychologia*, 36, 25–36.

Jacoby, L. L., Allen, L. G., Collins, J. C. and Larwill, L. K. (1988). Memory influences subjective experience: noise judgements. *Journal of Experimental Psychology: Learning, Memory and Cognition*, 14, 240–247.

Jacoby, L. L., Woloshyn, V. and Kelley, C. M. (1989). Becoming famous without being recognised: unconscious influences of memory produced by dividing attention. *Journal of Experimental Psychology: General*, 118, 115–125.

Jakobson, L. S. and Goodale, M. A. (1989). Trajectories of reaches to prismatically-displaced targets: evidence for 'automatic' visuomotor recalibration. *Experimental Brain Research*, 78, 575–587.

Kellogg, R. T. (1982). When can we introspect accurately about mental processes? *Memory and Cognition*, 10, 141–144.

Kelso, J. A. S. (1982). *Human motor behaviour: an introduction*. Hillsdale, NJ: Lawrence Erlbaum Associates, Publishers.

Kelso, J. A. S. (1995). *Dynamic patterns*. Cambridge, USA: MIT Press.

Kemp-Wheeler, S. M. and Hill, A. B. (1988). Semantic priming without awareness: some methodological considerations and replications. *The Quarterly Journal of Experimental Psychology*, 40A, 671–692.

Law, J., Masters, R., Bray, S., Eves, F. and Bardswell, I. (in press). An explicit example of supportive audience disruption to skilled performance. *Journal of Sport & Exercise Psychology*.

Lees, A. J. (1998). Abnormal movement disorders. In B. D. Jordan (Ed.), *Sports Neurology* (2nd ed.) Philadelphia, PA: Lippincott-Raven.

Liao, C. and Masters, R. S. W. (2001). Analogy learning: a means to implicit motor learning. *Journal of Sports Sciences*, 19, 307–319.

Liao, C. and Masters, R. S. W. (2002). Self-focused attention and performance failure under psychological stress. *Journal of Sport & Exercise Psychology*, 24, 289–305.

Light, L. L. and Singh, A. (1987). Implicit and explicit memory in young and older adults. *Journal of Experimental Psychology: Learning, Memory and Cognition*, 13, 531–541.

MacPhail, E. M. (1998). *The evolution of consciousness*. Oxford: Oxford University Press.

Magill, R. A. (1993). *Motor learning: concepts and applications*, 4th edn. Wisconsin: Brown & Benchmark.

Marcel, A. J. (1983). Conscious and unconscious perception: experiments on visual masking and word recognition. *Cognitive Psychology*, 15, 197–237.

Masters, R. S. W. (1992). Knowledge, knerves and know-how: the role of explicit versus implicit knowledge in the breakdown of a complex motor skill under pressure. *British Journal of Psychology*, 83, 343–358.

Masters, R. S. W. (2000). Theoretical aspects of implicit learning in sport. *International Journal of Sport Psychology*, 31, 530–541.

Masters, R. S. W., Polman, R. C. J. and Hammond, N. V. (1993). 'Reinvestment': a dimension of personality implicated in skill breakdown under pressure. *Personality and Individual Differences*, 14, 655–666.

Masters, R. S. W., Maxwell, J. P. and Eves, F. F. (2001). Implicit motor learning: perception of outcome feedback without awareness. Proceedings of the 10th World Congress of Sport Psychology.

Mathews, R. C. and Roussel, L. G. (1997). Abstractness of implicit knowledge: a cognitive evolutionary perspective. In D. C. Berry (Ed.), *How implicit is implicit learning?* (pp. 13–47) New York: Oxford University Press.

Maxwell, J. P. and Masters, R. S. W. (submitted). Reinvestment: a propensity to turn one's attention to the mechanics of one's movements – further validation of the Reinvestment Scale.

Maxwell, J. P., Masters, R. S. W. and Eves, F. (1999). Explicit versus implicit motor learning: dissociating selective and unselective modes of skill acquisition via feedback manipulation. *Journal of Sport Sciences*, 6, 559.

Maxwell, J. P., Masters, R. S. W. and Eves, F. (2000). From novice to no know-how: a longitudinal study of implicit motor learning. *Journal of Sport Sciences*, 18, 111–120.

Maxwell, J. P., Masters, R. S. W., Kerr, E. and Weedon, E. (2001). The implicit benefit of learning without errors. *Quarterly Journal of Experimental Psychology*, 54A, 1049–1068.

Mullen, R. and Hardy, L. (2000). State anxiety and motor performance: testing the conscious processing hypothesis. *Journal of Sport Sciences*, 18, 785–799.

Newell, A. and Rosenbloom, P. (1981). Mechanisms of skill acquisition and the law of practice. In J. R. Anderson (Ed.), *Cognitive skills and their acquisition*. Hillsdale, NJ: Lawrence Erlbaum.

Ohlsson, S. (1996). Learning from performance errors. *Psychological Review*, 103, 241–262.

Orrell, A., Eves, F. F. and Masters, R. S. W. (2002). 'Reinvestment': a dimension of the stroke personality? Paper presented at the 3rd World Congress of Neurological Rehabilitation, Venice, Italy.

Pall, P. S., Masters, R. S. W. and MacMahon, K. M. A. (2001). Reinvestment as an aspect of personality in Parkinson's disease. Paper presented at the First World Congress of Neurology, London, England.

Potter, S. (1947). *The theory and practice of gamesmanship*. Harmondsworth, Middlesex: Penguin.

Prather, D. C. (1971). Trial-and-error versus errorless learning: training, transfer and stress. *American Journal of Psychology*, 84, 377–386.

Reason, J. and Mycielska, K. (1982). *Absent-minded? the psychology of mental lapses and everyday errors*. Englewood Cliffs, NJ: Prentice-Hall.

Reber, A. S. (1993). Implicit learning and tacit knowledge: an essay on the cognitive unconscious. New York: Oxford University Press.

Reber, A. S., Walkenfeld, F. F. and Hernstadt, R. (1991). Implicit and explicit learning: individual differences and IQ. *Journal of Experimental Psychology: Learning, Memory and Cognition*, 17, 888–896.

Robinson, P. W. and Storm, R. H. (1978). Effects of error and errorless discrimination acquisition on reversal learning. *Journal of Experimental Analysis of Behaviour*, 29, 517–525.

Salmoni, A. W. (1989). Motor skill learning. In D. H. Holding (Ed.), *Human skills*. Chichester, UK: Wiley & Sons.

Schacter, D. L. (1987). Implicit memory: history and current status. *Journal of Experimental Psychology: Learning, Memory and Cognition*, 13, 501–518.

Schneider, W. and Schiffrin, R. M. (1977). Controlled and automated human information processing: I: detection, search and attention. *Psychological Review*, 44, 627–644.

Schneider, K. and Zernicke, R. F. (1989). Jerk-cost modulations during the practice of rapid arm movements. *Biological Cybernetics*, 60, 221–230.

Scully, D. M. and Newell, K. M. (1985). Observational learning and the acquisition of motor skills: towards a visual perception perspective. *Journal of Human Movement Studies*, 11, 169–186.

Seger, C. A. (1994). Implicit learning. *Psychological Bulletin*, 115, 163–196.

Servos, P., Carnahan, H. and Fedwick, J. (2000). The visuomotor system resists the horizontal–vertical illusion. *Journal of Motor Behaviour*, 32, 400–404.

Singer, R. N. (1977). To err or not to err: a question for the instruction of psychomotor skills. *Review of Educational Research*, 47, 479–498.

Summers, J. J. (1998). Has ecological psychology delivered what it promised? In J. P. Piek (Ed.), *Motor behaviour and human skill: a multidisciplinary approach*. Champaign, IL: Human Kinetics Publishers.

Todd, P. M. and Gigerenzer, G. (2000). Precis of simple heuristics that make us smart. *Behavioural and Brain Sciences*, 23, 727–741.

Tooby, J. and Cosmides, L. (1990). On the universality of human nature and the uniqueness of the individual: the role of genetics and adaptation. *Journal of Personality*, 58, 17–67.

Tooby, J. and Cosmides, L. (1992). The psychological foundations of culture. In J. Barkow, L. Cosmides and J. Tooby (Eds), *The adapted mind: evolutionary psychology and the generation of culture*. New York: Oxford University Press.

Tracy, J. I., Pinsk, M., Helverson, J., Urban, G., Dietz, T. and Smith, D. J. (2001). Test of a potential link between analytic and nonanalytic category learning and automatic, effortful processing. *Brain and Cognition*, 46, 326–341.

Weinberg, R. S. and Hunt, V. (1976). The interrelationships between anxiety, motor performance, and electromyography. *Journal of Motor Behaviour*, 8, 219–224.

Wulf, G. and Weigelt, C. (1997). Instructions about physical principles in learning a complex motor skill: To tell or not to tell…*Research Quarterly for Exercise and Sport*, 68, 362–367.

Wulf, G., Shea, C. H. and Whitacre, C. A. (1998). Physical-guidance benefits in a complex motor skill. *Journal of Motor Behaviour*, 30, 367–380.

Wulf, G., McNevin, N. H. and Shea, C. H. (2001). The automaticity of complex motor skill learning as a function of attentional focus. *Quarterly Journal of Experimental Psychology*, 54A, 1143–1154.

Young, R. P. and Marteniuk, R. G. (1997). Acquisition of a multi-articular kicking task: Jerk analysis demonstrates movements do not become smoother with learning. *Human Movement Science*, 16, 677–701.

Part II

The expertise approach

11 Deliberate practice and expert performance

Defining the path to excellence

Paul Ward, Nicola J. Hodges, A. Mark Williams and Janet L. Starkes

Like their sporting heroes, many young athletes aspire to greatness. The lure of an exciting lifestyle and an exponential increase in wealth is, for some, sufficient to warrant pursuing this dream. For others, motivation to endure the rigor and commitment of elite-level sport is provided by the 'love of the game'. However, regardless of the underlying motives few individuals reach the required level of performance to be deemed an expert, whilst an even smaller minority achieve greatness. The obvious question is 'why'? Is greatness, or even expertise, reserved for the select few who are born with the credentials that ensure that they stand out from their less 'gifted' counterparts or are only a handful of individuals able to withstand the challenges that they are confronted with along the road to excellence? Scientists have been trying to map out the route to excellence for many centuries and, perhaps not surprisingly, the notion that some performers are 'born to be great' has carried with it an almost mystical context (for a discussion, see Sternberg and Wagner, 1999). More recently, however, Ericsson and colleagues (Ericsson, 1996; Ericsson and Charness, 1994; Ericsson and Lehmann, 1996) have espoused the importance of practice in the development of elite performers. They have advocated that commitment to practice and practice itself are more important than 'natural ability' in defining the road to excellence. According to their deliberate practice theory, expertise results from the development of domain-specific knowledge structures and skills acquired through the process of adaptation to practice.

In this chapter, we review current knowledge regarding the importance of deliberate practice in developing elite performers. A critical review of the methods employed to examine the importance of deliberate practice is provided and recent work that has addressed some of these concerns presented. In particular, we focus on the role of chronological age in mediating the capability to predict performance from accumulated practice hours and examine other factors, such as the time spent in general fitness activities and match play, which may help account for the variance in performance between individuals.

The theory of deliberate practice

There has been considerable debate in recent years regarding the identification of those acquirable and/or pre-dispositional factors that can guide an individual through this adaptive process towards skilled levels of performance, and ultimately to attaining expertise (e.g. Howe *et al.*, 1998). The most prevalent theory to address these issues was presented by Ericsson *et al.* (1993). The theory of deliberate practice offers a somewhat controversial, environmentally-driven explanation for the development of expertise. This account was built on two propositions. First, extensive involvement within a domain is necessary before expert levels of performance can be achieved (i.e. the 10-year rule; Simon and Chase, 1973). The view that long and intensive periods of training are a precursor to the attainment of expertise has received considerable support across various domains (e.g. see Bloom, 1985; Charness *et al.*, 1996; Starkes *et al.*, 1996). Second, Ericsson *et al.* (1993) proposed that the defining characteristics of expertise are acquired through engagement in relevant activities. Ericsson and colleagues rejected the need to include talent as an explanatory mechanism for attaining excellence. Although these authors conceded that individuals differ in their predisposition to engage in hard work or that individual differences may influence motivational processes, they highlighted a general lack of support for fixed innate characteristics directly contributing to the development of expertise. For those of us who have engaged in activities for numerous years, observation of personal performance indicates that an elite level or status is not automatically achieved after the critical '10-year' marker has been surpassed. The implication is that attained levels of performance are not limited by those factors associated with innate talent but are acquired through sustained investment in practice and deliberate efforts to improve (Ericsson *et al.*, 1993).

Ericsson *et al.* (1993) suggested that effective learning occurs when activities are well defined, are pitched at an appropriate level of difficulty, when useful feedback is presented, and the opportunity for repetition, error detection and correction is provided. When these conditions are met, the term 'deliberate' is used to characterize practice. Ericsson and colleagues highlighted three different constraints that are inherent to attaining expert performance. First, there is no immediate financial reward from early investment in deliberate practice and frequently, a substantial number of *resources* (e.g. equipment, facilities) are required, often at significant expense to the performer and/or parents. Second, deliberate practice places considerable demand on physical and mental resources, both of which are typically assumed to be limited to some degree (e.g. Kahneman, 1973; Powers and Howley, 2001). The high degree of *effort* necessary for participation in these activities determines the extent to which an individual can sustain engagement and adapt to increased task demands over time. Finally, deliberate practice is assumed not to be inherently enjoyable and consequently, the *motivation* to sustain participation is largely determined by ones intent to improve. Without the goal of improving performance, the motivation to engage in such practice is likely to diminish (Ericsson *et al.*, 1993).

Ericsson and colleagues differentiated deliberate practice from work/competition and play. In work or competitive environments, individuals are under pressure to perform rather than learn and therefore are likely to use current effective, yet potentially sub-optimal, strategies as opposed to investing time in learning new, or refining old, methods. Playful activities are primarily engaged in for enjoyment, not necessarily skill development. Ericsson *et al.*'s (1993) principal hypothesis is that deliberate practice is monotonically related to the attainment of expertise. According to the monotonic benefits assumption, and in accordance with the power law of practice (Anderson, 1983; Newell and Rosenbloom, 1981), the amount of accumulated practice is directly related to current levels of performance. The greatest improvements in performance should occur with the largest amounts of deliberate practice. Those performers who have accumulated the largest number of practice hours throughout their career and consistently and deliberately engaged in high levels of practice for sustainable periods are more likely to attain expert status.

Evidence from the original performance domain: music

When the deliberate practice framework was first presented, Ericsson and colleagues supported their claims with empirical data from musicians (both violinists and pianists). Practice alone was the only variable to sufficiently meet the criteria laid out for deliberate practice. Although music lessons with an instructor were also rated highly relevant for improving performance, practice alone was the only activity where its duration was directly under the control of the individual. The tasks in which individuals engaged during this activity and the respective practice goals are typically supervised by a teacher and consequently, meet the criteria for deliberate practice.

Predominantly through questionnaire and diary methods, Ericsson *et al.* (1993) showed how hours spent in deliberate practice (i.e. practice alone) consistently differentiated performers of varying skill levels. The two best groups of skilled violinists (best and good students) reported spending an average of 24.3 hours per week in practice alone, compared to 9.3 hours for music teachers. The similarity in length of practice sessions across groups (i.e. 80 minutes) suggested that the skill-based differences were a reflection of the number of practice sessions in which participants engaged. Moreover, the limited duration of each session and the rating of practice alone as effortful provide support for the original definition of deliberate practice with respect to the effort constraint. Retrospective estimates of accumulated practice hours suggested that after 10 years of practice the best violinists had accrued a greater amount of practice (7,410 hours) than the good violinists (5,301 hours), and the music teachers (3,420 hours). After 10 years, the level of practice reported by the best students was comparable to that of professional middle-aged violinists who were members of the internationally reputed Berlin Philharmonic and Radio Symphony Orchestras. Expert and amateur pianists reported similar practice history profiles to the violinists. Experts spent 26.7 hours in solo practice per week and had accrued 7,606 hours of practice by the age of 18 years (14 years into their career), 6,000 more hours than their amateur counterparts. Both expert violinists and pianists conformed to the 10-year, 10,000-hour approximation for attaining excellence within their domain of expertise (see Ericsson *et al.*, 1993; Simon and Chase, 1973).

Evidence from the domain of sport

Researchers in the sports domain have been keen to examine the validity of deliberate practice theory. The question of whether high levels of good quality practice in sport are sufficient to bring about expert performance is of vital importance to practitioners and athletes. The answer to this question has major implications for training and selection. Ericsson has argued that a high quantity and quality of deliberate practice is sufficient to account for sporting excellence. In the absence of unequivocal evidence in favour of differences in innate capacities, the limitations in attaining exceptional levels of performance are attributed to a lack of appropriate training. There is no question that practice is a necessary vehicle for attaining exceptional levels of performance in sports. Individuals who appear 'talented' at a young age still need to invest considerable practice hours to compete at an adult level. If the propensity for expertise is predominantly biologically based, the relevant genes would still require some environmental interaction (e.g. practice) in order to be appropriately expressed. The question of importance to performers and practitioners is whether practice alone is enough to attain expertise, and more specifically, to produce improvements in performance?

Starkes and colleagues (e.g. Starkes *et al.*, 1996) were the first to undertake work on deliberate practice in sport. Athletes who participated in individual sports reported spending on average more than 10 years in practice before reaching an international level. At the age of 25 years, wrestlers reported reaching their peak, some 12 years into their career. Whilst commencing in practice activities at a relatively late age (13–14 years of age) compared to Ericsson's musicians, differences began to emerge in the amount of time that international-level wrestlers (M = 38.7 hours/week) estimated spending in practice compared to club-level wrestlers (M = 20.9 hours/week) after 6 years of practice. Interestingly, however, these athletes spent less time in practice than the 10,000-hour benchmark proposed by Ericsson and colleagues. The international group had accumulated 5881.9 hours compared to 3571.1 hours by the club-level wrestlers. Importantly, skill groups were not differentiated on practice alone but on time spent practicing with others (see also Hodges and Starkes, 1996). Figure skaters on the other hand, began participating in this activity much earlier at the age of 5 years, and were performing at an international level by the age of 21 years. The weighted average number of hours per week for national and junior national team members spent practicing alone (M = 21.2 hours) was similar to that reported by Ericsson *et al.* for the best and good violinists (see also, Starkes *et al.*, 1996).

Helsen *et al.* (1998) extended this initial work to team sport athletes by examining the practice histories of international, national and provincial level soccer players from Belgium. Typically, soccer players began participating within the domain at approximately 5 years of age and commenced regular systematic practice 2 years later. After 15 years into their career, the two elite groups (national and international) reached their peak and on the average spent 13.3 and 9.9 hours per week, respectively, in combined individual and team practice, compared to 6.9 hours for the lower skilled players (provincial). In the period between the sixth and twelfth year of their career, the players in the international group engaged in more weekly individual practice than provincial level players. However, from the end of this period onwards, all players reduced the amount of individual practice, to a point where no differences could be observed between skill groups. After 10–12 years into their career, the international group could be differentiated from the national and provincial level players in both weekly team practice and accumulated practice (individual and team practice combined) suggesting that deliberate 'team' practice rather than practice alone may be more discriminating in team-oriented sports, particularly where the content of training is fixed by a coach.

In a second team-sport domain, Helsen *et al.* (1998) examined the practice habits of players at similar levels of skill in field hockey. Players started practicing regularly in the sport at a relatively early age (M = 8.9 years). After 12 years into their career however, both international (M = 8.2 hours/week) and national (M = 7.9 hours/week) level players engaged in significantly more team practice than provincial level players (M = 3.7 hours/week). Statistically significant differences in the amount of accumulated practice did not emerge until 16 years into their career where provincial level players had accrued 5,341 hours compared to the international players who had accrued 8,541 hours. Furthermore, these players did not reach their peak until around 18–20 years into their career. Whilst each of the individual and team sport examples generally conform to the 10-year rule for attaining expert levels of performance, the number of hours in which athletes engaged in practice, as well as the number of accumulated practice hours, and the specific practice activities undertaken indicates that there may be far greater task dependence with respect to attaining expertise than originally presumed.

Sports-related revisions to the original theory: some outstanding issues

As a result of some of the discrepancies with the original findings highlighted above, a number of qualifications have been made to Ericsson *et al.*'s theory of deliberate practice. Research in non-sporting domains, specifically music, has indicated that practice alone is the activity most likely to reflect deliberate mastery attempts and improve performance (see Ericsson *et al.*, 1993; Howe *et al.*, 1998; Sloboda, 2000). Yet, the sports research illustrates that time spent in team and/or group practice might be a more appropriate predictor of expert–novice differences (e.g. Helsen *et al.*, 1998; Hodges and Starkes, 1996). Moreover, the nature of the activities undertaken, specifically with respect to the effort and motivational constraints, suggests that definitions of deliberate practice may need to be re-examined. For instance, in Ericsson *et al.*'s (1993) original outline, participation in deliberate practice activities was described as particularly effortful.

However, some physically effortful activities do not require the high levels of concentration that has since been shown to be a primary constituent of deliberate practice (see Hodges and Starkes, 1996; Starkes *et al.*, 1996). While these issues have received much attention in recent years and have been reviewed elsewhere (see Starkes, 2000), several questions remain unanswered.

Although hours of deliberate practice have differentiated across skill levels, there is a need to evaluate the sensitivity of deliberate practice estimates. There has been little empirical verification as to whether deliberate practice differentiates between performers in the same skill class (cf. Ericsson *et al.*, 1993). Objective performance measures are needed so that comprehensive analyses can be performed to determine how much variance can be accounted for by deliberate practice hours alone. It is not understood whether the processes responsible for attaining high levels of performance are equivalent to those for attaining the best or elite levels of performance in the same sport. Clarification of the nature of the activities that are considered deliberate practice would help researchers measure this construct in a consistent manner and have implications for best coaching practice. Although Ericsson's operational definition of deliberate practice is not tied to specific activities, but rather by its intent to improve certain aspects of performance, difficulties arise when assessing practice amounts. In sports, many activities are performed to maintain a certain level of fitness, rather than to improve performance *per se*. These activities have typically not been differentiated in current sport-specific studies of deliberate practice, although issues of performance maintenance have been considered with Master-level athletes (e.g. Weir *et al.*, 2002).

Contrary to Ericsson *et al.*'s proposal that practice is not inherently enjoyable, the typical finding in the sports' literature is that deliberate practice activities are perceived to be enjoyable. Subtle differences in how this rating of practice is obtained might be at least partly responsible for these discrepancies. While Ericsson *et al.* requested that musicians rate their perceptions of practice enjoyment irrespective of final outcome, researchers in sport have typically asked for a general rating of enjoyment from each activity, such that it is not possible to determine whether enjoyment ratings are based upon participation *per se* or from the appraisal of the activity's outcome.

Singer and Janelle (1999) recently suggested that, given the prevalence of sporting performance under competitive and/or stressful conditions, experience in match play, or practice-like match play may be an appropriate predictor of performance and an important constituent of optimal practice environments. However, Ward *et al.* (submitted) found that time in this activity, while important, is not as crucial for the development of expertise as time in practice activities designed to improve performance (e.g. technical and tactical/strategic skills training and the receipt of coaching in general). Many of the above characteristics have not always been given due consideration when deliberate practice has been measured. Unless there is some consensus as to which hours are included when determining accumulated practice, the prefix 'deliberate' to describe practice may become somewhat redundant.

Objective measures of performance and testing the sensitivity of deliberate practice

Typically, expert and novice performers across a variety of domains have been differentiated with respect to the amount of practice hours accumulated. While differences as a function of skill are informative, objective measures of expertise are required to determine the extent to which deliberate practice is able to predict performance. In their original investigation, Ericsson *et al.* (1993) were able to predict performance on domain-specific tests through hours practising alone with the violin. However, when Ericsson's theory was initially tested in sport with Olympic-style wrestlers (unpublished data, Hodges, 1996), it was not possible to predict individual performance rankings based on practice for the international wrestlers. Although these were subjective ratings of individual's perceived ability or talent, it does raise the question as to what makes someone the best in a sport, and whether deliberate practice is enough to account for variance within a skill class?

More recently, Hodges *et al.* (submitted) have examined practice in activities that have objective performance measures. International and varsity swimmers and triathletes who engaged in three sports: swimming, cycling and running were the participants. Although the primary issues concerned how much variation could be accounted for by deliberate practice hours, the sport-specific nature of practice and how much additional variation in performance times could be captured by time in related activities (e.g. fitness, active leisure) was also determined. Using performance and practice data from triathletes pertaining to each event, the issue of how well generic practice across all three sports could predict performance times beyond sport-specific practice was examined. For example, do hours spent in swimming and cycling practice contribute to predictions of running times based only on running practice?

In general, the most important type of practice (i.e. predictor of performance times) was sport specific. Sport-specific practice accounted for between 30 and 50 per cent of the variance in performance times. Very little additional variation in performance was explained by the inclusion of non sport-specific practice although, some transfer benefits were observed (i.e. predominately for the male rather than the female athletes). A similar lack of predictability was found for time spent in other fitness-related activities and active leisure pursuits, although only weekly estimates were available. As before, fitness activities had more predictive validity for the male rather than female athletes. For triathletes, approximately 10 per cent of the variance in triathlon performance times and the individual events of swimming and cycling could be accounted for by hours in fitness/active leisure pursuits. For the male swimmers, approximately 20 per cent of additional variance was explained by fitness activities, rising to 50 per cent for the butterfly event.

This information has both descriptive and predictive value. Whereas typically, hours in deliberate practice have successfully differentiated across skill groups (see Helsen *et al.*, 1998; Hodges and Starkes, 1996), the analyses reported above show how deliberate practice hours are able to account for a significant proportion of the variance in performance times across individuals (rather than groups), in addition to highlighting the sport-specific nature of practice in predicting performance. Although there is some transfer benefit across non-sport specific practice, particularly for male athletes, perhaps unsurprisingly, the greatest amount of variance is accounted for by practice in the event most related to performance (i.e. swim hours for swim times). This type of analysis has important implications for the sport's practitioner who might use this information to guide his or her athletes to activities where maximum performance benefits are to be gained. Due to the predictive nature of regression analyses, it is also possible to calculate the number of hours of practice that are necessary to improve by 1 second, or 1 minute (as a function of event) and as such this measure can be used as a guide for practice.

In a similar vein, albeit at a group level of analysis, Ward *et al.* (submitted) used a series of discriminant analyses to determine the amount of team practice a player would need to participate in order to reach an age-specific skill level. Based upon the most recent year of participation, practice estimates of elite and sub-elite soccer players increasing in age from 9 to 18 years were analysed and their data fitted to a model that could predict skill–group membership for between 72.9 and 100 per cent of the players. These types of predictive models might prove to be important tools for coaches and talent development scouts responsible for charting or predicting the future development of existing 'talented' players.

Developmental considerations

One of the underlying assumptions of the deliberate practice framework is that practice is equivalent across all ages and therefore independent of chronological age. However, recently a number of researchers have questioned the validity of this assumption. Although Ericsson *et al.*'s (1993) original thesis was primarily used to understand the factors (i.e. the type of practice) that led to the development of skilled performance, an important extension of this research is to determine how, once a high level of skill is reached, continued investment in deliberate practice can potentially delay any age-related decline in performance (see Ericsson and Charness, 1994). The fact that individuals generally become slower with age necessitates an extension to the deliberate practice theory to account for the fact that more hours accumulated within an activity do not necessarily result in performance improvement.

Pre-peak practice: practice, play, diversity and specialization

In Ericsson *et al.*'s (1993) theory of deliberate practice, age is not explicitly considered an important factor mediating the effects of practice on performance. Although Ericsson *et al.* note that in order to acquire the requisite number of hours of practice participants typically begin at an early age, practice estimates at a young age are not weighted differentially to those accrued as the performer develops. However, when Starkes *et al.* (1996) compared the accumulated practice hours across individual and team activities, both in music and sport, they found that practice increased in a monotonic fashion, irrespective of the type of domain and starting age in the sport. Despite this consistency, a qualitative analysis of practice as a function of age has pointed to considerable developmental differences. For example, Côté and Hay (2002) showed that if an individual is to become skilful in a particular domain, engagement in playful pursuits and practice in non domain-specific activities may be valuable in the early stages of an individual's career. Using semi-structured interviews, Baker *et al.* (in press) examined the participation histories of elite players who held an international or world-class ranking in a variety of different team sports. Rather than domain-specific, deliberate practice, these authors found that expert and world-class athletes engaged in considerably more 'deliberate play' during the sampling years (i.e. 7–12 years) than non-experts. The 'sampling years' were proposed to be a period where deliberate play and diversity were both encouraged and beneficial to the development of skilled performance (Côté, 1999; Côté and Hay, 2002; Côté *et al.*, 2001). Following Piaget's description of play development, 'deliberate play' was defined by Côté and colleagues as rule-based play that is primarily engaged in for fun, and is largely determined by the age at which participation occurs (i.e. after 7 years of age).

Whilst Côté and colleagues' description of athletes' initial participation is consistent with Bloom's (1985) delineation of the 'early years', Ericsson and colleagues (Ericsson, 1996, 1998; Ericsson *et al.*, 1993) have contested whether engagement in playful activities, where there is no explicit goal to improve, is productive in developing expert levels of performance. As detailed earlier, within the deliberate practice framework, playful activities have been differentiated from practice activities, where only a deliberate investment in the latter would lead to increases in performance. While arguments might arise as to the predictive ability of play and non-sport specific practice early in a person's career, there is agreement that as a foundation to skilled performance, playful activities may be fundamental for learning initial cognitive and movement skills, which enable the development of preliminary mental representations necessary for expert performance (Beamer *et al.*, 1999; Ericsson, 1998). Moreover, both agree that the engagement in intrinsically motivating behaviours early in an individual's career is likely to increase a performer's eagerness to pursue more externally controlled activities such as deliberate practice (Deci and Ryan, 1985; Ryan and Deci, 2000).

Although there is potential for reconciliation of the research findings, conflict arises as to the practical implications of the two models for sport development with respect to the most effective type of participation during early skill development. On the one hand, Ericsson and colleagues' monotonic benefits assumption suggests that engaging in deliberate domain-specific practice from an early age leads to associated increases in performance, and ultimately the attainment of expertise. On the other hand, Côté and colleagues recommend later specialization (i.e. specialization years; age 13–16/17 years) within a specific domain, preceded by deliberate play and sporting diversity in the early years. Not only do Côté and colleagues claim that early specialization in a sport is not necessary for the development of expertise, but they also claim that the decision to specialize late (e.g. 13–15 years of age) is an important predictor of later skill level (see Côté and Hay, 2002).

Baker *et al.* (in press) have shown that, in addition to more substantive engagement in deliberate play, world-class team players who demonstrated greater diversity across several domains had also accrued less practice hours within the specialist domain prior to national selection compared to those who exhibited a less diverse participation profile and were not of world class standing. The implication is that individuals can benefit via some mechanism of transfer from engaging in non-domain activities that require similar skills, or at least possess relevant attributes to those in their domain of expertise. Research in the domain of problem solving suggests that early specialization and lack of diversity may result in functional fixedness, where individuals may struggle to find an appropriate solution to a problem (Seifert *et al.*, 1995). Greater diversity across sports at an earlier age may, therefore, manifest itself in more flexible perceptual-motor and perceptual-cognitive solutions to a broader range of existing, as well as novel problems and ultimately, to the attainment of adaptive expertise (Hatano and Inagaki, 1986); a likely constituent of elite-level sport.

Whilst the idea of transfer from one domain to another is conceptually appealing, the research evidence tends to suggest that expertise is typically domain specific (see Allard and Starkes, 1991; Ericsson and Smith, 1991; Hodges *et al.*, submitted). The conflicting nature of the findings might be somewhat linked to the methods involved in collecting these data. While detailed profiles of elite athletes collected through interview techniques might elucidate on early diversity and qualitative differences in early practice experiences, cross-skill comparisons of practice estimates only inform as to quantitative differences in the area of specialization.

To address these methodological problems Ward *et al.* (submitted) compared the domain-specific and non-domain-specific participation histories (hours per week and accumulated hours) of nine age-matched groups of elite and sub-elite soccer players from 9 to 18 years of age. More specifically, the relative contributions of deliberate practice, play and diversity throughout development were ascertained through questionnaires administered under high levels of supervision.

Consistent with research from adult team players (Helsen *et al.*, 1998), only deliberate 'team' practice from the most recent year of practice consistently discriminated across skill groups. This variable was predictive of skill level from as early as 9 years of age. Time spent in soccer-related match play, deliberate 'individual' practice and playful activities also made some, yet not consistent contributions to skill-based differences. In Figure 11.1 the hours accumulated in these various soccer-related activities for the elite (top panel) and sub-elite (bottom panel) soccer players from the age of 8 years (U-9) to 17 years (U-18) has been illustrated. Where these variables played a role in predicting performance, elite players typically spent more time in match play and individual practice and less time in playful activities compared to sub-elite players. Although both groups spent a substantial amount of time in playful activities (e.g. kicking a ball around for fun), these activities did not discriminate between skill groups during the

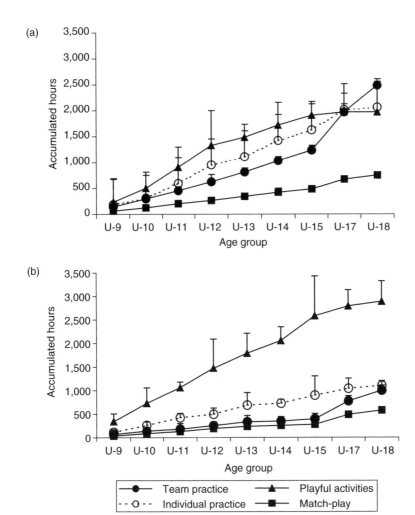

Figure 11.1 Accumulated hours spent in domain-specific (soccer) activities by elite players (a) and sub-elite players (b). Figure adapted from Ward *et al.* (submitted).

sampling years (7–12 years). Rather, contrary to Côté and colleagues, the data showed that those individuals who had spent less time in playful activities by their adolescent years were more likely to have achieved a higher skill level. Domain-specific practice (in particular, deliberate 'team' practice) from an early age accounted for 56 per cent of the variance between skill groups, increasing to 76 per cent for the oldest group.

With respect to diversity, Ward *et al.*'s (submitted) comparisons of time accumulated in non-domain-specific practice, play and match play (i.e. in sports other than soccer) has been plotted in Figure 11.2. Analyses of these data showed that elite (top panel) and sub-elite (bottom panel) soccer players did not differ on the

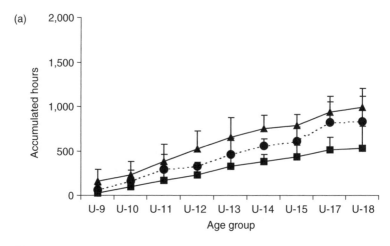

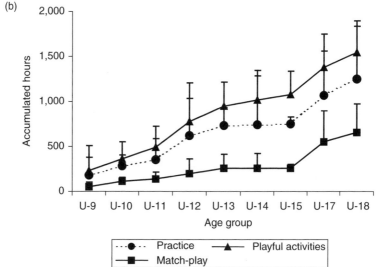

Figure 11.2 Accumulated hours spent in non-domain-specific activities (e.g. sports other than soccer) by elite players (a) and sub-elite players (b). Figure adapted from Ward *et al.* (submitted).

amount of time invested in each of these activities. Even when the total time accumulated in all other sporting activities was combined there were no significant differences between skill groups. In addition, both elite and sub-elite players tended to participate in a similar number of sports ($n = 3$) and both groups only specialized in an average of one sport upon leaving school or joining a professional soccer club on a full-time basis (i.e. at 16 years of age).

To examine whether there were any differences between sports as a function of their similarity to soccer, a descriptive analysis of time spent in similar team (e.g. field hockey), dissimilar team (e.g. cricket) and individual activities (e.g. swimming) was conducted. Surprisingly, sub-elite players appeared to spend approximately three times the amount of time in play, practice and match play activities in similar team sports when compared to elite players. There was no evidence that an investment in other activities (even similar activities) was in any degree comparable to investing in similar amounts of deliberate practice within the specialist domain itself. While these results are clearly at odds with Côté and colleagues' emphasis upon deliberate play and diversity during the sampling years, it is possible that discrepancies in findings primarily reflect the differences in the seasonal nature of the sports examined and/or cultural differences in the talent development systems examined by the respective researchers. Ward *et al.*'s research focused specifically upon English soccer where, although seasonal, the sport is typically played and practised by children all year round. In contrast, Côté and colleagues examined athletes from Canada and Australia where the sports concerned are far more seasonally distinct, often marked by the prevalence of other major sports competing for television 'air time'. Subsequently, non-domain-specific practice in the off-season may be more common and relevant to performance predictions in North American and Australian athletes.

Past performance peaks: age- or practice-related declines

Research has also been conducted into the practice habits of Master athletes and whether qualitative differences exist in the nature of activities that predict continued success, past peak as people age. Starkes *et al.* (1999) and Weir *et al.* (2002) have shown that declines in practice among track athletes and swimmers, respectively, are magnified with age as a function of distance. Longer distance events that require higher levels of endurance appear to be more affected by ageing. Although these declines are likely to be the result of the normal ageing process, associated with loss in physiological capacity (i.e. $\dot{V}O_2$max), examination of practice estimates showed that Master athletes decreased their hours of practice with age by about one-fourth of the rate reported by highly skilled, younger peers. The practice session for the Master athlete, however, was defined by a relatively increased amount of time in activities designed to improve endurance in comparison to their younger peers whose practice time was devoted to activities related to power and strength (Weir *et al.*, 2002). These findings suggest that the focus of deliberate practice for the older athlete changes, such that potential physiological declines can be somewhat delayed. Many researchers have shown that Master athletes are far fitter than their sedentary, age-matched counterparts (e.g. Rogers *et al.*, 1990). Greater declines (i.e. quadratic trends) in performance are typically reported when cross-sectional data are compared with longitudinal analysis (i.e. linear trends). The implication of these differential declines as a function of the type of comparison is that individuals who maintain engagement within an activity are not subject to accelerated declines that are somewhat artificially observed through comparisons of mean data across different athletes. Starkes *et al.* (2003)

have recently analysed practice histories of Master athletes as old as 90 years of age and have failed to find any quadratic declines of performance as a function of practice. These data generally highlight the importance of taking into account developmental changes when assessing deliberate practice (see also Krampe and Ericsson, 1996). The decline in performance through ageing can be somewhat circumvented by the amount and type of practice undertaken.

Methodological issues: reliability and validity of estimates of deliberate practice

When attempting to measure practice, two issues are of immediate concern; the validity and reliability of the data. Although the issue of reliability has received the most attention and attempts have been made in the majority of studies to ensure that estimates are reliable (e.g. Ericsson *et al.*, 1993; Helsen *et al.*, 1998; Hodges and Starkes, 1996), less attention has been devoted to the validity of practice estimates. We briefly address these two issues and present some data that addresses some of the limitations of previous investigations.

Reliability of practice data

The use of diaries to, assess the reliability of practice estimates was a method first employed by Ericsson *et al.* (1993). The practice estimates provided in the most recent year of participation were compared to those obtained from weekly activity diaries. Generally, across studies, high correlations were observed, such that those who retrospectively estimated more hours also recorded more hours in their weekly diaries. However, a little more disappointingly, the number of hours of practice was quite substantially overestimated in the retrospective records in comparison to the hours reported in the diaries. For example, Hodges and Starkes (1996) found correlations for international athletes of $r = 0.50$, even though the diary estimates were 4 hours/week less than those reported for the current year. A relatively high correlation, at least for the most skilled group, along with overestimations of practice of about 3–5 hours per week have been typical across studies. There are generally two methods for increasing the reliability of these estimates and these have been adopted in the most recent investigations of deliberate practice.

The first is to collect longitudinal or quasi-longitudinal data, whereby estimates of practice are collected at the time of practice, not merely retrospectively. The study by Ward et al. (submitted) is a first attempt to try and improve the reliability and validity of these estimates by collecting data across nine age groups (i.e. quasi-longitudinal), in addition to the typical retrospective estimates from each group. Comparisons of current estimates with retrospective estimates provide a strong indicator of retrospective reliability. Generally, no significant differences were found between the current (e.g. 12-year-olds) and retrospective reports of practice (e.g. at the age of 12 years, for the players aged between 13 and 18 years). More specifically, current and retrospective reports of playful activities, individual practice, and match play did not differ, irrespective of the age at which comparisons were made. The only significant age effects were found in the number of hours spent in team practice at 9, 10, and 11 years of age compared to those who provided retrospective estimates from age 12 to 18 years. The 9–11-year-olds typically reported spending on average 1.5 additional hours per week in team practice than the older groups. These differences could be explained by prevalent changes in the structure of the soccer academies in the United Kingdom as a result of the Football Association's Charter for Quality (Wilkinson, 1997), or equally, as a consequence of the overzealous nature of response by the younger cohorts. On the whole, however, this quasi-longitudinal approach provided quite strong support for the use of retrospective methods in recalling practice hours. Because these are different cohorts, some discrepancy in practice hours was expected.

A second method for improving the reliability of practice estimates employed by Hodges *et al.* (submitted) and Ward *et al.* (submitted) has been to change the technique of collecting practice data, based on the assumption that estimates closer to the current year will be more reliable than those at the start of a person's career. Rather than requiring individuals to recall estimates from the start of practice through to the present date, these researchers have obtained estimates from the most recent 3 years initially, on a year-by-year basis. From then on, estimates are provided in 3-year intervals (to mirror the decreasing reliability of the estimates as the performer reflects back in time). This method of recollection also prevents or decreases the tendency for a performer to gradually increase hours from the start of practice to the current date, lessening the probability that current estimates of practice within a questionnaire will be different from diary estimates. Hodges *et al.* (submitted) found that the difference between questionnaire and diary estimates for triathletes (collapsed across skill level) was approximately 2 hours ($r = 0.60$).

A third method for improving the reliability of practice estimates has been employed by Starkes *et al.* (2003) and Young and Starkes (submitted). They have used the training journals kept by Master athletes to plot the amount and type of practice engaged in throughout their training career. Thankfully, there are many top athletes who keep very detailed journals outlining their practice activities. For Master athletes, these journals may span 40–50 years of training and provide a wealth of longitudinal practice data.

Validity of deliberate practice estimates

In the empirical verification of the deliberate practice framework to date, the majority of the research in sport has tested quantitative aspects of the theory (i.e. the monotonic benefits assumption). What has been somewhat lacking, however, is a test of deliberate practice theory in such a way that only hours are counted that have the constituent qualities to be called deliberate practice. Although researchers have gained some insight into activities that would be defined as deliberate practice through attribute ratings of these acts in questionnaires, these have not always been the hours that have been used to predict performance. This problem has been somewhat linked to the method of collecting data, such that ratings of activities in terms of deliberate practice criteria are collected concurrently with the estimates of practice hours. Not all activities that could potentially fall under the umbrella of 'deliberate practice' have fulfilled the original criteria proposed by Ericsson *et al.* concerning the level of effort, relevance to improvement and enjoyment. Consequently, the practice data do not always provide a valid measure of deliberate practice.

To illustrate, Helsen *et al.* (1998) and Hodges and Starkes (1996) asked wrestlers, field hockey and soccer players to recall the number of hours in practice activities (both alone and with others) in addition to rating these different practice activities for effort, enjoyment, concentration and relevance. Although the wrestlers only rated mat-work highly in terms of relevance and concentration (thus fitting the criteria for deliberate practice), all types of practice activities, including those performed alone and with others, were entered into the analyses. This was due partly to the fact that individual hours in mat-work across the wrestler's career were not available and likely very difficult for the wrestlers to recall given its specific nature. As we have remarked previously, the 10,000 hours of deliberate practice usually quoted as a ball-park figure needed to reach a high level of skill (see Ericsson *et al.*, 1993), is likely to be highly overestimated, or at least somewhat domain dependent.

Helsen *et al.* (1998) reported that, at 18 years of age and after 13 years into their career, international, national and provincial level soccer players had accrued approximately 6,200, 5,000 and 3,900 hours, respectively, in combined estimates of team and individual practice. However, even these relatively low estimates included both maintenance- and improvement-type activities indicating that time spent in actual deliberate practice *per se* may have been overestimated. Ward *et al.* (submitted) reported a considerably lower estimate after distinguishing the actual number of hours spent in practice (e.g. improvement-type activities) from other domain-specific (i.e. play, match play) and domain-related (e.g. fitness work, talking about soccer) activities. After comparable levels of training to the participants reported in Helsen *et al.*'s study (i.e. 13 years of participation, including 12 years of systematic training), the 18-year-old elite players had accumulated 4,542 hours in combined team and individual practice (of which 2,484 were from team practice) compared to 2,100 total hours accumulated by sub-elite players. Low amounts of accumulated practice have also been reported by Soberlak (2001) (cited in Côté *et al.* 2001) and Baker *et al.* (in press). These authors noted that professional and world-class elite athletes had accrued only 3,072 and 4,000 hours, respectively, after investing 13 and 14 years in sport-specific deliberate practice. It appears that expert levels of performance can be attained with considerably fewer hours deliberately invested (e.g. approximately 2,500–4,500 hours) than previously believed, particularly where estimates are based on those actual practice hours which are predictive of performance.

Researchers have been accused of bean-counting when trying to apply Ericsson *et al.*'s deliberate practice framework across various sporting domains, due to the fact that only hours in practice are ascertained. In efforts to rectify this problem, Starkes and colleagues (Cullen and Starkes, 1997; Deakin *et al.*, 1998;

Starkes, 2000) have attempted to validate the practice estimates by examining qualitative aspects of the practice session. Questions such as whether an hour of practice for the beginner is as 'deliberate' in nature as an hour of practice for the more skilled performer and how much deliberate practice (i.e. effortful and designed to improve performance) is actually spent in a typical practice session has led to time motion analyses of practice in wrestling, ice hockey and ice skating. Ericsson (1996) echoed concerns regarding the quality issue and indicated that the nature of activities as one progresses from novice through intermediate, towards elite levels of skill may need to be differentiated.

Quite surprisingly, both skilled and less skilled skaters, ice-hockey players and wrestlers spent time on practice aspects that were already well learnt and that were not rated high for relevance to improving performance. This was despite the fact that the figure skaters estimated spending more time practising difficult and relevant activities. Although this does not necessarily mean that the practice was not effortful and designed to improve performance, it may be that it was not as effortful, or at least as attention demanding, as it could have been. Additionally, Cullen and Starkes (1997) found that relatively skilled ice-hockey players spent a long time resting and watching during a practice session, which would suggest that actual practice hours have been overestimated when accumulated hours have been counted.

As Starkes (2000) has suggested, because of the high amount of effort which needs to be devoted to improving performance, this might be one of the reasons why within a typical practice session only a comparatively small amount of time is spent practising more difficult activities. There are likely to be other psychological variables that mediate the type of practice engaged in by a performer, related to motivation and commitment to the activity. Practice at activities that a person is good at will likely reinforce the person's belief in their competence, perhaps providing enjoyment and feelings of worth that will be necessary for continued practice.

At a more global level, Hodges *et al.* (submitted) found evidence that less skilled triathletes (i.e. slower finishers) tended to devote more practice sessions to events that they perceived were their best, in comparison to their faster counterparts whose practice was more equally distributed (see Figure 11.3). Therefore, differences within one practice session might not capture the variety in practice sessions across a training week, or even within a season. Hodges *et al.* (submitted) also found that the intensity of practice across a season was sustained at a higher level for a longer period for the faster male triathletes in comparison to their slower counterparts, as illustrated in Figure 11.4.

The motivational constraint

In their original definition of deliberate practice, Ericsson *et al.* suggested that individuals might not necessarily gain any inherent enjoyment from participating in these activities. Given this constraint, individuals would likely be motivated by the instrumental nature of the activity to improve performance

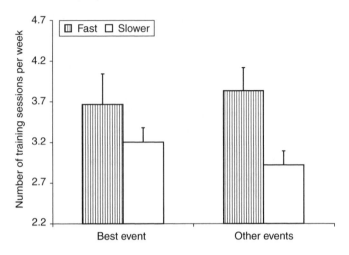

Figure 11.3 Mean number of training sessions per week for the fast and slower triathletes as a function of event (either best event, or mean of the other two events).

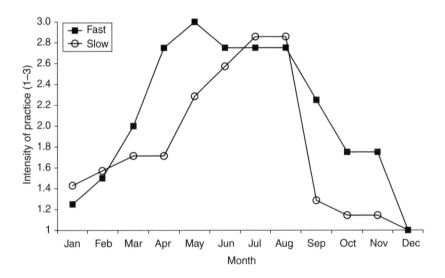

Figure 11.4 Intensity of practice for the fast and slower triathletes as a function of training month. Figure adapted from Hodges *et al.* (submitted).

(Ericsson, 1996). Ericsson argued that motivation was a pre-requisite for sustained engagement in deliberate practice over days, years and even decades. This view is consistent with the notion that individuals who possess high levels of intrinsic motivation are typically most committed to their domain of expertise (see

Csikszentmihalyi *et al.*, 1993). In a recent model of expertise, Sternberg (2000) suggested that its development occurs as an interaction between a number of elements: meta-cognitive, learning and thinking skills, as well as knowledge, motivation and their contextualization. Importantly, motivation was viewed as the pivotal and activating component within this interaction. Without its presence, the residual contributory factors were predicted to remain dormant.

Although different types of motivation (e.g. achievement, competence) have been examined in a number of contexts, Amabile (1996) indicated that a belief in their own ability (e.g. self-efficacy/perceived competence) is necessary for the development of expertise. In order to find an appropriate resolution to difficult tasks or problems, and hence, to progress along the skill continuum, experts need to develop or possess a sense of their own efficacy and/or competence (Sternberg, 2000). An individual's level of perceived competence is an important factor in ensuring continued participation beyond recreational levels of performance and sustaining commitment within an achievement domain. When an individual can expect to master a challenging task they are likely to invest considerably more effort and become far more motivated than when engaging in a non-challenging task or when they have a low perception of self-competence (Lens and Rand, 2000). Lens and Rand (2000, p. 199) proposed that 'individuals like to do things they are good at and they also become good at things they like to do'. Consequently a detailed examination of factors such as desire, dedication and competence within a domain are likely to bolster our understanding of the development of expertise. To gain greater insight into the motivational elements driving the development of expertise, Ward *et al.* (submitted) asked participants to provide ratings of time/effort spent in each activity, dedication to soccer compared to other 'favourite' activities and to identify reasons for participation. Elite players' higher ratings of time/effort and dedication from the onset of participation suggest that these players develop a 'rage to master' from an early age (cf. Winner, 1996, 2000). Moreover, such characteristics, not surprisingly, coincide with parents being rated as the most important influence on continued participation in soccer. The early levels of high perceived competence and environmental support may be indicative that these characteristics are acquired, potentially as a consequence of high levels of encouragement and successful mastery attempts in the early stages of learning. When a task is challenging and successful mastery is achieved, the increased intrinsic motivation that accompanies greater perceived competence is likely to mobilize commitment toward the domain, where opportunity for, and engagement in, deliberate practice monotonically affects performance.

An individual's commitment to deliberate practice is one of the factors that distinguish skilled participants from everyday individuals who may struggle to meet lesser practice demands (Ericsson *et al.*, 1993). To examine motives for participation, Scanlan *et al.* (1993) proposed a model of sports commitment, developed largely from Rusbult's (1980) investment model of commitment. This model highlights five factors that impact the desire to sustain participation and includes enjoyment, involvement alternatives, personal investment, social constraints and involvement opportunities. Scanlan *et al.*'s (1993) model indicates that enjoyment is positively related to commitment, which opposes Ericsson *et al.*'s (1993) conception of deliberate practice activities. In research examining the motives for participation in individual and team sports (e.g. wrestling, ice-skating, field hockey, soccer), Helsen *et al.* (1998) and Starkes *et al.* (1996) both found support for the claims of Scanlan and colleagues. Athletes rated practice activities as extremely enjoyable questioning Ericsson *et al.*'s prediction, particularly within domains that involve a large perceptual-motor component. As Starkes *et al.* (1996) suggested, individuals who excel in physically oriented domains are more likely to rate participation in such activities as enjoyable. It is still debatable, however, to what extent an individual's ratings of enjoyment are biased by outcome (i.e. product oriented) or truly reflect actual participation (i.e. process oriented). Without an appropriate behavioural index or some innovative method to tease these issues apart, the ratings of enjoyment in previous studies will remain a moot point. A shift from process- to product-based enjoyment with increased participation and/or success, for instance, might lend support to both Ericsson *et al.*'s (1993) and Scanlan *et al.*'s (1993) research. That is, enjoyment from actual participation during the early years might explain an individual's commitment. In later years, the enjoyment gained from an individual's assessment of the outcome (i.e. win/lose, observable skill improvement) says nothing about the inherent enjoyment of the practice process and may even bolster commitment further where a successful outcome is obtained.

In their analysis of the ratings attributed to various activities, Ward *et al.* (submitted) required soccer players to give additional ratings that were designed to differentiate the enjoyment gained from actual participation from enjoyment as a result of the activity's outcome. At a younger age, the athletes reasons for enjoyment were more process focused, however, as age increased, ratings of enjoyment became more outcome driven. At an older age, individuals may gain enjoyment from the activity, albeit based upon the outcome (e.g. good performance) or result (e.g. win), though may not find actual practice inherently enjoyable as they progress toward expert levels of performance. The transition in the nature of the ratings may well be a consequence of the competitive and ego-centred environment in which the elite players progress.

In the past, deliberate practice activities have been defined based on general ratings of various activities using a questionnaire. Rather than obtaining values associated with various practice activities after the event, ratings have been obtained all at once. There are a couple of problems associated with this method. First, the time lag between the event and the rating of that event is likely to influence an individual's perception of its relevance, effort, concentration, enjoyment and satisfaction. Proximity of the rating to the actual event is likely to moderate ratings for enjoyment in particular. As the time interval is increased, there is a greater chance that other factors such as physical benefits will impact on the evaluation of an activity. Second, given that within a week the same activity (e.g. a run) is unlikely to be judged equally in terms of relevance to improving performance, it is necessary to determine whether the session judged as most important is also perceived to be the most effortful and enjoyable and whether this is related to other factors such as time of day and length of the practice session. To overcome these problems, Hodges *et al.* (submitted) required athletes to provide ratings of all physical activities engaged in during a week in diaries. In this way, all activities were evaluated as soon as possible after the event and individual sessions analysed.

In general, there was no relation between the ratings and the duration of the activity. The activities judged to be most important for improvement were also rated high for effort and concentration, supporting previous research (e.g. Hodges and Starkes, 1996; Helsen *et al.*, 1998). Enjoyment, however, was found to be a relatively unimportant attribute, failing to covary with relevance of the activity to improving performance in a consistent fashion (cf. Ericsson *et al.*, 1993; Starkes *et al.*, 1996). Although the results of practice were judged to be satisfying, enjoyment was not consistently related to relevance of the activity to improving performance and in some cases showed a negative correlation. The primary conclusion was that deliberate practice should consist of those activities designed to improve performance that are effortful and mentally demanding with perhaps lesser emphasis on the enjoyment construct, particularly as the players' age increases.

Applications of deliberate practice to coaching: cultural and societal influences

Bloom's (1985) demarcation of the early, middle and late years in an athlete's development demonstrated the complex and dynamic relationship between athlete, parent and coach. The role of the coach in this model changes with respect to the attitude, instruction and goals they impart as individuals mature and increase their skill level (Samela and Moraes, 2003). However, the emphasis within the middle years on deliberate practice was largely based upon a middle class population of at least moderate to good, socio-economic standing. That is, both Bloom and Ericsson's assumptions were drawn from middle to upper class sports or activities such as swimming, tennis and music. Few researchers have examined whether this model provides an accurate reflection of populations from working or relatively poorer socio-economic classes or underdeveloped countries who might not be able to overcome the resource constraints, such as a high level of coaching, upon which deliberate practice is so contingent. In a recent study by Moraes *et al.* (2000), the practice activities of pre-elite 16–18-year-old Brazilian soccer players was examined, in addition to the degree of coaching that each individual had received. Athletes, parents and coaches were interviewed and the latter two cohorts were specifically asked to detail their experiences with these players prior to their selection in to three different junior professional development teams. Despite receiving very little familial support and receiving little, if any, high-level, quality coaching these athletes improved to a level that would be considered exceptional. In contrast to the typical coaching and supervisory practice activities received by the European soccer players studied by Helsen *et al.* (1998) and Ward *et al.* (submitted), these players were able to substitute sufficient quality for phenomenal quantities of practice, to the point that most waking hours, or at least 100 per cent of their leisure time, were spent playing soccer.

These conclusions are not only cultural but also reflective of soccer participation in general across the world. In the United Kingdom (UK), soccer has traditional roots in working class society and many of the elite and sub-elite youngsters in the Ward *et al.* study were inner city children whose parents were employed in what would be considered blue collar professions. Although these children experience less deprivation than their counterparts from inner cities in Brazil (evidenced by comparison of income and standard of living; for a discussion see Samela and Moraes, 2003) many of the children's families were financially 'challenged'. Although a high percentage of the UK-based participants also reported spending a considerable amount, if not all of their free time in soccer-related activities, what differentiated the skill-groups in the study by Ward *et al.* (submitted) was not time spent in the activity per se, but their access to higher level coaching and subsequent engagement in team practice. The question to ask in this context is whether the additional coaching and team practice received by the European children is an advantage compared to countries that are relatively underdeveloped? At a senior level, Brazil has a superior record in world-class soccer than either England or Belgium. This 'hands-off' approach to learning, albeit in an unintentional manner in this context, has been shown to be beneficial to learning when compared to approaches using explicit instruction (for a discussion, see Handford *et al.*, 1997; Williams *et al.*, 2002).

Criticisms of the deliberate practice approach

Despite its appeal, particularly from a 'talent' development perspective, the theory of deliberate practice has been heavily criticized. Sternberg (1996, 1998) has been the biggest critic of the theory. He suggested that the tendency to practice may well be genetically mediated, and shape the degree to which an individual practices. Moreover, heritabilities of practiced skills tend to increase with age, as opposed to decrease as one might expect from an environmental viewpoint. In a recent review, Singer and Janelle (1999) suggested that it would be a mistake to ignore the potential influence of genetic phenotypes on the acquisition of expertise, particularly in a sports domain, where both perceptual-cognitive and perceptual-motor skills are necessary constituents of achieving skilled levels of performance. As long as individuals recognize the fact that they may not be 'cut out' for success within a particular domain and subsequently drop out, it will be almost impossible to determine whether greater amounts of practice by experts is truly the defining characteristic of expertise (Sternberg, 1996). In the main, these critics objected to Ericsson *et al.*'s (1993) polar stance on expertise achievement, when in reality the relative contribution of nature and nurture is open to debate (see Sternberg, 1998). The view that deliberate practice is a causal mechanism has often been central to the environmental vantage point. In support of this doctrine, Ericsson and colleagues argued that many laboratory tasks have demonstrated lawful improvements in performance with increased practice according to the power law of practice (Anderson, 1982; Newell and Rosenbloom, 1981). The improvements in domains such as music and sports noted here and elsewhere, indicate that similar mathematical relationships exist between attained level of performance and engagement in deliberate practice (Ericsson, 1996).

Summary and conclusions

The original conception of the deliberate practice theory (Ericsson *et al.*, 1993) explicitly claimed that expert levels of performance could be acquired through sustained investment in activities deliberately designed to improve performance. These activities were proposed to be severely constrained, not simply by the necessity of high-level coaching to guide the learning process, and the associated financial resources that such commitment would consume, but also by critical motivational and effort constraints. Those individuals who are motivated to overcome the demands of prolonged engagement and subsequently accrue a greater number of hours in deliberate practice were predicted to acquire the necessary skills for attaining excellence. Expertise was viewed as a long-term adaptation process where, according to the power law of practice, monotonic improvements in performance would result as a consequence of such investment. In the absence of unequivocal evidence in favour of innate talents mediating attained skill level, research from the domain of music provided clear support for these claims, and the necessity of 10 years and approximately 10,000 hours of investment before achieving expert levels of performance. Starkes and colleagues were the first to test this theory in the sports domain and although support was found for the 10-year rule and the monotonic benefits assumption, these authors provided a number of qualifications. Whereas Ericsson suggested that 'practice alone' most accurately captured the definition of deliberate practice in music, in the sports domain, team practice or practice with others were often a more accurate predictor of attained skill level. In contrast to the original definition of deliberate practice as 'not inherently enjoyable', Starkes and colleagues also suggested that participation in deliberate 'sports' practice was likely to be highly enjoyable, particularly where there is a large perceptual-motor component.

　　Since the first examination of Ericsson's theory and subsequent qualifications, a number of conceptual, developmental, methodological, and motivational issues have come to the fore. First, the discrepancy in the true constituents of deliberate practice across domains has been highlighted as a potential concern. The current evidence suggests that whilst an additional 10–20 per cent of the variance in skill level among triathletes could be explained by maintenance-type activities (e.g. fitness work), not surprisingly, the majority of the variance was explained by sport-specific practice (i.e. 30–50 per cent) (Hodges *et al.*, submitted). Although individual practice and match play contribute to the development of elite athletes and contribute towards the variance explained, Ward *et al.*

(submitted) highlighted that the variable most valuable in predicting skill group membership for soccer players was the amount of time spent in team practice. In fact, investment in this activity in particular, accurately predicted elite and sub-elite levels of performance for over 85 per cent of the players.

Once appropriately defined, the question of whether engagement in deliberate practice can predict individual rather than group performance becomes important. This area of research may have the greatest application, particularly for talent scouts and coaches. If one can predict the amount of practice that an individual would need to improve performance times, say by one second or even a fraction thereof, or can delineate the quantity as well as the quality of practice needed to warrant progressing to the next skill level (i.e. from U-9 to U-10 Academy-level soccer), then according to the theory, one should be able to ensure appropriate skill development for a given individual. While this information is useful, it is not the case that any individual can partake in a specific quantity of practice and make incremental steps towards expertise. On the contrary, the resource, effort and motivational constraints indicate that only where sufficient learning opportunity is provided, and where individuals are motivated to conquer the demands of the adaptation process will monotonic improvements ensue. Without the pre-requisite motivation, increments in skill are likely to dissipate and level off rather than continue to develop (see Ericsson, 1998).

The nature of activities in which athletes engage throughout development has also been a topical issue over the last few years. Côté and colleagues have maintained that deliberate play is fundamental to providing the necessary foundations upon which expertise can be built. Côté's research demonstrated that elite players spent more time in playful activities, were more diverse in their pursuit of other activities prior to specialization, and also specialized at a relatively late age (e.g. approximately 16 years of age). However, none of these findings were supported by the research of Ward and colleagues, who concluded that although both elite and sub-elite groups spent a considerable amount of time in playful activities, players could not be discriminated on this activity. Irrespective of age, elite players tended to apportion their time so that they invested more time and effort into deliberate practice compared to sub-elite players. The observed differences between cohorts may well be explained by cultural biases and further research is needed to clarify this issue. These findings are likely to have significant impact upon the way in which talent is developed. According to Côté's view, spending time in deliberate play may reduce the amount of practice needed to achieve expert status. However, our research suggests that whilst play may be an integral part of skill development, engagement in this activity is not necessarily predictive of later expert performance, nor does it necessarily play a causal role in the acquisition of expertise. Rather, investment in team practice from an early age, with some experience in match play and individual practice, is likely to be the vehicle by which excellence is attained.

The way in which deliberate practice is measured, and the reliability and validity of the measurement established, is of utmost concern given the original claims for quantities of practice being predictive of performance. Typically, diaries and test–retest methods have been used to validate retrospective estimates using 'forward-recall' (e.g. recall starting with first year of participation). However, to increase the reliability of such estimates, and the inherent bias in forward-recall, recent research has taken a quasi-longitudinal approach by collecting retrospective data for current and preceding years using backward-recall (see Hodges *et al.*, submitted; Ward *et al.*, submitted). Generally, comparisons of current and retrospective reports revealed no significant differences between estimates by Ward *et al.* (submitted). This quasi-longitudinal methodology provides an excellent tool for cross-validating retrospective reports and detailing the development of elite-level players with respect to the amount and type of deliberate practice. By clearly differentiating between improvement-type activities from maintenance activities, the relative contribution of these activities throughout development can be examined.

Lastly, in order to move the current experimental paradigm away from a process of merely number crunching, researchers have attempted to detail the qualitative aspects of performance within a practice session and determine whether deliberate practice activities conform to the original definitions, when examined at a more micro level of analysis. Although deliberate practice was conceptualized as necessitating effortful attempts to improve performance, the research suggests that, surprisingly, much of the effort during a training session is directed toward activities that are already well learnt. The mere fact that deliberate practice activities are so effortful may well be the mediating factor in limiting the time invested in solving difficult problems or practising complex movements. Consequently, it is highly likely that time spent in actual effortful deliberate practice is likely to have been substantially overestimated in previous research.

In conclusion, although criticisms of the theory of deliberate practice have been raised, only exceptions to the monotonic benefits assumption are likely to cause any serious concerns for this theory, as remarked by Ericsson himself (personal communication). It is only with well-defined practice hours and strong support for the reliability of retrospective methods can any potential deviations in practice–performance profiles, either at an individual or group level, be reliably attributed to other factors, such as talent.

References

Allard, F. and Starkes, J. L. (1991). Motor-skill experts in sports, dance, and other domains. In K. A. Ericsson and J. Smith (Eds), *Toward a general theory of expertise: prospects and limits* (pp. 126–152). Cambridge, UK: Cambridge University Press.

Amabile, T. M. (1996). *Creativity in context*. Boulder, CO: Westview.

Anderson, J. R. (1983). *The architecture of cognition*. Cambridge, MA: Harvard University Press.

Baker, J., Côté, J. and Abernethy, B. (2003). Sport-specific practice and the development of expert decision making in team ball sports. *Journal of Applied Sport Psychology*, 15, 12–25.

Beamer, M., Côté, J. and Ericsson, K. A. (1999). A comparison between international and provincial level gymnasts in their pursuit of sport expertise. Paper presented at the 10th Annual European Congress of Sport Psychology, July 7–12. Prague, Czech Republic: FEPSAC.

Bloom, B. (1985). *Developing talent in young people*. New York: Balantine.

Charness, N., Krampe, R. and Mayr, U. (1996). The role of practice and coaching in entrepreneurial skill domains: an international comparison of life-span chess skill acquisition. In K. A. Ericsson (Ed.), *The road to excellence: the acquisition of expert performance in the arts and sciences, sports, and games* (pp. 51–80). Mahwah, NJ: Erlbaum.

Côté, J. (1999) The influence of the family in the development of talent in sports. *The Sports Psychologist*, 13, 395–417.

Côté, J. and Hay, J. (2002). Children's involvement in sport: a developmental perspective. In J. M. Silva and D. Stevens (Eds), *Psychological foundations in sport* (pp. 484–502), Boston, MA: Merrill.

Côté, J., Baker, J. and Abernethy, B. (2001) Stages of sport participation of expert decision-makers in team ball sports. In A. Papaioannou, M. Goudas and Y. Theodorakis (Eds), Proceedings of the 10th World Congress of Sport Psychology: Vol. 3. In the dawn of the new millennium (pp. 150–152). Skiathos, Hellas: International Society of Sport Psychology.

Csikszentmihalyi, M., Rathunde, K. and Whalen, S. (1993). *Talented teenagers: the roots of success and failure*. Cambridge, UK: Cambridge University Press.

Cullen, J. D. and Starkes, J. L. (1997). Deliberate practice in ice hockey. Paper presented at the Canadian Society for Psychomotor Learning and Sport Psychology. Niagara Falls, Canada.

Deakin, J. M., Starkes, J. L. and Allard, F. (1998). The microstructure of practice in sport. Sport Canada Technical Report. Ottawa, Canada.

Deci, E. L. and Ryan, R. M. (1985). *Intrinsic motivation and self-determination in human behaviour*. New York: Plenum Press.

Ericsson, K. A. (1996). The acquisition of expert performance: an introduction to some of the issues. In K. A. Ericsson (Ed.), *The road to excellence: the acquisition of expert performance in the arts and sciences, sports, and games* (pp. 1–50). Mahwah, NJ: Erlbaum.

Ericsson, K. A. (1998). The scientific study of expert levels of performance: general implications for optimal learning and creativity. *High Ability Studies*, 9, 75–100.

Ericsson, K. A. and Charness, N. (1994). Expert performance: its structure and acquisition. *American Psychologist*, 49, 725–747.

Ericsson, K. A. and Lehmann, A. C. (1996). Expert and exceptional performance: evidence of maximal adaptation to task constraints. *Annual Review of Psychology*, 47, 273–305.

Ericsson, K. A. and Smith, J. (1991). *Toward a general theory of expertise: prospects and limits*. Cambridge, UK: Cambridge University Press.

Ericsson, K. A., Krampe, R. T. and Tesch-Römer, C. (1993). The role of deliberate practice in the acquisition of expert performance. *Psychological Review*, 100, 363–406.

Handford, C., Davids, K., Bennett, S. and Button, C. (1997). Skill acquisition in sport: some applications of an evolving practice ecology. *Journal of Sports Sciences*, 15 (6), 621–640.

Hatano, G. and Inagaki, K. (1986). Two courses of expertise. In H. Stevenson, H. Azuma and K. Hakuta (Eds), *Child development and education in Japan* (pp. 262–272). San Francisco, CA: Freeman.

Helsen, W. F., Starkes, J. L. and Hodges, N. J. (1998). Team sports and the theory of deliberate practice. *Journal of Sport and Exercise Psychology*, 20, 12–34.

Hodges, N. J. (1996). Wrestling with the nature of expertise: a sport-specific test of Ericsson, Krampe and Tesch-Römer's (1993) theory of 'deliberate practice'. Unpublished data from a master's thesis, McMaster University, Hamilton, Ontario, Canada.

Hodges, N. J. and Starkes, J. L. (1996). Wrestling with the nature of expertise: a sport-specific test of Ericsson, Krampe and Tesch-Römer's (1993) theory of 'deliberate practice'. *International Journal of Sport Psychology*, 27, 400–424.

Hodges, N. J., Kerr, T., Weir, P. and Starkes, J. L. (submitted). Predicting performance from 'deliberate practice' hours for the multi-sport athlete: issues of transfer, validity and reliability of practice estimates.

Howe, M. J. A., Davidson, J. W. and Sloboda, J. A. (1998). Innate talents: reality or myth? *Behavioural and Brain Sciences*, 21, 399–442.

Kahneman, D. (1973). *Attention and effort*. Englewood Cliffs, NJ: Prentice-Hall.

Krampe, R. and Ericsson, K. A. (1996). Maintaining excellence: deliberate practice and elite performance in young and older pianists. *Journal of Experimental Psychology: General*, 125, 331–359.

Lens, W. and Rand, P. (2000). Motivation and cognition: their role in the development of giftedness. In K. A. Heller, F. J. Monks, R. J. Sternberg and R. F. Subotnik (Eds), *International handbook of giftedness and talent* (2nd ed.) (pp. 193–202). Amsterdam, Netherlands: Elsevier.

Moraes, L. C., Samela, J. H. and Rabelo, A. S. (2000). O desenvolvimento de desemprenho exceptional de jogadores jovens do futebol mineiro. Anais do premero conresso científico Latíno-Americano: Fundep: São Paulo: p. 22.

Newell, A. and Rosenbloom, P. S. (1981). Mechanisms of skill acquisition and the law of practice. In J. R. Anderson (Ed.), *Cognitive skills and their acquisition* (pp. 1–55), Hillsdale, NJ: Lawrence Erlbaum Associates.

Powers, S. K. and Howley, E. T. (2001). *Exercise physiology* (4th ed.). New York: McGraw-Hill.

Rogers, M. A., Hagberg, J. M., Martin, W. H., III, Ehsani, A. A. and Holloszy, J. O. (1990). Decline in VO_2max with aging in master athletes and sedentary men. *Journal of Applied Physiology*, 68, 2195–2199.

Rusbult, C. E. (1980). Commitment and satisfaction in romantic associations: a test of the investment model. *Journal of Experimental Social Psychology*, 16, 172–186.

Ryan, R. M. and Deci, E. L. (2000). Self-determination theory and the facilitation of intrinsic motivation, social development, and well being. *American Psychologist*, 55, 68–78.

Samela, J. H. and Moraes, L. C. (2003). Coaching expertise, families, and cultural contexts. In J. L. Starkes and K. A. Ericsson (Eds), *Expert performance in sport* (pp. 225–294). Champaign, IL: Human Kinetics.

Scanlan, T. K., Carpenter, P. J., Schmidt, G. W., Simons, J. P. and Keeler, B. (1993). An introduction to the sport commitment model. *Journal of Sport and Exercise Psychology*, 15, 1–15.

Seifert, C. M., Meyer, D. E., Davidson, N., Patalano, A. L. and Yaniv, I. (1995). Demystification of cognitive insight: opportunistic assimilation and the prepared mind perspective. In R. J. Sternberg and J. E. Davidson (Eds), *The nature of insight* (pp. 65–124). Cambridge, MA: MIT Press.

Simon, H. A. and Chase, W. (1973). Skill in chess. *American Scientist*, 61, 394–403.

Singer, R. N. and Janelle, C. M. (1999). Determining sport expertise: from genes to supremes. *International Journal of Sport Psychology*, 30, 117–150.

Soberlak, P. (2001). A retrospective analysis of the development and motivation of professional ice-hockey players. Unpublished thesis. Queen's University, Kingston, ON, Canada.

Sloboda, J. A. (2000). Individual differences in music performance. *Trends in Cognitive Sciences*, 4, 397–403.

Starkes, J. L. (2000). The road to expertise: is practice the only determinant? *International Journal of Sport Psychology*, 31, 431–451.

Starkes, J. L., Deakin, J., Allard, F., Hodges, N. J. and Hayes, A. (1996). Deliberate practice in sports: what is it anyway? In K. A. Ericsson (Ed.), *The road to excellence: the acquisition of expert performance in the arts and sciences, sports, and games* (pp. 81–106). Mahwah, NJ: Erlbaum.

Starkes, J. L., Weir, P. L., Singh, P., Hodges, N. J. and Kerr, T. (1999). Aging and the retention of sport expertise. *International Journal of Sport Psychology*, 30, 283–301.

Starkes, J. L., Weir, P. L. and Young, B. W. (2003). The retention of expertise: what does it take for older athletes to continue to excel? In J. L. Starkes and K. A. Ericsson (Eds), *Expert performance in sports: advances in research on sport expertise* (pp. 251–272). Champaign, IL.: Human Kinetics.

Sternberg, R. J. (1996). Costs of expertise. In K. A. Ericsson (Ed.), *The road to excellence: the acquisition of expert performance in the arts and sciences, sports, and games* (pp. 347–354). Mahway, NJ: Erlbaum.

Sternberg, R. J. (1998). If the key's not there, the light won't help. *Behavioural and Brain Sciences*, 21, 425–426.

Sternberg, R. J. (2000). Giftedness as developing expertise. In K. A. Heller, F. J. Monks, R. J. Sternberg and R. F. Subotnik (Eds), *International handbook of giftedness and talent* (2nd ed.) (pp. 55–66). Amsterdam, Netherlands: Elsevier.

Sternberg, R. J. and Wagner, R. K. (1999). Readings in cognitive psychology. Fort Worth, TX: Harcourt Brace.

Ward, P. and Williams, A. M. (2003). Perceptual and cognitive skill development in soccer: the multidimensional nature of expert performance. *Journal of Sport and Exercise Psychology*, 25 1, 93–111.

Ward, P., Hodges, N. J., Starkes, J. L. and Williams, A. M. (submitted). The road to excellence in soccer: a quasi-longitudinal approach to deliberate practice.

Weir, P. L., Kerr, T., Hodges, N. J., McKay, S. M. and Starkes, J. L. (2002). Master swimmers: how are they different from younger elite swimmers? An examination of practice and performance patterns. *Journal of Aging and Physical Activity*, 10, 41–63.

Wilkinson, H. (1997). *The charter for quality*. London: The English Football Association.

Williams, A. M., Ward, P., Knowles, J. M. and Smeeton, N. J. (2002). Anticipation skill in a real-world task: measurement, training, and transfer in tennis. *Journal of Experimental Psychology: Applied*, 8, 259–270.

Winner, E. (1996). The rage to master: The decisive role of talent in the visual arts. In K. A. Ericsson (Ed.), *The road to excellence: the acquisition of expert performance in the arts and sciences, sports and games* (pp. 271–302). Mahwah, NJ: Erlbaum.

Winner, E. (2000). The origins and ends of giftedness. *American Psychologist*, 55, 159–169.

Young, B. W. and Starkes, J. L. (submitted). Lifespan analysis of track performance: continued training moderates the age-related performance decline.

12 A life-span model of the acquisition and retention of expert perceptual-motor performance

Janet L. Starkes, John D. Cullen and Clare MacMahon

In this chapter, we present a life-span descriptive model of the acquisition and retention of perceptual-motor skill. The goal of descriptive modelling is to present a concise synopsis of observed behaviours. However, observed behaviours are often quite discrepant because laboratory and real-world findings differ, tasks are novel, and experimental designs are variable. Therefore, a central task for a descriptive model of skill acquisition is to reconcile those findings based on what is most commonly seen. If a comprehensive theoretical model of expertise is to be derived, it can only happen once a good descriptive model is able to capture details of performance change typically seen with the development of expertise. Elsewhere authors have noted the lack of, the need for and the difficulty in developing a generalized theory of expertise (Abernethy *et al.*, 2003; Ericsson and Smith, 1991; Starkes and Allard, 1993). It is our hope that this descriptive model of skill acquisition and retention may assist.

The model

Our model attempts to capture the constant transition that occurs in perceptual-cognitive and perceptual-motor behaviour as skill acquisition occurs, as well as how skilled behaviours may be retained following peak performance. The inclusion of post-peak performance considerations is a unique feature of the model, as this 'stage' of performance, while previously rarely considered, is increasingly of interest to many who conduct skill acquisition/expertise research (Krampe and Ericsson, 1996; Starkes *et al.*, 1999, 2003; Weir *et al.*, 2002). The model is presented in Figure 12.1, and will be referred to throughout the chapter. Performance is viewed as being in constant transition with phases denoting the types of behaviours that are characteristic at certain times. Two streams, labelled A and B influence behaviours. There is constant interaction and exchange between what one is able to perceive and understand (Stream A: perceptual-cognitive stream) and what one is able to perceive and do (Stream B: perceptual-motor stream). Performance emerges as a product of these streams and is either constrained or facilitated by their interaction.

We have identified anchor points that characterize the behaviours normally observed. These anchor points are labelled Phase 1 through Phase 4. It must be

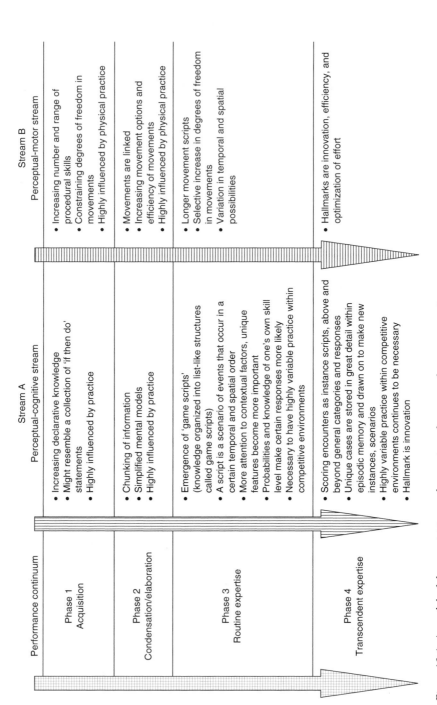

Figure 12.1 A model of the acquisition and retention of perceptual-motor expertise.

Stream A
Perceptual-cognitive stream

Stream B
Perceptual-motor stream

Performance continuum

Phase 1
Acquisition

- Increasing declarative knowledge
- Might resemble a collection of 'if then do' statements
- Highly influenced by practice

- Increasing number and range of procedural skills
- Constraining degrees of freedom in movements
- Highly influenced by physical practice

Phase 2
Condensation/elaboration

- Chunking of information
- Simplified mental models
- Highly influenced by practice

- Movements are linked
- Increasing movement options and efficiency of movements
- Highly influenced by physical practice

Phase 3
Routine expertise

- Emergence of 'game scripts' (knowledge organized into list-like structures called game scripts)
- A script is a scenario of events that occur in a certain temporal and spatial order
- More attention to contextual factors, unique features become more important
- Probabilities and knowledge of one's own skill level make certain responses more likely
- Necessary to have highly variable practice within competitive environments

- Longer movement scripts
- Selective increase in degrees of freedom in movements
- Variation in temporal and spatial possibilities

Phase 4
Transcendent expertise

- Scoring encounters as instance scripts, above and beyond general categories and responses
- Unique cases are stored in great detail within episodic memory and drawn on to make new instances, scenarios
- Highly variable practice within competitive environments continues to be necessary
- Hallmark is innovation

- Hallmarks are innovation, efficiency, and optimization of effort

acknowledged that the model owes much to an early version of cognitive development proposed by Schmidt *et al.* (1990), which was designed to describe the development of expertise in medical diagnoses. Our model is necessarily more complex in order to accommodate skill development in children and Master athletes, and the complex acquisition of motor skill. Nevertheless, Schmidt *et al.*'s formulations on the cognitive side of skill have profoundly influenced parts of this model.

In this chapter, we first discuss typical behaviours associated with each phase of development in the model (1–4) and use examples from various studies as illustrations. Since this is a model of acquisition and retention, we follow presentation of the model with considerations of how well expertise is retained in skilled performers who continue to train and compete long after their peak performance years. Finally, we ask whether it is possible to reconcile the disparate views of expertise seen through the lens of various theoretical models.

Phase 1: development of declarative knowledge and procedural skills

Our model proposes two major contributors to sport performance: a perceptual-cognitive stream (Stream A in Figure 12.1), and a perceptual-motor stream (Stream B in Figure 12.1). While these streams may develop at different rates, they are inextricably linked, and mutually influence an athlete's performance. Phase 1 of skill development is one in which there is a great *accumulation of declarative knowledge* (in Stream A) that is domain specific. At the same time the learner acquires a growing repertoire of domain related *procedural skills* (in Stream B). Physical practice permits the novice to 'try out' these movement skills and determine the conditions under which they are most appropriate. Initially, we might expect that this knowledge would be stored as a collection of 'if then do' statements. For example: as a basketball player, *if* the defense is too close *then* I would choose not to shoot but rather to go around the player, or pass off. *If* I am wide open with the ball, as on a fast break, *then* I would continue to the basket. These are fairly simple scripts that the learner employs. In order to carry out the actual movements involved, and thus combine both the perceptual-cognitive and perceptual-motor streams, one may have to constrain degrees of freedom (i.e. motor and cognitive choices or alternatives) in order to be successful. An example would be a young basketball player who is fairly successful at dribbling the ball down the court but is likely to lose control if forced to change pace, direction or dribbling hand.

The model describes constraining degrees of freedom when one stream develops faster than the other. In the case described above, the perceptual-cognitive stream is ahead of the perceptual-motor stream. We also speculate that *lack of progress* in one stream constrains an athlete's overall progress. Nevett and French's (1997) study of young baseball shortstops illustrates this point. The many stoppages in play during the course of a baseball game make it an ideal sport to study planning and tactics. In order to examine how these strategies change through development, the authors recruited male baseball shortstops from four age groups: 8-, 10- and 12-year-olds, and high school-aged. An added feature of this study was that data collection took place *during the course of games*. Nevett and French (1997) looked specifically at defensive planning, and used talk-aloud verbal protocols to elicit responses.

The development of the perceptual-cognitive stream was described in the analysis of players' strategic planning (i.e. action plans) and showed that the more experienced players planned in advance, had higher quality plans, higher quality rehearsal of plans and made modifications as conditions changed across pitches to the same batter. In contrast, younger players '...monitored more irrelevant game information, and accessed less tactical conditions, actions and goals' (Nevett and French, 1997, p. 212). In addition, the younger players were found to make more 'chatter' statements (e.g. 'hey batter, batter...swing!').

The most striking finding for a discussion of our model is that the younger players' action plans were constrained by their skill level. Younger players were not concerned with defending against a runner scoring from second base as their motor skills were not developed enough to counter this move with a throw to home plate. Young players' tactical solutions and knowledge development are thus influenced by the development of their motor skills. Once their motor skills are in place to facilitate a particular strategy they are more likely to employ that strategy. In this case, the perceptual-cognitive stream is necessarily constrained by the players' lack of motor competence.

Nevett and French (1997) proposed that actually playing in different game contexts influences planning as well as the range of procedural skills acquired. The game rules of baseball differed by age group in this study. Thus, where the 10-year-olds encountered stolen bases, they did not have exposure to bunting (a strategic play in which a batter deflects the pitched ball such that it falls just in front of home plate, usually done to move a runner closer to a scoring position while sacrificing the batter), as was the case for the 12-year-olds. The younger age groups were not exposed to defending a bunt situation, and did not plan for this scenario. This relationship proposes that actually performing the choice motorically will reinforce its development as part of the game-planning repertoire. The findings from this study support our view that perceptual-cognitive and perceptual-motor streams are developmentally linked in the overall performance of the athlete, and may serve to both facilitate or constrain performance.

We would add that there is no assumption within the model that knowledge is necessarily acquired through explicit instruction. Knowledge and procedural skill are often acquired implicitly, and for some tasks this form of acquisition may be superior to explicit coaching. Magill (1998) provides strong evidence that implicit learning is as important if not more important than explicit learning within what we term the perceptual-motor stream. The work of several researchers indicates that for open motor skills (i.e. skills in which the goal is different than the skill itself, typically within a continuously changing environment – in basketball, your team is not rewarded points for how well your shot is performed but whether or not the ball goes into the basket), acquiring the environmental regulatory features of a skill through implicit means is at least as effective as acquiring the information through explicit coaching (Green and Flowers, 1991; Magill and Clark, 1997). In situations where the environmental regulatory cues occur less than 100 per cent of the time, relying on explicit instructions may actually hinder performance.

After Phase 1, the development of knowledge and skills required for performance, access, retrieval and refinement become a focus for improved efficiency and superior performance outcomes. We now turn to the developments characteristic of Phase 2.

Phase 2: condensation and elaboration of content

The second phase of development involves *both condensation of knowledge as well as elaboration*. One might ask how these seemingly contradictory directions can happen simultaneously and an example will illustrate. Jack *et al.* (2003) studied how three groups of ballet dancers of varying skill recall dance steps. In their study, Canadian National Ballet students and semi-professional dancers (both with 10–13 years ballet training) were compared with novices (2–3 years experience) on their ability to recall choreographed dance sequences. Participants viewed a series of choreographed sequences of eighteen steps and then performed them. Absolute recall performance of the steps showed typical primacy–recency effects amongst the two high skill groups. Both National Ballet and semi-professionals showed almost perfect recall of the steps at the beginning and end of the sequence and roughly 40 per cent recall mid-sequence. As expected, National Ballet students were slightly better overall than the semi-professional dancers. Novices recalled a couple of steps at the beginning of the sequence and little thereafter.

What was most informative from this study was *how* experts and novices recalled the steps. National Ballet students placed the steps into 4.6 chunks of information with an average of 2.7 steps per chunk. Semi-professional dancers used 2.5 chunks with 4.1 steps per chunk, while novices simply recalled individual steps. This is evidence that with skill and experience, dancers first encode information into more chunks and then the relative size of chunks increases (this is described in Stream A of Phase 2, Figure 12.1). This strategy reduces the cognitive load for short-term memory while accessing long-term working memory, in turn facilitating recall. At the same time, each chunk is likely to contain more detailed information. For example, rather than performing four separate movements forward, backward and to each side, experts recall this entire sequence as a 'grand jetté', thus there is greater linking and elaboration of individual movements, a case of both condensation *and* elaboration.

Prior to this experiment we would have predicted that the most skilled dancers would encapsulate information in more chunks and each chunk would contain a number of elements. The National ballet students do employ more chunks (4.6) but each chunk has relatively fewer elements (2.7) than the chunks created by semi-professional dancers (4.1). We speculate that this may reflect a ceiling effect since the most skilled dancers recall ~75 per cent of the dance sequences as opposed to ~57 per cent by the semi-professional dancers. Alternatively, it may be that the creation of new associations or chunks is an earlier stage of skill and the 'filling' of the chunks follows secondarily. Thus the National level dancers have created new associations and are in the process of adding elements to those. If this is the case, then we would hypothesize that were we to test older professional dancers we would expect both a large number of chunks and chunks that contained 5–9 elements.

These findings are not unique to motor skill. The chunking phenomenon has been a robust finding in environments that are more cognitive in nature. For example, in chess, Chase and Simon (1973) have demonstrated superior memory for chess pieces structured by functional groupings. Likewise, Ericsson and Polson (1988) demonstrated how structure assists waiters in the recall of dinner orders.

An elegant study by Williams and Davids (1995) is used to illustrate the impact of different forms of sport exposure and experience on the development of the two streams. Williams and Davids (1995) studied the soccer knowledge/skills of high skilled players, low skilled players and physically disabled spectators. All of the participants had accumulated similar amounts of time soccer spectating, and all were tested on soccer-specific anticipation, recall and recognition tasks. Both player groups had the same amount of playing experience and differed only in the level of performance attained.

Our model proposes that an expert athlete (e.g. at Phase 3 or 4) is highly developed in both the perceptual-motor and the perceptual-cognitive systems. However, at different points during skill acquisition, the two systems may vary in stage of development, thus limiting overall performance. Differences between the two streams in Phase 2, as well as Phase 1, will be illustrated by comparing the groups in this study: individuals with (1) advanced development of both streams (high skill group); (2) moderate development in both streams (low skill group); and (3) development of the perceptual-cognitive stream only (disabled spectators). Thus, a task in which low-skill players perform better than disabled spectators points to perceptual-motor stream underdevelopment as a constraining factor for performance. Where there are no differences between groups, the perceptual-cognitive stream is seen to provide sufficient compensation for performance. Where high skill players are better than low skill players, we assume that both streams contribute; however, we cannot be clear which, if either is dominant. Thus, to illustrate the two streams of the model, our emphasis will be to compare the disabled spectator group to the low-skill player group. To illustrate the development of these two streams (or development of specific tasks) with expertise, we will compare the high skill with the low skill players.

For all tasks, participants viewed soccer game footage projected onto a large screen. For the anticipation test, participants saw a game film in which the ball was passed to a highlighted player, and then anticipated that player's pass destination. In tests of recall, participants were shown both structured and unstructured game footage and then recalled player positions. In the recognition task, participants viewed film clips and indicated whether these had been seen in the previous recall test.

Not surprisingly, high skill players were superior to low skill players on all measures except anticipation response time. Comparing low skill players and disabled spectators, low skill players had better recall accuracy and anticipation response time, but were no better in anticipation accuracy, recognition speed or recognition accuracy. Seen through the model, these findings point to the perceptual-motor system as central in recall accuracy and anticipation response time.

For the anticipation response test, high and low skill players did not differ and both were superior to disabled spectators. Whereas players anticipated pass destination prior to the ball being kicked, the disabled spectators responded after ball contact. Thus, players with experience reacting motorically to a ball kick exhibit speedy anticipation to facilitate movement initiation. In contrast, disabled spectators do not have experience initiating soccer movements, and do not need to 'save time' for a more complex response. For this group, a lack of perceptual-motor stream development holds back overall performance.

In recall accuracy, the results were differentiated based on whether the clips contained game structured or unstructured information. Recall of unstructured clips was the same across groups but high skill players made fewer errors on structured clips than low skill players, who were superior to disabled spectators. In recall accuracy for structured information, then, a disparity between the low skill players and disabled spectators once again points to the contribution of the perceptual-motor stream for this skill.

We speculate that Phase 2, the condensation/elaboration stage, is both lengthy and very significant in the acquisition of skill. This stage is also significant in that it precedes the first 'expert' stage: routine expertise.

Phase 3: routine expertise

What is an expert?

Phase 3 is the first time performers are considered 'experts'. Before describing this phase, we will turn to a question posed by our model: How good does one have to be to be considered an expert? This would seem to be a fairly straightforward question and yet it has plagued expertise research because it has proven impossible to answer. The easy answer is that for research purposes it is important to choose skills for which there is some metric of performance and then concentrate on the top performers (i.e. top 10 per cent of performers, or those who fall two or more standard deviations above average performance) (Starkes and Allard, 1993). This does not really help in skills for which 'best' cannot be metrically determined or for which 'best' is often presumed from social standards (e.g. medical diagnoses, judiciary decisions, figure skating judging, soccer officiating or visual artists). Some authors (Sloboda, 1991) are of the opinion that expertise is, in part, defined by the typical environmental demands of the task. Performance on some tasks plateaus such that most adults are eventually able to reach expert levels of performance (i.e. driving a car or tying one's shoes). There are other tasks, including most sports and musical performances, for which it takes several thousand hours of training and many years to attain expert levels of performance (for a more detailed discussion, see Ericsson *et al.*, 1993; Starkes *et al.*, 2000). In this case, the task appears much more complex and fewer individuals attain expert performance levels. An alternative view is that performance even on relatively simple tasks, such as cigar rolling (Crossman, 1959) still benefits from continued practice over the long term.

Another issue that impacts who is declared an expert is the breadth of field and relative participation levels. For example, it is likely that for 'new' sports such as skeleton or freestyle snowboarding, the participation base is so comparatively small at the inception of the sport that most 'experts' in that sport have only specialized over the short term. It is likely that as a sport ages and participation base increases, it becomes more difficult to become an expert in that sport.

Much of the existing literature that has purported to test expert–novice differences (including most of our own) has involved the testing of athletes that would fall within the model's Phase 3 of development and be considered routine experts. Within the expertise literature there is a large range of performance levels that have variously been termed 'expert'. Some studies have referred to high-school athletes as 'experts'; in other studies, experts have been World Cup soccer players. Because we see performance as a broad based continuum with phases that have certain identifying behaviours, not isolated points, the issue of who exactly is or is not an expert is of relatively little concern. It is more important for us to understand where an athlete fits along this continuum of behaviours. Likewise, if one is testing different ability groups with the goal of discussing expert–novice differences it becomes important to have distance between the groups along the performance continuum. It is to a description of Phase 3 of the model, and its markers along this continuum that we now return.

Routine expertise and the use of scripts

We hypothesize that during the routine expertise phase of performance 'game scripts' and 'movement scripts' are employed, wherein performers use previous experience and knowledge to map out a sequence of actions expected to lead to a desired outcome. While the term 'script' has the potential to be misunderstood, we feel it best represents our intent. 'Script' does not imply that these plans are necessarily verbally mediated or sequential. Take, for example, an expert skier in giant slalom. The racer has a plan in place prior to a competitive run that takes into account the layout of the course, the intended approach to each gate, fall-line and pace (use of the perceptual-cognitive stream). On the movement side (perceptual-motor stream) the approach to each gate is carried out using a particular movement script or sequence of well-practised movements. In very skilled performers it is unlikely that movements are verbally mediated, as movement procedures do not appear to be accessible from episodic memory (e.g. Beilock and Carr, 2001; Beilock *et al.*, 2002).

For expert racers, context plays a very important role. The racer's plan may be altered by weather changes occurring while waiting prior to the run, or if other racers have found a certain gate extremely icy. During the race things happen.

For example, the skier catches an edge, or slips into a gate. Part of expertise as a racer is dependent on how quickly and efficiently one can alter intent and actions, or 'rescript', in order to finish the race. McPherson and Kernodle (2003) would term this updating the *current event profile* for the race and have determined that it is unique to very skilled athletes.

We have termed Phase 3 'routine expertise', and discussed the use of scripts, which may be altered according to context. However, once again, our model poses a question: is 'routine' a part of expertise? Or, rather, is automaticity reflective of expertise? Fitts and Posner (1967) first suggested that as skill is acquired the performer goes through three stages. At first performing a task involves a great deal of cognitive load and the performer is therefore at the 'Cognitive' stage. With practice one evolves to an 'Associative' stage, very similar to what we propose as a period in which knowledge networks are condensed and elaborated. Finally, skilled performers reach an 'Automatic' stage in which complex procedures are run in the absence of conscious attention to individual components of execution. The fact that skilled athletes are often unable to explain how they do a certain move, or report that they simply do it 'by feel', has lent anecdotal support to Fitts and Posner's theory. Their theory has probably remained popular first, because it is parsimonious; and second, because it fits very well the kinds of transitions athletes experience with improvements in skill.

Until now, there was not a great deal of empirical support for the model put forward by Fitts and Posner (1967). Recently, Beilock and Carr (2001) found that novice golfers have very detailed episodic memories of the steps involved in individual putts, in spite of their general lack of declarative knowledge about putting. Expert golfers, on the other hand, have a wealth of generic knowledge about putting (e.g. how to putt, how to adjust a putt based on condition of the green, slope), yet have a very difficult time remembering details involving the actual execution of their putts. The best golfers simply cannot tell you how they just dropped a curling 25 foot putt. This is a phenomenon the authors have dubbed, 'expertise-induced amnesia'. At this level of skill, attention is no longer required for the step-by-step details of movements involved in performance, resulting in a loss of episodic memory for these steps and a proceduralization of performance.

The transition from storing performance as a series of steps to automating these steps and proceduralizing the skill is illustrated by a task manipulation. If expert golfers are placed in a novel putting situation (i.e. an unusually shaped and weighted putter), they will be required to pay attention to the steps involved in performance, and will store this information in episodic memory. This process reverts experts to novice levels, and they now become capable of reporting putting procedures in great detail. A question that remained following this study was whether these effects were unique to discrete skills or would the same phenomena apply for athletes performing repetitive movements, movements in more open sports, or movements that are highly time constrained. Beilock *et al.* (2002) conducted two experiments to address this, one on golf putting, the other on soccer dribbling. In both experiments, experienced performers putted or dribbled under dual-task conditions designed to distract attention from putting and dribbling and under skill-focused conditions that prompted attention to step-by-step procedures involved in the skills. As might be expected from the previous experiments, performance in the dual task conditions was more accurate than the skill-focus condition. Putting and dribbling were proceduralized for expert performers, and no longer required explicit attention to the details of the movements. Therefore, allocating this 'freed up' attention to a second task did not reduce accuracy. In contrast, requiring experts to focus upon the skill and its step-by-step components disrupted the automatic and proceduralized nature of the skill and its performance (i.e. reduced putting accuracy).

Additionally, when expert soccer players were required to dribble using their less proficient left foot, a reversal in experimental effects was observed. The experts now performed better in the skill-focused condition. Whereas novices and the less-proficient performances of experts benefit from continuous attentional focus on step-by-step performance, high-level skill performance is harmed.

In terms of our model, the view is that proceduralization of skills begins at the level where complex knowledge networks are condensed/elaborated (Phase 2 of the model) continues throughout routine expertise (Phase 3), and is certainly apparent within the last phase of the model (Phase 4), termed 'transcendent expertise'. It may be that secondary distraction and skill-focused tasks such as described above could eventually lead to a 'metric of proceduralization'. Essentially the more details one is able to recall about procedural steps, the less proceduralized the skill and the more cognitive load attached to encoding and retrieval of those steps. The extent to which procedures are 'lost' in terms of recall is probably a good indication of how automated those skills have become.

Not only does Phase 3 of the model describe increased efficiency of performance through proceduralization and automation of skills, but this freeing up of resources with skilled performance also allows for allocation of attention for other performance related processing. For example, an expert performer has a greater amount of attentional capacity to devote to higher level probabilistic decisions, a feature of expert performance which we now discuss.

How do experts make use of probabilities?

The more skilled a player is the more likely he or she will make use of situational probabilities. Sports are filled with examples of certain behaviours being more probable than others. Examples might include a batter facing a pitcher who is known for his fastballs when the count is three and two (a critical point in baseball when a poor pitch will allow the batter to reach base safely, while a good pitch will get the batter out). Another example is the likelihood of a basketball team attempting a three-point shot when they are down by four points with 20 seconds remaining in a game. In ice hockey a goalie is faced with a particular offensive player who always shoots right handed and prefers a wrist shot when close to the goal. All of these are situations where certain events have a higher probability and as such expert athletes will capitalize on these features.

One empirical example of experts' use of probabilities comes from international squash match play. Pollard (1985) determined that winning rallies at certain score configurations were more important in predicting the outcome of the game. In general, rallies near the end of a game (i.e. where one or both players have seven or eight points) were more important than those earlier in a game (i.e. where both players had six or less points). Pollard assumed that by 'trying harder' during a rally an individual could increase the probability of winning, while 'taking it easy' would decrease probability of winning. Conserving energy on certain points thus reduces the athlete's total effort output.

To test this, Pollard investigated first grade squash. Top ranked players won only 3.9 per cent more points in the first half of each game than the bottom ranked players, however; this difference was increased in the second half to 5.3 per cent in each game. The best players were able to increase their probability of winning at more important states of the game. As skill improves both in the perceptual-motor stream and the perceptual-cognitive stream, additional resources become available for more difficult tasks. At elite levels of performance, the extra resources available can be used to develop innovative strategies and motor sequences/linkages that push performance even further.

Phase 4: transcendent expertise

There are individuals in every human endeavour who are the geniuses of their field, whose performances in some way, shape or form, transcend all other performances to date. In music we think of the likes of Beethoven or Brahms; in art – Picasso or Rembrandt; in dance – Nureyev or Baryshnikov. In sport, we have many examples of athletes whose performances transcend what has gone before: Michael Jordan, Tiger Woods, Martina Navratilova, Muhammad Ali and Wayne Gretzky to name a few. To say that the performance of these individuals is at the same level as other national or international athletes in their respective sports is to deny the genius that characterizes their performances. Unfortunately, most of the skill and expertise research to date has been performed on those individuals who certainly exhibit levels of routine expertise, but only in rare cases broach transcendent levels of expertise. The scarcity of such individuals and the difficulty of accessing them as experimental participants means that we will probably never truly understand what makes these experts so remarkable.

Having acknowledged the difficulty in accessing these individuals, it is nevertheless important that we characterize aspects of performance that make them unique. The hallmarks of this phase of performance are the efficiency and optimization of effort as well as innovation. Innovation may be as 'simple' as being faster than anyone else (e.g. Marion Jones), or having better technique (e.g. Dick Fosbury) or as 'complex' as being stronger, faster, more agile and more sophisticated strategically (e.g. Ali, Gretzky and Jordan). We suggest that one characteristic of this level of performance is that, in addition to the declarative knowledge built up from Phases 1 to 3, a skilled athlete stores information based on specific sport experiences or instances in memory, called long instance scripts (Schmidt *et al.*, 1990). For example, a wrestler may remember the last time he or she encountered a particular opponent and style of wrestling, or a dancer may remember a particular dance sequence from a given performance. A long instance script thus stores both generic (or declarative) information and unique aspects of performance, with both sources of knowledge readily accessible and available as sources of inspiration.

An example will serve to illustrate the use of knowledge and scripts as sources for innovation in transcendent experts. In 1987, we published a study of young expert ballet dancers (Starkes *et al.*, 1987) and at the end of the article we recounted our good fortune during this research to be able to watch a prima ballerina (at that time one of the best in the world) learn a new piece of choreography. This was a piece she was seeing for the first time and consisted of a series of ninety-six steps. The choreographer first played the music and then demonstrated the series of steps to the music. The music was then restarted and she performed the piece. Her preparation to perform this series is most telling. Having seen the choreographed piece once, she remarked that it had obviously been designed so the first half was 'staged left' and then repeated 'stage right'. The choreographer agreed. This meant that the first forty-eight steps proceeded from centre back to the left front of the stage; the dancer returned to middle stage; then the steps were repeated to right front (but leading with the opposite foot). This simple acknowledgement meant that the ballerina had reduced the number of steps for recall by half. Next she commented that a portion of the series reminded her of a choreographed portion in another ballet she had performed 3 years earlier, but the tempo was slower and more melancholic. Once again the choreographer acknowledged this. Through this observation she had reduced the number of steps to be recalled by another eighteen, and decided on both tempo and tone. After viewing the piece once, she had recognized both the overall structure of the piece, connected it with a prior performance piece, and confirmed tempo. Remarkably, she had also reduced the cognitive load from ninety-six steps to less than thirty with one viewing. If we assume that each chunk may consist of seven, plus or minus two items (Miller, 1956), all remaining items could easily be retained within short-term memory, and have been aided by access to long-term working memory. In essence, one viewing of ninety-six steps provides sufficient information for recall. This example is a good illustration of the use of instance scripts and unique details to assist with learning new information. The agility and grace that accompanied the performance, however, was what made it most memorable!

How well is performance retained with ageing and post-peak?

Our model has several advantages when describing performance over extended periods of time within an individual (e.g. performance over an entire career). One advantage is the ability to explain maintenance of performance, particularly in highly physical tasks. Throughout a sport career, the relative importance of each stream (perceptual-motor, perceptual-cognitive) can and does change. As one ages, and certain physical abilities decline (e.g. flexibility, physiological recovery time), adaptations within the perceptual-cognitive stream can 'make-up' for losses within the perceptual-motor stream. Several anecdotal examples from North American professional sport demonstrate this phenomenon. Michael Jordan (in basketball) and Mario Lemieux (in ice hockey) both retired from their respective sport only to return several years later. In both cases, the players were not physically performing at the same level as when they retired; however, after only a brief conditioning period, they were able to return to play at the highest levels of competition and not only contribute to successful team performances, but in the case of Lemieux, also dominate the sport once again. Perhaps these players, realizing their reduced physical abilities, changed their style of play to focus on or maximize the use of the skills that were relatively unchanged over time.

Another advantage of the model we propose is that there is no specific time-frame during which peak performance is 'normally' attained. The anchor points for skill are descriptive only in terms of performance *behaviours*, not age. This is important because regardless of what age one begins a sport (i.e. 5 years for figure skating and soccer or 14 years for wrestling and field hockey) the career pattern of practice is similar. Generally, by 15 years into their respective training careers, athletes in all sports are putting in 25–30 hours per week training (a more extensive review of this issue is provided in Starkes, 2000). Athletes necessarily progress to expert levels very early in some sports (such as women's gymnastics) and are often able to maintain expert performance levels much longer in others (i.e. wrestling or long-distance running). The age of peak performance in sports is generally between 20 and 30 years of age, although the precise ages differ by sport. In swimming, for example, peak performance occurs around 20 years of age; whereas, short-distance running is around 23 and long-distance running around 27 years of age (Ericsson, 1991). As coaching, facilities and training systems improve, we might expect athletes to reach peak performance earlier. On the other hand, since athletes are now continuing to train and compete at older ages, in future peak performances are likely to plateau for longer periods. We have found that the study of Master athletes presents a unique opportunity to study the retention of expertise since the number of highly skilled athletes who train throughout a lifetime and continue to compete into old age is increasing.

Masters' athletics is on the rise worldwide and age-related competition is now extremely popular. In track and field, the World Association of Veteran Athletes (WAVA) sponsors World Championships, where performance is prorated based on age-related performance tables, known as WAVA tables (WAVA, 1994). In terms of competitive level, Masters athletics does accommodate those occasional weekend athletes, but increasingly is focused on those who train regularly and compete nationally and internationally.

Since the vast majority of our knowledge on expertise is based on skill acquisition up to peak performance, how then should we model the *retention* of expertise?

For example, in order to stay competitive, does someone who has trained for a life-time need to maintain the same level of training? What impact do increases or decreases in training volume have on Master athletes? Does continued physical training help stave off the inevitable physical and cognitive declines associated with aging? Does *what* is practiced or the *relative amount and importance* of certain components of practice change in ageing experts? Finally, contrary to popular belief, is it possible to continue to *improve* performance with training, later in life?

One of the few studies available on the maintenance of movement performance was by Krampe and Ericsson (1996). In their examination of ageing and young expert and amateur pianists they found that age-related decline for the older experts was negligible for domain-specific tasks. In fact, the older experts per-formed at levels nearly equal to their younger expert counterparts. The authors concluded that it was the amount of deliberate practice invested during the later phase of the older experts' careers that moderated the 'normal ageing' decline. On average, older experts maintained 10.8 hours per week of deliberate practice and, although this was less than the younger expert pianists' total (26.7 hours), they still invested more time in practice than the younger (1.9 hours) and older amateurs (1.2 hours). The authors coined the term 'maintenance practice' to reflect the preservative role of such training and found that it was most pivotal when a performer was aged between 50 and 60 years old.

The extent of performance retention in older experts is somewhat 'muddied' by the fact that those studies which have employed longitudinal or semi-longitudinal designs (following the same athletes and their training over long periods of time) invariably show better performance retention than traditionally found in studies that have employed cross-sectional designs (i.e. comparing performance of sepa-rate groups of 50-, 60- and 70-year-olds) (Hartley and Hartley, 1984; Starkes *et al.*, 1999, 2003; Stones and Kozma, 1982, 1984; Weir *et al.*, 2002). In general, we know that age-related decline in performance is tempered in those that have engaged in systematic practice throughout their competitive careers. We recog-nize that some athletes present a profile of *performance maintenance* in old age, while others may even show *performance improvement*. For the purposes of our model we present two case studies that illustrate how expert performance may be maintained and even improved at older ages, once again highlighting the fact that the retention of expertise is not dependent on chronological age.

Case Study 1: *performance is retained through 'maintenance practice'*

From Krampe and Ericsson (1996) we know that pianists are quite able to main-tain performance over extended periods of time, provided they continue to engage in sufficient maintenance practice. Through analysis of life-long training journals we were able to study performance of older runners and their career progress on a longitudinal basis for periods of between 20 and 50 years (Starkes *et al.*, 2003). A case study of one runner, BM, illustrates the concept of skill retention through continued long-term domain-specific practice (Figure 12.2a). BM ran his fastest 10 kilometre times at 29 years of age (29:49); however,

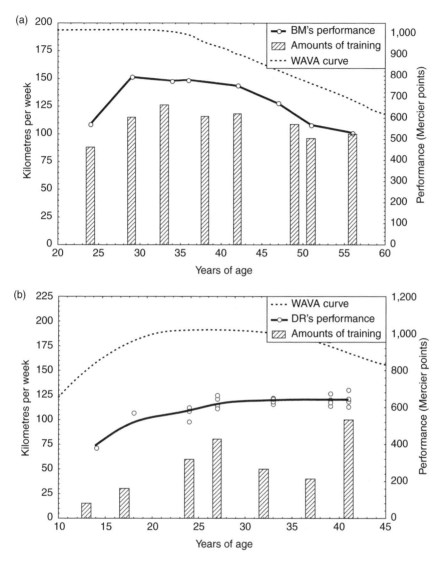

Figure 12.2 (a) Kilometres per week run by BM and performance scores (in Mercier points) across his career. (b) Kilometres per week run by DR and performance scores (in Mercier points) across his career. Best possible performances at each age are illustrated by the WAVA curve. (Reprinted from Starkes *et al.*, 2003, with permission of Human Kinetics Publishing.)

at the age of 56, BM established a 10 kilometre performance time of 34:23 (531 Mercier points, equivalent to 92 per cent on the WAVA age-graded tables and indicative of international-level Master's status) (WAVA, 1994).

BM's profile relates well to Krampe and Ericsson's (1996) notion of *selective maintenance* in older age. His profile from 52 to 56 years underscores the potential for 'trainability' and the moderation of age-related decline in older athletes. From Figure 12.2a we see that he trained the same amount at age 56 (8.33 hours and 100 km per week) compared to 30 years earlier (8.0 hours and 115 km per week). Despite a nagging injury at 53 years of age, BM was able to rebound and once again increase training volume at ages 54–56. As a consequence, he tempered the effects of age-related decline. Most importantly, his decline in running performance was noticeably less than the decrements demarcated by the WAVA curve, a curve derived from cross-sectional data.

Case Study 2: performance may continue to improve in middle age

By contrast, athlete DR recorded his career-best performance of 4:20 for the mile (equal to 697 Mercier points) at 41 years of age (from Schulz and Curnow, 1988), we know that peak performance in the mile is most often attained around 24.8 years of age). This performance truly qualifies him as an international-level Master athlete (92 per cent on the WAVA tables). In fact, DR achieved his absolute *best* performance at a time in life when many experience age-related decline and compromised trainability. The WAVA performance curve indicates that performance scores typically decrease after 35 years of age, yet DR's performance has improved across his running career. This trend is one indicator of 'trainability', even into the middle ages of life and runs contrary to the *preserved differentiation account* for aged expertise. According to the preserved differentiation account, the ability of older expert athletes to continue to perform at higher levels relative to age-matched non-expert athletes is the result of pre-existing, general abilities, stable throughout the expert athletes' athletic careers (Krampe and Ericsson, 1996; Salthouse *et al.*, 1990). DR's investment in increasingly greater amounts of sport-specific training across his career-span, as well as his heavy investment in training (ages 40–41 years), may provide a plausible explanation for his substantial improvement in performance. DR invested 8.0 hours and 100 km per week in training at the age of 41, which is substantially more than he devoted (5.9 hours, 60 kilometre per week) around the expected age of peak performance (Figure 12.2b).

Longitudinal studies on Master athletes have influenced our model of acquisition and retention in several ways. First, we know that performance retention is a function of continued domain specific practice. Second, it is important to consider longitudinal and not just cross-sectional data when determining performance retention post peak. Longitudinal studies show a more optimistic view of expertise retention and trainability. Some of our research shows that international level Master athletes continue to perform well with as little as 6–8 hours training per week. A greater proportion of training is often focused on endurance, and less on technique than is typical in young international level athletes (Starkes *et al.*, 1999, 2003; Weir *et al.*, 2002). It may also be that part of the reason Masters athletes can stay competitive with less training is that the size of the overall competitive field is reduced, or alternatively that a lifetime of training has certain payoffs in terms of the decreased need to practice game skills that have been learned and rehearsed over decades.

Our supposition is that athletes who continue to train post-peak eventually regress to levels of routine expertise and their performances may no longer be as innovative. As physical prowess declines, Master athletes appear to retain much of what had been gained within the perceptual-cognitive stream, while movement possibilities are more limited in terms of temporal–spatial options. We speculate that game strategies and use of probability information may be well retained, although the vast array of movement options once available may be reduced (primarily for physical reasons such as a decline in speed, flexibility and agility). Movement sequences that may have been very efficient at peak eventually become less so and may once again need to be constrained by selectively reducing degrees of freedom. Another possibility is that declines may be due to the age-related changes in the perceptual-motor stream (e.g. increased reaction time) requiring the perceptual-cognitive stream to adapt to novel motor parameters. Domain specific practice may then become more important at this stage, as it provides the opportunity for the perceptual-cognitive stream to learn how to adjust to the ageing perceptual-motor stream. Because continued high levels of training and competition for Master athletes is a relatively new phenomenon, it is likely to be some time before our understanding of skill retention is more advanced. Nevertheless, this is an exciting area of future development for the model.

Can we reconcile disparate theoretical approaches and their views of expertise?

To date the directions pursued by information processing, neural networks, ecological psychology and dynamical systems approaches have remained quite disparate. This has in part been due to information processing and neural network's reliance on the computer analogy and/or complex cognitive structures; and second, due to ecological psychology and dynamical systems' reluctance to invoke mediating cognitive structures. As a result, the first two approaches invariably encounter problems explaining the relatively quick adaptations often characteristic of athletic performance. Specifically, athletes are able to respond to changes in the sporting environment in times that would negate the use of feedback/feedforward loops and infer a more direct relationship between perception and action. Likewise, the latter approaches have largely avoided consideration of the role of intent and performance in highly open non-repetitive tasks. Here we regard the disparate approaches for their metaphoric value in explaining the model, and purposely avoid strict theoretical interpretations.

To illustrate, we turn to Phase 2 of our model, wherein content in both the perceptual-motor and perceptual-cognitive streams are elaborated and condensed. Interestingly, in previous literature such a phase has been observed through the lenses of many theoretical perspectives. If one views skill acquisition from a dynamical perspective, this is a period of parameterization and development of attractor states with dominant modes of behaviour given certain task constraints (Kelso, 1995). From an ecological perspective, it is when perceptual invariants are established (e.g. Gibson, 1966). In information processing, it is when cognitive load is reduced through more efficient encoding and retrieval processes. In the neural network approach, it is a time of increasing linkages between nodes and development of coordinative synergies (e.g. Fodor and Pylyshyn, 1988). Thus, the kinds of behaviours seen in learners during this period are consistent regardless of the theoretical metaphor used to describe them.

Our model can also serve as a tool in examining the emphases of research conducted with regards to sport expertise. The perceptual-cognitive stream accommodates the vast majority of research that has been done to date on expert performance, in part because most prior research has either employed the information processing approach or inferred complex cognitive structures. By comparison, less has been done on the perceptual-motor stream. This is a condition that has been lamented in the past (see Abernethy *et al.*, 1993) and continues to be an issue (Abernethy *et al.*, 2003). In these papers, Abernethy and colleagues suggest that other approaches such as ecological psychology and dynamical systems have not been employed extensively enough to examine expertise. They also suggest that the inherent 'motor' complexities of sport performance have largely been ignored in sport expertise research, in part because of the heavy usage of recipient paradigms from cognitive psychology. A recent paper by Beek *et al.* (2003) is unique in this regard. They propose ways in which ecological psychology and dynamical systems' approaches can be used to further our understanding of expert sport performance through a combination of the two approaches.

Beek and colleagues contend that one very important component of ecological psychology has been the education of attention, first proposed by Gibson (1966). Basically this involves learning to pick up higher order invariants, as opposed to non-specifying information. In general, the assumption has been that experts gradually converge on the information that is best suited to the demands of the task at hand and are thus able to exploit higher order informational variables (i.e. those variables that serve to organize into coherent structure of multiple interactive components). Based on this stance, most approaches to training suggest that we find which variables are attended by skilled performers and then transmit this information to novices (for experiments where this technique has been employed see Helsen and Starkes, 1999; Williams and Grant, 1999). Beek and colleagues however, suggest that knowing which variables are non-specifying, non-relevant or non-informative is equally as important in the design of training systems, as knowing which variables are more relevant to experts.

Beek *et al.* (2003) also indicate that dynamical systems can contribute to our understanding of expertise in rhythmic or polyrhythmic skills. On these kinds of tasks, experts exhibit multistability as well as flexibility. Within dynamical systems, there is a general assumption that experts reduce the dimensionality of the task by harnessing control of the degrees of freedom while abandoning

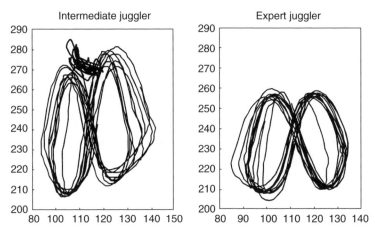

Figure 12.3 Examples of ball movements (in the form of the figure of eight that is characteristic for the cascade pattern) and PG (the trajectories near or above the zeniths of the ball trajectories) in an intermediate and an expert juggler. Whereas the PG of the intermediate juggler moves from ball to ball, the expert shows a clear 'gaze through' or 'distant stare'. (Reprinted from Beek *et al.*, 2003, with permission of Human Kinetics Publishing.)

non-essential degrees of freedom (Mitra *et al.*, 1998). For example, Diedrich and Warren (1995) demonstrated that novice runners do not have inherent correlations between their step cycle and breathing, whereas expert runners employ specific respiration/step ratios (1:4, 1:3, 2:5, 1:2, 2:3, 1:1) and these can be readily altered at different grades and running speeds. Novices continue to employ non-essential degrees of freedom in running. Skilled runners, on the other hand, present a more economic profile where respiration and step cycles share inherent patterns.

More recently, Post *et al.* (2000) demonstrated differences in expert, intermediate and novice jugglers for three-ball cascade juggling. They used principal component analysis (PCA) to determine the optimal description of the juggling patterns by means of the least number of correlated variables. As skill increased, fewer components were needed to describe patterns and only experts could readily deal with imposed tempo changes. Huys and Beek (2002) went on to study the role of eye movements for expert jugglers. They examined the point of gaze (PG) and ball movements, again for three-ball cascade juggling for intermediate and expert jugglers. Their results are illustrated in Figure 12.3.

Skilled jugglers constrain their eye movements to one central area and appear to use a 'gaze through' strategy. The authors suggest that hand movements are probably much more controlled by peripheral vision and haptic information at this stage of skill. They suggest that these expert jugglers show a 'task-specific harnessing of the degrees of freedom' in the task and as such have reached a very efficient solution to the 'motor problem' (a term after Bernstein, 1967). One thing that is very apparent from this demonstration is the relative economy of effort exhibited for PG and hand movements that is characteristic of expert jugglers. Unfortunately, and as Beek and colleagues are quick to point out, we do not know how degrees of freedom are harnessed with skill improvements, and we do not know how long an individual stays at a plateau of constrained degrees of freedom prior to their selective release. They suggest that the selective release of degrees of freedom accompanies the highest levels of performance, and may be one key to innovation in performance. This notion fits very well with our view of routine and transcendent expertise. We would add that while the dynamical systems approach and PCA are extremely valuable for analyzing repetitive tasks they cannot deal with the vast majority of sport skill seen in very open, discrete movements made in response to constantly changing environmental demands.

In conclusion, we have presented a descriptive model of the acquisition and retention of perceptual-motor performance. The development of skill is seen as a continuum, with four specific points used to anchor characteristic changes in the perceptual-cognitive and perceptual-motor behaviour of performers on the road to transcendent expertise. A unique aspect of this model is its consideration of post-peak performance, and the retention of expert skills. As well, the model considers different theoretical perspectives and interpretations. Our hope is that this work will guide further research efforts in this area and assist in the development of a generalized theory of expertise.

References

Abernethy, B., Farrow, D. and Berry, J. (2003). Constraints and issues in the development of a general theory of expert perceptual-motor performance: a critique of the deliberate practice framework. In J. L. Starkes and K. A. Ericsson (Eds), *Expert performance in sports: advances in research on sport expertise* (pp. 349–369). Champaign, IL: Human Kinetics Publishers.

Abernethy, B., Thomas, K. T. and Thomas, J. T. (1993). Strategies for improving understanding of motor expertise [or mistakes we have made and things we have learned!!]. In J. L. Starkes and F. Allard (Eds), *Cognitive issues in motor expertise* (pp. 317–356). Amsterdam: North-Holland.

Beek, P. J., Jacobs, D., Daffertshofer, A. and Huys, R. (2003). Expert performance in sport: views from the joint perspectives of ecological psychology and dynamical systems theory. In J. L. Starkes and K. A. Ericsson (Eds), *Expert performance in sports: advances in research on sport expertise* (pp. 321–342). Champaign, IL: Human Kinetics Publishers.

Beilock, S. L. and Carr, T. H. (2001). On the fragility of skilled performance: what governs choking under pressure? *Journal of Experimental Psychology: General*, 130, 701–725.

Beilock, S. L., Carr, T. H., MacMahon, C. and Starkes, J. L. (2002). When paying attention becomes counterproductive: impact of divided versus skill-focused attention on novice and experienced performance of sensorimotor skills. *Journal of Experimental Psychology: Applied*, 8, 6–16.

Bernstein, N. (1967). *The coordination and regulation of movements*. Oxford: Pergamom Press.

Chase, W. G. and Simon, H. A. (1973). Perception in chess. *Cognitive Psychology*, 4, 55–81.

Crossman, E. R. F. W. (1959). A theory of the acquisition of speed skill. *Ergonomics*, 2, 153–166.

Diedrich, F. J. and Warren, W. H. (1995). Why change gaits? Dynamics of the walk–run transition. *Journal of Experimental Psychology: Human Perception and Performance*, 21, 183–202.

Ericsson, K. A. (1991). Peak performance and age: an examination of peak performance in sports. In P. B. Baltes and M. M. Baltes (Eds), *Successful aging: perspectives from the behavioural sciences* (pp. 164–196). Cambridge: Cambridge University Press.

Ericsson, K. A. and Polson, P. G. (1988). An experimental analysis of the mechanisms of a memory skill. *Journal of Experimental Psychology: Learning, Memory and Cognition*, 14, 305–316.

Ericsson, K. A. and Smith, J. (1991). Prospects and limits in the empirical study of expertise: an introduction. In K. A. Ericsson and J. Smith (Eds), *Toward a general theory of expertise: prospects and limits* (pp. 1–38). Cambridge: Cambridge University Press.

Ericsson, K. A., Krampe, R. T. and Tesch-Romer, C. (1993). The role of deliberate practice in the acquisition of expert performance. *Psychological Review*, 100, 363–406.

Fitts, P. M. and Posner, M. I. (1967). *Human performance*. Belmont, CA: Brooks/Cole.

Fodor, J. A. and Pylyshyn, Z. W. (1988). Connectionism and cognitive architecture: a critical analysis. *Cognition*, 28, 3–71.

Gibson, J. J. (1966). *The senses considered as perceptual systems*. Boston, MA: Houghton Mifflin.

Green, T. D. and Flowers, J. H. (1991). Implicit versus explicit learning processes in a probabilistic, continuous fine-motor catching task. *Journal of Motor Behaviour*, 23, 293–300.

Hartley, A. A. and Hartley, J. T. (1984). Performance changes in champion swimmers aged 30–84 years. *Experimental Aging Research*, 10 (3), 141–148.

Helsen, W. F. and Starkes, J. L. (1999). A new training approach to complex decision making for police officers in potentially dangerous interventions. *Journal of Criminal Justice*, 27 (5), 395–410.

Huys, R. and Beek, P. J. (2002). The coupling between point of gaze and ball movements in three-ball cascade juggling: the effects of expertise, pattern and tempo. *Journal of Sport Sciences*, 20, 171–186.

Jack, R., Starkes, J. L. and Salter, J. (2003). Memory for dance sequences in expert and novice ballet dancers (under review).

Kelso, J. A. S. (1995). *Dynamic patterns: the self-organization of brain and behaviour.* Cambridge, MA: MIT Press.

Krampe, R. T. and Ericsson, K. A. (1996). Maintaining excellence: deliberate practice and elite performance in young and older pianists. *Journal of Experimental Psychology: General*, 125 (4), 331–359.

McPherson, S. L. and Kernodle, M. W. (2003). Tactics, the neglected attribute of expertise: problem representations and performance skills in tennis. In J. L. Starkes and K. A. Ericsson (Eds), *Expert performance in sports: advances in research on sport expertise* (pp. 137–168). Champaign, IL: Human Kinetics Publishers.

Magill, R. A. (1998). Knowledge is more than we can talk about: implicit learning in motor skill acquisition. *Research Quarterly for Exercise and Sport*, 69, 104–110.

Magill, R. A. and Clark, R. (1997). Implicit versus explicit learning of pursuit-tracking patterns. Paper presented at the annual meeting of the North American Society for the

Psychology of Sport and Physical Activity, Denver; CO. [Abstract: *Journal of Exercise and Sport Psychology*, 19, S85.]

Miller, G. A. (1956). The magical number seven, plus or minus two: some limits on our capacity for processing information. *Psychological Review*, 63, 81–97.

Mitra, S., Amazeen, P. G. and Turvey, M. T. (1998). Intermediate motor learning as decreasing active (dynamical) degrees of freedom. *Human Movement Science*, 17, 17–65.

Nevett, M. E. and French, K. E. (1997). The development of sport-specific planning, rehearsal and updating of plans during defensive youth baseball game performance. *Research Quarterly for Exercise and Sport*, 68, 203–214.

Pollard, G. H. (1985). A statistical investigation of squash. *Research Quarterly for Exercise and Sport*, 56, 144–150.

Post, A. A., Daffertshofer, A. and Beek, P. J. (2000). Principal components in three-ball cascade juggling. *Biological Cybernetics*, 82 (2), 143–152.

Salthouse, T. A., Babcock, R. L., Skovronek, E., Mitchell, D. R. D. and Palmon, R. (1990). Age and experience effects in spatial visualization. *Developmental Psychology*, 26, 128–136.

Schmidt, H. G., Norman, G. R. and Boshuizen, H. P. A. (1990). A cognitive perspective on medical expertise: theory and implications. *Academic Medicine*, 65 (10), 611–621.

Schulz, R. and Curnow, C. (1988). Peak performance and age among superathletes: track and field, swimming, baseball, tennis and golf. *Journal of Gerontology: Psychological Sciences*, 43, 113–120.

Sloboda, J. (1991). Musical expertise. In K. A. Ericsson and J. Smith (Eds), *Toward a general theory of expertise: prospects and limits* (pp. 1–38). Cambridge: Cambridge University Press.

Starkes, J. L. (2000). The road to expertise: is practice the only determinant? *International Journal of Sport Psychology*, 31 (4), 431–451.

Starkes, J. L. and Allard, F. (Eds) (1993). *Cognitive issues in motor expertise*. Amsterdam: North-Holland.

Starkes, J. L., Helsen, W. and Jack, R. (2000). Expert performance in sport and dance. In R. Singer, H. Howsenblas and C. Janelle (Eds), *Handbook of research in sport psychology* (2nd ed.) (pp. 174–201). New York: Macmillan.

Starkes, J. L., Weir, P. L. and Young, B. (2003). Retaining expertise: what does it take for older expert athletes to continue to excel? In J. L. Starkes and K. A. Ericsson (Eds), *Expert performance in sports: advances in research on sport expertise* (pp. 251–272). Champaign, IL: Human Kinetics Publishing.

Starkes, J. L., Deakin, J. M., Lindley, S. and Crisp, F. (1987). Motor versus verbal recall of ballet sequences by young expert dancers. *Journal of Sport Psychology*, 9, 222–230.

Starkes, J. L., Weir, P. L., Singh, P., Hodges, N. J. and Kerr, T. (1999). Aging and the retention of sport expertise. *International Journal of Sport Psychology*, 30 (2), 283–301.

Stones, M. J. and Kozma, A. (1982). Cross-sectional, longitudinal, and secular trends in athletic performances. *Experimental Aging Research*, 8, 195–198.

Stones, M. J. and Kozma, A. (1984). Longitudinal trends in track and field performances. *Experimental Aging Research*, 10 (2), 107–110.

Weir, P. L., Kerr, T., Hodges, N. J., McKay, S. M. and Starkes, J. L. (2002). Master swimmers: how are they different from younger elite swimmers? An examination of practice and performance patterns. *Journal of Physical Activity and Aging*, 10, 41–63.

Williams, A. M. and Davids, K. (1995). Declarative knowledge in sport: a byproduct of experience or a characteristic of expertise? *Journal of Sport and Exercise Psychology*, 7 (3), 259–275.

Williams, A. M. and Grant, A. (1999). Training perceptual skill in sport. *International Journal of Sport Psychology*, 30, 194–220.

World Association of Veteran Athletes (WAVA) (1994). *1994 Age-graded tables*. Van Nuys, CA: National Masters News.

13 Psychophysiological and related indices of attention during motor skill acquisition

Christopher M. Janelle, Aaron R. Duley and Stephen A. Coombes

Numerous book chapters and reviews have been written on the topic of *attention*. Despite the abundant philosophical, narrative, empirical and theoretical efforts devoted to describing attention, current understanding, especially as related to motor skill learning, is certainly not complete. William James is oft cited quote provides a logical starting point from which to discuss attention.

> Everyone knows what attention is. It is the taking possession by the mind in clear and vivid form, of one out of what seem several simultaneously possible objects or trains of thought...It implies withdrawal from some things in order to deal effectively with others, and is a condition which has a real opposite in the confused, dazed, scatterbrained state.
>
> (James, 1890, p. 403)

Given James is claims over a century ago, it is somewhat ironic that we do not yet understand 'what attention is' from a scientific perspective. This lack of scientific comprehension has been appropriately verbalized by Lawton *et al.* (1998), who noted, 'The term attention is not an explanation for anything. It is the name of a set of phenomena that require explanation' (p. 48). The importance of understanding attention and identifying the numerous influences on attentional allocation is exemplified by the wealth of data accumulated in disciplines ranging from motor behaviour and sport psychology to experimental cognitive psychology, social psychology and human factors. Given the vast literature base on the topic of attention and skill acquisition, the following discourse cannot serve alone as a comprehensive review of attention as it relates to learning. Other recent works by Abernethy (2001), Laberge (1999), Parasuraman (1998) and Pashler (1998) provide complimentary reviews in this regard.

In this chapter, we have attempted to provide a unique perspective on an 'old' topic, with a focus on contemporary research concerning attentional processing as related to skill acquisition and performance. The literature reviewed reflects the realization that the tools with which researchers investigate attention continue to evolve, confirming many of the predictions that have emanated from traditional cognitive perspectives, while offering promising avenues for future research.

The objectives of the chapter are to provide a short discussion of attentional theory and to assess the role of attention in motor learning with specific emphasis on psychophysiological methodology. Insight will be provided into how physiological substrates of attention evolve according to experience and skill level. In the final sections, we provide practical recommendations for sport scientists and movement practitioners and address unresolved issues in attention research as they relate to skill acquisition in sport. These objectives are addressed within a framework of attention that was delineated by Posner and Boies (1971) three decades ago. They characterized attention by: (a) its *limited capacity*, (b) its involvement in *selecting* what information will be processed and (c) its relation to the overall *alertness and preparation* of the learner.

Theories of attention

Human performance capabilities are fundamentally dictated by the information load and response demands associated with a particular task (Fitts, 1954; Hick, 1952; Hyman, 1953). As the level of response uncertainty and information load increases, so too does reaction time (RT). Importantly, laboratory research indicates that RT to a single unanticipated stimulus is in the order of 180–220 milliseconds, with this delay composed of latencies in stimulus detection, response preparation and neural and muscular activity associated with the response (e.g. Wood, 1983). This core RT issue helped shape research during the past century and has been foundational to the questions that now guide a large portion of psychological research.

The ability to acquire and react to relevant environmental (external) and organismic (internal) cues while minimizing distraction is critical to human performance in virtually any domain, and is indeed essential for human survival. As one strives to acquire a skill and, in some cases, strives for motor expertise, the individual must learn to attend to the most salient and critical information for effective response programming. In addition, the individual must often do so in a brief amount of time through attentional allocation to and efficient extraction of the most pertinent information. As such, most would agree that the successful acquisition of motor skills is reliant upon the refinement of attention-related skills. A wide variety of conceptual models have been posed to account for the psychological mechanisms underlying attentional shifts (Fernandez-Duque and Johnson 1999). The filter and the resource analogies have been dominant in this regard and are briefly summarized.

Filter models

Early concepts of attention, beginning with the seminal work of Welford (1952), suggested that due to the wide barrage of potential stimuli that could be used for information processing, a filter was necessary to remove irrelevant cues from further processing, thereby preventing the system from becoming overloaded. Future variations of dichotic listening and related protocols, however, led to the realization that attentional demands at each of the processing stages could impinge upon the ability to generate appropriate and speedy responses. Accordingly, researchers progressively moved the filter further along the sequential processing stages (e.g. Broadbent, 1957; Deutsch and Deutsch, 1963; Keele, 1973; Norman, 1968; see Figure 13.1), or introduced attenuator concepts (Treisman, 1960). In spite of modifications to Welford's original single channel hypothesis, by the early 1970s the filter metaphor was largely discarded in favour of capacity and resource models.

Capacity/resource models

Attention theorists who popularized the 'capacity' or 'resource' analogies viewed attention as a form of *fuel* that was exhaustible, thereby leading to the economic metaphor of 'paying' attention and 'investing' effort in tasks (Moran, 1996). As an example, Kahneman (1973), through his flexible attention model, suggested that the pool of undifferentiated resources from which attention could be drawn varied as a function of the task demands and the current arousal state of the organism. In contrast to Kahneman's notions, Navon and Gopher (1979) and

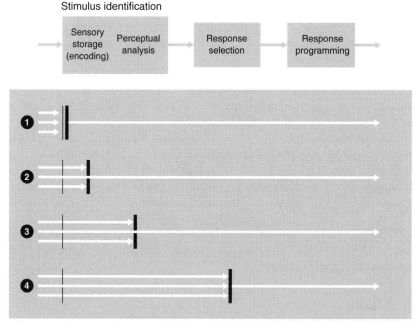

Utilization of attention in various stages of processing, according to various theories. [Line 1 represents the original single-channel theory (Welford, 1952); line 2 represents Broadbent's (1957) filter theory; line 3 represents the Deutsch and Deutsch (1963) and Norman (1969) theories; and line 4 represents Keele's (1973) theory.]

Figure 13.1 Variations of filter placement according to attention theorists (adapted from Schmidt and Lee, 1999).

then Wickens (1984) proposed that attentional capabilities were regulated by the existence of separate and differentiated resource pools. Despite initial support for these models as well as continued adherence to resource theories by attention researchers, advances in technology have illuminated the physiological substrate of attention as it relates to skill acquisition, and have thereby questioned the utility of resource metaphors that do not entail biological explanations.

In summary, early emphases in the study of attention were rooted in cognitive concepts of information processing that involved filters and notions of capacity limitations. Two separate themes sequentially dominated the theoretical inquiry that emanated from the filter and resource models: that concerning how information would be excluded from processing, and that describing how much information from different tasks could be processed at the same time.

Selective attention, divided attention and attention as alertness

Posner and Boies (1971) described the 'contemporary' psychology of attention as being organized under three primary orientations. These categorical distinctions are based on the attentional properties of selection, limited capacity and associated concepts of divided attention, and alertness or preparedness.

Selective attention

Theeuwes (1994) defined selective attention as 'the process of selecting part of simultaneous sources of information by enhancing aspects of some stimuli and suppressing information from others' (p. 94). Selective attention capabilities evolve with motor skill acquisition (see Abernethy, 1993, 2001) and these changes arguably occur with regard to the manner of perceptual analysis as well as the assignment of importance (pertinence) to cues. Selective attention has often been measured through indirect means, such as RT differences as a function of cue availability. Cue availability is commonly manipulated in the context of occlusion paradigms in which some aspect of the display has been hidden (spatial occlusion) and/or the duration of exposure to a particular event varies (temporal occlusion) across stages of skill learning (for reviews, see Starkes *et al.*, 2001; Williams *et al.*, 1999). Visual search patterns, as understood through the measurement of eye movements, have traditionally been used to infer critical aspects of the display that are attended or 'processed' more than others. Measurement of search patterns, as well as behavioural responses in occlusion paradigms and verbal reports have routinely shown reliable differences between experts and novices, in the manner by which the visual display is searched. These differences have been corroborated by performance changes in anticipation skills and decision-making capabilities that implicate selection of visual information as critical to effective performance. Currently, notions of selective attention tend to be relatively congruent with the idea that as skill level increases, so too does the tendency and ability to allocate attentional focus appropriately, as reflected in the search strategies that evolve with enhanced motor skill.

During the early 1970s, a shift in research emphasis among attention theorists began to emerge, with the 'hot topics' being centred on divided attention. This shift was largely spurred by Kahneman's (1973) influential work. His notion of a flexible pool of attentional resources had direct implications for the development of protocols designed to establish the limits of attentional processing. As such, theoretical interest increasingly moved away from the perceptual aspects of selective attention and towards a more functional orientation (Moran, 1996).

Divided attention

Divided attention is characterized by the ability to attend to several simultaneously active messages or tasks, or to distribute attention effectively to concurrent tasks. These capabilities generally increase with experience and practice on the task of interest (Eysenck and Keane, 1995; Hawkins and Presson, 1986). In addition to selective attention skills, learners must develop the ability to 'do more than one thing' at a time to attain proficiency in even the most basic movement contexts. In turn, the information load imposed on the individual and the combined demands of potentially numerous involved tasks will influence the capability to perform these tasks simultaneously.

Assimilating the recommendations of Eysenck (1984), Hirst (1986) contended that attention can be divided (i.e. attentional capacity can be used) in four primary ways: (a) coordinating two (or more) tasks so that they combine into a more complex unitary task, (b) practicing one task to an automatic level and then doing another task in addition to it, (c) learning how to do two or more tasks by figuring out how to minimize interference between them, mainly with a focus on their different stimulus characteristics and/or (d) finding time to do both tasks by sharing available time effectively between them. Empirical support exists for each of these explanations (e.g. Allport, 1980; Norman and Bobrow, 1975; Schneider and Shiffrin, 1977). However, upon re-examination of these possible accounts, it becomes quite evident that each can by accommodated within a *skills* approach to understanding attentional capabilities. That is, as individuals become capable of doing two tasks at once, they do so by allocating attentional resources more appropriately (Hirst, 1986; Moran, 1996). This notion of *attention as a skill* will be revisited later.

Divided attention capabilities have traditionally been assessed by observing the RT costs of performing different tasks simultaneously, and evaluating performance across stages of skill learning (e.g. Ogden *et al.*, 1979, Wickens, 1992). According to this view, the attentional costs associated with performance of any task can be determined by understanding the RT difference in task performance when a secondary task is introduced. Dual task performance issues are obviously germane to describing skill acquisition. Motor performance, even at its crudest level, necessitates the dual ability to *move* and *think* simultaneously. Proficient motor performance usually relies upon some level of dual task mastery. However, the dual task paradigm has been criticized by researchers (e.g. Fisk *et al.*, 1986), who have suggested that a number of potential confounds preclude the ability to establish firm baseline levels of attentional demand and then control the amount of learning that takes place on secondary tasks. It is, therefore, difficult if not impossible to reliably determine the 'amount' of resources consumed by either the primary or the secondary task.

The corpus of relevant literature illustrates that skill acquisition depends upon divided attention capabilities, with rich evidence that as skills are refined, observable improvements in dual task performance result. Underlying these skill improvements is a reduction in processing time needed to programme and execute the movement, as well as an overall increase in the degree of automaticity associated with involved tasks (Abernethy, 1993, 2001; Desimone and Duncan, 1995; Pashler, 1994; Treisman and Gelade, 1980). The capability to divide attention effectively is also intricately interwoven with the learner's capacity to selectively attend to the most information-rich cues in an efficient manner.

Alertness as attention

Of the three primary dimensions of attention that were outlined by Posner and Boies (1971), alertness has received the least interest from motor learning researchers. Indeed, much of the research dealing with alertness and related concepts has not been considered within the scope of mainstream motor learning research but rather in the context of human factors (e.g. stress and performance) and sport psychology topics (e.g. studies of motivation and anxiety). Strictly speaking, the alertness construct should most properly be treated as an influence on attention, rather than as attention itself (for a recent review of the attentional mechanisms that underlie performance variability when anxious, see Janelle, 2002). As such, making concrete recommendations for how this area might be related to attention in the context of skill acquisition requires a degree of caution.

With respect to alertness and arousal, Abernethy (1993) has suggested that the ideal learning environment would consist of one in which (a) arousal is optimized and the learner is taught ways of resisting overarousal, (b) the temporal pattern of alertness development is a focus of training and (c) strategies are formed for dealing with changes in arousal and sensitivity to environmental demands. Many of the possible negative influences of overarousal and maladaptive emotionality (e.g. attentional narrowing, see Janelle *et al.*, 1999), can be remedied through the implementation of arousal regulation techniques such as relaxation and meditation, among other interventions (Hanin, 2000). Situational perceptions and appraisals can be altered to yield more appropriate and positive interpretations that mobilize adaptive coping mechanisms (Jones, 1995).

Emotional and physiologically based fluctuations in systemic homeostasis have been empirically documented to influence attentional processing (Parasuraman, 1998). Given that arousal influences physiological activation levels, arousal levels are typically assessed by psychophysiological measures. Haemodynamic methods of arousal assessment such as positron emission tomography (PET) and functional magnetic resonance imaging (fMRI) provide spatially accurate information about oxygen concentration/metabolism in brain structures, blood flow in brain tissue and blood volume in brain areas (Andreassi, 2000). High-fidelity spatial resolution, however, is typically traded for poor temporal resolution. Specifically, haemodynamic measures provide accurate localization of brain function and activation, but are limited in their ability to portray that activation across fine time gradients (i.e. milliseconds). Alternatively, heart rate (HR), electroencephalography (EEG) and skin conductance methods provide physiological indices of arousal that can accurately coincide with modulating behaviours over extended periods, and can be observed in millisecond-to-millisecond changes.

Because fluctuations in alertness (and arousal) continuously alter performance through the mechanism of attention, the ability to maintain alertness over long periods becomes paramount. For example, in auto racing, drivers must continuously guard against concentration lapses that could lead to devastating consequences. Often this extremely focused state of concentration must occur over extended periods of time, and under potentially stressful conditions. Since alertness (and arousal), broadly speaking, has been the subject of much contemporary psychophysiological investigation, this fascinating body of research will be extensively discussed later as related to skill acquisition.

The psychophysiology of attention as related to skill acquisition

Understanding the dynamics of attention during skill acquisition and performance remains a fundamental challenge. The process that allows athletes to attend to an ever-present changing sensory stream and to select essential information is astonishing. Sport provides an exquisite context where the sophistication of the brain and its management of competing attentional demands may readily be appreciated. While numerous examples exist to illustrate the challenge of diverse and complex environments, perhaps in no other human endeavours do we so overtly notice the breakdown of this system or its remarkable resiliency than in the sport setting. The driving question for sport scientists and motor behaviourists, therefore, is to determine how elite performers learn to deal with competing attentional demands. Consideration of how to 'probe' attention may help researchers to determine how to implement learning strategies to best maximize performance. To achieve this objective, methods that allow direct quantification of attention are necessary (Posner, 1996).

Motor learning and sport psychology researchers have increasingly begun to rely upon neuroscientific means to understand the acquisition of motor skills. This progression is not surprising considering the extensive evolution towards 'the spotlight on the brain' metaphor as described by Fernandez-Duque and Johnson (1999). In other words, interest has now shifted to describing and accounting for the specific areas of the brain involved with different attentional tasks. Although fMRI, PET and other imaging technologies are still rarely employed by motor learning researchers, the use of EEG is relatively popular. An overview of EEG and other psychophysiological concomitants of attention and skill acquisition is provided next. Details of signal acquisition and processing cannot be described here, but the interested reader can find comprehensive information on EEG methodology from the following sources: Birbaumer *et al.* (1990), Davidson *et al.* (2000) and Fabiani *et al.* (2000).

Electroencephalography: an overview

Electroencephalography is used to measure the brain's electrical activity, which is thought to originate from summated postsynaptic potentials in the cerebral cortex (Davidson *et al.*, 2000). Despite restrictions in spatial precision, considerable information about psychological processes can be inferred from EEG. Recorded data, however, must progress through specific signal processing steps before inferences can be drawn (Lawton *et al.*, 1998). Methods used to reduce EEG data vary according to the goal of the researcher, in addition to the paradigm employed. Evaluating an EEG signal for frequency components (e.g. alpha and beta frequency) or amplitude (i.e. the magnitude of a signal) are both commonly used analytic strategies (Davidson *et al.*, 2000). In essence, the researcher is always interested in amplitude. What differs, however, is whether amplitude is investigated in the time domain [e.g. slow cortical potentials, event related potentials (ERP)] or the frequency domain. A trade-off exists between time domain analyses that provide no frequency specific information and frequency specific information that sacrifice accurate temporal resolution.

Once data within the frequency domain are clustered according to its frequency characteristics, these spectral elements can be used to provide information related to psychological or physiological processes. Modulations in amplitude within specified frequency bands can shed light onto the cortical location of, and extent to which, specific processes are engaged (e.g. attention, task difficulty, Gevins *et al.*, 1997). Variant frequency and site-specific activation patterns are mapped onto simultaneous variations in performance. As such, performance ability can be described and associated with characteristic cortical 'templates'.

With respect to the temporal domain, researchers have also been interested in examining amplitude variation in raw EEG data when coupled with a specific event in time (Kutas and Federmeier, 1998). The ERP is a broad term used to describe brain activity time-locked to some event, internal or external, that is thought to reflect discrete psychological states or processes (Andreassi, 2000). Specific ERP findings are described later.

Psychophysiology and motor skill acquisition

Psychophysiological protocols simultaneously assess physiological and psychological components of specific tasks, and then associate the modulations in one (physiology) with the cognitive–behavioural components of the other (psychology). Sport scientists have long used psychophysiological tools to explore the neural substrates of athletic performance (for a review, see Hatfield and Hillman, 2001). As early as 1967, radio-telemetered EEG was used to evaluate head impacts in American football during the course of competition (Hughes and Hendrix, 1967). Subsequent application of psychophysiology to the sport domain has focused on associating elite performance with the evolution of cortical networks (e.g. Elbert *et al.*, 1995), and with recognizable cortical activation patterns (e.g. Etnier *et al.*, 1996; Haufler *et al.*, 2000; Janelle *et al.*, 2000). Despite advances in modern technology, there remain obvious limitations in monitoring physiological systems during the course of motor performance. The resulting artefacts from movement native to most sporting environments pose constraints on the types of paradigms one may employ. In spite of this inherent limitation, researchers have taken advantage of psychophysiological tools and techniques to advance our understanding of attention, specifically within sports tasks that require minimal movement. Skills such as marksmanship (e.g. Hatfield *et al.*, 1984; Janelle *et al.*, 2000), golf putting (Crews and Landers, 1993) and archery (Landers *et al.*, 1994) have received most coverage with regard to cortical activation patterns.

Cortical indicies of attention as activation or information processing in skill acquisition and expertise?

Gruber *et al.* (1999) note that cerebral blood flow (via PET) is magnified in a focused fashion when an individual attends to a specific stimulus, or shifts spatial attention to visual stimuli in varying visual fields. For example, PET evidence has indicated that the superior parietal and superior frontal cortex activate when attention is shifted to peripheral locations rather than when maintained at the centre of gaze (Corbetta *et al.*, 1993). Similarly, fMRI evidence indicates that metabolic activity in specific cortical regions increases when participants attend to dynamic stimuli as compared to when this stimuli is ignored (Beauchamp *et al.*, 1997; Haug *et al.*, 1998). It may be assumed that attention results in a salient magnification of neuronal activity in cortical regions or pathways that are associated with the demands that are required to process the attended stimulus (Hillyard *et al.*, 1998).

The development of skill results in more efficient allocation of resources (Busk and Galbraith, 1975). Cortical representation has been shown to increasingly localize with training, and this physiological alteration has been associated with more proficient performance; a finding exemplified by the elegant work of Thomas Elbert and colleagues. Elbert *et al.* (1995) proposed that neural plasticity (i.e. a greater cortical representation of limbs) evolves via repeated exposure to similar stimuli. This allows greater task-related information processing specific to the corresponding body part or limb segment. For example, string musicians, as compared to non-musicians, were found to display enlarged cortical representations for digits in the left hand (i.e. the string hand), but not for the right hand (Elbert *et al.*, 1995). Additionally, a correlation was noted between the age at which string players began playing their instrument and the extent of change in the cerebral cortex. Neural plasticity has also been associated with the rehabilitation of motor skills in stroke patients (Liepert *et al.*, 2000). Exposure to consistent but progressively more complex stimuli over a prolonged period results in the repeated activation of the cortical areas that deal with these stimuli. Much like the physiology of a muscle, it is posited that these cortical areas adapt and respond to the increasing difficulty of the logically progressive stimuli (Hatfield and Hillman, 2001; Karni *et al.*, 1998; Sanes and Donoghue, 2000).

In general, decrements in cognitive and motor performance have been associated with a less specific pattern of cortical activation, which has been interpreted as indicating increased physiological effort to less effect (for examples using reading tasks, see Andreassi, 2000; for motor tasks, see Etnier *et al.*, 1996). Alternatively, a more focused activation pattern has been associated with accurate performance. Necessary cortical activation combined with performance improvement, therefore, signifies a more efficient transaction between an individual and the demands placed on him/her from environmental requirements. Hatfield and Hillman (2001) have proposed that a more exact activation pattern is the result of a pruning of neural regions that are not necessary to successfully process task-specific information. They summarize this notion by proposing a principle of psychomotor efficiency (see Figure 13.2).

$$\text{Efficiency} = \frac{\text{Work}}{\text{Effort}} \quad \Longrightarrow \quad \text{Efficiency} = \frac{\text{Psychomotor behaviour}}{\text{Neural resource allocation}}$$

Figure 13.2 The principle of psychometer efficiency (adapted from Hatfield and Hillman, 2001).

The principle of psychomotor efficiency holds that as skill level increases, the organism becomes increasingly capable of performing more psychomotor work with relatively less neuromuscular activity. This occurs due to a more precise pairing of resource allocation to psychomotor demand. Arguably, therefore, activation alone cannot index attention. Knowledge of the magnitude and exact cortical locations of activity across multiple sites (a mission that is enhanced but never exact with an increase in the number of electrode sites available) is required if one is to attempt to associate attention with cortical activation.

The EEG spectrum

Because the EEG is captured in the time domain, a commonly used analytic strategy is to derive the frequency structure of the EEG by applying a Fourier transformation (FT). The FT essentially decomposes one wave into a sum of sinusoidal waves of different frequencies, amplitudes and phases (Smith, 1997). Once the original EEG signal is decomposed into its spectral counterparts, its relative activity can then be grouped into frequency bands (e.g. alpha, beta, theta) that can be used to infer ongoing psychological processes (see Figure 13.3).

Theta waves typically occur during the first stage of sleep, but they can also be detected when awake. Theta waves traditionally display a frequency of 4–8 Hz,

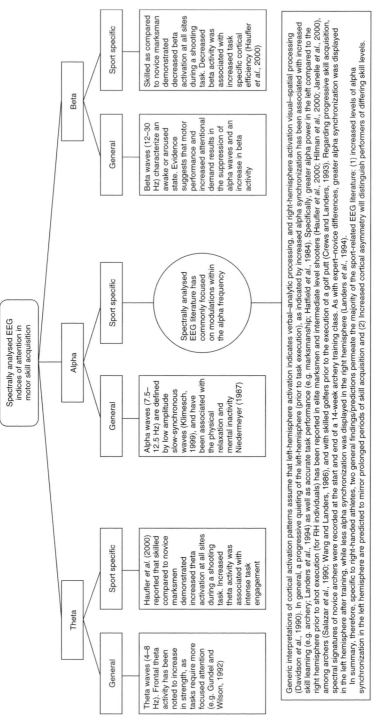

Figure 13.3 Summary of the EEG spectrum, associated frequency components and the identities of behavioural processes indexed by spectral components.

and as tasks require greater focused attention, frontal theta activity, in contrast to alpha activity, typically increases in strength (e.g. Gundel and Wilson, 1992).

The *alpha* rhythm is generally associated with physical relaxation and mental inactivity (Niedermeyer, 1987). This rhythm is characterized by slow-synchronous waves that are low in amplitude and occur at a frequency between 7.5 and 12.5 Hz (Klimesch, 1999). Criticism of this traditional broad alpha band has emerged following studies that have split the band into three narrower sub-bands of approximately 2 Hz each. These narrower, often individually defined frequency bands have provided greater insight into the subtle components that comprise attentional processes (for a comprehensive review of this issue, see Klimesch, 1999).

More irregular than the alpha waves, *beta* waves coincide with an awake or aroused state, and are characterized by frequencies in the range of 12–30 Hz. Suppression of alpha activity has been termed 'event-related desynchronization' (ERD) (Pfurtscheller and Klimesch, 1991), and typically coincides with motor performance, increased attentional demands (Sterman *et al.*, 1994) and an increase in beta activity.

Event related desynchronization

ERD is a measure of the relative power change in the alpha and theta bands over the time course of measurement (for a detailed explanation, see Nunez, 1995). In general, theta activation increases with increased alpha desynchronization (Andreassi, 2000). When compared to simple tasks, complex and difficult tasks commonly show significantly greater alpha desynchronization of longer lasting durations, and more widespread topographical distribution. These desynchronization characteristics have been reported for motor (Pfurtsheller and Berghold, 1989; Pulvermüller *et al.*, 1995) and cognitive tasks (Gevins *et al.*, 1997; Klimesch, 1999).

An increase in task-related alpha power (synchronization) should correspond to a decrease in cortical activation specific to that site. This relationship has been interpreted in polar opposite ways. In one view, alpha synchronization has been termed 'cortical idling' and is explained by Pfurtscheller *et al.* (1996) as a deficient ability to recruit cortical areas to complete a task. An alternative interpretation is that an increase in task related alpha reflects a general quieting of areas not related to task performance (Hatfield and Hillman 2001; Janelle *et al.*, 2000). Finally, widespread alpha synchronization has also been interpreted as indexing increased task automaticity and a more efficient processing state (e.g. Etnier *et al.*, 1996). Contemporary interpretations of alpha activity, therefore, seem problematic. Relative alpha power can be likened to a chameleon in that alpha activity is underpinned not exclusively by the activation of adjacent sites, but additionally by the relative success or failure of the associated and corresponding performance measures (e.g. Janelle *et al.*, 2000).

Frequency characteristics of the EEG associated with motor learning and performance

In light of variable experimental procedures and samples employed, findings within the spectrally analysed sport-related EEG literature should be interpreted with caution (Lawton *et al.*, 1998). However, specific to right-handed performers, two general findings permeate the majority of the sport-related EEG literature: (a) levels of alpha synchronization in the left hemisphere (e.g. Hatfield *et al.*, 1984) and (b) cortical asymmetry observed among performers of differing skill levels (e.g. Janelle *et al.*, 2000). In essence, a progressive quieting of the left-hemisphere (prior to task execution), as indicated by increased alpha synchronization, has been associated with increased skill learning (e.g. Landers *et al.*, 1994) as well as accurate task performance (e.g. Hatfield *et al.*, 1984). The generic notion guiding the interpretation of cortical activation patterns assumes that left-hemisphere activation is indicative of verbal–analytic processing, and right-hemisphere activation of visual–spatial processing (Davidson *et al.*, 1990). Evidence of hemispheric differences in elite marksmen, as indicated by a progressive quieting of the left-hemisphere prior to trigger pull, was first noted by Hatfield *et al.* (1982). In an elite population of marksman, Hatfield *et al.* (1984) showed a progressive quieting of the left-hemisphere during a 7.5-second pre-shot interval which was associated with increasing alpha synchronization in the left relative to the right temporal lobe. Asymmetric activation patterns were suggested to represent cortical efficiency and successful task performance.

The basic methodology used by Hatfield *et al.* (1984) and others is limited in detail concerning the psychological processes involved in skill acquisition and performance. Therefore, it is perhaps no surprise that very general hypotheses have commonly been supported across a range of sports, at the expense of generating more specific hypotheses intended for testing psychological processes involved with learning and performance. Likewise, although spectral activation clearly reflects attention, the intertwined nature of attention with arousal, for example, makes it impossible to absolutely decouple these constructs. Nevertheless, hemispheric asymmetry has been reported in elite marksmen and intermediate-level shooters (Haufler *et al.*, 2000; Hillman *et al.*, 2000; Janelle *et al.*, 2000), among archers (Salazar *et al.*, 1990; Wang and Landers, 1986) and with skilled golfers prior to the execution of a golf putt (Crews and Landers, 1993).

Recently, Haufler *et al.* (2000) implemented a comprehensive design to investigate cortical differences among skilled marksmen and novice shooters. In addition to a shooting task, a verbal task (word finding task) and spatial task (dot localization) were administered, with the latter two tasks having been matched for difficulty (Davidson *et al.*, 1990). Skilled marksmen demonstrated less activation at all sites during the shooting task (indicated by increased alpha power and decreased beta and gamma power), and corroborating previous findings (e.g. Hatfield *et al.*, 1984), this pattern was magnified in the left hemisphere. Novice participants, conversely, displayed similar cortical activation patterns during all three tasks in addition to a relative increase in left hemisphere activation (compared to experts) during the shooting task. No differences were found between the performances or the corresponding cortical patterns of the two groups for the visual and spatial tasks. The notion of task specificity as a product of responsiveness to training was supported (Elbert *et al.*, 1995; Hatfield and Hillman, 2001).

Theta activation has been associated with task difficulty and sustained attention (Gevins *et al.*, 1997; Smith *et al.*, 1999); hence, it is interesting that the majority of studies within the motor domain focus exclusively on the alpha and beta frequency bands. Haufler *et al.* (2000), however, also reported modulations within the theta band, noting that theta activation increased in experts during all tasks at all sites with group differences magnified during the shooting task. Apparently, experts were more intensely engaged in each task (Gundel and Wilson, 1992), but were simultaneously more efficient in their distribution of cortical resources (Smith *et al.*, 1999). Inclusion of theta band power within this domain of research should be encouraged.

Practice results in increased automaticity, which has been associated with increased alpha synchronization during performance of novel motor tasks (Etnier *et al.*, 1996). The relationship between modulations in alpha power and practice was clearly seen in a 14-week longitudinal study conducted by Landers *et al.* (1994). Spectral signatures of novice archers were recorded at the start and end of the study. Consistent with the profile generated by expert shooters, greater alpha synchronization was displayed in the left hemisphere after training, while less alpha synchronization was displayed in the right hemisphere. The EEG pattern that evolved among the archers progressed to approximate patterns that were evident among relative experts tested in other motor skills. With regard to skill acquisition, this remains among the most convincing evidence for how cortical activation evolves through extended practice.

Combined with haemodynamic (fMRI, PET) activation patterns (Corbetta *et al.*, 1993), the general trends reported in the spectrally analysed EEG literature can be interpreted as indicating an efficient transaction with the environment as motor skill improves. More specifically, as skills are acquired and refined, attention is not reduced but rather is directed away from irrelevant cues/information and towards task-relevant stimuli (Hatfield and Hillman, 2001). This process requires repetitive exposure to task-specific stimuli over a prolonged period.

Event-related potentials

Event-related potentials (ERPs) differ from spectrally analysed EEG data in that the latter provides frequency-specific information whilst ERPs are derived directly from temporally indexed EEG data. As mentioned, ERPs refer to a broad class of waveforms that occur specifically in response to actual or anticipated stimuli (Andreassi, 2000). ERPs are extracted from the raw EEG data while being temporally indexed. The term ERP includes many specific waveform classifications that include, for example, long-latency potentials, sensory ERPs (auditory, visual, somatosensory) and steady-potential shifts (contingent negative variation, readiness potentials, far-field potentials), each varying in their latency and response characteristics. Because ERPs are quite small in comparison to the ongoing EEG from which they are extracted, multiple trials are generally averaged to remove the background EEG activity not time-locked to the stimulus or event. Once averaged, a waveform can be visualized as consisting of a series of peaks and troughs that represent its polarity, latency and, in some cases, location (see Fabiani *et al.*, 2000, Picton *et al.*, 2000).

ERPs have been used extensively to examine human information processing, with latency and amplitude response characteristics thought to vary with the attentional requirements of a task (for a comprehensive review, see Birbaumer *et al.*, 1990; Hillyard and Hansen, 1986). However, the application of ERPs to examine attention in motor skill acquisition or in sport populations is limited. As mentioned previously, the inherent movement requirements of many motor tasks introduce artefact into the acquired signal, thereby rendering data collection impractical. However, because ERPs may be recorded prior to a movement, the use of ERPs to evaluate attention or processing efficiency during the preparatory period before overt action is appropriate for many sport-related tasks. Slow cortical potentials, for example, have been successfully used to evaluate visuomotor processing in marksmen (Konttinen and Lyytinen, 1992, 1993; Konttinen *et al.*, 1999, 2000) and more specifically, as an index of attentional focus in sports such as golf and archery (Crews and Landers, 1993; Landers *et al.*, 1991).

The P300 (or P3: named for a positive deflection in the ERP waveform that occurs approximately 300 milliseconds after an obligatory stimulus) has also been used to evaluate attention among experts and relative intermediates in other sport situations. For example, Radlo *et al.* (2001) evaluated P3 latency and amplitude among baseball players. Longer latency typically implies increased time to classify stimuli, and greater amplitude implicates greater attentional resources devoted to the stimulus. The obtained P3 characteristics were used to evaluate the influence of skill level on the ability to discriminate between fastballs and curveballs. Participants sat in front of a large projection screen where they viewed 400 randomly occurring pitches (200 fastballs, 200 curveballs). Prior to 300 of the pitches, a verbal precue was provided to indicate the type of pitch. For all 400 pitches, participants were required to indicate, via a button press, what type of pitch they had witnessed (i.e. fastball or curveball). Stimulus onset was determined to be the point of ball exposure (i.e. the release point of the pitch).

Intermediate batters were found to produce shorter P3 latencies, larger P3 amplitudes, longer reaction times and less accuracy compared to advanced batters. This effect was more pronounced for curveballs. Increased P3 latency in the advanced batters was interpreted as indicating greater detail in stimulus processing. This interpretation appears logical given that advanced athletes often have the luxury of processing a stimulus for longer periods because the speed and accuracy of their subsequent movement patterns are superior to those of the intermediate athlete. Murray and Janelle (2002) have also employed an ERP paradigm to evaluate the influence of competitive stress on attentional processing in a race car driving simulation. They found a reduction in P3 amplitude in competitive sessions for both low and high trait anxious individuals, indicating that greater attentional demands were dedicated to the central driving task, particularly when competitively anxious.

Similarly, researchers examining the function of attention in skill acquisition and performance have employed contrived laboratory-based studies as an alternative to the problems posed in more naturalistic sport settings or simulated sport situations in the laboratory environment. In their analysis of the sub-specialties of clay-pigeon shooting, for instance, Rossi and Zani (1991) hypothesized that the temporal characteristics of information processing and the emergence of a specific attentional style would functionally relate to the different task characteristics required for skeet and trap shooting. In skeet shooting, there is no ambiguity in the origination and trajectory of the target, but a short random delay (0–3 seconds) is present between the 'pull' command and the release. Trap, on the other hand, has no delay between the command and the release, but the target can vary in position and slope. Because of the nature of these two tasks, Rossi and Zani describe a bottom–up (or data-driven) attentional style for trap shooters, and a top–down (or knowledge-driven) style for skeet shooters. More importantly, they suggested that these attentional styles may transfer to other tasks.

To investigate their hypothesis, Olympic level skeet and trap shooters were instructed to depress a lever to a high-pitched tone, occurring in 20 per cent of the total trials during an easy (1,000 Hz/2,000 Hz tones) and difficult (1,000 Hz/ 1,050 Hz tones) laboratory-based auditory discrimination task. Early electrocortical data (see Ritter *et al.*, 1972) had indicated that the latency of the P3 component, in addition to reaction times, were longer when participants were required to make pitch discriminations and even longer when those discriminations increased in difficulty (Andreassi, 2000). Rossi and Zani's rational was that in a knowledge-driven processing mode, the uncertainty in the difficult auditory discrimination condition would result in a trade-off of speed in favour of accuracy, while a data-driven processing mode should be relatively unaffected by task difficulty. The researchers evaluated N2 and P3 latency in addition to reaction time, with N2 described as a reflection of sensory discrimination, and P3 latency reflecting the timing of stimulus evaluation processes as well as reaction time.

Despite a limited sample (three skeet and, three trap shooters), the researchers reported that although the latency of the N2 (a negative deflection approximately 200 ms after a stimulus) and P3 components of the ERP were significantly shorter in skeet shooters compared to trap shooters in the easy condition, skeet shooters exhibited a similar reaction time as trap shooters. However, reaction time was significantly reduced for skeet shooters during the difficult auditory discrimination condition, while trap shooters remained consistent across both conditions. As forwarded by Rossi and Zani, these findings suggest a distinct information processing strategy to deal with the repetitive exposure to and practice of skeet versus trap shooting.

Although the notion that shooters, or skilled performers in any domain, develop a specific attentional strategy to deal with task demands is intuitively appealing, Rossi and Zani's evidence that shooters develop distinct attentional styles that then transfer to laboratory tasks is relatively weak, and should be interpreted with caution. In contrast, the task and sport specificity of attentional skills is highlighted by the more routine finding that attentional expertise does not readily transfer from one domain to another (Ericsson *et al.*, 1993). Czigler *et al.* (1998) conducted a related project in which the ERP characteristics of shooters were assessed in a laboratory task designed to interrogate attentional allocation. Although significant effects were found for some measures, the investigation yielded largely inconclusive findings, suggesting that the cortical activation characteristics of attention associated with highly practiced motor skills does not transfer to novel laboratory tasks. As such, attentional strategies that underlie and develop through motor skill acquisition appear to be specific to the skill for which these strategies have been developed, and are relatively non-transferrable.

In summary, rapidly advancing technologies combined with more elegant experimental designs have supplemented our understanding of attentional processes as they correspond to the motor skills domain. EEG and ERP literature specific to motor learning, however, is relatively sparse. The inherent nature of motor skills as necessitating movement deems that the collection of salient data is impractical and often impossible. Consequently, one should be cautious when interpreting and attempting to generalize previous EEG-related findings between and within sport tasks. The need for caution is magnified when taking into account variable experimental procedures and populations (Lawton *et al.*, 1998).

Mindful of these concerns, results suggest that learners match neural resources with environmental demands in a more effective way as they acquire and refine skills. An efficient transaction with the environment has been interpreted as being reflected by two basic findings that permeate the majority of the sport-related EEG literature. Greater task-related alpha synchronization in the left hemisphere (e.g. Hatfield *et al.*, 1984) along with greater cortical asymmetry (e.g. Janelle *et al.*, 2000) characterizes those who attain superior skills. Likewise, as learners progress to incrementally higher levels of expertise, they adopt task-specific attentional strategies, and have a greater ability to flexibly implement these strategies. These developmental changes can be reflected in ERP measures as well. ERP data collection provides an exquisite view of the chronometry of the brain at a time scale not afforded by many measurement systems, and appears to be a fruitful method for future research.

Recommendations for future research and practice

The preceding discourse has provided a glimpse into the electrocortical characteristics that reflect the development of attentional specialization, and the proficiency that accompanies motor skill acquisition. Questions obviously remain concerning how to maximize attentional aptitude. A list of questions might be generated to specify this general concern. These queries might include, but are certainly not limited to: How does one develop the ability to selectively attend to the most critical internal and external cues? As divided attention capabilities are desirable, what capabilities permit learners to progress to performing more complex motor skills? Do learners develop a more refined capability to maximize selective and divided attention capabilities as they become more skilled? If so, do they achieve this by effectively regulating arousal to perform under an emotional state that is more representative of the state that was present when they learnt the task? Alternatively, do learners develop a more refined capability to perform effectively even in situations where arousal and emotional levels are variable?

The progression from higher demanding attentional stages to relative automaticity defines the expert performer in motor domains. Though its form is debated (i.e. Fitts and Posner, 1967; Hampson, 1989; Logan, 1988; Schneider and Shiffrin, 1977; Singer, 2002; Singer *et al.*, 1991) highly skilled performers apparently display greater attentional *efficiency* as skills are systematically practiced (Hatfield and Hillman, 2001; Janelle and Hillman, 2003). Most researchers and practitioners would agree that to be able to execute an action in an automatic fashion is desirable. Definitions of automaticity (e.g. Kahneman and Triesman, 1984; Logan, 1985; Pashler *et al.*, 2001; Singer, 2002) are all somewhat reliant upon ill-defined and vague terms such as 'processing' and 'resources'. Merely describing that skilled performers become more capable of performing efficiently by involving less attentional resources and processing information more efficiently does very little to address the mechanism(s) by which attentional skills are coordinated. As a result, these terms have become increasingly unacceptable among motor behaviourists; especially considering the proliferation of instrumentation that allows strong inference to more concrete interpretations of what a 'resource' is and how it is used for 'processing'.

Hirst (1986) and Moran (1996) have advocated the notion of *attention as a skill*. However, this perspective has not received systematic examination by the research community. Considering attention as a 'skill' itself is perhaps most appropriate, nevertheless, when discussing attention in the context of motor skill acquisition. Taking into account both traditional and contemporary literature, *motor* skill acquisition is intricately tied to and reliant upon *attentional* skill acquisition. One could assert that attentional skill develops in parallel with motor skill and domain-specific knowledge. However, a stronger contention would be that motor skill learning and eventual motor skill automaticity occurs *because of* attentional skill development. For example, the relative novice beginning the skill acquisition process does not know what movements to perform or when to perform them. Even if novice performers know when to execute a particular behaviour, they typically do not know how to do so. These relative deficits in skill level render performance of even the most basic movements extremely attention-demanding (Fitts and Posner, 1967). As the learner becomes attuned to the more relevant environmental and internal cues for motor performance (i.e. develops selective attention skill), the attentional effort that once governed choice of what action to perform, and when and how to perform it, is freed. Attention can then be directed to the most informative aspects of the performance context. Strategic decision making and accurate skill execution can then coexist and divided attentional capabilities are maximized, allowing cognitive and motor skill acquisition to develop. Practical application of this issue is interesting given that skill in the motor domain mandates an attentional component, while attention does not require motoric skill. Therefore, can attentional skills be trained independently of the motor domain, and if so, can these skills significantly progress motor skill learning?

Training programmes that include such protocols as perceptual cue training, implicit learning, external attentional focus, observational learning and attentional style have been shown to be relatively effective means towards developing attentional skills. The recent popularity of applied research and the findings emerging from recent training studies are encouraging (e.g. Farrow et al., 1998; Singer et al., 1994). At the same time, further research is needed to enable concrete recommendations for training attentional skills; especially considering the less than robust transfer of training that has been characteristic of these findings. Other practical recommendations for training attentional skills have been articulated by Abernethy (1993, 2001).

Any training method or programme developed to facilitate attention must alleviate the potential detrimental effects of distraction. Brown (1993) defines distraction as situations, events and circumstances that divert one's mind from some intended train of thought or from some desired course of action. This definition is somewhat different from James (1890) is original conceptualization of distraction, which he characterized as the experience of 'scattered' thoughts. Each of these views of distraction can be more easily understood if categorized in the context of internal and external types of distractors (Moran, 1996; Singer et al., 1991). Internal distractors refer to mental processes that interfere with one's ability to maintain attention, while external distractors are environmental or situational factors that divert attention from the task. The typical effect of distraction is a decrease in performance effectiveness. Distracters theoretically reduce the ability to attend to task-relevant information. This idea is supported by studies that have shown that distraction increases with task complexity and is greater as the similarity of distractors to relevant cues increases (Graydon and Eysenck, 1989). Current efforts are addressing distraction in its many forms (e.g. Janelle et al., 1999), with the end result anticipated to be a better understanding of under what conditions distraction is more likely and, therefore, what measures should be implemented for distraction control.

The paradigm shift away from behaviourist approaches and toward an emphasis on cognitive psychology that occurred in the late 1950s and early 1960s brought with it a greater understanding of the specific processes that are involved with attending to and processing information. However, the research has been criticized due to its reductionist nature. In other words, the primary focus of traditional cognitive psychology paradigms has been on identifying and manipulating cognitive variables within the framework of relatively simple information processing models. Typically, experiments within the cognitive psychology domain have been undertaken in contrived, highly controlled and benign laboratory environments using simple tasks. Largely ignored have been other relevant factors, particularly emotions (one exception being anxiety), that influence attentional processes and subsequent achievement (Kremer and Scully, 1994; Moran, 1996). By not studying the interaction of emotions, attention and performance in (complex and situation specific) action, the generalizability of research on attention is somewhat limited. A related criticism is that attention has been studied in virtual isolation from the performance of complex skilled movement. Particularly, our understanding of attentional contributions to motor response proficiency has evolved primarily using simple tasks, void of ecological validity.

Aside from the issue of ecological validity, researchers are currently challenging long-standing notions of attention by re-examining findings obtained from relatively simple tasks. Pashler *et al.* (2001) recently reviewed contemporary literature and found strong evidence against commonly accepted notions of automaticity. Traditionally, theorists have largely accepted the idea that exogenous (bottom–up or stimulus driven) attentional orientation occurs relatively automatically. That is, when a loud sound or prominent visual stimulus is presented, the stimulus 'pops out' and is attended without substantial cognitive effort. However, upon reviewing the work of Folk and Remington (1998) and Yantis and Egeth (1999), among others, they discovered that 'mental set' (i.e. expectations) significantly mediated the typical attentional capture seen in exogenous cueing experiments. That is, if participants were 'mentally set' for specific target attributes, the onset of distracters did not involuntarily capture attention. They also found evidence refuting the proposal that practice dramatically influences the capability to attain automaticity. After reviewing extensive empirical work using both continuous and discrete dual task paradigms, they make a strong contention that enhanced performance of dual tasks is likely due to attentional switching, or time sharing, rather than task automization, as has been typically assumed. This point has been echoed by Temprado *et al.* (1999) who reported that the cost of attentional shifting during task performance (as indexed via reaction time) is often a function of the dynamics of the task being performed as opposed to the level of task automaticity. Using the highly replicated HKB task (Haken *et al.*, 1985), they reported that reaction times were shorter during in-phase bimanual tasks as compared to anti-phase bimanual tasks. Manipulations of attention led to a trade-off between reaction time and pattern stability. The authors concluded that performing an intentionally stabilizing coordination pattern results in an attentional cost that depends on the dynamic properties of the coordination pattern, rather than task automaticity, per se. Pashler *et al.*'s (2001) conclusions are remarkably consistent with those offered by Hirst *et al.* (1986), again implicating the notion of *attentional skill development* as the primary means through which skilful performance results. By becoming skilled at attending to the most critical cues, and doing so quickly, attentional switching occurs very rapidly, thereby allowing dual task performance to improve.

A popular idea that may warrant reconsideration is the commonly held belief that attention is *limited*. Such an assertion may seem contemptuous considering the vast literature indicating, though not 'proving' such. Theoretically, the notion that attention is limited is attractive as it provides a convenient explanation for task variability. However, practical attentional limits are routinely exceeded with extensive practice. If contemporary notions of attentional efficiency are indeed accurate, then the precision of the pairing between environmental demand and neurological activation could potentially become so refined that the progression of skill acquisition and performance (at least from an attentional perspective) would be hypothetically limited only by the parameters of the neurological structures that govern attentional processes.

A final challenge for attention researchers is to translate empirical findings effectively, and to disseminate the wealth of knowledge in this domain to the individuals who may benefit from it. Recent publications (e.g. Coker, 2004) have begun to bridge this important translation gap in the motor learning literature. Whether the elite athlete, the recreational sports enthusiast, the recovering stroke victim, the fighter pilot, or the human factors engineer, translational research must be conducted and findings must be converted to pragmatic recommendations that can be effectively disseminated for use in training and rehabilitation. Continued and increased efforts towards this mission will yield motor performance improvements and inform future theory in this rich area of inquiry.

References

Abernethy, B. (1993). Attention. In R. Singer, L. K. Tennant and M. Murphey (Eds), *Handbook of research on sport psychology* (pp. 127–170). New York: Macmillan.

Abernethy, B. (2001). Attention. In R. Singer, H. Hausenblas and C. Janelle (Eds), *Handbook of sport psychology* (2nd ed, pp. 53–85). New York: Wiley.

Allport, D. A. (1980). Attention and performance. In G. Claxton (Ed.), *Cognitive psychology: new directions* (pp. 112–153). London: Routlege & Kegan Paul.

Andreassi, J. L. (2000). *Psychophysiology: human behaviour & physiological response* (4th ed.). Mahwah, NJ: Lawrence Erlbaum Associates.

Beauchamp, M. S., Cox, R. W. and DeYoe, E. A. (1997). Graded effects of spatial and featural attention on human area MT and associated motion processing areas. *Journal of Neurophysiology*, 78, 516–520.

Birbaumer, N., Elbert, T., Canavan, A. G. M. and Rockstroh, B. (1990). Slow potentials of the cerebral cortex and behaviour. *Physiological Reviews*, 70, 1–41.

Broadbent, D. E. (1957). A mechanical model for human attention and immediate memory. *Psychological Review*, 64, 205–215.

Brown, L. (1993). *The new shorter Oxford English dictionary*. Oxford: Clarendon Press.

Busk, J. and Galbraith, G. C. (1975). EEG correlates of visual-motor practice in man. *Electroencephalography and Clinical Neurophysiology*, 35, 415–422.

Coker, C. A. (2004). Motor learning and control for practitioners. New York: McGraw-Hill.

Corbetta, M., Miezin, F. M., Shulman, G. L. and Peterson, S. E. (1993). A PET study of visuospatial attention. *Journal of Neuroscience*, 13, 1202–1226.

Crews, D. J. and Landers, D. M. (1993). Electroencephalographic measures of attentional patterns prior to the golf putt. *Medicine and Science in Sports and Exercise*, 25, 116–126.

Czigler, I., Balazs, L. and Lenart, A. (1998). Attention to features of separate objects: an ERP study of target-shooters and control participants. *International Journal of Psychophysiology*, 31, 77–87.

Davidson, R. J., Chapman, J. P., Chapman, L. J. and Henriques, J. B. (1990). Asymmetrical brain electrical activity discriminates between psychometrically-matched verbal and spatial cognitive tasks. *Psychophysiology*, 27, 528–543.

Davidson, R. J., Jackson, D. C. and Larson, C. L. (2000). Human electroencephalography. In J. T. Cacioppo, L. G. Tassinary and G. G. Bernston (Eds), *Handbook of psychophysiology* (2nd ed., pp. 27–52). New York: Cambridge University Press.

Desimone, R. and Duncan, J. (1995). Neural mechanisms of selective visual attention. *Annual Review of Neuroscience*, 18, 193–222.

Deutsch, J. A. and Deutsch, D. (1963). Attention: some theoretical considerations. *Psychological Review*, 70, 80–90.

Elbert, T., Pantev, C., Weinbruch, C., Rockstroh, B. and Taub, E. (1995). Increased cortical representation of the fingers of the left hand. *Science*, 270, 305–307.

Ericsson, K. A., Krampe, R. T. and Tesch-Römer, C. (1993). The role of deliberate practice in the acquisition of expert performance. *Psychological Review*, 100, 363–406.

Etnier, J. L., Whitwer, S. S., Landers, D. M., Petruzzello, S. J. and Salazar, S. J. (1996). Changes in electroencephalographic activity associated with learning a novel motor task. *Research Quarterly for Exercise and Sport*, 67, 272–279.

Eysenck, M. W. (1984). *A handbook of cognitive psychology*. London: Erlbaum.

Eysenck, M. W. and Keane, M. T. (1995). *Cognitive psychology: a students handbook*. London: Erlbaum.

Fabiani, M., Gratton, G. and Coles, M. G. H. (2000). Event-related brain potentials: methods, theory, and applications. In J. T. Cacioppo, L. G. Tassinary and G. G. Bernston (Eds), *Handbook of psychophysiology* (2nd ed., pp. 53–84). New York: Cambridge University Press.

Farrow, D., Chivers, P., Hardingham, C. and Sachse, S. (1998). The effect of video-based perceptual training on the tennis return of serve. *International Journal of Sport Psychology*, 29, 231–242.

Fernandez-Duque, D. and Johnson, M. L. (1999). Attention metaphors: how metaphors guide the cognitive psychology of attention. *Cognitive Science*, 23, 83–116.

Fisk, A. D., Derrick, W. L. and Schneider, W. (1986). A methodological assessment and evaluation of dual task paradigms. *Current Psychology Research and Reviews*, 5, 315–327.

Fitts, P. (1954). The information capacity of the human motor system in controlling the amplitude of movements. *Journal of Experimental Psychology*, 47, 381–391.

Fitts, P. M. and Posner, M. I. (1967). *Human performance*. Belmont, CA: Brooks/Cole.

Folk, C. L. and Remington, R. W. (1998). Selectivity in distraction by irrelevant feature singletons: evidence for two forms of attentional capture. *Journal of Experimental Psychology: Human Perception and Performance*, 18, 1030–1044.

Gevins, A., Smith, M. E., McEvoy, L. and Yu, D. (1997). High-resolution EEG mapping of cortical activation related to working memory: effects of task difficulty, type of processing and practice. *Cerebral Cortex*, 7, 374–385.

Graydon, J. and Eysenck, M. W. (1989). Distraction and cognitive performance. *European Journal of Cognitive Psychology*, 1, 161–179.

Gruber, T., Müller, M. M., Keil, A. and Elbert, T. (1999). Selective visual–spatial attention alters induced gamma band responses in the human EEG. *Clinical Neurophysiology*, 110, 2074–2085.

Gundel, A. and Wilson, G. F. (1992). Topographical changes in the ongoing EEG related to the difficulty of mental tasks. *Brain Topography*, 5, 17–25.

Haken, H., Kelso, J. A. S. and Bunz, H. (1985). A theoretical model of phase transition in human movements. *Biological Cybernetics*, 51, 347–356.

Hampson, P. J. (1989). Aspects of attention and cognitive science. *Irish Journal of Psychology*, 10, 261–275.

Hanin, Y. (Ed.) (2000). *Emotions in sport.* Champaign, IL: Human Kinetics.

Hatfield, B. D. and Hillman, C. H. (2001). The psychophysiology of sport: a mechanistic understanding of the psychology of superior performance. In R. N. Singer, H. A. Hausenblas and C. M. Janelle (Eds), *Handbook of sport psychology* (2nd ed., pp. 362–388). New York: Wiley.

Hatfield, B. D., Landers, D. M. and Ray, W. J. (1984). Cognitive processes during self-paced motor performance: an electroencephalographic profile of skilled marksmen. *Journal of Sport Psychology*, 6, 42–59.

Hatfield, B. D., Landers, D. M., Ray, W. J. and Daniels, F. S. (1982). An electroencephalographic study of elite rifle shooters. *The American Marksmen*, 7, 6–8.

Haufler, A. J., Spalding, T. W., Santa Maria, D. L. and Hatfield, B. D. (2000). Neurocognitive activity during a self-paced visuospatial task: comparative EEG profiles in marksmen and novice shooters. *Biological Psychology*, 53, 131–160.

Haug, A. B., Baudewig, J. and Paulus, W. (1998). Selective attention of human cortical area V5A by a rotating visual stimulus in fMRI; implications of attentional mechanisms. *Neuroreport*, 9, 611–614.

Hawkins, H. L. and Presson, J. C. (1986). Auditory information processing. In K. R. Boff, L. Kaufman and J. P. Thomas (Eds), *Handbook of perception and human performance* (pp. 26–1–26–44). New York: Wiley.

Hick, W. E. (1952). On the rate of gain of information. *Quarterly Journal of Experimental Psychology*, 4, 11–26.

Hillman, C. H., Apparies, R. J., Janelle, C. M. and Hatfield, B. D. (2000). An electrocortical comparison of executed and rejected shots in skilled marksmen. *Biological Psychology*, 52, 71–83.

Hillyard, S. A. and Hansen, J. C. (1986). Attention: electrophysiological approaches. In M. G. H. Coles, E. Donchin and S. W. Porges (Eds), *Psychophysiology: systems, processes, and applications* (pp. 227–243). New York: Guilford Publications.

Hillyard, S. A., Vogel, E. K. and Luck, S. J. (1998) Sensory gain control (amplification) as a mechanism of selective attention: electrophysiological and neuroimaging evidence. *Philosophical Transactions of the Royal Society Series B*, 353, 1257–1270.

Hirst, W. (1986). The psychology of attention. In J. LeDoux and W. Hirst (Eds), *Dialogues in cognitive neuroscience* (pp. 105–141). Cambridge: Cambridge University Press.

Hughes, J. R. and Hendrix, D. E. (1967). Telemetered EEG from a football player in action. *Electroencephalography and Clinical Neurophysiology*, 24, 183–186.

Hyman, R. (1953). Stimulus information as a determinant of reaction time. *Journal of Experimental Psychology*, 45, 188–196.

James, W. (1890). *Principles of psychology.* New York: Holt, Rinehart, & Winston.

Janelle, C. M. (2002). Modification of visual attention parameters under conditions of heightened anxiety and arousal. *Journal of Sports Sciences*, 20, 1–15.

Janelle, C. M. and Hillman, C. H. (2003). Expert performance in sport: current perspectives and critical issues. In K. A. Ericsson and J. Starkes (Eds), *Recent advances in research on sport expertise* (pp. 19–48). Champaign, IL: Human Kinetics.

Janelle, C. M., Singer, R. N. and Williams, A. M. (1999). External distraction and attentional narrowing: visual search evidence. *Journal of Sport & Exercise Psychology*, 21, 70–91.

Janelle, C. M., Hillman, C. H., Apparies, R., Murray, N. P., Meili, L., Fallon, E. A. and Hatfield, B. D. (2000). Expertise differences in cortical activation and gaze behaviour during rifle shooting. *Journal of Sport & Exercise Psychology*, 22, 167–182.

Jones, J. G. (1995). More than just a game: research developments and issues in competitive anxiety in sport. *British Journal of Psychology*, 86, 449–478.

Kahneman, D. (1973). *Attention and effort*. Englewood Cliffs, NJ: Prentice-Hall.

Kahneman, D. and Triesman, A. (1984). Changing views of attention and automaticity. In R. Parasuraman and D. R. Davies (Eds), *Varieties of attention* (pp. 29–61). London: Academic Press.

Karni, A., Meyer, G., Rey-Hipolito, C., Jezzard, P., Adams, M. M., Turner, R. and Ungerleifer, L. G. (1998). The acquisition of skilled motor performance: fast and slow experience-driven changes in primary motor cortex. *Procedures from the National Academy of Science*, 95, 861–868.

Keele, S. W. (1973). *Attention and human performance*. Pacific Palisades, CA: Goodyear.

Klimesch, W. (1999). EEG alpha and theta oscillations reflect cognitive and memory performance: a review and analysis. *Brain Research Reviews*, 29, 169–195.

Konttinen, N. and Lyytinen, H. (1992). Physiology of preparation: brain slow waves, heart rate, and respiration preceding triggering in rifle shooting. *International Journal of Sport Psychology*, 23, 110–127.

Konttinen, N. and Lyytinen, H. (1993). Individual variability in brain slow wave profiles in skilled sharpshooters during the aiming period in rifle shooting. *Journal of Sport & Exercise Psychology*, 15, 275–289.

Konttinen, N., Lyytinen, H. and Era, P. (1999). Brain slow potentials and postural sway behaviour during sharpshooting performance. *Journal of Motor Behaviour*, 31, 11–20.

Konttinen, N., Landers, D. M. and Lyytinen, H. (2000). Aiming routines and their electrocortical concomitants among competitive rifle shooters. *Scandinavian Journal of Medicine Science & Sports*, 10, 169–177.

Kremer, J. and Scully, D. (1994). *Psychology in sport*. London: Taylor & Francis.

Kutas, M. and Federmeier, K. D. (1998). Minding the body. *Psychophysiology*, 35, 135–150.

Laberge, D. (1999). Attention. In B. Bly and D. E. Rumelhart (Eds), *Handbook of perception and cognition* (2nd ed., pp. 43–97). San Diego, CA: Academic Press.

Landers, D. M., Han, M., Salazar, W., Petruzzello, S. J., Kubitz, K. A. and Gannon, T. L. (1994). Effect of learning on electroencephalographic and electrocardiographic patterns on novice archers. *International Journal of Sport Psychology*, 25, 313–330.

Landers, D. M. Petruzzello, S. J., Salazar, W., Crews, D. J., Kubitz, K. A., Gannon, T. L. and Han, M. (1991). The influence of electrocortical biofeedback and performance in pre-elite archers. *Medicine and Science in Sports and Exercise*, 23, 123–129.

Lawton, G. W., Hung, T. M., Saarela, P. and Hatfield, B. D. (1998). Electroencephalography and mental states associated with elite performance. *Journal of Sport & Exercise Psychology*, 20, 35–53.

Liepert, J., Bauder, H., Miltner, W. H. R., Taub, E. and Weiller, C. (2000). Treatment-induced cortical reorganization after stroke in humans. *Stroke*, 31, 1210–1216.

Logan, G. D. (1985). Skill and automaticity: relations, implications, and future directions. *Canadian Journal of Psychology*, 39, 367–386.

Logan, G. D. (1988). Automaticity, resources, and memory: theoretical controversies and practical implications. *Human Factors*, 30, 583–598.

Moran, A. P. (1996). *The psychology of concentration in sport performers: a cognitive analysis*. London: Taylor & Francis.

Murray, N. M. and Janelle, C. M. (2002). Psychophysiological evidence for the processing efficiency theory. *Journal of Sport & Exercise Psychology*, 24, s99.

Navon, D. and Gopher, D. (1979). On the economy of the human processing system. *Psychological Review*, 86, 214–255.

Niedermeyer, E. (1987). The normal EEG of the waking adult. In E. Niedermeyer and F. Lopez da Silva (Eds), *Electroencephalography. Basic principles, clinical applications and related fields* (pp. 97–117). Baltimore: Urban & Schwarzenberg.

Norman, D. A. (1968). Toward a theory of memory and attention. *Psychological Review*, 75, 522–536.

Norman, D. A. (1969). *Attention, memory and attention: an introduction to human information processing* (2nd ed.). New York: John Wiley and Sons Inc.

Norman, D. A. and Bobrow, D. (1975). On data limited and resource limited processing. *Cognitive Psychology*, 7, 44–60.

Nunez, P. L. (1995). Neuromodulation of neocortical dynamics. In P. L. Nunez (Ed.), *Neocortical dynamics and human EEG rhythms* (pp. 591–627). New York: Oxford University Press.

Ogden, G. D., Levine, J. M. and Eisner, E. J. (1979). Measurement of workload by secondary tasks. *Human Factors*, 21, 529–548.

Parasuraman, R. (1998). *The attentive brain*. Cambridge, MA: MIT Press.

Pashler, H. (1994). Dual-task interference in simple tasks: data and theory. *Psychological Bulletin*, 16, 220–244.

Pashler, H. (1998). *The psychology of attention*. Cambridge, MA: MIT Press.

Pashler, H., Johnston, J. C. and Ruthruff, E. (2001). Attention and performance. *Annual Reviews of Psychology*, 52, 629–651.

Pfurtscheller, G. and Berghold, A. (1989). Patterns of cortical activation during planning of voluntary movement. *Electroencephalography & Clinical Neurophysiology*, 72, 250–258.

Pfurtscheller, G. and Klimesch, W. (1991). Event-related desynchronization during motor behaviour and visual information processing. In C. H. M. Brunia, G. Mulder and M. N. Verbaten (Eds), *Event-related brain research, EEG Supplement* 42, 58–65.

Pfurtscheller, G., Stancak, A. and Neuper, C. (1996). Event-related synchronization (ERS) in the alpha band- an electrophysiological correlate of cortical idling: a review. *International Journal of Psychophysiology*, 24, 39–46.

Picton, T. W., Bentin, S., Berg, P., Donchin, E., Hillyard, S. A., Johnson, R., Jr., Miller, G. A., Ritter, W., Ruchkin, D. S., Rugg, M. D. and Taylor, M. J. (2000). Guidelines for using human event related potentials to study cognition: recording standards and publication criteria. *Psychophysiology*, 37, 127–152.

Posner (1996). Attention in cognitive neuroscience: an overview. In M. Gazzaniga (Ed.), *The cognitive neurosciences* (pp. 615–625). Cambridge, MA: MIT Press.

Posner, M. I. and Boies, S. J. (1971). Components of attention. *Psychological Review*, 78, 391–408.

Pulvermüller, F., Lutzenberger, W., Preissl, H. and Burbaumer, N. (1995). Spectral responses in the gamma band: physiological signs of higher cognitive processes. *Neuroreport*, 6, 2059–2064.

Ritter, W., Simpson, R. and Vaughn, H. G. (1972). Association cortex potentials and reaction time in auditory discrimination. *Electroencephalography and Clinical Neurophysiology*, 33, 547–555.

Radlo, S. J., Janelle, C. M., Barba, D. A. and Frehlich, S. G. (2001). Perceptual decision making for baseball pitch recognition: using P300 latency and amplitude to index attentional processing. *Research Quarterly for Exercise and Sport*, 72, 22–31.

Rossi, B. and Zani, A. (1991). Timing of movement-related decision processed in clay-pigeon shooters as assessed by event-related brain potentials and reaction times. *International Journal of Sport Psychology*, 22, 128–139.

Salazar, W., Landers, D. M., Petruzzello, S. J., Han, M., Crews, D. J. and Kubitz, K. A. (1990). Hemispheric asymmetry, cardiac response, and performance in elite archers. *Research Quarterly for Exercise and Sport*, 61, 351–359.

Sanes, J. N. and Donoghue, J. P. (2000). Plasticity and primary motor cortex. *Annual Review of Neuroscience*, 23, 393–415.

Schmidt, R. A. and Lee, T. D. (1999). *Motor control and learning: a behavioral emphasis* (3rd ed.). Champaign, IL: Human Kinetics.

Schneider, W. and Shiffrin, R. M. (1977). Controlled and automatic information processing: I. Detection, search, and attention. *Psychological Review*, 92, 424–428.

Singer, R. N. (2002). Pre-performance state, routines, and automaticity. What does it take to realize expertise in self paced events? *Journal of Sport and Exercise Psychology*, 24, 359–375.

Singer, R. N., Cauraugh, J. H., Chen, D., Steinberg, G., Frehlich, S. and Wang, L. (1994). Training mental quickness in beginning/intermediate tennis players. *The Sport Psychologist*, 8, 305–318.

Singer, R. N., Cauraugh, J. H., Tennant, L. K., Murphey, M., Chen, D. and Lidor, R. (1991). Attention and distractors: considerations for enhancing sport performance. *International Journal of Sport Psychology*, 22, 95–114.

Smith, M. E., McEvoy, L. K. and Gevins, A. (1999). Neurophysiological indices of strategy development and skill acquisition. *Cognitive Brain Research*, 7, 289–404.

Smith, S. W. (1997). *The scientist's and engineer's guide to digital signal processing* (2nd ed.). San Diego, CA: California Technical Publishing.

Starkes, J. L., Helsen, W. and Jack, R. (2001). Expert performance in sport and dance. In R. N. Singer, H. A. Hausenblas and C. M. Janelle (Eds), *Handbook of Sport Psychology*, (2nd ed., pp. 174–201). New York: Wiley.

Sterman, M. B., Mann, C. A., Kaiser, D. A. and Suyenobu, B. Y. (1994). Multiband topographic EEG analysis of a simulated visuomotor aviation task. *International Journal of Psychophysiology*, 16, 49–56.

Theeuwes, J. (1994). Visual selective attention: a theoretical analysis. *Acta Psychologica*, 83, 93–154.

Temprado, J. J., Zazone, P. G., Monno, A. and Laurent, M. (1999). Attentional load associated with performing and stabilizing preferred bimanual patterns. *Journal of Experimental Psychology: Human Perception and Performance*, 25, 1579–1594.

Treisman, A. (1960). Contextual cues in selective listening. *Quarterly Journal of Experimental Psychology*, 12, 242–248.

Treisman, A. M. and Gelade, G. (1980). A feature integration theory of attention. *Cognitive Psychology*, 12, 97–136.

Wang, M. Q. and Landers, D. M. (1986). A psychophysiological investigation of attention during imagery performance. *Psychophysiology*, 23, 449.

Welford, A. T. (1952). The 'psychological refractory period' and the timing of high-speed performance – a review and a theory. *British Journal of Psychology*, 43, 2–19.

Wickens, C. D. (1984). Process resources and attention: In R. Parasuraman and R. Davies (Eds), *Varieties of attention* (p. 81). New York: Academic Press.

Wickens, C. D. (1992). *Engineering psychology and human performance*. Columbus, OH: Charles E. Merrill.

Williams, A. M., Davids, K. and Williams, J. G. (1999). *Visual perception and action in sport*. London: Spon.

Wood, G. (1983). *Cognitive psychology: a skills approach*. Monterey, CA: Brooks/Cole.

Yantis, S. and Egeth, H. E. (1999). On the distinction between visual salience and stimulus driven attentional capture. *Journal of Experimental Psychology: Human Perception and Performance*, 25, 661–676.

14 From novice to expert performance

Memory, attention and the control of complex sensori-motor skills

Sian L. Beilock and Thomas H. Carr

From the naissance of systematic skill acquisition research in the late 1800s (see Bryan and Harter, 1899) to the present day, investigators of human skill have explored differences in expert and novice task execution in an attempt to shed light on the variables mediating high-level performance. These investigations have not only been concerned with the measured success of overt performance at various levels of task experience, but also with changes in the cognitive mechanisms, such as memory and attention, that underlie performance improvements as learning progresses (Allard and Starkes, 1991; Anderson, 1982, 1983; Beilock and Carr, 2001; Ericsson *et al.*, 1993; Fitts and Posner, 1967; Reimann and Chi, 1989).

What makes expert performance different from novice execution? At first glance, one might suggest that the answer is simple. It is the quality of overt behaviour that separates exceptional performers from those less skilled. We can all point to many 'real-world' examples of such performance differences; just try comparing any professional athlete to his or her recreational counterpart. Although actual performance is one component that differentiates experts from novices, researchers who approach skill acquisition from a cognitive perspective believe that these overt performance distinctions are only part of the picture. Indeed, they are viewed as merely the surface manifestation of skill level differences. The cognitive control structures that support planning and drive execution are what is thought to truly distinguish novice from expert performance. These control structures rely on particular forms of memory and vary in the demands they place on attention. Both the memorial substrate and attentional demands of these control structures change as practice accumulates and skill proficiency increases.

Theories of skill acquisition

Cognitive theories of skill acquisition and automaticity suggest that performance proceeds through identifiably different phases as learning progresses, characterized by both qualitative changes in the cognitive substrate governing execution and in performance itself. A number of different frameworks have been proposed to capture these skill level differences. Fitts and Posner's (1967) three-stage model of skill acquisition suggests that early in learning, novices use explicit cognitive processes to control execution in a step-by-step fashion. Because of the involvement of conscious cognitive processes early in learning, Fitts and Posner termed this initial stage of skill learning the *cognitive phase*. Once learners understand the nature of the task, they are thought to enter an *associative phase* in which the need to consciously control real-time performance diminishes, and task representations are established that directly connect stimulus situations to actions. With extended practice, performance reaches the *autonomous phase*. In this final stage of learning, skill execution is based on a fully automatic task representation in which conscious attentional control is no longer required to execute a particular action when confronted by a particular stimulus situation.

While Fitts and Posner's (1967) characterization of skill level differences has been extremely influential to the study of human skill acquisition, their framework is mostly descriptive in nature. In an attempt to assign specific knowledge structures to Fitts and Posner's stages of learning, Anderson (1982, 1983, 1993) has developed a formal simulation model of skill acquisition most recently known as ACT-R (Anderson and Lebiere, 1998). In this model, skill learning is thought to progress from a *declarative phase* (similar to Fitts and Posner's cognitive phase) to a *procedural phase* (corresponding to Fitts and Posner's autonomous phase), through a process known as *knowledge compilation*. In ACT-R's early declarative phase, performance is thought to be based on declarative knowledge (i.e. facts and information about skill execution) that must be held in working memory during online execution. Working memory can be thought of as a short-term memory system that maintains, in an active state, a limited amount of information with immediate relevance to the task at hand (Proctor and Dutta, 1995). This information is used small amounts at a time by limited-capacity control processes, which guide performance in a step-by-step fashion. As learning progresses, declarative knowledge is said to be converted or compiled (through the process of knowledge compilation) into procedural knowledge that captures the instructions for performing the task at hand in a new form. Procedural knowledge is made up of 'productions' which represent knowledge about how we do things, for example, knowledge about how to kick a soccer ball. Unlike declarative knowledge, procedural knowledge does not require the active maintenance of each step of task execution in working memory. This more implicit type of knowledge is thought to run-off from one production to the next without explicit attentional control. When experienced soccer players kick a ball, for example, they do not think consciously about every component involved in kicking, they 'just do it' – supported by an automatic procedural control structure.

Thus, in general, cognitive theories of skill acquisition and automaticity suggest that novel skill performance is based on explicitly retrievable declarative knowledge that is held in working memory and consciously attended in real time (Anderson, 1983, 1993; Fitts and Posner, 1967; Proctor and Dutta, 1995). As learning progresses, information is restructured into a new type of skill representation, usually called a 'procedure' in the domain of cognitive skills, but often called a 'motor program' in the domain of sensori-motor skills (Brown and Carr, 1989; Keele, 1986; Keele and Summers, 1976). This new skill representation does not mandate the same degree of attention and control that was necessary at lower levels of practice, and is supported by different neural structures than were active early in learning (Raichle *et al.*, 1994).

In this chapter, we explore some of the implications of these differences in the representation and operation of the control structures supporting performance at various levels of skill learning and expertise. Specifically, we examine how the memory structures and attentional demands associated with task execution differ as a function of skill level. Such an investigation will not only make salient those variables distinguishing novice and experienced performance processes, but may also aid in the development of strategies for enhancing the acquisition and maintenance of high level skills across a variety of attention-demanding and pressure-packed situations. We focus on sensori-motor skills of the type required by sports performance, and we believe that theories like those of Fitts or Anderson describe such sensori-motor skills fairly well. At the end of the chapter, we will briefly consider how widely these theories of 'automatization via proceduralization' might generalize to other domains of skilled performance.

Memory and skill acquisition

One of the most widely discussed characteristics of expert performance is the ability of highly skilled individuals to recall task-relevant stimuli within their domain of interest (Proctor and Dutta, 1995). In their classic chess studies, Chase and Simon (1973) found that chess masters were better able to recall briefly presented structured chess positions than were less experienced players (for confirmatory data, see De Groot, 1978). Similarly, expert computer programmers have been shown to have greater memory for realistic programming code sequences than less experienced individuals (McKeithen *et al.*, 1981). In sensori-motor skills such as dance, Starkes *et al.* (1987) have demonstrated that when expert and novice ballet dancers are presented with a series of choreographed movement sequences and asked to recall these movements either verbally or physically, expert dancers are better able to do so than their novice counterparts.

Why do experts show this superior memory ability in comparison to their less skilled counterparts for structured stimuli within their domain? Ericsson and Polson (1988) have developed a theory of skilled memory in an attempt to answer this question. Skilled memory theory suggests that experts encode stimuli in a style that allows them to store this information as associations of patterns in long-term memory. In essence, experts have learned to organize knowledge in their domain in a manner that allows them to easily take in new information about the stimuli they act on and subsequently retrieve it (for a review of skilled memory theory, see Ericsson and Polson, 1988; Staszewski, 1988).

But do experts have superior memory for all aspects of performance? Highly skilled performers may have better episodic recollection for the stimuli in the environment that they operate on (e.g. chess game configurations, basketball play scenarios or choreographed dance sequences). They may also have better memories for the outcomes or results that their operations produced. That is, the new stimulus configurations that were created by their activities and whether these results achieved the desired goals (did the knight end up in the right space to hem in the queen or did the jump shot go in the basket?). But what about the mental events that led to these outcomes or the details of the actions the mental events controlled? It has not been demonstrated that experts have better memories than novices for all aspects of execution. In particular, this applies to the sequences of thought processes and executed actions that were responsible for changing the initial stimulus situation into the outcome situation. Indeed, from the theories of skill acquisition and automaticity presented in the previous section, it could be concluded that experts should actually have *worse* memories for these aspects of performance in comparison to less skilled individuals.

The theories of skill acquisition we have reviewed suggest that highly practised or overlearned performances are automated, supported by procedural knowledge that operates without the need for explicit or attended monitoring (Anderson, 1983, 1993; Fitts and Posner, 1967). It has been demonstrated that the successful explicit retrieval of information from memory is dependent on attention to this material at the time of encoding (Craik *et al.*, 1996; Naveh-Benjamin *et al.*, 1998). Thus, if experts are not explicitly attending to online performance, their memories for the step-by-step components involved in achieving a performance outcome as it actually unfolds in real time may be impoverished. Diminished memories of how a performance was actually achieved may make it difficult for experts to reflect and introspect on past performance decisions, strategy choices and execution processes implemented during task execution (Abernethy *et al.*, 1993). This information is not only needed to learn and improve from past performances, but also utilized in the dissemination of knowledge to others when high-level performers assume the roles of teachers or coaches. Thus, the very cognitive changes that accompany becoming an expert performer could make it more difficult to teach one's skill to another person.

In an attempt to examine the memory structures supporting performance at different levels of learning, Beilock and Carr (2001) assessed the generic knowledge and episodic memories of expert and novice golfers. 'Generic' knowledge captures prescriptive information about how a skill is typically carried out. 'Episodic' knowledge on the other hand, captures an autobiographical record of a particular performance, a memory for a specific instance of skill execution. Experienced golfers may well give longer, more detailed generic descriptions of the steps involved in a typical or 'generic' putt compared to the accounts given by novices because experts know more about how their skill should be performed and can call this declarative knowledge to mind when reflecting 'offline'. However, if the real-time performance of well-learned golf putting is supported by procedural knowledge, as theories of automaticity and skill acquisition would predict, then experienced golfers may give shorter, less detailed episodic recollections of any particular putt in comparison to less skilled golfers. Proceduralization reduces the need to attend to the specific processes by which skill execution unfolds, and reduced attention to performance decreases the likelihood of an explicitly accessible episodic performance memory.

Experienced golfers with more than 2 years of high-school varsity golf experience or a Professional Golfers' Association (PGA) handicap less than eight and novice golfers with no previous experience of the game served as participants. Individuals performed a golf putting task on a carpeted indoor putting green $(3\,m \times 3.7\,m)$. They were instructed to putt a golf ball as accurately as possible, making it stop at a target marked by a square of red tape. All participants alternately putted from nine different spots, located at varying angles and distances from the target. Participants took part in a pre-test condition consisting of twenty putts, a practice condition consisting of thirty putts, and two post-test conditions. The first post-test consisted of twenty putts while the second post-test consisted of ten additional putts. Putting accuracy was recorded after every putt and an average accuracy score was computed for each condition (for details, see Beilock and Carr, 2001). Following the pre-test and practice conditions, participants produced generic knowledge protocols – what one ought to do on a typical putt. Individuals were instructed: 'Certain steps are involved in executing a golf putt. Please list as many steps that you can think of, in the right order, which are involved in a typical golf putt.' Following both the first and second post-test conditions, participants were asked to describe, in as much detail as possible, their episodic memories of the last putt – their memory of what they actually did on that specific putt. In order to obtain episodic performance memories participants were instructed: 'Pretend that your friend just walked into the room. Describe the last putt you took, in enough detail so that your friend could duplicate that last putt you just took in detail, doing it just like you did' (for detailed protocol instructions, see Beilock and Carr, 2001; Beilock *et al.*, 2002c). The first episodic memory protocol was a surprise. The second was expected. Prior to the last putt taken before the second episodic memory protocol, participants were warned to keep track of their putting performance, as they would be asked to produce an episodic memory of the next putt.

Memory protocols were first analysed in terms of the number of steps given in each protocol. Three expert golfers and a 'how to' golf putting book (Jones *et al.*, 1998) were employed to establish a master list of steps involved in a successful golf putt that could be used as a guide in coding the protocols. The statements in each participant's protocol were compared with this master list. If a step given by a participant referred to the same action or the same biomechanical principle as a step on the master list, it was counted as one step.

As can be seen in Figure 14.1, novice golfers gave short generic descriptions and longer episodic recollections. Experts produced an opposite pattern. Experienced golfers gave longer and more detailed generic descriptions than novices, yet shorter episodic recollections in comparison to both their generic descriptions and the episodic recollections of novices. Experts' impoverished episodic memories for online execution demonstrate what Beilock and Carr (2001) called 'expertise-induced amnesia'. Highly skilled online performances are controlled by automated procedural knowledge that operates largely outside

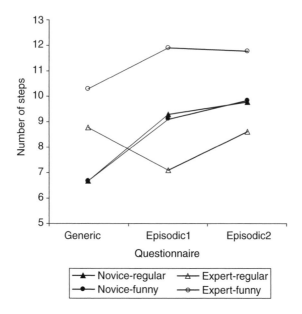

Figure 14.1 Mean number of steps for the generic questionnaire and the two episodic questionnaires for the novice and experienced golfers using the regular putter and the funny putter. Adapted from Beilock and Carr (2001).

the scope of attention and, therefore, is substantially closed to explicit analysis and report. As a result, memories for the step-by-step processes involved in performance are diminished in comparison to less skilled individuals.

The second episodic memory test, in which participants knew in advance that they would be required to recall an episodic memory of their last putt, generated the same results. Experts gave diminished episodic recollections in comparison to novices. Thus, it is not just that experts choose not to pay attention to skill execution in a manner that allows them to explicitly remember their perform-ance. It is as if experts *cannot* pay enough attention to remember as well as novices, at least when performing under heavily practised conditions.

Is it *always* the case that experts do not explicitly attend to step-by-step performance and, as a result, memories for skill execution are impoverished? If experienced individuals were never able to pay attention to real-time execu-tion, one might imagine that they would have trouble correcting performance flaws or altering skill execution parameters (e.g. revamping a golf swing or learning to throw a new type of baseball pitch) in such a way needed to main-tain or improve their high skill level. In situations where new task constraints are explicitly introduced as a means to disrupt or suspend automated procedures and allow performance patterns to be altered, experts should be able to attend to performance in a way that permits them to make desired performance corrections. Furthermore, once experts start attending to task performance, their expert knowledge may allow them to remember more of what they are attending to than novices; not less as the pattern of data seen above in which experts are attempting to achieve high-level performance by relying on their well-practised procedures.

In order to explore this kind of situation, Beilock and Carr (2001) had novice and experienced golfers perform the same putting task as described above, with the exception that a specially constructed 'funny putter' was substituted for the regular golf putter. The funny putter consisted of a regular putter head attached to an 's' shaped and arbitrarily weighted putter shaft. The design of the funny putter was intended to require experienced golfers to alter their well-practiced putting form in order to compensate for the distorted club, perhaps forcing them to allocate attention to the new skill execution processes in much the same way as they might need to be able to do in a practice situation designed to revise or correct a component process of performance.

If the 'funny putter' prompts attention to execution, then experienced individuals' memories for specific instances of performance may be enhanced, as the funny putter is now directing the attention needed to create episodic performance memories back to controlling the step-by-step execution of the putting skill. In contrast, the funny putter should not affect novice performers in the same way as more experienced golfers. Novices are already thought to attend to performance (Fitts, 1964; Fitts and Posner, 1967), and have not yet adapted to putting under normal conditions, performance should not be drastically influenced by an altered putting environment.

Comparisons of putting performance across the novice and experienced golfers demonstrated that the type of putter did not significantly affect novices' putting accuracy, although novices using the funny putter did generally perform at a slightly lower level than their regular putter counterparts (Figure 14.2). This result is not surprising considering that the novice golfers were not experienced with either type of putter prior to the experiment. Experts' putting accuracy was superior to novices and was more accurate with the regular putter than with the funny putter, especially during the practice condition and post-tests.

Although experienced golfers using the funny putter performed at a lower level than regular putter experts during the pre-test, this difference was not as large as in the later practice and post-test conditions. It may be that in the pre-test condition, expert golfers, regardless of putter type, were adjusting to the novel experimental demands of having to land the ball on the target rather than in a hole. Thus, experts using the regular putter were not performing up to their potential in the pre-test. The difference between the regular and funny putter experts widened quickly however, as practice proceeded. Due to the fact that experienced golfers often encounter novel putting greens, and must adapt to these situations in order to maintain a low handicap, it is not surprising the experts using the regular putter were able to rapidly adjust to our indoor green. In contrast, as can be seen from Figure 14.2, those experts using the funny putter were unable to adapt to the demands of the new putter within the time frame of the experiment, performing at a similar level of accuracy across experimental conditions.

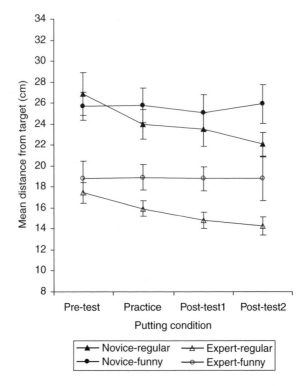

Figure 14.2 Mean distance (cm) from the target that the ball stopped after each putt in the pre-test condition (pre-test), practice condition (practice), first post-test condition (post-test1), and second post-test condition (post-test2) for each group. Error bars represent standard errors. Adapted from Beilock and Carr (2001).

In terms of the memory protocols, while novices, regardless of the type of putter, produced shorter generic descriptions of putting and longer episodic memory protocols than experienced golfers using the regular putter, this was not the case for the experts using the funny putter. As can be seen in Figure 14.1, experts using the funny putter provided the most elaborated generic and episodic protocols. From our theoretical perspective, attention to the novel constraints of the funny putter prompted these golfers to allocate more attention to skill execution processes, enhancing generic descriptions and leaving explicit episodic memory traces of performance. Additionally, the episodic recollections of the experts using the funny putter were longer than their generic descriptions, not shorter as produced by the regular putter experts. Thus, when a proceduralized skill is disrupted by the imposition of novel task demands, 'expertise-induced amnesia' disappears. Furthermore, once experts start attending to task performance, their expert knowledge allows them to remember more of what they are attending to than novices. Note that it is not an easy thing for an expert to achieve this level of attention to the step-by-step control of performance. Consider again the second episodic memory protocol of experts using the regular putter – the results shown in Figure 14.1. Despite the fact that these experts had just experienced the first memory test and were warned that the second test was coming, they still did not recall as much about their putts as the novices. Therefore, simply wanting to pay attention and to remember, or knowing that this is expected, may not be enough to overcome expertise-induced amnesia.

In an attempt to further explore memory protocols across putter type (i.e. regular versus funny putter) and skill level (i.e. novice versus experienced golfers), we performed a qualitative analysis of the type of putting steps that individuals remembered and compared these steps across the generic and first episodic memory protocols. Memory protocol steps were divided into three categories: assessment or planning referred to deciding how to approach a particular putt, what problems it might present, and what properties the putt ought to have. Examples are 'read the green', 'read the line' (from the ball to the hole or target), 'focus on the line', and 'visualize the force needed to hit the ball'. Mechanics or execution referred to the components of the mechanical act that implement the putt. Examples are 'grip the putter with your right hand on top of your left', 'bring the club straight back', and 'accelerate through the ball', all of which deal with the effectors and the kinesthetic movements of the effectors required to implement a putt. Finally, ball destinations or outcomes referred to where the ball stopped or landed and hence to the degree of success.

As can be seen in Figure 14.3, assessment steps decreased in number from the generic to episodic protocol for the two experienced groups, regardless of the type of putter. The two novice groups showed similar numbers of assessment steps in their generic and episodic protocols. In terms of mechanical steps, the experienced golfers using the funny putter gave more steps that referred to putting mechanics than any other group. The experienced golfers with the regular putter highlighted fewer steps relating to mechanics. The two novice groups did not differ and fell between the two groups of experts with regard to the number of mechanics reported.

It is interesting to note that while expert golfers using either the regular or funny putter included fewer assessment steps in their episodic protocols than in their generic descriptions, a different pattern emerged for mechanics. Experienced golfers using the regular putter highlighted fewer steps related to mechanics in their episodic protocols in comparison to their generic descriptions. The funny putter experienced golfers provided more steps which related to mechanics (see Figure 14.3). The design of the funny putter was intended to specifically distort the mechanical act of implementing the putt. As a result, attention to the assessment and planning of the putt should not have been significantly influenced by putter type. The fact that the experienced golfers did not differ in terms of assessment steps included in their episodic memory protocols as a function of type of putter, yet did vary in their accounts of the mechanical actions involved in putting, is consistent with the notion that increased attention to performance as a result of novel task constraints serves specifically to enhance episodic memories for the altered parameters and components of skill execution.

In conclusion, the memory data reviewed above suggests that novices have sparse general putting knowledge, yet detailed episodic memories for performance

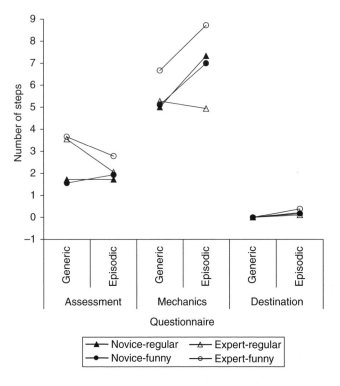

Figure 14.3 Mean number of steps in each category for the generic and first episodic questionnaire for each group. Adapted from Beilock and Carr (2001).

processes and procedures. Experts show the opposite pattern. Expert golfers have high levels of general knowledge but reduced episodic memories (i.e. 'expertise-induced amnesia') for heavily practiced phases of task activity in familiar skill execution situations (e.g. when using the regular putter). However, this pattern changes with the introduction of novel task constraints (i.e. the 'funny putter') that force experts to attend to the step-by-step processes of performance.

Attention and skill acquisition

The notion that different cognitive processes underlie various stages of skill acquisition, with a trend toward increased proceduralization at higher levels of expertise, not only carries implications for the quality of experts' and novices' generic and episodic performance memories, but also for the types of attentional manipulations that may influence performance at different levels of learning. Because novices must devote attentional capacity to task performance in ways that experts do not (Fitts, 1964; Fitts and Posner, 1967), novice and expert performers may be differentially affected by conditions that either draw attention away from, or toward, skill execution. Specifically, the capacity-demanding performance of novices may not afford these individuals the attentional resources necessary to devote to secondary task demands if required by the situation. However, the proceduralized performances of experts, that normally run outside of working memory, should leave attention available for the processing of other aspects of the stimulus situation, even stimuli not related at all to primary skill performance (Allport *et al.*, 1972; Leavitt, 1979; Smith and Chamberlin, 1992). Because the well-practised and proceduralized components of expert performance are not explicitly attended in real time, however, attention prompted toward skill execution may actually serve to break down or disrupt automated performance processes that normally run without such explicit attention or awareness (Beilock and Carr, 2001; Beilock *et al.*, 2002a; Lewis and Linder, 1997; Masters, 1992; Masters *et al.*, 1993; Marchant and Wang, 2001). In contrast, the novice, who must attend to the steps of skill execution in order to succeed, might not be harmed or could perhaps be helped by conditions that focus attention more squarely on the skill and prevent it from wandering.

In order to explore these possibilities, we conducted another putting study in which novice and experienced golfers performed the same task as described above under either dual-task or skill-focused attention conditions (see Beilock *et al.*, 2003). The dual-task attention condition involved putting while simultaneously listening to a series of recorded tones being played from a tape recorder. Participants were instructed to monitor the tones carefully, and each time they heard a specified target tone, to say the word 'tone' out loud. Tones (500 milliseconds each) occurred at a random time period once within every 2-seconds time interval. The target tone occurred randomly, once every four tones on average. In the skill-focused attention condition, participants were instructed to attend to a particular component of their golf putting swing. Specifically, individuals were instructed to monitor their swing and attempt to keep the club head straight, travelling towards the target along the same path as the ball, during the swing and follow through. Participants were informed that in order to assure that they were attending to the motion of the swing during the putt, they should say the word 'straight' out loud as they made contact with the ball. This particular component of the putting swing was chosen as the basis for the skill-focused manipulation because a straight club head is thought to be an important component of a successful golf putt (Jones *et al.*, 1998).

Individuals performed thirty-five initial putts, designed to familiarize them with our altered putting task requiring individuals to land the ball on a target rather than in a hole. Participants then took twenty practice putts in a single-task environment, twenty putts in a dual-task attention condition and twenty putts in a skill-focused attention condition. The order of the two attention conditions was counterbalanced across participants. The mean distance from the target that the ball landed after each putt for the twenty putts in the skill-focused and dual-task conditions was used as the measure of that condition's putting performance.

Novice golfers performed significantly worse in the dual-task condition in comparison to the skill-focused condition, as illustrated in Figure 14.4. Experienced

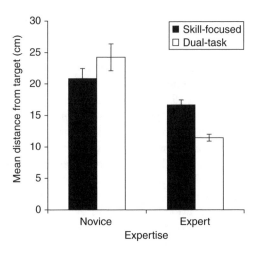

Figure 14.4 Mean distance (cm) from the centre of the target that the ball stopped
after each putt in the skill-focused and dual-task conditions for the
novice and experienced golfers. Error bars represent standard errors.
Adapted from Beilock *et al.* (in press).

golfers showed the opposite pattern, putting more accurately in the dual-task than
skill-focused attention condition. This pattern of results supports the notion that
the control structures driving performance differ as a function of skill level. Novice
performance is thought to be attended in real time (Fitts, 1964; Fitts and Posner,
1967). Thus, dual-task situations that draw attention away from performance harm
execution in comparison to conditions that prompt attention to online control.
Experienced performers, on the other hand, are thought not to explicitly attend
step-by-step execution. Consequently, attentional capacity is left over to devote to
secondary task demands, if the situation requires, without significantly disrupting
primary skill execution. However, if experts are asked to attend to performance in a
way that they are not accustomed (e.g. the skill-focused condition), this attention
serves to break down or disrupt execution, resulting in a less than optimal skill outcome. These negative effects of enhanced attention to skilled performance can not
only be seen in complex skills such as golf putting, but in more basic skills we use
everyday. For example, Wulf and colleagues have suggested that directing performers' attention to their movements through 'internal focus' feedback on a dynamic
balance task interferes with the automated control processes that usually control
balance movements outside of conscious scrutiny (Wulf and Prinz, 2001).

Implications for practice and instruction

The findings outlined in this chapter suggest that the effects of attention
on performance are dependent on an individual's skill level. This has obvious

implications for skill acquisition at lower levels of learning, as well as for performance at high levels of task proficiency across a variety of attention-demanding and pressure situations.

Attention and performance

Given the attentional demands of newly acquired performances, for example, it may be beneficial to limit the number of cues novices must attend to as they are learning to perform a specific task. This type of simplification for the sake of learning is often characterized as part-task practice in the motor learning literature (Magill, 1998) and has been proposed rather generally as a means to manage the heavy attention demands of learning new skills, whether sensori-motor or intellectual (e.g. Carlson *et al.*, 1990; Carr, 1984; Mattoon, 1994; Whaley and Fisk, 1993).

There are a number of different ways of instantiating part-task training regimens. Wightman and Lintern (1985) have suggested three: *fractionization* involves practicing separate components of an entire skill. *Simplification* is characterized by reducing the difficulty of the skill and practicing it in a unitary fashion. In a juggling task, for example, one might practice juggling with scarves prior to shifting over to flaming torches as a means to reduce the overall complexity of the juggling skill execution. Finally, *segmentation* involves separating a skill into separate components and progressively adding new components to skill practice. The segmentation approach is often seen in 'real-world' sports contexts.

In baseball, for example, children first learn to play 't-ball'. In this simplified form of baseball, a stationary 'tee' is substituted for a pitcher and the child's goal is to hit the ball off of the 'tee', which supports the ball at about waist height. Hitting the ball from the 'tee' eliminates the pitcher and the moving ball, limiting the number of stimuli that must be attended to by the novice batter. Given that novices are harmed by situations in which they must attend to many concurrent stimuli (e.g. the dual-task situations described above), the single-task t-ball situation allows the unpractised batter the attentional resources necessary to devote to learning an efficient and consistent swing pattern. Drawing on theories of skill acquisition and automaticity, with extended practice the swing may become proceduralized, freeing up attentional resources to be devoted to other aspects of the game situation. At higher levels of practice, a baseball player is able to successfully bat from a real pitcher as attention is not required for the step-by-step control of the swing and is thus available for attending to other components of play, such as tracking the movements of the pitcher and the ball. As we have seen above, attention to swinging the bat at this later stage of learning may not only be unnecessary, it may actually be detrimental to that aspect of performance. That is, attempting to explicitly attend to the step-by-step execution of a well-learned swing may actually hurt performance by slowing down or disrupting the proceduralized or automated swing movement. Theories of 'choking under pressure', to which we will return momentarily, propose just this effect.

At high levels of skill, however, there may be situations in which attention to performance is beneficial. When the goal is to explicitly alter performance processes in order to change execution parameters for the purpose of improving long-term skill performance, or in an attempt to achieve a different outcome, attention to performance may be beneficial. Attending to performance in this fashion has been proposed to be an important component of deliberate practice (Ericsson *et al.*, 1993), and may benefit both novice and experienced performers. In this type of situation, one might imagine that an experienced baseball player is interested in altering their swing pattern. In order to achieve this goal, the player must explicitly attend to the specific parameters of the swing. Because this process requires attention, the baseball player may not have the resources necessary to effectively deal with other stimuli in the environment (such as inconsistent or unpredictable pitches).

Furthermore, the act of paying attention may in itself be difficult for the expert. Turning back to the first experiment described in this chapter (Beilock and Carr, 2001), even when experts putting under normal conditions (i.e. experts using the regular putter) knew they were going to be expected to recall their memories of putting performance (in the second episodic memory test), they still showed a degree of expertise-induced amnesia. Because episodic performance memories are dependent on attention at encoding, this lack of memory suggests that even when experts are instructed to attend to their performance and are trying to follow the instructions, they may have difficulty doing so. Our baseball player interested in altering swing parameters then, may also need to expend additional executive resources concentrating and maintaining attentional focus on step-by-step control. To deal with these attentional demands, the batter may use a machine that produces predictable pitches, thereby reducing the total amount of information to be attended in the situation and affording the player the attention necessary to devote to correcting the swing process. Once the swing is corrected and the control structures of performance return to a proceduralized state, the batter may once again have the attention necessary to devote to a live pitcher, while ignoring or not explicitly attending to the more mechanical aspects of swinging the bat.

Choking under pressure

When the goal is to alter execution parameters, attention to performance may be beneficial. However, when optimal real-time performance is desired, attention to step-by-step execution may instead serve to slow, disrupt or dismantle high-level performance. 'Explicit monitoring' or 'execution focus' theories of choking under pressure suggest that sub-optimal performance of a well-learned skill under pressure results from an attempt to exert explicit monitoring and control on proceduralized knowledge that is best run-off as an uninterrupted and unanalysed structure (Baumeister, 1984; Beilock and Carr, 2001; Beilock *et al.*, 2002b; Lewis and Linder, 1997; Masters, 1992, 2000). Thus, high-level skills based on an automated or proceduralized skill representation may be more susceptible to the negative consequences of performance pressure than less practiced performances. This is due to the fact that the former, but not the latter, operates largely outside of working memory and pressure-induced attention may harm processes that are normally devoid of step-by-step attentional control.

Beilock and Carr (2001) have found support for the notion that well-learned, but not novice, sensori-motor skill execution is susceptible to performance decrements under pressure via this mechanism of inappropriate explicit monitoring or execution focus. Participants learned a golf putting skill to a high-level and were exposed to a high pressure situation both early and late in practice. Early in practice, pressure to do well actually facilitated performance. At later stages of learning, performance decrements under pressure emerged. It appears that the proceduralized performances of experts are negatively affected by performance pressure. Novice skill execution, however, is not harmed by pressure-induced attention to execution as less skilled performance is already explicitly attended in real time. This finding is consistent with Marchant and Wang's (2001) assertion that most of the evidence for choking under pressure has been derived from well-learned sensori-motor tasks that automate via proceduralization with extended practice.

Support for explicit monitoring theories can also be seen in training studies that serve to inoculate individuals against the negative effects of performance pressure by adapting them (during training) to the type of explicit attention to execution that pressure is thought to induce. For example, both Beilock and Carr (2001) and Lewis and Linder (1997) have found that learning a golf putting skill in a self-awareness-heightened environment inoculates individuals against the negative effects of performance pressure at high levels of practice. In both of these studies, participants were trained on a golf putting task under either a self-awareness condition (in which individuals putted while being videotaped for later analysis by golf professionals) or under a normal, single-task condition and then exposed to a high-pressure situation. The self-awareness manipulation was designed to expose performers to having attention called to themselves and their performance in a way intended to induce explicit monitoring of skill execution. In both the studies by Beilock and Carr and Lewis and Linder, it was found that pressure caused choking in those individuals who had not been adapted to self-awareness, a finding consistent with explicit monitoring theories. Furthermore, in the Lewis and Linder study, it was found that the introduction of a secondary task (counting backward from 100) while performing under pressure helped to alleviate performance decrements (for confirmatory data, see Mullen and Hardy, 2000). Because the secondary task served to prevent the pressure-induced instantiation of maladaptive explicit attention to automated or proceduralized performance processes, choking under pressure was alleviated.

Choking under pressure at high skill levels, then, may be alleviated by the instantiation of a secondary task during the actual high-pressure performance. A 'key word', that takes a golfer's mind off of the step-by-step mechanics involved in a simple 3-foot putt, or a song that a batter hums while up to bat, may prevent the type of maladaptive explicit attentional control that performance pressure is thought to induce. Further work on the judicious adoption of such self-distraction techniques seems quite worthwhile.

Summary and conclusions

While overt performance is one component that separates novice from well-learned skill execution, the cognitive control structures governing execution appear to distinguish unpractised from high level skills as well. Theories of skill acquisition and automaticity have proposed that distinct cognitive processes are involved at different stages of skill execution. Early in learning, individuals are thought to attend to the step-by-step processes of performance. However, once a high level of performance has been achieved, constant online attentional control may not be necessary (Anderson, 1983, 1993; Fitts and Posner, 1967; Logan, 1988).

While a progression from a declarative knowledge base to proceduralization is a powerful conception of the cognitive processes governing skill acquisition, alternative explanations of skill acquisition are available and have merit. Some of these alternatives propose differences in the type of representation that underlies skills early in learning, with implications for the type of training conditions that are beneficial to the novice. For example, it has been suggested that explicit declarative knowledge is not necessary in the acquisition of highly structured sequential knowledge analogous to the syntax of language production. Research in artificial grammar, for example, has demonstrated that in some cases learning may benefit from a lack of explicit instruction (for a review, see Reber, 1989). Masters has exported such an argument to the domain of sensori-motor skill execution (e.g. Masters, 2000).

Additional alternatives to the conceptualization of proceduralization have also been suggested as a means to describe well-learned performance. Logan (1988) has proposed an instance-based theory of automaticity in which highly practised performance is based on the direct retrieval of specific past episodes or instances of execution from long-term memory, rather than relying on a procedure or programme that can generate new performances in an effective, efficient manner. Performance based on retrieval of instances is thought to differ from earlier, less practiced stages of execution in which problem solutions and task performances are derived through the implementation of an explicit rule-based algorithm. It is not likely, however, that sensori-motor skill execution is governed by instance-based answer retrieval, as instance-based theories of automaticity do not allow for transfer of performance to novel situations, something that can occur in practiced sensori-motor skills (Koh and Meyer, 1991), albeit often with some cost. In our laboratory, we are currently comparing instance-based (e.g. mathematical problem solving) versus proceduralized skills (e.g. golf putting) in terms of their susceptibility to performance decrements in high pressure and attention-demanding situations (Beilock et al., 2002b).

In conclusion, in this chapter we have presented evidence concerning the differential attentional demands and changing memory structures that underlie performance at various skill levels. The present findings highlight the notion that one must look beyond overt performance measures in order to truly understand the variables mediating skill execution across levels of expertise. A continued exploration of the processes and procedures underlying performance at different levels of learning will not only serve to enhance our understanding of the skill acquisition process, but will add to our knowledge base concerning the ability to maintain high-level performance in situations where incentives for optimal task performance are at a maximum.

References

Abernethy, B., Thomas, K. T. and Thomas, J. T. (1993). Strategies for improving understanding of motor expertise [or mistakes we have made and things we have learned!!]. In J. L. Starkes and F. Allard (Eds), *Cognitive issues in motor expertise* (pp. 317–356). Amsterdam: Elsevier Science.

Allard, F. and Starkes, J. L. (1991). Motor-skill experts in sports, dance and other domains. In K. A. Ericsson and J. Smith (Eds), *Toward a general theory of expertise* (pp. 126–152). Cambridge: Cambridge University press.

Allport, D. A., Antonis, B. and Reynolds, P. (1972). On the division of attention: a disproof of the single channel hypothesis. *Quarterly Journal of Experimental Psychology*, 24, 225–235.

Anderson, J. R. (1982). Acquisition of a cognitive skill. *Psychological Review*, 89, 369–406.

Anderson, J. R. (1983). *The architecture of cognition*. Cambridge, MA: Harvard University press.

Anderson, J. R. (1993). *Rules of mind*. Hillsdale, NJ: Erlbaum.

Anderson, J. R. and Lebiere, C. (1998). *The atomic components of thought*. Mahwah, NJ: Erlbaum.

Baumeister, R. F. (1984). Choking under pressure: self-consciousness and paradoxical effects of incentives on skillful performance. *Journal of Personality and Social Psychology*, 46, 610–620.

Beilock, S. L. and Carr, T. H. (2001). On the fragility of skilled performance: what governs choking under pressure? *Journal of Experimental Psychology: General*, 130, 701–725.

Beilock, S. L., Carr, T. H., MacMahon, C. and Starkes, J. L. (2002a). When paying attention becomes counterproductive: impact of divided versus skill-focused attention on novice and experienced performance of sensorimotor skills. *Journal of Experimental Psychology: Applied*, 8, 6–16.

Beilock, S. L., Feltz, D. L. and Carr, T. H. (2002b). More on the fragility of skilled performance: choking under pressure is caused by different mechanisms in cognitive versus sensorimotor skills. Poster presented at the Annual Meeting of the Psychonomic Society. Kansas City, Missouri.

Beilock, S. L., Wierenga, S. A. and Carr, T. H. (2002c). Expertise, attention, and memory in sensorimotor skill execution: impact of novel task constraints on dual-task performance and episodic memory. *The Quarterly Journal of Experimental Psychology: Human Experimental Psychology*, 55, 1211–1240.

Beilock, S. L., Bertenthal, B. I., McCoy, A. M. and Carr, T. H. (in press). Haste does not always make waste: expertise, direction of attention, and speed versus accuracy in performing sensorimotor skills. *Psychonomic Bulletin and Review*.

Brown, T. L. and Carr, T. H. (1989). Automaticity in skill acquisition: mechanisms for reducing interference in concurrent performance. *Journal of Experimental Psychology: Human Perception and Performance*, 15, 686–700.

Bryan, W. L. and Harter, N. (1899). Studies on the telegraphic language: the acquisition of a hierarchy of habits. *Psychological Review*, 6, 345–375.

Carlson, R. A., Khoo, B. H. and Elliott, R. G. (1990). Component practice and exposure to a problem-solving context. *Human Factors*, 32, 267–286.

Carr, T. H. (1984) Attention, skill, and intelligence: some speculations on extreme individual differences in human performance. In P. Brooks, C. McCauley and R. D. Sperber (Eds), *Learning, cognition, and mental retardation*. Hillsdale, NJ: Lawrence Erlbaum.

Chase, W. G. and Simon, H. A. (1973). Perception in chess. *Cognitive Psychology*, 4, 55–81.

Craik, F. M., Govini, R., Naveh-Benjamin, M. and Anderson, N. D. (1996). The effects of divided attention on encoding and retrieval processes in human memory. *Journal of Experimental Psychology: General*, 125, 159–180.

De Groot, A. (1978). *Thought and choice in chess*. The Hague: Mouton (original work published in 1946).

Ericsson, K. A., Krampe, R. T. and Tesch-Romer, C. (1993). The role of deliberate practice in the acquisition of expert performance. *Psychological Review*, 100, 363–406.

Ericsson, K. A. and Polson, P. G. (1988). An experimental analysis of the mechanisms of a memory skill. *Journal of Experimental Psychology: Learning, Memory & Cognition*, 14, 305–316.

Fitts, P. M. (1964). Perceptual-motor skill learning. In A. W. Melton (Ed.), *Categories of human learning*. New York: Academic Press.

Fitts, P. M. and Posner, M. I. (1967). *Human performance*. Belmont, CA: Brooks/Cole.

Jones, B. T., Davis, M., Crenshaw, B., Behar, T. and Davis, M. (1998). *Classic instruction in golf*. New York: Broadway.

Keele, S. W. (1986). Motor control. In K. R. Boff, L. Kaufman and J. P. Thomas (Eds), *Handbook of perception and human performance*, Vol. 7. New York: John Wiley.

Keele, S. W. and Summers, J. J. (1976). The structure of motor programs. In G. E. Stelmach (Ed.), *Motor control: issues and trends* (pp. 109–142). New York: Academic Press.

Koh, K. and Meyer, D. E. (1991). Function learning: induction of continuous stimulus–response relations. *Journal of Experimental Psychology: Learning, Memory and Cognition*, 17, 811–836.

Leavitt, J. (1979). Cognitive demands of skating and stick handling in ice hockey. *Canadian Journal of Applied Sport Sciences*, 4, 46–55.

Lewis, B. and Linder, D. (1997). Thinking about choking? attentional processes and paradoxical performance. *Personality and Social Psychology Bulletin*, 23, 937–944.

Logan, G. D. (1988). Toward an instance theory of automatization. *Psychological Review*, 95, 492–527.

Magill, R. A. (1998). *Motor learning concepts and applications*. Boston, MA: McGraw-Hill.

Marchant, D., and Wang, J. (2001). Choking: Current Issues in Theory and Practice. Paper presented at the 10th World Congress of Sport Psychology. Skiathos, Greece.

Masters, R. S. W. (1992). Knowledge, knerves and know-how: the role of explicit versus implicit knowledge in the breakdown of a complex motor skill under pressure. *British Journal of Psychology*, 83, 343–358.

Masters, R. S. W. (2000). Theoretical aspects of implicit learning in sport. *International Journal of Sport Psychology*, 31, 530–541.

Masters, R. S. W., Polman, R. C. J. and Hammond, N. V. (1993). 'Reinvestment': a dimension of personality implicated in skill breakdown under pressure. *Personality and Individual Differences*, 14, 655–666.

Mattoon, J. S. (1994). Designing instructional simulations. Effects of instructional control and type of training task on developing display-interpretation skills. *International Journal of Aviation Psychology*, 4, 189–209.

McKeithen, K. B., Reitman, J. S., Reuter, H. H. and Hirtle, S. C. (1981). Knowledge organization and skill differences in computer programmers. *Cognitive Psychology*, 13, 307–325.

Mullen, R. and Hardy, L. (2000). State anxiety and motor performance: testing the conscious processing hypothesis. *Journal of Sports Sciences*, 18, 785–799.

Naveh-Benjamin, M., Craik, F. I., Guez, J. and Dori, H. (1998). Effects of divided attention on encoding and retrieval processes in human memory: further support for an asymmetry. *Journal of Experimental Psychology: Learning, Memory, and Cognition*, 24, 1091–1104.

Proctor, R. W. and Dutta, A. (1995). *Skill acquisition and human performance*. Thousand Oaks, CA: Sage.

Raichle, M. E., Fiez, J. A., Videen, T. O., Macleod, A. M. K., Pardo, J. V., Fox, P. T. and Petersen, S. E. (1994). Practice-related changes in human brain functional-anatomy during nonmotor learning. *Cerebral Cortex*, 4, 8–26.

Reber, A. S. (1989). Implicit learning and tacit knowledge. *Journal of Experimental Psychology: General*, 118, 219–235.

Reimann, P. and Chi, M. T. (1989). Human expertise in complex problem solving. In K. J. Gilhooly (Ed.), *Human machine and problem-solving* (pp. 161–189). New York: Plenum.

Smith, M. D. and Chamberlin, C. J. (1992). Effect of adding cognitively demanding tasks on soccer skill performance. *Perceptual and Motor Skills*, 75, 955–961.

Staszewski, J. J. (1988). Skilled memory and expert mental calculation. In M. T. H. Chi, R. Glaser and M. J. Farr (Eds), *The nature of expertise* (pp. 71–128). Hillsdale, NJ: Lawrence Erlbaum Associates.

Starkes, J. L., Deakin, J. M., Lindley, S. and Crisp, F. (1987). Motor versus verbal recall of ballet sequences by young expert dancers. *Journal of Sport Psychology*, 9, 222–230.

Whaley, C. and Fisk, A. D. (1993). Effects of part-task training on memory set unitization and retention of memory-dependent skilled search. *Human Factors*, 35, 639–652.

Wightman, D. C. and Lintern, G. (1985). Part-task training strategies for tracking and manual control. *Human Factors*, 27, 267–283.

Wulf, G. and Prinz, W. (2001). Directing attention to movement effects enhances learning: a review. *Psychonomic Bulletin and Review*, 8, 648–660.

15 Perceptual and cognitive expertise in sport

Implications for skill acquisition and performance enhancement

A. Mark Williams, Paul Ward and Nicholas J. Smeeton

Sport has become the largest entertainment industry in the world. For example, an estimated television audience of over three billion people, around half of the world's population, watched the final of the 2002 soccer World Cup in Japan and Korea. As sport continues to play a significant role in popular culture, there is increasing interest in the personal and professional lives of sporting superstars. The riches available to those who are successful in the sporting domain have also risen markedly in recent years and many sports performers now enjoy the lifestyle and media attention once the sole preserve of stars from the popular music and film industries. An issue of significant intuitive interest is what makes these athletes 'great'? Why are these performers at the peak of their sport whereas others have fallen by the wayside at various points in the journey from tentative beginner to supreme international superstar?

In recent years there has been growing acceptance that skill in sport is not merely a by-product of physical prowess. As in other domains such as architecture, physics, mathematics and music, expert athletes are typically characterized by superior perceptual and cognitive skills compared to their novice counterparts (Williams *et al.*, 1999). The ability to 'read' an opponent's intentions and to formulate an appropriate response based on strategic, tactical and technical considerations would appear crucial to successful performance in sport. Anticipation and decision-making skills are presumed to be particularly important as performers reach higher levels of excellence since athletic groups become more homogenous with regard to their physical and physiological characteristics (Reilly *et al.*, 2000; Williams and Reilly, 2000). In this chapter, we review contemporary research and theory on perceptual and cognitive expertise in sport, with a particular focus on anticipation skill. Key research findings that have emerged over the last 20 years are highlighted and implications for future research discussed.

Whilst the importance of perceptual and cognitive skills to elite performance is now more widely accepted, there is still speculation as to the extent to which these skills are amenable to practice and instruction. Historically, the widespread view held by sport practitioners was that athletes' propensity to acquire such skills is genetically determined and that it is too difficult or even impossible to enhance the acquisition of these skills via structured training programmes. More recently, there is at least tacit acceptance that such factors may be enhanced through suitable training interventions. For example, we know that performance on sport-specific tests of perceptual and cognitive skill improves with domain-specific practice rather than maturational age, even for novice performers (Abernethy, 1988; Ward and Williams, 2003). A reasonable number of researchers have also shown improvements in anticipatory performance following the implementation of training programmes designed to enhance perceptual and cognitive skill (see Williams and Grant, 1999; Williams and Ward, 2003). In the final section of this chapter, we explore the importance of research on perceptual and cognitive expertise for performance enhancement in sport. We review recent empirical work and highlight implications for the design, implementation and assessment of training programmes to develop anticipation skill.

Perceptual and cognitive expertise in sport: some key findings

We begin by reviewing some of the major findings that have emerged over the last two decades of research endeavour in the area of expertise in sport. The intention is to highlight the perceptual and cognitive, characteristics that differentiate skilled from less-skilled performers. More comprehensive reviews of the literature are provided elsewhere (see Starkes and Ericsson, 2003; Starkes *et al.*, 2001; Williams *et al.*, 1999).

Pattern recognition

Experts are better than novices at recognizing and recalling patterns of play from within their domain of expertise. The initial work by Allard *et al.* (1980) involved basketball, but findings have subsequently been extended to a variety of sports such as volleyball, rugby, field hockey and soccer (see Williams *et al.*, 1999). Typically, experts and novices are presented with 'structured' (i.e. sequences taken directly from match play) and 'unstructured' (e.g. teams warming up prior to a match) film clips. Following a short viewing period, participants are required to recall players' positions at the end of each action sequence (recall paradigm) or to indicate whether they had viewed the action sequence previously (recognition paradigm). The experts' superiority in recall and recognition performance is expected on structured trials only. Although a small expert advantage may occasionally be observed on the unstructured viewing sequences (see Gobet and Simon, 1996), these clips are intended as a control condition to ensure that there are no differences between skill groups in visual short-term memory.

Williams *et al.* (1993) employed the recall paradigm to examine expert soccer defenders' perceptual and cognitive superiority over novices. Players were presented with structured trials containing offensive patterns of play ending with a shot at goal or a pass into the attacking third of the field, whilst the control trials included unstructured film clips involving players walking on and off the field, teams warming up prior to a match, or a stoppage in play whilst an injured player received treatment. Following each 10-second action sequence, participants were required to recall players' positions on a computer-generated image of the field of play. Recall error was determined by comparing the degree of correspondence between the presented and reconstructed player positions. Expert players had smaller recall errors than novices on the structured trials, whereas, as predicted, no differences were observed between groups in the unstructured condition. In a follow-up study, Williams and Davids (1995) used the recognition paradigm to show that expert soccer defenders are faster and more accurate than their novice counterparts in recognizing previously viewed action sequences. Original theoretical proposals suggested that experts can circumvent the capacity limits of short-term memory on structured trials by clustering or grouping individual elements (e.g. individual player positions) into larger and more meaningful units (e.g. game configurations) (see Chase and Simon, 1973). More recently, empirical evidence suggests that experts are able to extend working memory to include storage of task-related information in long-term memory by associating these retrieval cues (e.g. perceptual features or chunks) with higher-level cognitive retrieval structures (see Ericsson and Kintsch, 1995; Richman *et al.*, 1996).

Although the ability to recall and recognize structured playing sequences is regarded as the strongest predictor of anticipation skill in team games such as soccer (see Williams and Davids, 1995), no attempt has been made to determine the minimal essential information underlying the pattern recognition process. What sources of information define and shape the emerging pattern of play? Does the expert defender need to be aware of the positions of all the opposing players or is each pattern of play defined by a few unique features? It may be that each pattern is defined by the relationship between a few select players such as the central midfield and forward players and that, in the majority of instances, the positions of other players such as the opposing defenders and goalkeeper provide redundant or at best confirmatory information. The use of visual search, point light and event occlusion paradigms may offer practical utility in attempting to answer such questions.

Advance cue usage

The ability to anticipate future events based upon information emanating from an opponent's postural orientation is essential in fast ball sports where the speed of play often dictates that decisions must be made in advance of the action. Jones and Miles (1978) are credited with having undertaken the original work in this area using the temporal occlusion technique in tennis. In this approach, the action under investigation (e.g. return of serve in tennis) is filmed from the performer's customary perspective. This film is then selectively edited so that a varying extent of advance and ball flight information is presented. In this seminal work, expert, intermediate and novice tennis players were presented with filmed images of an opponent's serve and were required to indicate where the ball would land within the service court area using a pen and paper response.

A repeated measures design was employed whereby each serve was presented under three different temporal occlusion conditions: 336 milliseconds after impact of the ball on the racket (condition A), 126 milliseconds after impact (condition B) and 42 milliseconds (condition C) before contact. The results showed that expert tennis players were more accurate than their less expert counterparts in anticipating the ball's intended destination at the earliest occlusion periods (conditions B and C). The expert players' scores were better than chance even at the earliest occlusion condition (condition C), signifying that the ability to predict the direction of an opponent's serve based on postural orientation prior to ball/racket contact is an important characteristic of high-level performers. The importance of advance cue utilization has subsequently been demonstrated in a variety of sports using laboratory-based procedures such as the temporal occlusion and response time paradigms, and field-based techniques involving high-speed film analysis and liquid crystal occlusion glasses (for a review, see Starkes *et al.*, 2001; Williams *et al.*, 1999).

A recent suggestion is that the ability to extract meaningful information from an opponent's postural orientation may be due to experts being more attuned than novices to the biological or relative motion presented in movement kinematics rather than the extraction of a specific information cue. Ward *et al.* (2002) showed that expert tennis players' superiority over novices was maintained even when the task required that they anticipate the direction of forehand and backhand shots presented in point-light form (i.e. dots of light representing the positions of the major joint centres filmed against a black background) rather than under 'normal' viewing conditions. The experts' visual search behaviours were also fairly stable across the two conditions, in contrast to novices, implying that the expert group extracted similar sources of information under point-light and 'normal' viewing conditions. Background and structural information are removed when the display is presented under point-light compared with normal viewing conditions. The suggestion is that skilled performers use the relative motion between joints (intralimb kinematics), limbs (interlimb kinematics) and/or body segments (e.g. relative to the centre of moment) to guide skillful action rather than a specific information cue(s) (cf. Abernethy *et al.*, 2001; Johansson, 1975). Point-light displays therefore offer a potentially fruitful approach when attempting to identify the invariant sources of information underlying perceptual skill (e.g. see also Horn *et al.*, 2002).

Visual search behaviour

Sophisticated eye movement registration systems have been employed to determine the orientation of visual gaze during sports performance. Although data have been collected *in situ* in sports like tennis (Singer *et al.*, 1998), table tennis (Rodrigues *et al.*, 2002) and basketball (Vickers, 1996), the majority of researchers have examined visual behaviour using film simulations of sport situations. Whilst there is some contradictory evidence (see Abernethy and Russell, 1987), the consensus is that experts focus their gaze on more informative areas of the display compared to novices, enabling them to more effectively anticipate action requirements (for a detailed review, see Williams *et al.*, 1999).

The search behaviour employed is determined by a range of factors in addition to the performer's skill or experience level, such as the nature of the task and the physical and emotional stress created by the competitive environment. For example, in team sports such as soccer, different search strategies are employed when viewing the whole field (i.e. eleven versus eleven simulations) compared to micro-situations within the game (e.g. three versus three or one versus one duels), and when participants are presented with offensive compared with defensive simulations (e.g. see Helsen and Pauwels, 1993; Williams and Davids, 1998; Williams *et al.*, 1994). Similarly, marked changes in search behaviour are commonly observed when performers are placed under emotional or physiological stress, due to the effects of peripheral narrowing or hypervigilance (e.g. see Janelle *et al.*, 1999; Vickers *et al.*, 1999; Williams and Elliott, 1999).

The visual search behaviour employed by sports performers may also reflect the unique role played by the peripheral visual system in extracting task-relevant information to guide performance. To this end, the distinction between visual search behaviour and cue usage should be highlighted. The visual search strategy employed by the performer highlights the way in which the eyes move around the display to extract task-relevant information, whereas, in contrast, cue usage refers to the specific source(s) of information used by the performer to guide action. Although cue usage can often be inferred from point-of-gaze data, in certain situations skilled performers fixate gaze (i.e. the fovea) centrally and extract information via peripheral vision. The use of such 'visual pivots', which have been observed in a variety of sport tasks (e.g. see Williams and Davids, 1998; Williams and Elliott, 1999), may offer the expert several advantages. For instance, a visual pivot strategy reduces the number of eye movements employed during task performance and, since there is a reduced threshold for information processing when the eyes move from one fixation to the next (i.e. saccadic suppression), this would likely lead to an increase in processing efficiency. Attention can be switched from one area of the display to another covertly using peripheral vision rather than via overt eye movements (see Nougier *et al.*, 1991; Posner and Raichle, 1994). Another suggestion is that information may be processed more quickly through peripheral vision, which is particularly sensitive to motion, rather than via the fovea (Milner and Goodale, 1995).

Situational probabilities

As well as their enhanced ability to extract contextual information from the display, experts are proposed to use knowledge stored in long-term memory to establish accurate expectations of likely events as the pattern of action unfolds. The underlying assumption is that experts dismiss many events as being 'highly improbable' and attach a hierarchy of probabilities to the remaining events, thus facilitating anticipation (see Williams *et al.*, 1999). Alain and colleagues (e.g. Alain and Proteau, 1980; Alain *et al.*, 1986; Alain and Sarrazin, 1990) carried out the initial work in this area. Alain and Proteau (1980) examined the extent to which defensive players in various racquet sports made use of situational probabilities to anticipate the shots available to their adversaries. The decision-making behaviour of squash, tennis, badminton and racquetball players was studied in the game situation by filming some of the rallies, allowing participants to view the film and then asking them specific questions regarding shot selection during the rally. Players were asked to comment on the subjective probabilities they had assigned to their opponent's shots. The results showed that players evaluated the probability of each possible event that could occur and then used this information to maximize the efficiency of subsequent behaviour. Players' initial anticipatory movements were guided by their expectations with subsequent corrective or confirmatory movements being made on the basis of current information or contextual cues.

In a more recent study, Ward and Williams (2003) asked elite and sub-elite soccer players to assign probability values to the 'best passing options' available to a player in possession of the ball. Film sequences were paused immediately prior to the ball being passed and participants were required to highlight likely passing options. The elite players were better than the sub-elite group at identifying those who were in the best position to receive the ball and were more accurate in assigning an appropriate probability to players in threatening and non-threatening positions, as determined by a panel of expert coaches. It appears that experts 'hedge their bets' judiciously applying their expectations and processing contextual information more effectively than novice participants. The sub-elite players, in contrast, were less efficient in their selection of critical and non-critical players and were not as adept at assigning a hierarchy of probabilities to likely events. Further research is required to determine how expert athletes use situational probabilities to guide their search for contextual information during skilful perception.

To summarize, when compared to their less skilled counterparts, skilled performers are faster and more accurate in recognizing and recalling patterns of play, are better at anticipating their opponents' actions based on contextual information (e.g. pick-up of postural information cues), have more effective and pertinent visual search strategies and are more accurate in their expectation of what is likely to happen given a particular set of circumstances. The consensus seems to be that expert performers develop knowledge and skills that enable them to deal effectively with a variety of related performance scenarios. Experts are able to encode information in memory more effectively such that they can anticipate future retrieval demands and access relevant knowledge more rapidly than novices (Ericsson and Delaney, 1999; Ericsson and Kintsch, 1995). An important question considered in the next section is whether these skills develop through maturation and practice or whether skilled players are endowed with superior 'game reading' capabilities than less skilled performers.

Maturation and practice

The majority of researchers have used adult participants to identify the important characteristics underlying perceptual and cognitive skill in sport. Few researchers have examined if these skill-based differences are apparent at an early age and whether they improve as a function of maturation and practice. Abernethy (1988) showed that the ability to anticipate an opponent's intentions based on postural cues improves with age using 12, 15 and 18 year old badminton players, whereas Tenenbaum et al. (2000) reported comparable conclusions with groups of 8–10, 11–13, 14–17 and 18 year old tennis players. Findings were less conclusive with regard to the age at which these skill-based differences in advance cue utilization emerged. In Abernethy's (1988) study no differences in anticipation skill were apparent between expert and novice participants across the three age categories. However, in a previous study using the same test procedures, skill-based differences were apparent with adult performers. Similarly, in the absence of any significant skill effects, Tenenbaum et al. (2000) reported only low to moderate effect sizes between skill groups for the three youngest age categories, whilst larger effect sizes were evident for the older age groups.

Ward and Williams (2003) showed that differences in perceptual and cognitive skills were apparent between groups of elite and sub-elite soccer players as early as 8–9 years of age. The elite soccer players were superior to their sub-elite counterparts in predicting key player involvement when observing attacking plays and in assigning more accurate probability values to each player. The elite players were also able to use advance information available within emerging patterns of play and from postural cues more effectively than sub-elite players. These findings suggest that 8–9 year old elite soccer players possess a comprehensive knowledge of the relationships between players, readily perceive the relative importance of each player and can pick up on their intended actions to a greater extent compared to sub-elite players. Although skill-based differences were apparent at an early age, the older age groups (i.e. 10–11, 12–13, 14–15, 16–17 years) generally showed better performance on various measures of perceptual and cognitive skill compared to their younger counterparts (cf. Abernethy, 1988; Tenenbaum et al., 2000).

In a follow-up study, Ward et al. (submitted) attempted to determine whether the differences in perceptual and cognitive skills between the elite and sub-elite 8–9 year olds were related to the players' practice history profiles (i.e. a function of domain-relevant practice rather than innate talent). Semi-structured interviews and performance dairies were employed to determine the age at which players commenced participation in the sport and the typical amount of time devoted to deliberate practice activities. Figure 15.1 indicates that although both groups of players commenced participation at a similar age, by 9 years of age the elite players had accumulated around an extra 200 hours of team and individual practice and match play. In the absence of any growth-related differences between skill groups at each age, it seems likely that the additional degree of

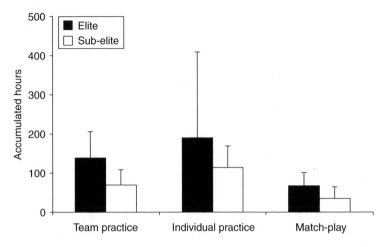

Figure 15.1 The total number of accumulated practice hours in team and individual practice as well as match play for elite and sub-elite soccer players between 6 and 9 years of age (data from Ward *et al.*, submitted).

deliberate practice contributed to the skill-based differences in performance observed on the tests of perceptual and cognitive skill.

Although perceptual and cognitive skills develop with age and sport-specific experience, there is evidence to suggest that these adaptations may at least be partly determined by genetics. Williams and Davids (1995) tested the perceptual and cognitive skills of experienced high- and low-skill soccer players. Participants were matched on experience (e.g. number of competitive matches played, amount of practice undertaken, degree of coaching to which they had been exposed and number of matches watched both 'live' and on television), but differed in their respective skill levels (i.e. amateur\recreational players compared with semi-professional players). The high-skill players demonstrated superior performance compared with low-skill participants on measures of anticipation, recall and recognition skill. These findings imply that the high-skill players' superior perceptual skill may be a constituent of skill or ability rather than purely a byproduct of their greater experience or exposure to the task. These conclusions should be viewed cautiously given the potentially confounding effect caused by differences between the two groups in the quality rather than quantity of practice exposure (Ericsson, 1996; Ericsson *et al.*, 1993). However, a player's genotype is likely to influence and potentially determine responsiveness to practice or training (cf. Bouchard *et al.*, 1997). This latter observation does not undermine the presumption that perceptual and cognitive skills are highly amenable to environmental influences such as practice and instruction, rather performance is likely determined by a complex interaction between initial ability and the quality and quantity of experience (Singer and Janelle, 1999).

Whilst the opportunity to influence a player's genotype profile is rather limited, at least for the time being, there would appear to be considerable potential in attempting to determine the nature of the practice activities that may facilitate gene expression, shape the phenotype and are most likely to elicit improvements in perceptual and cognitive skill development. In the final section of this chapter we consider the issue of training in greater detail. The important question, both practically and theoretically, is what type of instruction is likely to facilitate the acquisition of perceptual and cognitive skills?

Developing perceptual and cognitive skills in sport: the role of practice and instruction

In this section, we consider empirical evidence in favour of training programmes designed to enhance perceptual and cognitive skill. First, we review the typical approach used to train players to more effectively pick up postural information cues. We then consider evidence supporting the trainability of other perceptual and cognitive skills such as pattern recognition and use of situational probabilities. Finally, we highlight some avenues for future research by considering what type of instruction is most likely to facilitate the acquisition of perceptual and cognitive skills.

Advance cue utilization

The majority of researchers have attempted to improve anticipation skill by highlighting the important information cues underlying performance. The typical approach is to film the action (e.g. return of serve in tennis) from the performer's customary perspective and then to highlight important postural cues using various combinations of real time and slow motion video replay, instruction as to the expected response requirements and feedback on task performance. The information to be highlighted is normally identified from previous literature or using eye movement recording, verbal reports and/or film occlusion techniques (see Williams et al., 1999). Performance is assessed pre- and post-intervention, typically using an established film-based test of anticipation skill. The improvement observed on the post-test relative to the pre-test is assumed to indicate the effectiveness of the intervention. This approach, for example, has been used successfully to improve soccer goalkeepers' performance at penalty kicks and tennis players' ability to return serve effectively (e.g. see Farrow et al., 1998; Singer et al., 1994; Williams and Burwitz, 1993).

Although researchers have reported improvements in performance following such interventions, several methodological shortcomings have been highlighted. In particular, researchers have neglected to employ placebo (e.g. technical skill training) and/or control (e.g. complete pre- and post-test only) groups and, consequently, the improvements observed might be due to increased test familiarity or confirmation bias rather than a meaningful training effect. Other major problems include the absence of any measure of transfer to determine whether improvements observed in the laboratory transfer to the performance setting and the omission of a delayed retention test to establish long-term training effects. A more detailed and critical review of early perceptual training literature is provided elsewhere (e.g. see Abernethy *et al.*, 1998; Williams and Grant, 1999; Williams and Ward, 2003).

Williams and colleagues have recently addressed many of these concerns. In one study, Williams *et al.* (2003) attempted to improve the anticipation skills of field-hockey goalkeepers in the penalty-flick situation. Twenty-four novice goalkeepers were separated into three groups of similar ability. A training group was exposed to 45 minutes of video simulation training whereby the key information cues underlying anticipation of the penalty flick were highlighted under normal viewing and using a 'freeze-frame' facility, and an opportunity was provided to practice under progressively shorter viewing conditions. A control group merely completed the pre- and post-tests, like the placebo group, which also viewed a 45-minute instructional video focusing on the technical skills involved in hockey goalkeeping. A laboratory-based anticipation test required participants to respond to near 'life size' images of the hockey flick presented on film, whereas a measure of transfer was obtained by requiring goalkeepers to respond to actual penalty flicks in the field taken by the same players as employed in the test film. In order to facilitate the comparison of scores between the field and laboratory settings, split-screen, digital video analysis was employed to measure the initiation of movement relative to ball contact by the penalty taker. The findings are presented in Figure 15.2.

Participants who received perceptual training significantly improved their response times beyond that of the control and placebo groups on both the laboratory- and field-based tests of anticipation. Moreover, significant pre- to post-test improvements were observed in response times for the training group only. No differences in response accuracy were observed across groups. It appears that field-hockey goalkeepers' anticipation skills can be improved following only

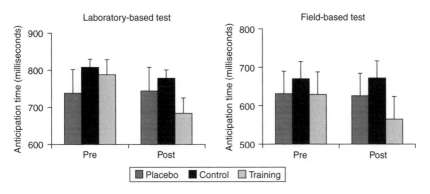

Figure 15.2 The anticipation time data for each group on the laboratory- and field-based pre- and post-tests (from Williams *et al.*, 2003).

45 minutes of instruction, practice, and feedback and that this improvement represents a meaningful training effect rather than the result of increased familiarity with the test environment or confirmation bias. This training effect also transfers from the laboratory to the field, highlighting the practical utility of video-based training programmes as a method of enhancing anticipation skill in sport.

Savelsbergh *et al.* (in prep.) reported similar conclusions in a study involving soccer goalkeepers. A group of novice goalkeepers significantly improved their performance on laboratory- and field-based measures of anticipation following 6 × 20 minute sessions of perceptual training low compared to matched control and placebo groups. A particularly innovative aspect of this study was the collection of visual search data on the pre- and post-tests. As predicted, participants exposed to perceptual training altered their search behaviour from pre- to post-test to more closely mirror the search patterns employed by expert soccer goalkeepers, highlighting the effectiveness of the training intervention employed. In future, process-oriented measures of performance, such as the recording of visual search behaviour, or protocol analysis of concurrent verbal reports, may provide a clearer indication as to the mechanisms underpinning improvements in performance as a result of perceptual training.

Pattern recognition

Few researchers have attempted to train perceptual and cognitive skills other than advance cue utilization. A suggestion is that pattern recognition skills can be improved through repeated exposure to a variety of related action sequences. For example, Christina *et al.* (1990) used such a training intervention to successfully develop pattern recognition skill in American football, whereas Wilkinson (1992) reported long-term retention of pattern recognition skills in volleyball following perceptual training. It seems likely that exposure to specific patterns of play results in the development of specialized receptors or detectors through a process termed imprinting (Goldstone, 1998). These detectors are proposed to develop and strengthen with exposure to the stimulus or stimuli resulting in increased speed, accuracy and general fluency with which stimuli are processed. An interesting question is whether repeated exposure to different types or categories of offensive sequences in team ball games, potentially using video simulation, can facilitate the recognition of similar patterns of play from within that sport and, for that matter, from one related sport to the next? This issue would appear worthy of further investigation.

Situational probabilities

There would appear to be no published studies concerning the issue of whether knowledge of situational probabilities can be trained, despite its perceived importance in guiding the recognition of, and search for, contextual information

(Williams, 2000). Video technology, perhaps coupled with quantitative match analysis data, may have some value in attempting to develop this skill. Major sports teams and individual athletes now routinely use video to review recent performances and to scout on forthcoming opponents. Although this is often a rather informal process that relies mainly on edited video footage of matches, players and coaches are now familiar with this type of intervention and, consequently, may be amenable to the presentation of more quantitative information on game performance. Players could be provided with detailed dossiers including statistical data on the moves and actions typically performed by their forthcoming opponents. For example, analysis may reveal that the opposition typically plays to a certain pattern or that attackers are consistent (i.e. predictable) in their movement patterns. Awareness of such points is likely to improve players' abilities to make accurate predictions regarding their opponents' actions. This information could be reinforced on the training field using specific coaching practices or drills.

Type of instruction

An important question for coaches and practitioners is how should information be conveyed to the learner? This issue has attracted considerable recent interest with various scientists proclaiming the superiority of one approach over another. Perhaps the two most vibrant debates relate to the effectiveness of explicit compared with implicit learning strategies and the importance of maintaining close functional links between perception and action during practice.

Implicit versus explicit learning

The relative effectiveness of implicit and explicit learning strategies has attracted considerable interest in recent years (e.g. see Masters, 2000; Maxwell *et al.*, 2000; Maxwell *et al.*, 2001). The suggestion is that skills learnt explicitly are more likely to breakdown under pressure than those learnt through implicit strategies since performers may 'reinvest' in controlled processing and shift attention away from external cues towards internal monitoring of feelings, thoughts and movements. Another potential benefit is that skills learnt implicitly are likely to be more resilient over time, leading to better long-term performance and learning (Allen and Reber, 1980).

Whilst the effectiveness of implicit and explicit learning strategies have been debated in the motor learning literature for some time (e.g. see Masters, 1992), few researchers have attempted to determine whether the typical conclusions reported for motor skills also relate to perceptual and cognitive skills. In a recent exception, Farrow and Abernethy (2002) compared the relative merits of explicit and implicit strategies in learning to anticipate the direction of an opponent's serve in tennis. Players were assigned to one of four equal ability groups based on their scores on an initial pre-test. The explicit learning group received instructions as to which postural cues they should focus upon when trying to anticipate service direction. Participants in the implicit group were given no instruction as to the important postural cues underlying performance, but rather, in an attempt to prevent the formation of explicit rules, were required to predict the speed and direction of serve while viewing the video footage. The explicit and implicit learning groups participated in 2 × 20 minutes sessions of video sim-ulation training and 1 × 20 minutes of on-court training per week over a 4-week period. The placebo group watched video footage of elite tennis matches for an equivalent time period, whereas a control group merely completed the pre- and post-test and a delayed (32 days after the post-test) retention test. A field-based temporal occlusion paradigm was used to examine players' ability to predict the direction of an opponent's service in an *in situ*, on-court setting.

The implicit learning group demonstrated a significant improvement in per-formance on the post-test compared to the other three groups, particularly in regard to the ability to anticipate service direction immediately prior to ball–racket contact. The implicit learning group also reported that they had learnt fewer explicit rules compared to the explicit learning group, implying that the interven-tion employed had been successful in creating a 'rule free', implicit learning envi-ronment. However, in contrast to the original prediction, the implicit group's newly acquired performance advantage was not maintained on the delayed reten-tion test, where no differences were reported across groups. The contradictory findings may be due to the apparent lack of measurement sensitivity, highlighted by the comparatively small improvements observed between conditions. Moreover, closer inspection of the data suggests that the placebo group showed similar improvements to that reported for the implicit participants, providing some concern as to the validity of the conclusions drawn by the authors.

Several researchers have highlighted the practical difficulties involved when trying to employ implicit learning strategies (see Maxwell *et al.*, 2000). Perhaps the biggest problem is trying to find a suitable secondary task that the learner can perform during practice so as to prevent the formulation of explicit rules whilst, at the same time, not detrimentally affecting task performance. Although the use of non-sense syllables or random number generation may be effective in the con-text of a classical laboratory-based experiment, it is difficult to imagine how coaches could implement such strategies on the practice ground. It may be that 'guided discovery' instructional techniques have more practical utility for coaches and practitioners than implicit learning strategies, particularly in relation to per-ceptual learning. In the guided discovery approach learners are merely directed towards relevant areas so that they can discover for themselves the regularities between various postural orientations and eventual response requirements (e.g. racket and ball orientation for different type of serves). The presumption is that through a process of learning by 'trial-and-error' the performer becomes progres-sively attuned to the invariant sources of information that guide anticipation skill. Guided discovery may be more effective than traditional explicit instruction strategies because the learner is likely to rely upon fewer explicit rules, implying that guided discovery may offer similar advantages to implicit learning. Moreover, the guided discovery approach may encourage learners to explore a variety of different solutions to the problem at hand, enabling them to abstract important solution principles from multiple exemplars and increasing response flexibility and adaptability (see Gick and Holyoak, 1983).

In a recent study, Williams *et al.* (2002) compared the effectiveness of guided discovery with explicit instruction when attempting to develop the ability to anticipate the direction of forehand and backhand drive shots in tennis. In one group of novice tennis players, the key information cues were highlighted using video simulation and on court practices, whereas participants in the guided discovery group were merely directed towards potentially informative areas of the display such as the trunk or hips, encouraging them to discover meaningful relationships between various postural cues and shot outcome. In the laboratory, players were required to respond in an interceptive manner to filmed images involving tennis forehand and backhand shots presented on a large screen, whereas in the on-court transfer test the players anticipatory responses to a 'live' model feed were filmed. The results are presented in Table 15.1.

The two experimental groups significantly reduced their response times on the laboratory and on-court post-test relative to matched placebo (watched tennis instructional videos) and control (completed pre- and post-tests only) groups. There were no differences in response accuracy across groups or test sessions. No differences were observed between the two training groups, both groups were significantly faster in responding as a result of training and this improvement transferred to the field setting. It appears that the guided discovery approach was at least as effective as more traditional, prescriptive approaches to instruction. It would be interesting to determine whether the improvements in performance are maintained over prolonged periods of time and whether the performance of the guided discovery players is more robust to changes in the emotional state, as proposed by Masters and colleagues (e.g. Masters, 1992; Maxwell *et al.*, 2000). A more direct comparison between guided discovery and implicit learning strategies is necessary to determine how mechanisms underpinning learning may differ across the two approaches.

Table 15.1 The anticipation time data for each group across the pre- and post-tests in both laboratory and field settings (data from Williams *et al.*, 2002)

| | | Anticipation time (milliseconds) | | | |
| | | Laboratory | | Field | |
		Pre	Post	Pre	Post
Explicit instruction (n = 8)	M	3,954	3,835	2,210	2,017
	SE	39	71	60	81
Guided discovery (n = 8)	M	3,999	3,880	2,169	1,985
	SE	93	74	31	22
Placebo (n = 7)	M	3,918	3,890	2,264	2,154
	SE	56	60	40	77
Control (n = 5)	M	3,901	3,943	2,248	2,231
	SE	86	93	30	93

Perception versus perception–action coupling

An important question is to what extent should the close functional links between perceptual and physical (action) variables be maintained during practice and performance? Several authors (e.g. E. Gibson, 1969; J. Gibson, 1979; Michaels and Carello, 1981) have argued that these functional couplings should be maintained by requiring the learner to physically respond to the action during practice. More recently, Milner and Goodale (e.g. Goodale and Milner, 1992; Milner, 1998; Milner and Goodale, 1995) have suggested that different functional streams of processing sub-serve perception and action. The ventral stream that runs from the striate cortex to the inferotemporal region is presumed to be crucial to the visual perception and identification of objects, whereas the dorsal stream that runs from the striate cortex to the posterior parietal lobe is responsible for the visual control of action. An implication may be that video simulations place much heavier demands on the ventral stream, whilst virtual environments, simulators and field-based practices are able to effectively train both the ventral and dorsal roots (Williams and Grant, 1999).

Williams *et al.* (in press) examined whether perceptual training that required the learner to physically respond to the action by attempting to return the serve (perception–action group) was more effective than training that merely necessitated the learner to make a judgement as to an opponent's intentions (perception only group). Participants who received technical instruction as to how to play forehand and backhand returns were included as controls. Anticipatory performance was assessed pre- and post-test using established on-court measures involving frame-by-frame video analysis, as described previously. The findings are presented in Figure 15.3.

The perception–action and perception only training groups significantly reduced their response times from pre- to post-test compared with the technical instruction control group. No significant differences were observed between the perception–action and perception only training groups. The mean improvement

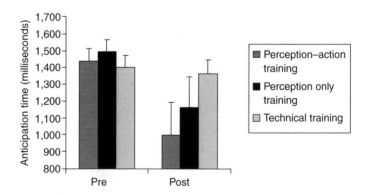

Figure 15.3 The anticipation time scores for each group on the pre- and post-tests (data from Williams *et al.*, in press).

for the two training groups was 384 milliseconds compared with 42 milliseconds for the control group. No differences in response accuracy were observed. It appears that anticipation skill can be improved through appropriate instruction regardless of whether the learner has to physically respond to the action or merely make a perceptual judgement as to the likely destination of an opponent's serve. It may be that the process of reading an opponent's intentions based on postural cues may rely mainly on ventral rather than dorsal processes and, consequently, these perceptual skills can be trained outside of the actual performance setting.

Although these findings need to be verified through further investigation, there are important potential implications for those interested in developing perceptual and cognitive skill in sport. If anticipation skill can be improved equally with or without an action response, then one possible implication is that video simulation training may be at least as effective as on-court instruction, allowing coaches to make alternative use of on-court practice time. The advantages of using video simulation rather than on-court practices for perceptual training is that learning can occur at a self-regulated pace, in and outside of regular practice time, or when the performer is injured or fatigued. Video images can also be more easily manipulated for training purposes, providing greater flexibility than that offered by on-court practices, by, for example, highlighting or occluding relevant or irrelevant sources of information (Williams and Grant, 1999). Further investigation is required to determine under what circumstances perception only training may be more effective than perception–action training and vice versa. It may be that perception only training is at least as effective as perception–action training when the task emphasizes judgement or object identification such as when attempting to pick up postural cues or recognize patterns of play in team sports. Alternatively, perception–action training may offer an advantage in situations where perceptual variables (e.g. optic variables) need to be mapped directly onto various action parameters (e.g. timing and force of stroke production) in, for example, interceptive tasks such as catching, or drive shots in table tennis, squash or tennis. Clearly, such issues provide potentially fruitful areas of investigation for those interested in skill acquisition in sport.

In summary, in this chapter we provided a brief overview of current knowledge on perceptual and cognitive expertise in sport. It appears that experts demonstrate a number of perceptual and cognitive advantages over novices. In particular, they are able to process contextual information from the evolving display more effectively than novices, with this superiority being partly due to more accurate expectations of forthcoming events based on situational probabilities. The experts' superior knowledge and skills are developed through sport-specific practice, rather than as a result of maturation, although it is likely that genetic factors may ensure that they are more inclined to benefit from exposure to the sport than novices. Regardless, perceptual and cognitive skills can be developed through appropriate interventions using various forms of instruction and feedback. The key factors underpinning the design, implementation and evaluation of such training programmes have yet to be adequately outlined, although significant progress has been made in recent years. It appears that video simulation coupled with instruction as to the important information cues underlying performance, and feedback, offers much practical utility in this regard. As highlighted in the final section of this chapter, several questions remain unanswered and further investigative effort is required before this area can make a more substantive contribution to performance enhancement in sport. However, in ending on a positive note, a number of exciting opportunities exist for those interested in the acquisition of perceptual and cognitive skills in sport.

References

Abernethy, B. (1988). The effects of age and expertise upon perceptual skill development in a racquet sport. *Research Quarterly for Exercise and Sport*, 59, 210–221.

Abernethy, B. and Russell, D. G. (1987). Expert–novice differences in an applied selective attention task. *Journal of Sport Psychology*, 9, 326–345.

Abernethy, B., Wann, J. and. Parks, S. (1998). Training perceptual-motor skills in sport. In B. Elliott and J. Mester (Eds), *Training in sport* (pp. 1–69). Chichester, West Sussex: John Wiley & Sons.

Abernethy, B., Gill, D. P., Parks, S. L. and Packer, S. T. (2001). Expertise and the perception of kinematic and situational probability information. *Perception*, 30, 233–252.

Alain, C. and Proteau, L. (1980). Decision making in sport. In C. H. Nadeau, W. R. Halliwell, K. M. Newell and G. C. Roberts (Eds), *Psychology of motor behaviour and sport* (pp. 465–477). Champaign, IL: Human Kinetics.

Alain, C. and Sarrazin, C. (1990). Study of decision-making in squash competition: a computer simulation approach. *Canadian Journal of Sport Science*, 15, 193–200.

Alain, C., Sarrazin, C. and Lacombe, D. (1986). The use of subjective expected values in decision making in sport. In D. M. Landers (Ed.), *Sport and elite performers* (pp. 1–6). Champaign, IL: Human Kinetics.

Allard, F., Graham, S. and Paarsalu, M. L. (1980). Perception in sport: basketball. *Journal of Sport Psychology*, 2, 14–21.

Allen, R. and Reber, A. S. (1980). Very long term memory for tacit knowledge. *Cognition*, 8, 175–185.

Bouchard, C., Malina, R. M. and Pérusse, L. (1997). *Genetics of fitness and physical performance*. Champaign, IL: Human Kinetics.

Chase, W. G. and Simon, H. A. (1973). Perception in chess. *Cognitive Psychology*, 4, 55–81.

Christina, R. W., Barresi, J. V. and Shaffner, P. (1990). The development of response selection accuracy in a football linebacker using video training. *The Sport Psychologist*, 4, 11–17.

Cutting, J. E. and Proffitt, D. R. (1982). The minimum principle and the perception of absolute, common and relative motions. *Cognitive Psychology*, 14, 211–246.

Ericsson, K. A. (Ed.) (1996). *The road to excellence*. Mahwah, NJ: Erlbaum.

Ericsson, K. A. and Delaney, P. F. (1999). Long-term working memory as an alternative to capacity models of working memory in everyday skilled performance. In A. Miyake and P. Shah (Eds), *Models of working memory: mechanisms of active maintenance and executive control* (pp. 257–297). Cambridge: Cambridge University Press.

Ericsson, K. A. and Kintsch, W. (1995). Long-term working memory. *Psychological Review*, 102, 211–245.

Ericsson, K. A. and Smith, J. (1991). Prospects and limits of the empirical study of expertise: an introduction. In K. A. Ericsson and J. Smith (Eds), *Toward a general theory of expertise: prospects and limits* (pp. 1–38). Cambridge: Cambridge University Press.

Ericsson, K. A., Krampe, R. T. and Tesch-Römer, C. (1993). The role of deliberate practice in the acquisition of expert performance. *Psychological Review*, 100, 363–406.

Farrow, D. and Abernethy, B. (2002). Can anticipatory skills be learned through implicit video-based perceptual training? *Journal of Sports Sciences*, 20, 471–485.

Farrow, D., Chivers, P., Hardingham, C. and Sachse, S. (1998). The effect of video-based perceptual training on the tennis return of serve. *International Journal of Sport Psychology*, 29 (3), 231–242.

Gibson, E. J. (1969). *Principles of perceptual learning and development*. New York: Appleton Century Crofts.

Gibson, J. J. (1979). *An ecological approach to visual perception*. Boston, MA: Houghton-Mifflin.

Gick, M. L. and Holyoak, K. J. (1983). Schema induction and analogical transfer. *Cognitive Psychology*, 15, 1–38.

Gobet, F. and Simon, H. A. (1996). Templates in chess memory: a mechanism for recalling several boards. *Cognitive Psychology*, 31, 1–40.

Goldstone, R. L. (1998). Perceptual learning. *Annual Review of Psychology*, 49, 585–612.

Goodale, M. A. and Milner, A. D. (1992). Separate visual pathways for perception and action. *Trends in Neuroscience*, 15, 20–25.

Helsen, W. and Pauwels, J. M. (1993). The relationship between expertise and visual information processing in sport. In J. Starkes and F. Allard (Eds), *Cognitive issues in motor expertise* (pp. 109–134). Amsterdam: North-Holland.

Horn, R., Williams, A. M. and Scott, M. A. (2002). Learning from demonstrations: the role of visual search during observational learning from video and point-light models. *Journal of Sports Sciences*, 20, 253–269.

Janelle, C. M., Singer, R. N. and Williams, A. M. (1999). External distraction and attentional narrowing: visual search evidence. *Journal of Sport and Exercise Psychology*, 21, 70–91.

Johansson, G. (1975). Visual motion perception. *Scientific American*, 232, 76–88.

Jones, C. M. and Miles, T. R. (1978). Use of advance cues in predicting the flight of a lawn tennis ball. *Journal of Human Movement Studies*, 4, 231–235.

Masters, R. S. W. (1992). Knowledge, knerves, and know-how. *British Journal of Psychology*, 83, 343–358.

Masters, R. S. W (2000). Theoretical aspects of implicit learning in sport. *International Journal of Sport Psychology*, 31, 530–541.

Maxwell, J. P., Masters, R. S. W. and Eves, F. F. (2000). From novice to know-how: a longitudinal study of implicit motor learning. *Journal of Sports Sciences*, 18, 111–120.

Maxwell, J. P., Masters, R. S. W., Kerr, E. and Weedon, E. (2001). The implicit benefit of learning without errors. *Quarterly Journal of Experimental Psychology* 54A, 1049–1068.

Michaels, C. F. and Carello, C. (1981). *Direct perception*. Englewood Cliffs, NJ: Prentice-Hall.

Milner, D. A. (1998). Streams and consciousness: visual awareness and the brain. *Trends in Cognitive Science*, 2 (1), 25–30.

Milner, D. A. and Goodale, M. A. (1995). *The visual brain in action*. Oxford: Oxford University Press.

Nougier, V., Stein, J. F., and Bonnel, A. M. (1991). Information processing in sport and orienting attention. *International Journal of Sport Psychology*, 22, 307–327.

Posner, M. I. and Raichle, M. E. (Eds) (1994). *Images of mind*. New York: Scientific American Library.

Reilly, T., Williams, A. M., Nevill, A. and Franks, A. (2000). A multidisciplinary approach to talent identification in soccer. *Journal of Sports Sciences*, 18, 668–676.

Richman, H. B., Gobet, F., Staszewski, J. J. and Simon, H. A. (1996). Perceptual and memory processes in the acquisition of expert performance: the EPAM model. In K. A. Ericsson (Ed.), *The road to excellence: the acquisition of expert performance in the arts and sciences, sports and games* (pp. 167–187). Mahwah, NJ: Lawrence Erlbaum Associates.

Rodrigues, S., Vickers, J. and Williams, A. M. (2002). Eye, head and arm coordination in table tennis. *Journal of Sports Sciences*, 20, 187–200.

Savelsbergh, G. J. P., Williams, A. M., Van der Kamp, J. and Ward, P (in prep.). Developing anticipation skill in soccer goalkeepers.

Singer, R. N. and Janelle, C. M. (1999). Determining sport expertise: from genes to supremes. *International Journal of Sport Psychology*, 30, 117–151.

Singer, R. N., Cauraugh, J. H., Chen, D., Steinberg, G. M., Frehlich, S. G. and Wang, L. (1994). Training mental quickness in beginning/intermediate tennis players. *The Sport Psychologist*, 8, 305–318.

Singer, R. N., Williams, A. M., Frehlich, S. G., Janelle, C. M., Radlo, S. J., Barba, D. A. and Bouchard, L. J. (1998). New frontiers in visual search: an exploratory study in live tennis situations. *Research Quarterly for Exercise and Sport*, 69, 290–296.

Starkes, J. L. and Ericsson, K. A. (Eds) (2003). *Expert performance in sports: advances in research on sport expertise*. Champaign, IL: Human Kinetics.

Starkes, J. L., Helsen, W. F. and Jack, R. (2001). Expert performance in sport and dance. In R. N. Singer, H. A. Hausenblas and C. M. Janelle (Eds), *Handbook of sport psychology* (pp. 174–201). New York: John Wiley.

Tenenbaum, G., Sar-El, T. and Bar-Eli, M. (2000). Anticipation of ball location in low and high-skill performers: a developmental perspective. *Psychology of Sport and Exercise*, 1, 117–128.

Vickers, J. N. (1996). Visual control when aiming at a far target. *Journal of Experimental Psychology: Human Perception and Performance*, 22, 342–354.

Vickers, J. N., Williams, A. M., Rodrigues, S. T., Hillis, F. and Coyne, G. (1999). Eye movements of elite biathlon shooters during rested and fatigued states. *Journal of Sport and Exercise Psychology*, 21, S116.

Ward, P. and Williams, A. M. (2003). Perceptual and cognitive skill development in soccer: the multidimensional nature of expert performance. *Journal of Sport and Exercise Psychology*, 25 (1), 93–111.

Ward, P., Williams, A. M. and Bennett, S. J. (2002). Visual search and biological motion perception in tennis. *Research Quarterly for Exercise and Sport*, 73, 107–112.

Ward, P., Hodges, N. J., Starkes, J. L. and Williams, A. M. (submitted). The road to excellence in soccer: a quasi-longitudinal approach to deliberate practice and deliberate play.

Wilkinson, S. (1992). Effects of training in visual discrimination after one year: visual analyses of volleyball skills. *Perceptual and Motor Skills*, 75, 19–24.

Williams, A. M. (2000). Perceptual skill in soccer: implications for talent identification and development. *Journal of Sports Sciences*, 18, 737–750.

Williams, A. M. and Burwitz, L. (1993). Advance cue utilisation in soccer. In T. Reilly, J. Clarys and A. Stibbe (Eds), *Science and football II* (pp. 239–244). London: E. & F. N. Spon.

Williams, A. M. and Davids, K. (1995). Declarative knowledge in sport: a byproduct of experience or a characteristic of expertise? *Journal of Sport and Exercise Psychology*, 7, 259–275.

Williams, A. M. and Davids, K. (1998). Visual search strategy, selective attention, and expertise in soccer. *Research Quarterly for Exercise and Sport*, 69 (2), 111–128.

Williams, A. M. and Elliott, D. (1999). Anxiety and visual search strategy in karate. *Journal of Sport and Exercise Psychology*, 21, 362–375.

Williams, A. M. and Grant, A. (1999). Training perceptual skill in sport. *International Journal of Sport Psychology*, 30, 194–220.

Williams, A. M. and Reilly, T. (2000). Talent identification and development in soccer. *Journal of Sports Sciences*, 18, 657–667.

Williams, A. M. and Ward, P. (2003). Developing perceptual expertise in sport. In K. A. Ericsson and J. Starkes (Eds), *Recent developments in expert performance in sport* (pp. 220–249). Champaign, IL: Human Kinetics.

Williams, A. M. Davids, K., Burwitz, L. and Williams, J. G. (1993). Cognitive knowledge and soccer performance. *Perceptual and Motor Skills*, 76, 579–593.

Williams, A. M., Davids, K., Burwitz, L. and Williams, J. G. (1994). Visual search strategies of experienced and inexperienced soccer players. *Research Quarterly for Exercise and Sport*, 5, 127–135.

Williams, A. M., Davids, K. and Williams, J. G. (1999). *Visual perception and action in sport*. London: E. & F.N. Spon.

Williams, A. M., Ward, P., Knowles, J. M. and Smeeton, N. J. (2002). Perceptual skill in a real-world task: Training, instruction, and transfer in tennis. *Journal of Experimental Psychology: Applied*, 8, 259–270.

Williams, A. M., Ward, P. and Chapman, C. (2003). Training perceptual skill in field hockey: is there transfer from the laboratory to the field? *Research Quarterly for Exercise and Sport*, 74, 98–104.

Williams, A. M., Ward, P., Allen, D. and Smeeton, N. J. (in press). Training perceptual skill using on-court instruction in tennis: perception versus perception and action. *Journal of Applied Sport Psychology*.

Part III

Ecological/dynamical systems approach

16 The evolution of coordination during skill acquisition

The dynamical systems approach

Raôul Huys, Andreas Daffertshofer and Peter J. Beek

Practice makes perfect, so they say. However, what does 'perfect' refer to, what does it entail, and how does practice lead to perfection? In the context of perceptual-motor skills, 'perfect' may be taken as 'dexterous', 'the ability to find a motor solution for any external situation, that is, to adequately solve any emerging motor problem correctly, quickly, rationally and resourcefully' (Bernstein, 1996: p. 228). This intuitively appealing statement has several important implications. We mention two that are at the core of Bernstein's thinking.

First, solving a motor problem implies exerting adequate control (while solving *any* motor problem implies the ability to cope with a large range of initial conditions). Bernstein (1984) framed the problem of control in terms of motor redundancy and degrees of freedom. Given the huge number of individual degrees of freedom of the human motor apparatus (e.g. muscle activation levels, joint configurations), what are the principles by which control is exerted over the highly complex apparatus of the human body? How is this seemingly uncontrollable system converted into a controllable one? Bernstein sought to answer this question through the concept of synergy or coordinative structure. In the execution of motor actions, temporary, soft-moulded linkages or constraints are operative that effectively reduce the number of degrees of freedom to be controlled. The next question then, which has stayed with the notion of coordinative structure ever since it was coined, is how are such task-specific constraints assembled and de-assembled?

Second, the adjective 'resourcefully' implies the existence of task-specific resources, that is, a functionally (sub)optimal 'global' organization defined over a large collection of interacting subsystems that can be flexibly brought to bear on the task at hand. By necessity, dexterity implies that bodily parts and processes are coordinated, both with each other and with the requirements of the environment. This is captured by the notion of coordinative structure or motor synergy. But how are coordinative structures rendered flexible and resilient? In his visionary study of the development of dexterity, Bernstein (1996) emphasized time and again that movements are 'constructed', as he called it, at multiple functional levels constituting a motor hierarchy, ranging from 'lower level' control of muscle tone and muscular–articular synergies to the formation of action plans and sequences at the highest control level. This was a tantalizing, exciting idea, but it has not been elaborated theoretically nor pursued experimentally, at least not in any rigorous or systematic fashion. Today, no one would probably deny the importance of functional cooperation among nested subsystems, but nevertheless the issue has remained largely neglected in the study of skilled motor behaviour.

In sum, Bernstein highlighted two key problems for the scientific study of the acquisition of perceptual-motor skills: (a) the formation of coordinative structures and (b) the promotion of the flexibility, adaptivity and resourcefulness of coordinative structures. Since the first translation of Bernstein's ideas into the English language (Bernstein, 1984), these problems have been addressed by introducing a variety of new concepts and methods. In a 'state-of-the-art' review, Turvey (1990) distinguished between Round 1 and Round 2 of theorizing on Bernstein's problem. Round 1 encompassed the works of Greene (1972) and Turvey (1977), which emphasized notions such as hierarchical and heterarchical control, perceptual tuning, ballpark responses and mass-spring models. Round 2, in contrast, entailed the study of coordinative structures in terms of their dissipative, self-organizing dynamics, using concepts and tools borrowed from dynamical systems theory and synergetics (Haken, 1977, 1983). Whereas Round 1 has lost momentum, or, on reading Turvey (1990), has come to an end, research in Round 2 continues to bloom (see, Beek *et al.*, 1995; Kelso, 1995).

In the present chapter we critically discuss and evaluate various approaches that are currently pursued in the study of perceptual-motor learning from a dynamical systems perspective. We examine their merits and limitations in addressing the two Bersteinean problems outlined in the preceding discussion, and explore implications for the understanding and promotion of the acquisition of sport skills. To achieve these goals, we have to strike a balance between the need for an informal yet precise explanation of key concepts (which are often of a formal nature) and the need to include sufficient concrete examples from the world of sports. Only in this way will we be able to convey the main gist of the ideas and methods presented to an interested reader with no specific background in dynamical systems theory. The discussion of the dynamical systems approach to the acquisition of coordinated movement is structured according to the two problems of Bernstein. First, after a brief characterization of dynamical systems theory, we discuss two ways of studying the formation of coordinative structures in terms of low-dimensional order parameter dynamics and reduction of the number of degrees of freedom (i.e. potential landscape and dimensionality/component analysis). Subsequently, we discuss two more recent lines of inquiry aimed at understanding issues of flexibility, adaptiveness and resourcefulness, namely the so-called UnControlled Manifold approach, and our own efforts to examine adaptive couplings and decouplings between heterogeneous subsystems in the course of skill acquisition.

Brief characterization of coordination dynamics

An important feature of biological systems is that they are in permanent contact with their environment through energy, matter and information fluxes. In thermodynamics, such systems are called open systems, as opposed to closed systems in which such contact is absent. Due to the interaction among their (microscopic) subsystems, open systems may organize themselves by forming coherent, that is, ordered spatial and temporal patterns and/or structures (Haken, 1996). The resulting patterns are macroscopic in nature and may be described by a small number of collective variables, conventionally referred to as order parameters. Spontaneous switches between macroscopic patterns are called non-equilibrium phase transitions in equivalence with similar qualitative, structural changes in thermodynamical systems (where the term 'phase' refers to a system's state). Switches in macroscopic patterns are a hallmark property of self-organization, as they involve no external agents imposing order from the outside. Phase transitions abound in both the inanimate and animate world. Well-known examples in the inanimate world are cloud formation due to temperature gradients (e.g. a mackerel or fleecy sky) and the formation of convection roles and hexagonal patterns in a layer of oil heated from below (in the so-called Bénard experiment). Apart from the examples of phase transitions to be discussed later in this chapter, the example par excellence in the science of biological movement are the spontaneous shifts in gait patterns that are observed when velocity of locomotion gradually increases (e.g. from trot to canter in the horse or from walking to jogging in humans).

The importance of non-equilibrium phase transitions can be appreciated when one realizes that qualitative changes in macroscopic patterns are accompanied by loss of the stability of the original pattern. The stability of a system's state (or phase) implies that every perturbation out of that state causes the system to return to it; when stability is lost the system does not return but rather switches to another stable state (or phase). Close to points of (macroscopic) instability the time to return increases tremendously. As a result, the macroscopic state evolves rather slowly in response to perturbation, whereas the underlying microscopic components maintain their individual time scale. From the perspective of the slowly evolving macroscopic state, the microscopic components change so quickly that they can adapt instantaneously to macroscopic changes. Thus, even though the macroscopic patterns are generated by the subsystems, they order the subsystems or, put metaphorically, they 'enslave' their generating microscopic structures (Haken, 1977). Ordered states can always be described by very few variables (at least in the close vicinity of macroscopic changes), and consequently the state of the originally high-dimensional system can be summarized by a few or even a single collective variable, the order parameter(s). The relationship between the subsystems and the macroscopic structure, in which the subsystems generate the macroscopic structure and these structures enslave the subsystems, implies a circular causality, which effectively allows for a low-dimensional description of the dynamical properties of the system under study. The notion of circular causality and the corresponding possibility of finding low-dimensional dynamical descriptions for self-organizing phenomena are at the heart of Haken's synergetics, an interdisciplinary approach to the study of pattern formation in physical, chemical and biological systems. The low-dimensional dynamical descriptions may be cast in the (here one-dimensional) form:

$$\frac{d\phi}{dt} = N(\phi, \text{[fixed] parameters, noise})$$

where $d\phi/dt$ represents the time evolution of the state variable (i.e. the order parameter $\phi = \phi(t)$), which is a function N of the order parameter itself, certain fixed parametric influences, which may either come from the environment or from the system's interior, and random fluctuations stemming from the microscopic components. In general, the function N will be non-linear as the focus of the approach is on qualitative changes in macroscopic patterns of behaviour induced by gradual changes in relevant system parameters (i.e. non-equilibrium phase transitions). Notice that order parameter equations like the one above are designed to capture the main dynamical properties of pattern formation phenomena in nature and may therefore be viewed as formal analogies. An explicit formal identification of the order parameter dynamics is important to pursue whenever feasible. It allows tight relations to be built between the experiment and the synergetic theory of pattern formation, which posits that very similar forms of pattern formation are present in very distinct material systems. In this sense, the phenomena of pattern formation and self-organization are viewed as universal. Nevertheless, it is evident that there are some profound differences between inanimate and living systems. For instance, in living systems meaningful information may originate from self-organizing processes and, in turn, may modify, guide and direct these processes, as is clearly the case in skill acquisition. Therefore, the study of coordinated movement patterns in terms of low-dimensional dynamics is not simply a matter of borrowing concepts and tools from the physics of self-organization and the corresponding mathematics of non-linear dynamical systems and applying them to biological movement. In what is called the dynamical systems approach to coordinated movement, coordination dynamics for short, concepts and tools borrowed from physics and mathematics are built upon and modified to develop an encompassing theory of coordination. A theory that describes, explains and predicts how patterns of coordination form, persist and change in animal behaviour as well as in the neural, physiological and muscular–skeletal subsystems supporting it. Coordination dynamics seeks to identify the laws, principles and mechanisms underlying coordinated behaviour at different levels of description and explicitly addresses, when feasible, the connection between levels. A key question for the approach as a whole is how the interaction among the parts of biological systems can produce coordinated behaviour, even though the individual parts of the system may preserve a certain degree of autonomy. Answering this question will ultimately lead to a demystification of the concept of self-organization, which is often erroneously taken to imply that coordination comes 'out of the blue', not seldom to make a mockery of the approach.

Although the study of real-time coordination forms a large portion of the research on motor behaviour conducted from the perspective of coordination dynamics, especially in the context of rhythmic interlimb coordination, the approach is also pursued in the study of motor learning and development, which are both characterized by a combination of transient change in behaviour over time. Potentially, there are many indices of changes in motor behaviour, many time scales over which these changes occur and many forms that these changes may take. Recently, Newell *et al.* (2001) re-addressed the age-old issue of learning curves from the perspective of dynamical systems theory, focusing on outcome rather than coordination measures. They showed that a variety of processes evolving at different time scales might be implicated in motor learning and development, leading to exponential, power law or sigmoidal learning curves. In the present chapter, we approach the dynamics of skill acquisition from a different perspective, namely by asking how movement coordination evolves during the acquisition of complex perceptual-motor skills. To this purpose, we review several lines of inquiry within the dynamical systems approach that address this issue. We do so according to the steps mentioned in the introduction and identify strengths, limitations and implications for practice and instruction as we go.

Learning as changes in coordinative structures

Intrinsic dynamics and behavioural information

Besides cursory mention of its potential relevance to the theoretical study of gait transition in quadrupeds (Haken, 1977), the order parameter concept was introduced to the field of motor control by Haken *et al.* (1985) in their formal modelling of Kelso's (1981, 1984) data on bimanual finger wiggling, subsequently referred to as the HKB model. In these experiments, the participants' task was to oscillate their index fingers in either an in-phase pattern (simultaneous activation of homologous muscle groups) or an anti-phase pattern (simultaneous activation of non-homologous muscle groups) while cycling frequency (paced by a metronome) was gradually increased. Kelso observed that when the participants started in the anti-phase pattern, a spontaneous switch occurred to the in-phase pattern at a certain critical frequency. Above this frequency, only the in-phase pattern could be stably performed. Conversely, if the participants started in the in-phase pattern, no phase transition was observed with increasing frequency. In modelling these results, Haken *et al.* (1985) identified the relative phase between the oscillating fingers as the order parameter and captured its dynamics by a potential function, along whose gradient the order parameter evolves (see Figure 16.1). In this theoretical representation, the order parameter's evolution is conceived as over-damped movement of a particle in the potential landscape, which shows the order parameter's stationary solutions in the form of 'valleys' (local minima) and 'peaks' (local maxima) representing stable and unstable fixed points, respectively. This is illustrated in the top left panel of Figure 16.1. When positioned on a finite slope ($\neq 0$), the order parameter evolves towards a stable solution in accordance with the underlying gradient. The steepness of the corresponding valley reflects the order parameter's stability, that is, its resistance against perturbations. Increases

The HKB potential that accounts for the switch from anti-phase to in-phase coordination in rhythmic limb movements reads

$$V_{HKB}(\phi) = -a\cos\phi - b\cos 2\phi$$

The (local) minima or valleys in the potential landscape represent stable solutions. The evolution of the coordinative state is represented as a ball rolling overdamped along that landscape. The ball will always return to the closest stable solution, i.e. the closest valley (e.g. left panel). A variation of the control parameter, movement frequency, results in a change of the potential's shape so that eventually the anti-phase position ($\phi = \pm\pi$) can no longer be maintained (middle panel). The coordination switches to the in-phase mode (right panel) as this mode is still stable.

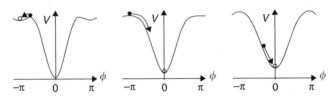

Along this line of thought, processes of learning can be viewed in terms of additional (potential) factors. Below, this is indicated as different potentials, each of which represents a to-be-learned pattern as specified by the behavioural information (BI; the dashed and dotted line show minima a different phase values of $\psi_{\text{to-be-learned}}$, left panel):

$$V_{BI}(\phi) = -c\cos\left(\frac{\phi - \psi_{\text{TO-BE-LEARNED}}}{2}\right)$$

Superimposing these potentials on the already present landscape (HKB potential; solid line in the left panel) results in modifications as is indicated in the right panel.

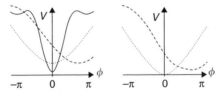

If the value of the behavioural information coincides with a readily stable solution (dotted line with minimum at $\phi = 0$), then its stability is increased ('cooperation'). In contrast, if the behavioural information does not match a previously stable state, the latter may be affected and even lose stability ('competition'). The already present landscape ('intrinsic dynamics') deforms more as the parameter c in the equation above increases, which may occur as learning proceeds.

Figure 16.1 Intrinsic dynamics, behavioral information and learning.

in the movement frequency, or more generally, changes in the control parameter, deform the potential landscape, thus affecting the order parameter's stability (without specifying desired values for the order parameter). As shown in the top right panel of Figure 16.1, these deformations lead to the annihilation of the anti-phase valley, resulting in an abrupt switch of the particle to the in-phase valley, that is, a phase transition. Since the paradigmatic experiments of Kelso, numerous studies of rhythmic interlimb coordination have shown that, without special additional practice, only the in-phase and anti-phase pattern are intrinsically stable modes of coordination.

Building on the notion of a potential landscape, Schöner *et al.* (1992) (see also Schöner, 1989; Schöner and Kelso, 1988; Zanone and Kelso, 1992) modelled the acquisition of an intrinsically unstable coordination mode by introducing the complementary concepts of intrinsic dynamics and behavioural information. The intrinsic dynamics reflect the learner's inherent coordination tendencies (resulting from a mix of innate biological constraints, development and previous learning) as he or she starts out to learn a new coordination or task. Experimentally, the intrinsic dynamics may be assessed by means of a scanning procedure, in which the performance of 'all' possible phase relations, in terms of the deviation from the required phasing and the relative phase variability, is probed in a systematic and often step-like manner. The behavioural information represents a specific parametric influence on the order parameter dynamics that may originate from the perceptual environment or from a person's memory, attention and/or intention. Importantly, the behavioural information is still described in terms of the order parameter(s) characterizing the coordination pattern (i.e. relative phase between the two oscillating limbs), allowing for a formalization of its interplay with the intrinsic dynamics. Accordingly, one can easily appreciate that if the intrinsic dynamics and the behavioural information 'constructively cooperate', learning will enhance the stability of an already stable coordination pattern. If, on the other hand, the behavioural information corresponds to an unstable coordination, such as a 90° phase difference, the behavioural information and the intrinsic dynamics are at odds with each other and thus 'compete'. In the latter case, the intrinsic dynamics has to be modified in the direction of the to-be-learned pattern, which occurs as the behavioural information becomes memorized. The learning of a new coordination pattern under the guidance of behavioural information may eventually lead to the development of a new 'valley' in the intrinsic dynamics, which corresponds to the newly acquired pattern. In this sense, learning may be understood as a kind of phase transition. To test these theoretical notions, Zanone and Kelso (1992) examined how participants with an initially bi-stable intrinsic dynamics (i.e. with in-phase and anti-phase as stable solutions) learned to oscillate their index fingers at a phase difference of 90°. In accordance with the predictions, performance of the 90° phase relation improved in that both the deviation from the required coordination pattern and the standard deviation of relative phase decreased with practice. This was taken as evidence that a new 'valley' had emerged in the potential landscape and that its steepness had increased in the course of learning. However, learning effects were not confined to the 90° phase relation. Even though its symmetrical coun-terpart, 270° phase relation (i.e. where the left rather than the right finger leads) was not practiced, performance of this phase relation improved. Thus, as a result of learning, the entire attractor layout had changed. Furthermore, in at least one of the participants the acquisition of the new coordination pattern could be inter-preted as a non-equilibrium phase transition.

The impact of the HKB potential is beyond dispute. Due to its pedagogic value and the relative simplicity of the associated measures (relative phase and its vari-ability), the HKB model motivated an enormous amount of research. However, the use of gradient dynamics in the study of movement coordination and learn-ing has some intrinsic limitations. First, in many cases, the order parameters are unknown and a potential function cannot be derived. This is, for instance, the case in polyrhythmic tapping and other forms of multi-frequency coordination, where the number of stable performance patterns may become overwhelmingly large (e.g. Daffertshofer *et al.*, 2000). Second, in many instances of motor learn-ing, the task goal is not defined in terms of a particular coordination, but in terms of a particular environmental effect (e.g. hitting a target in pistol-shooting or throwing a basketball through a hoop). As a consequence, it is hard, if not impossible, to assess the intrinsic dynamics for such tasks as no equivalent to the scanning procedure is available. Third, the notion of assessing the intrinsic dynamics presupposes that one is already able to perform the task to a sufficient degree so that the intrinsic dynamics can be assessed. However, when learning complex skills from scratch this requirement is not met. In situations such as these, one must address the question of how coordination is wrestled out of the many heterogeneous subsystems of the human action system.

Besides these methodological limitations, the distinction between intrinsic dynamics and behavioural information is not devoid of certain logical problems. Where the concept of intrinsic dynamics refers to the fact that patterns may arise spontaneously due to non-specific changes in a control parameter, the concept of behavioural information refers to specific parametric influences acting on those dynamics, including intentional influences (Kelso, 1995). Yet, to assess the intrin-sic dynamics, using, for instance, the scanning procedure, the participants must engage in a particular intentional behaviour, implying that behavioural (inten-tional) information always pervades the intrinsic dynamics to a certain degree. A second problem is that the concept of behavioural information allows for differ-ent interpretations of learning. On the one hand, one can say that a pattern is learned to the degree that the behavioural information is recalled or memorized, thus emphasizing changes in the local attractor associated with the behavioural information (see Schöner and Kelso, 1988). On the other hand, one can say that the intrinsic dynamics are modified in the direction of the to-be-learned pattern, thus emphasizing the global form of the intrinsic dynamics (Kelso, 1995).

However, notwithstanding its limitations, several insights have been obtained in this line of inquiry that are highly relevant for sports (wo)men and their coaches, most notably with regard to the notion of intrinsic dynamics. First, the conceptual-ization of learning as a modification of the intrinsic dynamics implies that learning a new coordination pattern not only leads to improved performance of the learned pattern, but may affect the performance of other patterns as well. In other words, learning a particular coordination pattern may have both positive and negative transfer effects. Although, admittedly, little is known about such transfer effects in the context of the learning of everyday skills, coaches should be aware that such effects may occur, especially when their pupils engage in skills or activities involving similar coordination patterns (e.g. squash and tennis). Second, all learning processes operate from existing coordination tendencies, never from a tabula rasa. Although one can measure those coordination tendencies only under special circumstances, they always affect the dynamics of learning. As a consequence, some coordinations or skills are easy to learn by some individuals but hard to acquire by others. This is especially true if the intrinsic dynamics are pronounced, as will be the case when one has already intensively practiced a particular coordination or technique for solving a particular motor problem.

Consider, for instance, an athlete with a strongly 'automatized' coordination pattern say a free-style swimmer whose breathing pattern is characterized by an inhalation every fourth stroke that is performed repeatedly on the same side of his or her body. Assuming that this technique is inferior, the swimmer may decide to replace it with an alternative, superior technique; such as inhaling every third stroke to avoid running out of breath. This would then require the acquisition of a bilateral breathing pattern. In such cases, it could be expected that the athlete would encounter difficulty in achieving the adopted aim as the inferior technique may remain present as a ghost or remnant of a stable solution in the attractor layout, and thus may continue to affect coordination. This implies that the newly required coordination must be intensively practiced to alter the existing intrinsic dynamics. Even so, already existing coordination patterns may be very hard to get rid of entirely, and may pop up every now and then, especially under special circumstances (e.g. arousal). Therefore, as a rule, coaches should be aware of the fact that one's learning history determines one's future performance and learning possibilities, and thus be reluctant to try to replace existing coordination patterns by others that are deemed superior. Of course, this should not be taken to imply that deliberate changes in coordination or technique should always be avoided. There may certainly be situations in which such changes are needed, especially when it is evident that a particular technique or coordination forms an obstacle for reaching higher levels of performance in competitive sports. Coaches should remember, however, that deliberate interventions in coordination or technique are always demanding and risky.

Degrees of freedom, principal component analysis and dimensionality

In view of the redundancy of the action system, Bernstein (1984) formulated the problem of motor control in terms of degrees of freedom and highlighted the need to master 'the redundant degrees of freedom of the moving organ' (p. 355). This perspective implies that motor redundancy is a curse, a point of view that still prevails in the field of motor control. Bernstein defined 'degrees of freedom' in the conventional anatomical/biomechanical sense of planes of rotation. He speculated that learning entails a process of initially 'freezing out' degrees of freedom that are subsequently harnessed to form a coordinative structure, that is, 'a group of muscles often spanning a number of joints that is constrained to act as a single functional unit' (cf. Kugler *et al.*, 1980: p. 17). This suggestion inspired various experimental studies on the formation of coordinative structures, which focused on the variability of joint excursions and their cross-correlations (e.g. Arutyunyan *et al.*, 1968, 1969; Newell and van Emmerik, 1989; Temprado *et al.*, 1997; Vereijken *et al.*, 1992). For example, Vereijken and colleagues studied the acquisition of slalom-like ski-movements and reported small amplitude but strongly correlated movement excursions between the lower limbs and the torso early in learning. As learning progressed, however, movement amplitudes increased and cross-correlations decreased. These results were interpreted to imply that in the course of learning functional synergies were assembled and disassembled.

Whereas these studies were instrumental in advancing the notion of coordinative structures, they are, in retrospect, open to criticism, both methodologically and conceptually. Methodologically, these earlier attempts suffered from the fact that sophisticated techniques for the detection of patterns of variation in multivariate data sets were not yet available or unknown among movement scientists. Typically, analyses were restricted to a combination of non-coordinative measures (such as joint angles and variations therein) and statistical correlations between two signals taken arbitrarily from a much larger set (e.g. Newell and van Emmerik, 1989; Temprado *et al.*, 1997; Vereijken *et al.*, 1992). As a consequence, profound properties of coordination, such as functional relations among multiple components and hidden structures in the variance, remained unaddressed. Conceptually, the earlier work was based on the assumption that 'freezing out' degrees of freedom would imply that they are released from control, which is unwarranted (see Scholz *et al.*, 2000).

With the advent of dynamical systems theory and synergetics, the notion of coordinative structure received a new definition, namely that of a coherent, macroscopic (spatio-)temporal pattern, generated under non-equilibrium constraints in open systems. Accordingly, the (active) degrees of freedom problem was re-defined in terms of the identification of the number of order parameters minimally needed to describe a system's state. The identification of synergies and the formation thereof during skill acquisition required a method for the detection of similar dynamical patterns among multi-dimensional sets. A generic method for this purpose was found in Principal Component Analysis (PCA), because this method requires no a priori assumptions regarding the kind of variables to be controlled or implicated in coordination.

PCA is an unbiased, statistical method used to identify a smaller set of linear independent combinations of the original variables. This new set of variables, or principal components, captures most of the variance of the original variables (for an explanation of this method, see Figure 16.2). Using PCA, Haas and Haken (see Haken, 1996) studied the formation of synergies in the acquisition of riding the pedalo, a curious contraption allowing forward propulsion by making cyclical

PCA

Let $\{q_i(t)\}$ be a set of time series $(i = 1, 2, \ldots, N)$ represented as N-dimensional vector $q(t) = [q_1(t), q_2(t), q_3(t), \ldots, q_N(t)]$. Using PCA, one seeks for a set of M different vectors $\{v^{(k)}\}$, which allows for the following approximation:

$$q(t) \approx \xi_1(t)v^{(1)} + \xi_2(t)v^{(2)} + \cdots + \xi_M(t)v^{(M)} = \sum_{k=1}^{M} \xi_k(t)v^{(k)}.$$

If the number of vectors or modes $v^{(k)}$ matches the dimensionality of $q(t)$, that is, for $M = N$ this approximation is exact. Whenever the time series $q_i(t)$ have joint properties, however, one can expect that the number of modes required to represent the data is smaller than its original dimensionality, that is $M < N$. In this case, however, the quality of the approximation strongly depends on the explicit forms of $v^{(k)}$, which can be obtained by minimizing the least square error:

$$E_M = \int_T \left[q(t) - \sum_{k=1}^{M} \xi_k(t)v^{(k)} \right]^2 dt = \min$$

To illustrate this minimization we consider a set of three sampled time series and plot each data point in the corresponding three-dimensional space. The resulting cloud of points is distributed along every direction (see figure below). The shape of this point distribution can be quantified in terms of variances along its main or principal direction. In detail, the direction of maximal variance defines $v^{(1)}$ and projecting all the data onto this first mode yields the evolution along this direction, i.e. $\xi_1(t)$. The residual (orthogonal) space results from subtracting the first mode from the data, here providing a two-dimensional data set. This set can be treated equivalently and one obtains an iterative definition of modes $v^{(2)}$ and $v^{(3)}$ that are ranked by means of decreasing variance or their contribution to the entire data set.

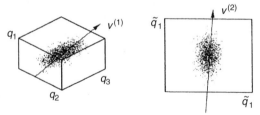

Given this geometrical construction via iterative variance maximization, the aforementioned least square fit can readily be realized using the covariance that is defined between every pair of the original time series, i.e. the covariance matrix. The eigenvectors of this matrix already coincide with the desired vectors $v^{(k)}$ and the corresponding eigenvalues λ_k reflect the variances explained above. Finally, the projection of the data onto each individual mode is simply given as product

$$v^{(k)} \cdot q(t) = \xi_k(t)$$

which yields time-dependent coefficients $\xi_1(t), \xi_2(t), \ldots, \xi_M(t)$ as optimal representation of the system's dynamics.

Figure 16.2 Principal component analysis.

stepping movements while standing on two small wheeled platforms. By sticking markers on specific anatomical landmarks distributed over the entire body, the whole body kinematics could be registered as a twenty-two-dimensional system. PCA revealed that, early in practice, this twenty-two-dimensional system could be effectively reduced to five components (i.e. a five-dimensional system). During practice, a gradual reduction of dimensionality was observed, resulting in a system that could be represented as a two-dimensional system. In other words, learning led to a marked reduction of the dimensionality of the underlying control structure.

In a similar vein, Huys *et al.*, (2003) recently showed (using different though related techniques) that the dimensionality of the overall ball patterns in three-ball cascade juggling reduces in the course of learning. This finding is consistent with research indicating that dimensionality reduces with learning a skill (Mitra *et al.*, 1998), and suggesting that reduced dimensionality is associated with improved rather than reduced control. However, the conclusion that early and intermediate stages of learning are characterized by a decrease in dimensionality of control may be premature. Newell and Vaillancourt (2001) proposed that the directional change of the dimensionality depends on the required change of the task-relevant intrinsic dynamics in order to meet new task demands. For instance, reduced dimensionality also seems to be a characteristic feature of many movement disorders and impairments (cf. Longstaff and Heath, 2003; Newell *et al.*, 2001). This observation shows that reduced dimensionality does not necessarily imply improved rather than reduced control, as suggested by Mitra *et al.* (1998). In general, PCA and dimensionality analysis provide no information about the control design of the system, and thus neither about the quality nor the flexibility of control.

In view of the preceding considerations, it may prove to be essential to distinguish between the acquisition of a prescribed, single task performance, as typically used in laboratory settings, and the acquisition of 'true' skill, which in general requires the individual to be able to meet a task goal from a range of 'initial conditions', including perturbations. As it stands, it seems reasonable to conclude that PCA provides a useful technique for extracting coordinative patterns from multidimensional movement data and that reductions in dimensionality are common in early and intermediate stages of learning of some tasks, but not necessarily in others. With regard to the understanding of the modus operandi of coordinative structures, and changes therein due to learning, however, the use of PCA and dimensionality analyses seems limited. As a consequence, immediate implications of this type of research for practice and instruction are few.

Learning as changes in coordinative flexibility

Flexibility within synergies

Whereas PCA is a powerful tool for detecting patterns of co-variation among multiple 'elements' involving a minimal set of assumptions, it provides no information with regard to the functionality of the covariance assessed. In contrast, the UnControlled Manifold (UCM) approach, introduced and developed by Schöner (1995) (see also Scholz and Schöner, 1999; Scholz et al., 2000), specifically aims at decomposing the variability in a multi-dimensional array of data into two distinct subspaces. The variability in one subspace leaves task performance unaffected, and is therefore called Goal Equivalent Variability (GEV), whereas the variability in the other subspace deteriorates task performance, the Non-Goal Equivalent Variability (NGEV; Tseng et al., 2003). For instance, in trying to hit the bull's-eye in rifle shooting, success critically depends on the alignment of the barrel of the gun with the target. A biathlete may adopt a range of joint combinations (which across trials constitutes a space of variability) that leave this critical alignment unaltered, whereas other joint configurations will lead to a miss due to mis-alignment of the barrel with respect to the target (see Figure 16.3). A proficient marksman will show a higher GEV-to-NGEV ratio than a less proficient marksman. Thus, importantly, the UCM approach is based on the notion that people learn to exploit the redundancy of the motor apparatus to achieve success in the face of ever-present fluctuations, thus lending flexibility to their performance. In contrast to Bernstein's interpretation of motor redundancy as a major problem for control, the UCM approach emphasizes that motor redundancy is a necessity for successful control.

A distinct difference between UCM and PCA is that the former necessarily involves explicit hypotheses regarding the variables controlled in a given task, whereas the latter requires no such hypotheses. Where PCA may be said to have

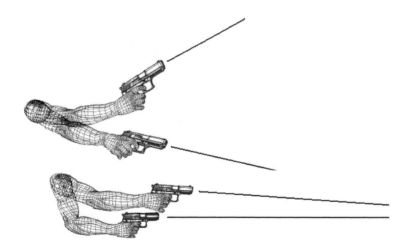

Figure 16.3 Joint configurations during pistol shooting. Certain configurations change the alignment of the barrel with respect to the target, deteriorating performance – the variability in this subspace is NGEV (upper panel). In contrast, alternative configurations leave the (relevant) alignment unaltered, hence do not affect performance since the mark will still be hit – the variability in this subspace is GEV (lower panel).

the advantage of allowing for an unbiased search for underlying coordinative structures (see Post *et al.*, 2000), UCM may be said to have the advantage of allowing for an objective test of explicit hypotheses regarding controlled variables (e.g. the orientation of the barrel in the example given; see Scholz *et al.*, 2000). In a sense, therefore, the two methods may be seen as complementary. A distinct limitation of the UCM approach is that a decomposition of the variance into GEV and NGEV is possible only if the relation between the goal-state and the variability of the 'elements' under scrutiny is explicitly known. Explicit knowledge regarding such relations may be obtained through the relating of multi-dimensional kinematics to a spatially defined goal, as in tasks like pistol-shooting and pointing (cf. Scholz *et al.*, 2000; Tseng *et al.*, 2003), but is impossible to obtain in many other tasks. How, for instance, should one explicate the relation between EMG activity and propulsion velocity in competitive cycling, or between joint rotations and pole-vaulting performance? Further, decomposing the multi-dimensional variability throughout the entire movement in GEV and NGEV requires the introduction of a specific goal criterion at every temporal instance. In a pointing task, for instance, such a criterion could be operationalized in terms of movement direction. However, an explicit, continuous match between the goal criterion and hand position is not required for the hand to reach the target. To avoid this problem, a reference or 'desired' path has to be introduced, representing an idealized path, which as such incorporates the required continuous changes of the goal criterion. Hence, to be able to apply the UCM approach, the invariant properties of coordinative structures have sometimes to be re-introduced through the backdoor.

Despite these restrictions, UCM is a very promising approach that opens up the possibility to come to terms with the so far much neglected, but theoretically highly significant notion of coordinative flexibility. After all, variability is an inherent property of movement patterns, and biological systems in general. From a functional perspective, it is therefore worthwhile to examine not the degree of variability as such, but rather the structural properties of the variability of movement data. For instance, an increase of GEV relative to NGEV may characterize the development of dexterity, rather than the entire amount of variability in itself, because GEV reflects functional variability.

The motor control literature already contains several indications that the variability of the motor performance of experts possesses a more intricate, sophisticated underlying structure than that of non-experts. For instance, Pressing and Jolley-Rogers (1997) found that an expert musician used a second-order error correction function to perform a synchronized tapping task, whereas a non-musician only used a first-order error correction function. Put differently, the expert musician used information about synchronization errors of the last and penultimate tap whereas the non-expert adjusted each tap on the basis of the last synchronization error only. These relatively new insights into the nature of variability can be readily translated into a general recommendation for coaches and trainers, namely, that the development of dexterity will probably be hampered by training methods that are strongly geared towards reducing variability in movement (e.g. as in methods of tennis training emphasizing stereotypical, idealized movement forms rather than outcome). To a certain extent it is true that becoming an expert implies becoming less variable, but in the end the difference between an expert and an intermediate performer is not so much in the degree of the variability as such, but rather in the way in which it is structured relative to a given task goal. To acquire a properly structured variability, it is necessary that the pupil or learner is able to relate changes in the configuration of the components of the motor apparatus to motor outcome; for reasons having to do with the issue of explicit versus implicit learning, this is probably best achieved through augmented knowledge of results in the absence of explicit instructions.

Flexibility across synergies

In the preceding sections, we have discussed the identification and formation of coordinative structures, as well as their flexibility as realized through the exploitation of motor redundancy. Without exception, the focus of the studies cited was on the synergies directly involved in the realization of a given coordination or task goal. However, to be economical, reliable and resourceful, the synergies directly implicated in task execution must be adequately embedded in a task-specific 'global' organization consisting of both supporting and performatory subsystems. Consider again the biathlete. Regardless of the quality of the aiming synergy defined over shoulder, elbow and wrist, the biathlete will have a hard time hitting the mark while randomly swaying around the ankle and/or hip joints, or when respiration interferes with shooting. For the biathlete to be a proficient marks(wo)man, the multi-joint synergy defined over shoulder and arm must be functionally integrated with postural and respiratory synergies. As a rule, the realization of any motor goal involves the 'execution' of several simultaneous subtasks that have to be coordinated with each other in a flexible, adaptive manner. The importance of this aspect of proficiency and expertise was explicitly recognized by Bernstein (1996) in his treatise on the development of dexterity, but has received little attention in the modern literature.

The manner in which multiple synergies are brought together is in itself a task-specific process. In order to ski, the biathlete's arms and legs have to be coordinated in a completely different manner, requiring a different type of postural control, as well as another kind of coordination with respiration to meet the higher metabolic demands of skiing. It follows from this task-specificity that the assembly of heterogeneous components of the human action system into distinct 'global' organizations is a 'soft', flexible process. This adaptive feature is extremely important from a functional point of view as it allows biological organizations to engage in a huge diversity of activities, and endows them with the capability to realize the same goal in a variety of ways. Nevertheless, relatively little is known about how the subsystems of the human action system cooperate in realizing specific task goals, let alone about how their interaction evolves during skill acquisition.

As mentioned previously, Bernstein (1996) theorized about 'levels in the construction of movement'. In this book, Bernstein started out from the observation that the functional behavioural repertoire of organisms has expanded explosively in the course of history, and that new classes of motor behaviour were added in a layer-like manner upon phylogenetically older ones. According to Bernstein, these new classes emerged through the mutually interdependent evolution of perceptual systems, effector systems and 'corresponding' neural tissue. As a result, the human nervous system is more or less hierarchically organized, both anatomically and functionally. Bernstein addressed the functional aspect of this hierarchy by distinguishing four levels of control in the construction of movement: the level of tonus (i.e. muscular tone), involved in all movements; the level of synergies (i.e. muscular–articular linkages), allowing for the production of coarse-grained coordination patterns (co-developed in concordance with interoceptive perceptual systems); the level of space, responsible for manual discrete movements as well as coarse-grained movements that need to be coordinated in relation to the environment (co-developed in concordance with exteroceptive perceptual systems); and the level of actions, responsible for the planning, sequencing and steering of goal-directed actions in an adaptive and creative manner. According to Bernstein, the lower levels are supportive, whereas either the level of space or the level of action may take the lead, depending on the task to be performed and the degree to which it has been practiced. The hierarchical nature of control is reflected in the recruitment and control of the lower levels by the leading level.

During skill acquisition, control is delegated to lower levels that are tuned to carry out specific (sub)functions, thus alleviating the task of higher control levels. In this context, sensory 'background' correction mechanisms evolve, which reduce the necessity for feedback control by the higher control levels, a process commonly called 'automatization'. Bernstein thus drafted a picture of skill learning involving the task-specific delegation and distribution of control over dedicated functional subsystems. During this process, the relative importance of perceptual modalities may change, depending on the task demands at hand.

Empirical support for such a shift was already reported a long time ago by Fleishman and Rich (1963), who showed that novices learning to operate a two-handed pursuit rotor device initially rely predominantly on vision and later predominantly on kinesthesis. In a similar vein, Huys and Beek (2002) found that expert jugglers more often exhibit a so-called 'gaze through' than less-expert jugglers when performing a three-ball cascade, in that their point-of-gaze remained confined to a small, but strategically chosen spatial location. This observation may be taken to imply that the role of vision decreased in importance relative to that of kinesthesis. Importantly, the expert jugglers could still track the motion of the balls when invited to do so, implying that they acquired the ability to flexibly switch between different coordination modes. Thus, in the course of learning, subsystems may couple and/or decouple in a task-dependent fashion. An important question is how do such couplings and decouplings come about. In addressing this question, Bingham (1988) distinguished between the inherent dynamics of the human action system and its components or subsystems and the incidental dynamics following from the constraints imposed by the task at hand. According to Bingham (1988), the coupling between subsystems may either be dictated by incidental constraints or by inherent dynamical properties. In all likelihood, the coupling between ball movements and looking behaviour in novices, and its decoupling in experts, reflects an accommodation of incidental, task-specific constraints. In order to elucidate how distinct constraints may mediate couplings between subsystems, we discuss some examples of recent research on this exciting topic and show how concepts and methods discussed in the preceding contribute in attempting to uncover mechanisms mediating couplings.

Task-specific constraints and adaptive coupling between subsystems

A well-documented and common form of coupling between physiologically distinct subsystems is that between locomotion and respiration. Locomotor–respiratory coupling (LRC) has been reported for cycling (Bernasconi and Kohl, 1993; Kohl *et al.*, 1981), running (Bramble and Carrier, 1983; Bramble and Jenkins, 1993), wheelchair propulsion (Amazeen *et al.*, 2001) and rowing (Mahler *et al.*, 1991a,b; Siegmund *et al.*, 1999). In re-examining Siegmund *et al.*'s (1999) data on LRC in rowing, we formulated a model to account for the transition from $1:1$ to $1:2$ frequency locks between locomotion and breathing observed in the data (see Figure 16.4; Daffertshofer *et al.*, submitted). This model was based on the consideration that cyclical abdominal pressure (Manning *et al.*, 2000) modulates self-sustained breathing (Del Negro *et al.*, 2002) and, in super-imposing the total lung pressure, causes (local) effective $\dot{V}_{O_2}$ maxima at integer frequency ratios between the rowing strokes and respiration. In the derived dynamical model, a 'free' limit cycle oscillator ('respiration') and a periodically forced oscillator ('rowing') are coupled according to the maximization of effective $\dot{V}_{O_2}$ in the lungs. The model was shown to account for the experimentally observed bifurcations, thus lending support to its implicit hypothesis that the coupling between both subsystems comes about through a single physiological, albeit mechanically constrained, measure.

In view of the importance of the incidental dynamics, it is interesting to note that, in tasks in which the breathing dynamics are constrained to a lesser degree than in rowing, such as cycling, wheel-chair propulsion, walking and running, a wider range of stable frequency ratios between respiration and locomotion has been observed (e.g. $1:1$, $1:2$, $2:3$, $1:4$ and $2:5$). The general picture emerging from the LRC literature is that in the course of practice locomotion becomes entrained to respiration. In all likelihood, the resulting form of entrainment represents (local or global) optimal solutions that are more effective and economical than non-entrained modes (see Bernasconi and Kohl, 1993; Garlando *et al.*, 1985). It appears that well-trained athletes have acquired the ability to opt for distinct LRC modes, rendering them more flexible.

As a final example, we refer to a recent juggling study in which we examined changes in the coupling between ball evolutions and hand movements, on the

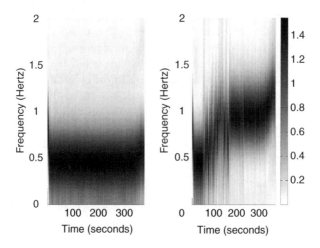

Figure 16.4 Time-resolved frequency distributions (spectrograms) of handle speed ('rowing stroke'; left panel) and respiration (right panel). Interestingly, after approximately 80 seconds the 1:1 locking between movement and respiration appears to become unstable finally leading to an change of respiration speed by means of a 1:1 → 1:2 transition in frequency locking – see the switch from maximal spectral power at about 0.5 Hertz to ca. 1 Hertz in the right panel in contrast with an almost constant rowing frequency.

one hand, and body sway patterns, on the other, as novices learned to perform the three-ball cascade (Huys *et al.*, 2003). By using a combination of cross-spectral techniques, relative phase and PCA, we observed that sway patterns were frequency locked with the ball/arm movements in two qualitatively distinct modes, albeit that the strength of these locks varied markedly across trials and participants (note that the task constraints in juggling require locking between ball and arm movements). Specifically, the centre-of-pressure cycled with the same or with twice the movement frequency of the arms. Using a mechanical model we showed that these qualitatively distinct sway modes could be attributed to different combinations of arm movement amplitudes, angles and relative phase relations. In other words, the sway dynamics appeared to be shaped by the mechanical consequences of the arm movements. Interestingly, in the course of learning, the stability of the juggling pattern evolved asymptotically, whereas the dynamics of both postural sway components progressed in qualitatively distinct manners. These components were characterized by gradual appearances and disappearances as well as abrupt changes between both sway oscillations. These observations hint at the existence of distinct, relatively autonomous dynamical processes in learning, and as such, may be taken as evidence for a multi-levelled 'construction' of movement.

In sum, when performing perceptual-motor tasks, a variety of heterogeneous subsystems are assembled, and movements constructed as distinct functional coordination patterns become embedded in a task-specific global organization.

The explicit form of coordination patterns is governed to a large extent by the constraints imposed onto the action system, be it from within (inherent dynamics) or from without the system (incidental dynamics). During skill acquisition, specific couplings develop and the number of stable coordination modes available to the performer seems to increase, endowing the sports (wo)man with the flexibility required 'to find a motor solution for any external situation, that is, to adequately solve any emerging motor problem correctly, quickly, rationally and resourcefully' (Bernstein, 1996: 228).

Although, admittedly, the study of flexibility across synergies is still in its infancy, several relevant implications for practice and instruction may be distilled from the ideas and findings discussed. A general observation is that the interactions between oscillatory subsystems may result in frequency locking at a variety of $p:q$ ratios (with p and q representing small integer numbers). In general, these entrained solutions can be considered as more effective and economical than non-entrained or transient solutions. However, which particular frequency ratio is the most optimal for a given situation is unknown, and may depend on the prevailing internal and external conditions. Given this state of affairs, coaches are probably best served by the advice to let their pupils explore the full spectrum of possible coordination solutions in this regard and to encourage them to attempt to settle down on any solution that is found appealing during the exploration (i.e. 'go with the flow' rather than prescribing solutions that are considered to be optimal a priori), thus avoiding dwelling long on non-entrained or transient solutions. However, it is important to realize that this advice is based on considerations of economy and stability, which may not always apply (e.g. during the final sprint of a race only maximal velocity matters, not the efficiency of energy expenditure).

Conclusions

In this chapter, we discussed a number of generic concepts and methods that, collectively, are representative of the currently evolving theoretical and empirical understanding of coordination dynamics. In view of space limitations, we chose to bring out the main gist of the approach and to explore its possible implications for practice and instruction in sports instead of presenting a full-blown tutorial. However, for interested readers who wish to learn more about the concepts and methods discussed the chapter contains many key references, which, invariably, will be a challenge to read for people without a background in the exact sciences.

Being fully aware of the intrinsically abstract nature of coordination dynamics, we have included several concrete examples of possible implications of the fundamental concepts of coordination dynamics for practice and instruction in sport settings. As such, this is a potentially dangerous endeavour. Concepts such as phase attraction, intrinsic dynamics and attractor states are easy to use methaphorically, but very hard to apply in a strictly operationalized way in the experimental study of coordinated movement. Whereas the endeavour of coordination dynamics explicitly attempts to achieve the latter, there are several examples of methaporical applications of coordination dynamics, not only in informal speech but also in a host of scientific studies. This is unfortunate because the power of coordination dynamics resides in its strict, quantitative operationalization of key concepts, resulting in close links and intensive interactions between theory and data. Although it is not, of course, forbidden to use the concepts of coordination dynamics metaphorically, as indeed we have done on several occasions in the present chapter, it is essential to keep on making a sharp distinction between metaphorical use and strict operationalization. After all, one has to know chalk from cheese.

The preceding remarks are also important when evaluating or predicting the potential of coordination dynamics for the study of coordinated movement and skill acquisition in sports. To reiterate, the fundamental concepts of coordination dynamics are operationally defined, allowing for rigorous tests when applied to the study of motor control and learning. As a consequence, the concepts in question are only applicable to situations (i.e. coordination tasks and problems) that fit their operationalization. In the preceding discussion, we have seen that especially the concepts of intrinsic dynamics and uncontrolled manifold are vulnerable in this regard as they cannot be applied to a broad range of perceptual-motor skills. Obviously, this situation limits the possibilities of developing a coordination dynamics of sport skills. Fortunately, however, other methods such as PCA as well as various kinds of cross-spectral and relative phase analyses are quite robust and can be readily applied to the study of complex perceptual-motor skills of the kind encountered in sports.

Obviously, a formidable amount of work remains to be done in this regard. In fact, there is a farrow research ground here waiting to be cultivated, with many exciting, urgent and unresolved questions. Simply extending the issues addressed in this chapter already leads to a respectable and challenging list: How do coordination patterns arise and evolve in the acquisition of functional skills? How is flexibility of task performance insured, as skill learners become more and more proficient? When are excessive degrees of freedom a curse and when a blessing? How are postural and respiratory subsystems integrated with performatory synergies, and how does this integration evolve in the course of learning? In principle, coordination dynamics offers some exciting and, we believe generic, new concepts to pursue such questions in the sports domain, but we are only just beginning to test and widen their scope of application.

References

Amazeen, P. G., Amazeen, E. L. and Beek, P. J. (2001). Coupling of breathing and movement during manual wheelchair propulsion. *Journal of Experimental Psychology: Human Perception and Performance*, 27 (5), 1243–1259.

Arutyunyan, G. A., Gurfinkel, V. S. and Mirskii, M. K. (1968). Investigation of aiming at a target. *Biofizika*, 13, 536–538.

Arutyunyan, G. A., Gurfinkel, V. S. and Mirskii, M. K. (1969). Organisation of movements by man of an exact postural task. *Biofizika*, 14, 1103–1107.

Beek, P. J., Peper, C. E. and Stegeman, D. F. (1995). Dynamical models of movement coordination. *Human Movement Science*, 14, 573–608.

Bernasconi, P. and Kohl, J. (1993). Analysis of coordination between breathing and exercise rhythms in man. *Journal of Physiology*, 471, 693–706.

Bernstein, N. A. (1984). Some emergent problems of the regulation of motor acts. In H. T. A. Whiting (Ed.), *Human motor actions: Bernstein reassessed* (pp. 343–371). Amsterdam: North-Holland.

Bernstein, N. A. (1996). On dexterity and its development. In M. L. Latash and Turvey, M. T. (Eds), *Dexterity and its development* (pp. 3–244). Mahwah: NJ: Erlbaum.

Bingham, G. P. (1988). Task-specific devices and the perceptual bottleneck. *Human Movement Science*, 7, 225–264.

Bramble, D. M. and Carrier, D. R. (1983). Running and breathing in mammals. *Science*, 219 (4582), 251–256.

Bramble, D. M. and Jenkins, F. A., Jr. (1993). Mammalian locomotor–respiratory integration: implications for diaphragmatic and pulmonary design. *Science*, 262 (5131), 235–240.

Daffertshofer, A., Peper, C. E. and Beek, P. J. (2000). Spatio-temporal patterns of encephalographic signals during polyrhythmic tapping. *Human Movement Science*, 19, 475–498.

Daffertshofer, A., Huys, R. and Beek, P. J. (submitted). An account for the dynamics underlying locomotor–respiratory coupling.

Del Negro, C. A., Morgado-Valle, C. and Feldman, J. L. (2002). Respiratory rhythm: an emergent network property? *Neuron*, 34 (5), 821–830.

Fleishman, E. A. and Rich, S. (1963). Role of kinesthetic and spatial–visual abilities in perceptual-motor learning. *Journal of Experimental Psychology*, 66, 6–11.

Garlando, F., Kohl, J., Koller, E. A. and Pietsch, P. (1985). Effect of coupling the breathing- and cycling rhythms on oxygen uptake during bicycle ergometry. *European Journal of Applied Physiology and Occuppational Physiology*, 54 (5), 497–501.

Greene, P. H. (1972). Problems of organisation of motor systems. In R. Rosen and F. M. Snell (Eds), *Progress in theoretical biology*, Vol. 2 (pp. 303–338). New York: Academic Press.

Haken, H. (1977). *Synergetics. An introduction: nonequilibrium phase transitions and self-organisation in physics, chemistry, and biology*. Berlin, New York: Springer.

Haken, H. (1983). *Synergetics: an introduction: nonequilibrium phase transitions and self-organisation in physics, chemistry, and biology* (3rd rev. and enl. edn). Berlin, New York: Springer.

Haken, H. (1996). *Principles of brain functioning. A synergetic approach to brain activity, behaviour and cognition*. Berlin, Heidelberg, New York: Springer.

Haken, H., Kelso, J. A. S. and Bunz, H. (1985). A theoretical model of phase transitions in human hand movements. *Biological Cybernetics*, 51 (5), 347–356.

Huys, R. and Beek, P. J. (2002). The coupling between point-of-gaze and ball movements in three-ball cascade juggling: the effects of expertise, pattern and tempo. *Journal of Sports Sciences*, 20 (3), 171–186.

Huys, R., Daffertshofer, A. and Beek, P. J. (2003). Learning to juggle: on the assembly of functional sub-systems into a task-specific dynamical organisation. *Biological Cybernetics*, 88 (4), 302–318.

Kelso, J. A. S. (1981). On the oscillatory basis of movement. *Bulletin of the Psychonomic Society*, 18, 63.

Kelso, J. A. S. (1984). Phase transitions and critical behaviour in human bimanual coordination. *American Journal of Physiology*, 246 (6 Pt 2), R1000–R1004.

Kelso, J. A. S. (1995). *Dynamic patterns: the self-organisation of brain and behaviour.* Cambridge, MA: MIT Press.

Kohl, J., Koller, E. A. and Jager, M. (1981). Relation between pedalling and breathing rhythm. *European Journal of Applied Physiology and Occupational Physiology*, 47 (3), 223–237.

Kugler, P. N., Kelso, J. A. S. and Turvey, M. T. (1980). On the concept of coordinative structures as dissipative structures: I. Theoretical lines of convergence. In G. E. Stelmach and J. Requin (Eds), *Tutorials in motor behaviour* (pp. 3–47). Amsterdam: North-Holland.

Longstaff, M. G. and Heath, R. A. (2003). The influence of motor system degradation on the control of handwriting movements. *Human Movement Science*, 22, 91–110.

Mahler, D. A., Hunter, B., Lentine, T. and Ward, J. (1991a). Locomotor–respiratory coupling develops in novice female rowers with training. *Medicine & Science in Sports & Exercise*, 23 (12), 1362–1366.

Mahler, D. A., Shuhart, C. R., Brew, E. and Stukel, T. A. (1991b). Ventilatory responses and entrainment of breathing during rowing. *Medicine & Science in Sports & Exercise*, 23 (2), 186–192.

Manning, T. S., Plowman, S. A., Drake, G., Looney, M. A. and Ball, T. E. (2000). Intra-abdominal pressure and rowing: the effects of inspiring versus expiring during the drive. *Journal of Sports Medicine and Physical Fitness*, 40 (3), 223–232.

Mitra, S., Amazeen, P. G. and Turvey, M. T. (1998). Intermediate motor learning as decreasing active (dynamical) degrees of freedom. *Human Movement Science*, 17, 17–65.

Newell, K. M. and van Emmerik, R. E. A. (1989). The acquisition of coordination: preliminary analysis of learning to write. *Human Movement Science*, 8, 7–32.

Newell, K. M., Liu, Y.-T. and Mayer-Kress, G. (2001). Time scales in motor learning and development. *Psychological Review*, 108, 57–82.

Newell, K. M. and Vaillancourt, D. E. (2001). Dimensional change in motor learning. *Human Movement Science*, 20 (4–5), 695–715.

Post, A. A., Daffertshofer, A. and Beek, P. J. (2000). Principal components in three-ball cascade juggling. *Biological Cybernetics*, 82 (2), 143–152.

Pressing, J. and Jolley-Rogers, G. (1997). Spectral properties of human cognition and skill. *Biological Cybernetics*, 76 (5), 339–347.

Scholz, J. P. and Schöner, G. (1999). The uncontrolled manifold concept: identifying control variables for a functional task. *Experimental Brain Research*, 126, 289–306.

Scholz, J. P., Schöner, G. and Latash, M. L. (2000). Identifying the control structure of multijoint coordination during pistol shooting. *Experimental Brain Research*, 135, 382–404.

Schöner, G. (1989). Learning and recall in a dynamic theory of coordination patterns. *Biological Cybernetics*, 62 (1), 39–54.

Schöner, G. (1995). Recent developments and problems in human movement science and their theoretical implications. *Ecological Psychology*, 7, 291–314.

Schöner, G. and Kelso, J. A. (1988). A synergetic theory of environmentally-specified and learned patterns of movement coordination. I. Relative phase dynamics. *Biological Cybernetics*, 58 (2), 71–80.

Schöner, G., Zanone, P. G. and Kelso, J. A. S. (1992). Learning as change of coordination dynamics: theory and experiment. *Journal of Motor Behaviour*, 24, 29–48.

Siegmund, G. P., Edwards, M. R., Moore, K. S., Tiessen, D. A., Sanderson, D. J. and McKenzie, D. C. (1999). Ventilation and locomotion coupling in varsity male rowers. *Journal of Applied Physiology*, 87 (1), 233–242.

Temprado, J., Della-Grasta, M., Farrell, M. and Laurent, M. (1997). A novice–expert comparison of (intra-limb) coordination subserving the volleyball serve. *Human Movement Science*, 16, 653–676.

Tseng, Y. W., Scholz, J. P., Schöner, G. and Hotchkiss, L. (2003). Effect of accuracy constraint on joint coordination during pointing movements. *Experimental Brain Research*, 149 (3), 276–288.

Turvey, M. T. (1977). Preliminaries to a theory on action with reference to vision. In R. Shaw and J. Brandsford (Eds), *Perceiving, acting and knowing: toward and ecological psychology* (pp. 211–265). Hillsdale, NJ: Erlbaum.

Turvey, M. T. (1990). Coordination. *American Psychologist*, 45 (8), 938–953.

Vereijken, B., Whiting, H. T. and Beek, W. J. (1992). A dynamical systems approach to skill acquisition. *Quarterly Journal of Experimental Psychology A*, 45 (2), 323–344.

Zanone, P. G. and Kelso, J. A. (1992). Evolution of behavioural attractors with learning: nonequilibrium phase transitions. *Journal of Experimental Psychology: Human Perception and Performance*, 18 (2), 403–421.

17 Perceptual learning is mastering perceptual degrees of freedom

Geert J.P. Savelsbergh, John van der Kamp,
Raôul R.D. Oudejans and Mark A. Scott

Peak performance requires a vivid awareness of the environment. To have such awareness, attention should be focused on aspects of the environment relevant for one's actions. According to Weinberg and Gould (1999), situation awareness is 'One of the least understood but most interesting and important aspects of attentional focus in sport' (p. 328). The ecological approach to visual perception and action (Gibson, 1979) may offer a useful starting point for understanding situation awareness in sport as this issue is a core theme of this approach: perceiving the environment by detecting those sources of information that are relevant for one's actions. The control of movement, according to ecological psychology, is based on a continuous coupling to available perceptual information. Given the relevance of information detection, it is no surprise that perceptual skill is part and parcel of peak performance in sport (see Williams *et al.*, 1999). For instance, research has demonstrated differences in visual search behaviour between expert and novice performers, where experts are superior in using predictive information (i.e. advance visual cues) to guide their anticipatory responses (e.g. Abernethy, 1987; Savelsbergh *et al.*, 2002; Williams and Burwitz, 1993).

Although skill-related differences are often found, the underlying processes that lead to these differences in perceptual skill are largely unknown. Using an analogy to the earlier work of Bernstein (e.g. 1967), we argue that the observed differences in perceptual skill between novices and experts can be understood as the reflection of the process of mastering *perceptual* degrees of freedom (Savelsbergh and van der Kamp, 2000). In doing so, we propose different phases in detecting and using sources of information during the acquisition of perceptual-motor skill, and illustrate these with data from soccer goalkeeping. We conclude the chapter with some implications of the idea of perceptual degrees of freedom for research and practice.

Freezing and exploiting perceptual degrees of freedom

The study of movement coordination is highly influenced by the writings of Bernstein (1967). Bernstein formulated one of the central issues in the study of motor coordination: the 'degrees of freedom problem'. He argued that the complex interactions between the different components of the movement apparatus (e.g. muscles, tendons, joints) make separate control of all these components impossible. Therefore, the large number of individual degrees of freedom has to be reduced in order to make control possible. This reduction in degrees of freedom is a process of '...mastering redundant degrees of freedom of the moving organ, in other words its conversion to a controllable system. More briefly, coordination is the organization of the control of the motor apparatus' (Bernstein, 1967, p. 127).

Bernstein distinguished three phases in the process of mastering the degrees of freedom, namely *freezing*, *freeing*, and *exploiting*. The work of Vereijken and colleagues nicely illustrates these phases. Vereijken (Vereijken *et al.*, 1992a,b) examined Bernstein's propositions in novices practising slalom-like ski movements on a ski-simulator. They found that in the early practice trials, the joint angles of the lower limbs and torso displayed little movement (i.e. relatively small range of motion), whereas at the same time the inter-joint couplings (i.e. as indicated by cross-correlations) were high. During practice, angular movement in the joints, in particular the knee joints, increased and the coupling between the joints weakened (Vereijken *et al.*, 1992a). These results support Bernstein's ideas of an initial *freezing* in the early practice phase followed by a *freeing or releasing* of the degrees of freedom during later phases of learning. In a subsequent paper, Vereijken and co-workers (Vereijken *et al.*, 1992b) observed that during early practice, novices applied force to the ski-simulator's platform, which is attached to a spring, at a biomechanically inefficient moment. That is, the novices did not benefit from the available elastic forces stored in the stretched springs. With experience, however, participants learned to *exploit* the characteristics of the apparatus, postponing their force production until after the platform had passed the centre of the apparatus and started to slow down. With this strategy, participants made use of the elastic forces that gave them a 'free ride' back to the centre of the apparatus and beyond, allowing them to reduce their active muscle forces. This neatly illustrates Bernstein's idea of exploiting degrees of freedom during skilled performance.

Savelsbergh and van der Kamp (2000) have recently proposed, analogous to Bernstein's ideas, that during the process of learning to detect and use perceptual information to control movements three mutually overlapping phases of freezing, freeing and exploiting of *perceptual* degrees of freedom may be distinguished.

During the initial phase of *freezing* perceptual degrees of freedom, one source of information out of a multitude of available sources is used to control movement. In other words, within a certain set of constraints, a particular coupling between information and movement emerges that fits the local task requirements – mostly this would not be the most optimal fit. The selection of this perceptual information source is induced by the interaction of constraints (i.e. environmental, task and organismic; see Newell, 1986). In other words, in the freezing phase (Figure 17.1a), the actor selects one of multiple information sources that will enable him to more or less successfully perform the task at hand. For example, in the case of controlling a ground-level ball in soccer, distance information might

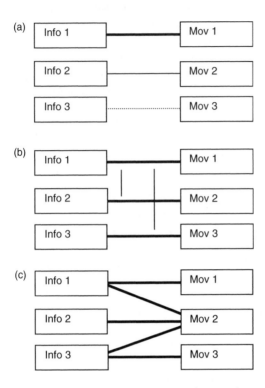

Figure 17.1 The phases of perceptual-motor learning: (a) freezing: the coupling
between information (Info 1) and movement (Mov) gets stronger during
practice, but not for Info 2 and Mov etc.; (b) freeing: one can switch from
one strong coupling to another; and (c) exploiting: information (Info 1)
can be used for different actions (Mov 1 and Mov 2) and different information (Info 2 and Info 3) for the same movement (Mov 2). (Adapted
from Savelsbergh and van der Kamp (2000).)

be used to position the foot in time more or less correctly. With practice, the
strength of the coupling increases: the movement gets intricately tuned to information, which enhances the probability that this particular coupling re-occurs
under the same set of constraints. Eventually, this would result in a pruning of
other potential couplings, and an increasing stability of the selected coupling.
However, a change within the particular set of constraints during this early phase
will disrupt the information–movement coupling. Because an alternative coupling is not available or too weak, this could lead to a breakdown of action. Only
after practice can an alternative information–movement coupling emerge, specific for the new set of local constraints.

The second phase involves the *freeing or releasing* of perceptual degrees of
freedom (Figure 17.1b). During this phase, practice under different sets of constraints (e.g. controlling a ground-level ball on a wet pitch or an 'over hit' pass)
eventually leads to a whole repertoire of possible information–movement

couplings for a certain task (e.g. timing the positioning of the foot by coupling it to information specific for distance, speed or time). Hence, if the local constraints change, the actor will be able to realize an alternative coupling, without the need to learn it from scratch and without a complete breakdown of the action.

Finally, expert performance is characterized by the ability not only to use different information couplings, but also to *exploit* the different information–movement couplings (Figure 17.1c). The expert can now draw from a whole repertoire of information–movement couplings that can be exploited under different sets of constraints. Information (e.g. about ball approach) may be tuned to the original movement (e.g. controlling a ground-level ball) but may also be exploited for other movements in different conditions (e.g. one-touch-play or heading). In short, the original information–movement coupling forms the foundation for new couplings to emerge under similar or different sets of constraints, that is, the available perceptual degrees of freedom can be exploited.

In sum, we have proposed that improvements in perceptual skill by learning to couple information to movement may be captured by three mutually overlapping phases of freezing, freeing and exploiting of the available perceptual degrees of freedom. Individual differences in performance would, at least in part, reflect the phase of learning for an individual.

Evidence for freezing between information and movement can be found in a learning experiment by Savelsbergh and Whiting (1992, Experiment 2). In their experiment, relatively poor catchers (i.e. less than six successful catches out of thirty attempts) were trained under monocular and binocular viewing conditions in order to examine the effects of learning with binocular and monocular vision on spatial predictions in catching (putting the hand at the right place). In Experiment 1 more spatial errors were observed under the monocular condition than under the binocular condition while no differences were found for temporal predictions. Savelsbergh and Whiting (1992) suggested that the superiority of performance in the binocular viewing condition might be attributed to the fact that participants simply have more experience with binocular viewing than they do with monocular information. In other words, it is the lack of experience and not the insufficiency of the monocular information that was thought to result in more spatial errors. To explore such a contention, it is necessary to allow participants to spend an equal amount of time training under both viewing conditions in order to become attuned to the information available. This would enable participants the opportunity to freeze perceptual degrees of freedom and converge onto specific information and movement couplings.

Participants received training in the dark where only the ball was visible. One group practised for five sessions under the binocular condition and switched over in session 6 to training under the monocular condition (binocular to monocular). For the second group, sessions were reversed (monocular to binocular). The results showed a significant improvement in spatial prediction under the monocular condition up to the level reached under binocular conditions (Figure 17.2). No significant improvement in spatial predictions were observed when transferred from

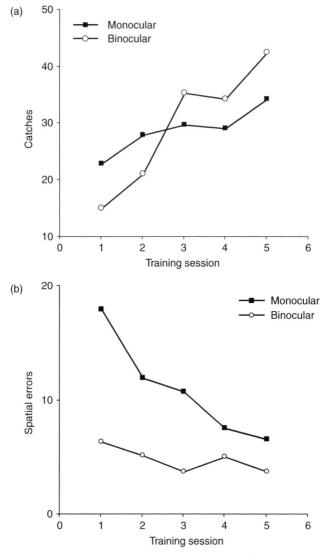

Figure 17.2 The results of the training for the monocular and binocular groups as a
function of session with respect to successful catches (a) and spatial
errors (b). (Adapted from Savelsbergh and Whiting, 1992.)

monocular to binocular, while when transferred from binocular to monocular
significantly more spatial errors were made (Figure 17.3).

The first finding, as illustrated in Figure 17.2, demonstrates that under the
monocular condition, catchers became attuned to the monocular information that
was available, while they were unable to use binocular information when it became

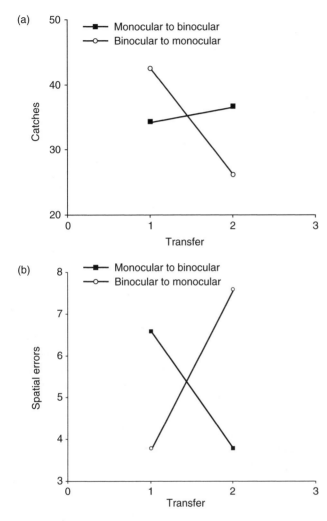

Figure 17.3 The transfer results from monocular to binocular and reverse for successful catches (a) and spatial errors (b). (Adapted from Savelsbergh and
Whiting, 1992.)

available under binocular viewing. The performance increments across sessions in
the monocular condition, attributed to a decrease in spatial errors, suggest that participants used monocular information for their spatial predictions (i.e. a freezing
between monocular information and movement). The asymmetrical transfer effects
are interesting, particularly because they show no adverse effects of training under
monocular viewing when required to perform and continue training under binocular viewing. In contrast, transfer from binocular to monocular did produce adverse
effects. Arguably, this effect was due to the freezing of binocular information with

movement and the subsequent absence of this information under monocular conditions. This finding suggests that participants in the experimental monocular to binocular training group simply continued to make use of the monocular information (frozen) that had been used during the first five sessions when transferred from the monocular to binocular condition. Alternatively, they may have transferred back to using binocular information immediately as they had experienced this coupling previously, which could be either an example of freeing or exploiting the degrees of freedom. The participant uses whichever source of information is available and is the most optimal for the present situation. In both cases, no new coupling was necessary. Participants who were trained under binocular viewing, however, showed a decrement in performance when they were required to perform under monocular viewing. This could be the result of (exclusively) making use of binocular spatial information (freezing of perceptual degrees of freedom) without being able to use monocular information for the catching movement.

Perceptual degrees of freedom and the education of attention

According to proponents of the ecological approach, the perceptual array surrounding an actor is extremely rich in information. The actor has to select from all available information sources which is relevant to control one's movement. This process, by which information is selected, is called 'attention' (Gibson, 1966). The process of coming to attend to the source of information that is most useful in the control of movement is what is commonly referred to as the 'education of attention'. J. J. Gibson described the process of education of attention as 'a greater *noticing* of the critical differences with less noticing of irrelevancies' and 'a progressive focusing or centering of the perceptual system' (Gibson, 1966, p. 52). In other words, the education of attention is the process by of learning which sources of information to attend to in which situation and when to attend to these variables. Recently, Jacobs and Michaels (2002; see also Michaels and Beek, 1995) have argued that this education of attention entails a change from detecting non-specifying to specifying sources of information. Specifying information sources are specific to the to-be-perceived properties of the environment. This means that detecting a certain information source that specifies a property of interest in the environment allows one to make reliable judgements about this property (Beek *et al.*, 2003). A non-specifying information source might be related to the to-be-perceived property, but it is not specific to this property as its value does not under all circumstances veridically predict the value of the to-be-perceived environmental property (Beek *et al.*, 2003). Thus, with practice actors converge from sources of information that are only partly useful in one particular situation to sources of information that are more useful (i.e. specifying), perhaps even under different circumstances.

The proposal that perceptual learning should be considered as a mastering of perceptual degrees of freedom is inextricably bound up with the process of education of attention, as the study of Savelsbergh and Whiting (1992) shows. Novices will make use of a source of information they are exposed to, such as either monocular or binocular sources of information in the catching example above. In catching a fly ball in baseball, to provide another example, the information a novice experiences may well be the peak optical velocity or the maximum height of the ball. These sources of information do not exactly specify in which direction and how fast the fielder should run and hence would not always result in successful interception (Michaels and Oudejans, 1992; see also Scott, 2000). To control their movements, novices stick to the non-specifying information source as a way to freeze several perceptual degrees of freedom; they have only a very limited range of alternative couplings available and do not easily switch to other sources of information. Only during later phases of learning, and depending on the success of its use, the performer may converge to other more useful or even specifying variables such as vertical optical acceleration (Michaels and Oudejans, 1992). This would be related to freeing the perceptual degrees of freedom as the possibility is created to use other sources of information that would lead to more successful catches. At the highest levels of skill, one can exploit several sources of information in a given situation, using whichever information is available and is suited to the situation. Experts have learned to attend to and detect those information sources that are most useful in the control of movement, while leaving unattended and undetected those sources that are less useful, irrelevant or potentially distracting (e.g. Abernethy, 2001; Williams and Grant, 1999).

The free(z)ing of perceptual degrees of freedom: an example from soccer goalkeepers

Recently, we have examined in our laboratory differences in perceptual skills of goalkeepers during attempts to stop penalty kicks in soccer (Savelsbergh *et al.*, 2002). Goalkeepers of different levels of expertise were required to move a joystick in response to penalty kick situations presented on a large screen. Participants had to anticipate the direction of each penalty kick quickly and accurately by moving the joystick as if to intercept the ball. If the joystick was positioned in the correct location the very moment the ball crossed the goal line, the penalty was judged a successful save. The use of the joystick allowed the participants to make corrections to their initial decision as the run up to the penalty kick evolved. It was found that the near-expert goalkeepers were generally more accurate in predicting the direction of the penalty kick, waited longer before initiating a response and made fewer corrective movements with the joystick compared to novices.

We also assessed visual search behaviour using an eye movement registration system. Data presented in Table 17.1 and Figure 17.4 are from the successful trials only, that is, those trials in which the penalties were stopped by the goalkeepers as indicated by the spatio-temporal pattern of the joystick movement.

Table 17.1 illustrates, as is often found in similar studies, that with expertise the number and duration of fixations change. As a function of expertise, there is a decrease in the number of fixations which are compensated for by longer fixation

Table 17.1 The number and duration of fixations as a function of level of expertise (data from Savelsbergh *et al.*, 2002)

	Number	Duration (milliseconds)
Novice	4.3	389
Near-experts	2.9	530

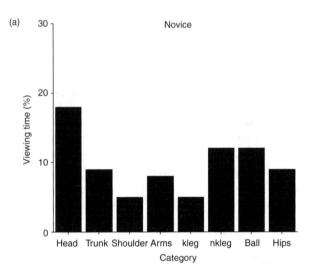

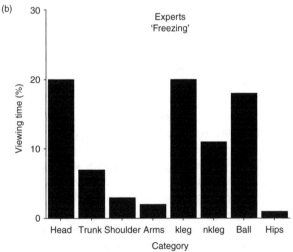

Figure 17.4 The percentage of time of eye fixations on different regions of the body for the penalty taker during the run-up to the ball. In the top panel, the mean eye fixation of novice performers has been plotted. In the bottom panel, the same information for near-expert goalkeepers is illustrated (data from Savelsbergh *et al.*, 2002).

durations. This change in visual search may be interpreted as a freezing of the perceptual degrees of freedom, from being a complete novice to being a near-expert goalkeeper (or intermediate penalty stopper). That is, the near-expert goalkeepers may stick longer to fewer sources of information, as would be found in the first phase of mastering the perceptual degrees of freedom. A similar interpretation is reached after inspection of Figure 17.4.

Figure 17.4 depicts the regions of eye fixation of the opponent's body during the run up to the ball (e.g. head, trunk, shoulder, kicking leg). The percentage of time within each region as a function of total time for both the novices (top panel) and the near-experts (bottom panel) is illustrated. The novices seem to 'visit' all possible regions, the percentages of time within each region are quite evenly distributed (between 5 and 12 per cent except the head area). The near-experts, on the other hand, show a different pattern. Apparently, they found the head, the kicking leg and ball to be the most informative areas. A possible interpretation is that the novices' fixations wander around without selectively attending to one of the possible sources of information. The near-expert goalkeepers (who are not necessarily expert penalty stoppers), however, have learned to attend to a few probably more informative regions. Still these do not appear to be the most useful or specifying sources of information given the observation that even the near-expert goalkeepers only stopped about one-third of penalties. Again, this points to an initial freezing of the perceptual degrees of freedom.

Obviously, such an interpretation is speculative and needs careful scrutiny. However, the prediction is that since *expert* goalkeepers would have released or already exploited the degrees of freedom, they would visually search more or more useful (i.e. specifying) regions of the opponents body during the run up to the ball. This type of analysis might provide a window into how the commonly observed changes in eye-movement and eye-fixations reveal something about the underlying processes of perceptual learning.

Perceptual degrees of freedom and its implications

The proposal that the road to perceptual expertise is characterized by a mastering of perceptual degrees of freedom has some important implications for both the design and interpretation of research into perceptual learning. First, previous investigations often included conditions (e.g. the occlusion paradigm) in which potentially useful or specifying information sources were either removed or perturbed in order to determine their contribution in the control of action. Depending on the phase of learning (i.e. the freezing, freeing or exploiting phase), the effects of such manipulations may be quite different. For instance, the performance of an individual in the freezing phase is likely to be completely disrupted, whereas the performance of a participant in the exploitation phase is much more likely to be unaffected by the removal of information due to their ability to adapt faster and more easily to different circumstances. This makes it methodologically difficult to pinpoint the source of information experts would use when performing at their very best. Moreover, it is likely that every participant will have experienced different perceptual constraints when learning how to regulate movements, and hence, a wide variety of information–movement couplings is likely to exist between individuals. This could result in individual participants responding in different ways to the same experimental conditions, even when they are in the same learning phase. This suggests that individual differences (and perhaps learning history) need to be taken into account when interpreting empirical findings (cf. Zanone and Kelso, 1992). The lack of consideration of individual differences could explain why some other research areas (e.g. investigations into the timing of interceptive actions) have produced such equivocal findings (Savelsbergh and van der Kamp, 2000; Scott, 2000).

Second, it should be emphasized that the education of attention implied by our perceptual learning phases is not exclusively a matter of the convergence to most useful information sources. It also involves *an accurate timing of attention to moments* at which the most useful sources are available. Information is by definition dynamic rather than static, that is, it is defined by persistence under change (in time) (Gibson, 1979). As an example, research into gaze behaviour during dart throwing has revealed that it is not just the duration of looking at the target but also the timing relative to the execution of the throwing movement that is important (Vickers *et al.*, 2000). This finding has recently been corroborated by the results of Oudejans *et al.* (2002; see also Oudejans *et al.*, submitted). These authors demonstrated that in the visual control of a basketball jump shot, success of the shot is dependent on the time when the shooter looks at the target (either early or late, depending on the style of shooting). Not only the particular source of information, but also the moment at which it is available and thus detected is a perceptual degree of freedom that may or may not be frozen, released or exploited.

A final remark concerns the possibility that further exploitation of perceptual degrees of freedom may sometimes be impossible, simply because all possible sources of information are 'visited'. As an example, Oudejans *et al.* (2000) have recently demonstrated that errors in judging offside in soccer appear to be the result of assistant referees' using an information source that does not specify who is closer to the goal (i.e. attacker or defender). The assistant referee appears to judge offside on the basis of the optical angle between defender and attacker, which specifies who is closer to the defender's goal line. However, this is only correct if the assistant referee is on the offside line. Oudejans *et al.* (2000) showed that (experienced) assistant referees are frequently not positioned on the offside line when they administer their judgements, giving them a point of observation from which errors are optically inevitable. The assistant referees respond to what they see from their position, that is, the relative retinal position of attacking and defending players. However, they have trouble taking into account the differences in depth between players, probably due to the lack of information about differences in depth beyond 10 metres (Cutting and Vishton, 1995). Therefore, Jacobs' (2001) assumption that assistant referees could 'learn not to use the commonly used non-specifying variable and, perhaps, come to rely on variables that lead to fewer errors' (p. 205) is doubtful. In the current system, with the assistant referee next to pitch at the same height as the players, alternative sources of information are unlikely to be available. In other words, it is not by necessity that expert performance enters the phase of exploiting perceptual degrees of freedom, or even when it does it may not always lead to the use of specifying sources of information.

Practical applications: examples from soccer and basketball

Specificity of practice in soccer

In order to further illustrate our model of perceptual degrees of freedom, we use soccer training and practice. Typically, expert players have acquired excellent ball control skills in a variety of circumstances, which has taken them years of (regular) practice. As argued earlier in this chapter, perception is also an important component of practice. Information specifies to a player what he or she should do. For instance, it 'tells' them how and when to move when the player wants to head the ball at a corner kick. To be successful, the attacker should arrive in the correct place at the right time. Visual information about ball flight trajectory 'tells' the player how and when to run. When the player fixates the point of projection of the ball, a moving image of the ball will form on the player's retina. Michaels and Oudejans (1992) (see also Chapman, 1968; Babler and Dannemiller, 1993; McBeath *et al.*, 1995; McLeod and Dienes, 1993) showed that the player should run in such a way that they cancel out the acceleration of the ball's image on the retina. If this is achieved, the ball will be intercepted. Hence, information and movement are tightly coupled.

As perception and movement are inseparably and specifically coupled, practice should also be *specific*. That is to say, what should be learned during practice is to couple information and movement. Soccer training, therefore, should match the game situation as closely as possible. The visual information available during training should correspond with the information during the match. Heading should be trained by running and jumping for the ball. Jumping from a standing start, or tossing a ball to a stationary player will not help in getting the head to the right place at the right time during an actual match.

From the present perspective, learning is considered to be the result of establishing and further refining information–movement couplings. We have argued that the learning process of coupling information to movement consists of a sequence of mutually overlapping phases. We are now in the position to deal with the specificity of practice proposition in this context. Particularly during the early phase of learning, specificity of practice is implied, where information is only coupled to movement under specific conditions. During latter phases, practice should take place under more variable conditions such that a repertoire of couplings can be formed and further exploited. What does this mean for coaching and the organization of practice?

First, the coach should create a certain set of conditions that pushes the player to attune to a specific information–movement coupling. Instead of forcing the player, the coach needs to create a facilitative environment (Buekers, 2000). For instance, when teaching very young players to kick a ball to each other, accuracy can be facilitated by constraining the environment. Cones can be used to create 'a goal' 2 metres apart. Asking children to pass the ball between them forces them to become more accurate. By reducing the distance between the cones, the demands on accuracy of kicking through the goal, and thereby of passing to each other, can be increased. Ball control can also be facilitated in this manner. By gradually making the playing area smaller and smaller, the constraints become similar to those in a match situation.

Specificity of practice will also remain important during the later phases of learning. However, the player should now build on the established coupling to exploit other information–movement couplings under different conditions. For instance, the stopping of the ball should be practised under different circumstances; with and without pressure, with two or more defenders or with the ball approaching from many different directions. In all cases, specificity of practice is crucial as information–movement couplings should be established that are the same as the player will be confronted with in real matches.

In general, many coaches and trainers already use different types of environmental facilitators (e.g. cones, other players). However, these 'environmental facilitators' should always simulate the circumstances in the games situation, otherwise the relevant information–movement coupling will not be established.

Occlusion in basketball shooting

An interesting constraint that may prove to be highly effective in perceptual training in sports in order to facilitate information–movement couplings is occlusion. Although occlusion paradigms do not elucidate effectively on the specific information used by players to perform various skills, the occlusion technique might encourage athletes to converge onto the use of particular information sources. Occlusion may help in freezing certain perceptual degrees of freedom. One example is learning to dribble the ball in basketball while wearing glasses which prevents sight of the dribbling hands and the ball. This simple device forces a player to become attuned to the haptic information that is available, and to couple this information to the dribbling action, so that one learns to dribble without constantly looking at the ball (see also Williams *et al.*, 2002).

Another example, which we have investigated, concerns the use of occlusion in improving the skill of basketball jump shooting. Oudejans *et al.* (2002) have shown that expert shooters who use a high shooting style bring the ball above their head before making the final extension movement with the shooting arm. As a result, they can look at the basket until ball release. Oudejans *et al.* (2002) have also shown that with this style it is necessary and sufficient to be able to look at the basket during the final instance before ball release (looking late). As it may be the case that young basketball players do not optimally use the information that is available to them during these final moments. Oudejans *et al.* (submitted) investigated whether shooting performance could be improved by providing specific perceptual training during which players were only given the opportunity to see the basket when they were hanging in the air for the jump shot (ball release takes place at about peak jump height). Two methods of occlusion were used, whereby vision was only available during the final moments before ball release. The other method involved shooting from behind a screen so that the basket would only be visible during the jump, and thus, again, during the final moments before ball release.

Several national-level junior shooters were perceptually trained during a period of 2 months. Although it is difficult to draw firm conclusions because of individual differences, the overall shooting performance of the experimental participants improved, both during practice and games, while the performance of a small control group (players of the same team who did not receive the perceptual training) did not. Perceptual training using event occlusion offers a promising way of improving performance of even already skilled athletes. Just as with the environmental facilitators described above for soccer, these constraints guide the learners to converge onto the use of specific sources of information, thereby freezing certain degrees of freedom.

Conclusions

In this chapter, we have argued that perceptual learning in the context of action can be understood as three mutually overlapping phases. Initially, one out of multiple sources of information is attended to and coupled to a particular movement, that is, the redundant perceptual degrees of freedom are frozen. After some practice, the perceptual degrees of freedom are slowly released and several separate information–movement couplings are available to the actor. Expertise is reached only when the actor is able to exploit all available perceptual degrees of freedom, and is able to detect the most useful information source(s) given the particular set of constraints.

The idea that perceptual expertise is characterized by a mastering of perceptual degrees of freedom has implications for the design of investigations and their interpretation. The effect of perceptual manipulation(s) depends on the phase of learning the participant is in at that time, which suggests that individual history of learning needs to be taken into account when interpreting empirical findings. In addition, we emphasize that the education of attention implied by our perceptual learning phases means that the time at which attention is directed to the most useful information sources is important in order to facilitate the detection of these sources.

With respect to practical implications, we emphasize that information and movement are tightly and specifically coupled. This implies that practice should also be specific in order to achieve appropriate couplings between information and movement. The required couplings can be achieved across all phases by the coach creating a set of conditions that pushes the player to attune to the appropriate information–movement couplings. Different types of environmental facilitators (e.g. cones, occlusion) can be used to ensure that information available during training corresponds with the information used during the game. Later in the learning process (freeing and exploiting phases), practice should take place under more variable conditions so that a repertoire of information–movement couplings can be formed and further exploited.

References

Abernethy, B. (1987). Anticipation in sport: a review. *Physical Education Review*, 10, 5–16.

Abernethy, B. (2001). Attention. In R. N. Singer, H. A. Hausenblas and C. M. Janelle (Eds), *Handbook of research on sport psychology* (2nd ed., pp. 53–85). New York: John Wiley & Sons.

Babler, T. G. and Dannemiller, J. L. (1993). Role of image acceleration in judging landing location of free-falling projectiles. *Journal of Experimental Psychology: Human Perception and Performance*, 19, 15–31.

Beek, P. J., Jacobs, D. M., Daffertshofer, A. and Huys, R. (2003). Experts performance in sport: view from the joint perspective of ecological psychology and dynamical systems theory. In J. L. Starkes and K. A. Ericsson (Eds), *Experts performance in sport: advances in research on sport expertise* (pp. 321–344). Champaign: Human Kinetics.

Bernstein, N. A. (1967). *The coordination and regulation of movements*. Oxford: Pergamon Press.

Buekers, M. (2000). Can we be so specific to claim that specificity is the solution for learning sport skills? *International Journal of Sport Psychology*, 31, 485–489.

Chapman, S. (1968). Catching a baseball. *American Journal of Physics*, 36, 868–870.

Cutting, J. E. and Vishton, P. M. (1995). Perceiving the layout and knowing distances: the integration, relative potency and contextual use of different information about depth. In W. Epstein and S. Rogers (Eds), *Perception of space and motion* (pp. 69–117). San Diego: Academic Press.

Gibson, J. J. (1966). *The sense considered as perceptual systems*. Boston, MA: Houghton Mifflin.

Gibson, J. J. (1979). *The ecological approach to visual perception*. Boston, MA: Houghton Mifflin.

Jacobs, D. M. (2001). On perceiving, acting, and learning: toward an ecological approach anchored in convergence. Doctoral dissertation, Vrije Universiteit Amsterdam. Utrecht: Digital Printing Partners Utrecht.

Jacobs, D. M. and Michaels, C. F. (2002). On the apparent paradox of learning and realism. *Ecological Psychology*, 14, 127–139.

McBeath, M. K., Shaffer, D. M. and Kaiser, M. K. (1995). How baseball outfielders determine where to run catch fly balls. *Science*, 268, 569–573.

McLeod, P. and Dienes, Z. (1993). Running to catch the ball. *Nature*, 362, 23.

Michaels, C. F. and Beek, P. J. (1995). The stae of ecological psychology. *Ecological Psychology*, 7, 259–278.

Michaels, C. F. and Oudejans, R. R. D. (1992). The optics and actions of catching fly balls: Zeroing out optical acceleration. *Ecological Psychology*, 4, 199–222.

Newell, K. M. (1986). Constraints on the development of coordination. In M. Wade and H. T. A. Whiting (Eds), *Motor development in children: aspects of coordination and control* (pp. 341–360). Dordrecht: Martinus.

Oudejans, R. R. D., Bleijendaal, I., Koedijker, J. M. and Bakker, F. C. (submitted). Training visual control in basketball jump shooting.

Oudejans, R. R. D., van de Langenberg, R. W. and Hutter, R. I. (2002). Aiming at a far target under different viewing conditions: visual control in basketball jump shooting. *Human Movement Science*, 21, 457–480.

Oudejans, R. R. D., Verheijen, R., Bakker, F. C., Gerrits, J. C., Steinbrückner, M. and Beek, P. J. (2000). Errors in judging 'offside' in football. *Nature*, 404 (6773), 33.

Savelsbergh, G. J. P. and van der Kamp, J. (2000). Information in learning to coordinate and control movements: is there a need for specificity of practise? *International Journal of Sport Psychology*, 31, 476–484.

Savelsbergh G. J. P. and Whiting, H. T. A. (1992). The acquisition of catching under monocular and binocular conditions. *Journal of Motor Behaviour*, 24, 320–328.

Savelsbergh, G. J. P., Williams, A. M., van der Kamp, J. and Ward, P. (2002). Visual search, anticipation and expertise in soccer goalkeepers. *Journal of Sports Sciences*, 20, 279–287.

Scott, M. A. (2000). Perceptual degrees of freedom: some potential implications. *International Journal of Sport Psychology*, 31, 490–495.

Vereijken, B., van Emmerik, R. E. A., Whiting, H. T. A. and Newell, K. M. (1992a). Free(z)ing degrees of freedom in skill acquisition. *Journal of Motor Behaviour*, 24, 133–142.

Vereijken, B., Whiting, H. T. A. and Beek, W. J. (1992b). A dynamical systems approach towards skill acquisition. *Quarterly Journal of Experimental Psychology*, 45A, 323–344.

Vickers, J. N., Rodrigues, S. T. and Edworthy, G. (2000). Quiet eye and accuracy in the dart throw. *International Journal of Sports Vision*, 6, 30–36.

Weinberg, R. S. and Gould, D. (1999). *Foundations of sport and exercise psychology* (2nd ed.). Champaign, IL: Human Kinetics.

Williams, A. M. and Burwitz, L. (1993). Advance cue utilization in soccer. In T. Reilly, J. Clarys and A. Stibbe (Eds), *Science and football II* (pp. 239–243). London: E. & F.N. Spon.

Williams, A. M., Davids, K. and Williams, J. G. (1999). *Visual perception and action in sport*. London: E & FN Spon.

Williams, A. M. and Grant, A. (1999). Training perceptual skill in sport. *International Journal of Sport Psychology*, 30, 194–220.

Williams, A. M., Weigelt, C., Harris, M. and Scott, M. A. (2002). Age related differences in vision and proprioception in a lower limb interceptive task: the effects of skill level and practice. *Research Quarterly for Exercise and Sport*, 73, 386–395.

Zanone, P. G. and Kelso, J. A. S. (1992). Evolution of behavioural attractors with learning: Nonequilibrium phase transition. *Journal of Experimental Psychology: Human Perfromance and Perception*, 18, 403–421.

18 Musculoskeletal constraints on the acquisition of motor skills

Jonathan Shemmell, James R. Tresilian,
Stephan Riek and Richard G. Carson

It is often said that the human motor system possesses surplus degrees of freedom or redundancy. This redundancy bestows upon the system a great deal of flexibility, enabling the same goal outcome to be achieved in a wide variety of different conditions – if one method for achieving the goal will not work, another can be used instead. This kind of flexibility is essential for an animal that interacts with a changing, dynamic environment, but it necessarily involves the problem of having to determine, in each instance, the particular method (of the potentially infinitely many possible) by which an outcome is to be achieved. Most theorists have supposed that this problem is solved by the nervous system using an hierarchical control architecture: the intention to achieve a particular goal outcome is progressively transformed into an appropriate pattern of efference to the contributing muscles in a sequence of stages (Saltzman, 1979). Saltzman (1979), for example, suggests a seven-stage (or level) architecture in which the first (highest) level represents the goal outcome to be achieved, such as a change in the location of an object (say from on the floor to on top of the table). Subsequent levels then progressively determine how this will be done, starting with a plan for how the object should be moved (its trajectory specified in an extrinsic set of coordinates) and culminating in the efferent commands sent to the contributing muscles.

The number of component stages of the action planning process and what these stages actually do is a matter that awaits resolution, and different accounts of how the motor system is organized give rise to a number of different alternatives (Bizzi, 1993; Sternberg *et al.*, 1988; Tresilian and Stelmach, 1997; Wolpert and Kawato, 1998). That which appears most firmly established is that there exists a stage in which the motion of the working point is specified in an extrinsic set of coordinates that are independent of the actual system of effectors (muscles, body segments and tools) that will be used to execute the action, and which appear to correspond to the coordinates of the visually perceived environment. The working point is defined to be that part or element of the effector system that actually performs the task (Latash, 1993): for example, when reaching out to press a switch, the working point would be the distal segment of the finger that presses the switch; in the case of hammering a nail, the working point is the hammer-head, in the case of a tennis stroke, the working point is the racquet head.

The specified motion of the working point is subsequently transformed into patterns of efference that cause the working point to be driven along the specified trajectory. The evidence for the specification of the working point trajectory in an extrinsic, effector independent set of coordinates comes largely from the study of point-to-point reaching tasks in which a working point (e.g. the distal finger segment) is moved from one spatial location to another. In these tasks, it has been found that the human motor system prefers to have the working point move between the two locations in a straight line with a smooth, asymmetrically bell-shaped tangential speed profile (Flash and Hogan, 1985; Figure 18.1). In normal (i.e. familiar) conditions, the motor system will use the rest of the effector system – in a reaching task, this will be the arm and hand – in whatever way is necessary to achieve the preferred motion of the working point (Cruse et al., 1993). If the conditions are unlike any previously experienced, either because the effectors are exposed to a novel force environment (Shadmehr and Mussa-Ivaldi, 1994) or because the relationship between the visually perceived and actual motion of the working point has been altered (Flanagan and Rao, 1995;

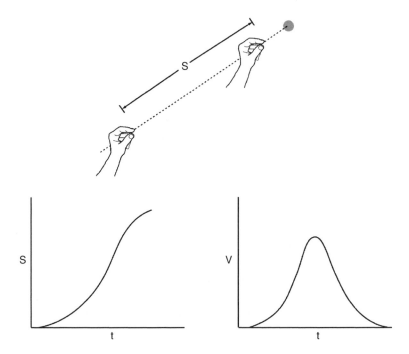

Figure 18.1 Typical displacement and velocity profiles for reaching movements (adapted from Flash and Hogan, 1985). Point-to-point movements are generally performed with smooth end-point trajectories (left panel) and bell-shaped velocity profiles (right panel), regardless of the limb segments involved. In this example, s represents the distance travelled by the hand from its starting position, v represents the instantaneous velocity at which the hand travels and t is the time elapsed from the beginning of the movement.

Wolpert *et al.*, 1995), the motor system quickly learns how to make the current working point move in the preferred manner. Thus, the trajectory of the working point is invariant, but the trajectories of the individual segments of the effector system are not invariant, neither are the muscles used nor are the torques developed at the joints. Any or all of these things may vary in order to achieve the invariant characteristics of the working point trajectory.

Exactly how the nervous system is able to transform a representation of the motion of the working point into an appropriate pattern of efference to contributing muscles is unknown. Theoretical approaches to this issue have proposed different types of representation of the working point motion: an explicit preformed plan of the trajectory kinematics (Flash and Hogan, 1985; Hollerbach and Flash, 1982), a generative process that produces the trajectory representation in real time rather than pre-planning it (Bullock and Grossberg, 1988, 1991) or the specification of an abstract dynamics which when realized by the effector system causes the working point to move in the preferred manner (Saltzman and Kelso, 1987). The type of representation will determine, in part, the kind of transformation required. One thing is certain, however, such a transformation demands knowledge of the effector system that is to perform the action. This knowledge is typically referred to as an internal model, and it has been suggested that it includes a complete inverse of the effector system dynamics (Kawato, 1999; Shadmehr and Mussa-Ivaldi, 1994; Wolpert and Kawato, 1998). Whatever the precise nature of the knowledge involved and its representational format, it must be acquired through experience – that is, through a process of learning.

In order to get an effector system to do something – such as move its working point along a desired trajectory – it is necessary to know how the system responds to control signals (efference) and what the system can and cannot do, that is, how the system is constrained. Musculoskeletal systems are constrained by their morphological structure: for example, some movements and postures are not possible because the joints are limited in their range of motion, as with gymnastic manoeuvres – more subtle examples are described later. Low-level neural connectivity also constrains what musculoskeletal systems can and cannot do. A well-established example of this is eye movements. The extraocular muscles that move the two eyes could, in principle, make the eyes move independently of one another – one eye could move up (elevation) whilst the other moved down (depression), for example. However, this type of eye movement cannot be achieved by a normal person who is constrained by the neural connectivity of the extraocular muscles, such that the eyes move together and only in certain ways. The neural circuity forbids, as it were, certain types of eye movements that the extraocular muscles are, in principle, quite capable of producing – no amount of practice and effort will allow you to elevate one eye whilst depressing the other. Skilled action involves working with a complex set of constraining factors – anatomical, mechanical and neural – and in order that this be done the higher levels of the nervous system require knowledge (internal models) of these constraints. Such knowledge is acquired with experience and, as will be argued in this chapter, it is an essential component of skill acquisition.

Muscle synergies

In the acquisition of motor skill, joint and limb kinematics are adjusted through practice by altering the neural input to muscles. Although the neural structures that are modified as a result of learning are distributed through both cortical and sub-cortical regions, the consequences of such changes must necessarily be expressed via the quantal unit of motor output, the motor unit (Liddell and Sherrington, 1925). It is clear that not all parameters of muscle activation are equally suscepti-ble to change through learning. Modification must occur in the context of constraints imposed by the structure of the neuromuscular–skeletal system.

Natural tasks, such as walking, reaching or grasping, seldom involve a single classically defined motoneuron pool and its muscle units. More often a group of muscles or muscle units will be involved. Bernstein (1967) introduced the con-cept of a muscle synergy to describe a means by which the control of movement could be simplified, and the problem of kinematic redundancy alleviated, at least in part. Synergies are defined operationally as mechanisms employed by the central nervous system (CNS) to coordinate groups of motor units or muscles into functional assemblies (e.g. Windhorst *et al.*, 1991), thus simplifying the central control requirements (e.g. Loeb, 1987). As originally conceived, they represent scalable patterns of control signals, directed to a number of muscles in order to initiate movement or respond to postural disturbances. During elbow flexion movements, for example, the flexor muscles (i.e. biceps brachii, brachialis and brachioradialis) are activated approximately in proportion to their capacity to contribute to the action.

While muscle synergies appear to represent an elegant solution to the problem of musculoskeletal redundancy, a balance must exist between the need to reduce the number of parameters to be controlled and the facility for adaptation in a dynamic environment. In many movement systems, a predisposition towards the use of specific muscle synergies is expressed, at least upon initial exposure to a novel task. Yet the patterns of behaviour that arise do not always result in the most effective solution of task demands. It is often the case, therefore, that the acquisition of motor skill requires the adaptation of muscle synergies, through changes to the relative magnitude of contractions across the muscles involved, or the temporal organization of those contractions. The present chapter deals with the organization of muscle synergies and with the stability and adaptability of these synergies in relation to the acquisition of motor skills. In order to deter-mine the extent to which muscle synergies are amenable to modification through learning, it is first necessary to characterize the context of the anatomical, mechanical and neural constraints which bear upon their composition and re-composition.

Morphometric and mechanical properties of muscle

Muscles are the actuating level of the neuromuscular–skeletal system. Associated with each muscle is a set of constraints arising from its structure, and its orientation in relation to the action performed. The specific properties of muscle that constitute constraints on action are those relating to length, physiological cross-sectional area (PCSA), line of action, fibre-type morphology and fibre pennation angle. The morphological and mechanical properties of a muscle determine its capacity for torque production about each joint that it spans (i.e. the greater the PCSA of a muscle, the greater its capacity for torque production at each joint). Consequently, both morphometric and mechanical muscular properties impact upon CNS strategies for movement control, and upon the adaptation that occurs during the learning of motor acts. The degree to which these properties are amenable to adaptation, and the sensitivity of performance to these adaptations, ultimately govern the extent to which they serve to facilitate or constrain the acquisition of skill. Long-term adaptations (over weeks or months) may occur in many of these morphometric and mechanical properties as a result of task repetition. The extent to which these adaptations contribute to skill acquisition will depend upon the nature of the task. For example, the execution of many gymnastics skills places high demands on the capacity of muscles to produce force, as well as requiring precise intermuscular coordination. In order to become an expert gymnast, therefore, both neural adaptations which promote improvements in the specification of motor commands, and muscle adaptations that mediate increases in force generating capacity are required. In general, muscle hypertrophy and the associated changes in fibre-type morphology occur over a longer time period than the initial neural adaptations that accompany overload training. Nonetheless, given that muscle force generating capacity is often a limiting factor in relation to the performance of specific gymnastic routines, the time course of skill acquisition in these tasks will be heavily dependent upon the time course of muscular adaptations. This situation stands in contrast to skills in which the emphasis of performance is solely upon dexterity, such as juggling, or spin bowling in cricket. The time course of skill acquisition in this type of task is almost exclusively determined by the rapidity of improvement in neural structures associated with the specification of motor commands.

Muscle articularity

In recent years, it has become clear that the activation relationships between muscles that ostensibly perform the same function (i.e. rotation of a particular joint) are complex, and are not simply determined by their action at that joint (Buchanan et al., 1989; Jamison and Caldwell, 1993, 1994). Rather, the functional role of a given muscle within the overall activation strategy for a specific movement is influenced by its mechanical action at every joint that it spans. As such, its contribution will also be determined by the nature of the interactions occurring at adjacent joints. As a result, the precise role of any single muscle acting at a specific joint will be influenced by the contributions made by surrounding muscles, which are, in turn, formulated within the broader context of simultaneous joint actions. The recruitment of muscles that have the potential to act around more than one joint, or in more than one degree of freedom, will therefore have a significant influence on the activation profiles of muscles that are more restricted in their functions.

The capacity of a muscle to generate torque at more than one joint, or to generate motion in more than one mechanical degree of freedom, is determined by the respective locations of the origin and insertion. Muscles that span a single joint are termed monoarticular, whereas those that cross multiple joints are referred to as polyarticular. The ankle plantarflexor muscle group contains examples of both muscle types: the monoarticular soleus muscle spans the ankle joint only, whereas the biarticular (a muscle that spans two joints) gastrocnemius muscle spans both the ankle and knee joints. The recruitment of polyarticular muscles is commonly combined with the activation of monoarticular muscles in order to produce actions that would be impossible or less effective using a single class of muscle. For example, the simultaneous ankle plantarflexion and knee extension observed during vertical jumping results in near-isometric contractions of the gastrocnemius which serves to transfer power generated by the monoarticular knee extensor muscles to the ankle joint (van Ingen Schenau, 1989; Figure 18.2). As a consequence, the functional role of gastrocnemius in this context is more akin to that of a tendon. The unique action of polyarticular muscles allows power to be generated more effectively at distal joints than would be possible with

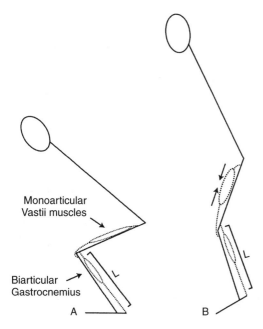

Figure 18.2 Interactions between monoarticular and biarticular muscles during jumping actions (adapted from van Ingen Schenau, 1989). The amount of plantarflexion torque produced in the transition from jump preparation (A) to take-off (B) is due to the concentric contraction of the knee extensors and the concurrent near-isometric contraction of the gastrocnemius. The constant length of the gastrocnemius during this action serves to transfer more force to the ankle joint from the knee extensors than could be produced with isolated concentric contractions of the plantarflexor muscles (gastrocnemius and soleus).

the activation of monoarticular muscles alone. The specialized mechanical properties of polyarticular muscles, therefore, have a large bearing on the composition of muscle synergies during multi-segment movements. In many cases, coactivation of mono- and polyarticular muscles that are apparently antagonistic at one joint may be necessary to effectively utilize the work capacity of each muscle.

Is there evidence to suggest that the facility to utilize muscle articularlity in an optimal fashion is learned during the acquisition of motor skill? Although there have been a number of studies which have examined improvements in the performance of vertical jumping over time, in most instances these have simply focussed on increases in the force generating capacity of the muscles involved (e.g. Maffiuletti *et al.*, 2002; Matavulj *et al.*, 2001). It is likely, however, that a substantial portion of the improvement in performance that occurs at least initially, is attributable to neural adaptations. In particular, these are likely to take the form of refinements in the sequencing of muscle recruitment within a synergistic group, and greater precision in the combined utilization of mono- and polyarticular muscles. To the best of our knowledge, however, there have been no studies which have directly addressed this issue (cf. Bobbert, 1990).

Multifunctional characteristics of skeletal muscles

In many instances, the anatomical configuration of a muscle is such that it may contribute to motion in more than one mechanical degree of freedom at joints that permit such rotations. The elbow–forearm complex provides an example of a joint that accommodates rotation in two degrees of freedom (flexion–extension of the elbow; pronation–supination of the forearm). A number of the monoarticular muscles which cross the elbow joint are capable of producing torque in both degrees of freedom. Muscles which produce torque/motion in more than one degree of freedom at a joint are termed multifunctional (muscles that generate torque in two degrees of freedom are referred to as bifunctional). The bifunctional biceps brachii muscle, for example, has moments of force such that it can contribute to flexion of the elbow and to supination of the forearm (see Figure 18.3). In contrast, the monofunctional brachialis muscle (by virtue of its line of action) can produce a flexion moment only. It is important to note that the articularity of a muscle does not dictate its functionality at a specific joint. It is common to have monoarticular muscles that are multifunctional at a specific joint or joint complex (e.g. pronator teres acts to pronate and flex the elbow joint complex), and it is also possible to have polyarticular muscles that are monofunctional at one or more of the joints that they cross (triceps brachii acts as a monofunctional extensor at the elbow joint).

The differences in the roles played by monofunctional and multifunctional muscles are analogous in some respects to the distinctions between monoarticular and polyarticular muscles. The bifunctional muscles of the elbow–forearm complex may in some task contexts act as agonists in both degrees of freedom. Alternatively, they may act as an agonist in one degree of freedom and as an antagonist in the other, or as an antagonist in both degrees of freedom. It has been observed that

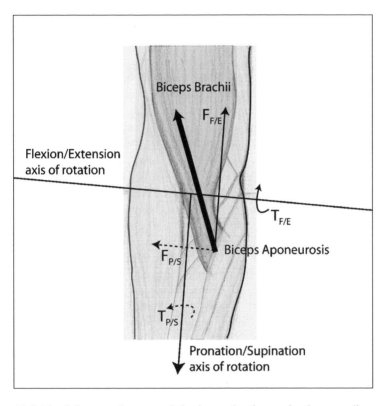

Figure 18.3 The bifunctional action of the biceps brachii at the forearm–elbow joint complex. Due to the relative positions of its origin and insertion (biceps aponeurosis), the bifunctional biceps brachii muscle is capable of generating force components that cross both the flexion/extension ($F_{F/E}$) and pronation/supination ($F_{P/S}$) axes of the elbow/forearm joint complex. The fact that the line of action of the biceps brachii crosses two axes of rotation means that it is capable of contributing to torque production in both flexion ($T_{F/E}$) and supination ($T_{P/S}$).

during the course of a single discrete action, requiring simultaneous motion in both degrees of freedom at the elbow (flexion/extension and pronation/supination), the bifunctional biceps brachii and pronator teres muscles display discriminable bursts of electrical activity that are characteristic of both agonist and antagonist actions. For example, during tasks requiring simultaneous flexion and pronation, such as a golf backswing, biceps brachii is activated synchronously with brachioradialis (a flexion agonist), and with triceps brachii (a flexion antagonist), during separate phases of the movement (Sergio and Ostry, 1995). The timing of these bursts coincides approximately with activity in the pure (monofunctional) agonist and antagonist muscles, which produce motion in a single degree of freedom. During simultaneous flexion and supination (e.g. during a bicep curl in resistance training), the amplitude of the agonist burst generated in biceps brachii during the combined movement is approximately the sum of the amplitudes exhibited during movements in each single degree of freedom. Several of the monofunctional muscles acting at the elbow, such as triceps brachii and pronator quadratus, display patterns of electrical activity that are not influenced appreciably by motion in a second degree of freedom. The magnitude of electrical activity in the triceps brachii, for example, is invariant for a given amount of elbow extension torque, regardless of the amount of pronation or supination torque required (Jamison and Caldwell, 1993). In contrast, the activity of other monofunctional muscles, such as brachialis and brachioradialis, is influenced directly by such motion. Muscles of this latter type appear to act in a compensatory fashion when the level of activity in the bifunctional muscles (e.g. biceps brachii) is attenuated by a requirement to produce motion simultaneously in flexion–extension and pronation–supination.

These findings suggest at least two ways in which patterns of activation within these muscle synergies may be amenable to change through learning. In the first instance, there may occur a refinement of the relative phasing between the agonist and antagonist bursts in the bifunctional muscles, and the activity in the monofunctional agonists. Adaptation may also occur through the modulation of activity in those monofunctional muscles which have a compensatory function. In particular, a significant role is likely to be afforded to monofunctional muscles (e.g. brachialis, pronator quadratus) in circumstances in which the organization of the bifunctional muscles represents an impediment, rather than an aid, to the solution of task goals. During pure flexion movements about the elbow joint, the activation of the biceps brachii contributes a significant amount of flexion torque, but also produces supination torque that must be compensated for through the concurrent activation of pronating muscles. In this case, the desired outcomes of the task may be achieved most effectively with less relative activity in the biceps brachii and more from monofunctional flexors, such as brachialis and brachioradialis. In a similar vein, MacConaill and Basmajian (1977) have proposed that, in single degree of freedom movements at least, the development of expertise is accompanied by an attenuated level of engagement of multifunctional muscles.

While a differentiation of the roles performed by monofunctional and multifunctional muscles appears to represent a fundamental organizing principle of neuromuscular control, very little research has been conducted which specifically addresses the implications of this disposition for the acquisition of motor skill. Clearly, however, this intrinsic property of the neuromuscular–skeletal system defines the context within which motor learning must occur, regardless of whether the ultimate objective is rehabilitation and therapy, sporting prowess or occupational capability. As such, the detailed exploration of this class of constraint is another important avenue for future research.

Muscle task groups

While a contraction may involve a group of muscles, it may also involve only part of a complex multifunctional muscle. It is well known that each motoneuron innervates a discrete population of muscle fibres, and it has been proposed that the pools of motoneurons which innervate a muscle may be organized into purely functional 'task groups' (cf. Loeb, 1985). Task groups can be viewed as intramuscular synergies, based on specialized circuitry in the spinal cord that can be utilized selectively by the CNS in response to environmental contingencies (Loeb, 1987).

Multifunctional muscles may be expected to have more complicated motoneuronal pool organizations than single function muscles (Windhorst *et al.*, 1991). It is now clear that many of the muscles that contribute to the rotation of the elbow and forearm, for example, have distinct sub-populations of motor units (ter Haar Romeny *et al.*, 1984; van Zuylen *et al.*, 1988b). These observations force a reassessment of the degree of flexibility that is available to the CNS with respect to the formation of muscle synergies.

In humans, intramuscular task groups comprising three types of task-specific motor units have been identified in the long head of the biceps brachii (ter Haar Romeny *et al.*, 1984; van Zuylen *et al.*, 1988b). These motor units were categorized on the basis of their critical firing level, defined as the level of flexor, supinator or combination of flexor and supinator torque necessary to recruit the unit. The three types of motor units were found to have different spatial distributions. Those units recruited only during flexion were located along the lateral border of the muscle, those recruited only during supination were located medially and those recruited during the production of a combination of flexor and supinator torque were located centrally and medially. These local patterns of organization appear to be related to slight variations in mechanical advantage. This is expressed as a direct relationship between the functional recruitment of motoneurons and the force vector of their muscle unit (Windhorst and Kokkoroyiannis, 1991). In the long head of the biceps, for example, the medially located motor units have a mechanical advantage toward supination because of their attachment to the medial aspect of the biceps tendon (ter Haar Romeny *et al.*, 1984). Further evidence for neuromuscular compartmentalization has also been obtained through anatomical investigations (Segal, 1992; Segal *et al.*, 1991). Dissections have revealed that bifurcations of the musculocutaneous nerve innervating long and short heads of the biceps brachii branch further to innervate both heads at several discrete points. These discrete innervation points divide the biceps brachii into medial to lateral in-parallel neuromuscular compartments, which are likely to form the basis of the functional specialization revealed by single motor unit recordings.

In recent years, there has been a gradual accumulation of both functional and anatomical evidence which supports the view that the allocation of task-specific roles to separately innervated compartments is an integral feature of most skeletal muscles (Segal *et al.*, 2002; van Zuylen *et al.*, 1988a,b). Given the common function of the upper limb in performing discrete movements, it is perhaps not surprising that multiple distinct sub-populations of motor units have been distinguished in the brachialis, brachioradialis, biceps brachii and triceps brachii muscles (van Zuylen *et al.*, 1988a,b). In the supinator (monofunctional) and pronator teres (bifunctional) muscles, however, there appears to be no indi-cation of inhomogeneous activation. Anatomical evidence which suggests parti-tioning of neuromuscular control has also been obtained for the extensor carpi ulnaris, flexor carpi ulnaris and flexor digitorum profundus muscles (Segal, 1992). As with biceps brachii, these local patterns of organization appear to be related to slight variations in mechanical advantage. In the extensor digitorum communis muscle, task-specific motor units have been identified for extension of either the middle finger or the ring finger. During extension of the wrist, how-ever, these motor unit task groups are 'pooled' to act together as synergists (Riek and Bawa, 1992).

The presence of functionally specific task groups, which can be engaged selec-tively, appears to represent an additional means by which the CNS can alter pat-terns of muscle activation in response to changing task requirements and during the acquisition of new motor skills. A question that remains to be addressed is whether the neural connections that form the basis of functional task groups are also subject to remodelling (Purves, 1988). Although there have been reports that sprouting and terminal branching of the motor nerve endings may occur in association with repeated intense and rapid muscle contractions (Perciavalle *et al.*, 1990), the issue of whether such adaptations also occur during the process of skill acquisition has not yet been examined.

The recomposition of muscle synergies during discrete movement tasks

Thus far we have given consideration to a number of anatomical, mechanical and neural constraints, which may bear upon the composition and re-composition of muscle synergies. In spite of a widespread recognition that such factors are likely to be of critical importance in determining the nature and time course of motor learning, there have been very few investigations which have focussed on the impact of specific musculoskeletal constraints (e.g. joint configuration, muscle size, and orientation) on skill acquisition. There have been many studies which have examined the alterations in muscle synergies that occur during the learning of motor tasks, or upon exposure to novel variants of a task (Shadmehr and Mussa-Ivaldi, 1994; Thoroughman and Shadmehr, 1999, for a review of mus-cle synergy flexibility see Macpherson, 1991). In most instances, however, it is not possible on the basis of these studies to identify the impact of specific musculoskeletal constraints upon the processes of adaptation. Nonetheless, they do provide some insight concerning the features of muscle synergies which are amenable to change in response to altered task demands.

While muscle synergies are defined typically in terms of their spatial organiza-tion (i.e. the specific muscles involved), it is apparent that changes in their tem-poral organization (i.e. the sequence of activation) will also result in quite distinct behavioural outcomes (Macpherson, 1991). The acquisition of motor skill is, therefore, likely to be based upon task-specific modification of both the spatial and temporal organization of muscle synergies. In a recent study designed to examine this issue (Thoroughman and Shadmehr, 1999), individuals were required to complete reaching movements following the introduction of a novel dynamic field which forced the hand in a direction perpendicular to that of the intended movement. In the period following the imposition of the external force field, the activation profiles of the muscles involved were altered in a manner that compensated precisely for the effects of the imposed force. This adaptation took the form of changes in both the magnitude of activation of individual muscles and their relative timing. The onset of muscle recruitment also occurred progressively earlier as task performance improved. Thus, in response to alterations in external dynamics (i.e. during movements in water as opposed to air, or changes in the camber of the road while driving), neuromuscular adaptation may be mediated by modification of both the spatial and temporal organization of muscle synergies. It is not yet clear, however, whether the alterations in neuromuscular control that occur in order to compensate for intrinsic musculoskeletal constraints (i.e. when performing a novel skill) are of a similar nature.

During flexion at the elbow of a neutral forearm (the mid-point between maximum pronation and maximum supination), biceps brachii is considered an agonist. Its additional action of supination of the forearm may be counteracted by recruitment of a pronator muscle (e.g. pronator teres). In this context, biceps brachii and pronator teres act as functional synergists. During elbow flexion and supination, however, biceps brachii acts in conjunction with supinator. In this case, pronator teres is an antagonist muscle. In tasks that require the generation of isometric torque at the elbow (e.g. when performing an arm lock in wrestling), as emphasis is shifted from a maximum voluntary contraction (MVC) in the direction of flexion, to the requirement that a pronation torque be produced in addition to maximum flexion, a reduced overall level of flexion torque ensues (Jamison and Caldwell, 1993, 1994). Although pronation is not antagonistic to flexion, the reduced flexor torque arises from a tendency towards reciprocal inhibition of the biceps brachii during pronation. Reflex reciprocal inhibition is a fundamental characteristic of the motor system, is instantiated in a relatively simple mechanism which is functionally efficient, and gives rise to what Sherrington referred to as a 'singleness of action'. One might anticipate that muscle synergies based upon reflex reciprocal inhibition will be fairly robust in the face of changing task demands. Indeed, Jamison and Caldwell's (1993, 1994) analysis of the muscle activity patterns obtained in the task described above revealed that the activation levels of both monofunctional and multifunctional muscles were altered in a highly stereotypical fashion when the direction of the required torque was altered. The activity of the bifunctional muscles was generally greatest when they acted as agonists in both degrees of freedom, and was reduced when they acted as an agonist in only one degree of freedom. The activity of the monofunctional muscles was modulated in a manner that compensated for any unwanted torque generated by the bifunctional muscles. These findings suggest that the alterations in neuromuscular control that occur in compensation for intrinsic musculoskeletal constraints may be rather different in nature from those which occur in response to an alteration of the external dynamics.

This view is supported by recent observations obtained in our laboratory (Shemmell *et al.*, 2002). A variation of the isometric torque generation task introduced by Jamison and Caldwell (1993, 1994) was employed to assess the acquisition of skill (measured in terms of the speed and accuracy of torque production in two skeletal degrees of freedom) over a 5-day learning period. Improvements in the performance of the task, which required the rapid generation of torque in various directions at the elbow, were mediated primarily by increases in the rate at which the muscles were activated at the onset of a voluntary contraction (see Figure 18.4). There were few alterations in the overall pattern of muscle activation, or changes in the relative timing of muscle recruitment. In short, both the spatial and temporal aspects of the muscle synergies remained largely invariant, even though there were substantial improvements in the rapidity with which the targets were acquired. These findings suggest that compensation for intrinsic musculoskeletal constraints may not be mediated by substantial changes in either the spatial or temporal organization of muscle synergies. At least

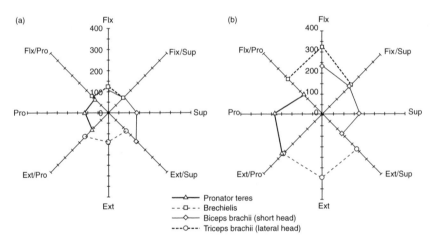

Figure 18.4 The magnitude and rate of muscle activations during a rapid isometric target acquisition task in two degrees of freedom. Adapted from Shemmell *et al.* (2002). Post-test values for (a) the rms amplitude of EMG signals and (b) the rate of onset of muscle activation expressed as a percentage of pre-test values. A value of 100% on either panel, therefore, represents no change in the measured variables after 5 days of practice. Data are displayed for those torque combinations in which each muscle acted as an agonist. The small changes in amplitude values after practice show that adaptations in the spatial organization of the muscle synergies involved were not the primary mechanism through which performances on the experimental task were improved. Similarly, few changes were observed after practice in terms of the temporal organization of the synergies employed (data not shown). The rate of onset of muscle activation appeared to be the factor most responsible for the improvements as large changes in this variable were observed inagonist muscles for each torque combination (b). The closed symbols in each panel represent differences from pre-test values that were statistically reliable ($p < 0.05$).

in the context of certain classes of task, improvements in performance are brought about by adaptations in other aspects of neuromuscular control.

The recomposition of muscle synergies during rhythmic movement tasks

Neuromuscular-skeletal constraints on the stability of coordination are expressed prominently in rhythmic movements such as walking, running and playing the piano (e.g. Carson *et al.*, 2000). Such movements, therefore, provide an excellent basis upon which to study the organization of muscle synergies, and the stability and adaptability of these synergies during the acquisition of motor skill.

It is apparent that only a small subset of all possible muscle combinations are employed by the CNS in the regulation of movement. The robust muscle synergies represented by these combinations appear particularly sensitive to the force generating capabilities of the individual muscles acting upon the limb (Loeb *et al.*, 2000). It is evident, therefore, that the subspace of possible muscle combinations that may be accessed by the CNS during the process of skill acquisition will also be constrained by the forces that can be produced by individual muscles.

In a study conducted recently in our laboratory (Carroll *et al.*, 2001), we demonstrated that changes in the strength of specific muscles, brought about by a resistance training program, have a systematic influence upon the stability of rhythmic movement tasks. Specifically, increases in the strength of the muscles that extend the index finger enhance the stability of a syncopation task, in which individuals are required to perform a finger extension movement between the beats of an auditory metronome. As alterations in force-generating capacity, brought about either through changes in limb posture (Carson and Riek, 1998), or as a result of resistance training (Carroll *et al.*, 2001), have consistent and predictable effects on the stability of rhythmic movements, the potential force output of the component muscles engaged in a motor task may be identified as a relevant source of constraint. These findings also suggest that the modifications in neuromuscular control that occur during skill acquisition may serve to compensate for variations in the intrinsic force-generating capacities of the muscles engaged in the movement task.

In order to examine this possibility, we examined the learning of a coordination task that required rhythmic abduction–adduction movements of the index finger (Carson and Riek, 2001). Upon initial exposure to this task, most individuals exhibit involuntary spontaneous transitions to rotary motion and to flexion–extension, as the frequency of movement is increased (Kelso *et al.*, 1993). These transition phenomena necessarily arise from the intrinsic properties of the musculoskeletal system. In particular, the recruitment of additional mechanical degrees of freedom appears to be contingent upon the force-generating capabilities of the individual muscles acting upon the finger. Side to side movements of the finger can be brought about by the action of muscles intrinsic to the hand: the first dorsal interosseus and the first volar interosseus. We hypothesized that in the initial stages of learning individuals may be incapable of directing sufficiently focal motor commands to the interossei without also engaging muscles, originating in the forearm, that act primarily to flex and extend the finger. As the force-generating capacity of the extrinsic muscles is substantially greater than that of the interossei, their recruitment may result in motion that is either rotary, or is dominated by flexion and extension. In order to assess the changes in muscle recruitment that occur during skill acquisition, we sought to determine the muscle combinations that are employed by the CNS, upon initial exposure to the task, and when individuals became more adept in their performance.

Five experimental sessions were conducted on successive days, during which the participants attempted to produce abduction–adduction movements of the index finger in time with an auditory metronome. During each experimental trial, the metronome frequency was increased in eight steps from an individually determined base frequency. Electromyographic activity was recorded from first dorsal interosseus (FDI), first volar interosseus (FVI) (both small muscles located in the hand, producing abduction and adduction, respectively, of the index finger), flexor digitorum superficialis (FDS) and extensor digitorum communis (EDC) (larger muscles located in the forearm acting to, respectively, flex and extend the fingers and wrist). Upon initial exposure to the task, while the movements intended were abduction–adduction, those produced were punctuated by extended periods of rotary motion and by flexion and extension. By the final day of the learning period, the movements more accurately matched the required profile, and exhibited greater spatial and temporal stability than those generated during initial performance. In the early stages of skill acquisition, an alternating pattern of activation in the intrinsic hand muscles (FDI and FVI) was maintained, even at the highest frequencies. In contrast, as the pace of the movements was elevated, the activity in FDS and EDC increased in overall intensity, and became either sustained or intermittent. As learning proceeded, and performance improved, alterations in neuromuscular control were expressed primarily in the extrinsic muscles (EDC and FDS). These changes took the form of increases in the postural role of these muscles, shifts to phasic patterns of activation, or selective disengagement of these muscles (Figure 18.5).

Early in learning, the extrinsic muscles were recruited involuntarily, and inappropriately, as the demands of the task were accentuated by increases in pacing frequency. This organization was clearly maladaptive, as the increased neural drive to the stronger extrinsic muscles resulted in the dominance of their primary (flexion–extension) actions. The participants simply appeared incapable of directing sufficiently focal motor commands to both the interossei and the extrinsic muscles. Although functional clusters of motoneuronal projections and the synergies to which they give rise form the basic repertoire of voluntary movements, the acquisition of fine motor skill is necessarily based upon the recomposition of these groupings. In the context of a task that requires rhythmic abduction–adduction of the index finger, the modifications in neuromuscular control that occur during skill acquisition compensate specifically for variations in the intrinsic force-generating capacities of the muscles engaged in the movement task. The more general conclusion that can be drawn is that in some instances there is considerable flexibility in the composition of muscle synergies which may be exploited during the acquisition of motor skill. In other cases, for example, those in which specific patterns of muscle recruitment are supported by

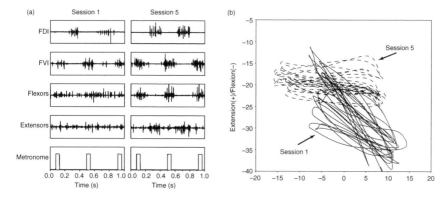

Figure 18.5 Electromyographic and kinematic adaptations during a rhythmic finger flexion– extension task. Adapted from Carson and Riek (2001). Panel (a) EMG recordings from FDI, FVI, EDC (extensors) and FDS (flexors). For each muscle, the data are shown for a 1-second epoch within a single experimental trial. Session 1 data are shown in the panels on the left while session 5 data are shown on the right. Panel (b) Single kinematic records from one participant obtained during the initial and final sessions of the skill acquisition regime. Angular displacement in the flexion/extension direction is shown on the ordinate with downward (negative) deflections representing flexion and upward (positive) deflections representing extension. Positive deflections along the abscissa represent abduction, while negative deflections represent adduction. All angular deflections are measured with respect to the plane of the dorsum of the hand. The data records shown correspond to the final 5 seconds of the trial (frequency = 2.625 Hz). The solid curve indicates data obtained during session 1. The dashed curve indicates data obtained during session 5.

neural circuitry that promotes the reciprocal activation of agonist–antagonist pairs, intrinsic muscle synergies may prove to be rather more robust.

Summary

In the present chapter, we have given consideration to a number of anatomical, mechanical and neural factors which impact upon the acquisition of human motor skill. All motor acts are performed within contexts which are defined by a complex of these factors. As a necessary consequence, the transformations of internal models that occur with experience and during learning are driven by the specific nature of these constraints. Ultimately, however, the consequences of such changes must be expressed via the final common pathway. Unfortunately, we presently have a very poor understanding of the way in which specific musculoskeletal constraints impact upon the changes in neuromuscular control that occur during skill acquisition. There are preliminary indications that these changes may be quite different in nature from those which occur in response to alterations of external dynamics. In addition, it seems logical to assume that the various factors which have been discussed, including muscle articularity, morphometric and mechanical properties, the multifunctional characteristics of skeletal muscle, and the presence of functional task groups, will each have quite different effects on the timescale of the adaptations that occur during skill acquisition. The practical significance of these differences will, in turn, depend on the extent to which each factor is influential in the context of a specific motor task. The association between the physical characteristics of the motor system and the flexibility of CNS control have implications for rehabilitation and therapy, sporting prowess and occupational capability, in that the strategies employed to enhance motor performance must be developed with specific consideration of the musculoskeletal structures involved and their influence upon the time course of adaptation. In spite of these practical implications, there have thus far been very few investigations which have focussed on these issues. The impact of musculoskeletal constraints on the acquisition of motor skills is, therefore, a topic worthy of extensive further study. The time scale of adaptations leading to improvements in performance will influence expectations for improvement and strategies for enhancement of performance.

Acknowledgement

This work was supported by the Australian Research Council.

References

Bernstein, N. (1967). *The coordination and regulation of movements*. New York: Pergamon.

Bizzi, E. (1993). Intermediate representations in the formation of arm trajectories. *Current Opinion in Neurobiology*, 3 (6), 925–931.

Bobbert, M. F. (1990). Drop jumping as a training method for jumping ability. *Sports Medicine*, 9 (1), 7–22.

Buchanan, T. S., Rovai, G. P. and Rymer, W. Z. (1989). Strategies for muscle activation during isometric torque generation at the human elbow. *Journal of Neurophysiology*, 62 (6), 1201–1212.

Bullock, D. and Grossberg, S. (1988). Neural dynamics of planned arm movements – emergent invariants and speed accuracy properties during trajectory formation. *Psychological Review*, 95 (1), 49–90.

Bullock, D. and Grossberg, S. (1991). Adaptive neural networks for control of movement trajectories invariant under speed and force rescaling. *Human Movement Science*, 10 (1), 3–53.

Carroll, T. J., Barry, B., Riek, S. and Carson, R. G. (2001). Resistance training enhances the stability of sensorimotor coordination. *Proceedings of the Royal Society of London Series B – Biological Sciences*, 268 (1464), 221–227.

Carson, R. G. and Riek, S. (1998). The influence of joint position on the dynamics of perception– action coupling. *Experimental Brain Research*, 121 (1), 103–114.

Carson, R. G. and Riek, S. (2001). Changes in muscle recruitment patterns during skill acquisition. *Experimental Brain Research*, 138 (1), 71–87.

Carson, R. G., Riek, S., Smethurst, C. J., Parraga, J. F. L. and Byblow, W. D. (2000). Neuromuscular-skeletal constraints upon the dynamics of unimanual and bimanual coordination. *Experimental Brain Research*, 131 (2), 196–214.

Cruse, H., Bruwer, M. and Dean, J. (1993). Control of 3-joint and 4-joint arm movement – strategies for a manipulator with redundant degrees of freedom. *Journal of Motor Behaviour*, 25 (3), 131–139.

Flanagan, J. R. and Rao, A. K. (1995). Trajectory adaptation to a nonlinear visuomotor transformation – evidence of motion planning in visually perceived space. *Journal of Neurophysiology*, 74 (5), 2174–2178.

Flash, T. and Hogan, N. (1985). The coordination of arm movements – an experimentally confirmed mathematical model. *Journal of Neuroscience*, 5 (7), 1688–1703.

Hollerbach, M. J. and Flash, T. (1982). Dynamic interactions between limb segments during planar arm movement. *Biological Cybernetics*, 44 (1), 67–77.

Jamison, J. C. and Caldwell, G. E. (1993). Muscle synergies and isometric torque production – influence of supination and pronation level on elbow flexion. *Journal of Neurophysiology*, 70 (3), 947–960.

Jamison, J. C. and Caldwell, G. E. (1994). Dual degree-of-freedom tasks – flexion effect on supination pronation response. *Journal of Electromyography and Kinesiology*, 4 (3), 143–152.

Kawato, M. (1999). Internal models for motor control and trajectory planning. *Current Opinion in Neurobiology*, 9 (6), 718–727.

Kelso, J. A. S., Buchanan, J. J., DeGuzman, G. C. and Ding, M. (1993). Spontaneous recruitment and annihilation of degrees of freedom in biological coordination. *Physics letters [Part A]*, 179, 364–371.

Latash, M. L. (1993). *Control of human movement*. Champaign, IL: Human Kinetics.

Liddell, E. G. and Sherrington, C. S. (1925). Recruitment and some other factors of reflex inhibition. *Proceedings of the Royal Society of London Series B – Biological Sciences*, 97 488–518.

Loeb, G. E. (1985). Motoneuron task groups: coping with kinematic heterogeneity. *Journal of Experimental Biology*, 115, 137–146.

Loeb, G. E. (1987). Hard lessons in motor control from the mammalian spinal cord. *Trends in Neuroscience*, 10, 108–112.

Loeb, G. E., Giszter, S. F., Saltiel, P., Bizzi, E. and Mussa-Ivaldi, F. A. (2000). Output units of motor behaviour: an experimental and modeling study. *Journal of Cognitive Neuroscience*, 12, 78–97.

MacConaill, M. A. and Basmajian, J. V. (1977). *Muscles and movements: a basis for human kinesiology* (new revised edition). Huntington, NY: R. E. Krieger.

Macpherson, J. M. (1991). How flexible are muscle synergies? In D. R. Humphrey and H. J. Freund (Eds), *Motor control: concepts and issues. Report of the Dahlem Workshop on Motor Control: concepts and issues*, Berlin, December 3–8, 1989 (pp. 33–47). Chichester: John Wiley and Sons Ltd.

Maffiuletti, N. A., Dugnani, S., Folz, M., Di Pierno, E. and Mauro, F. (2002). Effect of combined electrostimulation and plyometric training on vertical jump height. *Medicine and Science in Sports and Exercise*, 34 (10), 1638–1644.

Matavulj, D., Kukolj, M., Ugarkovic, D., Tihanyi, J. and Jaric, S. (2001). Effects of plyometric training on jumping performance in junior basketball players. *Journal of Sports Medicine and Physical Fitness*, 41 (2), 159–164.

Riek, S. and Bawa, P. (1992). Recruitment of motor units in human forearm extensors. *Journal of Neurophysiology*, 68 (1), 100–108.

Perciavalle, V., Casabona, A. and Polizzi, M. C. (1990). Adaptation of motor nerve fibers to physical activity. *Bolletina Della Societa Italiana di Biologia Sperimentale*, 66, 1121–1128.

Purves, D. (1988). *Body and brain: a trophic theory of neural connections*. Cambridge, MA: Harvard University Press.

Saltzman, E. (1979). Levels of sensorimotor representation. *Journal of Mathematical Psychology*, 20 (2), 91–163.

Saltzman, E. and Kelso, J. A. S. (1987). Skilled actions – a task-dynamic approach. *Psychological Review*, 94 (1), 84–106.

Segal, R. L. (1992). Neuromuscular compartments in the human biceps brachii muscle. *Neuroscience Letters*, 140 (1), 98–102.

Segal, R. L., Catlin, P. A., Krauss, E. W., Merick, K. A. and Robilotto, J. B. (2002). Anatomical partitioning of three human forearm muscles. *Cells Tissues Organs*, 170 (2–3), 183–197.

Segal, R. L., Wolf, S. L., DeCamp, M. J., Chopp, M. T. and English, A. W. (1991). Anatomical partitioning of three multiarticular human muscles. *Acta anatomica*, 142 (3), 261–266.

Sergio, L. E. and Ostry, D. J. (1995). Coordination of multiple muscles in 2-degree-of-freedom elbow movements. *Experimental Brain Research*, 105 (1), 123–137.

Shadmehr, R. and Mussa-Ivaldi, F. A. (1994). Adaptive representation of dynamics during learning of a motor task. *Journal of Neuroscience*, 14 (5), 3208–3224.

Shemmell, J. P., Forner, M. J., Tresilian, J. R., Riek, S. and Carson, R. G. (2002). Effects of neuromuscular-skeletal constraints on the acquisition of skill in two kinetic degrees of freedom. Paper presented to the Society for Neuroscience, Orlando, FL, November 2002. Society for Neuroscience Abstracts, 28, Program No. 269.2.

Sternberg, S., Knoll, R. L., Monsell, S. and Wright, C. E. (1988). Motor programs and hierarchical organization in the control of rapid speech. *Phonetica*, 45 (2–4), 175–197.

ter Haar Romeny, B. M., van der Gon, J. J. and Gielen, C. C. (1984). Relation between location of a motor unit in the human biceps brachii and its critical firing levels for different tasks. *Experimental Neurology*, 85 (3), 631–650.

Thoroughman, K. A. and Shadmehr, R. (1999). Electromyographic correlates of learning an internal model of reaching movements. *Journal of Neuroscience*, 19 (19), 8573–8588.

Tresilian, J. R. and Stelmach, G. E. (1997). Common organization for unimanual and bimanual reach-to-grasp tasks. *Experimental Brain Research*, 115 (2), 283–299.

van Ingen Schenau, G. J. (1989). From rotation to translation – constraints on multi-joint movements and the unique action of bi-articular muscles. *Human Movement Science*, 8 (4), 301–337.

van Zuylen, E. J., Gielen, C. C. and Denier van der Gon, J. J. (1988a). Coordination and inhomogeneous activation of human arm muscles during isometric torques. *Journal of Neurophysiology*, 60 (5), 1523–1548.

van Zuylen, E. J., van Velzen, A. and Denier van der Gon, J. J. (1988b). A biomechanical model for flexion torques of human arm muscles as a function of elbow angle. *Journal of Biomechanics*, 21 (3), 183–190.

Windhorst, U., Burke, R. E., Dieringer, N., Evinger, C., Feldman, A. G., Hasan, Z. *et al.* (1991). What are the outputs of motor behaviour and how are they controlled? In motor control: concepts and issues D. R. Humphrey and H.-J. Freund (Eds) (pp. 101–119). New York: John Wiley and Sons.

Windhorst, U. and Kokkoroyiannis, T. (1991). Interaction of recurrent inhibitory and muscle spindle afferent feedback during muscle fatigue. *Neuroscience*, 43 (1), 249–259.

Wolpert, D. M. and Kawato, M. (1998). Multiple paired forward and inverse models for motor control. *Neural Networks*, 11 (7–8), 1317–1329.

Wolpert, D. M., Ghahramani, Z. and Jordan, M. I. (1995). Are arm trajectories planned in kinematic or dynamic coordinates – an adaptation study. *Experimental Brain Research*, 103 (3), 460–470.

19 Emergence of sport skills under constraints

Duarte Araújo, Keith Davids, Simon J. Bennett,
Chris Button and Graham Chapman

A key factor in understanding the emergence of skilled behaviour in sport concerns the role of the coach in structuring task constraints and organizing practice environments (for a review, see Schmidt and Lee, 1999). Perhaps the most significant task constraints include the nature of the equipment used by learners during practice and the structure and organization of activities that coaches use to simulate strategic sub-phases of sports, such as attacking or defending in team ball games. From a dynamical systems theoretical standpoint, contemporary work on motor behaviour in sport has been influenced by concepts such as self-organization, constraints, emergence, variability and stability of motor patterns in developing and learning movement systems (see Davids *et al.*, 2002; Handford *et al.*, 1997; Kelso, 1995). Dynamical systems are complex, highly interconnected systems that are capable of acquiring rich patterns of behaviour due to the potential for interaction between system components.

In human movement systems learners are able to assemble functional coordination patterns from numerous peripheral motor system degrees of freedom (broadly speaking, these are the many different components of the human body) during practice. Dynamical systems theory views influential factors within the practice environment as constraints on the acquisition of movement coordination (Newell *et al.*, 2001). The proposition is that movement coordination emerges under interacting constraints, which harness the mechanical degrees of freedom of the movement system during learning. Due to the abundance of mechanical degrees of freedom available in the human motor system, Bernstein (1967) argued that the acquisition of movement coordination was 'the process of mastering redundant degrees of freedom' (p. 127), or the conversion of the human movement apparatus to a more controllable, stable system. With learning, functional groupings or coordinated states emerge from the available degrees of freedom, which stabilize the motor system from the random fluctuations that can occur between system components (Mitra *et al.*, 1998).

In recent years, increasing research activity has led to the characterization of a *constraints-led approach* (Davids *et al.*, 1999; Handford *et al.*, 1997) to explain the process of change in movement behaviour that can be imputed to processes of learning and development (e.g. see Newell, 1986; Newell *et al.*, 2001). It has been argued that motor system reorganization can result in an increasing and decreasing number of mechanical degrees of freedom (and increasing/decreasing attractor dimensions) being involved, due to the changing nature of the constraints that individuals need to satisfy (Newell and Vaillancourt, 2001). The emphasis on a constraints-led approach has led researchers to consider the effect of identifying and manipulating key constraints under which skilled behaviour emerges in sport (see Davids *et al.*, 2003a,b). It has also been argued that a key role for the coach is to understand the nature of the constraints that each individual athlete needs to satisfy during sport performance. Coaches need to manipulate these constraints during practice in order to enhance learning (Handford *et al.*, 1997).

There have also been a number of recent attempts to map out how key constraints may channel motor skill acquisition in sport (see Davids *et al.*, 1999; Handford *et al.*, 1997). Perusal of the extant motor behaviour literature reveals various *ad hoc* proposals in favour of a *constraints-attunement* hypothesis as an explanation for specific aspects of behaviour such as perceptual learning (Gibson, 1969, 1991; Greeno, 1994), the memory recall basis of expert performance in different domains (e.g. Vicente and Wang, 1998), and the beneficial effect of an external focus of attention (compared to an internal focus) in feedback and instructions (e.g. Wulf *et al.*, 2000).

Our goal in this chapter is to explore how a constraints-led perspective can provide a theoretical rationale for manipulation of key task constraints by coaches/teachers, such as equipment and the organization of practice contexts. For this purpose, we use as a task vehicle some recent research examining strategies for understanding and manipulating key practice constraints such as sports equipment, in order to facilitate the emergence of skilled movement behaviour in young children; and practice structure, to facilitate emergence of tactical decision-making skills in adults during sub-phases of team ball sports. We conclude by discussing the implications of a constraints-led perspective for the behaviours adopted by the coach/teacher during practice.

Constraints on dynamical systems

The role of constraints in channelling motor behaviour has become prominent in the last two decades because it is realized that the stability of functional coordination patterns can be altered by constraints imposed on performers, such as the nature of the information available to channel movement dynamics, the nature of equipment used for performing an activity and the structural organization of the performance environment including intentions and instructions to act (e.g. see Kugler *et al.*, 1982; Newell, 1996).

In order to understand the importance of the concept of constraints in a theoretical explanation of skilled behaviour in sport, one needs to understand the relationship between stability and flexibility in the behaviour of natural dynamical systems. As we noted earlier, the learner in sport may be conceptualized as a dynamical movement system searching for stable and functional states of coordination (or 'attractors') during goal-directed activity (Handford *et al.*, 1997). The term 'functional' in this description signifies a pattern of behaviour that will support the performer in achieving a specific task goal such as performing a *pas-de-deux* in ballet, balancing on a beam in gymnastics or intercepting an approaching ball in cricket. Dynamical systems have been modelled as complex systems that are continuously evolving over different timescales (Newell *et al.*, 2001). van Gelder and Port (1995) defined a dynamical system as 'any state-determined system with a numerical phase space and a rule of evolution (including differential equations and discrete maps) specifying trajectories in this space' (p. 9). The term phase space refers to all the hypothetical states of organization into which a dynamical system can evolve. For example, the phase space of molecules of water adhering as a dynamical system involves just three attractor states or forms of organization, characterized as liquid, steam or ice. Dynamical systems can evolve along different pathways, primarily because they are 'open' systems, meaning that their form can be influenced by many factors in the environment. In studying open, dynamical systems, it has become clear that the influences that guide the form emerging from the system should be considered as constraints on system behaviour (Newell, 1986).

Constraints on movement systems

The phase space of a dynamical human movement system attempting to perform specific task goals such as a forward defensive stroke in cricket or a tumble-turn in swimming has been metaphorically described as a perceptual-motor landscape with many attractors or regions of stability (see Davids *et al.*, 2003a,b; Glazier *et al.*, 2003). The term 'perceptual-motor' captures well the idea that human movement systems are very flexible and can adapt to dynamic environments because they are sensitive (open) to information surrounding them and can use the information to plan and organize actions. Constraints act to pressurize the flow of a dynamical movement system around the perceptual-motor landscape. Both internal (e.g. the anatomical organization of the body) and external constraints (e.g. auditory or haptic information) act to channel the emergence of functional movement patterns (e.g. Bernstein, 1967; Warren, 1990). For example, in skiers, changing environmental conditions could act as a significant pressure on existing patterns of movement coordination. A steepening gradient encountered on a mountain slope would typically force a skier to adopt a pattern of traversing from side to side on the piste. When a steepening gradient is encountered by skiers, they can adapt by shifting the distribution of their weight over the inside ski and changing the alignment of the skis. In this way, the skier does not generate excessive downhill speed, providing a task-specific solution without a significant loss in postural stability. This example illustrates how information from a performer's equipment can constrain the motor patterns that emerge during performance. We explore this issue in more detail later in the chapter.

From a constraints-led perspective, skill acquisition may be viewed as a process of stabilizing a functionally appropriate attractor that a movement system can settle into during task performance. A state of coordination emerges which is *relatively resistant* to the environmental forces or constraints that might perturb the stability of the motor system during goal-directed activity. States of coordination or attractors are constantly subjected to potentially perturbing forces, which often arise from random fluctuations within the abundant motor system degrees of freedom (Mitra *et al.*, 1998).

Learning is a process in which athletes search for specific, functional coordination states, that they assemble and stabilize over extended periods of time. Athletes typically develop a repertoire or landscape of stable, functional attractors to satisfy the constraints of complex environments. For example, a perceptual-motor landscape for a gymnast might include a number of different skills involved in floor exercises as well as the actions forming a high or asymmetrical bar routine, and the landscape of a golfer might include attractor regions for putting and driving. According to Newell (1986), constraints can be classified into three distinct categories to provide a coherent framework for understanding how movement behaviours emerge during performance (see Figure 19.1).

Organismic constraints

Organismic constraints refer to the existing structural characteristics of the individual, such as height, weight, body mass composition and the functional characteristics such as connective strength of synapses in the brain, cognitions, motivations and emotions. Customary patterns of thought (exemplified in self-talk) by an athlete, levels of practice or defects in the visual system can act as constraints to channel the way that a particular performance goal is approached. Such unique characteristics represent resources that are brought to bear on the task problem or limitations that lead to individual-specific adaptations by the performer.

Environmental constraints

Many environmental constraints are physical in nature and include energy flows such as the auditory information available to the performer or the ambient light in

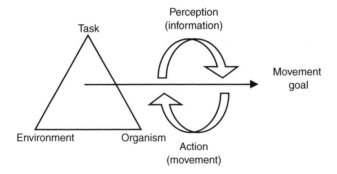

Figure 19.1 A model of constraints depicting how organismic, task and environmental constraints all interact to channel behaviour (adapted from Newell, 1996).

a performance context. Gravity is a key environmental constraint on movement coordination in all tasks, as our example of a skier traversing down a steep mountain slope showed. Considering our skier once more, the visual flow presented by a mogul field can be used to regulate the torques generated across the hip, knee and ankle joints. Larger mounds of snow will require the skier to bend the hips and knees in order to absorb the reaction imparted to the legs as the skis travel over them. Of course, some environmental constraints are social rather than physical. Socio-cultural factors are key environmental constraints including family support networks, peer groups, societal expectations and values as well as cultural norms.

Task constraints

Task constraints are usually more specific than environmental constraints and include goals, rules of a sport, implements or tools to use during performance, pitch and boundary markings, augmented information sources and other instructional aids such as video. In sports, task constraints are significant because coaches/teachers can manipulate them to help learners search for functional and individualized coordination solutions. Adaptive learning allows athletes to cope with novel task constraints as performance conditions change. To encourage flexibility and adaptability in athletes, sport coaches often manipulate task constraints, particularly where the playing environment is dynamic and unpredictable. For example, a soccer dribbling drill might be conducted within an enclosed area in an attempt to improve close ball control of learners. Such practices also encourage the performer to explore alternative movement solutions, and hence optimize techniques in competition.

It needs to be emphasized that the *interaction* of the main classes of constraints on the neuromuscular system during goal-directed activity results in the emergence of optimal behaviours. For example, how a basketball dribbler decides to act in a one versus one sub-phase depends on relevant constraints at any one time, including the information available on court, current fitness levels, physiological status, the nature of the practice surface and intentions (e.g. to score points quickly or to maintain possession of the ball, and the interaction with the opponent).

To summarize so far, skilled behaviour can be characterized as movements that are adaptable yet resistant to environmental forces, which could perturb the stability of the motor system. Movement solutions evolve over time as a consequence of the constraints on system behaviour in any given context. Clearly, intra-individual variability in the perceptual-motor landscape reflects the constraints on each individual performer, supporting the need to adopt a constraints-led perspective on skill acquisition.

In the following sections, we build on this theoretical overview of the basis of the constraints-led perspective by elucidating how constraints may guide or channel emergent behaviour in athletes. The examples highlighted provide specific insights into how movement patterns and decision-making processes can be viewed as emergent behaviour in team ball sports. The constraints chosen to exemplify our analysis include many common features of skill performance that coaches and athletes encounter in sport: equipment design and practice structure.

Equipment design

One of the most important task constraints during practice is the size and mass of a piece of equipment (e.g. a ball) relative to relevant limb segments (e.g. arm or leg). This type of task constraint has implications for the implementation of coaching strategies during practice and training, particularly, but not exclusively, with children. Motor development theorists have also been concerned with the dimensions of sports equipment and playing areas, and their effects on children's skill acquisition (e.g. Gallahue, 1987; Haywood and Getchell, 2001). Konczak (1990) proposed children's skill acquisition would be enhanced if sports equipment were correctly scaled to body dimensions. In dynamical systems theory, invoking the Principle of Similitude from biology supports this proposal. This principle underscores the fact that a particular movement form, such as a lower limb coordination pattern, facilitates achievement of a particular function (e.g. kicking a soccer ball), as long as the magnitudes of key system properties do not vary beyond a critical value (e.g. lower limb length, foot size relative to ball size and mass). In soccer, the ball and lower limb form a *striking system* and if the magnitudes of relevant properties within this system are changed in scale (e.g. ball coefficient of restitution or ball size), then stable movement forms may not achieve the desired function and there may be a need for a different functional pattern (Kugler *et al.*, 1982). The implication of this idea is that appropriate scaling of key system properties can facilitate the emergence of skilled behaviour. Despite this theoretical rationale, commercialized sports equipment is rarely engineered to facilitate skill acquisition in young children. Previous work has shown that tennis rackets specifically designed and manufactured for use by 10-year-old children are too universal and do not take into account the huge variation in the moments of inertia of the upper limb segments at that age (Beak *et al.*, 2002).

With respect to upper and lower limb interceptive actions, motor development research has revealed decrements in skill acquisition when practice occurred with balls that are too large or too heavy for grasping, throwing or kicking by children (e.g. Herkowitz, 1984). The literature has recommended the use of appropriately scaled equipment for school children, including reduced size of playing field/court dimensions, changed height/width of goals/baskets and use of balls/implements scaled to key limb dimensions (e.g. see Pangrazi and Dauber, 1989; Siedentop *et al.*, 1984; Wright, 1967). Children are able to perceive clear preferences based on small differences between items of sport equipment (for an example with junior tennis rackets, see Beak *et al.*, 2002). In basketball, Regimbal *et al.* (1992) looked at the preferred size of ball by 10-year-olds in shooting. A large proportion of the children (66 per cent) preferred using the smaller ball compared to an adult-sized ball, with accuracy of motor responses correlating with the improvement of fit between ball and hand.

The anthropometrical scaling of sports equipment is also important for medical reasons. In soccer, there have been recent reports linking repeated heading of leather balls during practice to degenerative brain diseases in high-profile players (http://news.bbc.co.uk/2/hi/health/2441569.stm), leading to concerns over the safety of ball design for heading practice in young children (Kirkendall *et al.*, 2001). Similar health and safety issues exist over children's impact-related sports injuries in distal limb segments during soccer goalkeeping practice. Boyd *et al.* (2001) found that children who practiced soccer goalkeeping with oversized footballs were at greater risk from injuries, like distal radial fractures, compared to children who played with scaled balls. Despite these health and safety implications, research on manipulation of task constraints, such as ball weight and size, and their effect on the emergence of skilled behaviour, is negligible (Klebez, 1978; Launder, 1973).

The 'Futebol de Salão'

Over the last decade, a ball designed in South America, the Futebol de Salão (FDS), has been used increasingly during soccer practice. The FDS ball is smaller (i.e. similar in size to a size three ball) and heavier than a regulation size five soccer ball. A regular size five ball has a coefficient of restitution between 45 and 48 per cent with a recommended pressure of 11.4 psi (pounds per square inch), whereas the FDS has a circumference of 0.52–0.54 m and weighs approximately 0.465 kg. It has a rebound resilience ranging from 10 to 15 per cent and pressure maintained at 8.5 psi. The density of the FDS ball is manipulated by filling the bladder with a specific type of foam, and is intended to reduce its bounce characteristics, thereby ensuring more playing time on the ground. Very little scientific research exists on the FDS ball as a constraint on the emergence of soccer skill. An exception to this was a study by Williams (2000). He compared the effects of practising with an FDS ball to a regulation size five ball on the emergence of ball juggling skills in adult males of intermediate skill level. Pre- to post-test comparisons revealed that the group practising with the FDS ball significantly improved ball juggling skills compared to the control group who used a size five soccer ball.

It is unclear from the current literature on adults whether the emergence of ball skills in children could be facilitated by use of the FDS ball, and whether any observed skill changes may be a function of learners' existing skill level. An interesting question is whether scale changes in key properties of a soccer ball (i.e. size and mass) can facilitate development of ball control in novice children who have not already acquired a coordination pattern for juggling a soccer ball. Recently, experimental work has begun to tackle these issues, with a view to investigating two specific questions: (a) Since the FDS ball has a lower coefficient of restitution than regulation practice soccer balls (e.g. size five), does practising with it lead to better ball control in children? (b) Does the size of the FDS ball, relative to regulation size four and five soccer balls, support better ball control in children? Comparisons across adult and child populations facilitate an analysis of how ball characteristics, such as size and coefficient of restitution, interact with skill level of learners.

Button *et al.* (1999) examined these questions with 11-year-old children who were beginners at soccer and, therefore, more likely to be sensitive to practice over a short period of time. After a pre-test to equate basic skill level, one group practised dribbling and juggling skills with the FDS, while a control group practised with a regulation size five soccer ball. The aim of the juggling test was to keep the ball in the air for as long as possible using any legal body parts under the laws of association football. The aim of the dribbling test was to examine the participant's ability to complete a course of four cones in a zigzag formation as fast as possible, whilst keeping the ball under control. The FDS and control groups practised separately over a 5-week training programme; 2 × 40 minute sessions per week. Each session formed part of a standardized training programme delivered by a qualified coach. All participants undertook post-tests employing the juggling and dribbling skills, conducted 1 week after the programme. The size five soccer ball was used for both groups in the pre- and post-tests.

Both groups significantly improved in terms of juggling and dribbling performance over the course of the programme. For the juggling test, results indicated that the FDS experimental group were juggling the conventional ball more successfully than the control group in the post-test (see Figure 19.2). Button *et al.* (1999) suggested that children using a smaller, heavier ball could be guided towards relevant information (such as haptic and proprioceptive sources) for establishing functional coordination solutions, enabling effective transfer to other task constraints (see also Handford *et al.*, 1997).

Button *et al.* (1999) and Williams (2000) provided some insights into the relative effects of ball coefficient of restitution as a task constraint on ball skill

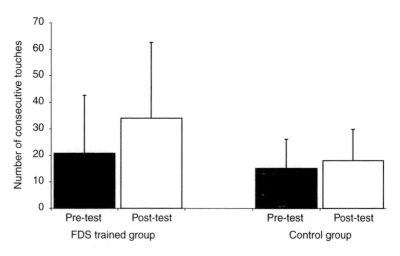

Figure 19.2 Pre- and post-test data from Button *et al.* (1999) on a ball-juggling test for groups using a FDS and a size five soccer ball.

acquisition of children and adults. However, the data from these studies do not help us to differentiate between the relative effects of *specific* task equipment constraints such as ball size and coefficient of restitution and to understand how each constraint may interact with learners' skill level. For example, better performance with the FDS ball on the juggling task may have been the result of using a smaller, rather than a less resilient, ball for practice. Chapman *et al.* (2001) extended the work of Button *et al.* (1999) and Williams (2000) by attempting to dissociate the effects of ball size and coefficient of restitution on juggling and dribbling skills. A sample of completely novice players, aged between 8 and 11 years, were investigated. Similar procedures to Button *et al.* (1999) were employed; however, Chapman *et al.* (2001) also included a retention test in order to examine the effects of ball characteristics on learning. After the pre-tests, all participants were divided into one of three equal, randomly stratified groups. One group practised with the FDS ball, another with the size three soccer ball and a third group was assigned to the size four soccer ball. Since the FDS ball approximates the size three soccer ball, the comparison of learning to juggle and dribble relative to a group practising with a size four soccer ball permitted dissociation of the effects of ball size and ball coefficient of restitution on ball skill acquisition in the children. Means and standard deviations for the dribbling and juggling tests can be seen in Table 19.1.

All three groups significantly improved their juggling and dribbling performance between the pre- and post-tests. The results revealed no significant relative benefits for the acquisition of ball control skills among novice children when practising with the FDS ball, compared to size three and four soccer balls.

The findings extended the work of Button *et al.* (1999) and Williams (2000) by investigating the effects of ball characteristics on acquisition of ball control in completely novice children. However, the fact that no differences between groups were revealed in the study by Chapman *et al.* (2001) points to differences in skill level between the groups of children involved in the studies. Pre-test means for the groups in the separate studies suggest that the participants were at different stages of learning. Button *et al.* (1999) reported higher pre-test mean values for juggling and dribbling than Chapman *et al.* (2001), implying that the

Table 19.1. Means and standard deviations of the juggling and dribbling tests across the time phases (data from Chapman *et al.*, 2001)

	Juggling (touches)			Dribbling (seconds)		
	Pre	*Post*	*Ret*	*Pre*	*Post*	*Ret*
FDS	2.48	4	3.89	27.62	23.4	25.35
	(±1.19)	(±1.63)	(±2.18)	(±3.84)	(±2.48)	(±3.49)
Size three	2.66	3.85	3.42	28.05	24.35	25.64
	(±0.98)	(±1.46)	(±1.53)	(±6.13)	(±3.39)	(±3.35)
Size four	4.38	6.33	5.33	26.30	24.21	24.84
	(±3.77)	(±4.83)	(±2.78)	(±3.11)	(±2.83)	(±2.90)

children were at a more advanced stage of skill acquisition. In the study by Button *et al.* (1999), the participants were at the control stage (Newell, 1985), having already assembled a basic coordination pattern for juggling and dribbling a ball. In the Chapman *et al.* (2001) study, the lower pre-test means implied that they were at the coordination stage because they had not yet assembled a stable coordination pattern for successfully juggling and dribbling a ball. It seems that manipulating the characteristics of soccer balls can enhance children's ball control, as long as the learners are already at the control stage of skill acquisition. Stability of task constraints is important so that new coordination patterns can be assembled, whereas manipulation of equipment characteristics can fine-tune established actions. Although the attempt to dissociate effects of the equipment constraints (i.e. ball size and coefficient of restitution) did not affect the emergence of ball control skills in completely novice children, further work is needed to ascertain whether such a manipulation can enhance skills of more advanced learners. Determining how skill level and task constraints mediate the emergence of skilled behaviour poses important challenges for future work. Moreover, refined analyses should assess how movement coordination changes with learning.

To summarize so far, the studies on task constraints on the emergence of ball control skill in adults and children show how the equipment constraints of ball characteristics, such as size and coefficient of restitution, interact with organismic constraints such as learners' skill level. A constraints-led perspective is also useful for investigating the emergence of cognitive skills relevant for selecting actions. To exemplify our arguments, in the next section of this chapter, we report research that is beginning to examine decision-making in team ball sports as an emergent process under constraints. We focus on the sport of basketball as a task vehicle for our analysis and briefly discuss the implications of this approach for coaching and the organization of practice conditions.

Decision making as an emergent process under constraints

Whereas traditional theories have emphasized the role of organismic constraints in attempting to understand decision-making skill as a normative rational process (e.g. Mellers *et al.*, 1998), from a dynamical systems perspective, skilled behaviour consists of intentional adaptation to the interacting constraints imposed by the environment during task performance (e.g. Newell *et al.*, 2001). From this standpoint, the role of cognitions and intentions is viewed as 'setting up self-assembly (i.e. leading to the emergence of self-organized behaviour), not explicitly controlling such processes during movement coordination' (Davids *et al.*, 2001, p. 144). Self-organization of movement systems is constrained but not determined by important cognitive processes. Intentions in humans are based in the real world (environment) and are constrained by mind, body, social and biological contexts, and it is misleading to refer to the internal generation of a willed action as if intentional behaviour could exist separate from an environment and the movement system (Davids *et al.*, 2001). There is little sense in proposing a hierarchical relationship between intentions and actions because it is not possible to separate their influence on movement system behaviour (Thelen and Smith, 1994). To intend a goal (i.e. a final condition) means that the performer selects the initial condition that permits attainment of the specified final condition under the existing (physical) law domain. With each step closer to the goal, the information must become ever more specific, narrowing the possible action paths, until ultimately, at the last moment of goal accomplishment, the path becomes uniquely defined (Kugler *et al.*, 1990). Logically, therefore, intentional action is influenced by the instantaneous movement capabilities of the system, which in turn are constrained by intentions, and '...decisions emerge for the system depending on fluctuations in the initial task conditions and any higher-order goals impinging on action' (Davids *et al.*, 2001, p. 156).

Intrinsic metrics in decision making

Decision making is also constrained by information in performance environments. During learning and development, movement capabilities are clearly constrained by contextual information. To detect such information, the performer needs an *intrinsic metric* specified by dimensions of his/her perceptual-motor system. That is, the athlete perceives the properties of the environment not in extrinsic units (such as meters, inches), but in relation to his/her own body or body parts, action capabilities and relative location to important objects and surfaces in the environment (Konczak *et al.*, 1992). For example, the climbability of a stair is perceived in relation to a performer's leg length. In a landmark study addressing intrinsic metrics in humans (Warren, 1984), it was observed that young adults of a wide range of statures could, by visual inspection alone, decide which in a series of stairs of varied riser heights afforded bipedal climbing or quadrupedal locomotion. A ratio smaller than the critical ratio (the one where bipedal locomotion transits to quadrupedal locomotion) specifies bipedal climbability. Using the words of Ulrich *et al.* (1990, p. 2), this study showed that 'Individual *choices* varied but were body-scaled; subjects' *choices* were the same mathematical function of the leg length, regardless of stature' (our emphasis). Similarly, van der Kamp *et al.* (1998, p. 352) argued 'body-scaled ratios can be used as a critical determinant of *action choice* – a change beyond the critical ratio value demands a new class of action' (our emphasis). Later, Konczak *et al.* (1992) showed that in stair climbing, one's action capability is subject to multiple constraints, some of which relate to anthropometric (body) dimensions and others to kinematic and kinetic factors. It can be concluded that a person-action scaled metric incorporates all of these constraints and, theoretically, decision-making behaviour can emerge from within this framework.

From a constraints-led perspective, therefore, it seems that in selecting behaviours, individuals might not always engage in conscious and rational mental calculations, using internal representations of critical ratios and deciding which action to execute. For example, in judging stair climbability, at the point of bifurcation (i.e. the critical ratio) the probability of using bipedal and quadrupedal locomotion is the same. An accidental fluctuation or perturbation to the system, constrains the decision such that one or the other mode of locomotion is selected, so no 'agent' inside the system 'decides' which mode to use. Bifurcations (i.e. points where different paths can be taken) show how open systems have several functional options for the same environmental conditions, a redundancy which parallels that seen at other levels of the motor system (Davids *et al.*, 2003a,b).

According to Davids *et al.* (2001), skill acquisition in ball games may be seen as the emergence of movement solutions based on a better tuning to the constraints on action. Cognitive factors related to 'game intelligence' such as anticipation, decision making and creativity could constrain learner's intentions, guiding their search for optimal task solutions. Thus, practice should provide the opportunity to search for solutions to the movement problem in a perceptuo-motor workspace that is generated by the combined constraints of the learner, task and environment.

Emergent decision making in team ball games

An interesting question is whether emergent processes characterize decision-making performance in specific sport activities, such as dribbling in team ball games. As recently noted (Gréhaigne *et al.*, 1997; Hodges *et al.*, 1998; McGarry *et al.*, 2002), sport competition in general, and team ball sports in particular, can be considered as a dynamical system composed of many interacting parts (e.g. players, ball, referees, court dimensions). Macroscopic patterns of behaviour from such a system spontaneously emerge from nonlinear interactions of various components at a more microscopic level of organization (see McGarry *et al.*, 2002). In the study of dynamical movement systems, discontinuous changes in the macroscopic order of a system, induced by continuous changes in value of a control parameter (i.e. a variable that can act as an important source of information for a particular system and exerts considerable influence over system stability), is called a phase transition and is based on a symmetry-breaking process (Kelso, 1995; Mitra *et al.*, 1998). McGarry *et al.* (2002) argued that sport competition should (a) be described in terms of control and order parameters (i.e. variables that characterize the collective state of the system); and (b) exhibit a general tendency to stability.

The studies from McGarry and colleagues have primarily focused on dyatic sports such as squash, although we can refer to an example from basketball to understand the application of these ideas to the study of decision-making processes in team ball games (see also Schmidt *et al.*, 1999). Consider the relative positioning of an attacker with the ball and a marking defender near the basket. Such a one versus one sub-phase of invasive team ball games is very common and can be referred to as a dyad. The dyad formed by an attacker and defender, plus the basket, comprises a system. The aim of the attacker is to 'destroy' the stability of this system. When the defender matches the movements of his/her opponent and remains in position between the attacker and the basket/goal, the form or symmetry of the system remains stable. When an attacking player dribbles past an opponent, near the basket, he/she creates a break in the symmetry of the system. Even though the defender may run to stay in front of him/her, it will be after the attacker has moved the ball towards the basket. This constant adjustment between the positioning of the opposing players is a characteristic of dribbling tasks in many team ball games, and can be understood as a type of interpersonal coordination.

Interpersonal coordination in decision making in team ball sports

The study of interpersonal coordination is relevant in examining the constraints on decision making in basketball dribbling. Consider the attacker–defender dyad in team ball sports as forming a sub-system. Sub-phase work (e.g. one versus one; two versus two; three versus three) is typical of the practice organization in many ball sports including basketball, soccer, hockey, lacrosse and rugby union. The assumption is that changes in the stability of such sub-systems are based on the dynamics between individuals involved in the sub-phase context (Schmidt *et al.*, 1990). The cooperative nature of the relationship between an attacker and defender is highlighted because 'the two individuals can be thought of as a single organism, a dyadic synergy' (Schmidt *et al.*, 1990, p. 227). A dyadic synergy demonstrates properties of nonlinear dynamic systems, including emergent behaviour and entrainment (i.e. the spatial and temporal aspects of interacting movements become mutually related). Creation, maintenance and dissolution of a dyad rely on information about its ongoing coordinative state, that is, its kinematics and its kinetics. The self-organizing dynamical pattern of between-person rhythmic coordination investigated by Schmidt and colleagues (e.g. Schmidt *et al.*, 1994) not only models the equilibrium of coordinative states but also how these coordinative states can spontaneously change form. For the purposes of this chapter, it is important to note that modes of interpersonal coordination are specific to task constraints. It is clear that both intentional and informational constraints are instrumental in the assembly of interpersonal coordinated movements (Kugler and Turvey, 1987).

Interpersonal coordination is not just a function of the continuous rhythmical movements typically studied by Schmidt and colleagues. In ball games, inter-passing between teammates involves discrete movements. Moreover, as we noted above, attackers and defenders form closely interacting dyads in which both parties do not typically seek to coordinate actions. In basketball and soccer, dribbling attackers want to 'get rid' of defenders to score, while defenders seek to remain between attackers and the net/goal in order to stop the attacker from scoring and to recover the ball. Defenders typically are comfortable with stable dyads formed with attackers in non-critical spaces of the pitch or court (note that an exception to this 'rule' may occur during 'catch up' situations when defenders need to gain possession of the ball from attackers in order to score during the closing moments of a match). From a dynamical systems perspective, in these circumstances, attackers are faced with a challenging decision: When and where to break the symmetry created by the unwanted interpersonal system formed with the marking defender? Due to the dynamics of competitive games, there is typically not enough information to specify a goal path completely in advance for attackers. Consequently, goal path selection or decision making in de-stabilizing dyads is an emergent process. In order to exemplify this argument, a model of a symmetry breaking process is presented next in which attackers try to increase system instability and defenders try to maintain system stability.

Situational constraints for decision making in team sports

Of particular interest is the intrinsic metric or specific measurement system that attackers use for making fundamental decisions, such as their critical location on court, relative to the defender's position, at which point they need to change direction during the approach to the basket. The decision would not occur at an absolute critical distance every time (e.g. 1.5 metres from the defender), but rather would emerge from the intrinsic metric of the specific system formed by each individual attacker and defender. Analysis of the coaching literature in basketball (e.g. Bain *et al.*, 1978) reveals that a candidate control parameter for an attacker–defender system could be the intrinsic metric of the *interpersonal distance* between the attacker and defender in a one-on-one situation. This metric system is 'action-scaled' (Konczack *et al.*, 1992) because the dimensions formed by each individual attacker–defender dyad will differ. The use of an intrinsic metric signifies that the value of the control parameter might change depending on the action-scaled features (e.g. limb sizes) of a specific attacker–defender system. Additionally, analysis of the coaching literature reveals that a critical order parameter could be the median point of the distance of both players to the basket. In order to test these assumptions, it is necessary to investigate whether the equilibrium in attacker–defender dyads is broken when a critical value of interpersonal distance is reached. Obviously, during competition, other factors will constrain the strength of interpersonal coordinative states formed on the court or pitch (e.g. skill level, fitness levels, injuries, relying on non-functional information), but the proposal remains that a basic principle of decision making in dribbling during team ball games is a symmetry-breaking process.

The case of basketball one-on-one dribbling

In this section, we present some preliminary findings from pilot work (Araújo *et al.*, 2002). Araújo *et al.* (2002) predicted that the order parameter (the distance between the median point of the dyad and the basket) would change dramatically as a consequence of the attacker successfully exploring the constraints on deciding when to 'attack' the basket. Ten players participated in the experiment and formed five dyads of attackers and defenders. Each dyad started on the free throw line, with the other members of both teams located on court based on the 'attack system 1:2:2' (see Figure 19.3). Instructional constraints were for the attacker to score and the defender to prevent a score, within the rules of basketball. The eight other players were passive players, only participating in the play 5 seconds after the beginning of the task, and keeping the positions described in

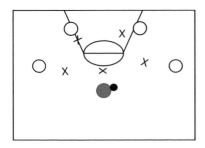

Figure 19.3 Starting position of the dyad (in grey), based on the 'attack system 1:2:2'.

Note
X = defenders; O = attackers.

Figure 19.3. To elucidate our examination of symmetry breaking, the trials chosen for analysis were those where the attacker did not shoot immediately after receiving the ball, and instead, tried to dribble past the defender.

The horizontal plane trajectory (two-dimensional) of the mass centre of each player in the dyad was recorded by one digital camera placed behind and above the dyad's position on the court. The main question concerned whether phase transitions occurred in the interpersonal system formed by the attacker–defender dyads. Dyad transitions were assumed to occur at emergent decision points, identified as the moment when the attacker attempted to dribble past the defender. To illustrate this point, we report data from a number of typical situations in basketball dribbling.

In Figure 19.4, the attacker–defender–basket system exhibited initial symmetry (during the first seconds), which was broken during transition to a new state (just before 4 seconds) at a specific value of the control parameter (i.e. interpersonal distance). In other words, the attacker was trying to dribble past the defender, but the defender was attempting to maintain the initial system state. The attacker increased the number of dribbling actions (fluctuations) in order to create information on the emergence of a system transition (i.e. a decision 'when to go'). Suddenly, the decision emerged in the 'intending–perceiving–acting cycle' (Kugler *et al.*, 1990). Importantly, the emergence of the decision was a result of the breaking of symmetry between the dyad.

Future work using this approach may be able to answer questions that a theory of expert decision making must address including: (a) When (and where) do decision points occur during specific sports? (b) What effect does expertise have on decision making? (c) What factors determine the extent of these effects? An approach to exploring these questions is to find a way to produce deeper insights into the differences between successful and unsuccessful dribbling attempts. In Figure 19.5, we can see that very early the attacker abruptly breaks the symmetry. In this case, the symmetry lasts for a very short period compared with Figure 19.4. Also, we see that the defender, after being passed, could not follow the progression of the attacker towards the basket. In contrast, in Figure 19.6, where the defender has supremacy, the system maintains its symmetry.

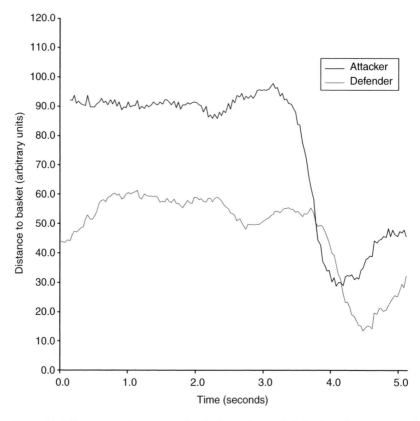

Figure 19.4 Distinction between individual attacker and defender's distance to basket, showing a slight attacker's advantage.

In sum, the emergence of decision making in basketball dribbling was a result of the break of symmetry between the attacker–defender dyad. This break was more abrupt in situations when there was a clear supremacy of the attacker, compared to instances in which defenders maintained supremacy and there was no symmetry breaking in the system. The role of symmetry breaking in the acquisition of decision-making skill merits further investigation.

Implications of a constraint-led perspective for coaching behaviours in sport

We conclude the chapter by providing some insights into the practical issues raised by a constraints-led perspective for sport practitioners and athletes. In sports and physical activities, there are many constraints on motor behaviour that coaches and sport practitioners can manipulate in order to enhance learning. According to Newell's (1986) model, these key constraints include: *Organismic*

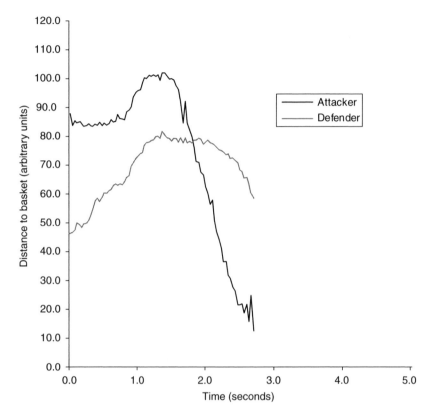

Figure 19.5 Distinction between individual attacker and defender's distance to basket, showing attacker's supremacy.

constraints – learners' intentions, cognitions and beliefs, fatigue and injury status; *Task* constraints – equipment, artificial aids, surfaces and boundaries of practice area, practice organization, types of feedback, task instructions; *Environmental constraints* – presence of spectators, ambient lighting and temperature, background texture, performance incentives. The role of the coach is to manipulate the task and environmental constraints on the learner in order to facilitate skill performance. This aim can be achieved in many ways and below we highlight how a constraints-led perspective can impact on coaching behaviours.

Influence of scaling task constraints on emergent behaviour

In sport, experience gained in acting on objects and developing expectancies (e.g. texture, rigidity and mass) affords better multisensory information from objects, surfaces and implements for athletes. Changes in body dimensions and physical abilities inherently affect the object–person relationship (Ulrich *et al.*, 1990).

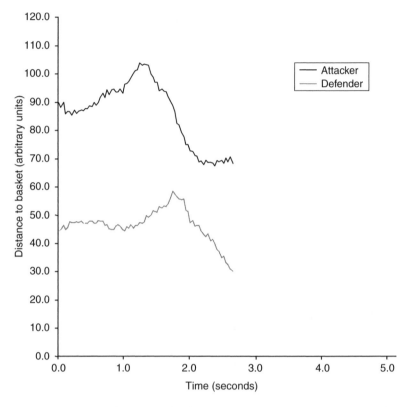

Figure 19.6 Distinction between individual attacker and defender's distance to basket, showing defender's supremacy.

Planning a practice session that includes a variety of practice with equipment of different scaling dimensions for early learners may be important to develop perceptual awareness of informational constraints on movement. The data on the role of the FDS ball as an equipment constraint on soccer skill acquisition suggest it could be safer and more advantageous for children to use appropriately sized equipment, particularly if they have an established coordination pattern to support the performance of specific ball skills.

In relation to dribbling in ball games, a constraints-led perspective suggests that it may be useful to analyse which body dimensions of defenders are appropriately scaled for the attacker to be quickly tuned to symmetry-breaking potential. For example, inexperienced attackers will need to learn that different arm lengths in defenders afford different 'standing reach' distances. After successful attempts to break the symmetry formed with marking defenders, advanced learners should be required to play against opponents with different body scaling. Special attention should be paid to the interpersonal distance between attackers and defenders during dribbling practice. Identifying the most stable intrinsic metric used by learners and increasing the variability of this specific variable through exploration and discovery learning may train this aspect of perceptual and decision-making skill in dribbling. Coaches could ensure that learners have experience of practising with a number of systems varying in intrinsic metric values. A similar approach could be taken with regard to the approach velocity of dribblers, as well as to the effects of changes in velocities (e.g. acceleration, jerk). Also, interpersonal coordination in dyads may allow the exploration of variability in 'between-person' entrainment. Analysis of characteristic signatures of critical fluctuations could help defenders learn to anticipate the proximity of the transition point in the system.

The coaches' role in manipulating constraints: what can a constraints-led perspective tell us?

From this standpoint, the role of the coach during practice can be viewed as directing each individual learner's search for emergent movement task solutions (for a full explanation, see Davids *et al.*, 2003b). Following Newell's (1986) constraints model, coaches should consider three directions for organizing practice and their interventions: (a) using environmental constraints; (b) constraining the performer and (c) changing task constraints (for an example in sailing, see Araújo and Rocha, 2000).

It is not simple to manipulate environmental constraints. A possible solution is to vary the practice location to change the social (e.g. spectators) or physical (e.g. temperature, humidity, light) characteristics of the practice setting, in order to let environmental constraints influence a situation like the one-on-one in basketball. It is the coach and the players who should move towards the environmental conditions that must be explored in order to improve decision-making skill (see Hardy *et al.*, 1996; Williams *et al.*, 1999).

In directing the intervention on the performer, it is important to attend to the link between perception and action, as well as variability in motor behaviour (see Davids *et al.*, 2001). It is possible to focus more on perception (i.e. in detecting action possibilities) or on actions (i.e. in the execution of action possibilities), but keeping the link present. A third possibility is to provide the formation of new links between perception and action (i.e. creating new action possibilities).

Detecting action possibilities

Systematic video-based viewing (and anticipation) is a way to recognize patterns of play and the competition scenario (cf. Abernethy *et al.*, 1998). Also, competition statistics of different play options of the opponent are helpful if attained at the system level (e.g. look for key variable relations between players). These activities should be combined with the real or imagined execution of these action possibilities. A different approach is to use virtual environments and simulators. However, simulators should maintain the link between perception and action, as well as the intentional demands of the real task. The use of simulators is relevant (Abernethy *et al.*, 1998) because it implies lower risks and costs for: (a) anticipating an opponent's action and executing a response; (b) recognizing patterns and acting accordingly; (c) tailoring information to allow the guided acquisition of cognitive skills.

Executing action possibilities

In team ball sports, decision making can be enriched if deception skills are developed (e.g. Abernethy *et al.*, 1998). Deception skills relevant to the athlete can be detected by videotape analyses or by objective statistical investigations focusing on the interactions between individual players or groups of players. After this preliminary assessment, the development of these skills can be made by masking the critical information sources; presenting false cues; increasing the number of 'possibly relevant' information sources; or presenting critical sources as late as possible (see Glencross and Cibich, 1977). These skills should be prac- tised in a very realistic manner in training to simulate situations where the deceptions are most applicable. Another possibility for developing decision- making is the establishment of pre-performance routines, in order to focus on the goals of the competition, attending to the specific constraints of the competi- tion. Decision making is improved not only because of a better tuning to the relevant constraints, but also because of the avoidance of non-functional thoughts (e.g. cognitive anxiety), distractions and the reduction of the warm-up decrement effect (e.g. Hardy *et al.*, 1996).

Creating action possibilities

The establishment of new links between perception and action can be made when the coach asks for new solutions (for several recommendations about coaches' instructions, see Hodges and Franks, 2002). Another important coach- ing strategy is to use other athletes' solutions in demonstrations of decision- making behaviour (see also Williams *et al.*, 1999). The viewing of competitions and a concomitant analysis can clarify the search for different solutions, namely if motor or imagined practice can be made immediately after. A different possi- bility is to change the athlete's psychological states by showing videos that induce emotions, by recalling past experiences with the associated emotions or by inducing fatigue. Naturally, these states must be related to the sporting expe- riences of the athlete (see Hardy *et al.*, 1996). These different states act as situa- tional constraints, which channel the way intention and intrinsic dynamics interact (see Davids *et al.*, 2001).

Another direction for training decision making is to change task constraints. The task can be presented in ways that allows exploration of emergent behav- iour. Thus, the manipulation of task constraints can direct the search process. Manipulations could relate to materials and surfaces, spatial and temporal con- straints and also instructions, namely how the goals, the rules and relevant strategies to complete the task are presented by coaches (see Davids *et al.*, 2001; Williams *et al.*, 1999). When considering a one-on-one situation in basketball, the characteristics (e.g. morphology) of specific opponents represent an important manipulation that should be considered to permit the emergence of body-scaled action solutions.

Feedback provision and skill acquisition: implications of emergent processes under constraints

The coaches' use of feedback and instructions as constraints on learning is an important consideration. Feedback can be used to direct observers' attention towards relevant information sources during performance and learning. Sport coaches are challenged with the task of providing feedback in forms that are understandable by the learner and which address the tuning of intrinsic dynamics in each individual by information. From this perspective, verbal instructions and visual demonstrations are seen as constraints on the search process during learning and performance of movement skills (Newell, 1986). Consequently, attention has been focused on the instructional constraints used to direct observers' attention during practice (e.g. Al-Abood *et al.*, 2001). An important issue that Vereijken and Whiting (1990) demonstrated was that augmented verbal feedback is much more effective if it were directed towards the order parameter, for example, the relative phasing of limb segments during different forms of locomotion.

An interesting question concerns how coaches can constrain the search of learners for emergent movements and tactical behaviours. An issue of particular relevance to coaching behaviour is: Can performance be enhanced when learners *view* movement dynamics in an effort to imitate a model's movement topology or form? Based on Bernstein's (1967) insights, Whiting and Den Brinker (1982) proposed that learning is constrained by information about the *image of the act* (focus on movement dynamics or topological form) and the *image of achievement* (focus on the movement effects to be achieved in the environment). More recently, research has also shown beneficial effects of instructions and feedback as a function of an external focus of attention (emphasis on movement effects on the environment) compared to an internal focus (focus on movement of specific body parts) (e.g. Wulf *et al.*, 2001).

It has been proposed that an external focus on the image of achievement (i.e. an emphasis on task outcomes) provides better opportunities to constrain learners' search for emergent task solutions during discovery learning (e.g. see Wulf *et al.*, 2000). In previous work, Vereijken and Whiting (1990) argued that an external focus allowed discovery learners to focus on an image of achievement alone, facilitating performance and learning of a slalom skiing task. It appears that an external focus of attention may not interfere with self-organization processes of the movement dynamics as athletes explore the task (Davids *et al.*, 2002). Interestingly, Wulf *et al.* (2000) have found that an external focus that directed performer's attention towards the movement effects, rather than to other external sources of information, yielded better learning and performance of a tennis forehand drive. That is, the effects of instructions towards an external focus of attention were not due to distracting performers from an explicit focus on their movement dynamics, but were influential in allowing emergent processes to inherently regulate task performance and learning. It seems that visual feedback can be used to direct learners' search of emergent solutions. Al-Abood *et al.* (2002) found that an external focus of attention on the effects of a model's performance leads to better task performance by observers than an internal focus on the same model's movements. These findings, therefore, can be related to the use of models and video-taped images in the coaching context.

In conclusion, the theoretical analysis of skill acquisition in sport as an emergent process under constraint is in its infancy, but it is becoming clear that concepts such as body-scaling of actions, symmetry-breaking in order to seek phase transitions are potentially useful ideas that need to be fully investigated in future research programmes. In particular, the role of practice structure and organization and the nature of equipment used during learning are key factors in understanding the emergence of skilled behaviour. These, and many other issues, are likely to form the basis of a theoretico-practical programme of work on a constraints-led approach to skill acquisition for many years to come.

References

Abernethy, B., Wann, J. and Parks, S. (1998). Training perceptual-motor skills for sport. In B. Elliott (Ed.), *Training in sport: applying sport science* (pp. 1–68). Chichester: John Wiley & Sons.

Al-Abood, S. A., Davids, K. and Bennett, S. J. (2001). Specificity of task constraints and effects of visual demonstrations and verbal instructions in directing learners' search during skill acquisition. *Journal of Motor Behaviour*, 33, 295–305.

Al-Abood, S. A., Bennett, S. J., Moreno Hernandez, F., Ashford, D. G. and Davids, K. (2002). Effect of verbal instructions and image size on visual search strategies in basketball free throw shooting. *Journal of Sports Sciences*, 20, 271–278.

Araújo, D., Davids, K., Sainhas, J. and Fernandes, O. (2002). Emergent decision-making in sport: a constraints-led approach. Communication to the International Congress on Movement, Attention and Perception, Poitiers, France.

Araújo, D. and Rocha, L. (2000). The trainability of decision-making in sport: the example of the Portuguese Olympic sailing team. In B. Carlsson, U. Johnson and F. Wetterstrand (Eds), *Proceedings of the Sport Psychology Conference in the New Millenium* (pp. 94–98). Halmstad, Sweden: CIV, SSHS.

Bain, B., Hayes, D. and Quance, A. (1978). Coaching certification manual – level two. Canada: J. Seaman, Basketball Canada.

Beak, S., Davids, K. and Bennett, S. J. (2002). Child's play: children's sensitivity to haptic information in perceiving affordances of rackets for striking a ball. In J. E. Clark and J. Humphreys (Eds), *Motor development: research and reviews*, Vol. 2. Reston, VA: NASPE.

Bernstein, N. A. (1967). *The control and regulation of movements*. London: Pergamon Press.

Boyd, K. T., Brownson, P. and Hunter, J. B. (2001). Distal radial fractures in young goalkeepers: a case for an appropriately sized soccer ball. *British Journal of Sports Medicine*, 35, 409–411.

Button, C., Bennett, S., Davids, K. and Stephenson, J. (1999). The effects of practicing with a small, heavy soccer ball on the development of soccer related skills. Invited Communication to British Association of Sports and Exercise Sciences Annual Conference. Leeds Metropolitan University, UK, 9–12 September.

Chapman, G., Bennett, S. J. and Davids, K. (2001). The effects of equipment constraints on the acquisition of juggling and dribbling in soccer. Communication to 6th Annual Congress of European College of Sports Science (Perspectives and Profiles), Cologne, Germany.

Davids, K., Bennett, S. J., Handford, C. and Jones, B. (1999). Acquiring coordination in self-paced extrinsic timing tasks: a constraints-led perspective. *International Journal of Sport Psychology*, 30, 437–461.

Davids, K., Savelsbergh, G. J. P., Bennett, S. J. and Van der Kamp, J. (2002). *Interceptive actions in sport: information and movement*. London: Routledge, Taylor & Francis.

Davids, K., Williams, A. M., Button, C. and Court, M. (2001). An integrative modeling approach to the study of intentional movement behaviour. In R. Singer, H. Housenblas and C. Janelle (Eds), *Handbook of sport psychology* (2nd ed., pp. 144–173). New York: John Wiley.

Davids, K., Button, C. and Bennett, S. J. (2003a). *Acquiring movement skill : a constraints-led perspective*. Champaign, IL: Human Kinetics.

Davids, K., Glazier, P., Araújo, D. and Bartlett, R. M. (2003b). Movement systems as dynamical systems: the role of functional variability and its implications for sports medicine. *Sports Medicine*, 33(4), 245–260.

Gallahue, D. L. (1987). *Developmental physical education for today's elementary school children*. New York: Macmillan.

Gibson, E. J. (1969). *Principles of perceptual learning and development*. New York: Appleton-Century-Crofts.

Gibson, E. J. (1991). *An odyssey in learning and perception*. Cambridge, MA: MIT Press.

Glazier, P. S., Davids, K. and Bartlett, R. (2003). Dynamical systems theory: a relevant framework for performance-oriented sports biomechanics research? *Sportscience*, 7, sportsci.org/jour/03/psg.htm

Glencross, D. and Cibich, B. (1977). A decision analysis of games skills. *Australian Journal of Sports Medicine*, 9, 72–75.

Greeno, J. G. (1994). Gibson's affordances. *Psychological Review*, 101, 336–342.

Gréhaigne, J. F., Bouthier, D. and David, B. (1997). Dynamic-system analysis of opponent relationships in collective actions in soccer. *Journal of Sports Sciences*, 15, 137–149.

Handford, C., Davids, K., Bennett, S. and Button, C. (1997). Skill acquisition in sport: some applications of an evolving practice ecology. *Journal of Sports Sciences*, 15, 621–640.

Hardy, L., Jones, J. and Gould, D. (1996). *Understanding psychological preparation for sport*. Chichester, England: Wiley.

Haywood, K. M. and Getchell, N. (2001). *Life span motor development* (3rd ed.). Champaign, IL: Human Kinetics.

Herkowitz, J. (1984). Developmentally engineered equipment and playgrounds. In J. R. Thomas, (Ed.) *Motor development during childhood and adolescence* (pp. 139–173). Minneapolis: C. C. Brown.

Hodges, N. J. and Franks, I. M. (2002). Modelling coaching practice: the role of instruction and demonstration. *Journal of Sports Sciences*, 20, 793–811.

Hodges, N. J., McGarry, T. and Franks, I. M. (1998). A dynamical system's approach to the examination of sport behaviour: implications for tactical observation and technical instruction. *Avante*, 4, 16–34.

Kelso, J. A. S. (1995). *Dynamic patterns: the self-organization of brain and behaviour.* Cambridge, MA: MIT.

Kirkendall, D. T., Jordan, S. E. and Garrett, W. E. (2001). Heading and heading injuries in soccer. *Sports Medicine*, 31, 369–386.

Klebez, G. A. (1978). Learning and improving selected soccer skills with different pressure and size soccer balls. Unpublished Thesis, University Microfilm.

Konczak, J. (1990). Towards an ecological theory of motor development: the relevance of the Gibsonian approach to vision for motor development research. In J. E. Clark and J. H. Humphrey (Eds), *Advances in motor development research 3* (pp. 201–224). New York: AMS Press Inc.

Konczak, J., Meeuwsen, H. and Cress, M. (1992). Changing affordances in stair climbing: the perception of maximum climbability in young and older adults. *Journal of Experimental Psychology: Human Perception and Performance*, 18 (3), 691–697.

Kugler, P. N., Kelso, J. A. S. and Turvey, M. T. (1982). On the control and coordination of naturally developing systems. In J. S. Kelso and J. Clark (Eds), *The development of movement control and coordination* (pp. 5–78). New York: Wiley.

Kugler, P. N., Shaw, R. E., Vincente, K. J. and Kinsella-Shaw, J. (1990). Inquiry into intentional systems I: issues in ecological physics. *Psychological Research*, 52, 98–121.

Kugler, P. N. and Turvey, M. T. (1987). *Information, natural law, and the self-assembly of rhythmic movement.* Hillsdale, NJ: Lawrence Erlbaum Associates.

Launder, A. (1973). Soccer for school: a modern approach. *Journal of Health, Physical Education and Recreation*, 44, 25–27.

McGarry, T., Anderson, D., Wallace, S., Hughes, M. and Franks, I. (2002). Sport competition as a dynamical self-organizing system. *Journal of Sports Sciences*, 20, 771–181.

Mellers, B., Schwartz, A. and Cooke, A. (1998). Judgement and decision making. *Annual Review of Psychology*, 49, 447–477.

Mitra, S., Amazeen, P. G. and Turvey, M. T. (1998). Intermediate motor learning as decreasing active (dynamical) degrees of freedom. *Human Movement Science*, 17, 17–65.

Newell, K. M. (1985). Coordination, control and skill. In D. Goodman, R. B. Wilberg and I. M. Franks (Eds), *Differing perspectives in motor learning, memory and control* (pp. 295–317). Amsterdam: Elsevier Science, North Holland.

Newell, K. M. (1986). Constraints on the development of coordination. In M. Wade and H. T. A. Whiting (Eds), *Motor development in children: aspects of coordination and control* (pp. 341–360). Dordrecht, Netherlands: Martinus Nijhoff.

Newell, K. M. (1996). Change in movement and skill: learning, retention and transfer. In M. L. Latash and M. T. Turvey (Eds), *Dexterity and its development* (pp. 393–430). Mahwah, NJ: Erlbaum.

Newell, K. M. and Vaillancourt, D. (2001). Dimensional change in motor learning. *Human Movement Science*, 20, 695–715.

Newell, K. M., Liu, Y.-T. and Mayer-Kress, G. (2001). Time scales in motor learning and development. *Psychological Review*, 108 (1), 57–82.

Pangrazi, R. P. and Dauber, V. P. (1989). *Dynamic physical education for elementary school children.* New York: Macmillan.

Regimbal, C., Deller, J. and Plimpton, C. (1992). Basketball size as related to children's preference, rated skill and scoring. *Perceptual and Motor Skills*, 75, 867–872.

Schmidt, R. A. and Lee, T. D. (1999). *Motor control and learning* (3rd ed.). Champaign, IL: Human Kinetics.

Schmidt, R. C., Carello, C. and Turvey, M. T. (1990). Phase transitions and critical fluctuations in the visual coordination of rhythmic movements between people. *Journal of Experimental Psychology: Human Perception and Performance*, 16, 227–247.

Schmidt, R. C., Christianson, N., Carello, C. and Baron, R. (1994). Effects of social and physical variables on between-person visual coordination. *Ecological Psychology*, 6, 159–183.

Schmidt, R. C., O'Brien, B. and Sysko, R. (1999). Self-organization of between-persons cooperative tasks and possible applications to sport. *International Journal of Sport Psychology*, 30, 558–579.

Siedentop, D., Herkowitz, J. and Pink, J. (1984). *Elementary physical education methods.* Englewood Cliffs, NJ: Prentice-Hall.

Thelen, E. and Smith, L. (1994). *A dynamical systems approach to the development of cognition and action.* Cambridge, MA: MIT Press.

Ulrich, B., Thelen, E. and Niles, D. (1990). Perceptual determinants of action: stair-climbing choices of infants and toddlers. In J. Clark and J. Humphrey (Eds), *Advances in motor research*, Vol. 3 (pp. 1–15). New York: AMS Press.

van der Kamp, J., Savelsbergh, G. and Davis, W. (1998). Body-scaled ratio as a control parameter for prehension in 5- to 9-year-old children. *Developmental Psychobiology*, 33, 351–361.

van Gelder, T. and Port, R. F. (1995). It's about time: an overview of the dynamical approach to cognition. In R. F. Port and T. van Gelder (Eds), *Mind as motion: explorations in the dynamics of cognition* (pp. 1–43). Cambridge, MA: MIT Press.

Vereijken, B. and Whiting, H. T. A. (1990). In defence of discovery learning. *Canadian Journal of Sport Psychology*, 15, 99–109.

Vicente, K. J. and Wang, J. H. (1998). An ecological theory of expertise effects in memory recall. *Psychological Review*, 105, 33–57.

Warren, W. (1984). Perceiving affordances: visual guidance of stair climbing. *Journal of Experimental Psychology: Human Perception and Performance*, 10, 683–703.

Warren, W. (1990). The perception–action coupling. In H. Bloch and B. Bertenthal (Eds), *Sensory-motor organizations and development in infancy and early childhood* (pp. 23–37). Amsterdam: KAP.

Williams, A. M. (2000). Transfer of learning in football: from juggling to ball control. *'Insight' – The F.A. Coaches Association Journal*, 4(3), 30–31.

Williams, A. M., Davids, K. and Williams, J. G. (1999). *Visual perception and action in sport.* London: E & FN Spon.

Whiting, H. T. A. and Den Brinker, B. P. L. M. (1982). Image of the act. In J. P. Das, R. F. Mulcahy and A. E. Wall (Eds), *Theory and research in learning disabilities* (pp. 223–241). New York: Plenum Press.

Wright, E. J. (1967). Effects of light and heavy equipment on acquisition of sports-type skills by young children. *Research Quarterly for Exercise and Sport*, 38, 705–714.

Wulf, G., McNevin, N. H., Fuchs, T., Ritter, F. and Toole, T. (2000). Attentional focus in complex motor skill learning. *Research Quarterly for Exercise and Sport*, 71, 229–239.

Wulf, G., Shea, C. H. and Park, J.-H. (2001). Attention and motor performance: preferences for and advantages of an external focus. *Research Quarterly for Exercise and Sport*, 72 (4), 335–344.

Index